The Middle East and the Making
of the Modern World

# The Middle East and the Making of the Modern World

## CYRUS SCHAYEGH

Harvard University Press

Cambridge, Massachusetts, and London, England    2017

Library of Congress Cataloging-in-Publication Data
Names: Schayegh, Cyrus, author.
Title: The Middle East and the making of the modern world /
Cyrus Schayegh.
Description: Cambridge, Massachusetts : Harvard University Press, 2017. |
Includes bibliographical references and index.
Identifiers: LCCN 2017001309 | ISBN 9780674088337 (alk. paper)
Subjects: LCSH: Middle East—History—1517- | Human geography—
Middle East. | Rural-urban relations—Middle East—History. | Civilization,
Western—Middle Eastern influences.
Classification: LCC DS62.4 .S33 2017 | DDC 956—dc23
LC record available at https://lccn.loc.gov/2017001309

*To Dalia and Leo*
*and to Tsolin*

# CONTENTS

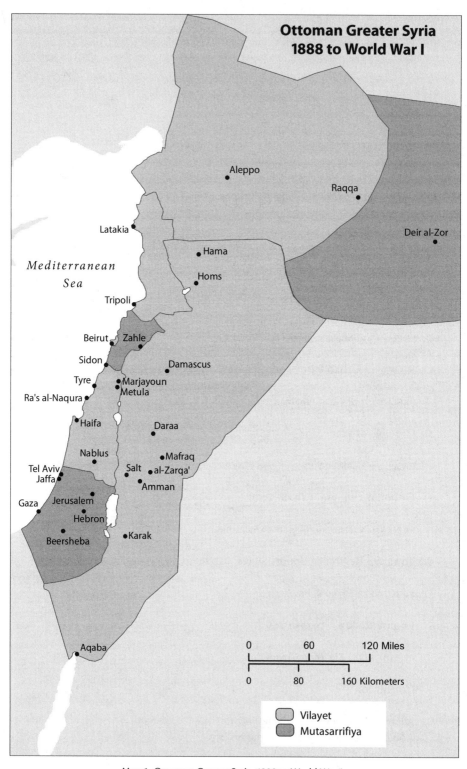

Map 1  Ottoman Greater Syria, 1888 to World War I.

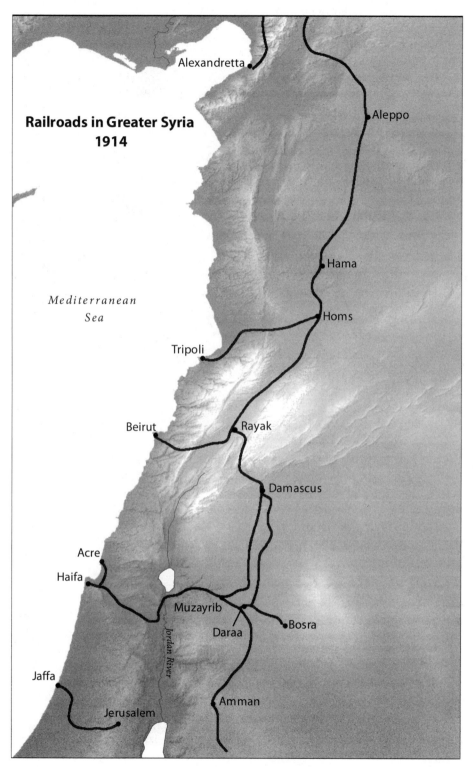

**Railroads in Greater Syria 1914**

Alexandretta

Aleppo

*Mediterranean Sea*

Hama

Homs

Tripoli

Beirut

Rayak

Damascus

Acre

Haifa

Muzayrib

Daraa

Bosra

*Jordan River*

Jaffa

Amman

Jerusalem

Map 2  Railroads in Greater Syria, 1914.

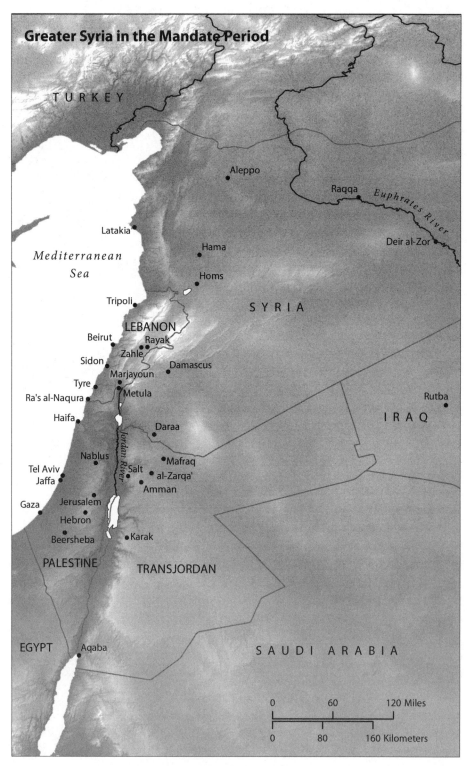

Map 3  Greater Syria in the Mandate Period.

# INTRODUCTION

This book is an interpretation of the socio-spatial making of the modern Middle East. Why, how, and in which stages, it asks, did well-rooted cities and regions mold a dynamic modern world economy and powerful modern states? How, in return, were cities and regions remolded? And what does the Middle Eastern case tell us about the world as a whole?

To answer these questions, the book focuses on a transformative stretch of time. It starts in the middle third of the nineteenth century, when a now clearly West-centric form of economic globalization, and modern state formation in the Ottoman Empire and elsewhere, began in earnest. Rather than concluding in 1918 with the Ottoman Empire's dissolution and the expansion of European rule in the Middle East, it continues until the 1940s, when a number of Middle Eastern states gained independence. A postscript traces the story to the present. Further, this book has a pivot: Bilad al-Sham, a region central to the Middle East. Its European name was Syria until 1918; thereafter it became known as Greater Syria, in distinction from the new country Syria, because that region was divided into French Lebanon and Syria and British Palestine and Transjordan following World War I. From Bilad al-Sham, the book looks beyond: to neighboring Egypt, Iraq, and Turkey, to diaspora communities, and to a variety of imperial and transnational connections. And it peers deeply into the region, at cities, at their ties, and at the global economic forces, the Ottoman and European empire-states, and the post-Ottoman nation-states at work within Bilad al-Sham.[1]

What the book finds is that the socio-spatial making of the modern world cannot be fully grasped by studying globalization *or* state formation *or* urbanization. Certainly, the world's accelerated interdependence, states' unprecedented ability to penetrate their territory, and record urban growth all have been instrumental in creating the modern world, distinguishing it from premodern times. But no single one of these developments has been clearly dominant. Hence, neither has any single one been *the* distinguishing feature of the socio-spatial making of the modern world. This is the case not the least because these developments were inherently interlaced.

It is indeed this fact—that cities, regions, states, and global circuits reconstituted and transformed each other much more thoroughly and at a much faster rhythm than at any other point in history—that is the primary distinguishing feature of the socio-spatial making of the modern world. I call that feature transpatialization.[2] It is not one single process. (Neither are globalization, state formation, and urbanization, for that matter.) Rather, it denotes a set of processes: of socio-spatial intertwinements. Put differently, transpatialization is not an empirical unit. It is a heuristic umbrella. Its use, by a historian, makes sense because the processes it bundles unfolded in tandem. Also, it does not assign artificial primacy to any one presumably unitary process or to any one seemingly distinct scale like "the global" or "the urban." As such, this book picks up the "real challenge" to scholars that global historian Sebastian Conrad recently identified: To "shift between, and articulate, different scales of analysis rather than sticking to fixed territories. . . . In many cases," Conrad added, "historians have opted for novel geographies, but in the end have tended to then treat these spaces as given."[3]

This chapter introduces this book's story, argument, and implications. I start with a first look at Bilad al-Sham. I then outline how transpatialization evolved in the Middle East from the mid-nineteenth to the mid-twentieth century. Next, I comment on my choices in telling that story. And finally, I discuss that story's relevance for studying the modern world in general and the Middle East in particular, including the Yishuv, the Zionist state in the making in Palestine.

## Bilad al-Sham

The terms Syria and Bilad al-Sham have existed for a long time. The former, a Greek word with probable Semitic roots derived from "Assyria," dates back to the sixth century B.C. The latter has been in use since the region's Arab-Muslim conquest in the seventh century A.D. Both terms are primarily geographical. They denote the area circumscribed by the Mediterranean Sea in the west, the Anatolian high plateau in the north, Mesopotamia in the east, Arabia in the south, and the Egyptian Nile Valley in the southwest. French historian Dominique Chevallier could have been talking not only about the Middle Ages but about the time from the Arab-Muslim conquest as well, when stating that Bilad al-Sham's inhabitants had "the consciousness of belonging to a regional ensemble," one that was *not* Anatolia, Mesopotamia, Arabia, or Egypt. This "negative" definition was reinforced by "positive" ones. A crucial one took shape following the conquest, when the region's Arabic dialects, while not uniform, slowly became distinct from those of neighboring regions. Another crucial positive definition took root around the mid-nineteenth century, when intellectuals from Bilad al-Sham developed a regional form of "Arabism," imbuing the region with a cultural national meaning without, however, rejecting Ottoman rule. Some also started to call the region Suriya, influenced by Europeans who had never stopped using Syria. Moreover, during this same time, expanding Ottoman state administration and trade and communication infrastructures had the side effect of integrating the different bits of Bilad al-Sham, including its cities, more tightly than before.[4]

However, Bilad al-Sham has never been clearly defined or bounded. Only thrice in history was it a single province within an empire: under Rome from 64 B.C. to 194 A.D., during a spell of Egyptian rule from 1831/1832 to 1840/1841, and during World War I when its various provincial governors reported to a single Ottoman official headquartered in Damascus. (Also, it almost never served as the center of an empire, and the one exception, the Damascus-based Muslim Umayyad dynasty that ruled from 661 to 750, had come from Arabia.) Even as a geographical term, Bilad al-Sham is not precise. It is not plainly the land of Sham, which is how it translates into English. Both *bilad* and *Sham* are intricate words. *Bilad* is "a country" or "countries forming a whole," and is the plural form of *balad* (country, town, place). *Sham* stands for Syria as well as for Damascus, and its etymology is relational, meaning "left" or "north" as opposed to *yaman*, "right" or "south," from the viewpoint of the Arab-Muslim conquerors of Syria and Yemen.[5] In addition, Bilad al-Sham's physical geography is diverse and in many places difficult to access. Two north-south mountain ranges separate a desert in the east from a narrow coastal plain in the west; and the region lacks a unifying feature like a river. Hence it is no surprise that Bilad al-Sham has been a haven for minority sects and a religious mosaic. Nor is it a surprise that none of its cities has ever exerted the dominance of a city like Baghdad, established in the eight century A.D. in the Mesopotamian river plain, or like Cairo, founded in the tenth century on the banks of Egypt's Nile. Even stalwart advocates of Bilad al-Sham, like Damascene intellectual Muhammad Kurd 'Ali (1876–1953), recognized the region's soft boundaries. "Arab and Western geographers agree that *al-Sham* reaches from 'Arish, in Egypt, to the Euphrates, and from the Mediterranean to the Taurus. . . . [But] it confuses the mind whether all of Aleppo's actions today are inside Syria's borders or partly outside it, [in zones] counted as Asia Minor."[6] Last but not least, at times the region's very meaning and function shifted—a point detailed further below regarding the transformative stretch of time from the mid-nineteenth century to the mid-twentieth century.

In sum, rather than being sharply defined and unified, Bilad al-Sham / Suriya has always been a loose, somewhat shifting "super-identity." To quote Chevallier in full: "While having the consciousness of belonging to a regional ensemble," the people of Bilad al-Sham "entertained local particularisms, i.e. autonomies."[7]

## Bilad al-Sham's Cities before the Nineteenth Century

Front and center to those local autonomies were Bilad al-Sham's cities. They stood out for several reasons. Many were age-old: Damascus had been inhabited since the seventh millennium B.C., Jerusalem, since the fourth. A number played significant roles in the three monotheistic traditions—Judaism, Christianity, and Islam. Never did a single city dominate all others. And nonurban elites were never powerful enough to dominate cities. Although armed Arab-Muslim tribes commanded respect, neither they nor other nonurban groups possessed the powers of medieval Europe's feudal seigneurs.[8]

In 1516 / 1517 the Ottomans conquered Bilad al-Sham as well as its ruler from the mid-thirteenth century, Mamluk Egypt. In Bilad al-Sham, smaller cities such as Jerusalem were made capital of an Ottoman district (*sanjak*) while larger cities became capitals of a province (*eyalet* in Turkish, *wilaya* in Arabic): Damascus in 1516, Aleppo in 1521, Tripoli around 1570, and Sidon in 1614. Having been in the doldrums in the fifteenth century, the region profited from becoming part of an empire that was large and provided security. In particular, Aleppo's international trade and Damascus's pilgrimage-based trade to Mecca grew. And especially in the sixteenth and eighteenth centuries urban populations increased. Aleppo and Damascus even developed suburbs—improved security made city walls less necessary.[9]

For a good century and a half after 1516 / 1517, Istanbul governed Bilad al-Sham directly, appointing governors and judges and providing soldiers. Then, by the late seventeenth century, as part of an empire-wide process, the region's cities became more self-governing, though they remained loyal to Istanbul. Local notable families (*a'yan* in Arabic) became more influential. Although their sources of power differed—they bore arms, were wealthy and / or learned—all played a similar double role: They governed their city together with socio-administrative institutions including guilds, and they mediated between their city and Istanbul.[10]

## The First Stage of Transpatialization

This situation continued until the first third of the nineteenth century, whereafter two new macrohistorical developments reached Ottoman Bilad al-Sham. The world economy became more transformative and more firmly Eurocentric.[11] And modern state territoriality emerged, partly in reaction to economic globalization and to its political counterpart, the expansion of European empires. Egypt made a first stab when occupying Bilad al-Sham from 1831 / 1832 to 1840 / 1841. But it was some time following the Ottoman reconquest of the region, by the 1850s, that change started in earnest. Istanbul sought to project as much administrative energy into as much territory as possible. State and society and center and provinces became more enmeshed. This development was not extraordinary. From mid-century, states around the world reacted to "a series of parallel, simultaneous crises in the organization of power, production, and culture. . . . [These] arose from indigenous causes and had their own chronologies . . . [but] played out in the context of deeper and more competitive interactions among regions, the competitive [sic] driven largely (but not exclusively) by more vigorous European interventions." As part of modern Ottoman state territoriality, Ottoman nationalism rose, and in the Arab Ottoman provinces, especially in Bilad al-Sham, a cultural sense of Arabism was born and soon picked up and amplified by emerging diaspora communities.[12]

Although the modern Eurocentric world economy and modern Ottoman state territoriality reached Bilad al-Sham from the outside, both became deeply enmeshed with the region. The encounter of these new developments with Bilad al-Sham and its cities formed the first stage of transpatialization, lasting until the late 1910s. That stage began with a crisis-ridden transition in the 1830s–1840s: the Bilad al-Sham part of a global "saddle period" between the early modern and the modern world that started in different parts of the world as early as the 1770s and ended as late as the 1840s.[13]

Formed around mid-century, this stage featured three basic sociospacial intertwinements, which unfolded in tandem. One was, quite simply, that Bilad al-Sham's cities became part of the modern world: in the now Eurocentric world economy and in the now much more transformative Ottoman state. Moreover, cities started to grow more rapidly. This development fit into an "exceptional wave of [urban] transformations" across the Ottoman Empire, which in turn was part of a process begun in some parts of Europe in the mid-eighteenth century and which by the nineteenth century became palpable around the world. In consequence, urban forms changed. Cities spilled over their walls; new roads were paved, restructuring certain quarters; and new infrastructures, including tramways, appeared especially in the large cities. But precisely because Bilad al-Sham's cities were transformed, they remained central to their inhabitants' sense of belonging in a now rapidly globalizing world: the very "building blocks of their geographical imagination." Cities were not only remade, then, but constituted the place where their inhabitants actively lived and experienced the modern world. And while becoming more tightly integrated into the Ottoman state, cities also were the very centers from which officials and officers reached deep into Bilad al-Sham, exercising territoriality. Cities were the places, too, where state power was negotiated between, and shared by, Istanbul and notables. They became the hothouses for new collective identities: politically, Ottoman nationalism, and culturally, Arabism. And some cities tightened their economic grip on their rural hinterland, seeking to offset the drawbacks of being incorporated into a Eurocentric world economy.[14]

The second manifestation of transpatialization concerned interurban ties. Specific port and interior city pairs, such as Beirut and Damascus or Jaffa and Jerusalem, drew closer, partly due to improved roads and newly introduced railways and telegraphs. This trend formed part of economic globalization, and sometimes involved European capital. It also cemented social ties between city pairs, actively channeling the "tentacles" of Eurocentric world trade to the benefit of local merchants, some of whom were members of growing transnational family networks.[15]

Third and last, the region of Bilad al-Sham started to change. Its relationships with neighboring regions grew stronger. By the early twentieth century Egypt, for example, had attracted over 30,000 merchants and intellectuals from Bilad al-Sham. Further, within the region, cities and interurban ties linked up. Bilad al-Sham was becoming more integrated, a process that from the late nineteenth century comprised the Zionist Yishuv, modern Jewish settlements in Palestine. In the absence of a clearly dominant city, the region was a decentralized urban patchwork. But it had a gravitation point. Beirut, profiting most from Bilad al-Sham's incorporation into a now Eurocentric world economy, became a bustling commercial port city and a cultural and educational center. By 1888, it convinced Istanbul to grant it its own province. This made official the relative decline of other littoral cities such as Sidon, Tripoli, and Acre and of however still large interior cities like Damascus and

Aleppo. Last, intellectuals framed Bilad al-Sham not simply as a cultural-geographical region but increasingly as the homeland (*watan* in Arabic) of all "Syrians." Although loyalty to Istabul persisted, Bilad al-Sham, now also called Suriya, became nationalized. By the late nineteenth century, this entailed globalizing Suriya, analyzing it as part of a worldwide family of *awtan* (pl. of *watan*).[16]

World War I was a distinct phase in the first stage of transpatialization. An Allied naval blockade on Bilad al-Sham slashed its world trade links, hurting the port city of Beirut. By contrast, state territoriality peaked and was exercised from one center, the interior city of Damascus, by General Jamal Pasha, an iron-willed Turkish Ottoman statesman. He defended Bilad al-Sham against British forces massed in Egypt, and ruthlessly exploited the war to boost Ottomanization. This tied the region closer to the empire. Moreover, specific state policies such as the expansion of transport infrastructures within the region happened to further regional integration. This was the case doubly because the Ottomans lost only a sliver of the region to Britain until the fall of 1918—the southern half of Palestine up to Jerusalem. Even so, the region was not fully centralized. This was partly because even in wartime central state power knew its limits: some planning was flawed and local administrators were still needed. Most important, cities continued to be central to their inhabitants' sense of belonging, and even during a time of horrible scarcity, urban sociabilities, while reeling, did not disintegrate.[17]

## The Second Stage of Transpatialization

The persisting though deeply transformed relevance of cities, strengthened interurban ties, and firmed regional integration: after 1918, these processes deeply shaped the embryonic nation-states of Lebanon, Syria, Palestine, and Transjordan, as well as European imperial administrations and world economic forces operating within them. In return, cities, their ties, and the region were reshaped. The resultant interlinked socio-spatial intertwinements formed the second stage of transpatialization.

Like the first stage, the second stage did not happen overnight. The year 1918 was not quite a new dawn. Rather, the entire first post-Ottoman decade until 1929 was an Ottoman twilight: a transitional phase. To be sure, it was not as radical a departure from the period preceding it as the transitional phase of the 1830s–1840s. In the 1920s the world economy in Bilad al-Sham remained Eurocentric; territoriality as practiced by the European-ruled nation-states did not fundamentally differ from that of the late Ottomans; and urban notable elites persisted. Hence, in this book the 1830s–1910s and the 1920s–1940s are referred to as two stages, rather than two periods, of transpatialization.

Still, the 1920s did see momentous changes, with four new nation-states created in Bilad al-Sham. Post-Ottoman nationalisms—Zionism and various forms of Arab nationalism—became fully political and more vociferous, a development fanned by European imperial rule that triggered considerable violence especially in Syria and Lebanon. Although the Mandates system of the League of Nations—the world's first permanent international organization of states, created in 1919— set some bounds to British and French rule, its touch was light.[18] And Turkey's historic abolition, in 1924, of the almost 1,300-year-old Caliphate confounded Muslims also in Bilad al-Sham. Besides, like the transitional phase of the 1830s–1840s, the 1920s formed part of a wider pattern. The first years following World War I were unstable around the world— not the least in Europe, where the German, Austro-Hungarian, and Russian empires fell.[19]

How did this transition and further developments from the 1910s manifest themselves in space? What were the main interlinked facets of transpatialization until the 1940s? That is the question to which this book pays most attention. Bilad al-Sham was, on the one side, deeply marked by its fourfold division. In the 1920s, it began to slowly shift from being mainly a patchwork region of cities and interurban ties to becoming principally an umbrella region of nation-states. Each imperially ruled nation-state developed its own economic and administrative institutions and accumulated its proper experiences, giving people's lives in each of the four new countries a distinct texture. On the other side, Bilad al-Sham, having become quite integrated by 1918, forced the hand of the new French and British rulers. Just having quartered the region, the latter—what irony!—proceeded to uphold its integration. They created a regionwide customs-free zone, and within that zone the policy decisions of one imperial power had the unintended consequence of spilling over the border, affecting the other's policies. Further, incessant crossborder movements of people, animals, goods, and ideas impelled French and British Mandate administrators to cooperate systemically—in the region and beyond—on matters as varied as law enforcement and disease prevention. Regional integration was cemented by infrastructural investments and by a technological novelty, the car. In short, the region had tangible economic and administrative effects on the new nation-states and on their imperial rulers. This was also true for Bilad al-Sham's cultural-geographical framing. A flurry of Arabic texts on "Natural Syria" reinforced views of it as a naturally undivided *watan* in a global family of *awtan* (pl.). Even Zionists somewhat agreed.

Cities and their interurban relationships still mattered, too, and sociospatial intertwinements involving them continued to unfold in lockstep with intertwinements related to the region. No doubt, superimposed on a map made up of cities and their hinterlands, and cutting across it, was a map of national spaces. But in return, the latter were subdivided into cut-off bits of cities' hinterlands and interurban ties, many of which now straddled borders; that is, they were transnationalized. This transnationalization affected Bilad al-Sham's European-ruled nation-states, too. For instance, Damascus's trade with the port city of Beirut became more bureaucratized and hence more irksome. Conversely, Damascene merchants took advantage of a railway to another port city—Haifa, under British rule, beyond the reach of France—to force the French authorities to keep the Damascus-Beirut railway prices low.

Collective identities were reshaped in a similarly double-sided manner. Surging nationalist rhetoric meant that city dwellers, many of whom spearheaded that very rhetoric, reimagined their home as a place vital to the nation-state. Cities were "nationalized," as it were. In return, nation-states were not internally uniform but a conglomerate of competing cities: "urbanized," as it were. Overseas diaspora communities often saw new national identities through the lens of extant urban identities, too. Furthermore, to lionize their importance in the new nation-state, city dwellers often asserted their city's weight in fields that transcended the nation-state—the global economy, say, or the Muslim world, or Bilad al-Sham. As a result, nation-states were linked "upward" to various transnational spaces.

In the late 1920s, the Ottoman twilight ended.[20] The 1930s was a phase of its own in the post-Ottoman stage of transpatialization, distinct from the 1920s as well as from 1939–1945. A shift matured that had begun in the 1920s. Bilad al-Sham ceased being principally a patchwork region of cities and interurban ties, and became primarily an umbrella region of nation-states. In a sense, this was a story foretold—nation-states are powerful. But it was also contingent: sped up and shaped by an extraordinary confluence of events and trends in the late 1920s and early 1930s.

Perhaps most important, single-country (*watani* in Arabic) nation-state movements grew stronger institutionally and socioeconomically. Demands for independence began to set the European-ruled Mandates' political agenda. The years around 1930 saw the start of a drawn-out process of decolonization in the A (Middle Eastern) Mandates; from this viewpoint, the mandate period can be divided into two parts—the 1920s and the 1930s–1940s.[21] In Syria, a costly revolt, from 1925 to 1927, compelled France to finally recognize nationalists, doubly because the latter were headed by urban notable elites who had reinvented themselves as nationalists after 1918. The nationalists became institutionalized. In 1927 / 1928, they formed a notable-led alliance known as the National Bloc (*Kutla Wataniyya*). And in 1931, France held a parliamentary election that bent to nationalists' political demands enough for them not to boycott it. They entered the legislative, exerting considerable influence in it. Further, in 1933 and 1936, France offered Syria independence, however conditional. The second time the Bloc accepted. (In 1938, the French parliament refused ratification, though.) Lebanon also elected a parliament in 1929, the first since it had become the Lebanese Republic in 1926. Although France closed that parliament in 1932, new parliamentary elections were held in 1934. And already in the early 1930s a few politicians from Lebanon's two dominant denominations—the Maronite Christians and Sunni Muslims—opened a conversation that by 1936 matured into a vision of postcolonial coexistence. In Transjordan, the ruler Emir Abdallah strengthened his grip through a pact with Britain in 1928. Although the Yishuv had been recognized by Britain since the late 1910s, its strongest administrative actor, the Zionist Executive, was revamped and strengthened as the Jewish Agency in 1929. And from 1929 Britain even took more seriously Palestinian nationalist demands.[22]

This was because in that year Palestinian-Zionist tensions, simmering through 1921 to 1929, exploded into violence. The political stance of both sides hardened; also, many shawwam (sg., shami, an inhabitant of Bilad al-Sham) became more engaged in the conflict. Further, by the early 1930s, worsening European antisemitism boosted Jewish emigration and capital transfers to the Yishuv. Consequently, the Yishuv's population, purchasing power, and industry grew by leaps and bounds. But also Lebanon and Syria industrialized more, and cheap Syrian exports, including agricultural products, saturated Palestine. In addition, from the late 1920s pan-Arab nationalism (*qawmiyya* in Arabic) grew stronger. Its loudest advocates were members of a growing educated middle class, many of whom were young people, who saw Bilad al-Sham as the gravitation point of their politics and of the Arab nation. Finally, the Great Depression started. States near and far from Bilad al-Sham raised import tariffs, and global economic integration faltered after a hesitant recovery in the 1920s.

Together, those events and trends had a dual effect on how nation-states interacted within their regional framework in the 1930s. On the one hand, those nation-states grew stronger and turned inward, toward Bilad al-Sham. Competition rose. Almost every country's elite wanted to defend its national turf but also lead in the region politically (Syria, Transjordan) and/or economically (Syria, Beirut, the Yishuv). On the other hand, the competitors' economies differed the longer the more. Because these differences existed within a customs-free zone, they pulled the region's nation-states closer together. However, that transnational integration was now more unequal than before 1918. On a related note, French and British Mandate administrators continued to cooperate: The pattern set in the 1920s persisted.

Meanwhile, Bilad al-Sham's neighborly relations changed. Ties with Turkey, the Ottoman successor, were fraying. Trade suffered with Egypt and stagnated with Iraq, but social webs, *qawmi* affinities, and political ties with both and other Arabs grew. The contours of the contemporary Arab state system appeared. And international, including inter-imperial, administrative communications in and beyond Bilad al-Sham persisted and became more varied, also through the League of Nations.[23]

While Bilad al-Sham matured as an umbrella for nation-states, cities still mattered—and socio-spatial intertwinements continued to unfold in tandem. The nation-states' material and imagined space was still multi-urban and heterogeneous; vice versa, city dwellers still saw their cities as national bastions. Also economically, stronger nation-states did not necessarily equal weaker cities or enfeebled interurban ties. One reason was persistent inequalities among and within Bilad al-Sham's nation-states; people who acted on the resulting incentives often moved along well-established—from 1918 transnationalized—channels. Another reason was imperial interests. Following patterns created already in the late Ottoman period, France and Britain invested greatly in Beirut's and Haifa's infrastructure, respectively. This, and new French- and British-built roads between Bilad al-Sham and Iraq, buoyed the two cities.

World War II was another distinct phase in the post-Ottoman stage of transpatialization. Bilad al-Sham's nation-states were reaching for independence, and Lebanon and Syria actually obtained it in 1943 (though full independence would come only in 1946). This happened partly because Britain sought to keep the Axis powers from undermining the Middle East by supporting certain *watani* nation-state aspirations. At the same time, and to keep the Axis out militarily, Britain extended its rule across the Middle East. In consequence, Bilad al-Sham's countries huddled under their regional umbrella much less than in the 1930s. Those who had economically grown most in the 1930s—the Yishuv and Lebanon's capital Beirut—reached out most energetically to Middle Eastern markets. This was possible because of Britain's wartime economic policy. To balance out plummeting world trade, Britain—from headquarters in Cairo—turned the entire Middle East into one economic zone and massively invested in industries, communication, and transport.

"Reaching out from under the umbrella" took other forms, too. Some Arabs and Yishuvi Jews toyed with the idea of a postwar Middle East-wide customs-free zone. (It failed.) Also, shawwam's sense of cultural and political connectivity to other Arab countries increased, especially to Egypt, which by now considered itself the center of all Arabs. Related, the Arab state system started to take form. In 1945 Lebanon, Syria, and Transjordan acted like the independent governments they were, or were about to become, in helping to establish a moderate *qawmi* project, the Arab League. They did so with Britain's consent, led by Egypt, and together with Iraq, Saudi Arabia, and Yemen; Palestine had to make do with second-rate membership.

As for cities, they continued to assert their position in the material and imagined nation-state space. There was basic continuity here, though with a twist. As nation-states reached for independence, they became more distinct from one another, forcing cities to self-position in more country-specific ways. For example, Aleppines and Tripolitans asserted their cities more as other capitals vis-à-vis their countries' official capitals, Damascus and Beirut.

Last but not least, Beirut played in a league of its own. It continued to be Bilad al-Sham's global city par excellence, and in fact experienced a second golden age from the 1940s to the 1970s. Whereas the year 1918 had hurt Beirut, which had thrived in the nineteenth-century world of empires and few borders, following World War II it became the cultural and economic gravitation point not only of Arab Bilad al-Sham but also of Iraq and the Arabian Peninsula. Having slowly extended its reach in the Middle East, beyond Bilad al-Sham from the 1930s, it expertly linked West-centered global economic and cultural networks to recently decolonized, still fledgling Arab countries in the following three decades.[24]

## Authorial Choices

How would this book fare if one tinkered with its scaffolding? What would happen if, for instance, its pivot were not Bilad al-Sham but a single city, or a particular post-Ottoman nation-state with its late Ottoman roots? What if one included not only cities like Beirut and Damascus but also towns or villages? And what about systematically looking from the outside into Bilad al-Sham? Various perspectives come to mind. One would be the world of Islam, including transnational religious connections; another, neighboring countries; the sea, for instance the Mediterranean and the global circuits of which it formed part; or the international system including the League of Nations. Yet other perspectives would be diaspora communities—Syro-Lebanese-Palestinian ones overseas; the Armenian one in Bilad al-Sham—or bedouin nomads of the Syrian-Arabian Desert: a space that would turn from a periphery of Greater Syria into an expanse connecting that region with Egypt, Arabia, and Iraq.

I ask these questions to make explicit that conscious choices have shaped this book. When studying how cities, regions, states, and global circuits socio-spatially constituted each other, I pay most attention to intertwinements that involve the region of Bilad al-Sham and its cities. This choice is necessary. Not enough histories of the formation of the modern world as a whole have been written from the viewpoint of non-Western places. Such a choice is useful, too. It delimits this book—a total history of all transpatialization patterns from all perspectives would be an encyclopedia, not a history—and provides a structure: This book's chapter sections study transpatialization from the viewpoint of the region and of cities. A history, say, of globalization or of state formation in Bilad al-Sham would trace links from that region to other places outside or inside the Ottoman Empire, respectively. By contrast, this book, while in each chapter outlining the extra-shami contexts of states and global circuits, focuses on them in as far as they interplayed with the region and its cities.

## Conceptual Implications for Studying the Making of the Modern World

This book has two sets of conceptual implications. One concerns its underlying argument that the socio-spatial making of the modern world is characterized by cities, regions, states, and global circuits reconstituting and transforming each other much more thoroughly and at a much faster rhythm than before in history.

What were fundamental features of that process of transpatialization? The present answer to that question addresses diachronic and synchronic features; I will circle back to, and elaborate on, this answer in the book's Conclusion.

One diachronic feature was that the structure, function, and even very meaning of cities, regions, states, and global circuits changed over time—and that they did so hand-in-hand. None of these fields—not even cities, which at first glance may appear to be an obvious unit—can be clearly delimited in space or function, as geographers have long recognized. Instances abound. Bilad al-Sham shifted from a patchwork to an umbrella region; moreover, it was both nationalized and globalized in the late nineteenth century, and from the 1930s it was increasingly framed as an integral part of the Arab world. Cities became reframed—nationalized—from 1918, and some of their hinterlands became transnationalized. Meanwhile, new nation-states were framed and functioned as multiurban spaces, and furthermore were linked up to transnational spaces.

Moreover, the rhythm of diachronic changes in structure, function, and meaning accelerated compared to the premodern period. Thus, this book is divided into two stages—Ottoman and post-Ottoman. Both stages have phases, each with its own distinct hierarchies and interactive patterns. To make matters more complex, there were two transitional phases, the 1830s–1840s and the 1920s, and the two world wars were not inert interludes but phases of their own that gave transpatialization a distinct spin.

Finally, the accelerated rhythm of diachronic changes meant that characteristics of one phase easily affected later phases. For example, Ottoman state power and European capital at work in Beirut before World War I, together with the city's intense social networks, for all matters and purposes compelled France to choose Beirut as its Mandate capital. Similarly, Bilad al-Sham's prewar integration convinced Britain and France to create a customs free zone after 1918 and to coordinate policies, although the two had just divided the region. Such a sociospatial dialectic did not equal geographical determinism, however.[25] For instance, cities and interurban axes did not rise or fall because of their absolute location but because combined urban, state, and global interests and investments in them waxed or waned, as the shifting fates of Beirut, Haifa, Damascus, Aleppo, Amman, and other cities illustrate.

Two synchronic features of transpatialization stand out. One is that relations between the urban, the regional, the state, and the global were not a zero-sum game. For instance, a more intense presence of state power in a city did not mean less city. As a matter of fact, more intensity in one field often meant more intensity in others. The result was a wide range of mutually transformative dual relationships. Some linked a city and the region, for instance, or an interurban axis and world economic forces. Others involved the nation-state. From their very birth following World War I, Bilad al-Sham's nation-states were shaped by transnationalized—formerly urban, hinterland, and regional—ties. Similarly, the urbanization of nation-states and the nationalization of cities were two sides of the same coin. Moreover, the continued impact of cities' hinterlands on nation-states had its mirror image in the transnationalization of those hinterlands that now straddled a border. And nation-states' regionalization went hand-in-hand with the transnationalization of the region, its transformation from a patchwork into an umbrella. Accordingly, Bilad al-Sham's new nation-states did not simply evolve individually but also as one single set. In the region's central periphery—the mostly rural zone composed of northern Palestine, southern Lebanon, southwestern Syria, and northwestern Transjordan—this had an ironic effect. Although each post-Ottoman national bit was peripheral and marginalized in its own national economy, the fact that these four bits formed a transnationalized transport crossroad at the center of a still firmly integrated Bilad al-Sham somewhat attenuated their peripheral position within their respective nation-state.

All this has a crucial conceptual implication. It makes little sense to explicitly or implicitly choose any one scale—say, the national—as the "ground floor," as it were, of one's historiographic imagination, below and above which are local and global (and regional and imperial) floors.[26] The same goes with choosing "the global" as one's ultimate yardstick. There is no clear hierarchy among what we may call sociospatial fields. While focusing on one has advantages (as the below discussion of Christopher Bayly and Jürgen Osterhammel shows), it has just as many drawbacks, because the implied hierarchy and order obfuscates as much as it clarifies.

A second synchronic feature of transpatialization was the wealth of triple and quadruple linkages. These embody the above statement that city, region, state, and world economy are not mutually exclusive but enmeshed; hence, change in one affects all. Examples abound. The Ottoman state propped up cities to keep world economic forces at bay—and in the process affected the structure of the region. After 1918, cities exploited and indeed highlighted and built up both old transnational and newly transnationalized linkages to strengthen their position within their new nation-state. And European empire-states helped to open up Bilad al-Sham to neighboring regions and to international circuits of governance and administrative collaboration, and in the process helped to strengthen some cities while weakening others.

These conceptual observations draw on, and bring into conversation, the work of transnational historians and of historians of urbanization, historic regions, state formation, and globalization.

Transnational historians cover a wide range of themes and geographic areas.[27] Methods differ widely, too.[28] As the coeditors Akira Iriye and Pierre-Yves Saunier of the landmark *Palgrave Dictionary of Transnational History* have stated, transnational history is about various "links and flows," about "people, ideas, products, processes and patterns that operate over, across, through, beyond, above, under, or in-between polities and societies."[29] While emphasizing variety, this definition also reflects shared ground. Indeed, the transnational perspective has been said to constitute a collective "umbrella," a shared "angle," a common "perspective."[30] A sense of harmony is prevailing. In 2010, Middell and Naumann diagnosed a "pragmatic minimum consensus," and in 2012, Philipp Gassert averred that "the most important things have probably been said."[31] This book is part of that literature. But it also differs somewhat, for its most central question is how multiple socio-spatial fields constituted each other and how we can trace these developments in various sets of human actors, rather than how this or that set of actors moved across polities.

In urbanization, a fascinating tension reigns. On the one hand, to first take the example of Europe, whatever serious administrative autonomy or even independence some cities still possessed in the early nineteenth century, was thereafter lost to modern state territorialization.[32] On the other hand, certainly from mid-century, urbanization rates eclipsed any past precedent. As Andrew Lees and Lynn Hollen Lees have noted, cities became a "'third force' in modern European society," a key linkage space between individuals and nation-states. More specifically, "the growth of cities [was] a major force behind democratization and industrialization. . . . Cities brought together energy, information, and human and financial capital in the critical mass needed for social transformation. New forms of transportation, communication, employment, family, life, governance, and leisure within Europe . . . were also closely linked to urban development. . . . Cities were the place where modernity began and where it reached its zenith."[33]

Moreover, around the world, as historians like Jürgen Osterhammel have shown, cities were key arenas in nineteenth-century globalization. The century's "second half, in particular, was a period of intense urbanization." And "although the 'modern' city of European origin spread around the world"—also by means of colonialism—"it encountered indigenous urban cultures that usually did not give way before it." True, urbanization did not happen everywhere and progressed at various paces, urban forms continued to vary, and no single factor caused urbanization. But in a more rapidly and thoroughly globalizing world, cities became ever more intensely hubs for bureaucratic action and state territoriality, economic pivots, hothouses of knowledge, and centers of sociability.[34] In sum, this book builds on a fundamental lesson: Cities cannot be properly analyzed as independent units. They operate within wider contexts and hierarchies, some regional, others global; and their relationship with their state matters greatly, too.[35] At the same time, arguments such as the Lees', about cities as links between individuals and nation-states, or such as Osterhammel's, about cities as nodes of globalization, differ somewhat from this book's focus on the intertwinement among cities and multiple other fields—regions, states, and the world economy—and are distinct from this book's interest in how not only the function but also the very meaning of cities shifted over time.

This book's choice of a region as its pivot owes much to transnational historians' studies of regions. My reticence to exactly fix the region is inspired by how historians such as Peregrine Horden and Nicholas Purcell have treated the Mediterranean and other bodies of water.[36] The malleability of the region has long been noted by local and regional historians and, crucially, by geographers.[37] Moreover, transnational historians such as Ghislaine Lydon, working on the Sahara, have a renewed interest in large sweeps of land, sometimes characterized as recentralized borderlands. East Asian historians like Sebastian Conrad and Prasenjit Duara have reopened the question of how global processes play out regionally or whether they indeed are regional.[38] Finally, since the 1990s, interest has grown in rethinking

Europe as an object of historical study. Europeanists like Arnd Bauerkämpfer are revisiting the old conceptional question of "how and whether 'European history' can be identified and analyzed as distinct objects of historical study, especially in relation to traditional national history and to newer works on global history."[39]

In the process, Europeanists have fine-tuned a concept relevant to this book: the historical meso-region, which is "a region of relative historical uniformity," insofar as that it "over a long period of time is characterised by an individual cluster of social, economic, cultural and political structures." Such regions are "larger than a single state yet smaller than a continent—Scandinavia or the Balkans being classical examples."[40] This medium size makes meso-regions suitable for writing the history of Europe, which "has to avoid two things: splintering and being monolithic. Historical meso-regions are . . . one way between Scylla and Charybdis. They are compatible with the plurality of Europe without fragmenting and dividing it to the degree that ultimately, all that remains is an unmanageable hodgepodge of individualities and particularities."[41] This also means that such regions "do not form an area defined by permanent geographic borders, but constitute an abstract space constituted by structures—a space whose historical development is distinguished from its neighborhood and other historical regions by these structures. It is a fluid zone with flowing transitions."[42] Put differently, historical meso-regions are not fixed units. They are heuristic devices. Further, a historical meso-region should not be mistaken for a mental map.[43] Rather, as noted, it is defined by a combination of structural traits; and it is this combination, rather than any one trait, that distinguishes it from neighboring regions. Such a region is fluid in space—it always shares some traits with a neighboring region. For this reason, too, historians need to be wary of reifying the region.[44] This book hopes to avoid that trap. True, it recognizes Bilad al-Sham's long history. But its interest lies in explaining why it became more integrated during late Ottoman times, how that structural change after 1918 affected embryonic nation-states and their European imperial rulers, how the region was remolded in turn, and how people understood those changes.

Regarding territoriality, there is a go-to text: Charles Maier's "Consigning the Twentieth Century to History: Alternative Narratives for the

Modern Era," published in 2000. Looking back at the twentieth century, and pondering questions of periodization, Maier concluded that "to focus on [that century] as such obscures one of the most encompassing or fundamental sociopolitical trends of modern world development, namely the emergence, ascendancy, and subsequent crisis of what is best labeled 'territoriality.'" This was the case because modern state territoriality in fact had started around the 1860s. (Its crisis came in the 1970s.) While palpable in different ways and degrees, and unfolding at different speeds, its advent was a truly "global transition." This new, modern type of state territoriality eclipsed premodern states' grasp of, and interest in, their territory. Now, states became more concerned with demarcating and protecting borders. More important, they "emphasized that national power and efficiency rested on the saturation of space inside the frontier. National space was to be charged with 'energy' throughout, like the ether. . . . Administrative energy in the form of schools, prefectures, and railroads would pervade and 'fill' the nation's space."[45]

Sharpening Maier's text was an online conversation between him and various scholars. The one set of comments most pertinent to this book came from Jean Quataert and from a group of Dutch historians and their students. Quataert noted that an "international (human) community" emerged simultaneously with modern state territoriality, and argued that "the key theme" was not the former or the latter, but their "tension." In a different though ultimately related note, the Dutch scholars wrote that they "had difficulties with how you [Maier] used globalization and interdependence as the reasons for the end of the territorial era. Globalization was already there at the end of the nineteenth century."[46]

Moreover, other historians approached the issues Maier raised from the study of globalization. They have argued that modern state territoriality partly rose in interplay with, if not in reaction to, globalization. This is a crucial basis for this book's study of how different socio-spatial fields constituted each other. Sebastian Conrad demonstrated how the late nineteenth-century German nation-state emerged not the least in response to global challenges. And Matthias Middell and Katja Naumann folded modern state transformations into the very definition of globalization. They describe the latter as a "dialectical process of de- and re-territorialization," namely "the challenges to existing borders that limit economic, socio-cultural, and political activities, and the establishment of new borders as the result of such activities."[47]

Other scholars of globalization have framed it as interplay, though not only of states and transnational movements. Take Christopher Bayly's landmark *The Birth of the Modern World, 1780–1914: Global Connections and Comparisons*. It opened with a fascinating dialectic. Globalization, defined as a surging "interdependence of political and social changes across the world," made lives around the globe more similar. But in result, people also felt an urge to emphasize what made them distinct, to the point of "antagonism," which often entailed reframing an identity or even inventing one.[48] Moreover, because this process was one and the same around the world, distinctions had to be of the same genre and were measured by one yardstick. And—a point stressed also by Osterhammel—certainly in the long nineteenth century, Europe was that yardstick, was accepted around the world as providing models to be studied. Then again, as both Osterhammel and Bayly insisted, non-Westerners did not meekly swallow those models but adapted them to their needs.[49]

The crux in all of this, for our purposes, is the conclusion Bayly drew for the historian's craft. "All local, national, or regional histories," he maintained, "must be global history, too." Globalization did not entail the emergence of a new, autonomous sphere. Hence, "rather than being an object of study," it can be "a mode of studying objects" and their linkages.[50] That approach to historical study has been formative for how this book is conceptualized. Further, if Bayly started his oeuvre with a dialectic inherent in globalization, Osterhammel concluded his own tome with a note on five "angles of vision" that "characterized . . . [the] long nineteenth century . . . from the point of view of global history." These angles were asymmetrical efficiency growth, increased mobility, asymmetrical reference density, tension between equality and hierarchy, and emancipation.[51] Like Bayly's dialectic, these are central conceptual tools for thinking about how to study globalization. This book—while concerning not only globalization, and while finding that Bayly's dictum that "all local, national, or regional histories must also be global history" could and should be turned on its head—is deeply in debt to Bayly's,

Osterhammel's, and other historians' endeavor to dig beneath specific themes and to identity underlying patterns.[52]

## Conceptual Implications for Studying the Middle East, Including the Yishuv

This book's second set of conceptual implications concerns modern Middle Eastern historiography as a whole, and the Yishuv's place in it.

This book's point that cities and regions continued to matter even after 1918 is a corrective to the dominant historiography of the modern Middle East. Here, the nation-state often circumscribes the space of inquiry. To be sure, few scholars subscribe to the nationalist rhetoric or message of that narrative, and are aware of those new nation-states' multireligious and multiclass compositions. Still, for the most part, *histories involving* post-Ottoman Palestine, Israel, Jordan, Syria, or Lebanon are *histories of* Palestine, Israel, Jordan, Syria, or Lebanon. The same goes for other countries.[53] Also, most historians of Bilad al-Sham stick to the nation-state framework regarding time. Few straddle 1918. Most monographs study either the late Ottoman or the post-Ottoman period.[54] Tellingly, nationalism is the exception.[55]

No doubt, there are several good reasons for this historiographic situation. First, regarding periodization, the replacement of Ottoman with European rule and Bilad al-Sham's resultant division truly were historic events. As for space, nation-state-centered histories of the Middle East form an integral part of a powerful global pattern that dates back to the nineteenth century. Second, although the imperially ruled post-Ottoman states were created against popular will by France and Britain, they helped mold everyday life and collective action. In the name of nationalisms, politics was made, social tensions were fought out, revolts launched, and treatises signed. Third, like elsewhere in their colonies after 1918, imperial powers faced a rising nationalist tide. "Developing a convincing national story was part of the resistance to colonialism," doubly because in the Middle East, that tide had strong pre-war roots.[56] Fourth, this condition was strengthened by the fact that Palestine / Transjordan, Syria, and Lebanon were Mandates. Although governed rather like other colonies, they had, legally speaking, been bestowed on Britain and France by the League of Nations. And the stipulation that those countries were eventually to become independent helped push the imperial powers to accept nationalism. Last, most people in those new countries had, by the 1930s, in effect accepted the principle of territorial division. But the Palestinians, Israelis, and Lebanese, and in some sense Jordanians, have continuously been challenged by one or more neighbors. This pressure, oftentimes violent physically and / or symbolically, has accentuated nation-state identities.

Still, nation-state-centered stories are only part of a complex history, as Middle East historians know. For decades, some, like Yehoshua Porath or Adib Daweesha, have studied *qawmi* (Arab-wide / pan-Arab) ideological connections and political projects, which from the 1910s through the 1940s transcended the single Arab nation-states (*awtan*; sg., *watan*).[57] More recently, a good number have framed the Mandate countries (and period) as a whole as a possible object of study, like Peter Sluglett; posited and / or examined transborder and local and urban contexts of actions within post-Ottoman countries, like Keith Watenpaugh; or explored individual careers through those lenses, like Leila Parsons.[58] The 2000s also saw an increasing interest in global contexts and connections, including studies of diasporas in books like Andrew Arsan's *Interlopers of Empire*.[59] As for scholars of late Ottoman Bilad al-Sham, they look at the region not only or so much through national lenses, but through two key developments that reshaped it from the mid-nineteenth century: Ottoman state modernization and the post-Napoleonic transformation of a loose, multicentric world economy into a much more networked and Eurocentric one. Until the 1980s, most historians saw the former as a zero-sum game between an Istanbuli center and provincial peripheries. More recently and helpfully, they have been seeing synergies. Cities are one key site of studies, for instance by Jens Hanssen, Beshara Doumani, and Stefan Weber, who have focused on the agency of urban elites, their interactions with Istanbul, and their sense of Ottomanness, amongst other themes.[60] Although interurban relations, for instance between Beirut and Damascus, and their function in late Ottoman Bilad al-Sham are understudied, they are partly addressed by studies of specific cities. Some economic historians, too, focus on specific cities and their position in the world economy, or have delivered, like Roger Owen, overviews. Others, like James Reilly, have critically deconstructed regional settings.[61]

By focusing on how late Ottoman cities and regions shaped, and were reshaped by, European-ruled nation-states after 1918—that is, by applying a focal point of late Ottoman studies to the post-Ottoman era—this book builds on the work of the aforenoted historians. However, it also goes further. It does not focus on cities or regions or states or global networks, but on their intertwinement; it traces that development through a long stretch, from the Ottoman 1830s to the post-Ottoman 1940s; and it uses Bilad al-Sham as its pivot.

A second issue concerns the Yishuv. Its historians, perhaps even more than those of Arab countries, have adopted its national time and space as the temporal and spatial framework of their studies. They have good reasons. Besides those cited above concerning Middle Eastern history in general, Zionism positioned itself vis-à-vis its Arab neighbors. It sought to prove that Jewish life in the diaspora differed fundamentally from national life in Eretz Israel. Only here could one become a pioneer and hence mend one's presumably weak diasporic body and soul: *livnot we-lehibanot* (to build and be built), as the Hebrew maxim had it. At the same time, historians of the Yishuv, like those of Arab countries, do recognize ties beyond the nation-state. Zionism's roots in European history and profound ties between diasporic Jews and Yishuvi Zionists, most of whom after all were immigrants, have always been central for interpreting Yishuvi history. Also, transnational historians have of late reframed those profound ties, reinterpreting the Yishuv as simply one of multiple linked places of Jewish nation-building; in consequence, some scholars stress the Yishuv's heterogeneity, arguing it should not be seen as a single entity, certainly not before the 1920s. And in positing a "relational history" between the Yishuv and Arab Palestine, which explains the development of each through their ties rather than only through their own internal logic, Zachary Lockman has helped to open up our understanding of how the Yishuv functioned.[62]

Although or rather precisely because this book is not a study of the Yishuv, it can build on the above historiographic advances by showing that the Yishuv formed part of a larger, regional system of interactions.

In turn, and this is the other side of the same coin, the book shows that one cannot properly understand Mandate Syria, Lebanon, or Transjordan without heeding their interrelation with Zionist nation-state building. This pattern is about much more than politics. At its root stands the fact that the Yishuv per force formed part of a regional system of interactions.[63] In consequence, there are crucial similarities in periodization. During the late Ottoman period, World War I, the 1920s, the 1930s, and World War II, life in the Yishuv and among Arabs was shaped by similar processes (which of course does not mean they were identical or that there were not singular processes at play in the Yishuv). Hence, life unfolded roughly in tandem. A case in point was the strengthening of the (not only Arab but also Jewish) Jaffa—Jerusalem axis, which paralleled the Beirut—Damascus axis, around the same time, that is in the late Ottoman period, and for the same structural reasons. More important, being part of one regional system of interactions meant not only parallel, similar, and roughly simultaneous developments, but also interrelated developments and reciprocal influence. An example was the rising economic rivalry between, and the growing if unequal mutual economic integration of, the Yishuv and Syria in the 1930s. Yishuvi Zionists saw their nation-state project as an endeavor best pursued in isolation from their Arab neighbors. Yet they were deeply enmeshed in their region, a fact of life many understood well.[64]

## The Story to Come

This book is divided into five chronological chapters. Each one is preceded by a prelude, the story of a person or group, which serves as a "historical probe" for its immediately following chapter. Moreover, each has the same three-part structure. A historical contextualization is followed by an outline of the chapter's argument, which in turn is substantiated in the chapter's core part. Relying on secondary sources and on a wealth of primary sources—archival materials, newspapers, books, and open-ended oral history interviews collected in Lebanon, Syria, Israel/Palestine, Jordan, France, Britain, Germany, the United States, and Switzerland—those core parts work by way of illustration. They present examples that reflect on key dimensions of transpatialization and on their variations. Throughout, those examples concern three broad areas—culture, the economy, and administration.[65]

Chapter 1, "Rise of an Urban Patchwork Region," covers the late Ottoman period except for World War I, which is the focus of Chapter 2, "Crucible of War." Chapter 3, "Ottoman Twilight," moves on to the transformational decade of the 1920s. Chapter 4, "Toward a Region of Nation-States," studies the 1930s. Chapter 5, "Empire Redux," zooms in on World War II. Finally, the Postscript, "The More Things Change," shows that cities and regions mattered—if in yet again changing ways—even after Syria, Lebanon, Israel, and Jordan became independent nation-states in the 1940s and after Palestinian statelessness crystallized.[66]

# Khalil Sakakini Has a Dream

[New York] Monday, 20 January 1908. I dreamed I was in Jerusalem.... [W]ith the teacher Iliyas Halabi I was walking on a wire, like
a telegraph wire, and I started asking him about Dawud and his
disease and about whether he is in danger, whether it is possible to
stop [the disease]? He answered had you noticed it from the start
[Dawud] would be completely rid of it but now I do not think that
he will be saved, he will certainly die. And when I heard that I could
not walk on the wire anymore and I said let me down, let me down.

—Khalil Sakakini (2003)

"I dreamed I was in Jerusalem." Thus start dozens of entries in the
diary of Khalil Sakakini, a Palestinian educator and intellectual born
1878 in Jerusalem, during his stay from the fall of 1907 to the summer
of 1908 in New York City and Maine. By day he works in America; he
barely makes ends meet, translating Arabic texts for a Columbia
University professor, proofreading for a local Arabic journal, sweating
in a paper mill. By night he crosses the ocean; he visits his extended
family, including his best friend, Dawud Saidawi, other friends and
neighbors. Particularly after Dawud's death in January 1908 his
longing is dark; his dreams often plummet into anxiety, horror even.
And almost without fail the place that gives his dreams their shape is
his hometown.[1]

The family house is center stage. In April 1908 Sakakini dreams that
"I entered the house and asked about my mother and was told she had
died, then I asked about my brother Ya'cub and was told he had died,
then I asked about Shafiq and was told he had died and about Na'ifa
and was told she had died, and I started to slap my face in despair,
shouting oh mother, oh brother, oh Shafiq, oh Na'ifa." Around the
house twist and turn the alleyways of Jerusalem's Old City. Soon after

hearing of Dawud's death Sakakini writes that "I was in Jerusalem, walking in the Christian Quarter, opposite our shop, . . . When I got to the steps of Dayr al-Rum, women descended in a procession ordered in rows, in the first row girls wrapped in a white shawl, but their cloths and headscarves black and their forearms bare, behind them four rows of elderly women, all of them drowning in black." Beyond the Old City stretch new neighborhoods and buildings. Shortly before Dawud's death, Sakakini dreams that

> I was walking from place to place looking for Dawud, on my way I met the teacher Ya'qub Andria, then I suddenly met [Dawud] and anxiously greeted him and he greeted back. He carried a bolero on his shoulder and wore glasses. We walked together, I asked how he was and he answered me: like shit. We walked a bit further until we reached the train station and he said: hurry before the train leaves, and started to dance as fast as lightning and jumped onto one of the roofless wagons and before I got to [it] the train moved, tearing through the land with tremendous speed and I almost succeeded in jumping on the wagon but could not and I waved at him and bode him farewell and told him wait for me at the next train.[2]

There is no way to ascertain one true interpretation of these dreams, a fact compounded by our inability to tell Sakakini's dreams from his accounts thereof. Take the last dream. At its start, is Sakakini walking through a vague dream-world-Jerusalem or is he in particular places but does not care telling? And why does he meet the teacher just before seeing Dawud? We cannot know. Besides, are not these dreams unexceptional, timeless even, and hence useless to the historian?

Not quite. Sakakini's dream accounts are part of diary entries; in return, these form part of a larger range of texts like letters; hence they have contexts and in this sense are open to interpretation. Many letters are for Sultana—a neighbor's daughter, beautiful, and an educator and Greek Orthodox like him—with whom Sakakini fell madly in love the summer of his departure. They are always emotive and often come with more than one tear. (Sultana is more down-to-earth: "What's this,

Khalil?! Do not make crying all-consuming business!"[3]) And in these letters as in Sakakini's dreams, Jerusalem is the arena. At its center is, again, the family's house. In the last letter that Sakakini gives Sultana before leaving, he implores her "remember me when you visit the house, stand in your window that overlooks our house and say 'peace be upon you, oh Khalil.'" And beyond the house extend, again, the city and its environs. Sakakini asks Sultana "to visit as often as you can our beloved rock" in the Shaikh Jarrah neighborhood, and recalls the day "we . . . with my sister Milia walked on the road of the Mount of Olives and I felt like gaily striding on the peak of my happiness."[4]

Was the geography of Jerusalem that of Sakakini's longing, then? Put awkwardly, was "the local" all that mattered to the emotions of somebody who crossed an ocean and "went global," as it were? Yes and no. "The local" was key to Sakakini's emotions; it grounded them. But just like the "real" Jerusalem of bricks and stones started spilling beyond its old walls by the mid-nineteenth century, the Jerusalem of Sakakini's dreams and love was not walled in. It was not simply local. And the way it was not simply local was neither indistinguishably commonplace nor sakakinesquely idiosyncratic, but specific enough to tell us a thing or two about the time and place the writer lived in.

By the mid-nineteenth century Ottoman Jerusalem started interacting with the world in ways both new and transformative. (Outside worlds had of course been present in this city holy to Jews, Christians, and Muslims for millennia.) While the center of the Ottoman Empire—Istanbul—was not very present in its provinces from the late 1600s, from the mid-nineteenth century a new era of state formation bound center and provinces closer together. European powers, too, became more active. Interacting with these changes, Jerusalem's ties with its rural surroundings grew stronger. All these changes found reflection in Sakakini's Jerusalem, including that of his dreams. He may have dreamed of Dawud racing away on a train not simply because he was afraid to lose him but because Dawud—his very best friend—had moved from Jerusalem to Jaffa. From here, a French company had built a railway to Jerusalem in 1892. And it was here that Sakakini met Dawud for the last time, as it was in this port city that he commenced his maritime journey to America. Another dream, where he met the Empress of Germany as she was visiting Jerusalem, processed an event that actually happened in 1898. And he dreamed also of native Jerusalemite Ottoman officers. (And back in Jerusalem, he would proudly call a school he established *Madrasa Dusturiyya Wataniyya,* Constitutional National School.)[5]

The Jerusalem of Sakakini's dreams and love was "not simply local" in another sense, too. It was one of countless hometowns for which migrants longed during an era of unprecedented world-encompassing migration. Between 1860 and 1914 about 600,000 people emigrated from Bilad al-Sham to the Americas, a movement so massive that it inspired the Lebanese saying that "Would there be a road to the moon you would see a Lebanese ascending it." Sakakini did not quite go that far. But after his dream about Dawud moving away on a train that "tears through the land with tremendous speed," he dreamed about "my father and mother and I sometimes saw us in New York and sometimes in Jerusalem," moving back and forth and back and forth again. In fact, more than ever before in human history, myriad "locals"' were on the move. On board of the ship that took Sakakini from Marseille, where he had changed ship, to New York, a young Damascene woman who saw him shed tears over Sultana's picture sighed: "if you are crying, what shall I do, having left my betrothed behind me?"[6]

So much movement affected how one viewed oneself and was viewed. Take Sakakini and the woman he met en route to New York. In busy Marseille—a European migration hub—French bureaucrats (and the Ottoman consul) would have seen them not chiefly as a Jerusalemite and Damascene but as Ottoman citizens, and businessmen would have approached them as "Syrians." When in 1899 the Marseille-based merchant Melhem Elias advertised his *Hotel du Syrie* [sic] in the Beiruti newspaper *Lisan al-Hal,* he addressed "our Syrian brothers who are travelling to Europe and what is behind it [the Americas] and returning."[7] What's more, across the ocean Americans, too, talked about "Syrian" immigrants. Indeed, during crises American Syrians closed ranks. When the news of the *Titanic* catastrophe hit New York, community papers that loved to hate each other served as a collective clearing house for information about loved ones missed and found. Sakakini himself worked in New York for some time for a Syrian journal, *al-Jam'iyya*; ate meager meals in Syrian (and Greek) restaurants; and wrote about Syrians he met.[8]

But he was not in love with them.

> The Syrians in this country are in general a disgusting crowd—both morally and in their mannerisms [even though] they tend to show a great deal of respect towards me. Recently I have been attending some of their social get-togethers. I took my violin and played some Arabic tunes, and they went crazy [with delight]. What a miserable lot! What if Miss Mannana [Dawud's sister] shows up here? I will not be exaggerating if I tell you that even among the Americans you will not find a woman of her education and sophistication.[9]

Sakakini's snobbish remark was about place—he "missed his intellectual circle in Jerusalem." But he did not wait for his return to Jerusalem to be with Jerusalemites. In New York, too, much of his social life revolved around them. The apartment he rented in Brooklyn? Arranged by Jerusalemites. His friends? From Jerusalem. As a matter of fact, at the time such a close connection to people from one's home city, town and even village was the rule for migrants from Bilad al-Sham. Khalil Totah for instance, who in 1906 emigrated from Ramallah, a small town north of Jerusalem, to New York, stayed at Ramallah acquaintances on the way, in Alexandria, and in New York he often socialized with Ramallahis. Indeed, even the term "Syria" in the aforementioned ad by merchant Elias was at second look a composite. When referring to migrants "returning" from overseas, Elias talked of the *awtan* (places of birth, homelands; sg., *watan*) to which they were heading rather than of one *watan*.[10]

Sakakini's dream accounts and the larger tale of his migration can—predictably—be taken to illustrate how the global and local reshaped each other in the transformative nineteenth century. Within this changing situation, the local remained crucial to people. Jerusalem was the place and from here were the people Sakakini knew best and trusted most; this was the heart of his identity, the stuff of his dreams; this was home. Moreover, the local was becoming intertwined not only with the global. There was an imperial Ottoman aspect in Sakakini's story; an interurban link between Jerusalem and Jaffa made an appearance; and a region, Bilad al-Sham, mattered, too. How did these developments come to pass? And why did the meaning of various socio-spatial fields, and the way they interlocked, shift in the nineteenth century? These questions inform Chapter 1.

# 1

# RISE OF AN URBAN PATCHWORK REGION

### 1830s–1914

## Historical Context: The Premodern Period, Modern State Territoriality, and the Modern World Economy

For more than a century and a half after conquering Bilad al-Sham in 1516 / 1517, Ottoman Istanbul governed the region, its provinces and cities directly. Then, by the later seventeenth century, "political power emanating from the capital weakened . . . as local actors began to claim the right to serve the sultan in place of his own handpicked men." Cities became more self-governing, part of a trend palpable across the empire. On the coast, Sidon had a mamluk household, and Acre saw the rise of a quasi-autonomous governor, Ahmad al-Jazzar Pasha, from 1775 to 1804. In the interior, small Nablus and Jerusalem had a merchant and a composite notable (a'yan) elite, respectively. And Bilad al-Sham's two biggest cities, the international trade hubs Aleppo and Damascus, each had its notable elite. It was composed of families that possessed different if overlapping—economic, military, and cultural-religious— types of capital, but that were united in their sociopolitical role as the intermediary between the city's populace and Istanbul. Even in Aleppo, where Istanbul tried hardest not to lose its grip, "central control did weaken somewhat after 1760." Moreover, even here, where the elite had used to be welcoming to rich newcomers, from 1770 there was "a remarkable continuity among the families who already belonged to the upper class."[1]

By the late eighteenth century, Istanbul began to reform the state. This happened initially in the capital, and with some false starts. The first real milestone came in 1826, with the abolishment of the old, Janissary army. Reforms continued until World War I. Unfolding as they did over almost a century, their pace varied, as did their implementation in different parts of the empire. Still, with time they grew more pervasive. From the late eighteenth century to 1908 the Ottoman bureaucracy ballooned from 2,000 to 35,000 officials, and the army quintupled from 24,000 to 120,000 soldiers between 1837 and the 1880s. Throughout the century the state accumulated "infrastructural power," often through new transport and communication technologies such as the railway and the telegraph. Especially during the 1839–1876 *tanzimat* (reorganization) era, it passed a raft of societal and legal reforms, including decrees establishing basic equality between its hitherto legally privileged Muslim subjects, and Christians and Jews. From the 1860s, it "execut[ed] a comprehensive catalogues of measures, extend[ed] state power into basically autarkic regions, [and] unifi[ed] state policy towards all peripheries." In the later nineteenth century, it also tightened the military draft and strengthened its involvement in education. By 1900, the "central state exerted more power over its subjects and competing power clusters than ever before in Ottoman history." Modern Ottoman state territoriality was taking shape—one of two modern macrohistorical changes shaping the Ottoman Empire, including Bilad al-Sham.[2]

This process was a "defensive developmentalist" response to external threats. In the eighteenth century the Ottoman Empire's northern neighbors, Russia and Austria-Hungary, started nibbling at its European possessions. Then in the nineteenth century Europe's strongest empires, Britain and France, started posing a challenge, expanding aggressively around the globe; and indigenous nationalist movements developed in the Ottoman Empire's mainly Christian Balkan provinces, each supported by at least one European power. The Ottoman response to those threats was in some fateful ways a failure. Most painfully, by 1912 / 1913 Istanbul had lost all its wealthy southeast European provinces except for a sliver of land to its northwest, as well as all its

North African provinces: the former to Russia, Austria-Hungary, and independence movements; the latter to France, Italy, and Britain. Moreover, the Ottoman Empire, like many other nineteenth-century defensive developmentalist states, was stuck in a vicious circle. Its agrarian tax base was weaker than industrializing Europe's; hence, its revenues were insufficient to effectively defend itself; hence, from the 1850s it had to obtain European loans; on these loans, it eventually defaulted. In return, this allowed European companies backed by their governments in 1881 to impose on Istanbul the so-called Ottoman Public Debt Council, which took control of a quarter of Istanbul's fiscal revenues.[3]

Istanbul also had two signature successes, however. The just noted restrictions aside, it remained a sovereign polity, keeping its Asian territories, and its growing bureaucratic and infrastructural power helped transform society.[4] True, in Bilad al-Sham it was Egypt's quasi-independent, centralizing ruler Mehmed 'Ali Pasha (r. 1805/11–1849) who made a first stab at reforms that would implement modern state territoriality. His son Ibrahim Pasha occupied the region in 1831 and, among other measures, in 1832 united its four provinces—Aleppo, Damascus, Tripoli, and Sidon—into one Bilad al-Sham-wide province with Beirut as capital. Moreover, there was some popular resistance, which continued after Istanbul in 1840/41 drove Egypt out of Bilad al-Sham with Franco-British aid. That resistance formed part of a global transition that, in different parts of the world, started as early as the 1770s and continued to as late as the 1840s—what Jürgen Osterhammel has called a "saddle period" between the early modern and the modern world.[5]

By the 1850s, the Ottoman exercise of modern state territoriality in Bilad al-Sham began in earnest. Istanbul reestablished the old provinces and then, at various points between 1854 and 1888, rearranged them for political and economic reasons into six units. Beirut, Aleppo, and Damascus (from 1864 called Suriya) each was a regular province, *eyalet* in Turkish, *wilaya* in Arabic; and Mount Lebanon, Jerusalem, and Deir al-Zor each was a *mutasarrifiyya,* an autonomous district directly linked to Istanbul (see Map 1).[6] More crucially, Istanbul started to implement, also in Bilad al-Sham, state-building measures. It did so while knitting more complex ties to locals first in cities and the rural countryside, and from the 1860s also in less accessible and/or strongly bedouin areas.[7]

Exercising territoriality was not a zero-sum game. The center's "gain" was not the provinces' "loss." Rather, political-administrative patterns changed and intensified, becoming more interactive and denser. This was a two-pronged development. As Istanbul was penetrating its provinces more forcefully, and with more institutions, it also had to engage— with carrots as much as sticks—the deeply rooted urban notable elites. In the process, some families rose and others dropped out of their respective city's composite notable elite. And each city's elite became administratively and socioculturally more strongly intertwined with Istanbul, which many more than ever got to know first-hand. "The Ottoman state [and] . . . local elites" were tightly joined as "unequal parties to self-serving bargains."[8]

Before the Ottoman Empire started exercising modern state territoriality in Bilad al-Sham, another macrohistorical change started to take root. The region became incorporated into a now Eurocentric (rather than, as previously, multicentric) global world economy. To appreciate this development, we first need to take a glance back. Already in the eighteenth century Europeans, mainly France, started to somewhat improve their trade position vis-à-vis the Ottoman Empire as a whole. But the Ottomans were not unduly worried, all the more because Asia remained the principal Ottoman trading destination. Also, several Ottoman cities and their rural hinterlands cashed in on Europe's hunger for raw materials and food with the onset of industrialization in the late eighteenth century. In Bilad al-Sham it was the port city of Acre and the cotton and grain producing Galilee under al-Jazzar Pasha that profited most. The prices of Ottoman exports remained constant even during the Napoleonic Wars and Europe's subsequent economic contraction until the early 1840s. In short, Ottoman economic interaction with Europe grew, but production did not become exclusively agricultural and trade with non-European partners remained crucial.[9]

This changed substantively when a flourishing Eurocentric global capitalist market started incorporating the Ottoman Empire, a process that in Bilad al-Sham gathered pace circa 1840.[10] At its root, capitalist globalization was made possible by London's success in replacing the truly anarchic, war-prone European state system of 1648–1815 with a more stable concert of powers. Peace in Europe facilitated an aggressive,

Eurocentric global economy. Although Britain's empire was untidy and sprawling, its capitalist drive served enough powerful European interests for London to be its ultimate center and policeman during the nineteenth century.[11]

Throughout that time the Ottoman Empire preserved its independence. This mattered economically. European capitalist penetration involved next to no direct investments in artisanal or industrial production and—unlike in many colonies—only few investments in agriculture. Rather, it focused even more than in colonies on trade, including faster, mechanized shipping. After mid-century, loans to governments and investments in transport—in the ports of some big littoral cities, and in roads and railways from there into the interior—joined the mix: a timing typical for the world economy as a whole. Besides, in the Ottoman Empire as elsewhere, Britain replaced post-Napoleonic France as the leading European economic partner.[12]

Britain leveraged its political support of Istanbul from 1831 to 1840 against the Egyptian occupiers of Greater Syria. In 1838 Istanbul signed the Balta Liman trade treaty with Britain. Illustrating the "empire of free trade" approach then spearheaded by Britain, this treaty set import duties at 12 percent and export duties at 5 percent, and outlawed protectionism. Similar agreements with the United States and other European states followed rapidly. Around 1850 "the Ottoman Empire [was] Britain's second-largest export-market," with the "value of the exchanges between Britain and the Ottoman Empire . . . increas[ing] about sixfold" from the 1840s to the 1870s. By that time the empire was firmly part of the global capitalist market. It contributed mainly cash crops like cotton and silk, and grains, as well as other raw materials like yellow berries, for textile dyes, and opium, and from the late 1800s also tobacco and food stuffs like raisins and figs. In return, it imported finished products, firstly textiles. Economic incorporation into the Eurocentric world economy hit home when the prices of exported raw materials dropped during the global recession, from 1873 to 1896. It is not surprising then, that they rose with the recovery from 1896 to 1913.[13]

World economic incorporation affected socioeconomic relations within cities, beyond them, and between them. From the 1860s peasants came under increased pressure by urban merchants and notables, and even before journeymen had to start accepting lower wages. Also, the traditional Eurasian transit trade of Greater Syria's interior commercial hubs was bypassed by the steamship. Thus, Aleppo's international trade started sagging in the late 1700s, its ties with Mesopotamia by the 1830s. Matters grew worse when in 1869 Egypt opened a new world trade maritime shortcut, the Suez Canal.

But such substantive economic changes did not equal even or total change. First, while interior cities suffered, some cities on the littoral flourished. Most important, Beirut surged from a town of 10,000 in the 1840s to a city of 150,000 by World War I. A world trade port city, it became Greater Syria's economic gravitation point. Second, the European commerce of Beirut—and of two other littoral cities, Haifa and Jaffa, that started to rise a bit later than Beirut, in the late nineteenth century—was handled not by Western traders but in the main by Arabs, mostly Christians who from 1860 formed the city's majority. While some of the latter enjoyed Western consular protection, and while they were part of far-flung trade networks, sometimes with family members, Beirut remained Ottoman, a fact reinforced by Istanbul giving Beirut its own province in 1888. (See Map 1.) Third, while the interior cities of Aleppo, Damascus, and a third trading and production hub, Nablus, were hit, they—like the Ottoman Empire as a whole—did not simply become a periphery or semi-periphery of a supposedly clear European world economic core. Rather, Aleppo and Damascus managed to preserve bits of their long-distance Eurasian overland trade. Also, by the late nineteenth century they and Nablus had learned to maximize trade within their rural hinterland, to energize some transurban trade, and to keep and retool parts of their artisanal production to that commerce.[14]

Their success was not the least due to help from Istanbul, that is to the fact that the Ottoman Empire, while under severe political and economic pressure from Europe, remained sovereign. True, soon after Istanbul adopted a noninterventionist, liberal economic approach in the late 1830s, "the consequences . . . turned out to be [most] significant in terms of the effective limits they placed on the ability of the Ottoman state to supervise and benefit from this trade." But Ottoman opinions changed accordingly. The first countermeasures came in the early 1860s. Then, at the end of the following decade, a new protectionist generation of Ottoman economic writers battled liberals. And the autocratic sultan Abdul Hamid II (r. 1878–1909) abandoned *tanzimat* political reforms for a focus on economic development and made large-scale preemptive purchases of land especially in his Asian provinces, to stem deepening Western economic influences. This overall objective failed: the Ottoman trade deficit with Europe, having disappeared during a worldwide depression in 1873–1896, ballooned again thereafter; and the Ottoman Public Debt Council continued curtailing Istanbul's fiscal and budgetary sovereignty. Still, certain protective economic measures, also in Bilad al-Sham, helped cities to find and defend a niche in the Eurocentric world economy.[15]

## The Story to Come

The drawn-out intertwinement between the Eurocentric world economy and the territorially intrusive modern Ottoman state, and Bilad al-Sham and its cities: that intertwinement formed the first stage of modern transpatialization.

It had three linked socio-spatial manifestations. First, while those state and global economic transformations were powerful, the cities held up. They dealt with the global economic change of their age by penetrating their hinterlands more aggressively and by strengthening links with other cities. Also, because they were very well rooted, they and their interurban links succeeded to channel global economic and state forces. In Bilad al-Sham, cities became the centers from which the modern Ottoman state penetrated its territory more forcefully than before; the places where Istanbul's agents and urban notable elites met and meshed; and the hothouses for the growth of new collective identities, the most important of which were, politically, Ottoman nationalism, and culturally, Arabism. In sum, transformed by the changes of the nineteenth century as well as transformative, Bilad al-Sham's cities with their hinterlands were the place—as Sakakini's story in Prelude 1 shows—where people lived the modern age, and *the* place from and through which people were connected more tightly to various transnational worlds.[16]

Second, interurban ties thickened considerably. However, they did not form an evenly networked whole. Rather, Bilad al-Sham became a patchwork region of cities and interurban ties. The region's areas were unequally connected, and while one area's economic, political, and cultural actors often traveled to other areas and in a few cases even opened a branch, with few exceptions no business or party and no newspaper built a unified, multibranch, region-wide network. Even the newly soaring littoral city of Beirut could not unify and dominate the Bilad al-Sham patchwork. It was a newcomer—it had been tiny for centuries—and it was not sovereign. That two mountain ranges separated it from the interior did not help either. Perhaps most crucially, other cities were too well rooted to be dominated.[17]

Third, as Bilad al-Sham was interacting with the powerful economic and political changes of its age, it became closer knit. "An interconnected [Bilad al-Sham-wide] market . . . was developing." Within it, Beirut, although not hegemonic, outshone the formerly dominant interior cities of Damascus and Aleppo. It became the region's gravitation point: a melting pot of local initiative and money, of European capital, of Ottoman imperial interests, and by the late nineteenth century even of French imperialist stakes. Moreover, from mid-century the new scent of a region-wide identity was in the air. People—first Christians, soon also Muslims—started using the European term Suriya in addition to Bilad al-Sham, and writers assigned Bilad al-Sham a national meaning while also making broader cross-references reflective of tightening globalization.[18] Last but not least, some Ottoman imperial and Western economic actions had regional knock-on effects. Ottoman and missionary schools pulled together students from around the region; the surging Ottoman bureaucracy pushed men into careers that crisscrossed the region; and Western- and Ottoman-financed roads and railways, while principally connecting cities into interurban axes, together were starting to form a broader network. (See Map 2.)

## The Nationalization and Globalization of the
## Concept of Bilad al-Sham

From the mid-nineteenth century, Arabism started to take form as a cultural national identity.[19] While this process involved various places—emigrés especially in the Americas and Europe had a hand in it; some advocates had strong ties to or lived in Egypt—both its intellectual center and its reference point was Bilad al-Sham, or Suriya, an originally European term that now came into use among Christians but also Muslims.[20] Here, Arabism had two epicenters, where it assumed somewhat different meanings. One was Beirut. Some of its Christians—the majority in this city, but well aware of living in a mainly Muslim empire and of being linked to Bilad al-Sham's mainly Muslim interior—posited the cultural unity of Arabs, independent of creed, in that region. To them, such a territorial, supra-confessional identity was "essential for tranquility in the region and for the creation of common interests between [Christians] and the Muslims." Some also believed that Beirut and its adjacent Christian-majority Mount Lebanon could guide Suriya, and/or that they, like other areas in- and outside the Ottoman Empire, should become more autonomous as part of a proposed Ottoman federalization.[21] Arabism's second epicenter was Damascus. Here, it took root in popular strata, while its main carrier was some of those Muslim urban notables whose position had—unlike that of other notables—declined with Istanbul's extension of modern state territoriality. And here, though also in Beirut, some demanded a greater political role for Arabs within the Ottoman Empire. They did so in reaction to a partly real, partly perceived rise of Turkish nationalism from the very late nineteenth century but chiefly from the 1908 Young Turk revolution, an army-led uprising against sultan Abdul Hamid II's autocratic rule that ushered in a parliament in Istanbul. But they were not separatists. Until World War I, almost all Ottoman Arabs remained loyal to Istanbul or at least acquiesced in its rule.[22]

The most influential early intellectual entrepreneur of Arabism in Bilad al-Sham was Beirut-based Butrus al-Bustani (1819–1883), an independent-minded Maronite convert to Protestantism. As a writer, Bustani was most famous for his modern Arabic dictionary published in 1870, *Muhit al-Muhit,* and for editing the first Arabic encyclopedia, *Da'irat al-Ma'arif,* in 1876. These were two pillars of the so-called *nahda:* an Arab cultural and linguistic renewal, a veritable "Arab project of Enlightenment" indeed, which from the mid-nineteenth to the early twentieth century was driven by intellectuals in Arab cities—most important Cairo, but also Beirut, Damascus, and others—and in diaspora communities in Europea and the Americas.[23] Already in 1860–1861, Bustani also made the first public call to all Syrians, Suriyyun, to set aside their religious differences. He did so in *Nafir Suriya, The Trumpet of Syria,* a series of eleven leaflets that he anonymously distributed in Beirut during a bout of intercommunal warfare in Mount Lebanon and Damascus. Especially to Christians, that event drove home the need for a supra-religious, culturally territorially defined identity within the bounds, still, of the Ottoman Empire.[24]

*The Trumpet of Syria* made a twin move that was momentous doubly because it would catch on among Bilad al-Sham's interior as well as coastal Syrian Arabists.[25] First, it nationalized the geographical term Suriya. Its core concept was *watan:* homeland. Bustani called his leaflets *wataniyyat;* started each with "Ya abna' al-watan" (Oh sons of the homeland); and signed each with "Min muhibb li-l-watan" (From a lover of the homeland). The violence of their days was written all over them. The first opened by deploring the "horrors and atrocities that our villains have committed this year"; the fourth, distributed in the fall of 1860, warned of the imminent winter: "The ant tribes have already finished collecting [their] winter supplies . . . [but] as for . . . our brother, a human being and son[s] of our homeland, they barely make it to this evening. . . . [For] these of our miserable brothers 'time is life,' because each day the homeland claims the life of many of its sons." The experience of violence was built into the very core of the *wataniyyat,* too. Although all creeds ought to enjoy "the freedom of consciousness in matters of religion," their tensions need to be curbed, Bustani cried. "Of the rights that the homeland [owes] its sons is the security of their highest rights: those to their life, honor and possessions." Bustani's national unity was a remedy to the pernicious effects of politicized communal differences.[26]

Second, *The Trumpet of Syria* addressed Syria's geographical heterogeneities, indeed embraced them. Syria "is our homeland despite the difference(s) between her plains and rough areas, coasts and mountains," Bustani ruled about the region's physical geography. More than that—he incorporated those differences into his very definition of the *watan*'s make-up. "The homeland resembles an uninterrupted chain with multiple links: one end is our house or birthplace and those who are in it, and the other our country and those in it."[27] This view also appeared in Bustani's other writings. His dictionary noted that "watan is the house of residence of man and his (fixed) abode whether he was born in it or not," adding that "in modern times, love of the homeland is [an article] of faith." In his magnum opus, the encyclopedia, the evidence is not quite conclusive, because its last volume reached the letter *'ayn,* which precedes *watan*'s *waw,* and because Bustani died while preparing volume seven, which is why Suriya, in volume ten, was written by three of his sons. Certain, though, is that while Syria mattered—it boasted a twenty-six-pages long entry—other things did, too. During Bustani's editorship, he covered all continents and many cities of Bilad al-Sham. Indeed, to him the latter formed a human type of geographical heterogeneity, alongside the afore-noted physical geographical heterogeneity. Aleppo (*Halab*), Hama, Homs and Haifa appeared in volume seven; Damascus in volume eight, perhaps still written by him; and he for certain signed off on Beirut, in volume five. He loved these cities deeply, dedicating ten pages each to Beirut and to Aleppo and a whopping twenty-nine pages to Damascus.[28]

Bustani's double move, nationalizing the geographical notion of Suriya / Bilad al-Sham while recognizing the region's heterogeneities, caught on. Moreover, beside the physical and urban geographic heterogeneities, a third was picked out. From the late nineteenth century, some authors described Bilad al-Sham as containing two parts: in the south, Filastin (Palestine); in the north, Suriya.[29] Most insistent were authors who focused on the latter, including Lebanon and its presumably national Phoenician forefathers, who were seen as Syria's savvy spearhead. In 1912 Khairallah Tannous Khairallah, then a journalist for the French daily *Le Temps,* opined that while Palestine geographically belongs to Syria, its society is distinct, read inferior. "Israel has [always] seen an enemy in every foreigner while the subtle Phoenician, a world citizen, mixed with all people." Other authors, while not passing such judgment, made Khairallah's geographical distinction, too.[30]

In doing so, most talked inconsistently about the relationship between Filastin, Suriya, and Bilad al-Sham. This was not out of sloppiness, but because they were writing at a time when those very terms were in the midst of change, being suffused with new national meanings. Iqlimis Yusuf Dawud, the Damascus Metropolitan of the East Syrian church, in a historical-linguistic treatise sometimes called Suriya a part (like Filastin, but separate) of Bilad al-Sham; sometimes used Suriya and Bilad al-Sham interchangeably; and sometimes was ambiguous whether Filastin was included or excluded: "we use the term al-Sham . . . like the Arabs did, i.e. the large bit of Asia that the ancient Romans called Syria, stretching from the Euphrates in the east to the Mediterranean in the west." In a voluminous book titled *Ta'rikh Suriya* (*Syria's History*), Tripolitan educator Jurji Yanni called Filastin (like Lebanon) a part of Suriya, but also stated that Suriya has "two [administrative] parts, the Province Suriya . . . and the Province of Aleppo . . . [while] Jerusalem is a mutasarrifiyya." And Henri Lammens—a Belgian native and *the* professor of Syrian geography and history at Beirut's Jesuit Université de Saint Joseph (USJ) in 1886–1937, who shaped contemporaries as a teacher and a writer of both French and flawless Arabic—included Filastin *within* Bilad al-Sham, yet occasionally also talked about "al-Sham *and* Filastin."[31]

The treatment of cities and of physical geography, too, reflected that authors wrote during a time of transition. Regarding cities, a telling example is Yanni's *Ta'rikh Suriya*. Its introduction and first two parts— "Syria's situation," a sketch of Syria's location and an account of the Phoenicians as Syria's oldest and savviest inhabitants, and an "Overview of Syria's history" from the Chaldeans to the Ottomans—imbued Syria with national flavor and historical subjectivity. They framed Syria as a distinct arena with a distinct history, peopled it with a distinct people, the Phoenicians, who like their descendants were Syria's very own, and implicitly placed that people alongside other people (*umam;* sg., *umma*). But then, in part 3, Yanni created a second narrative, parallel to the one above. A "History of Syria's most famous cities," whose 230 pages equaled the "Overview of Syria's history," imbued cities with as much importance as the region. Yanni reinforced that point by dedicating the first part's opening section, "The geography of Ancient Syria," mostly to cities. This urban focus, echoing Bustani's, reflected cities' entrenched historical weight and their persistent grip on people's imagination of Bilad al-Sham / Suriya even as the region was being reframed as a national *watan*.[32]

The treatment of Suriya's physical geographical units reflected times a-changing, too—but in yet another way. Whereas Bustani and Yanni saw no problem in geographical heterogeneity, later authors did. To Khairallah, Syria's "physical setup has profoundly influenced its political destiny": "barriers" created "rival and often inimical statelets."[33] In this, he and others drew on Lammens. In a number of lessons serialized in USJ's well-known Arabic language journal *Mashriq*, Lammens stated that "nature has divided Syria into five or six different areas." Mountains "cross the country, keeping its factions from mingling and its elements from uniting." Worse, those mountains run its entire length, and the fact that Suriya is eight times as long as it is broad "hinder[s] communication and unity between the country's parts."[34] This view also signaled another change from Bustani: geographical determinism.[35] It was not value neutral. Rather, Lammens sorted nature into bad and good elements. The former were those instigating divisions in Syria. They were "disadvantages," "exaggerated," "vices" even, and constituted "geographical accidents." By contrast, elements producing unity were created by Providence and God, and "did good." This issue was related to a last change. Lammens and some of his contemporaries did not see Suriya's physical geographical units and cities as *awtan* (sg., *watan*) parallel to the region. They recognized only one *watan*: Syria. All other elements, as powerful as they may be, could by definition not be a *watan*. They had to be subsumed under Suriya.[36]

But truly subsumed, they were not. Indeed, Lammens's writings teemed with contradictions. On the one hand, he argued that Syria "possesses an invaluable benefice, that of territorial unity [and] clearly defined borders" vis-à-vis neighboring Anatolia, Mesopotamia, Arabia, and Egypt.[37] As crucial, the region was fortunate to be where Africa, Europe, and Asia overlap. This made it, most exaltedly, perhaps the place of "Paradise," and certainly an outstanding "crossroad of trade routes," the birthplace of monotheistic religions, and "the cradle of humanity." Lammens also described the Syrians as a distinct people. They were the original "carriers of ancient civilization" in human history and "the propagators of religion"; their ethos was crystallized in the Phoenicians; and their land was "the cradle of the Semites."[38] In fact, Lammens in his Arabic texts and more clearly in French argued for "a remarkably uniform race, a truly national type" in Syria. Even today Syrians look different from their neighbors, he claimed. Even Syria's many religions "could not modify the fixity of the race," and invaders "were absorbed by the locals" because of the latter's "vitality"—a fact manifest "principally vis-à-vis the Arabs" who differ from Syrians and for whose Islam Lammens had little respect.[39]

On the other hand—and herein lies the contradiction—Lammens stated that "if you consider the history of Syria, you find that region divided into separate provinces that are inhabited by segregated groups." A point in case was a counterexample, the Umayyad dynasty that governed the Muslim world from Damascus in 661–750, that is Lammens's interpretation of the Umayyads' long-term relevance. They—Syrian rather than Arab to him—proved that Syrians could be unified: a "lesson [that] was not lost" on Syrians. But there was a catch. Lammens acknowledged that "centuries passed before [that lesson] trickled into popular conscience." To be precise, more than 1,000 years: until the nineteenth century, which in reality simply shows that in Bilad al-Sham as elsewhere around the world, a nation in the modern sense of the word did not exist in the premodern past. Creating one required jumps of imagination, leapfrogging many centuries, bracketing them as pauses in a presumably uniform national history.[40]

To be fair, in making those jumps, Lammens and his contemporaries were in good company. Around the world, spaces were being reframed as national. Authors in Bilad al-Sham knew this, and wrote accordingly. Indeed, Bilad al-Sham / Suriya's nationalization was simultaneously its globalization. Sometimes, this twin process was implicit. In a book by the editor of the *nahdawi* journal *al-Muqattam*, Shahin Makaryus, a section titled "Syria's situation and boundaries" provided the region's coordinates. Never mind that "between 30' 34° and 30' 37° East and 10' 31° and 30' 43° North" was incorrect. What matters to us is that it mattered to Makaryus to show where Syria was situated on the map not simply of Islam or Christianity or the Ottoman Empire, but of the world. Lammens, too, put Suriya's nationalization in a global context. For one, he drew on the Frenchman Élisée Reclus's *La nouvelle géographie universelle: les terres et les hommes* [*A New Physical Geography*]. This work differed from earlier world geographies. It was up-to-date in its details and monumental, nineteen tomes long; it was based not only on personal travels in the Americas, Egypt, and Western Anatolia (the fourteenth-century Arab historian Ibn Khaldun, say, traveled widely too) but also on a "vast network of informants" around the world; and Reclus sought to reconstruct a unified "life of the globe."[41] More crucially and explicitly, Lammens compared Syria to contemporary polities around the world. Although separate from its neighbors, it was "unlike England not isolated from others [but] rather [like] open harbors to who demands [to come to] it." And unlike China, which was hunkered down "behind a wall," it did not suffer from "confusion and languor." On a different note, its long shape resembled Italy, which was struggling to transcend political divisions but whose relative success in 1870 may have suggested to Lammens that Syria might do the same. This was the case doubly because Lammens likened mountainous Syria also to Anatolia, which he may have seen, racially, as the Ottoman heartland, and to Switzerland, which succeeded to create a modern federal state in the nineteenth century.[42]

In sum, from mid-century and more intensely from the late nineteenth century, some intellectuals reframed Bilad al-Sham / Suriya. It ceased to simply be a cultural-historical region among others within the world of Islam, and was declared a national space alongside, and comparable to, other national spaces around the world. Still, writers conceded that it was complex and internally divided, and recognized if not extolled its cities' weight. Also, next to none demanded independence from Istanbul. Bilad al-Sham ultimately remained a "super-identity."[43]

## Change and Continuity in Bilad al-Sham's Cities:
## A First Approximation

Why did cities situated below that super-identity stay relevant? What follows is a first approximation to this question, focusing on three aspects: pride of place and its material underpinnings, sociability, and politics.

The lead case will be Sidon, "an ancient city [whose] beautiful memory is everlasting" but now is "wretched compared to the developed cities" according to one of its leading intellectuals, Ahmad 'Arif al-Zain (1884–1960), a Shiite who, born in the adjacent Jabal Amil, had moved to Sidon in his youth. Beirut had eclipsed this time-honored provincial capital economically and, adding insult to injury, swallowed it administratively. Still, its native al-Zain waxed lyrical about "its outstanding beauty and its wonderful grace . . . I invited one of my friends to make an outing," he wrote in 1909, and "the gentle breeze of the eastern wind (al-saba) blew around us with its tender scents and carried the aroma of the lemon tree blossoms." Al-Zain even used non-Saidawis (Sidonites) for validation. "Since ancient times Sidon has been famous for the many crops and delicious fruits of its lands," he proudly quoted an outsider.[44]

Al-Zain was not an exception. Others, too, praised the beauty and bounty of their *watan*. The people of the "oasis city" Damascus called it *al-Faiha'*, The Fragrant. They loved its endless surrounding gardens (*ghuta*) which, watered by the perennial Barada River, were their paradise on earth. Visitors echoed their sentiment—Egyptian 'Abd al-Rahman Sami called Damascus "the Eden of the East." Moreover, even writers from less central zones like the Jabal 'Amil, in today's southern Lebanon, underlined that their "air [is] good, water fresh, and earth fertile, making grow all fruits, produce, vegetables, herbs and grains, of the best taste."[45]

Beauty and bounty elicited praise for a reason. Agriculture was Bilad al-Sham's largest economic branch. City dwellers took pride in particular products grown there and in their respective hinterland. Damascenes boasted about their apricots. Saidawis could not stop talking about their citrus fruits, the "aromatic" lemon trees al-Zain loved and the orange groves whose description filled a good dozen pages of a book of his, *Ta'rikh Saida, Sidon's History.* Because cities continued to trade, and because imports from Europe were not agricultural, economic globalization did not nick that pride. On the contrary, it left untouched, strengthened, or even created the material underpinning of that pride. Damascene apricot products remained famous in Bilad al-Sham and neighboring Egypt as well as in the West; Sidon's citrus fruit were "desired by the inhabitants of Syrian" and "European cities"; the wider Damascene hinterland's grains were exported to Europe; and some places became newly famous for cash crops like silk, in Mount Lebanon, or tobacco, in the Jabal Amil.[46]

Moreover, people took pride in their place's history, for most cities of Bilad al-Sham were old in ways that mattered religiously and politically. Al-Zain did not have to scratch his head to draw up a long list of historic places in *Ta'rikh Saida*. He dedicated one-third of the book to Sidon's millennia-old past and its many monuments from the Phoenicians via the Muslim Conquest and the Crusaders to the present. Also, Sidon boasted seven mosques like the *Jami' al-Battah* and a Great Mosque, whose religious endowments (*awqaf* in Arabic) continued to be well-off enough to rebuild it "in a very beautiful manner" after a flood in 1820. Saidawis called it *'Umari*, dating it back to the seventh-century Muslim conquest of Bilad al-Sham by the second caliph, 'Umar; and the *Jami' al-Battah* dated back to Islam's dawn, too. Of Sidon's churches, two were run by the Franciscans and the Jesuits, while three others served the Maronites, Roman Orthodox, and Catholics. The latter continued to be strong enough a community to finance a new church, Sidon's "most amazing," in the 1870s. There were places of popular worship, too. *Maqam Sidun* served Muslims and Jews; the latter also frequented *Aba al-ruh* and *al-nabi Yahiya*; and *Mar Iliyas* attracted Christians. Saidawis called these places *maqamat*, abodes, associating them with persons of mostly religious fame. The Jews believed one of Ya'cov's sons, Zebulon, was buried in *Maqam Sidun*; and Christians claimed Saint Elias had turned a sun temple into a Christian site at *Mar Iliyas*, whose natural setting al-Zain proudly portrayed as "one of the world's most amazing sights."[47]

These sites were alive with locals coming and going, meeting and mingling, a sociability that in the late nineteenth century was supple-

mented by new educational institutions. Speaking in relative terms, ,
Sidon was left in the dust by nearby Beirut, but in absolute terms it advanced. Missionaries created institutions here. American Presbyterians
established the Patriotic Evangelic Service Society, ran a boys' and a girls'
school, and operated public reading rooms that had "a good number of
books and newspapers" and were "open to [everybody] who wants to
study on all days but Sunday." In 1878 fifteen leading Saidawi Muslims
founded the *Jam'iyyat al-Maqasid al-Khairiyya* and raised local money
for a *Maqasid* school, part of a private campaign in Bilad al-Sham to energize Muslim secondary education. (On a related note, the Great Mosque
had a religious library.)[48] There were also a school and orphanage run by
Catholic sisters, and since 1902 an *Alliance Israëlite Universelle* school. In
all, "immense sums were spent on these buildings, already producing a
developing spirit."[49]

Sidon's fate—growing yet still overtaken by Beirut—was not extraordinary. Other littoral cities near Beirut, for instance Tripoli, fared
similarly. Neither was Sidon's sustained sociability exceptional. Another, although quite different, example was Acre. It was not only, like
Sidon, eclipsed by Beirut but also challenged by its smaller neighbor,
Haifa. In reaction, 'Akawis lionized their old caravansaries and stores
and their Islamic character (far superior to mainly Jewish and Christian Haifa!) and their garrison, which Haifa lacked. They deprecated
Haifa as "a town that thinks of itself as a *watan* for any traveler and
migrant in the world and [i.e., but hence] is not *watani*." Only Acre was
a real *watan*. They also may have coined the deprecating saying "Haifa's
people—salty water, burning sun, dark faces." Haifawis retaliated. "The
ruined Acre was apparently coated with gold, but today," they sneered,
"when a respectable woman enters she will be raped."[50]

A last aspect of continued urban sociability concerned marriage
patterns. Even in the international trade city of Aleppo, whose notable elite had long been open to rich outsiders, only few "outsiders"
broke into the elite after 1770. This was typical for nineteenth-century
Bilad al-Sham. Although the notable elites of various cities were in
contact with each other, each city had a rather distinct elite, a fact reinforced not the least by intra-city marriages and by women rather
than men being married to families in other cities. It was internally

that a city's elite changed, with the rise of some families and the fall of others.[51]

Cities' pride of place, material underpinnings, and sociability was reflected in politics. Writing after the 1908 Young Turk revolution, al-Zain, while lamenting that some new political associations fell dormant fast, recognized that others were active. People "swarmed" to the local chapter of the Union and Progress Party in government. Also, the revolution itself was most intensely experienced locally rather than simply as an event in Istanbul. "When the Constitution was proclaimed we were in a village in the hinterland of Tyre," al-Zain recalled. "We came (back) to Sidon and found the ground utterly transformed . . . and on the third day the city appeared in its most wonderfully adorned dress and in the *Khairiyya* (*Maqasid*) school there was a celebration in which [many] orated." For Sidon the story ended here. It was too small to have its own deputies in the parliament that was opened in Istanbul in 1908. This, however, is precisely what happened for the larger cities in 1908 and again in 1912. In fact, already for a first, short-lived parliament that was convened in 1876, Bilad al-Sham had sent deputies to Istanbul not as a region. Rather, each province had sent its own delegation, which consisted of representatives of the "well-known families" of the largest cities.[52]

In sum, cities' emotional appeal, social ties and politics were deeply rooted; and also cities that faced economic challenges had a material base solid enough to at least protect their relevance to their own inhabitants.

But this was only one side of the coin. Cities were not self-contained islands. They were part of various well-established far-flung networks. Some networks were cultural and religious, a matter addressed further below, but about which one point can be made here. Cairo was as much as Damascus an educational center for Bilad al-Sham. Some Egyptians religious judges worked in cities like Nablus and towns like Hebron, Gaza, and Salt. And at Cairo's famed al-Azhar religious university one could find students from Aleppo, in Bilad al-Sham's north, down to the region's south. When Muhammad 'Abd al-Jawwad al-Qayati, a known Azhar-educated Egyptian scholar, toured Bilad al-Sham at the turn of the century, he effortlessly found and socialized with fellow Azharites up and down the region, from Beirut to Tripoli, Jaffa, Ramla, Jerusalem, Nablus, and Damascus.[53]

Furthermore, cities and their hinterlands did not stand a chance to survive the transformative nineteenth century untouched. Istanbul's territorial losses had dramatic demographic effects reverberating through the empire. As a result of the 1877–1878 Russo-Ottoman War up to 2,000,000 Muslims fled from the Balkans and the Caucasus. While many stayed in Istanbul, the state also sent some to the provinces. In peripheries like Transjordan or the Jawlan, the Golan Heights, it resettled Circassians, whom it valued as tough warriors, to help control bedouins, to further agricultural expansion, and thus to raise more taxes for a cash-hungry treasury. Hence, even hinterlands in the empire's south felt the shockwaves of global political changes that hit the empire most brutally in the north.[54]

Finally, Istanbul itself became a palpable force in Bilad al-Sham's cities. As center-provincial interactions grew tighter from about mid-century, Istanbul became more visible. Sometimes this was the case literally, like in wall paintings adorning Damascene elite families' homes that depicted Istanbul as the empire's capital and as a quintessentially modern place to which Damascenes belonged, too. More mundanely, the capital permeated newspapers. These regularly reported about the goings-on there—this now mattered much more than before the 1830s!—and about Syrians' exploits in the capital: new honors, recent degrees, fresh promotions. Besides, the strengthening of the Ottoman state had regional knock-on effects. The career of bureaucrats—of whom there were more and more—crisscrossed Bilad al-Sham. And not only Western missionary but also Ottoman state high schools and colleges were established in provincial capitals and Istanbul. All these, and the *Maqasid* schools, brought together students from across Bilad al-Sham. Here, they socialized—which also helped shape political views. Last but not least, Istanbul itself became a center of Arab student secret societies prior to the 1908 revolution and a political hothouse thereafter. Some students were Syria-oriented; others were interested in all Ottoman Arabs; and in both, shawwam (sg., shami, an inhabitant of Bilad al-Sham) played a key role.[55]

## Beirut as Bilad al-Sham's Cultural Gravitation Point

How did the generic urban traits outlined in the last section look like concretely? As Beirut was the region's cultural and economic gravitation point, we start here.

In 1909, the fifteen-year-old Jerusalemite 'Umar al-Salih Barghuti was sent by his father to study in Beirut's Ottoman *Sultaniyya* high school. Like Sakakini, he traveled via Jaffa, by ship. Out at sea, at night, he slept badly; his quarters were too cramped, the engines too loud. Then came dawn. "He heard clamor and shouts, and he knew he had arrived in the port of Beirut. He got up from his bed, washed his face and body, dressed, had breakfast, and climbed to the deck, and the city of Beirut presented itself. She is a great city that stretches along the coastline, propped up by the towering Mount Lebanon behind her that is covered by a lush dense forest, like armies lined up in invulnerable citadels."[56]

Barghuti was not the only arrival taken by Beirut's sight. And once inside, travelers were impressed by the rich city's "broad streets and splendid houses." They would have agreed with Bustani, who singled out Beirut for its sophistication when he wanted to draw the clearest possible distinction to whom he saw as Syria's lowest: its Bedouin (just like the "grand and noble of Paris and England" were the antithesis of "cannibalistic Africans"). One sign and reason for Beirut's worldly, intellectual attraction was the cause for Barghuti's journey: higher education. Around 1900, over 1,500 pupils were taught in a number of secondary schools, many in the neighboring quarters Zukak al-Blat and Basta; and there were colleges, too.[57]

Success bred success. Beirut's wealth attracted more and more people from near and far. And that success was coercive. Anybody with a stake in Bilad al-Sham had to mark his presence in highly competitive Beirut. Locals built up their own systems. Christian denominational schools like the Greek Catholic one, established in 1864, were followed by the Sunnis and their *Maqasid* system in 1878. Already in 1863, Bustani created a secular school, the *Madrasa Wataniyya*. Providing also some post-secondary education, it pushed American Protestant missionaries to open the Syrian Protestant College (SPC) in 1866. Built on extant educational initiatives, the SPC was the Protestants' educational crown jewel in the region. They had arrived in Beirut back in the 1820s, before the city's rise turned meteoric, partly because it was on the littoral but mainly because, exceptional for the region, Christians here formed a considerable part of the population. Competing with them was an even stronger missionary group, the Jesuits, most of whom were French here, who arrived in 1831 and moved an expanded and renamed college, the Université de Saint Joseph, to Beirut in 1875. Shortly thereafter, in 1878, the Alliance Israélite Universelle opened its first school, for girls. Istanbul also expanded its educational presence. Beirut's *Sultaniyya*, one of only three lycées empire-wide, opened as early as 1869; and among other schools, an Arts and Crafts School (*Sanaya*) was instituted in 1907. Even Cairo had a finger in the Beiruti pie with its *Tawfiqiyya* school, opened in the 1890s. All these schools attracted students from across Bilad al-Sham, other parts of the Ottoman Empire, and Egypt.[58]

Beirut was becoming Bilad al-Sham's cultural gravitation point because it was most firmly connected to the world beyond. Besides Istanbul, another close contact was to Egypt, more precisely Cairo and Alexandria. The *Tawfiqiyya* was only one example. Beiruti schools attracted Egyptian intellectuals like Muhammad 'Abduh, who worked in 1883–1884 and 1885–1888 at the Ottoman *Sultaniyya*. And crucially, from the 1870s Egypt hosted intellectuals from Bilad al-Sham, many from Beirut. Moreover, Beirut was culturally and intellectually linked to the world beyond the Ottoman Empire and Egypt. Western missionaries were one factor. Another was Muslim, diaspora, and global leftist networks. For sure, most networks connected with cities in Bilad al-Sham not only through Beirut. But that city was their key meeting point, where the most diverse intellectuals worked shoulder to shoulder—and from where they interacted with other parts of the region. Hence, sending his son to Beirut made sense for an enterprising father like 'Umar Barghuti's. He "summoned his son to his room and told him: we have agreed that you shall go to Beirut to enroll in the *Sultani* School. . . . Trust in God. I want you to make me proud among the people."[59]

Beirut's rich life, its part in networks near and far, and its role as a regional gravitation point mattered also in other cultural fields, like material culture and consumption or the press. These were vital because they reflected and drove the *nahda*. Beirut was the publication place of many—and some of the earliest—Arabic periodicals, including Khalil al-Khuri's 1858 *Hadiqat al-Akhbar*, Bustani's 1870 *al-Jinan* and *al-Janna*, 'Abd al-Qadir al-Qabbani's 1875 *Thamarat al-Funun*, and Bustani's nephew's, Khalil Sarkis's, 1877 *Lisan al-Hal*. "From 1852–1880, 25 nonofficial periodicals appeared in Beirut," read by a widening, sophisticated middle class. This development was driven by brains as well as brawn, of the financial kind. *Pecunia non olet*: the Latin proverb, which means money does not stink, could have been coined for Beirut, whose intellectuals worked hand in glove with the city's commercial elite. It's not simply that some merchants loved the occasional ode by a poet; were amateur novelists or, like Alfred Sursock, amateur painters; helped bankroll some schools; or joined *nahdawi* associations like the Syrian Society for the Acquisition of Sciences and Arts, *al-Jam'iyya al-Suriyya li-Iktisab al-'Ulum wa-l-Funun*. They also were leading financers of some papers like *Thamarat al-Funun* and consumers of newspapers as well as of other products like books and Bustani's encyclopedia, and by the late nineteenth century also of plays, concerts and exhibitions.[60]

But their influence knew limits, too. When sultan Abdul Hamid II turned autocratic in the 1880s, some intellectuals voted with their feet. Bilad al-Sham, although an increasingly integrated region, was not a sealed box. Some intellectuals left for far shores, mainly Europe and the Americas; many went in the footsteps of other Beirutis and shawwam who in the 1870s had followed the call of Egypt's cultural opening and economic dynamism. The result was a heady meeting of *nahdawis* from Bilad al-Sham and from Egypt in a place that now was not only a center of Islamic learning but a key world communication node formed around the Suez Canal, and that attracted non-Arab and Muslim intellectuals from places as far-flung as America, Spain, Italy, China, Indonesia and Iran. Beirutis formed part of this trend. In 1875, brothers Salim and Bishara Taqla founded in Alexandria *al-Ahram*, a leading Egyptian paper to this very day. A decade later the two "deans of Arabic journalism," Ya'qub Sarruf and Faris Nimr, saw themselves forced to relocate *al-Muqtataf* to Cairo. Other editors followed. Both their products and papers run by Egyptians were disseminated in Bilad al-Sham, too. On a related note, in the 1890s Bustani's sons moved the *Encyclopedia* to Egypt. Already two decades earlier Bustani had been able to secure his enterprise only when besides Beiruti subscriptions, and others from Bilad al-Sham, some Egyptians subscribed, too, and Egypt's Khedive Ismail "guaranteed the subscription for one thousand copies of the encyclopedia."[61] In short, Egypt did not simply attract a considerable number of shawwam—34,000 by 1907—but also, more specifically, became the epicenter of the Arabic press. "From 1880–1908 . . . Beirut produced 42 private papers . . . but Cairo and Alexandria together wielded an astonishing 627 newspapers and journals."[62]

Following the 1908 revolution's political opening, numerous editors returned to Bilad al-Sham. While a number settled in Beirut and while that city continued to play a key role in Bilad al-Sham's cultural and intellectual affairs, many did not go there. Muhammad Kurd 'Ali for instance would never have dreamed to move his *al-Muqtabas* anywhere else than to his hometown Damascus, an important center of a now increasingly political Arabism. Moreover, it was not only in Beirut but across the region that newspapers mushroomed in 1908–1914. Outside Beirut, 152 new publications were launched, 46 in what would after 1918 become Lebanon, 80 in Syria, and 26 in Palestine.[63] Similarly spread were newspapers that "explicitly supported the general Arab ideas or the particularist ideas—the Syrian and the Lebanese," political notions gelling from 1908. Of these papers, about half appeared outside Beirut: five in Damascus, three in Hama, two in Haifa and in Tripoli, and one in Homs, Jaffa, and in what today are the Lebanese towns of Jounieh, Sidon, and Zahle. Moreover, papers from one city found interested readers in others. A periodical published in Sidon by Ahmad 'Arif al-Zain, *al-Kawthar*, which featured a "Question and Answer" column, received attention not only in Sidon or Beirut. In 1911, of eighteen self-identified questioners, two each came from Jerusalem and Homs and one each from Salt, in today's Jordan, and from Dayr al-Qamar and Nabatiyya, both in today's Lebanon.[64]

Indeed, information sharing within Bilad al-Sham grew. But this trend unfolded in what still was a patchwork region of increasingly tight interurban ties. The region's newspapers could not afford to fund region-wide networks of journalists, for they were small one-man or family businesses. Their (mostly unpaid) correspondents were stationary locals, who often copied from each other. But this, in return, was possible only because transport and information exchange had quickened; and it made sense only because more than before the region's sundry locals felt that they ultimately sat in the same boat. In 1908–1914 this feeling ripened as part of empire-wide politics. A freer press, parliamentary elections, and the Committee of Union and Progress's (CUP) perceived or real Turkification tendencies, that is some shawwam's anger about it: all this helped to form the Bilad al-Sham patchwork region. Tellingly, in the embattled 1912 election campaign—that pitted an opposition critical of Turkification against the CUP, which ended up rigging the results—newspapers across the region reported avidly, citing each other as well as non-Arab Ottoman newspapers.[65]

This patchwork region was uneven, however. It was Beiruti newspapers like *al-Mufid* that were most distributed, cited, and read in Bilad al-Sham. Only Egyptian papers—some still published by shawwam—did as well.[66] Characteristically, the Jerusalemite Barghuti senior knew 'Abd al-Majid Bek Abu al-Nasr, of *Beirut,* and perhaps also Ahmad Hasan Tabbara, of *al-Ittihad al-'Uthmani,* well enough to entrust them with his son. Also, *Filastin* cited Beiruti papers not only for imperial and Beiruti affairs but for news of other cities like Haifa and even of its home turf, Jaffa, where for example Beirut's *al-Muraqib* had a correspondent. And the papers that the municipality of Nablus subscribed to were mostly Beiruti. Put in numbers, of 152 publications launched in Bilad al-Sham outside Beirut between 1908 and 1914, 60 saw the light there, almost twice the count of runner-up Damascus's 33. Nineteen of Bilad al-Sham's 36 pro-Arabist newspapers established during that period appeared in Beirut. And from that city came eight of *Kawthar*'s eighteen reader questions, besides the seven from other places in Bilad al-Sham and one each from Istanbul, Cairo, and Sao Paolo. The patchwork region of Bilad al-Sham was getting tighter knit and better linked to the world—and Beirut was central to that development.[67]

## Beirut as Bilad al-Sham's Economic Gravitation Point

This was the case also regarding Beirut's economy. Here, Ottoman politics, Western capital, and some Western, especially French, state imperialist interests were mixed with local initiative. This unique high-energy fusion of various interests—together with other places' neglect and with Beirut's longtime success in stunting potential rivals—boosted Beirut: as an urban space, as a center of a hinterland of its own, Mount Lebanon, and as its region's premier gateway to the Eurocentric world economy.

Beirut's growth was not preordained. Although it existed already in Antiquity, as Berytus, the roots of its modern success were shallow, dating to around 1800. It profited from the neglect of once powerful Sidon, to its south, by al-Jazzar, who in 1775–1804 was based in Acre, to Sidon's south; and from Acre's own subsequent weakening. What helped Beirut, too, was its protection by Mount Lebanon's autonomous Bashir II (r. 1788–1840) and Egypt's decision to make it Syria's capital from 1831 to 1840. Consequently, in the 1830s its population of about 6,000 started growing. By mid-century, it had quadrupled. Beirutis left the cramped Old City for new neighborhoods like Zokak al-Blat, Ashrafiyeh, Musaytbeh, and Ra's Beirut. They were on the up and up—and knew it. In a speech Bustani gave around 1850 to the local Syrian Society for the Acquisition of Sciences and Arts, he bragged how Beirut's "rank rose" and called it "the most beautiful place in the Turkish land."[68]

Bustani also understood how important it was that "Europeans' trade moved to Beirut" and that the city's "business expanded." This happened partly because Western consuls started settling in the city after it became Egyptian Syria's provincial capital in the 1830s. In return, this shows that economic success was due to the selfsame factors that made Beirut a cultural hothouse. Beirut was a littoral city—an advantage in a Eurocentric world trade system oiled by mechanized maritime transport. Unlike other cities in Bilad al-Sham from the 1840s, it was mainly Christian, which helped to attract Western merchants. Although few in number, foreign trading houses, principally French and British, played a certain role in business by the 1830s–1840s. Christian Beirutis often worked for them and under their consuls' protection. (Muslim traders would not and could not.) With Beirut rising fast, the local apprentice soon outshone his Western master—but happily remained under the legal umbrella that consuls nolens volens left open.[69]

Beirut's success was sealed by a calamity. The communal warfare of 1860–1861 that made Bustani write *Nafir Suriya* inundated the city with Maronite, Greek Orthodox, and Greek Catholic refugees from Damascus, Mount Lebanon, and the Bikaa Valley town of Zahle. Beirut's population doubled almost overnight to about 60,000. Of these, a majority, just under two-thirds, now was Christian. Some of the refugees were traders, helping to boost Beirut's commerce. Moreover, Ottoman punishment of Damascus and a protective French expeditionary force stationed for nine months in Beirut "tipped the balance firmly on the side of Beirut's political domination over Damascus," which joined Sidon and Acre as weakened cities, further strengthening Beirut.[70]

At this very time Beirut also saw advances in communication and transport. Partly in reaction to the 1860–1861 events, which had to be managed well to head off looming Western intervention, Istanbul connected Beirut by telegraph to Damascus in 1861 and these two cities via Aleppo to itself two years later. In transport, Western capital made its most forceful entry to date. (It would remain crucial, financing Beirut's port expansion and a railway to Damascus in the 1890s.) Like Beiruti merchants, Istanbul wished to modernize transport but lacked sufficient capital. Hence, in 1857 it gave a French resident of Beirut, Edmond de Perthuis, a concession for a 112-kilometer long road to Damascus. Built from 1859, that road was by 1863 serviced by two daily carriages each way. They slashed transport time from three to four days to thirteen hours, and this though they had to surmount two mountain chains, the Lebanon, whose lowest point is 1,540 meters, and the Anti-Lebanon. It was telling that of two alternative routes de Perthuis and his allies picked the one that bypassed nearby Sidon. Once on top, Beirutis kicked down. Knowing that Beirut's topology was problematic—Tripoli, Sidon, and Haifa had much easier access to Bilad al-Sham's interior, and port Beirut was open to northern and western winds—they stunted competitors as long as possible.[71]

De Perthuis's road did not only tie Damascus tighter to Beirut. Together with an Ottoman Land Law passed in 1858 that happened to facilitate merchants' land purchases, and with the empire's post–civil war subjugation of Mount Lebanese land holding elite families (*muqat-ajis*), it finalized Beirut's economic penetration of Mount Lebanon.[72] Starting in the 1830s, that process sped up by mid-century. It involved European and Beiruti capital and silk, a profitable cash crop that kept expanding until the early twentieth century. Mount Lebanon's economy was restructured by the hunger of European, and especially Lyonnais, manufacturers for raw material. At the same time, this incorporation into the world economy had momentous repercussions for nearby Beirut.

Here, many made a fortune. Beiruti merchant families used money earned in silk "for loans to members of other groups, like the *muqat-ajis*, or for other types of business like the purchase and sale of foreign goods, thus encouraging the use of money and the spread of commercialization far beyond the reaches of the silk sector itself." After 1860 "the number of European owned [silk spinning] factories remained more or less constant at around ten or eleven, [but] those established by local entrepreneurs (including members of leading commercial families like the Sursuqs and the Tuwaynis) rose from thirty-three in 1862 to forty-seven in 1867." By 1880, Europeans had sold half their factories to Beirutis and to some other merchants from Bilad al-Sham, who by then owned about one hundred establishments.[73] Beirut was "incontestably the most important city on the entire Syrian coast": Austro-Hungarian Consul-General Julius Zwiedinek von Südenhorst's statement from 1873 referred to an already well-established fact. It remained true for the rest of the Ottoman period.[74]

Although the bedrock of Beirut's wealth—silk—was productive as much as mercantile, the city soared when around mid-century it leveraged that wealth and its improving infrastructures to become the region's biggest trade hub. Certainly, its trade knew its downs, and it kept a nervous eye on the competition. But its relative preeminence persisted. The figures proved it; Beirut's look and its attraction to traders across Bilad al-Sham reflected it; and interactions with Istanbul's and European capitalist and imperialist interests explained it.[75] Consider Beirut's trade volume *versus* Jaffa's, an important secondary port. In 1872 / 1873, Beirut crushed Jaffa (£1,857,000 versus £385,000); and while it later gave ground, it continued to dominate (£2,718,000 versus £1,160,000 in 1906). It led also in transport. In 1903, the 865 steamships and 3,268 sailors docking there topped the sum total of Tripoli, Haifa, and Acre (266, 220, and 64 steamships and 1,249, 534, and 1,043 sailers, respectively). And while around 1850 Bilad al-Sham's two largest cities, Aleppo and Damascus, were about eight times more populous than Beirut, by 1890 the latter's 120,000 inhabitants had almost caught up.[76]

Beirut's urban space was transformed, too. Utterly unsentimental and quintessentially capitalist, Beirutis looked forward, razing without qualm whatever need be. "Travelers were astounded by the extent to which in Beirut entire neighborhoods are torn down and replaced by modern buildings," and in the 1930s a French geographer noted that "nothing of the past manages to survive" here. As the place in Bilad al-Sham where urban-imperial and urban-imperial-global interactions released most energy, Beirut turned itself into the economic gravitation point in the region as well as of the region, pulling cities closer together. It was crammed with merchant counters and warehouses, shipping agencies, insurances, banks and legal offices, as well as hotels, restaurants and department stores.[77] And the region's merchants kept coming. In 1911 a British trade report on Syria stated that "Retail as well as wholesale traders from Hama, Homs, Damascus, the Lebanon, Haiffa, Nablous, Jaffa, Jerusalem, &c., look to Beyrout for many of their supplies, and visit the town at least once a year in order to replenish their stocks. Many of these country tradespeople prefer dealing with wholesale Beyrout firms rather than order goods from abroad. In Beyrout they come into contact with merchants, are able to see a large and varied assortment of goods of all kind, can buy small quantities, they bargain for the best terms, get their goods at once, and obtain facilities of payment which could not be granted by European firms."[78]

How did this development affect Beirut's relationship with Istanbul? That relationship had its ups and downs, and the two sides brought different assets to their continuing negotiations: Istanbul its sovereign power; Beirut's merchants their global economic prowess. However, by the late nineteenth century their interests were largely aligned. Imperial support was doubly important because, as noted, Beirut's geography did not preordain it to be Bilad al-Sham's gravitation point. In 1888, Istanbul saw fit to accept a longstanding Beiruti request: the administrative restructuring of Bilad al-Sham, the creation of Province Beirut. An "Ottoman provincial capital," Beirut was more than ever the to-go place not only commercially, but for people up and down Bilad al-Sham's shore now also administratively, and the center of expanding state services like schools for people from across the region. Also, not the least to Westerners whom Istanbul wished to impress, it was Bilad al-Sham's premier showcase for Ottoman urban modernity. It featured tramway lines facilitated by an Ottoman concession, fancy government buildings, electrical lighting, a modern water supply, and new public spaces like the central Place des Canons and the Pine Forest promenade near town.[79]

The world economy, too, helped Beirut ascend in the region. The city was tightly linked to Egypt and its economic opportunities resulting from the Suez Canal and cotton production. Moreover, Beirut was Bilad al-Sham's key node in a global network in which, for instance in imported consumer goods, non-Europeans were active adapters rather than passive recipients of European trends. The city also profited from a fundamental problem besetting Western producers and merchants trading in the region. With the reach and volume of their business expanding by leaps and bounds, legal norms as well as transport and communication infrastructures and resultant social contacts could not keep pace. Only few European producers and traders dealt directly with the myriad small-time shami traders, just like the latter did not like to "order goods from abroad."[80] On both sides, trust and predictability were in short supply. An Austro-Hungarian trade report insisted that it is "absolutely necessary not to create any direct ties with the small, petty local [Levantine] customers"—"known to be *Routineschikaneure* [who] pay at a snail's pace and dump the prices" of goods bought—"but to have business be handled by an intermediary agent." Of the latter, some were Damascene, but many Beirutis. The "wholesale Beyrout firms" thrived as the solution par excellence to the trust problem that arose with the rapid expansion of trade in the nineteenth century.[81]

Finally, Beirut illustrated how crucial a role European, here mostly French, capital played in the world economy. Just like it financed the 1863 Beirut-Damascus road, it was indispensable for two later transport projects that underwrote Beirut's dominance: a port expansion and a

Beirut-Damascus railway, both fully operational by 1895. The former was 80 percent French financed, the latter "essentially French."[82] Even together, Beirut's merchants and Istanbul could not have bankrolled either project. There even was continuity between the capital invested in the 1860s and the 1890s. Both times, de Perthuis played a leading role. But while French capital was a necessary condition for these projects, it was not sufficient. The interest of the port city's mercantile elite and of the Ottoman state was a precondition. Thus, de Perthuis was deeply, and over decades, embedded in Beirut's socioeconomic elite. And it was a Beiruti, Joseph Moutran, and Moutran together with another Beiruti, Hasan Beyhum, who were the first parties to receive from Istanbul concessions, for the new port and a railway, respectively. True, both concessions were soon folded into French firms. But Beiruti merchants' long-standing lobbying for these initiatives, the indispensability of Istanbul's concessions to both, and the high ranking of a Syrian, Selim Malhamé, in the central government, all played a leading role in the port concession and the railway administration.[83]

Besides, French financiers were at first skeptical whether either project would be profitable. Their capital flowed only after the Quai d'Orsay applied some pressure and made financial guarantees. This reflected a French government attempt, by the 1890s, to establish an unofficial sphere of influence in Bilad al-Sham. This trend sharpened an older belief, dating back to the Crusades and best visible in French links to Maronite Christians, that France had a special relationship with what it called la Syrie française. Furthermore, France feared its big eastern neighbor, Germany, since its defeat in 1870–1871. When in the late nineteenth century Berlin became Istanbul's key European ally and German entrepreneurs became more active in the empire, Paris reacted. It increased its presence in Bilad al-Sham, not the least by demanding Istanbul to grant French companies concessions commensurate to those given to Germans. By the last prewar decade, this move and parallel British moves in the Palestinian backyard of 'its' Egyptian Suez Canal started creating unofficial spheres of influence in transport. This trend received a political tinge when in 1912 Britain assured France that is had "no political aspiration in Syria" north of Palestine, and was confirmed in early 1914 in a German-French understanding about the primacy of French railroad interests in Syria.[84]

In sum, the fusion of urban, imperial, and European capitalist and imperialist interests allowed Beiruti merchants to operate far outside their city, across Bilad al-Sham and beyond the sea. An example is the Bustros family, which "invest[ed] well in land, trade, and finance. They acquired real estate in Beirut and landholdings all over Syria and Egypt. They traded in agricultural products, since they owned large olive and mulberry plantations" for silk.[85] Another example, perhaps the best, is the Greek Orthodox Sursock family, whom we encountered above as silk entrepreneurs and, in Alfred Sursock's case, as a merchant and amateur painter. (He was an art collector, too.) The Sursocks made their fortune not simply by participating in Mount Lebanon's silk boom. From a "Beirut[i] . . . base of operations," they rode the wave of various large-scale capitalist ventures, investing in Egypt in the Suez Canal Company and in Bilad al-Sham in the Beirut-Damascus road company and the port company in Beirut, among other endeavors. They nurtured connections in the Ottoman capital. And they owned "extensive rural holdings, including whole villages, in Egypt and Palestine" as well as in in Mount Lebanon and in today's Turkey.[86] Letters by friends and family that were forwarded to Alfred Sursock illustrate how breathlessly he juggled his business on the move between Egypt, Bilad al-Sham, Istanbul and Europe. "Dear Alfred, you are still not here," his mother admonished him—as always in French—on New Year's Day 1914. "When do you intend to come? Have not you enough of this tiring life that you lead, I believe that it is already time that you come back to retire in Beirut. The New Year has already passed."[87]

## The Limits of Beirut's Influence

Although urban-imperial and urban-imperial-global interactions made Beirut Bilad al-Sham's economic gravitation point, the city did not control the region, for its cities were too well rooted. Especially the interior cities Aleppo and Damascus were simply too powerful to fall under Beiruti control. Regarding the littoral cities, the limits of Beirut's power owed also to its less than optimal geographical position. By the early twentieth century, its attempts to compensate this problem by stunting the growth of potential competitors started to fail. Although the cities nearest to Beirut, Sidon and Tripoli, remained in its shadow, others emerged from it. The best example was Beirut's ultimate failure to nix the railway from Haifa via Dir'a to Damascus, opened in 1905, which only had to climb the southern-most slopes of the Jawlan Heights.

Moreover, although no littoral city other than Beirut became a true port city—an important node in the world economy and truly transformed by that experience—some cities profited the longer the more from being keyed into world trade. Especially Jaffa, which lagged far behind Beirut throughout the nineteenth century, started catching up from 1905. By 1913, its total trade was worth £2,058,000 versus Beirut's £2,806,000.[88]

Last, Beirut's regional role was also limited by the selfsame actors that helped make it the region's gravitation point: Istanbul and European capital. The Ottomans tried to buttress Bilad al-Sham against Western encroachment by backing different provinces, not only Beirut's. Also, the empire's economic and strategic interests, while mostly in line with Beirut's, also differed in some ways. It was Istanbul that finally built the Haifa-Dir'a(-Damascus) railway as a supply route of the Hijaz Railway, which was constructed principally for a strategic reason, to facilitate Istanbul's political and military reach in Bilad al-Sham's interior and to keep out Western governments. Western capital, too, cared little about an integrated region. Its foremost interest was improving transportation between Beirut and its premier entry point into the region's interior, Damascus. That was the professed focus of the railroad constructors in the 1890s.[89] Beirut-Damascus: this indeed was the premier interurban connection for both cities. It was a real axis, that is a connection along which a comparatively great volume of people, goods, and information moved. Hence, it was the crux of the position of these two cities in late Ottoman Bilad al-Sham.

## The Perseverance of Interior Cities: Damascus

Before examining this interurban connection, however, we need to take a look at Damascus itself. How did that city deal with the challenges of the nineteenth century?

Before the nineteenth century Damascus was, after Aleppo, Bilad al-Sham's biggest market, with a substantial artisanal base and a strong presence in the surrounding *ghuta*. It also was a trade hub, mainly within the empire but also as "a center of trading networks that extended to Baghdad, the Hijaz, Palestine and Egypt." Some goods arrived from India, many from Iran and Iraq via a few massive yearly caravans from Baghdad. Many goods were reexported together with Damascene products to the Ottoman Empire or (mostly via Sidon) to Egypt, the Mediterranean and, least important, Europe. Damascus profited from the hajj, too. Every year, 15,000–20,000 Muslim pilgrims brought wares to, and spent money in, the city while traveling to Mecca and back.[90]

This picture was altered but not effaced by the Ottoman incorporation into the world economy. Incorporation started in the 1830s and 1840s, when Egypt opened Bilad al-Sham to Western trade, and when Istanbul, upon ousting Egypt in 1840 / 1841, applied the liberal commercial treaties then being signed with Western countries. Rising insecurity in the desert crippled the Damascus-Baghdad caravans, and from the 1840s steam ships from Egypt to the Red Sea started hurting the Damascus-Mecca caravans. Still, Damascene merchants persevered. Western goods sold to Damascus were not all consumed there. Rather, many were reexported via Aleppo to Iraq and southern Anatolia. Also, the Hijaz trade remained considerable. And although Europe remained a minor trading partner, Damascene merchants did increase artisanal and especially agricultural exports to that destination.[91]

A principal export to Europe and to neighboring areas like Mount Lebanon was grain. Luckily, Bilad al-Sham's biggest breadbasket, the Hawran, lay at Damascus's doorstep, to its south. The city's merchants started penetrating it in earnest in the 1850s, when the Crimean War—in which the Ottoman Empire, France, and Britain defeated Russia—stimulated agricultural demand, inflating prices in the Eastern Mediterranean. In the 1860s, they intensified efforts in response to rising consumption by Europe's growing population, which helped redress Damascus's growing trade imbalance. Many notables who did not jump on the bandwagon grew weaker. Conversely, big grain merchants rose into Damascus's notable elite. Together with "government-sanctioned political and fiscal brokers" in the Hawran, they formed an "informal cartel . . . [that] disrupt[ed] the autarkic pattern, extend[ed] agriculture, and 'free[d]' surpluses for external markets and for revenues for the Ottoman provincial treasury." By the 1880s and 1890s the strong leaders of the Hawran's beduin tribes and Druze communities, empowered by the difficult terrain of parts of the Hawran and by the state's decision to try tax peasants directly, loosened the cartel's grip. But the stream of grain from the Hawran via Damascus to the coast persisted. In this sense, incorporation into the world economy profited Damascene merchants and even created business.[92]

But that was only one side of the coin. Already in 1873, a Western observer noted that Damascus's pilgrimage "trade has been very much reduced, especially since the Suez Canal" in 1869 "opened the direct maritime connection with the Arabian coast." Arabs agreed. Indeed, Damascus's already sagging trade with Iraq and the Hijaz suffered further from 1869. Damascus ceased being a transregional trade hub. More generally, the expanding world economy and the underlying changes in transport routes and means made the city more vulnerable and dependent. Worse, just as this systemic challenge peaked in the 1870s, a world economic recession kicked in.[93]

Damascus wobbled—but then regained its balance. Like a short but shrewd boxer, it learned to make up lesser range by applying greater force at close quarter. In the city itself, already by the 1860s textile producers, the largest artisanal sector, had adjusted manufacturing mainly to a poor rural clientele reaching from Palestine to central Syria to southern Anatolia. Istanbul helped. Its decrees curtailed Western merchants and their Christian protégés especially in interior cities.[94] True, world economic incorporation made Damascus more dependent. Using European cotton thread, textile masters were subject to Western prize fluctuations. Social ties were subverted, too: Guilds lost power and masters were prone to cut journeymen's wages. Still, Damascus's economy was not wiped out. It adapted and survived, and by around 1900 thrived enough for numerous Damascenes to live honorably. Damascus's urban landscape reflected that continuity. The Ottoman state, some foreign capital, and local entrepreneurs changed the city from the mid-nineteenth century. They added buildings and neighborhoods, squares and thoroughfares, electrical and tramway infrastructures, and adjusted some houses even in the Old City. But unlike Beirut, where destruction and reconstruction was all the rage, in Damascus change was gentler. Deeply proud of their city's millennia-old past and rank, Damascenes had no intention to transform their city wholesale.[95]

## The Damascus-Beirut Interurban Axis

Damascus regained its balance by making two additional moves, one outside its hinterland, the other inside. Key to the former was its part in strengthening the interurban axis with Beirut. Although topologically inconvenient, that route was strengthened when Beiruti merchants became Bilad al-Sham's main connecting point to the world market in the 1830s and when de Perthuis built a new road from Beirut to Damascus in 1859–1863. Indeed, Beirut was the stronger party in this axis. "[R]elatively few Damascene merchant families had direct connections to Europe," but "rather seem mostly to have worked through Beirut-based wholesalers or agents." For trade with the world beyond the Mediterranean, Beirut had made itself indispensable.[96]

But Beirut was not all-powerful. Traders did not gain control over Damascus and its hinterland. This situation solidified after 1861. Damascus's Muslim merchants profited from the Christian exodus which, while inflating the ranks of Beirut's Christian traders, made them more dependent on Damascus's Muslim merchants and their contacts in Bilad al-Sham's interior. Foreign merchants, too, were rare in Damascus. Thus, Damascene merchants were able to use the axis to Beirut to their own benefit. Especially after the opening of the Suez Canal, this helped them to somewhat offset their city's decline as a transregional hub. In return, this shows that Bilad al-Sham's world economic incorporation did not transform shawwam into passive reactors. Because of Damascus's deeply rooted position and due to Istanbul's unwillingness to allow Western traders to gain access to Bilad al-Sham's interior, the Beirut-Damascus interurban axis was not simply a tool for global trade. Rather, it spatially channeled that trade in the region.[97]

Seen from Damascus, how did the unequal yet mutually dependent relationship with Beirut look like in practice? Consider two monumental tomes written in the late nineteenth century and early twentieth century, respectively—Muhammad Saʿid al-Qasimi's *Dictionary of the Crafts of Damascus* and Muhammad Adib Al Taqi al-Din al-Hisni's *Anthology of the Histories of Damascus*. To al-Qasimi, who toured Damascus's *suqs* (specialized markets) and manufacturers throughout the 1890s for the book on which he worked until his death in 1900, Damascus's close connection with Beirut, although relatively recent, had become quasi natural. He regularly mentioned the littoral city in the same breath as Homs and Hama, two interior cities with traditionally close ties to Damascus.[98] To him these were all "near cities." The ʿannabs—people selling grapes, of which the by far best (obviously!) are grown in Damascus's vicinity, in Darayya—"travel . . . to Beirut, Homs and Hama and other cities near Damascus." The sheer ordinariness, by the late nineteenth century, of Damascus's close connection to Beirut showed also in a Beirutization of sorts. Although many goods that *khardaji*s, import merchants, brought from Beirut were European, al-Qasimi distinguished between those goods and "goods imported from further away, including Europe."[99]

At the time of al-Qasimi's writing, the *khardaji*s were spreading beyond their original *suq*, ʿAsruniyya, into the larger *Hamidiyya*. While Damascus's trade with Beirut and via Beirut with Europe was blooming, the fact that the *khardaji*s were locals illustrates that Damascus did not relinquish control over its end of the axis with Beirut. This double impression is reinforced by al-Hisni. In a 110-page-long description of Damascus's leading families, he mentioned numerous Damascenes trading with Beirut and / or living there. He wrote at length, too, about Damascenes who moved to Beirut for other purposes, mostly to work in the expanding Ottoman bureaucracy in the new provincial capital.

But he listed only one Beiruti merchant family, the Beyduns, as having family members in Damascus. Although Beirut was securely on his radar, it did not dominate Damascus. Though it was Damascus's most important interurban partner in Bilad al-Sham, it was not its only reference point. Damascene traders lived also in Istanbul, underlining the Ottoman capital's continued mercantile importance.[100]

## Damascus's Tightening Grip on Its Rural Hinterland

What about Damascus's economic moves inside its own rural hinterland? The city did not simply maintain its role as "a clearing house for and reexporter of products of the Syrian interior." It also deepened the penetration of its hinterland and widened its hinterland's range, pushing harder into the Jawlan Heights southwest of Damascus, the Bikaa Valley in the northwest, the zone around Homs in the north, the western Syrian Desert in the east, and the Hawran and Transjordan in the south. Istanbul tended to back these moves.[101] The abolition of internal customs duties in 1874 was one example; another, infrastructural projects. Take the opening of the Medina leg of the Hijaz Railway in 1908. Since the opening of the Suez Canal in 1869, Damascene merchant had nimbly channeled the scraps of the once impressive Baghdadi caravans into markets in Damascus and in towns to its south. The railway bolstered this enterprise because now some Iraqi pilgrims to Mecca, near Medina, did not sail around the Arabian Peninsula but rode a camel westward to Damascus and then boarded a southbound train. Here, the steel horse and the camel created a profitable synergy. Damascus benefited also from earlier Ottoman concessions to French companies to build roads and railways in its hinterland, and from macadamized roads that the government finished by 1909 between Damascus and Quneitra in the Jawlan Heights, Homs, and the Hawran.[102]

We have seen how Damascene traders became more involved in the Hawran from the 1850s. In Transjordan penetration came later, was more directly a response to the Suez Canal. But it also appears to have been more direct: "Damascene merchants established themselves as distributors of goods to the peasants and pastoralists." They piggybacked on the expansion, from 1867, of Istanbul's territorial writ and taxation demands in Transjordan and on the Ottoman state's considerable success in "pacifying" bedouin and in settling certain tribes. Some Damascene merchants settled in a town. Others worked seasonally, roving from village to village and from tribe to tribe, sometimes with a pied-à-terre in a town. All, however, kept in touch with Damascus. They remained part of family networks and sold Damascene textiles and other goods, extending their city's writ, which was facilitated by the building of the Hijaz Railway from 1900 until 1908, when it reached Medina. Irbid for example became "an important point for the marketing, principally, of Damascene goods, and goods of other Syrian cities, [while] Western goods were absent. The merchants of Damascus' Meydan . . . [neighborhood] constituted most merchants settling in Irbid." In addition, they energized agricultural production, either directly by buying lands or indirectly; and they sold the produce grown back to Damascus. Some also moved further south. In Salt, a few—Christians—came as early as 1860–1861, fleeing from the massacre in Mount Lebanon and Damascus.[103]

## A Comparison with Damascus: The Interior City of Nablus

They were not alone. In fact, it was as "the second Nablus" that Salt became known in the late nineteenth century. In Transjordan, the expanded hinterland of Nablus overlapped with that of Damascus. It also offered a telling contrast. Nablus was pushed as well as pulled into Transjordan, like Damascus, but for a somewhat different mix of reasons. Being less mighty than Damascus before the nineteenth century, Nablus lost less in the nineteenth century and thus had less to compensate for. The Suez Canal did not affect it too greatly; its manufacturing and regional trade, which turned more and more around olive oil soap, continued to grow. Conversely, competition by Beirut and Damascus hurt some Nabulsi merchants. Hence, it was concern about the impending world economic recession in the 1870s as well as competitive pressure that helped propel them across the Jordan River. Moreover, they were attracted by Transjordan's improved security and opening markets, its proximity to Nablus, and the new Transjordanian Ottoman tax payers' rising demand for loans or hard currency in exchange for their products.

The end result, however, resembled that of Damascus. Nabulsis not only deepened their ties to their city's immediate surroundings. They also extended their hinterland, mainly north- and eastward, settling in a number of towns across the Jordan River, like Irbid and Salt. And again like Damascenes, Nabulsis who now lived across the Jordan kept close ties to their hometown. Families like the Bisharat, some of whom first moved to Salt in the 1880s, continued to commute between Nablus and Salt, married daughters back to Nablus, had some of their children educated back in Nablus—and increased cross-river trade. Nablus's municipality followed suit, helping to finance a permanent boat service across the Jordan and organizing the transport of telegraphs from its city to Salt. Besides, this pattern and the overlap between Damascus and Nablus repeated themselves further south. Nabulsi-Salti trade intersected with that between Salt and Jerusalem; and the latter also increased its contacts with cities to the south of Salt, like Karak.[104]

### Another Comparison: The Interior City of Aleppo

In sum, Damascus and Nablus expanded their hinterlands around the same time and for reasons that, while somewhat different in form, were similar in nature. This held for Aleppo, too—with the added difference that the latter, more than Damascus, made a minor comeback as an international trade city.

From the late Middle Ages to the nineteenth century Aleppo was the biggest Eurasian trade hub in Bilad al-Sham—and of true importance in world trade. This was due partly to its excellent position. It is situated half way between the western-most point of Iraq's Euphrates River and the Mediterranean; about half way between Istanbul and Cairo and Istanbul and Mecca; and on the Eurasian land trade route, of which one section skirted the Anatolian Highlands. Being the biggest city to Anatolia's south had an additional effect. The province of Aleppo reached deep into that region, and Aleppo's economic hinterland extended to northern Mesopotamia. Indeed, its mixed population, composed of Arabs, Turks, Turkmen, Kurds, Armenians, and seasonally bedouins, reflected Bilad al-Sham's fuzzy borders.[105]

When by the 1870s Aleppo, like Damascus and Nablus, was forced to deal with its incorporation into the world economy, it coped in a fundamentally similar way, penetrating its hinterland more deeply. Here, too, the Ottoman state facilitated that process by settling some nomadic bedouin tribes, which improved security and helped peasant populations grow. But unlike Damascus and Nablus, Aleppo did not broaden its hinterland. To the contrary, northern Anatolia reoriented itself to the Black Sea and to the steam ships serving its ports. Then again, Aleppo had no urban contender to its north and only a rather distant Mosul to its east—a great difference from Damascus, the expansion of whose hinterland was limited by the desert to its east, by sparsely populated Jordan to its south and by powerful littoral cities to its west. Also, Aleppo now fully cashed in on its geography as a "steppe city" whose hinterland is both bigger and more suitable to agriculture than Damascus, an "oasis city" close to the desert. More than Damascene merchants and notables, who traded with the Hawrani breadbasket but never truly owned it, Aleppines bought and expanded landed properties. By the 1880s agricultural goods were replacing lost long-distance commercial goods and helped reestablish Aleppo as an international trade city—though one whose standing had fallen and whose role had changed with its incorporation into the world economy.[106]

### Back to the Littoral: Jaffa in Comparison to Beirut

Having examined the interior cities of Damascus, Nablus, and Aleppo, we now return to the littoral: to Arab and Jewish Jaffa. Long overshadowed by Gaza to its south, Acre and Sidon to its north, and Jerusalem and Nablus in the interior, its time came in the nineteenth century—just like Beirut.

But it was not Beirut. Its character differed, a key economic contrast being that by the late nineteenth century local agriculture, mainly citrus fruit, helped energize it. Jaffa was less important than Beirut also in other ways. Beirut had a province; Jaffa was a district (*qada'* in Arabic) in the *mutasarrifiyya* Jerusalem. On the eve of World War I, Beirut had 150,000 inhabitants; Jaffa, 50,000. Jaffa received less European capital than Beirut; indeed, "European endeavors in the 'Holy Land'" as a whole "were principally non-economic." Istanbul facilitated less infrastructures in Jaffa than in Beirut—Jaffa's port was not modernized—mainly because Europeans were dangerously penetrating Palestine. Although Jaffa's trade started catching up with Beirut by the early twentieth century, in some ways it was dependent on Beirut. It received credit lines from Beirut, and some Beiruti absentee agricultural investors bought plots. Culturally, too, Beirut was in the lead. Its educational sector eclipsed Jaffa's. Some of its newspapers had a correspondent in Jaffa, but not vice versa. Jaffawi newspapers like *Filastin* reported with much greater care on Beirut than Beiruti papers on Jaffa, and did so citing Beirut's own newspapers. It was telling that the founder of the newspaper *Filastin*, Issa al-Issa, had studied at the Syrian Protestant College, in Beirut; and it was there, too, that he bought *Filastin*'s print letters. In sum, Beirut was a port city, Jaffa a city with a port.[107]

Still, Jaffa had come far by the early twentieth century. Although it did not rise as meteorically as Beirut, the two had much in common. Looking at them side by side, one appreciates how incorporation into the world economy and modern Ottoman state territoriality boosted some of Bilad al-Sham's littoral cities. (To Jaffa's luck, it was distant enough from Beirut not to pose a threat; Beirutis did not try to stunt its growth.) If Beirut was the bride of the littoral, Jaffa too made heads turn, as "one of the most interesting of the towns that rise above the Oriental shores of the Mediterranean." While Beirut developed earlier than Jaffa, which started to rise rapidly only from the late nineteenth century, both did so faster than the interior. Between the early nineteenth century and World War I Jaffa's population exploded about twentyfold. By contrast, Jerusalem's grew eightfold, to 80,000. Between 1841 / 42 and 1917 / 18, Jaffa's expansion, from 0.1 to 1.4 square kilometers, was double that of Jerusalem, which grew from 0.6 to 3.8 square kilometers. Like Beirut, Jaffa became a trade hub for its interior: southern and central Palestine including Jerusalem and the towns of Hebron and Nablus. Through both Beirut and Jaffa, exports were mainly agricultural and imports mainly of manufactured goods after their region's incorporation into the world economy. For both, Europe was an important but not the only trade destination. Egypt and the non-Arab parts of the Ottoman Empire were key customers, too. Both proved attractive. To Jaffa, Arabs migrated from neighboring towns like Lydda, from places like Jerusalem, Gaza, and Hebron, and from other parts of Bilad al-Sham and Egypt, among others. Moreover, although far less important than Beirut culturally, also Jaffa's cultural profile rose by the late nineteenth century. Several schools were established, and *Filastin* was a leading newspaper in Palestine.[108]

Similarly, while Jaffa attracted less European capital than Beirut, money flowed here too, not the least into the French Jaffa-Jerusalem railway that was finished in 1892. And although Istanbul did not facilitate a port, respective projects almost matured by the early 1910s. Also, Istanbul did grant the Jerusalem railway concession, and executed projects of its own, including schools, a 1864 telegraph line to Jerusalem that was via Jaffa connected to the Ottoman capital, and a modern road to Jerusalem in 1867. It took an active interest in Palestine, seeking to tie it firmly to itself to counteract European influence.[109]

### Jaffa's Jews, Zionism, and the Question of the Yishuv's Place within Bilad al-Sham

One group present in Jaffa was absent in Beirut: German Templer.[110] Another group was eventually much more numerous: Jews. Some were from Middle Eastern lands, who started arriving in the 1830s— very late, for Jaffa was of secondary importance in the old Yishuv, the age-old religious Jewish presence in Palestine concentrated in Jerusalem, Hebron, Tiberias, and Safed. Until the 1870s, Jaffa's Jewish community barely grew. But then it rose swiftly, from 1 percent of the population to 20 percent in 1915. This was due mainly to immigrants, drawn by opportunity. Some were Jews from old Yishuv towns. But from the 1880s, others were a new sort of Jewish immigrant from Europe and from new agricultural settlements in Palestine: Zionists.[111]

It was in the 1880s, indeed, that Zionism crystallized. It was part of a groundswell of nationalist movements that wished more autonomy in, or even exit from, the multinational empires that dominated nineteenth-century Central and Eastern Europe. But it was special, too. Its advocates belonged to a religiously exclusive group; Jews were scattered and everywhere a minority; and Zionism was principally a reaction to Jews' discontent with how their emancipation in Christian Europe had fared since its start in 1791, in France. In Western Europe, the 1894 French Dreyfus Affair suggested that social acceptance would never follow legal emancipation; in Eastern Europe, especially Russia, pogroms in 1881–1884 and 1903–1906 added injury to the insult of persistent legal restrictions. True, many West European Jews still believed in emancipation and many of their Eastern coreligionists emigrated to Germany, Britain, and the Americas. But even of these, some agreed with Russian Jewish intellectual Leon Pinsker's argument, in 1882, that "With the loss of their fatherland" in Roman times, the Jews had become a merely "spiritual nation," a "ghostlike apparition" scaring the gentiles into "Judeophobia"—which would disappear only if the Jews would again become a material nation, which in turn would happen only if "we have a *home,* if not a *country* of our own." That home, for most Zionists, was Palestine, to them their ancient fatherland. A few, most famously the celebrated author Ahad ha-'Am, doubtful a state could be built, saw that home as a cultural center for connecting and rejuvenating the world's Jewish communities. Of those who desired a state, some believed that winning the political support of a big power (first Istanbul, the sovereign of Palestine) should precede settling. Yet many of them, including Zionist leader Theodor Herzl, did not oppose those demanding practical action. And indeed in 1882 the first aliyah, immigration, initiated the new—Zionist—Yishuv.[112]

Organizationally, politically, and socioculturally, Europe was the center of Zionism until the 1930s if not 1940s. Also, most capital invested in the Yishuv came from European and eventually American Zionist individuals and organizations. (Non-Zionist Jews sent money, too; old Yishuv Jerusalem heavily relied on those funds, for example.) Yet the Yishuv did not live in splendid isolation.

This was true in two ways. Firstly, some Yishuvi patterns obeyed region-wide trends. Jaffa is a case in point. Whether together or alone both Arabs and Jews made Jaffa rise; for instance Jaffa's Jews like its Arabs built new neighborhoods extra muros, most famously Tel Aviv in 1909. And not only Arab Jaffa functionally resembled port city Beirut, but the port city of Jaffa as a whole did, Jews included. One aspect was migration. Some Jews from old Yishuvi centers, especially Jerusalem, moved to boomtown Jaffa; its port welcomed almost all Zionist immigrants to Palestine; some just stayed there; and while many founded agricultural settlements (the earliest, closest to Jaffa), some returned to that city. Another aspect was the considerable investment of capital from Europe in Jaffa, in this case, true, mostly Jewish. Jaffa also was the new Yishuv's demographic heavyweight and a cultural hub for it, boasting schools like the Hebrew Gymnasium Jaffo, libraries like the *Sha'ar Zion,* theaters, and newspapers. And it was an organizational center. Until 1909, it served as the headquarters of the leftist Po'alei Zion party's Palestine branch, founded in 1906 as part of the 1904–1914 second aliyah, which was socialist nationalist rather than capitalist like the first. And when in 1908 the World Zionist Organization, established in 1897 at the first Zionist Congress in the Swiss city of Basel, opened a Palestine Office, its head, Arthur Ruppin, determined that choosing Jaffa as its headquarters was "almost inevitable."[113]

Secondly, the Yishuv was an integral part of region-wide structures. No doubt, Zionist Jaffa was not subsumed under Beirut the way Arab Jaffa was, for the aforenoted reason that the Yishuv was tightly linked to Europe. But in some ways the Yishuv was linked to Beirut. Some infrastructural realities and Beirut's economic power and regional reach affected the Yishuv, too. Least important yet telling, in stormy weather steamships did not stop at Jaffa's rather dangerous port but continued to Beirut, where Palestine-bound passengers disembarked, to fold back by land or sea. Also, as the region's premier trade hub, Beirut had goods that were of use also to the Yishuv; thus, Ruppin bought U.S. drilling machines there. Because Beirut was a financial center, it was the only Arab city outside Palestine where the Zionist Anglo-Palestine Bank, which was founded in London in 1902 and opened its main Palestine branch in Jaffa in 1903, established a branch. And Zionists followed Beirut's economic development with care. Besides, Jews in Palestine were not deaf to Beirut's cultural attractions, and had personal connections to the city. Yosef Eliyahu Chelouche, scion of a rich Sephardi merchant Jaffawi family who became a (however critical) Zionist, in the 1880s studied at one of the new Jewish schools there; Ruppin was in touch with the head of the Syrian Protestant College; and even the socialist nationalist pioneer David Ben-Gurion (1886–1973), who in 1948 would become Israel's first prime minister, visited Bilad al-Sham's headquarters of world capitalism, in 1908. In the long run most important to Zionists, however, was Beiruti-owned property in Palestine. The Sursocks, among others, owned vast lands in the Marj Ibn 'Amir Valley, east of Haifa, some of which they would start selling in the 1920s. On a related note, in the late Ottoman period Zionists started pondering the Yishuv's economic place in the region. For now, such thinking was just that: thinking, with scant application. But that would change after World War I.[114]

## Jaffa as Part of the Bilad al-Sham Patchwork Region

Differences and similarities with Beirut aside, Jaffa illustrates two generic features of late Ottoman Bilad al-Sham. One was a view of the region not as a unit but a patchwork. This was clear, and relevant, especially for Jaffa's Arabs. The newspaper *Filastin* reflected that view well. One of its columns was *Akhbar al-jihhat* (News of the areas). It covered Beirut, Damascus, Haifa, and Jerusalem heavily; regularly, Nablus and two towns near Jaffa, Lud and Ramla; and sporadically, Beit Jala, Majdal, Betlehem (all three in Palestine), Dir'a, Hama, Hawran, Zahle, Lebanon, the now Turkish cities of Iskandarun and Mersin, Egypt, and Mosul, in today's Iraq.[115] That is, *Akhbar al-jihhat* united under one heading news from across Bilad al-Sham, with an emphasis on its center (Beirut and Damascus) and south (Palestine), with little regard to its north, and with an occasional glance at Egypt. The latter sat on the fence. Unlike the other places in *Akhbar al-jihhat*, it often appeared in *Akhbar shatta* (Mixed news) that reported on places as varied as Iran, the United States, Russia, Sudan, England, or Morocco.[116]

If *Akhbar al-jihhat* was a bit porous especially to Bilad al-Sham's southwestern neighbor, Egypt, its title—*jihhat* (area*s*)—and its diverse reporting styles illustrated that its region was not homogeneous, but comprised multiple areas. To be precise, four areas, from *Filastin*'s Jaffawi standpoint. On some towns—a few near, most far—it reported once in a blue moon, without giving a source or by citing another newspaper's report. Betlehem or Zahle, say, were of little import. The other extreme were Beirut and Damascus that, while relatively distant, mattered a great deal and on which *Filastin* reported in detail, consistently citing these two cities' own newspapers. With a stretch Haifa could be included in this group. Third, Gaza and Nablus, while not nearer to Jaffa than Haifa was, mattered enough for *Filastin* to have a *mukatib* (writing correspondent). Last, *Filastin* had two *murasils* (letter writing correspondents). One was in Lydda, close to Jaffa, which *Filastin* mentioned on and off. The other lived in Jerusalem, about which the newspaper wrote without fail. Just as Egypt straddled the border between international *Akhbar shatta* and regional *Akhbar al-jihhat*, Jerusalem sat on the fence between the latter and *Akhbar mahalliyya* (Local news), *Filastin*'s Jaffawi column that occasionally discussed the Holy City, too.[117]

## The Jaffa-Jerusalem Interurban Axis

Jaffa's and Jerusalem's ties thickened progressively from the late nineteenth century. This illustrates a second generic feature of late Ottoman Bilad al-Sham—the strengthening of interurban links that we have witnessed already in the Beirut-Damascus case, and the fact that these links channeled outside imperial political and global economic actors.

In trade, Jerusalem's economy was much smaller than that of Damascus, and focused much less on production than on services for visitors like pilgrims. Hence, its trade with Jaffa was much thinner than that between Damascus and Beirut. But relatively speaking, it mattered, because Jaffa imposed itself as the closest port for the many consumers of Jerusalem, which was Palestine's largest city. Moreover, the Jaffa-Jerusalem axis was powered by an infrastructure cluster unique for Palestine: a modern road, a railway, and a telegraph line. The railway in particular increased Jaffa's value and power. The axis found expression also in strong sociocultural ties between the two cities' Arab populations, discussed further below, and by two factors absent in the relationship between Beirut and Damascus.

One factor had to do with the Holy Land. In particular Jerusalem, a premier Jewish, Christian, and Muslim pilgrimage center, attracted from the 1830s more and more European and American visitors. With the opening of a British consulate in 1838, it also became the object of intense European competition. Many visitors were too poor to even rent a donkey to reach it. Thus, thousands of Russian peasant pilgrims walked from Jaffa to Jerusalem. (They were dedicated: In 1864, 150 of them rolled a large church bell all the way up to the Holy City.) Still, by the later nineteenth century almost all Christian and many Jewish and Muslim visitors to Jerusalem traveled via Jaffa. Put more forcefully, they had to travel via the port of Jaffa, from where they were channeled up the hill to Jerusalem; thus spent some money in Jaffa; and often paid for some sort of transport to and from Jerusalem.[118]

The other factor absent between Beirut and Damascus but present in the Jaffa-Jerusalem interurban connection was a sizable Jewish population. To be sure, few Jaffawi Jew married into a Jerusalem family: their community was too young and small for that. Also, in Jerusalem the Zionist "newcomers went unnoticed among the large majority of the old *yishuv*," and the leftist pioneer Zionists of the second aliyah (1904–1914) had little regard or patience for Judaism's holiest city. Ben-Gurion waited more than two years to visit Jerusalem after arriving in Jaffa in 1906 and being busy in politics and agriculture. It was working the land, and hence reworking one's presumably weak diasporic body and soul, that formed the material and symbolic crux of "practical" Zionism, an approach that by 1905 had become as influential as the "diplomatic" Zionism of Theodor Herzl. Besides, Zionism's original intellectual and political epicenters were Russian and European cities like Odessa, Warsaw, Berlin, and London.[119]

Nonetheless, the Jewish Jaffa-Jerusalem axis mattered for demographic, administrative-political, and cultural-political reasons. A number of Jerusalemite Jews migrated to booming Jaffa, some stores had a branch in both cities, and Jaffa shops and institutions posted ads in Jerusalem newspapers that were read also in Jaffa and across Palestine, for instance *Ha-Zvi* that was published by the father of modern Hebrew, Eliezer Ben Yehuda (1858–1922). Jaffa-based Zionist officials like Ruppin traveled for meetings with Jews and Ottomans to Jerusalem, also because it was the capital of the *mutasarrifiyya* Jerusalem. (Also, in 1914 the Zionist Office was moved from Jaffa to Jerusalem.) Certain leftists, many from traditional Eastern European and Russian Jewish families, discovered some feelings for Jerusalem. Ben-Gurion was touched after all when he first visited the Wailing Wall. A few Zionist politicians, too, worked in Jerusalem. In 1908 / 1909 the leader of the leftist Po'alei Zion party's Palestinian branch, Itzhak Ben-Zvi, "made [Jerusalem] his headquarters, believing [it] to be the best place for the party to grow and prepare a Jewish proletariat for its revolutionary mission." In 1910 Ben-Gurion moved to Jerusalem to work, until 1911, for the party's newspaper *Achdut*. And it may not have been by chance that Tel Aviv built its municipal building right next to the Jaffa-Jerusalem railway track, for all travelers to see.[120]

Jerusalem's and Jaffa's Arabs, too, became strongly tied together. Jaffa's meteoric rise from the late nineteenth century showed in Jerusalem's demography. "Jaffa . . . accounted for . . . 49% of all transregional ties through marriage and migration" into the Greek Orthodox community of Jerusalem's Sa'diyya neighborhood in 1905. For the neighborhood's Muslims, Jaffa was despite its very recent rise a more important origin point than giant Damascus, and it snapped at the heels of Jerusalem's old interior neighbors Hebron and Nablus.[121] Also, because Jerusalem was with Jaffa Palestine's principal cultural hub— featuring Western, Ottoman state, and Arab schools like Sakakini's *Madrasa Dusturiyya Wataniyya*, public libraries like the *Khalidiyya*, visiting Egyptian and Syrian musicians and story tellers, and various presses—the two cities developed a strong sociocultural synergy. It took form in the inclusion of news from Jerusalem in *Filastin's* Local News, and in events like a visit, in 1911, by Jaffa's athletic club to Jerusalem, the only other Palestinian city to found such a club before 1914. And it was not by chance that al-Issa bought *Filastin's* printers in Jerusalem, or that one of his closest friends was a Jerusalemite: Khalil Sakakini.[122]

The two were so close indeed that al-Issa attended Sakakini's small wedding in Jerusalem—and that the two and Sakakini's wife Sultana decided to move the nuptials to Jaffa. The reason was that in Jerusalem, Greek Orthodox priests, whom al-Issa and Sakakini were fighting as part of the so-called *nahda urtuduksiyya,* had conditioned their blessing on humiliating demands. Al-Issa's and the Sakakini's ensuing shenanigans—they had an al-Issa family member in Jaffa sequester Greek Orthodox priests to keep them incommunicado from Jerusalem and then perform the ceremony when the wedding party arrived— illustrate just how close Jaffa and Jerusalem had grown. They felt they *had* to pull that stunt because the Jaffa-Jerusalem telegraph had brought their cities, priests included, very close together. And they *could* pull it off because they, too, were able to use the telegraph, alerting al-Issa's accomplices, then take the train and get Khalil and Sultana married the very same evening.[123]

The question of Zionism and, partly related, of proto-national ideas about Palestinianness had an Arab Jaffa-Jerusalem dimension, too. Both cities were organizational and intellectual hotspots for Arabs concerned about Zionism. No doubt, there was by no means only enmity between Jews and Arabs but a range of interactions including friendships, cooperation, and coexistence. Also, conflicts mattered not only to Jaffa and Jerusalem. Zionists lived in a number of towns and agricultural settlements, and news about Arab-Zionist rows in the countryside, mostly about property rights, did make the rounds. And not only Jaffawis and Jerusalemites commented on Zionism. In Haifa for instance the editor of *al-Karmil,* Najib al-Khouri Nassar, warned that "Zionism . . . requires [one to be] alarmed and cautious."[124]

Even so, Jerusalem and Jaffa were hotspots for Arab concerns about Zionism. The two cities were the highest concentration of Arabs and Zionists (in Jaffa) and of non-Zionist Jews and some Zionists (in Jerusalem). Also, the two were Palestine's best connected, most audible and most visible communities. Jerusalem's Arab elite—notables like in other cities of Bilad al-Sham—was Palestine's most powerful. As for Jaffa, the gateway to Palestine, it saw hundreds and in peak years more than thousand Zionist arrivals. While many moved on or reemigrated, almost all received their first impression of Erets Israel here. "Hebrew spoken in the streets, shops and restaurants: buds of the [Hebrew] renaissance!," Ben-Gurion recalled his excitement. Many stayed, about 10,000 by 1914. Also, Zionist patterns like building and if possible living apart were ominously plain early on, with a particularly grating example at Jaffa's doorstep: Tel Aviv's "Jews only" policy interdicted land resale to Gentiles. Besides, the Jaffa region was one of two areas, the other being the Galilee, where most Zionist rural settlements were concentrated.[125]

Against this background, Jaffa's *Filastin* persistently attacked Zionists and, concerned about land purchases, distributed a free copy of each issue to every Jaffawi village. Its worries had precedents. Already in the early 1890s tensions rose in Jaffa, with a short riot in 1895, and another in 1908. Also, Arab Jaffawis protested to the Ottoman authorities against land sales. Jerusalemites criticized the Zionists, too. Mufti Tahir al-Husayni, of a prominent notable family, protested from the start of the first aliyah to sultan Abdul Hamid II; other Husaynis, most insistently Sa'id by the twentieth century, did so, too. (Others had no problem with Zionists.) In 1891, a letter to Istanbul drafted by leading Jerusalemites against Jewish immigration was apparently signed by 500 locals. A member of another notable family, Ruhi al-Khalidi, an intellectual who entered politics in the twentieth century and whose uncle Yusuf had for years voiced concerns about Zionism, tried stopping immigration, saw danger in the growing Jewish-only settlements, and was most alarmed about Zionism's "larger vision." Numerous Zionist texts he read proved to him that "the Zionists had a broader plan to first create a miniature state within the state, and then ultimately . . . take over Palestine."[126]

Is it a contradiction, then, that one of *Filastin*'s stated core missions was to "inform the people of *Jaffa*"? Or that Sakakini, although regarded not only by Jerusalemites as an important thinker and teacher, was deeply rooted in his city? Probably not. "The national" as a real and imagined space does not simply transcend the urban, interurban, and regional. It is built by them and builds onto and sometimes across them without, however, dissolving them. Toward the end of the Ottoman era, Jaffa and Jerusalem became centers of an emerging sense of (Ottoman) Palestinianness. As important, together they became a geographical and political-intellectual axis for that sense. This was the case doubly because Palestine's northern and southern bounds were vague and the Jaffa-Jerusalem axis was suitably situated in the middle; and because the *mutasarrifiyya* Jerusalem, which included Jaffa, served as an administrative core for Palestinianness, indeed often was referred to as "Palestine" *tout court.*[127]


## From Cities to the Countryside: The Central Periphery

Until now, this chapter has focused on socio-spatial intertwinements involving the region of Bilad al-Sham, cities, and their interurban relations. To round out this picture, I now turn to a rural area: Bilad al-Sham's central periphery, a zone composed of the Upper Galilee, Jabal Amil, Jawlan, and northwestern Transjordan. It is treated here partly because it will continue to matter to this story, for after World War I it would straddle the borders of Palestine, Lebanon, Syria, and Transjordan; but chiefly because it illustrates that there were limits to large cities' penetration of their hinterlands.[128]

Administratively divided between the provinces Beirut and Suriya, the central periphery is hilly, even mountainous, and hence was not easy to access in the late Ottoman period. While the time-honored Damascus-Cairo caravan route crossed its southern part, it had no modern roads, and the Haifa-Damascus railway skirted its southern border and arrived late, in 1905. Moreover, the zone was situated dead in the middle between Damascus, Beirut, Sidon, Acre, Haifa, and Nablus. No one city dominated it. Hence, it was peripheral despite its position at Bilad al-Sham's center. Zionist settlers of Metula, founded in 1896 south of Marjayoun, called it a "forlorn corner," "distant from the Yishuv" and "without connection to the civilized world."[129]

Reality was more complicated. The fact that the central periphery was not dominated by one large city did not mean that it was behind the moon. For one, neighboring cities actually did somewhat intervene. After the 1858 Ottoman Land Law, a few merchants from Beirut and Sidon bought some land in the Jabal 'Amil. More crucially, the central periphery had two small but active mercantile towns: Safad and particularly Marjayoun, a mixed Christian / Muslim tertiary Ottoman administrative center. Some Marjayouni merchants worked in their zone, with peasants and settled or seminomadic bedouin, as well as outside, mainly in Transjordan, with nomadic bedouin. This shaped some merchants' way of life, not only their business hours. The Roman Orthodox Jabbaras—who originated from the Hijaz and Transjordan, that is, had lived among bedouin for centuries before arriving in Marjayoun in 1613, and some of whom had converted to Islam—helped "administer the law to the Beduin Arabs. They were famous for their horsemanship and intimate social ties with the beduin." Another merchant, Ibrahim Dhiba, had a *madafa*—a free guest house, typical also of bedouin sheikhs—and "an open house" in Marjayoun. A third, Wahba Shadid, was famed to be so hospitable that like bedouin he "threatened to beat his guest if he would not eat."[130]

They were not exceptions. The list of Marjayouni trading families was long. In 1900, it included 106 merchants working in the Hula Valley north of the Sea of Galilee, the Jawlan, and the Hawran; 177 in Irbid, the Ghor, the Galilee, Nazareth, and the Marj Ibn 'Amir Valley; 118 among the Beni Hasan beduin tribes and / or in the Jabal 'Ajlun; and 148 among other peasant and bedouin populations, mainly in Transjordan. (Many worked in several places.) And as the Damascus-Cairo caravan route crossed their zone, a few even traded as far as Egypt. Especially those working among the bedouin returned home to Marjayoun only for a few months each year in winter. They bought their goods—some of which, like dyes, finished in Marjayoun—from the town's richest, wholesale merchants. Some also opened a branch in places like Quneitra, to easily interact with Damascene traders. And into the postwar period, Marjayoun was visited every year by caravans carrying agricultural and husbandry produce from places as far as the Najd. From Marjayoun, the goods were sold locally and to larger cities like Nablus and Damascus. And although they felt the attraction of big cities—Ilias Abu Murad, born in Marjayoun in 1906, studied female tailoring in Beirut in 1930, for example—local attachments endured. Abu Murad opened a shop back home in 1931. And it is said that when landowner and merchant Sa'ad Hourani was asked to buy land in a Beiruti neighborhood near the beach, he replied: "I'm king here, and you want me to leave and buy cacti and sand!?"[131]

At the same time, many Marjaouni families' origins and life destinies transcended the central periphery. Many Christians like the Barakat family traced their presence to an immigration wave from the Hawran in the early 1600s. The Shadids said that their ancestor was a Russian merchant who had settled in Homs, where one of his four sons stayed whereas the others moved to the Hawran, to Damascus, and to Marjayoun. Other Christian families arrived fleeing from the 1860–1861 massacres. Furthermore, by the late nineteenth century some inhabitants, like one Doctor As'ad Rahhal, moved to Beirut to get a higher education, just like other shawwam did at the time. Many more emigrated overseas, mainly to French West Africa and the Americas. A descendant, late New York Times correspondent Anthony Shadid who died in 2012 covering the Syrian civil war, wrote a fascinating memoir that turns around his ancestral home in Marjayoun. And back in the late nineteenth century, we know of various Marjayounis overseas. Thus, of the six Sammara brothers, four remained and traded in and around Marjayoun while two more emigrated, staying in contact with their family in the Old World but settling and working in New York—the very city where Prelude 1 started.[132]

## Conclusion

The time from the middle third of the nineteenth century to World War I was a first stage in the twin-faced process of transpatialization in Bilad al-Sham. The region and its age-old, from the late seventeenth century quasi-autonomous cities met and mingled with, shaped and were reshaped by, a now Eurocentric world economy and a resurgent, territorially intrusive Ottoman state.

This encounter transformed Bilad al-Sham's cities. They were administratively and socioculturally linked to the Ottoman state more than before. In particular, elites became more Ottomanized and more strongly tied to Istanbul—looking to it for cultural inspiration, socializing with its elites, and periodically sojourning there. Also, the composition and behavior of cities' economic actors shifted as they were being incorporated into a now Eurocentric world economy. Some actors folded; others survived by cutting manufacturing costs or adapting their products; yet others, merchants, traded with a wider range of destinations. Last, cities grew precipitously and turned recognizably modern, part of a most momentous trend reshaping life in the nineteenth century around the globe.

Despite these developments, cities remained central to their inhabitants and rural hinterlands. They had deep roots. More crucially, they remained hubs of sociability; retained their politics, including a distinct notable or other elite in each city; and preserved their pride of place and its (agricultural, mercantile, and/or artisanal) material underpinnings. This last feat underlines that although their economies shifted upon being incorporated into a Eurocentric world system, they did not crumble. This, in turn, was partly because Istanbul somewhat protected especially Bilad al-Sham's interior cities from outside pressures. Belonging to one of the few polities in Afro-Asia that were not colonized in the nineteenth century had its advantages—and produced a fascinating triangular, urban/state/world-economic aspect of transpatialization.

Cities' persistence showed in four distinguishable ways. All were interlinked; and in all, cities were transformative. First, as Sakakini's story showed so intimately, cities remained the place where shawwam lived the modern world, the arena to experience and perform being modern. Second, they functioned as staging points and channelers of the region-wide exercise of modern state territoriality. The Ottoman Empire's civil and military institutions penetrated Bilad al-Sham not directly from Istanbul but via provincial and sub-provincial capitals. Third, to tackle negative effects of being incorporated into the Eurocentric world market, some cities economically penetrated their surrounding hinterland more than before, even expanded their hinterland. They succeeded partly because Istanbul, for its own raison d'état, bit by bit pacified rural and tribal areas. This was another advantage, to urbanites, of living in a sovereign polity; and constituted another triangular, urban/state/world-economic aspect of transpatialization. Fourth and last, by fortifying interurban ties—between the coast and the interior chiefly Beirut-Damascus, Jaffa-Jerusalem, and Haifa-Damascus; within the interior, Damascus-Aleppo—pairs of cities helped channel world trade to their own advantage or, especially in interurban ties in the interior, to bolster trade alternatives. True, European capital built the transport infrastructure for two interurban ties, Beirut-Damascus and Jaffa-Jerusalem. But Istanbul agreed to them, and bankrolled the two others. As important, the two European ones could not have been built without resident mercantile and political elites being involved. And most crucial, despite the presence of some European traders and consulates in the coastal cities, it was resident merchants who dominated that expanding interurban trade, deepening their presence also overseas, sometimes through expanding mercantile family networks.

Regarding cities, a last note needs to be added: on Beirut. Secondary at best in the early modern period, by the early 1860s it had become Bilad al-Sham's economic-mercantile and cultural-educational gravitation point. This happened for two reasons. Beirut's exceptionally sizeable Christian population—a large minority until 1860; a majority thereafter—attracted European consulates and traders, which in the context of the now Eurocentric world economy gave Beirut an edge. And when Egypt occupied Bilad al-Sham in 1831/1832–1840/1841, it made Beirut its sole provincial capital; thereafter Istanbul, albeit at first reinstituting the old multi-provincial structure, paid more attention to Beirut and by 1888 agreed to create an entirely new province for that city. Beirut's development, including Istanbul's part in it, is fascinating doubly because it constituted a prominent quadrangular, urban/region/state/world-economic aspect of transpatialization.

Furthermore, Beirut's success epitomized the changing hierarchy between interior and coast. Interior cities—most important Damascus and Aleppo, whose old transcontinental trade suffered in the nineteenth century—became weaker, the coast stronger. But not all cities were equally affected. The coastal cities Tripoli, Sidon, Tyre, and Acre were eclipsed by Beirut; and they were demographically, economically, and administratively politically weaker than the big interior cities. Although Aleppo's chief port, Alexandretta, did reasonably well, and although Haifa and Jaffa rose from the late nineteenth century, none could hold a candle to Beirut; and they, too, were weaker than Damascus and Aleppo. This situation, in turn, helps clarify what it meant that Beirut became Bilad al-Sham's "gravitation point." Beirut's relative weight in the region grew. But it did not gain centralized control over it, for its rise was too recent; its topological disadvantages (difficult access to the interior; shallow waters at the port) were too grave; the interior cities were too big and agile in reacting to the challenges of the Eurocentric world economy; Istanbul was too invested in bolstering the interior; and Jaffa and Haifa, also them supported by Istanbul, were too capably rising as ports by the late nineteenth century.

In consequence, Bilad al-Sham's increasing sociocultural and economic integration took the shape not of a centralized region, but of a multi-urban patchwork. This process was driven mainly by strengthening interurban ties between multiple pairs of cities; partly, by Beirut functioning as a gravitation point and hence meeting point for shawwam from across the region; and lastly, by an uptick in region-wide interactions. The Jewish Yishuv, in Palestine, was an integral part of this development.

More integration in the region did not mean less outside contact, though. The opposite was true. Various premodern transnational ties—some socioreligious, to do with the Christian and the Muslim worlds; others mercantile, related to trade across Eurasia—persisted, if in shifting forms. As noted above, administrative, sociocultural, and commercial linkages grew with the Ottoman Empire and with Istanbul at its center. Commercial and sociocultural relations grew tighter also with Egypt, a trend dramatized by tens of thousands of shawwam migrating there. And an even more massive migration was overseas from the late nineteenth century. Some shawwam went to Europe and West Africa, most to the Americas; many stayed in contact with their hometowns, and some returned periodically or for good. Their movements formed part of the peak, from the 1880s to World War I, of one of history's most massive migration patterns, that across the Atlantic: mainly westward but also eastward, as remigration and multiple-stop migration.

The simultaneity and correlation of more regional integration and more outside contact had a fascinating parallel in shifts in the very concept of Bilad al-Sham or Suriya, the European name that was becoming fashionable from the mid-nineteenth century. At this time, intellectuals started assigning national meaning to Bilad al-Sham / Suriya, which before had been merely cultural-territorial terms; and by the late nineteenth century, some inserted this nationalized concept into a global context, framing Suriya as one *watan* in a worldwide family of homelands.

Nota bene: This shift in Bilad al-Sham's / Suriya's meaning and the shift in its functioning (i.e., its greater integration) together epitomize a key point underlying this book. Like all regions, Bilad al-Sham was not an unchanging geographic given, but a product of changing historical actors and processes. How it, its cities, and their internal and external linkages fared in World War I—this is the question to which we turn now.

# Rafiq al-Tamimi and Muhammad Bahjat Make a Tour

It is an undeniable truth that we are very much in need of useful publications that track and examine the general state of our country from a scientific and civilizational perspective, so that we may get to know the essence of our holy homeland. Without doubt, failure to do so will weaken [our] resolve and [make us] lose courage and activity.... His Excellency 'Azmi Bek Efendi, the Exalted Wali of Beirut, has recognized the importance of this matter, ... and sent [Rafiq Bek al-Tamimi and Muhammad Bahjat Bek] to the southern part of the province.

Beirut, 1917. Rafiq al-Tamimi and Muhammad Bahjat open *Wilayat Beirut,* a report on an official investigative tour in 1916 of the southern half of Province Beirut, with guns a-blazing. They are full of élan and young, in their late twenties; model products of the modern Ottoman state that allowed two boys born in Nablus and Aleppo to study for free in Istanbul, Salonika, and Paris; and loyal cogs of its machinery, as the principal of the Beiruti School of Commerce and the vice-principal of the *Sultani* School, respectively. Most crucially, they are living and working in the midst of Istanbul's toughest test to date, World War I. Stronger enemies than ever before—principally Britain and Russia, and France—are threatening the Ottoman Empire's very existence. Thus, more than ever before the state needs to shape society and make it do what the state needs to survive. 'Azmi Bek, since 1915 the governor (*wali*) of Province Beirut, dispatches al-Tamimi and Bahjat on their southbound mission in 1916 and has them publish their findings. He agrees with them that periodically published yearbooks (*salnamihs*) are not effective enough an information tool in wartime. This report is followed in 1918 by a second one, describing a 1917 inspection of the northern part of Province Beirut.[1]

During their two tours al-Tamimi and Bahjat observe the power of the state. Up and down the province the army builds roads, and Ottoman Turkish, until recently not well known, is in some places now understood by a number of people, especially the young. The two officials project state power, too. They go wherever they want and interrogate whomever they please, peasants, merchants, notables, and state officials high and low. And they speak the language of power. They rebuke and reprove, advise and advocate, and address their readers in the second person plural—"you!"—which makes for a doubly intense read.[2]

But with all that power comes the recognition of its limits. A heart-wrenching instance is al-Tamimi's and Bahjat's journey from Beirut to the province's northern half through Mount Lebanon, which since 1915 has been in the grip of a famine. The two find "many doors and windows shut"—some people have moved to the Bikaa Valley, between the Lebanon and the Anti-Lebanon Mountain ranges—and are beset by "black-faced children" begging for "a piece of bread." At night, cooped up in a room in the coastal town of Batrun, halfway between Beirut and Tripoli, they can't sleep. "We did not stop hearing the voice of a man from the Mountain (*jabali*) saying 'I am hungry, I am hungry' outside."[3]

What drives them up the wall are other things, though: statistics that are inadequate in their eyes, malfunctioning municipalities, and, worst, lassitude.[4] Although they do not talk about World War I often—combat would reach Bilad al-Sham only in 1917—they do impress on the reader that the empire is fighting for its very survival, and that it therefore is doubly lamentable that in places like Tripoli "you will not see in the Muslim neighborhoods a trace of initiative or activity. . . . This is an immense misfortune. For our age is far from being immaterial, and until today history's womb has not born . . . [such a] universal war that engulfs the entire world."[5]

Al-Tamimi and Bahjat's endeavor, and their book, is organized in a way that reflects the continuing weight of cities. To be sure, on their tour the two have to cross the countryside, and their book painstakingly details distances, villages, and beautiful scenes and ancient ruins. They observe peasants, too. On the way to Marjayoun for instance they note that every person they cross is a peasant woman; no man is in sight.[6] But they barely report contacts with peasants. The places where they stay, investigate, and socialize are administrative centers. Their book is ordered accordingly: not by topics, but by cities.

And how well established these still are! Al-Tamimi and Bahjat routinely report in a neutral tone on age-old local particularities. In Tripoli for instance they detail marriage and burial customs and relate stories about one of the city's most beloved, recently deceased sons, Shaykh 'Ali al-'Umari. Sometimes, they strike a more exasperated tone. Thus, Acre, a city with much historical pride, as Chapter 1 noted, worries al-Tamimi and Bahjat to no end. They find the 'Akawis poor, sick, and worst of all lazy, their women neurasthenic, and their town dirty.[7]

The queen of all those cities is Beirut. More than half a century of relentless growth and a quarter century as provincial capital have left their trace. It is not simply that 'Azmi Bek governs from there. Al-Tamimi and Bahjat describe Beirut as a civilizational lodestar for Bilad al-Sham. Tripoli for instance features two sorts of buildings— old-fashioned ones and those built "in the Beiruti style." Indeed, "because of Tripoli's situation on the littoral, its proximity to Beirut and its strong mixity, the life of its leading families has been palpably transformed." It is to Beirut, too, and to Istanbul, that Tripolitans send their children to acquire a higher education. Especially Bilad al-Sham's coastal cities take their cues from Beirut, which according to al-Tamimi and Bahjat stands at the forefront of modernization (*tajaddud*).[8]

A visit that al-Tamimi receives in Beirut confirms the impression that this city is a cultural capital also during the war. In April 1918 two Germans, Professor Gotthelf Bergsträsser, an Orientalist scholar, and Major Friedrich Trautz meet al-Tamimi as part of an official economic and statistical mission in Bilad al-Sham: Berlin is Istanbul's war ally together with the Austro-Hungarian Empire. With British imperial forces at this point already occupying the southern half of Palestine, al-Tamimi now "expresses great pessimism about Turkey's chances to get up again and about its human material." He also complains about his and Bahjat's difficulties in collecting statistics, and notes that to prepare their publications they used the library of Beirut's Université de Saint Joseph, which is currently under state control. This does not surprise Bergsträsser. During his and Trautz's stay in Beirut, they run into Muhammad Kurd 'Ali, the Damascene intellectual we met in Chapter 1, who has come to use that selfsame library, and they themselves are visiting Beirut to purchase books untraceable elsewhere. In short, in Bergsträsser's learned opinion Beirut is and remains Bilad al-Sham's "spiritual center."[9]

Then again, he and Trautz are only on a visit. Beirut, the city that for a good half century has been outshining all others in Bilad al-Sham, is not their base. Damascus is, and not by chance. German soldiers and civilians who are stationed across the region are headquartered here. Safely separated by two mountain ranges from the Mediterranean Sea, which is under absolute Allied control, this interior city is the wartime headquarters of the Ottoman Fourth Army. It is from Damascus that the Ottoman military defends all of Bilad al-Sham and the Hijaz, and that Jamal Pasha, its commander from December 1914 to January 1918, rules those regions, outranking civilian provincial governors like 'Azmi Bek.

Al-Tamimi and Bahjat's *Wilayat Beirut* can be read as a reflection and projection of Ottoman state power at its peak—a peak so high indeed that the text also feels like a towering searchlight which spots weaknesses without mercy. Moreover, the report, its authors' tour, and their German visitors give us a taste of how nineteenth-century socio-spatial changes developed in the crucible of war. In 1914–1918 Bilad al-Sham's cities continued to powerfully structure social action, while Bilad al-Sham's integration as a patchwork region sped up. Why was this the case? And what role did war conditions play? These questions underlie Chapter 2.

# 2

# CRUCIBLE OF WAR
## 1914–1918

### Historical Context: The Ottoman Empire in World War I

World War I was total like no conflict before. Citizen-soldiers were mobilized by the millions and civilians became part of war in a more organized form than ever, in both metropoles and colonies.[1] This showed most dramatically on the stalemated Western European front. Here, industrialized warfare was much more devastating, and reflected much greater state power, than on Ottoman fronts. But total war engulfed also Europe's east, European colonies, and the Ottoman Empire.[2]

In the empire, from 1913 the government had been headed by a dictatorial triumvirate—Talaat Pasha and officers Enver Pasha and Jamal Pasha (1872–1922)—who operated at the core of the Committee of Union and Progress (CUP) party. They had reacted to military defeats in Libya and the Balkans, in 1911–1913, by seeking to give their empire-state more nation-like coherence. Key to that endeavor was mass mobilization which, with roots in 1911–1913, grew during a German-supervised army reorganization in 1913 and ballooned in 1914–1918, partly with German assistance.[3] In these four years the Ottoman state mobilized a mindboggling 2,850,000 men, over 10 percent of the population, and extracted as many goods as possible from its population. As a result, Ottomans experienced World War I not so much as a rupture, like western Europeans accustomed to decades of peace, but as a shocking climax of wars starting in 1911. The Ottoman Empire had the by far the highest civilian death ratio of all major combatants: 15 percent of the overall population, versus Russia and Britain (both 2 percent) and Germany, Austria-Hungary, and France (all 4 percent). The war proved to be most traumatic for Armenians. Especially in the territories forming today's Turkey, the Ottoman state targeted them in a genocide that killed up to 1,500,000 people. The war massively affected other civilians, too, though the reason differed. In Bilad al-Sham, about one in six civilians died because—as al-Tamimi and Bahjat's story in Prelude 2 has illustrated—the state was not organized enough to properly distribute across the region food supplies that were dropping due to a strict Allied sea blockade. Still, the Ottoman state's tenacity in 1914–1918 was impressive. The acme of a century-long intermittent development of infrastructural power, it allowed Istanbul to keep fighting all the way until fall 1918.[4]

From a bird's-eye view of the world war as a whole, however, the Ottoman fronts were ultimately secondary and treated as such—as a *Nebenkriegsschauplatz*, a side show[5]—by the empire's closest ally, Germany, and by its opponents alike. In Britain's case, this showed, for one, in differing diplomatic approaches to Berlin and Istanbul. London never considered a separate peace with the former but repeatedly toyed with that idea regarding the latter. Although it did not envision Germany's occupation or division, it planned for just such an eventuality concerning the much weaker Ottoman Empire, including its Arab provinces. Thus, in 1915, letters by Sir Henry McMahon, High Commissioner of British Egypt, to Hussein, the Sharif of Mecca, promised support for an Arab kingdom in key parts of Bilad al-Sham after the war in return for a revolt. (Known as 'the Arab Revolt' and led by a son of Hussein, Faisal, it had little political resonance and even less military value during the war. The overwhelming majority of Ottomans remained loyalist in word if not deed.)[6] In 1916, the secret Anglo-French(-Russian) Sykes-Picot agreement divided Bilad al-Sham, Iraq and southeastern Anatolia between France and Britain, with some consideration also to other European, especially Russian, and Arab interests. And in 1917, the Balfour Declaration stated that "His Majesty's Government view with favour the establishment in Palestine of a national home for the Jewish people."[7]

Militarily, too, the Ottoman fronts were ultimately a side show. The biggest spectacle, and the place where the war was decided, was the eastern and especially the western fronts of Germany, the country most responsible for triggering the war, and the single strongest army in 1914–1918. The military might of Russia and the British Empire—and of the French Empire and from 1917 the United States—was concentrated here. It was firstly for victory in Europe, on the Western front against Germany, that Britain and France recruited men and materiel from across their respective empires and purchased goods from around the globe. And it was in Europe, too, that most soldiers died. Although horrendous, Ottoman military casualty figures—up to 771,844 killed and up to 763,753 wounded, a total of 1,535,597—paled compared to the totals of Russia (7,204,369), Germany (6,252,662), France (5,663,800), Austria-Hungary (5,114,200), and the United Kingdom (2,652,858), a fact Ottomans understood already during the war. And it was not by chance that the British Empire's largest (and failed) campaign against Istanbul, a seaborne attack on the Dardanelles in 1915, was waged not simply to reopen the Straits between the Mediterranean and the Black Sea, but also to thereby launch a southeastern front against Germany and its Austria-Hungarian ally.[8]

Again from a bird's-eye view of the world war as a whole, Bilad al-Sham was a side show within the Ottoman side show. Besides the Dardanelles, the Ottomans fought their toughest campaigns against Russia in the Caucasus in 1914–1917 and against Britain in Mesopotamia in 1915. By contrast, two Ottoman stabs at British Egypt, launched from Bilad al-Sham in 1915 and 1916, faltered quickly. Supply lines were stretched too thinly in the Sinai Peninsula. As a result, both Jamal Pasha and Britain adopted a defensive military posture: the former on land, in Bilad al-Sham, the latter in Egypt and along Bilad al-Sham's coast on which it imposed a tight naval blockade. It was only one year before the war's end, in the fall of 1917, after having completed a railroad through the Sinai, that British imperial troops broke through Ottoman lines at Gaza and Beersheba and swept through a small part of Bilad al-Sham, southern Palestine, up to Jerusalem. And only at the war's very end, in the fall of 1918, did Britain thrust its troops up to Aleppo.[9]

## The Story to Come

This strategic picture mattered for wartime Bilad al-Sham: the region barely experienced ground fighting and basically remained in Ottoman hands. Moreover, Jamal Pasha—a man ruthless and resourceful; and possessing "full powers in military and civilian affairs" in Bilad al-Sham[10]—and his officials did not just have roads paved and railway tracks laid for the military, did not merely mass-recruit men and mass-requisition food. Among other actions, they also had people moved around, new state schools established, and urban neighborhoods reordered. They did not only wage war, then, did not contend themselves with keeping Britain out of Bilad al-Sham. As al-Tamimi and Bahjat's story epitomized, they took advantage of the war to speed up one of the two macro-historical processes that had shaped Bilad al-Sham from the mid-nineteenth century: the exercise of modern state territoriality. They sought to give the Ottoman empire-state more nation-like coherence. And as they acted within the confines of Bilad al-Sham, over which Jamal Pasha had exclusive control, they deepened the region's integration.[11]

Regarding cities, two points stand out. First, the hierarchy between interior and littoral cities was reversed. For separate reasons the former grew stronger, the latter weaker. The command center of peak state territoriality was Damascus, and also economic production, including agriculture, was strongest in the interior. Contrariwise the war, including the Allied blockade of Bilad al-Sham, unmoored that region's place in the world economy, the other macro-historical process shaping Bilad al-Sham from the mid-nineteenth century. This hurt the littoral. Exports from Bilad al-Sham collapsed; imports dropped. Although European goods still were imported into the Ottoman Empire, they were much fewer than before and entered mainly by land, through Istanbul and Anatolia. Consequently, not many made it all the way to Bilad al-Sham, at the empire's southern end; and those that did, entered by road and rail from the north, via interior cities like Aleppo and Damascus, rather than by ship from the west, via port cities like Beirut.

Second, cities as a whole retained a powerful presence in wartime Bilad al-Sham. This was because officials headquartered in Damascus needed local administrative support to accomplish their goals. Moreover, although hundreds of thousands of people hit the road when hunger or state exactions became unbearable, most remained in Bilad al-Sham; and after 1918 many returned to their points of origin. The interurban ties that had been strengthened from the mid-nineteenth century persisted, too. While they saw less commercial activity than before 1914, some interurban and regional commerce by private individuals and the state persisted, and so did the traffic infrastructure.

In sum, transpatialization did not disappear. True, its facets functioned quite differently in 1914–1918 than before 1914, mainly because Bilad al-Sham's world economy inclusion was gravely weakened, and because the exercise of state territoriality was de facto regionalized within Bilad al-Sham. But principal factors integral to transpatialization persisted: cities, including their however shifting interurban ties; the region, whose integration indeed sped up in 1914–1918; and the exercise of modern state territoriality, irrespective of the fact that it became regionalized. And pre-1914 manifestations of transpatialization persisted, too. Some were weakened, echo-like, but extant; an example was how Beirut, though subordinated to Damascus, used its vast prewar economic, social, and cultural capital as an established port-city—as an urban / regional / state / world-economic fusion point (see Chapter 1)—to preserve some of its powers of attraction in 1914–1918. Other manifestations of transpatialization remained sturdy; an instance was the wartime expansion of modern road and rail infrastructures. Together, these continuities meant that by 1918 the region, its cities and their interurban ties were very recognizable versions of their prewar selves and of how they had in tandem helped to drive transpatialization before 1914.

## Bilad al-Sham's Wartime Regional Integration

Various factors catalyzed Bilad al-Sham's wartime regional integration. A particularly tangible one had to do with the Ottoman state's war logistics: road and rail expansion. From the army's overall perspective of fighting the British, this was ultimately too little, too late. "Measured by the enormous demands of modern warfare, the provisioning line was inadequate," stated Merkel, the Damascus-based head of German logistics in Bilad al-Sham.[12] But the view from Bilad al-Sham differed. It was not simply that the army had absolute priority in using the railway and the more widely spread road projects served military purposes, and that the premier railway construction connected headquarters in Damascus to the front in southern Palestine. More important, many roads and rails remained usable during the war and for the most part thereafter, too. After the war Arab scholars, not great admirers of the Ottomans, acknowledged that in 1914–1918 "many kilometers were added to the road system of the country and never before had roads been in such good conditions as they were in 1918."[13] To the Ottoman infrastructure expansion we need to add the British railway that connected Egypt to Palestine. It played a key logistical role in 1916–1918 and thereafter helped modernize transport between Egypt and Bilad al-Sham. In fact, in 1916 Jamal Pasha himself was "a friend of the plan of a railway connection between Syria and Egypt, which in his opinion could be of political and economic use."[14]

We, who know how the war ended, might see that comment as a historically irrelevant oddity. But it was nothing of the sort. Rather, it exhibited a muscular commitment to wartime state building inside the radius of Jamal Pasha's rule.[15] To him—and to the thousands of civilian and military bureaucrats who worked for him, including convinced Ottoman nationalists like al-Tamimi and Bahjat—respective policies transcended the here and now. They shaped up into a vision of things to come. In an extended conversation that Jamal Pasha had with a German-Ottoman delegation, "a main topic was Syria's economic future." Similarly, in an interview with a German visitor, he underlined that some economic undertakings "have to and will endure long after the war." The interviewer came away feeling that "with and especially after the war, a new life shall enter Syria." This impression was deepened by images the pasha used in the interview. He wished to bring "light and air" to Syria's cities, for instance. The impression was apparent, too, in the pasha's thirst for more knowledge about his territory. Thus, in 1915 he supported an economic tour through Bilad al-Sham by the German Jewish head of the Zionist Palestine Office, Arthur Ruppin, which together with previous studies by Ruppin formed the basis for a massive German publication in 1917.[16] In sum, war was more than battles. It was an opportunity to re-form Bilad al-Sham such that it could be plugged into a more centralized, nation-state-like empire.[17]

This development had considerable regionalizing side effects. Some, like the dispatch of bureaucrats from one part of the region to another, extended past patterns.[18] Others sped up such patterns. While not directly furthering regional integration, a now firmly state-controlled system of education made life across the region more similar. After all, Jamal Pasha's writ ended at Bilad al-Sham's borders; and after the British occupation of southern Iraq in 1915 and the start of the Arab Revolt in the Hijaz in 1916, Bilad al-Sham was the only major Arab Ottoman region left intact. "Re-ordering" education entailed not only the closure of all but the American Western schools and the insistence to keep them shut after the war, but "the duty [to] . . . open and encourage Turkish schools." Turkish signified state rule as well as the firm rooting of that language, now the central state's paramount "official tongue," in schools and official life.[19] Perhaps not by chance, even in Francophile Beirut private Turkish tutors proliferated. Certainly not by chance was the mentioning of Turkish instruction in an opening announcement for primary and secondary schools in thirty-one Lebanese towns. So many in one fell swoop: that was exceptional, yet still part of a trend. Among other institutions, in Beirut a new elementary girls' school was founded, the Jamal Pasha Girls' School, formerly French, reopened for 500 pupils, the 'Ain Tura Armenian Orphanage was revamped, the *Maktab al-Sina'i* was expanded, and a new medical school launched. Moreover, the Bikaa Valley received a reopened formerly French agricultural school, Latrun a new one; Tripoli and Aleppo got new teachers' colleges; Damascus obtained a new elementary girls school, its medical college was reopened a year after its closure in 1914, and it acquired a law school; and Jerusalem boasted the particularly prestigious *Salahiyya* secondary school, which was moved to Damascus after Jerusalem's occupation by Britain in late 1917.[20]

Bilad al-Sham's regional integration was furthered by two other factors. One was minor: the vision of an Arab state within the region but also including the Hijaz. It was given some form and meaning in the McMahon-Hussein correspondence; and from 1916 an assortment of Arabs fought a guerilla Arab Revolt for it. In a sense, that revolt gave expression to Arabs' mostly private indignation about what they saw as a "brusque Turkification policy that engulfed all areas of public life," which they believed was designed to advance the empire's Turks. Such feelings were fed by the execution of eleven Arabs accused of treason in 1915 in Beirut and of twenty-one in 1916 in Beirut and Damascus. However, only following the war did the vision underlying the Arab revolt become truly relevant. Until 1918 guerilla actions were contained in the Hijaz and south Transjordan. Fearfully resigned and loyal to the Ottoman state headed by Jamal Pasha *al-Saffah* (Shedder of Blood), only few shawwam, people from Bilad al-Sham, were involved.[21]

A major factor advancing Bilad al-Sham's integration was people on the move and people's perception of this phenomenon. For one, some traders continued working across the region.[22] Much more massive was the movement of hundreds of thousands of soldiers and civilians. Not by chance, the term *safarbarlik,* travel by land—which from the early 1910s had become a popular term for compulsory mass recruitment— came to describe wartime life as a whole.[23] This life was so miserable that a German officer stationed in Bilad al-Sham, Theodor Wiegand, invoked Albrecht "Dürer's woodcuts" like *Four Horsemen of the Apocalypse:* "wherever one looks, misery, disease and pestilence." He could have added 'hunger,' even famine, whose root causes were the Allied blockade and flawed Ottoman food policies. The man whose desperate cries kept al-Tamimi and Bahjat from falling asleep in Batrun probably was one of as many as half a million people of a population of just over 3,000,000 who died of starvation and starvation-related diseases in 1915–1918.[24]

Indeed, hunger was what drove most civilians to hit the road. Some used confessional ties to survive the famine; a reported 50,000 Druze from the Shuf Mountains, in today's Lebanon, moved to the Jabal Druze, in Syria. Many others, too, trekked to the food-producing interior from the coast, especially from Mount Lebanon where silk production had replaced subsistence farming by the later nineteenth century. Still others tried to survive in the coastal towns or traveled there to try obtain basic supplies. In 1918 a German, Range, who rode from Haifa northward "hourly met people who came from the north to buy grain in Haifa and Acre"; a year earlier in Jouniyeh, Wiegand was "shocked by the masses of Lebanese people who, emaciated to skeletons, had come from the mountains to beg."[25]

Seen as a result of Jamal Pasha's policies, hunger helped to make life feel somewhat similar across Bilad al-Sham (though far from wholly identical, as we will see later). Together with the broader experience of internal migration that it fed, it would after the war become part of a specifically Bilad al-Shami war remembrance, including the claim that the "Turks" had always oppressed the "Arabs."[26] But it had deep effects already in 1914–1918. Although the war brought misery to all parts of the Ottoman Empire, shawwam experienced that misery within Bilad al-Sham, that is as a regional problem. This sentiment built on similar (though not identical) experiences of hunger / famine; on all shawwam being part of one and the same polity ruled by Jamal Pasha; on similar (though again not identical) sentiments toward that rule; and on almost all people moving within Bilad al-Sham, and hence transmitting their stories within the region's boundaries. This was most palpable in large cities like Damascus, because they attracted people hoping to survive from across the region.[27]

Civilian shawwam were not the only civilians on the move. Groups of Armenians from Anatolia who had somehow survived the genocide there, including death marches to northern Bilad al-Sham, were scattered all over the region. While all were in a horrible state and many died of starvation, some survived, forming the nucleus of enlarged postwar Armenian communities. There also were innumerable military fugitives from the law: draft dodgers and soldiers so hungry that they deserted. (Germans ironically called Ottoman soldiers "starvation artists," *Hungerkünstler*.[28]) This state of affairs worried officials. Although in some places like the province (*wilaya*) of Beirut it was only around 1916 that the state really tried to recruit anybody it could, also here recruitment exemptions became rarer already in 1915, with the defense against the British attack in the Dardanelles and with preparations for a second stab at Egypt. The provincial governor (*wali*) threatened to deport the families of draft dodgers and of deserters. Similarly, newspapers habitually reported on deserters found, tried, and often executed, and on deserters turned bandits. Some civilians were on the run, too, people like Najib Nassar, the editor of the Haifawi newspaper *al-Karmil* whom we met in Chapter 1. He moved around and hid out for two years; in 1917, he gave himself up and was brought to Damascus.[29]

## The Inclusion of the Yishuv in Bilad al-Sham's Wartime Regional Integration

The Yishuv partook in the process of sped-up regional integration. To be sure, after 1918 wartime experiences would be sidelined if not erased by the need to frame the Yishuv as part of Britain's victory and by the monumental impact of the Balfour Declaration and of the Palestine Mandate Charter on the Yishuv's self-view. But in 1914–1918 key Yishuvi experiences were structurally similar, if not equal, to those of Arabs. Like before 1914 the Yishuv formed part of region-wide trends. The famine that ravaged Lebanon caused some harm also to Palestine, and in 1915–1916 a horrible locust attack hit not only Lebanon and the Syrian interior but also Palestine—first, indeed, as it originated from the Sinai. Also, Jews feared Jamal Pasha as much as Arabs. Both had to move when the pasha ordered the people of Gaza and of Jaffa / Tel Aviv to evacuate into the interior in March 1917. (Fearing that a British attack on Gaza would succeed and that London's troops would sweep up Palestine's coast, he apparently wished to keep for Ottoman Bilad al-Sham as many inhabitants as possible, even when losing territory.) Similarly, not only Arabs but also a few Jews were executed for treason and sent into internal exile for political reasons.[30]

Finally, not unlike Arabs, Zionists for a long time during the war did not oppose the Ottomans. Rather, they hedged their bets and continued working with Istanbul, although there were serious contacts with London, too, chiefly by Haim Weitzman. In 1914, many followed the World Zionist Organization's call to acquire Ottoman citizenship to prove their loyalty; among them were members of the leftist Po'alei Zion party such as David Ben Gurion, Israel's future first Prime Minister, who had immigrated to Palestine in 1906 and studied law in Istanbul in 1913–1914. A few young men enlisted in the Ottoman army. And Zionist officials sought to keep in touch with Ottoman officials in Istanbul and with Jamal Pasha and his officials in Bilad al-Sham. Jamal Pasha, ever the state builder, appreciated Zionist economic know-how. The idea for Ruppin's economic tour of the region was born in a 1915 meeting with the pasha. A letter of introduction from the Imperial German General Consulate in Jerusalem stated that Ruppin's tour had "the authorization and [was] by order of the High Commander, Dschemal Pascha," and Ruppin's Ottoman tour travel papers described its objective as *maslahat* (state's benefit).[31]

## Damascus: Bilad al-Sham's Wartime Center

The Ottoman administration of wartime Bilad al-Sham had a center: Damascus. It was from here that it "project[ed] . . . its influence northwards to the Tauris Mountains [and] southwards to the Sinai and the Hijaz." As a result, it also pulled in a wide range of people from across the region to Damascus.[32] This twofold centralizing trend was set in motion by Istanbul's choice of Damascus as the Fourth Army's headquarters. Istanbul presumably chose one headquarter for its military presence in Bilad al-Sham because here it faced one enemy on one front, the British Empire across the Sinai, in Egypt. But why Damascus? The provincial capital Beirut was on the Allied-controlled Mediterranean Sea and its large Christian population had Francophile tendencies; and the provincial capital Aleppo was far away from the Egyptian front. Damascus, on the other hand, was not only a provincial capital and removed from the sea, but centrally located in Bilad al-Sham and staunchly Muslim to boot. Once chosen, its centrality was hardened by three factors. Jamal Pasha's rule meant that anybody who needed something important done had to make a pilgrimage to try to gain personal access. Moreover, due to state centralization, the British blockade, and wartime conditions, the state became a key economic actor; hence, Damascus became central not only militarily and administratively but also economically. And as the blockade included food, Damascus's proximity to grain-growing Hawran and Transjordan was a vital advantage.

The centrality of Damascus showed in many ways. The city was swamped by forced and voluntary arrivals, merchants, exiles and prisoners, soldiers, and refugees. Final military and civilian administrative decisions for the region were taken here. Damascus became also an information center. Beiruti newspapers reported about it more than before, often referring to its publications. Similarly, the German army newspaper *Armee-Zeitung Jildirim* was printed in Damascus and from there transported to German troops who in return wrote letters back to the Damascus-based editor.[33] And as the blockade and wartime conditions turned the state into a key economic actor, Damascus became central economically. Manufacturing in general, and for the army in particular, was centered there. The main citadel was turned into an enormous army production site. A new conserve factory in its first thirteen months reportedly churned out "55,000 tins of vegetables, 2,400 tins of tongue, 12,200 tons of meat broth, 13,300 tons of soup, 10,600 bottles lemonade, 4,500 bottles orange lemonade, 12,000 kilogram vinegar and 3,000 kilograms pickles . . . [and] great masses of salted meat and durable Turkish sausages." In fact, Damascus's wartime economic centrality was quite existential. The city used its administrative force and proximity to wheat-growing Hauran and Transjordan to provision itself with food at levels of which especially littoral cities could only dream in 1915–1918.[34]

Damascus's centrality was further cemented and given a particularly despotic twist because Jamal Pasha was the commander of the Fourth Army for most of the war. As one of the three members of the dictatorial triumvirate, he wielded tremendous power from 1913. And once in Damascus in late 1914, he used his domineering character and presence and the absence of Enver Pasha and Talaat Pasha to run his own show. In fact, he was not accountable even to these two, did not take any orders from anybody unless he happened to agree with them. In 1917 for instance he rebuffed a proposal by Enver to attack Britain in southern Palestine. And in the same year the German ambassador in Istanbul advised Arthur Ruppin, whom he met to discuss Jamal Pasha's orders to evacuate Jaffa, to be cautious because "experience shows that Jamal Pasha only gets more enraged when a third party intervenes." "This," Ruppin concluded, "is indeed the pivot of the entire matter, as we know only too well: Jamal Pasha is the absolute ruler in Palestine and [Istanbul's] central government does not dare stop his actions. "[35]

This situation reinforced Damascus's new central role in the region. This showed, for one, in the pasha's power to force people to appear before him. Right upon his arrival in Damascus in December 1914 he summoned the administrator of the *mutasarrifiyya* Mount Lebanon—an administrative unit directly governed by Istanbul—and the Maronite patriarch, based near Beirut. Beirut's *wali* came to pay his respects soon thereafter, too. Similarly, Aleppo's *wali* periodically visited Damascus; and sometimes all *walis* were summoned. In fact, anybody who wanted anything important authorized had to come see Jamal Pasha. His German advisers met him in Damascus, and were based there. And when Arthur Ruppin embarked on his economic tour of Bilad al-Sham he first headed to Damascus, where he met the *wali*—whom he proceeded to impress by relating greetings from Jamal Pasha, whom he apparently had just met in Jerusalem.[36] Moreover, just as all roads led to Damascus, Jamal Pasha projected his Damascus-based rule outward. His orders, issued in Damascus, were reprinted—often as a *barqiyya* (telegram), to be delivered with maximum speed—in provincial newspapers, with the pasha addressing his subjects in the first person singular. Jamal frequently traveled, too, in 1915 to the Egyptian front, else to accompany delegations on a visit or to inspect the goings-on in the provinces.[37]

Damascus's increased regional weight was palpable also in the pasha's urban ambitions. In Jaffa he had an almost one-kilometer long avenue built, and in Beirut he boasted to a German-Ottoman delegation how he and Beirut's wali, Azmi, "had destroyed . . . entire quarters that had been the source of diseases . . . [and] had built wide, beautiful streets that recall French boulevards." But it was Damascus that to him, and to Ottoman municipal bureaucrats, was "exemplary" for Bilad al-Sham's urban restructuration and for the region's Ottoman postwar future.[38] "Work began on the drawing of a detailed map of the city. . . . The citadel received a facelift, and portions of existing city streets were renovated, widened, and extended both on the east-west and north-south axes. The most elaborate and best-known street construction was an avenue 45 meters wide and 650 meters long. Many buildings and shops were torn down to make this artery possible." Fittingly named Jamal Pasha Avenue, it soon became a popular gathering place.[39]

Thus, on the afternoon of March 8, 1918, we would have seen "walking up and down" that street somebody we know: Khalil Sakakini. He was in exile. In December 1917 the authorities in Jerusalem decided that because he was an enemy citizen—he had obtained a U.S. passport—he needed to be deported. By now married to his beloved Sultana, father of a son, Sari, and himself son of an ailing mother whom he feared he would not meet again, he was until August 1918 imprisoned and put under city arrest in Damascus. Here, he despaired to make ends meet but also enjoyed many an hour socializing.[40]

Such stark contrasts of life in wartime Damascus showed up time and again in Sakakini's diary, which he was still keeping, as he had in New York. On the one hand, war did not put life on hold. Customs persisted. Throughout the year, people were entertained by street impresarios and frequented cafés such as al-Kamal or al-Zahra. In winter, they watched bear tamers who had come down from the Lebanon Mountains. June was mulberry season, whose local-variant orchards Damascenes loved to visit, most of all mornings when their red fruit was still deliciously chill. And in the hot season they took time to cool down in those and other orchards: in their pride and paradise, the *ghuta*.[41] On the other hand, the famine that had started in 1915 on the littoral was felt as hunger in the interior, too. Poor people from the coast started arriving already in 1914, and Damascenes themselves suffered. In 1916 food was becoming scarcer and from late 1917 the city started to descend into famine. By the spring of 1918 a German soldier noted "children half-dead of hunger, I am not lying, every ten steps in the streets."[42] Sakakini's acquaintances got skinnier by the day, and he noted how everywhere "people talk only about bread, and nothing worries their thoughts as much as its rising price."[43]

Damascus's regional centrality, too, was written all over Sakakini's diary. "People rent some of their rooms furnished, like in Europe and America, [rental] prices are rising madly, and you knock on many houses before finding an empty room," he wrote upon arriving, and added, "Damascus the Fragrant is jam-packed with immigrants and exiles from all over the country." This situation was encapsulated by the varied provenance of friends old and new he met and made. Many were exiles like him. A few hailed from outside Bilad al-Sham, especially Turks, as well as an Iranian, an Iraqi who worked for the official newspaper, and a few Germans. Some were Damascenes, such as Muhammad Kurd ʿAli and others working at newspapers like *Sharq* and *Muqatabas*.[44] But most came from other areas in Bilad al-Sham. The closest to him were fellow Jerusalemites such as Tawfiq Jawhariyya, Hussein Khalidi, and Musa al-ʿAlami, with whom he shared a room for months and who, though born in Jericho, had been a student of his in Jerusalem. Close, too, was Alter Levine, an American Jew whom Sakakini had hidden from the Ottoman authorities for a time in Jerusalem and with whom he was imprisoned in Damascus. From Jaffa came a member of the Chelouche family who was there with a large group of Jaffawi Jews; Sakakini also corresponded with his Jaffawi friend Issa al-Issa, exiled in Ankara. And he made the acquaintance of the Haifawi Nassar and of a Nabulsi, Hasan Hammad; of a few people from Karak and Saida; and of a number of Beirutis, including, in prison, a Jewish trader named Musa al-Shatin, Nakhla Tarazi who was on a visit in Damascus, and a café performer, ʿAbd al-Rahim al-Safah.[45]

## Beirut's Declining Fortune

From Beirut, too, was Sakakini's barber, Tawfiq, who had moved to Damascus "to make a living": his "*rizq*."[46] That move and its rationale encapsulate the fact that while the strong Beirut-Damascus interurban tie analyzed in Chapter 1 persisted in 1914–1918, its balance changed. Damascus's rise was the reverse image of the decline, due to the British blockade, of the global trade port-city of Beirut. This shift reflected wartime state formation, too. Istanbul kept more soldiers in Bilad al-Sham's interior than on the coast.[47] And whereas Damascus was the Fourth Army headquarters, on the coast Allied ships—including spies and planes launched from them—exercised a certain military veto power. Although not invading the coast, they could nix Ottoman attempts to expand extant navy ports or airplane fields. And the only major isle on Bilad al-Sham's coast, Arwad, off Tartus, was from 1915 a French navy and intelligence base, which served to smuggle money into the country, too. The Allies indeed had very good intelligence, which they flaunted: "Every time [Jemal Pasha] comes . . . over from Damascus to visit Beirut . . . as his train pulls into the station, down by the port, a French patrol boat is steaming back and forth at the mouth of the harbor, just to give him a welcome."[48]

Even so, the Ottoman state did not forsake control of the littoral. We have seen that in Beirut, too, it intervened in education and urban rebuilding. More crucially, it "set up a military administration in which they took control of the public security agencies and imposed broad censorship controls; placed curbs upon the foreign community, including exiling enemy aliens; and implemented a wide-scale program of conscription and commandeering. These measures were backed by the personal authority of Ahmad Jamal Pasha . . . and the military tribunal in 'Alayh," a small mountain town above Beirut that became an extension of the Damascus-based will of Jamal Pasha.[49]

Similarly, the state now held the reins of the traffic of trains, animals, telegraphs, and—newly—cars between Beirut and Damascus. Take the railway. Before the war it had been a private company capitalized in France and based in Beirut. In 1914 the state confiscated it; its central administration moved to Damascus because that city had become "the sole source of all communication between Damascus, Hama and its extensions"; and the army ran it. Military needs came first, civilian passengers and goods, second. Beiruti newspapers regularly reported on how many trains the state in Damascus allowed to be used for whom and how many times a week. And they could not help noting that also in other matters such as postal services, Damascus now received preferential treatment.[50]

Worse, movement between Beirut and Damascus was at times a question of life and death. As early as November 1914 Beiruti officials traveled to Damascus to try to secure regular grain transports to the littoral. Newspapers reported pleas to Damascus, and particularly to Jamal Pasha, for aid; and when help was forthcoming the municipality sent telegrams effusively thanking its Damascene counterpart and invoking Beiruti-Damascene "brotherhood."[51] Also institutions were moved to Damascus, for instance a number of *Sultaniyya* schools in

1914. And although Beirut's traders did not disappear—a few even made very good money during the war—lucrative business now had to flow through contacts with state officials in Damascus and in other interior cities like Aleppo. Chapter 1 commented at length on their power, but they do not figure prominently in this chapter. Wartime Beirut was eating humble pie.[52]

## Limits to Beirut's Declining Fortune

Still, Beirut's prewar influence in the region did not quite evaporate. For one, the city remained preeminent in modern knowledge: Bilad al-Sham's "spiritual center," to quote the German Professor Gotthelf Berg-strässer, whom we have met in Prelude 1. Although the Ottoman state closed most Western schools, it reopened some as state schools to (re)educate the young. Also, the American Syrian Protestant College (SPC) enjoyed Jamal Pasha's almost uninterrupted support. Beirut's *wali* succeeded in bringing back to Beirut some schools that had been moved to Damascus.[53] And although many non-Beiruti students returned to their hometowns—in 1917, almost all SPC students were Beirutis or Lebanese—Beirut retained a modicum of regional relevance. Some students from outside the region, for instance Iran, stayed. And in a list of 144 youngsters studying in Beirut who were drafted in late 1915, about 70 percent (103) were from Beirut (85) and Mount Lebanon (18). Most of the remaining 30 percent came from elsewhere in Bilad al-Sham.[54]

Beirut's fame for culture and sophistication persisted, too. Jamal Pasha, together with Azmi Pasha, built new avenues and planned to construct in Beirut—rather than in Damascus—a new castle for the sultan. Azmi supported the building of a park and horse racing course in the Pine Forest just outside Beirut, a project led by Alfred Sursock, whom we met in Chapter 1 and who was a "friend" of Azmi's.[55] And with Jamal Pasha the Sursocks entertained ties—ties of some ambiguity. On the one hand, even rich Beiruti merchants like the Sursocks needed government contacts more than before. Also, Jamal Pasha and other Ottoman officials in Lebanon made the Sursocks and other rich Beirutis part with considerable sums. As SPC president Howard Bliss noted in his wartime diary, "if the government wants anything it just proceeds to get it. It has done my heart good to see how some of the people in the city have been held. . . . The Sursuk families . . . have just been held up again and again."[56]

But although Bliss gloated that "dinners *must* be given and other entertainment provided . . . [to] visit[ing] dignitaries," reality was more complicated. Certainly in the case of the Sursocks and Jamal Pasha, socializing reflected cultural affinities and social ties. Alfred had long before the war risen through the ranks of the Ottoman diplomatic service, was a known quantity in Istanbul, and in 1917 in Damascus received the second-highest Ottoman decoration.[57] His brother Michel was similarly well positioned. In the war, he was a Beiruti parliamentarian in Istanbul. When he, like other merchants in Beirut and other cities in Bilad al-Sham, made very profitable speculative business in grain in 1917–1918, he used his well-oiled social ties, striking a deal personally with Jamal Pasha. What is more, the two kept in touch.[58] In the summer of 1918 Michel Sursock traveled from Beirut to Austria and Switzerland to undergo medical cures. (He would pass away in 1920.) During his stopover in Istanbul, Jamal Pasha, who had already returned from Damascus, bothered to come to his Pera Palace hotel room to bid him goodbye before his departure. He even helped him to sort out his papers and organized a sleeping car train to Vienna for him, which was a veritable "affaire d'État" in war times.[59]

This story may also be read as a sign that the image of Jamal Pasha as an omnipotent centralizer is too facile and too disconnected from his prewar past and from a complex wartime present. No doubt, the pasha was of unusual energy and equally unusual ruthlessness. Being a terrifying bully was part of his persona, key to his way of trying to control Ottoman Bilad al-Sham in the trial of fire that was World War I. In the fall of 1916 a consultant, Wiegand, whom we have encountered above, dared tell him that "people everywhere are terribly afraid of you." "The Pasha," the German reported in a letter to his wife, "was extraordinarily amused."[60] That disposition and behavior, together with shawwam's need for an ultimate scapegoat to make sense of the war, turned Jamal Pasha from a mortal into a quasi-mythical figure. He saw everything, was everywhere. His eyes "pierce one's very core [kidneys and heart] and penetrate everybody's thoughts," reported a panicked Chelouche, a prominent Jew from Jaffa, who met him; he ruled from Beirut and Aley uninterruptedly from 1915 to 1916, insisted a Lebanese, wrongly. That figure belonged to the realm of fantasy. Jamal Pasha was powerful. But all-powerful, he was not.[61]

## Limits to Damascus's Centrality

This was the case, too, for the Ottoman wartime administrative center of Bilad al-Sham, Damascus. This situation had two related reasons. One was limits to the smooth region-wide projection and implementation of state policies devised in Damascus; the other, the continuing power of cities.

In early December 1917, Jamal Pasha decided to make one of his feared surprise visits. He descended on the Damascus citadel and—outrage!—caught soldiers urinating in "forbidden places." His retribution was swift. He "issued strict orders to keep the citadel clean." The soldiers trembled. But when the pasha left and "all soldiers of the citadel were united . . . [to watch] one [being] bastinadoed, [they] looked on as if at a carnival and then left, grinning." Jamal ruled with an iron hand and ruthlessly pushed through projects. But these required his presence. Once he moved on and focused on the next issue, a somewhat different reality set in.[62]

This reality looked somewhat different from place to place. Although Damascus was Bilad al-Sham's wartime decision-making center, implementation was another matter. Different cities and their hinterlands did not experience identical administrative practices. As a result, their experience of war, too, differed in some ways—and Jamal Pasha's inability to truly see and control everything was not the only explanation related to the state.

For one, Jamal Pasha's subordinates wielded their own, though more limited, despotic power. Access to higher level officials was often indispensable to get certain things done. When Sakakini's Jewish friend in Damascus, Levine, refused to go through a high official to avoid deportation to Ankara, he was promptly put on a train up north.[63] As painful was corruption, small and large. And then there was flawed centralized planning, particularly regarding the economic effects of war. Freiherr von Kress—a high-ranking German officer who worked with Jamal Pasha for more than two years and regarded him as hard headed in military and political matters—also noted that "like so many of his compatriots, [he had] only a very limited understanding of questions of financial economy." The worst manifestation was food and animal procurement policies, which helped feed the wartime famine whose root cause was the Allied maritime blockade of Bilad al-Sham. While nationwide macro-economic planning made a leap forward in wartime Western Europe, especially in Germany under Walther Rathenau, this was a domain in which the war's immensely complex requirements largely overwhelmed the Ottoman state (and other countries like Russia).[64]

As a result, while all areas in Bilad al-Sham experienced hunger, there were variations. "Amidst . . . starvation there was food"—in some hinterlands like parts of Transjordan and the Hawran and in interior towns like Homs there was a grain surplus even by 1918, which, although not benefitting everybody, made life less harsh.[65] By contrast, hunger was especially grave and started earliest on the coast, especially in Lebanon, in 1915–1918. Hit hardest was the Christian parts of Mount Lebanon and Beirut, the mountain's urban center since the mid-nineteenth century and hence the destination for many desperate mountain villagers. Here, World War I was called *harb al-juʻ* (the war of famine).[66] Wiegand's description of emaciated people in Juniyeh, north of Beirut, was echoed by countless writers.[67] Moreover, variations in war experience translated into variations in war perception. Although hunger was a theme in most places of Bilad al-Sham, a real trauma of mass starvation gripped principally Beirut and Mount Lebanon. Here, the gravity of the famine unhinged time—some children's "faces were so wrinkled from starvation that they looked like older people"—and broke fundamental norms governing human life.[68]

A last factor related to administration that explains variations in Bilad al-Sham war experience was the fact that even at such an extreme time like World War I and with such an extreme ruler like Jamal Pasha, the state's central organs and officials could not manage alone. Local administrators mattered, as even the Lebanese, who blamed "the Turks" for everything, recognized. "The qa'imaqam played an important role in requisitioning. If he was a good man, he could make it easy on the people by lightening their burden and then making excuses to the Turks."[69] While the war constituted the peak of the modern Ottoman state's exercise of territoriality that emerged from the mid-nineteenth century, central state actors did not simply apply more force but still, as before 1914, had to coopt local power holders and administrators who knew their way around their area. During the war this was true all the more because the stakes were so high and the state was in such desperate need of goods. Hence, to try to regulate the grain market the state from 1915 worked with merchants, many of whom got away with not paying the state back what they owed. Similarly, it entrusted loyal officials with deep local ties, like the Druze Shakib Arslan from the Shuf area of Mount Lebanon, with raising volunteer forces for the army. And then there were extreme cases of officials—people whom Jamal trusted, admittedly—who simply took over an area.

> Würthenau, King of Baalbek! There since two years, commander of the Depotregiment 13 . . . ; has without any means turned a totally decayed farm with two houses into a big casern, with bakery, artisanal rooms, etc. . . . Has erected stables in the ground floor of the [Antique] temples; big, 8-km long water carrier. . . . In the former hotel Ras al-Ain constructed a hospital with Borromaean Sisters, whom he once quarantined when they were coming through Baalbek because one was sick, until the head sister in Aleppo whom he brought to Baalbek . . . gave him permission to keep them. . . . [I]s responsible for the coastal protection in the area of Tripoli . . . has for that reason constructed defensive positions on the Lebanon's western slope and paved a road to Lebanon, done much for the city . . . ; organized agriculture in the Bika' [Valley], also with Jamal's help, whom he got interested . . . ; takes measures against robbery in the area; rules without constraints and like a patriarch, with beatings, cutting off the heads of robbers and impaling [those heads] on [top] of guns. Highly regarded in the area.[70]

## The Perseverance of Cities: A Jerusalemite in Damascus

Cities and their hinterlands clearly remained a key point of reference for their inhabitants' life. We have seen this fact at play already in the limits to Damascus's rise as a regional center and in the limits to Beirut's decline. We will now consider it further by looking at the importance of Jerusalemite connections for Sakakini's survival in his Damascene exile, and at Aleppo's wartime experience.

Although Sakakini had acquaintances and friends from across Bilad al-Sham, there were distinct patterns to his social universe in Damascus. He did not report on people from the region's Aleppine north. A majority of his contacts hailed from Palestine, and of these, the core group was made up of Jerusalemites. These included not only Tawfiq Jawhariyya but also Hussein Khalidi, the American Jew Alter Levine with whom he was imprisoned, and Musa al-'Alami, a Jericho-born former student of his with whom he shared a room for several months. Sakakini also was in touch with the Austrian consul in Jerusalem, who came to visit him in prison; nurtured relations with high officials from the Jerusalem patriarchate, then in Damascus; and was in contact with the *Salahiyya,* the school where he had taught in Jerusalem, when it was moved to Damascus. The core of his social universe in Damascus was, in his own words, a "small Jerusalem settlement"—a situation not unlike that in New York in 1908, described in Prelude 1. Moreover, that settlement was existential to his survival. While he earned a minimal income by teaching, he was able to make ends meet only because he repeatedly received money from Levine and the patriarchate. Similarly, Jawhariyya asked him to intercede with the patriarchate, and Ahmad Khalidi sent him a letter from Beirut asking him for help.[71]

Was Sakakini's social and existential reliance, in exile, on people from his own hometown typical? While we do not have the sources to satisfactorily answer that question, we can make two observations. The more destitute a war immigrant in Damascus, the more likely she relied on aid not only from people from her home but also from the state, which helped up to 80,000 poor to survive from late 1917 through 1918. Sakakini himself tried to obtain a stamp [*fisa*] from the Food Ration Administration, *idarat al-i'asha,* also on behalf of some of his Jaffawi friends from the al-Issa family, but apparently without success.[72]) At the same time, very few shawwam were displaced by fighting, and it was only from late 1917 to late 1918 that a few cities in Bilad al-Sham were somewhat disconnected from others. Sakakini's Damascus exile illustrates the latter point by counterexample. During those months, Jerusalem was already British-controlled; he was in Ottoman territory. While luckily for him Jerusalemite figures and institutions had moved to Damascus, securing him socially and existentially, he and his family were incommunicado. This depressed him deeply, and he tried various channels to contact them, including the International Red Cross in Geneva through whose services he received a letter from Sultana.[73]

Perhaps also because of this disconnection, Jerusalem continued being Sakakini's most central mental reference point in Damascus. This decidedly does not mean that he was a country bumpkin. He was a man of the world who had lived in New York, held a U.S. passport, and was well acquainted with the United States.[74] Moreover, he was socially and intellectually immersed in a wider Bilad al-Shami circle and, firmly embedded within it, in Palestine. Still, he was a man from Jerusalem, which was central for his sense of himself in the world at large. When he dreamed in Damascus, he was back in Jerusalem. When he was awake, he thought of that city as the opposite of his *ghurba* (exile) in Damascus. He wondered about the strange foods Damascenes sometimes ate. And although conceding that their fruit were as great as they boasted, he asserted that Jerusalem easily topped Damascus: for its "location and mountains and ravines and houses and streets and its four seasons," for its "vegetables and fruit," and certainly for "its people."[75] "I love a small spring that flows in a small garden with a few trees . . . more than the Barada River and Damascus 'the Fragrant,'" he noted one day in February 1918, and added "I do not like big cities jam-packed with people, where people are unable to know everybody, and known to everybody, in whichever [quarter] they live." And when on a walk in the *Salihiyya* neighborhood he had a "splendid view of Damascus," but immediately stressed "I prefer Jerusalem's views, especially on the Mount Olive Road."[76]

Sakakini's geographical vocabulary reinforces the above impression. To be sure, he did use Syria and Palestine, referring to their territory, talking of "the Palestine [war] front," and mentioning them as a couple, as "Syria and Palestine"—a reflection of their prewar description as Bilad al-Sham's two parts, noted in Chapter 1. He also used Palestine once regarding people, referring to "all the sons of Palestine in Damascus." But that was it. Everywhere else he used city names—Jerusalem, say, or Beirut—when referring to a person's place of origin.[77]

Everywhere? Not quite. There is one fascinating exception. It appears on the last page of Sakakini's Damascus diary. An undated text titled "escape from Damascus," it summed up what happened to him from August 1918 until the end of that year. That is, it was not a diary entry but a note written at some later point. At the end of 1918, the war was over, the Ottoman Empire gone, the postwar world emerging—and Sakakini back in Jerusalem. But although he had longed for that city so much, he did not mention it on that page. Rather, he spoke of *dukhul Filastin:* "entering Palestine." This may be an irrelevant detail. Then again, something else that Sakakini had never mentioned in his Damascene diary entries suddenly attained significance: "In August 1918 the cause of the Arab Revolt became strong. My dear friends' true *wataniyya* [nationalism] and their zeal for it would have been denied to them in Damascus, unless they joined it. They left Damascus on 10 August, and I had the honor to be with them. . . . We . . . crossed the desert to the camp of Amir Faisal."[78]

Following the Ottoman breakdown, political ideas and action developed fast. Or was that just how Sakakini chose to explain post facto why and how he left Damascus? We cannot know for sure. But two things are clear. After the war nationalism became very significant, and indeed dominant ideologically and politically. But it did not simply replace older focal points of people's life and identity. Rather, it fused with them in a protracted, messy process, as Chapter 3 will show.

## The Perseverance of Cities: Aleppo

I end this chapter with a look at a remarkable city and its hinterland in Bilad al-Sham: Aleppo. It was probably the most far-reaching example of how in 1914–1918 cities and their hinterlands remained relevant and continued drawing on their prewar strengths. For one, Aleppo was better off than littoral cities, a blessing it shared with Damascus. More important, its fate differed from that of Damascus, mainly because of its exceptional position. It was half way between the western most point of Iraq's Euphrates River and the Mediterranean, halfway between Istanbul and Cairo, and on the Eurasian land trade route. More vital in 1914–1918, when trade with the outside world decreased, it also straddled Bilad al-Sham and Anatolia. This geostrategic advantage turned Aleppo into an administrative and logistical staging ground for Ottoman and German operations in Bilad al-Sham and Iraq: It was the city closest to the point where the railway supply line from Anatolia branched off to those two regions. For that reason, in early 1918 it also became the new headquarters of the Second Army after its final retreat from most parts of northern Mesopotamia. In crucial ways Aleppo did form part of the Bilad al-Sham–wide wartime acceleration of regional integration. Perhaps most important, it underwent an administrative reorientation to Damascus and to its Damascus-based ruler Jamal Pasha. But this reorientation was qualified by its exceptional geostrategic position.[79]

That position was reflected in Aleppo's role in the Armenian genocide. Because of its proximity to Anatolia, by the summer of 1915—a few months after the Ottoman army started atrocities against the Armenians, worst in eastern Anatolia—the city turned into "a center for information" on those unfolding events. Until the genocide abated in 1917, the city "became a crossroads where the fate of [Armenian] deportees was decided. During the first month of the Armenian Genocide, those deportees who were lucky were sent south to the Hauran or towns like Hama, Homs, or Kerak. Many deportees managed to remain in Damascus or made their way to Jerusalem. The majority of deportees, however, were sent southeast from Aleppo and the railway line into the Syrian desert. Here the Ottoman authorities organized a network of concentration camps along the Euphrates toward the town of Der Zor and beyond."[80] Being a hub also meant that in places near Aleppo, most infamously in Katma, massive transit camps for tens of thousands of people living under horrible conditions were set up. In Aleppo itself many Armenians, as even rather unsympathetic observers like the Aleppine "jurist-historian" Kamil al-Ghazzi noted, arrived "kaashbah ba-la arwah," like ghosts, nay spirits. Most died; some tried to hide out, organize, and survive; but few succeeded. (The city's Armenian population would boom in 1921, when Cilicia's Armenians reemigrated after French troops retreated from that southcentral part of Turkey.)[81]

Aleppo's proximity to Anatolia also had advantages. Although in 1916 it suffered from supply problems, rising food prices, and hunger, by 1918 it was better off than even Damascus. Although by March 1918 about one hundred people died of hunger daily in Aleppo, most were Armenians survivors from Anatolia.[82] Around that time, visitors Bergsträsser and Major Friedrich Trautz noted that "the prosperity and activity of Aleppo's bazar was noteworthy [and] astonishing, in contrast to Damascus and Beirut. Hundreds of bedouins and fellahin pushed through the bazar's lanes, which were fully equipped with goods. . . . Clearly of import for Aleppo is [the fact] that, situated on the meeting point of Mesopotamia and Syria, it has a large hinterland to three sides," including Anatolia; "since the connection to Baghdad has been cut, Aleppo's transactions are reported to have grown even more."[83] German officials permanently stationed in the city confirmed this picture. "Nisbin, Mardin, Der ez-Zor, Urfa, Diarbekir [and] Biredschik" continued to send various goods, including wool, to Aleppo, reported one. Another, Walter Rössler, the German consul in town—who sent reams of documents on the Armenians' fate to Berlin—stated that in March 1917 meat prices in Aleppo fell by 100 percent. The immediate reason had nothing to do with Aleppo: sheep breeders sold for fear of a long dry spell continuing into the summer. But the city could profit only because most of those breeders lived in its Anatolian and northern Iraqi economic hinterland. Similarly, in the spring of 1918 a German logistics officer reported that while there had been a wheat supply problem earlier that year, the *wilayat*'s peasants were starting to sell considerable amounts of wheat—one reason why the city's markets looked as bountiful as Trautz and Bergsträsser described them at the time.[84]

## Conclusion

The war was a distinct phase within the late Ottoman-era stage of transpatialization in Bilad al-Sham. This had two underlying reasons. First, one of the two macro-historical processes integral to transpatialization before 1914, Bilad al-Sham's incorporation into a Eurocentric world economy, faded during the war, also because of a tight Allied maritime blockade of the region. Second and by contrast, the region's commander, Jamal Pasha, and his officials exploited the war to speed up another process integral to prewar transpatialization: the exercise of modern state territoriality. With Jamal Pasha unaccountable to Istanbul and in exclusive control of Bilad al-Sham, this region now was not only the target of territoriality. It also became the very place where policies for it were designed, substituting Istanbul. Central state territoriality was regionalized, and Bilad al-Sham's distinctiveness was amplified by the Allied blockade and by reduced interactions with British Egypt, with Iraq, most of it British from 1917, and with the Hijaz, the Arab Revolt's point of origin in 1916 / 1917.

Policy implementation was facilitated by Bilad al-Sham being the Ottoman front that saw least warfare. Until the fall of 1917 fully Ottoman and from then until the fall of 1918 shorn only of southcentral Palestine, it was a side-show within the Ottoman side-show to the eastern and especially western European fronts into which the war's strongest combatants poured their and their colonies' resources, and where the war's outcome, Germany's defeat, was settled. In sum, in 1914–1918 transpatialization was simpler than before 1914; it involved the interplay between cities, their interurban ties, and the region functioning as a quasi-autonomous unit for the exercise of state territoriality.

Under these circumstances, the state's tighter territorial grasp deepened Bilad al-Sham's level of integration in the most immediate way possible. This development was furthered by hundreds of thousands of starving people and deserters moving *within* the region and by shawwam's perception that they were experiencing a distinct war. Still, Bilad al-Sham did not become homogeneous. Crucial differences and variations persisted. The prewar littoral-interior hierarchy turned on its head in 1914–1918. Aleppo was doing well given the circumstances and Damascus was for all matters and purposes Bilad al-Sham's capital. By contrast, Beirut fell from grace, and starvation ravaged the coastal areas worst. More broadly, urban identities and solidarities continued to matter, as the fate of the Jerusalemite Sakakini in Damascus illustrated. Furthermore, although Jamal Pasha ruled the region from one headquarters, Damascus, he and his employees understood very well that they needed the administrative cooperation of urban political and administrative elite. Besides, some towns were under the quasi-absolute control of a military commander. Recall the German "Würthenau, King of Baalbek [who . . . ] rules without constraints and like a patriarch, with beatings, cutting off the heads of robbers and impaling [those heads] on [top] of guns."

In sum, the war, although traumatic and reducing Bilad al-Sham's exposure to the world economy, did not fundamentally alter interaction patterns between cities, the region, and the (temporarily region-centered) state. Transpatialization persisted. As a result, the region, cities and their respective rural hinterlands and interurban links would have a massive effect on postwar life.

## PRELUDE 3

# Alfred Sursock Keeps Busy

> On the evening of his arrival, [French] General [Henri] Gouraud was
> given a reception in the Park of Beirut. From the Damascus Road to
> the Porte du Cercle entrance, there were, on both sides of the street,
> posts [adorned with] flowers and banners and French flags, and each
> post carried an electrical lamp. Engineer[s] had installed electricity in
> the Park, in the circles, trees and fountains. The pathway of the
> Damascus Road to the Park Gate looked like the Avenue d'Opéra at
> night, and the Park like Magic City. Two 75' cannons had been placed
> in the park, and when [Gouraud] entered 101 shots were fired. It was
> beautiful, fairy-like, grandiose and magnificent, as the General
> [himself] said by the way. But I said loud and clearly, and many are
> those who said it with me: missing was somebody to preside over
> the General's reception, especially as he was received in the Park, and
> that somebody was you!

"You": this is Alfred Sursock, the Beiruti merchant we have met earlier
in this book. At the time he receives these lines from a Beiruti aide,
G. Fakhr, in late 1919, it has already been a year that Istanbul's army
and administration have left Bilad al-Sham (which some now also
called, in distinction from the new state of Syria, *Suriya al-tabiʻiyya,*
Natural or Geographic Syria, or *Suriya al-kubra,* Greater Syria).[1]
Britain is the strongest power in the region, which it has occupied all
the way to Iraq in order to take direct control of the larger perimeter
of the Suez Canal. Already by 1918, not only the Ottomans but also
their German and Austrian allies are down and Russia is out, in the
throes of a revolution. France has a very small presence only. But in
the fall of 1918 Britain agrees to hand over Lebanon to its principle
wartime ally. Paris asserts special rights in what it, for historical,
religious, and cultural reasons, calls *la Syrie française.* Besides, the war

underlined the weight of the Mediterranean, including its east, in its Eurocentric security strategy. Two years later, in the summer of 1920, France occupies also Syria with British concurrence, evicting the Hashemite Emir Faisal, the wartime leader of the Arab Revolt against Istanbul, who with London's approval ruled Syria in 1918–1920.[2]

Thus, direct European rule comes to encompass all of Bilad al-Sham. Britain is not only in Iraq, where it appoints Faisal king in 1921, but also in Palestine and Transjordan, and France in Lebanon and Syria: territories that at the San Remo conference, in the spring of 1920, are recognized by the war's victors, and which that same year are set up as Mandates by a new inter-state organization, the League of Nations.[3] Four hundred years of Ottoman sovereignty have come to an end. It is perhaps telling that when Sursock receives the above lines in late 1919, he is absent from Beirut because he has business not in Istanbul but in the capital of France, Paris. In the Middle East, a page has been turned; a new era has started. Or has it?

When Paris sends General Henri Gouraud (1867–1946) as its new political representative and troop commander to Lebanon in the fall of 1919, there is no doubt where he would alight and reside. Beirut is the obvious choice because of the powers it amassed in the last Ottoman decades. Its wartime dependence on Damascus is over. And although in the quote above, Beirut's Pine Park is compared to Paris—to the Avenue de l'Opéra; to the Magic City amusement park—it in fact was developed during Istanbul's rule. It is Sursock's park and horse racetrack, mentioned in Chapter 2. Beirut's modern Ottoman dimensions have not vanished with Istanbul's troops. Many physical traces like the Pine Park remain. And so do social ties.[4]

Sursock sustains his relationship with Azmi Pasha, from 1915 to 1918 Beirut's provincial governor, and by the Sursocks' own account a "friend" who has supported the park and race track construction.[5] After Azmi leaves for Istanbul in 1918, Sursock stays in touch with him.[6] Two years later Azmi surfaces in a somewhat ungrammatical French letter he sends from Berlin to Sursock, who at that moment was in Paris.

22, 1, [19]20. My very dear friend, . . . I was very pleased to
know your health and have heard something about Beirut. . . .
You know very well that I love Beirut and Beirutis much. I
always desire to hear news of my friends. I write you and
*mukhtar* Beyhum [another, Muslim, merchant] in Beirut
but I think that you did not receive. I would be very pleased to
receive your letters. If possible, write to me all the things that
interest me, and write also the health all the family and the
friends. . . . At the same time, tell me how the park is going
and the streets that I demolished [part of the destruction
and reconstruction of Old Beirut] and the Beiruti are they
pleased now. I want to go to Beirut I desire stay some time
amongst you but the present government, I believe, does not
allow. . . . When will be possible for me to leave for Beirut
write me. Please write greeting for all the friends, and if
possible write a letter to *mukhtar* Beyhum, I await his reply.
Awaiting your letter, I greet you again, Azmi.[7]

Like other high Ottoman officials, Azmi moves to Istanbul's wartime
ally Germany after 1918. Some do well—Jamal Pasha is a case in point.
(That is, until an Armenian assassinates him in Georgia in 1922.)
Others, like Azmi, do not. And hence, swallowing his pride, he takes
advantage of the ties he has woven in Beirut. He asks Sursock for
money, and receives it. The merchant expects him to eventually repay,
on which he himself insists too, if only to keep his honor. But the style
of his letters suggests that Sursock does not press him, probably due to
a sense of friendship, perhaps in the hope that Azmi may one day
again climb to administrative eminence and be of use to him.[8]

30, 5, [19]22. My very dear friend, I thank you very much for
your help and friendship. I am still in Smyrne [Izmir].
Without doing anything[;] my principle does not allow me to
accept such a post. I will have to wait until normal times, i.e.
another year. To wait and to live, one needs to do something
I am always embarrassed it is you who makes me live until
today. I have many friends here but all are like me. For this,

being shame and with remorse I ~~demand~~ [*sic*] make my last
request to you. Through another friend I would make a
commercial deal to live. Is it possible lend me 1,000 pounds
Sterling. After one year I will pay you all my debts. . . . My best
wished and friendship, Azmi.[9]

Azmi Pasha is not the only Ottoman official with whom Sursock stays
in contact, or who wants to be remembered. In Azmi's afore-quoted
letter he conveys greetings from one Tahsin—possibly the former
provincial governor of Damascus—and one Kenan. In 1920 he thanks
Sursock for greetings that the latter has conveyed to him through
other Ottomans then in Berlin, and he refers to a letter that Sursock
has sent to "Madame Djémal Pacha" and that the latter has shown
him. Indeed, Sursock's contacts not simply with Ottoman officials but
with some of their wives, including Madame Jamal Pasha, strengthens
the impression that these contacts are social relationships rather than
simply business.[10]

Sursock's ties with Turkish Ottomans are not the only part of his
past that keeps resonating after 1918. Consider the following note that
he, together with *mukhtar* (neighborhood head) Omar Beyhum and
three other leading Beiruti merchants, Habib Trad, Joseph Audi, and
A. Bassoul, write for Gouraud in the fall of 1919.

> Our unlimited trust in your person encourages us [to] ask you
> [to] help to realize the almost unanimous wish of the city of
> Beirut, to make it a Free City and free port, seat of the Man-
> date (sa création ville libre et port franc siège du mandat).
> Having envisioned all other hypotheses, we find that Free City
> and free port alone are capable [to] assure [the] future of
> Beirut, whose prosperity would benefit Lebanon. We hope you
> will join [this view] and assure you that consultation by ballot
> would obtain [a] virtual unanimity [of the] populations.[11]

Sursock & Co.'s unapologetic focus on Beirut and their appropriation
of the Free City model (then discussed in Europe to help manage
the post-imperial continent's nationalities questions) for their own

purposes underscore a crucial issue. At the dawn of colonized nation-states in Bilad al-Sham, Beiruti merchants very much want to preserve the weight their city acquired when that region was undivided and European imperialism at its peak.[12] Politically, this vision soon comes to naught. It is buried by the proclamation, on September 1, 1920, of *Grand Liban* including Beirut, which reflects the wishes of France and of considerable parts of Lebanon's Christian population, most important the Maronites, and which is accepted by Beirut's merchant elite. Administratively, however, it succeeds. Beirut becomes the capital of French Lebanon and Syria.

Beirut's economy, too, continues to enjoy preferential treatment. Government policies aside, one early instance is the creation, in April 1923 in Paris, of the Syndicat général d'études et de travaux publics et privés France et Orient (SGFO), of which Sursock is the leading Beiruti member. The name of this enterprise suggests that it would act across the Orient. In reality, it focuses on Beirut. Its key project is a FF 20,000,000 urban infrastructure package including, most prominently, a sewage system. It also plans to build hundreds of houses and villas in a 500,000 square-meter-large area in south Beirut, in St. Elie. And its third concrete project is a water supply canal from 'Ain al-Delbe, off Beirut, to the city.[13]

At the same time, Beirut's leading economic branch, trade, operates far beyond its own city limits and the boundaries of tiny Lebanon. Bilad al-Sham remains its key framework, with Beirut's elites (and France) interested also in long-range transport projects—and Sursock, with a nose for business, becomes involved. In the spring of 1924, he invests in the Nairn Transport Company, named after the two New Zealander brothers who—having served in the British army in World War I in the Middle East and having stayed in Beirut—in 1921 have launched the first Haifa-Beirut cab service, and in 1923 connected Haifa-Beirut-Damascus by car to Bagdad.[14]

While Sursock's Ottoman ties, his focus on the city of Beirut, and his interest in Beirut's wider economic sphere of action continue prewar trends, there are shifts and changes, too. These can be boiled down to one word: France. To be sure, in business it was already before 1914 that French capital had, as seen in Chapter 1, reinforced its presence. Characteristically, a key SGFO member, Edouard Coze is an old French Ottoman hand, ex-director of *Gaz de Beyrouth* and ex-general secretary of the Beirut-Damascus Railway and the Beirut Port Company. But after 1918 more than before, especially in large-scale construction and infrastructure projects, many companies are French. One example is the SGFO; another, the well-established Paris-based Société générale française d'entreprises et des travaux publics (SGFETP), the financial engine behind the SGFO. In March 1924 Sursock, in recognition of his influence, is appointed director of an "independent branch" of the SGFETP, of its section d'Orient. But he needs the SGFETP just as much. It facilitates access to capital, and the SGFETP's French bank agrees to lend money for projects in Lebanon and Syria only to the SGFETP, not to local companies.[15]

If business shifts toward France, politics truly pivots. After all, Paris is Lebanon's and Syria's new master. The 1919 telegram to Gouraud acknowledges this new reality. So does an exchange of letters between Sursock and Gouraud in 1922 in which the former raises the idea of an economic investment company (the one which in 1923 would take form as the SGFO); or the fact that the SGFO is constituted "according to instructions that have been fully approved by General [Maxime] Weygand," who in 1923 succeeds Gouraud as France's second High Commissioner in Mandate Lebanon and Syria.[16]

Especially for an influential businessman like Sursock, this new political reality makes connections to French government circles a must more than before 1918. It is not that Sursock thinks of the French as disinterested do-gooders. When his nephew Vlado writes from Marseille that he has overheard a French official refer to Lebanon as a "chien de pays" (and promptly dressed him down), his frankly expressed outrage suggests that his uncle is no stranger to such feelings. Moreover, Sursock has formal political complaints. He deplores the "incomprehensible political situation" in Lebanon in the first year of French rule, 1919, when it is yet unclear what final form it would take. A draft of a telegram from 1923—scribbled, likely in the presence of friends, on stationery of Beirut's *Restaurant & Dancing Tabaris*—shows concern about the meandering of French policy. And in a speech he gives to the French senate's Foreign Affairs Committee in 1924 he castigates "a hastily created administration."[17]

Yet French rule is not a problem for Sursock. If anything, the opposite is true. The 1919 telegram echoes this indirectly, as does Sursock's impassioned assurance to the French senate that Lebanon and Syria are of use to France. More directly if not aggressively, in 1918 he rebuffs an offer by Emir Faisal to join his government in Damascus. Also, at the latest from 1919 he is in good contact with the pro-French, Paris-based Comité Central Syrien and its head, Chekri Ganem. And in 1921 he discusses with Gouraud how to counter Lebanese and Syrian anti-French protests in Europe.[18]

Sursock's relationship with Gouraud is perhaps the best example of how deep his connections with the French government becomes. The two have overlapping political interests, which show for instance in their 1921 tête-à-tête, or in a private letter by Gouraud informing Sursock in early 1922 about successful Mandate budgetary negotiations with the French parliament. But if Sursock needs Gouraud, the reverse holds, too. The general has Sursock sit at a place of honor during the proclamation of Grand Liban (Lebanon) in 1920, and has that event held in the Pine Park; and invites him, his wife—the Italian aristocrat Maria Serra di Cassano, whom Sursock marries in 1920, four years before his untimely death—and several of their friends for dinner at his residence in Aley; and perhaps most indicative for the sort of relationship they had, sends that invitation to Sursock's wife, whom he clearly knows in person.[19]

Moreover, Sursock's contacts with the French government are not limited to Beirut. He frequently visits Paris to make sure his connections will be not only deep but broad. He is invited to address the French Senate. And he meets with an official working directly under French president Alexandre Millerand while in Paris for talks about the SGFETP and the SGFO in 1923. The two discuss Middle Eastern and European politics, and socialize. "I will have a few days of recreation after the 19th [of September]," the unnamed official writes, "and we will use them to make a few visits that will interest you, choose airplanes for the aeroclub." He ends, "Please lay my respectful deference at the feet of Madame Sursock, and always be certain, dear monsieur and friend, of my feelings of very sincere and loyal fondness."[20]

After the war even more than before, then, Alfred Sursock's life is by more than one measure extraordinarily intricate. Born in and devoted to Beirut, he becomes a European by marriage and status and ever more connected to France, yet remains in constant touch with Ottomans. His privileged access to government is reinforced by strong social ties, which are further tightened by marriage. And his business operations go beyond the Middle East, and in the Middle East beyond Beirut and Lebanon.[21]

The persistent complexity of Sursock's post-war life captures a fundamental fluidity at the heart of early post-Ottoman Bilad al-Sham. Although European rule began in 1918 with one loud bang, and although the following creation of four polities was no less dramatic, the content, meaning, and ramifications of these historic changes were in flux in the 1920s. What caused this situation? In how far did late Ottoman urban, interurban and regional socio-spatial fields continue to matter after 1918 in Bilad al-Sham? And how were they affected by the region's fourfold division? These questions are at the basis of Chapter 3.

# 3

# OTTOMAN TWILIGHT
## 1918–1929

### Historical Context: Nationalism, Imperialism, and Recovering World Trade

Bilad al-Sham in the 1920s was shaped by three key macro-historical processes: accelerating nationalism within each of the region's new countries as well as between and beyond them; a new type of European imperial rule within a new international framework; and reincorporation into world trade, which was recuperating from World War I.

Nationalism per se was not new in 1918. Chapter 1 explained the late nineteenth-century rise of Zionism; of Arabism, mainly as a cultural sentiment though eventually also as a demand for a greater Arab political role within the Ottoman Empire; and of Ottoman nationalism, a sense of belonging to the Ottoman polity held by many Arabs. New about the post-Ottoman era was that non-Ottoman nationalisms turned fully political and became more viable. In Zionism, the cultural strand, which before the war had seen Palestine not as a state to be but as a spiritual beacon for the world's Jews, declined. Predominant already before 1914, state-building Zionism now effectively became the only game in town, boosted by Britain's occupation of Palestine in 1917/1918, by Britain's 1917 Balfour Declaration, and in 1920/1922 by that declaration's incorporation into the League of Nation's Palestine Mandate Charter. And to Arabs, independent nation-statehood became the only viable political option after the Ottoman Empire's death.

Here, two traits stood out. Whereas before 1918 "the lines . . . between . . . different tendencies" of Arabism "were not yet clearly drawn,"—recall for instance how some Arabists saw Lebanon as Suriya's spearhead—after 1918 Arabs envisioned different nationalisms and different states. There was *qawmiyya* (pan-Arab nationalism), which came from *qawm* (people), a word now infused with national and even racial meaning. In the 1920s, its advocates for the most part still excluded Egypt but included Bilad al-Sham, Arabia, and Iraq, that is basically focused on the late Ottoman Arab provinces. *Qawmiyya* was distinct from, but for practical and ideological reasons also overlapped with, various single-country movements each one of which focused on one country, for example Syria. Its Arabic name, *wataniyya* (sg.), politicized the nineteenth-century nationalization of the word *watan* (homeland).[1]

*Watani* movements in Bilad al-Sham still walked on wobbly feet in the 1920s. Their fate is important enough to this chapter to be treated in some detail, which will happen as the need arises throughout this chapter, and which may be summarized as follows. Zionists were and felt weak in Palestine both demographically and socioeconomically. But they were recognized by Britain as a nation with political rights and built up a para-state institution, the Zionist Executive. The Palestinians were not recognized as a nation by Britain and politically sidelined. However, there were sturdy administrative links especially between their elites—mainly urban notables, a social stratum we have encountered in Chapters 1 and 2—and British officialdom. The Lebanese national movement was in the 1920s (and into the mid-1930s) not accepted by most Muslim Lebanese, who desired unification with Syria. But it was carried by Christians, especially Maronites, and underwritten by France; besides, also Muslim elites—whether notables, wealthy merchants, or big landowners based in the countryside—filled administrative posts. Syrian nationalists, led by a notable elite, were first ignored and then fought by France in the 1925–1927 Syrian Revolt, which touched also Lebanon. However, Syria's notables had some administrative contacts with France, and were overall more moderate than middle class nationalists. Last, in Transjordan there was no nationalist movement to speak of in the 1920s and Emir Abdallah, who had arrived only in 1920, was still a rather weak ruler, although he had Britain's support.[2]

What, indeed, about the British and French presence? It formed part of a broader Anglo-French imperial expansion after 1918, not only into ex-Ottoman Asia but into German African and Asian colonies, too. Just as the reach of both empires peaked, however, critics grew louder. This was doubly problematic for the empires because, bled white by the war, their expansion stood in reverse relation to their means.[3] They had to adjust. Britain did so for instance in India, where in the 1920s it started to devolve some power, and in Egypt, which it granted more autonomy (though not quite independence, as it claimed) in 1922. And both Britain and France did so in Bilad al-Sham. True, this ex-Ottoman region was the spoils of the victors of World War I. But it also became a new type of colonies: the Mandate system. It was "a bargain . . . struck between what Britain and France perceived to be their vital interests, and the internationalism and anti-imperialism then in vogue" and spearheaded by U.S. president Woodrow Wilson. Specifically, it was created by the League of Nations in 1920, and in the case of the ex-Ottoman territories—A Mandates—conclusively confirmed in 1922. The League itself had been founded as the until then most encompassing inter-state organization at the postwar Versailles Peace Conference in 1919; in 1920 it moved to Geneva, where it would be headquartered until its dissolution in 1946. It was firstly a "global system of collective security" meant to ascertain that the Great War would be the last. Nazi aggression revealed that it was unequipped for that task (for which it got undeservedly bad rap). But it also intensified international coordination in technical fields— and it helped to open imperialism up to questions.[4]

It was in this last regard that the Mandate system was crucial. Economically, an Open Door policy stipulated that League members, and the United States, were to have equal economic access to the Mandates. Other than in trade, this policy was not strictly applied. Four of Beirut's five leading banks, for example, were French-owned by the 1920s, and French firms led foreign investments in 'their' Mandate. However, trade was strictly policed by the Permanent Mandates Commission (PMC), protecting League member states' interests. As a result, the Mandates partook in the cautious revival of world trade from 1918 to the onset of the Great Depression in 1929.[5]

Politically, London and Paris were mandated to lead their subjects to independence. They owed a yearly report to the PMC, to which their subjects could complain. Most important, the PMC was a "political arena," whose delegates were contacted by lobbies like the Geneva branch of the Cairo-based Syro-Palestinian Congress, and where the Mandate powers could be criticized by other states and had to "legitim[ize]" themselves. In consequence, "the Mandate system became the laboratory based on which one was able, by extension, to judge the management of other colonies." However, softening imperialism did not mean abolishing it. The Mandate powers also were members of the League—which in a sense was a 'League of Empires'—with influential PMC delegates. And in the Mandates, they governed how they saw fit, were not formally accountable to the PMC. In this crucial sense the Mandates did not generically differ from regular colonies, and like these they did not come with an independence deadline attached. Lastly, the PMC's token influence on governing showed in its lack of executive power. It could not punish but only scold, which it did rarely, and subjects' complaints had to pass through the Mandate powers.[6]

Given the Mandate powers' wide prerogatives, it is unsurprising that their Mandate territories were not cut from the same cloth. Paris ruled French Lebanon as a unit, but divided Syria into autonomous regions, changing their shapes and numbers several times in the 1920s and 1930s. Also British Palestine and Transjordan and Iraq were different. The latter two had royal heads of state, the first did not. Also, Transjordan was technically part of the Palestine Mandate. And Palestine was truly special because its Mandate charter, incorporating the Balfour Declaration, recognized Jews as a people with collective political rights while defining the rest as people, as non-Jewish communities with civic and collective religious rights only.[7]

Policies differed, too. Whereas there was much continuity in British personnel, including the High Commissioner, and policy in the 1920s, the French were attacked even at home for the "astonishing waltz of High Commissioners" in and out of Beirut and the "uncertainty of conception, goals, and methods." Unlike London, Paris early on harbored illusions about a *Syrie française*. Until 1927 the French took greater distance from the (Sunni) urban notable elite, which we met in the last two chapters, and also thereafter ruled more directly and entrusted less powers to local authorities than the British. France used the support it enjoyed among many Christians, mainly Maronites, to appoint itself the protector of minorities and particularly in the 1920s practiced "divide and rule" between Sunni Muslims and Christian, Druze and Alawi minorities. Britain lacked France's bond with Christian Arabs; Palestine was not quite the religious-ethnic mosaic that Lebanon and Syria were; and both Muslim and Christian Palestinians saw the Zionists as their foremost problem. Last, Britain was less suspicious of Arab nationalists than France, which as noted battled them in the Syrian Revolt, all the more because it feared that their example may spread to French North Africa.[8]

French and British rule also had much in common, though. Economically, London and especially Paris discontinued Ottoman attempts to protect agriculture and manufacturing by laws meant to constrain Western competitors. And in the 1920s customs tariffs on manufactured goods and food items, while being raised, especially in the French Mandate did not adequately protect manufacturing or agriculture. This facilitated the Mandate countries' reincorporation into a recovering world trade system, a process driven also by the League of Nations' Open Door policy.[9]

Politically, both France and Britain made the self-serving claim that Istanbul had neglected the Arabs and that they alone harbingered progress. Also, both were influenced by, and indeed part of, imperial policies elsewhere, and ruled by officials and soldiers who often had served in other colonies. Both had a regular government structure with similar portfolios; and both had one executive head for their respective Mandate territories, a High Commissioner based in Jerusalem and Beirut, who reported to their Colonial and Foreign Minister, respectively. In security, both tried being proactive, busily gathering intelligence, but if need be they used brutal force, in the 1920s most violently in the Syrian Revolt. Both, too, systemically employed lower-grade coercive measures: a European imperial twist to modern state territoriality. Both France and Britain also engaged in state building on the cheap. While projecting their power and defending their interests in their territories by expanding certain infrastructures, in health and education Britain relied also on Jewish organizations (for Jews), and France, on Western missionaries and programs run by religious communities. On a related note, sooner (Britain) or later (France), both worked with their Mandates' well-rooted elites. Mandates were arenas of negotiations where the European rulers had the last word, but not the only one.[10]

## The Story to Come

Following World War I, Palestine, Transjordan, Syria, and Lebanon as well as British and French imperial infrastructures and policies were superimposed on, cut across, and hence transnationalized Bilad al-Sham, its interurban ties, and its cities' hinterlands. (See Map 3.) Thus began the second stage of transpatialization in the modern Middle East. It had a reverse side. From their birth the four new nation-states displayed two traits. Internally, they were divided into a number of subunits, each centered on a city; after all, many interurban ties and most cities' hinterlands did not match post-Ottoman borders but rather crossed them. Meanwhile, externally, those nation-states were strongly linked to Bilad al-Sham and to the world beyond; in other words, were transnational. This was for three reasons. Bilad al-Sham's late-Ottoman-time regional integration was not stopped but rather restructured by the region's postwar division. Also, any given nation-state's socio-spatial subunits now crossed borders, for they were cut-off bits of Ottoman-time cities-cum-hinterlands and of interurban ties. And many cities, although now part of a nation-state space, nurtured transnational ties not only within Bilad al-Sham but also to wider worlds like that of Islam or of the global economy. In sum, nation-states on the one side, and on the other side cities and the region, (re)shaped—transnationalized—each other in multiple interlinked socio-spatial intertwinements that involved transnational ties also beyond Bilad al-Sham.

What were the underlying causes of this second stage of transpatialization? With regard to the region's changes, an external reason was European imperial interests, which had the side effect of strengthening Bilad al-Sham's infrastructural links to other regions, some near, like Egypt and Iraq, others far. Moreover, waning Ottoman-ness and waxing Arab nationalisms caused a shift—slow in the 1920s; more rapid thereafter—in how the region was framed. It was increasingly seen as part of the Arab world, which was—again, first slow, then faster—being re-imagined: as broader, as more unified and linking all regions inhabited by Arabs, as national in nature rather than simply linguistic, and as having Egypt as a center. (However, the term *al-'alam al-'arabi*, the Arab World, would really become current only from the mid-1940s.) Also within Bilad al-Sham there were changes. Drastic ones, indeed, for a reason as simple as it was historic: Bilad al-Sham's fourfold division created distinct institutions and experiences. Lives started diverging. All this affected how Bilad al-Sham functioned, even its very nature. In the 1920s, it started to shift from being a patchwork region of cities and interurban ties to becoming an umbrella region of nation-states—a process that would mature in the 1930s.

The last paragraph, together with Alfred Sursock's story in Prelude 3, illustrates something crucial about the 1920s: many of its changes were gradual. Indeed, like the first stage of transpatialization, so the second stage started fluidly. The 1920s were a transitional phase, linking transpatialization's first (Ottoman, empire-state) stage to its second (for a while European imperially ruled, nation-state) stage. In Bilad al-Sham, 1918 did not truly signal a new dawn, then. It was not a sharp break from the late Ottoman world. Rather, the entire 1920s were an Ottoman twilight.

This showed also in the region's continued relevance. Here, three factors were at play. First, the protracted process of integration shaping Bilad al-Sham from the mid-nineteenth century was powerful enough to not simply vanish in 1918. In infrastructure, Ottoman-time regional integration even begot more integration after 1918. Rails and roads that the Ottomans had expanded before 1918 survived; and roads helped to channel a postwar technology, the automobile, within the region. Second, the relative strength of the decades-long process of regional integration stood in contrast to the relative weakness of two new sets of actors. One set—and this is my second factor—was nationalist movements and elites, which were quite weak in the 1920s. Third, the other set of actors was the French and British imperial administrations which, running the Mandates on a shoestring, had neither the means nor the will to totally undo the late-Ottoman regional reality. They even recognized that reality; made major policy decisions—for example regarding the economy—accordingly; cooperated administratively, partly also beyond the region; and thus strengthened the region's integration in some ways. What irony given their division of Bilad al-Sham!

Also regarding cities, the birth of new nation-states was crucial. Cities had to adapt: new nation-state became a crucial new framework for how they functioned and saw themselves. Also, in order to carve out their space and prove their relevance within a new nation-state, many cities sought to advance transnational ties both within and beyond Bilad al-Sham. Thus, the birth of nation-states did not create a zero-sum game. "More national" did by no means necessarily mean "less urban" or "less transnational."

Vice versa, cities structured nation-state spaces, for three sets of reasons. As Chapters 1 and 2 have shown, cities had grown considerably in the late Ottoman period and remained at the center of their inhabitants' sense of being in the world. Although the world looked different after 1918, cities' continued relevance in a globalizing world from the mid-nineteenth century was not simply replaced by post-Ottoman nation-states. This was the case doubly—my second point—because the new imperial rulers accepted extant cities. Britain and France did not build new imperial urban centers (as they earlier had done in some colonies); sooner (Britain) or later (France) accepted urban notable elites; and were not too effective in tightly controlling their territories' borders. Finally, the birth of nation-states did not create a zero-sum game with cities. Rather, cities sought to use transnational ties to prove their worth within the nation-state space—thereby shaping that very space, too.

The rest of this chapter has a two-tiered structure. It is divided into a section each on culture, on the economy, and on administration. Each section examines the multi-dimensional process of transpatialization through the lens of cities and the region. The section on administration is mainly concerned with the region's changing position also within imperial and international spaces. Applied also to Chapters 4 and 5, this two-tiered structure will facilitate tracking continuities and changes from the 1920s to the 1930s and from there to 1939–1945.

## Cultural Identities in Flux: A Snapshot

On September 17, 1919, Jerusalem woke up to find a new newspaper, *Mir'at al-Sharq,* on offer. Its first editorial opened by asking God to bless this endeavor. It then proclaimed that "today we publish amongst our *qawm* (nation, people) this newspaper and issue it from the city of Jerusalem (*al-Quds al-Sharif*)"; expressed its hope that through its service "this *umma* (community, nation) may live and join *al-shu'ub al-hayya* (the living people, pl.)" and promised to maintain correspondents "*fi atraf al-bilad* (across the country)." One article, on the ongoing negotiations at the Versailles Conference, was titled "the Syrian problem and the Zionist issue." The last page included a note on "the movement of ships" in Jaffa and the local news (*mahalliyya*). These reported on "emigrants from Palestine" returning "to us" from "America," "looking forward to the day when all sons of the country (*abna' al-bilad*) return to their mother, Suriya."[11]

It is not simply the changing nature and overlap of terms like *qawm, umma,* or *bilad* that is fascinating here, but the blurriness between various fields. *Mir'at al-Sharq* targeted "our *qawm*" yet was proud about being from *al-Quds al-Sharif,* the Exalted Holy place. Similarly, the only port of interest—in a note immediately following the *mahalliyya* (Local News) section on Jerusalem—was Jaffa. Gaza and Haifa, let alone Sidon and Beirut, remained unmentioned. And while *mahalliyya* used the word "us" and noted returnee Khalil Totah, from Ramallah next to Jerusalem, it in the same breath talked of Palestine and Syria. Also, Palestine was seen as a unit of sorts but also as a part of Bilad al-Sham.[12]

This blurriness persisted. During *Mir'at al-Sharq*'s first three months of publication, all correspondents were in Palestinian towns, none in Lebanon or Syria, and reports on the British administration of Palestine reflected an emerging territorial reality.[13] At the same time, the newspaper continued to define Palestine as part of Syria and included Beirut and Damascus as well as Palestinian towns in *Akhbar al-jihhat* (News of the areas).[14] Then again, *Akhbar Suriya* did not include Palestine; neither did *Akhbar al-Sham.*[15] Local and national affairs continued to be deeply entangled, too. It was *Mir'at al-Sharq*'s local section which reported that Jerusalem's *Nadi 'Arabi* (Arab Club) had sent a telegram to Damascus. Talking for all of Palestine, it conveyed to Emir Faisal that it had submitted to the U.S. King-Crane commission, which was then touring Bilad al-Sham on a fact-finding mission, a memorandum against the region's division and Zionist immigration. And it was again in *mahalliyya* that a note for prospective students at Damascus Law School was published.[16]

### The Persistence of Urban Identities: Aleppo, Homs, and Damascus

If the above snapshot conveys a sense of how cultural identities were reconfigured after 1918, it cannot make sense of that complex process. To do so, we have to slice that process into manageable parts, which now will happen, first, from the viewpoint of cities.

We begin in Aleppo, and with an acquaintance: Jamal Pasha. Many people in Bilad al-Sham saw the region's wartime Ottoman ruler as a rather sinister, omniscient character. It is surprising, then, that for Aleppo's premier chronicler-historian, Kamil al-Ghazzi (1853–1933), some of Jamal's actions were nothing less than "the greatest of good deeds, . . . immortalizing his memory in history." No doubt, al-Ghazzi had his reasons. In particular, Jamal had a water pipeline built just before a drought peaked in the summer of 1917, which saved Aleppo's mushrooming population from catastrophe. Also, the pasha's good deeds "atoned some of his bad deeds" like forcing Aleppines to march northward to help the army fix a supply road in late 1914, an order that flopped when the officers, undersupplied, had to send many back home and some died on the way. Still, the Aleppine al-Ghazzi portrayed Jamal differently from most other people of Bilad al-Sham. The reason cannot be the pasha's actions in Aleppo, for also in places like Damascus he saved untold souls, for instance by helping to establish the Food Ration Administration in 1917. Rather, al-Ghazzi's judgment mirrored the deeper geohistorical fact that his city was oriented to Anatolia as well as to Bilad al-Sham.[17] Cities continued to differ from each other also after becoming part of the same nation-state in the 1920s.

Those urban identities continued to matter, too. In Aleppo, a good starting point is the Muslim Muhammad Raghib al-Tabbakh's

(1877–1951) I'lam al-Nubala' bi-Ta'rikh Halab al-Shahba', *Information about the Noble Men in the History of Aleppo the Gray*. It was an over 2,000-page heavy labor of love: a chronological compendium of biographies of prominent Aleppines from the dawn of Islam to the present. Al-Tabbakh wrote it mostly before World War I but published it in the 1920s. His foreword was revealing. Why had he spent decades bent over a desk to write his book? "In service to my area (*biladi*) and to the sons of my hometown (*watani*)," he declared, to "acquaint them with the history of their homes (*awtan*) and the exploits of their forefathers." This focus on his hometown—his very own *watan* even in the nationalist 1920s, when *watan* meant homeland—stood out doubly because, as he noted, "I did not try to obtain [supporting documents] in the Syrian lands (*al-diyar al-suriyya*) because this is impossible."[18]

A similar bent characterized *Udaba' Halab Dhawu al-'Athr fi al-Qarn al-Tasi'-'Ashar, Influential Aleppine Writers in the Nineteenth Century*. Its author, the Christian Qustaki al-Humsi, used *watan* for Aleppo as a matter of course. He even called his work for an interim city administration that had formed in late 1918 in coordination with the departing Ottoman governor a *khidma wataniyya* (a service to the hometown). Aleppo's relevance to its inhabitants' social standing was thrown into relief by his own biographical entry. Right off the bat, he made sure to specify just how long his family had already been in Aleppo: "He is Qustaki *ibn* (son of) Yussif *ibn* Butrus *ibn* Yussif *ibn* Mikha'il *ibn* Butrus *ibn* Yussif *ibn* Ibrahim *ibn* Salim *ibn* Mikha'il Mas'ad al-Humsi, the great ancestor who settled in Aleppo[,] emigrat[ing] from Homs in the first quarter of the sixteenth century." And he asserted that both his father's and mother's families are among "Aleppo's most outstanding houses."[19]

Such continued attention to one's city was not unique. Take Homs, to Aleppo's south, and Damascus. *Hums*, the newspaper of the former city—whose inhabitants are to this day often belittled by their larger neighbors Aleppo and Damascus—hastened to allege that it had published "the first legally printed Arab newspaper" after the 1908 Young Turk revolution. It cared for the present, too. One of its main goals was to raise money, through subscriptions, to support male orphans. And it made sure to mention that although small, Homs had an educated class, including a group of graduates from the American University of Beirut (formerly, the Syrian Protestant College). Also, like Jerusalem's *Mir'at al-Sharq* it ran a *mahalliyya* local news section on events that mattered to the city. It covered the French governor's actions, for example, or visits like that by an Orthodox priest, Luis Sheikhu. He, *Hums* took care to detail, addressed students in two Homsi schools and in a third, Jesuit school gave a free lecture to the interested public about Homsi antiquities and old literary works.[20]

As for Damascus, its inhabitants were, and still are, famously proud of their city. Thus, the opening paragraphs of Muhammad Adib Al Taqi al-Din al-Hisni's massive, three-volume *An Anthology of the Histories of Damascus* were one uninterrupted, glowing declaration of love. Like Tabbakh, al-Hisni called his hometown a *watan*. And in a eulogy given at a funeral in 1926 that he reprinted, writer Muhammad Abu al-Su'ud Murad honored a famous Damascene religious scholar, Khalil Efendi al-Bakri, with a poem one of whose verses echoed Damascus's persistent value for its inhabitants: "oh scholars of Damascus, your loved one has died—and his voice pervaded sea and land" (*wa-ya 'ulama' al-sham mata habibukum—wa-min sautihi qad sha'a fi al-bahr wa-l-barr*).[21]

## The Persistence of Urban Identities: Old Transnational Dimensions

This verse also expressed something else, though. Damascus saw itself not at all in splendid isolation, but as a significant place in the world at large. For one thing, Islam was crucial for the city that from 661 to 750 had been the Umayyad dynasty's capital. Al-Hisni pointed out that some Muslim families had branches in "Damascus and other Islamic cities like Baghdad, Mosul, Diarbekir, Hama, Tripoli al-Sham and the Hawran," all part of a wide Islamic urban network. He took pride in the number of Damascene families who, like the al-Bakris or the 'Umaris, traced themselves back to Islam's crème de la crème, the Prophet's companions. And he believed that God favored his city: he had "made it the fortress of believers . . . [and] given it . . . good fortune in abundance." He wrote during difficult times: many Muslim Syrians rejected Paris because it was neither Arab nor Muslim, and saw the French-supervised education system as a particularly insidious vehicle for pro-Christian secularization. In Damascus, religious scholars (*ulama'*, sg. *'alim*, in Arabic) and pious laymen, many of whom were merchants, soon reacted. Starting in 1924, they built up the Islamic press and the *Gharra'* school system for poorer children that drew pupils from Damascus and—often through Damascene merchants—also from its wider hinterland, including the Hawran and North Jordan. This effort was spearheaded by two *ulama'*: 'Ali al-Daqr and Muhammad al-Khatib. They succeeded not the least by securing the support of Damascus's leading, extremely learned, and exceedingly humble *'alim*, Muhammad Badr al-Din al-Hasani (1850–1935). This man illustrated, too, how Damascus's Ottoman-time function as a center of Islamic learning echoed in post-Ottoman times. His father, an *'alim* too, had arrived from Morocco in the nineteenth century, and al-Hasani himself attracted students from all over Bilad al-Sham and beyond.[22]

The Islamic context mattered not only to Damascus. Take again the Aleppine Tabbakh. He was the first director, from 1922, of the reformist *Khosrowiyya* seminary that employed traditionalist Aleppine clergymen while also corresponding with a famous reformist seminary in India, Lucknow's *Nadwat al-'Ulama'*. Throughout his oeuvre he paid special attention to Aleppo's religious leaders. His introduction affirmed "that the tidings about the past that Allah told his greatest prophet (peace be upon him) confirm [its] usefulness and guide the *umma*," the Islamic community. And he insisted that "most important for a human being is to be aware of the history of the town in which he was born" but also of "the religious community to which he belongs."[23]

Moreover, Islam was not the only outside universe to which cities in Bilad al-Sham belonged and through affiliation with which they continued to define themselves. Aleppo was linked to various worlds. The Ottoman, centered on Istanbul, was the most important but by no means the only one. A good illustration is the various profiles of nineteenth-century writers compiled by al-Humsi. Many spoke and often composed literature not only in Arabic but in Turkish, French, Syriac, and/or Italian, too. One had toured "Asia, Europe and Africa" others had lived for a while, or printed works, in Egypt, Lebanon, Istanbul, Paris and Marseille, Baghdad, Mersin, Mecca, and London. And al-Humsi himself was so deeply in love with Paris, where he lived for four long spells, that he wrote "c'est là, c'est là que je veus [*sic*] vivre, aimer et mourir" (it is there, there that I want to live, love and die).[24]

Although Aleppo, until the early 1800s a Eurasian trade hub, was uniquely well-connected, it was not exceptional. The section *qudum*, "arrivals," in *Hums* conveys a sense of Homs' connection points. They resembled those of Aleppo, although much fewer people moved between them and the small city of Homs. Non-Homsi and expatriate Homsi visitors came from Istanbul, Sudan, Cairo and Alexandria, from Syrian cities including Hama, Aleppo, and Damascus, and from Lebanon and its capital Beirut. They arrived from the Americas, too, from émigré communities like Sao Paolo, Chile and New York. In fact, most people who received a yearly subscription to *Hums* as a gift from a friend or relative lived in the *mahjar*, the diaspora communities especially of South America.[25]

## Urban Identities in Flux:
## The Mutual Splicing of City and Nation-State

Damascus, too, positioned itself globally, profiting from becoming Syria's capital. A case in point was the establishment, in 1919, of *al-Majma' al-'Ilmi al-'Arabi*, the Arab Academy of Science, which researched Arab culture and history and Arabic and advised on modern challenges to the Quran's venerable language. Publishing academic articles, in Arabic, and proclaiming its scientific nature, the Academy wished to be an equal to other academies, especially in Europe. It published monthly notes on other academies, and it enlisted as members leading European orientalists. By 1928, luminaries like Louis Massignon and Christiaan Snouck-Hurgronje constituted a third of its 109 members. Many corresponded with it, and following its foundation many also stated why. Damascus was a center of learning, even if, Western orientalists thought, it had declined since the Middle Ages. The Academy itself signaled its will to perform a renaissance by choosing as its home a building that in the twelfth century had been a famous religious seminary, the *'Adiliyya*. It was in this spirit that Italian orientalist Ignazio Guidi honored it as "the center of the world and the lady of the land" and that the Prussian Academy of Science called it the "Scientific Academy in the City of Damascus."[26]

Damascus continued to matter also because it was reframed as Syria's core. The urban and the national were intertwined: a key dimension of the second, post-Ottoman stage of transpatialization.[27] This intertwinement had a transnational link-up: it was warped by Damascenes' assertions, discussed above, that their city mattered in spaces much wider than the Syrian nation-state. And it was greatly facilitated by what one may call a "capital effect." As Syria's capital, Damascus became home to various national institutions—which in return reinforced its sense of being the center of Syria. A case in point was the Academy's self-description—"service to the dear language and nation"—and its membership roster. In 1928, sixteen of its twenty-seven Syrian members lived in Damascus, only nine in Aleppo. The capital effect took concrete shape at the Academy also in weekly talks and lectures, in Damascus, by secular and also religious scholars from far and wide. Moreover, the Academy reflected and nurtured Damascus's sense that it was not only Syria's heart, but—interwoven with being a center of Islam—a well-networked Arab center. Its peers were not so much the Syrian city of Aleppo, but rather Cairo and Beirut, with twelve Academy members each.[28]

The urban was spliced with the national not only in institutions but in texts, too. An example is the monumental six-volume tribute to Bilad al-Sham by the Damascene Muhammad Kurd 'Ali, who was the Academy's first director from 1919 to 1933. "In 1317h (1899)," his *Khitat al-Sham, The Districts of al-Sham,* opened, "I published in the [Egyptian] journal *al-Muqtataf* nine chapters of [an article called] "Umran Dimashq' [The civilization of Damascus]. . . . That day it occurred to me to expand this inquiry and study the civilization of all of *al-Sham,* because the form of the capital alone is insufficient to make sense of the situation of the region (*qutr*). It is by controlling [all] parts that one may get to know the health of the body in general and of the heart in particular." The challenging, transitional nature of the 1920s showed in Kurd 'Ali's rationale for his oeuvre. Since the 1800s Westerners had written much more about Bilad al-Sham than its people, he stated, and he did

not have to name the French conquest of Syria for his readers to understand that to him, this had had fatal consequences. "The subject matter
of [this book] is sublime," he affirmed. "Everybody who loves his country
has the duty to know it in order to serve it and draw profit from it." Although to Kurd 'Ali Damascus was the capital and heart of Syria and
more broadly of Bilad al-Sham, which he believed ought to be one single
nation-state, it did not matter anymore on its own, especially because it
now was under European rule. "Who is interested in the portion," in
Damascus, "ought to be doubly interested in the totality," Kurd 'Ali
concluded.[29]

Another example of how the urban and national were spliced is al-
Hisni. The same man who boasted that God had blessed his Damascene
hometown, mentioned no single Damascene personality in his acknowl-
edgment, but rather praised Ahmad Nami Bek, the Beirut-born man
whom France had put in charge of a Syrian government in 1926. While
less anti-French than most Syrian notables, Nami challenged France
and, in al-Hisni's eyes, understood that "strengthening the place of
knowledge and the publication of history . . . was and remains the strongest foundation and the most splendid pillar on which the living nations concentrate in their renaissance." It was to further this selfsame
nation-state-wide aim that Nami had supported al-Hisni's work and
that the Damascene author presented his book to "the sons of the
watan," by which he meant all Syrians rather than only his fellow
townsfolk.[30]

Although Damascus's objectively central role in watani and qawmi
nationalisms and in Arab culture meant that in this city, the urban and
the national became particularly intertwined, that process unfolded
elsewhere, too. In Aleppo, Tabbakh—he who so loved his hometown,
who insisted that "most important for a human being is to be aware of
the history of the town in which he was born" and "the religious community to which he belongs"—also recognized that man ought to know
"the places he borders and the state of which he is a subject."[31] Al-
Humsi—he who talked about Aleppo's administration in 1918 as a service to his hometown, watan—on the very next page cursed Aleppines
who had assented to the French administrative separation of an Aleppine from a Damascene district, within Syria. They were "enemies of

nationalism (*wataniyya*) [and] worshipers of their [own material] interests," he thundered. Moreover, whereas Damascus barely appeared in his biographical profiles of Aleppine writers who had died before Syria's birth in 1918, after that date Syria's capital became more present. Al-Humsi himself lived there for a spell in 1919, during Faisal's rule. And he and three other out of the ten Aleppine writers who were alive when he profiled them were corresponding members of the Damascus-based Arab Academy of Science, which, he acknowledged, "played an important role . . . in the general development of the humanities" in Syria. Al-Humsi thought of Aleppo and Damascus as Syria's twin towers.[32]

Smaller cities like Homs were specially pressed to prove their relevance within the embryonic nation-state. Take one of the most famous Homsi products, a silken textile called *hatta*. *Hums* called it not simply Homsi but "national Homsi textiles"; claimed that it was superior to other similar Syrian products and thus had always sold well in Syria as well as in neighboring Egypt, Palestine, Iraq, and Anatolia, and Istanbul; and asserted that it could be of use to Syria's economy if present trade difficulties with Turkey and Iraq were solved. Homs tried to position itself favorably in education, too. In 1923, a new school opened its doors. It chose the name *Kulliyyat Hums al-Wataniyya* (Homs National College), and sought to show that Homs mattered to Syria including Lebanon, whom almost all Syrians saw as an integral part of Syria. An ad from the fall of 1923 started out by detailing that its students, Muslims and Christians, hailed from all of "Homs, Tripoli, Lebanon, Damascus (*al-Sham*), Hama, Aleppo, Palestine, and Baghdad." Its hymn, in poem form, echoed this message: "The repute of this house of science / reaches as far as the horizons / to Palestine and Egypt / and to the people of Iraq / and the people of Lebanon and Syria / have a friend / in you, oh Homs."[33]

## Old Hometowns as New National Conduits for Global Diasporas

Five months earlier, in the spring of 1923, halfway around the world, the Sao Paolo conservatory was the venue for the second anniversary of the Brazilian city's *al-Nadi al-Humsi* (Homs Club). Its members, which included the "crème de la crème of [its] merchants and writers," sang another hymn for Homs. It peaked in the sigh "I am still in love."[34] Syria remained unnamed. Not at all because it was irrelevant: for it clearly mattered, as did Syrian and Lebanese nationalism.[35] But for Homsis in Sao Paolo and elsewhere in the *mahjar*, Homs formed the social and emotional center for what Syria was. It was their original *watan* and hence their emotional and social reference point in and to Syria. The newspaper *Hums* itself reflected this merger of the meaning and relevance of city, nation, and global diaspora not only in its *qudum* (arrivals) section. It also insisted that it was crucial for "the sons of the one homeland in Hums and in the diaspora" to keep in touch. And when its Sao Paolo correspondent sent news "to bring joy to the sons of the *watan*," he first meant Homs but by extension Syria, too. For while his reports concerned specifically Homsis—the foundation of the new Homsi Women's Association; news of prominent Orthodox Christians— he also made it crystal clear that the Homsis saw themselves as part of the larger Syrian population. As another *Hums* correspondent in the Chilean Andes put it: "In Val Paraiso, where we, a good Syrian community, have settled, we have seen the Homsi community count as its successful and literary central leader."[36]

## Bilad al-Sham's Cultural-Geographic Reframing

If the question concerning the cultural relationship between old cities and new nation-states was not who won but how they became entangled (including old transnational and newly transnationalized ties), the same holds for the nation-states and Bilad al-Sham.

Indeed, these new nation-states were deeply enmeshed with the region. This development found a conceptual bedrock in the term *Suriya al-tabiʻiyya*, Natural, or Geographic, Syria. Rooted in the late Ottoman nationalization of Bilad al-Sham / Suriya, a development traced in Chapter 1, this term was supercharged with meaning when Bilad al-Sham was divided. Its advocates described Suriya as "natural" in two related ways. One was explicit: the region was geographically and geologically a unit of nature. This depiction was clearest in Arabic geography school textbooks, whose authors agreed that Syria's "natural geography" had three distinguishing features: a narrow coastal plane and two mountain ranges divided by a valley. All ran from the region's north to its south, that is, together were common to Palestine, Transjordan, Syria, and Lebanon.[37]

In consequence, the region's new countries' natural state of affairs, as it were, was to be part of one polity or at least to be solidly integrated. This second "natural" feature was written into the presumably neutral language used to describe Bilad al-Sham's natural geography. In the natural geography section of his school textbook, Lebanese Sa'id Sabbagh presented a drawing of all the sections of the two mountain ranges. At its bottom were lines indicating the lower ranges, at its top the higher ranges (Figure 3.1). The effect was, even more than a map, a single schematic frame of the region as a unit. Palestinian Khalil Totah and Habib Khuri stated in the natural geography section of their textbook that "the position of the Palestinian mountains in Palestine is like the position of the spine in the human body. We have no choice but *not* to consider this elevated part of our country as separate and independent. For it is only a link in a chain that extends from Mount Lebanon in Syria and ends in the Red Sea." They did not have to spell out what happens when a spine is snapped or what it means that the region resembles one human body. Also, they chose their words with purpose and care. Palestine's "position" was not the neutral *wad'* but *minzala,* which is derived from the same Arabic root as "home," *manzil.* And "independent," *mustaqill,* obviously was a political term, which they used for the entire region rather than for Palestine alone.[38]

With a natural region came natural borders. Those of Bilad al-Sham, authors agreed, were the Syrian-Arabian Desert, the Egyptian Sinai Peninsula, the Mediterranean, the Anatolian Taurus Mountains, and the Euphrates River. These borders differed, though. To Totah and Khuri, for instance, the Mediterranean was Syria's "open door," the Arabian-Syrian Desert its "closed door." The reason was so obvious that it remained unnamed. The sea led to the West, to civilization. By contrast, the "primitive" desert-dwelling bedouin were written out of the region, despite the fact that they enjoyed strong ties especially to Bilad al-Sham's interior cities.[39]

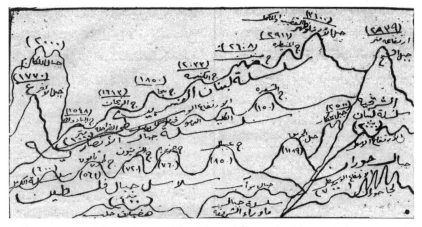

Figure 3.1 Sa'id Sabbagh's unified region. Sa'id Sabbagh, *Jughrafiyyat Suriyya al-'Umumiyya al-Mufassala* (Sidon: Matba'at al-'Irfan, 1923), 28.

This makes explicit something that already peeked from between the lines of the last paragraph. As it turns out, Natural Syria is not really natural. Like every geographical unit, it is made by and for man. Moreover, there were not only cultural and social but also political subtexts. Because the Syrian-Turkish boundary was contested, authors pointed out that Natural Syria's northern border, the Taurus Mountains, was inside Turkey. By contrast, nobody hesitated to call the international boundary between Palestine and Egypt Bilad al-Sham's natural southern border.[40]

Together with the general talk about the region's natural unity, those political subtexts were an answer to the problem of Bilad al-Sham's imperial division. This showed elsewhere, too. Consider how Palestinians referred to their new country. Totah and Khuri declared that it "can barely be called a country if we compare it to the expanse of Egypt or Iraq . . . or Russia or the United States or Brazil." They also explicitly refused to say how large it is; stated that its northern border is the Taurus Mountains (because it is part of Syria); and called its mountains the "completion" of Mount Lebanon in Syria.[41] More subtle was how both Palestinian and other authors broached the very theme of Bilad al-Sham's territorial division. Whether saying that the region now is composed of two (French and British) "areas" (*mintaqatain* in Arabic), or choosing to call the divisions "administrative" rather than "political," or downplaying the division by equating them with the region's Ottoman provincial divisions, the effect was one: to keep divisions within a regional framework and rhetorically protect Bilad al-Sham's unity. Authors recognized that this unity was man made, too. Bilad al-Sham's tightening transport links, the integrative role of cities like Beirut, and expansive economic ties: all demonstrated that the region was one.[42]

### The Yishuv and Bilad al-Sham's Cultural-Geographic Reframing

Zionists also thought about Bilad al-Sham and its relationship to the newly founded countries. They differed from most Arabs. They rejoiced in the creation of a separate country, Palestine, in which the Balfour Declaration foresaw a national home for the Jewish people; and their Yishuv formed part of the Jewish world, especially in Europe, Russia, and the United States. But what had been true before 1918 fundamentally still held in the 1920s, too. Some Yishuvi patterns echoed region-wide patterns, and the Yishuv was an integral part of region-wide structures. Zionists understood this. They could not, indeed did not want to, isolate themselves from Bilad al-Sham. They were a universe away from comparing their home to "a villa in the jungle" as Israeli general-turned politician Ehud Barak did in 1996. This was the case doubly because in the 1920s the Yishuv did not experience mass immigration, was still fledgling and not inward looking, although it was starting to build its own economy. Also, Arabs were not yet as hostile as they would become in 1929. The fact that Bilad al-Sham had been quite integrated by the end of the Ottoman era and was seen as a natural unit also after 1918, helped to frame the Yishuv and its view of its place in the world.

Like the Arabs' view of the region, the Zionists' was shaped by the Ottoman past—a past that had barely passed and that could not be neatly separated from the present. Take *Syrien als Wirtschaftsgebiet* (*Syria as an Economic Region*), by Arthur Ruppin, the German Zionist whom we have met earlier as the first director of the Palestine Office of the World Zionist Organization. A comprehensive oeuvre published in 1917 and an instant classic, his book was the fruit of extensive fieldwork across Bilad al-Sham from 1915 to 1916. Its tone and its publication by the Berlin-based *Kolonial-Wirtschaftliches Komitee;* Jamal Pasha's backing of the fieldwork; and Ruppin's correspondence with high-ranking German officials and state institutes: all this indicates that Ruppin wrote in the belief that Germany and the Ottoman Empire might survive the war.[43] To posit that "Syria, in the larger sense of the term," was "inclusive of Palestine"; to assert, just like Arab authors, that "geographically Syria may be divided into four longitudinal zones," a coast and two mountain ranges separated by a depression; to treat Palestine as an integral part of Ottoman Syria throughout the text: this was expedient, then. But was it only that? Note that the above quotes are not from the German original but from an English translation. Moreover, this translation appeared not in 1917 but in 1918—*after* Britain had issued the Balfour Declaration, occupied Palestine up to Jerusalem, and started nibbling at Ottoman Syria. And it was published not by a German colonial institute but by the Provisional Zionist Committee, in New York. Ruppin's portrayal of Syria as a region that included Palestine was not only expedient, then. It also reflected fundamental views.[44]

These views did not die with Ottoman Syria. They persisted and were expounded by leading Zionists in the 1920s. In economic geography, they referred to the fact that Syria, including Palestine, had been under one Ottoman rule, which meant that it had developed as one. Transport networks tied Palestine to what was now the French Mandate countries, be it by road to Beirut or by rail to Damascus; expansions that the French and British planned were welcomed. The region was described as a shared pool of various raw materials. Easy access to it was key for industrial and agro-industrial development, which started after the mid-1920s and would take off in the 1930s.[45] More crucially, the region was a home market and transit area (especially to Iraq) that comprised Palestine. This, however, also meant that Zionists worried about Beirut's powerful port and Syria's cheap industries and agriculture, for which Palestine was a premier export market. Palestine's tight regional connectivity was driven home by an economic downturn in 1926–1928, which affected Jews particularly hard. Its "causes lie principally abroad," affirmed an economist from Tel Aviv. It has to do with "the political conditions in

Syria," which, as noted, was in revolt from 1925 to 1927 and with which Palestine "is economically closely linked."[46]

But this was not the only external reason for the downturn. Another was "the economic crisis in Egypt."[47] Although Palestine was closely linked to Transjordan, Lebanon, and Syria, the Yishuv's industrialists, the Zionist Executive, and economists believed the Yishuv had to nurture wider connections and make the best of Palestine's exceptional geoeconomic position. Egypt and "the Oriental market" in general was a potential mass market for Zionist products. In fact, it was strongly linked to Palestine because of the low, 8 percent, customs franchise for products from all ex-Ottoman countries that it retained until 1930. Besides, Palestine's rail link with Egypt could easily plug its trade into the global trade highway, the Suez Canal. Also, Zionists thought that the Yishuv should exploit Palestine's inclusion in the British Empire to start market their wares also there, and expand connections to Europe.[48]

All this points to a crucial issue: Palestine, Erets Israel, was incontestably the heart of Zionism. While Bilad al-Sham helped frame the Yishuv and shape its inhabitants' view of their place in the world, the reverse was very much true, too. Bilad al-Sham's post-Ottoman division reshaped Zionists' views. The region was starting to turn from one (Ottoman) unit, in which they had to find a place, to an umbrella region composed of particularly tightly knit but separate polities, which moreover were tied to multiple outside worlds. In Ruppin's words, "there is a prospect that in ten or twenty years Palestine will become the most progressive land in the Near East."[49]

This, certainly, differed from how most Arabs saw Bilad al-Sham. But ultimately this difference was relative, not categorical. Arabs, too, started seeing Bilad al-Sham as an umbrella region of separate polities. Geography texts are a case in point. Totah and Khuri determined that Palestine's borders abutted the Taurus Mountain and declined to indicate its surface. However, their conclusions to these two passages matter-of-factly named British Palestine's political borders and stated that the country was 240 kilometers long and about half as wide. This, of course, allowed readers to calculate the country's surface. Sabri Sharif 'Abd al-Hadi explicitly defined Palestine as an integral part of Syria, but also talked of the ports and coasts of Syria and then of Palestine and had no compunction to name boundaries. Sabbagh, although covering all of Natural Syria, repeatedly singled out Lebanon: explicitly by paying more attention to it, for instance in a special note on tourism; and implicitly by foregrounding Lebanon. Thus, he talked about the western mountain range's central "Lebanese" section first, then moved north to the Alawite Mountains, and finished by leapfrogging southward, over Lebanon, to Palestine. And Kurd 'Ali, a diehard advocate of Bilad al-Sham's unity, noted that while some people see the region as "one sham," *shaman wahidan,* others "make it into *shams* (*shamat*) and turn Palestine and the Holy Land up to the Jordan into one sham," with other *shams* including the lands around Damascus and the lands up to Aleppo.[50]

Moreover, Kurd 'Ali underlined that Bilad al-Sham is "the close connection point between . . . the three old continents Asia, Europe and Africa." It is also "in the middle of the regions whose people speak Arabic," as well as of religious significance to Jews, Christians, and Muslims, and "the land of imagination and poetry." In other words, its unity did not imply isolation. To the contrary: it was a hub in and for the world, geographically and religiously culturally. Arab geography textbook authors shared this view.[51] Also in this regard, then, the Yishuv's Zionists and Arabs were not clearly distinct. Both believed that Bilad al-Sham, while a region, was not isolated but linked to other communities and areas.

### Bilad al-Sham's Cultural-Geographic Reframing and Transnational Connections

One such area was Egypt. Its proximity to Bilad al-Sham showed not the least in sociocultural contacts. Particularly in Palestine, Egyptian newspapers remained as well read as Syrian, Lebanese, and Palestinian ones in the 1920s. Egyptian authors and other personalities frequently visited Bilad al-Sham for conferences and readings. And people across Bilad al-Sham acknowledged the weight of that relationship. This stood out in moments of crisis. When in 1927 an earthquake hit central Bilad al-Sham, damaging most severely Nablus, the Egyptian government, Egypt's Red Cross, and a Cairene individual sent money and condolences to the Palestinian city. This was exceptional: Bilad al-Sham's other neighbors—Arabia, Iraq, and Turkey—stayed silent.[52]

Then again, Egypt's part needs to be seen in proportion. Egyptian donations all came from one place, Cairo, and were mostly governmental. By contrast, a much larger number of donations were sent from across Palestine—mostly from Arab municipalities, but also from several Jewish ones, as well as Jewish individuals—and from across Bilad al-Sham, including Amman (from Emir Abdallah), Beirut, Hama, Tripoli, and Damascus. Also, Bilad al-Sham's newspapers covered the event and its aftermath for months. But this setting has to be put in perspective, too. Most donations were Palestinian; and a place like Damascus, although less damaged than Nablus, took care firstly of itself. In sum, the response to the earthquake shone a light on one particularly close, Egyptian, transregional tie to Bilad al-Sham and on the increasing entanglement, in the 1920s, of urban, nation-state, and regional elements.[53]

## Bilad al-Sham's Continued Economic Integration: The Region-Wide Free Trade Zone and Transport Infrastructures

This trend—an increasing intertwinement and mutual reshaping of cities, nation-states, and various transnational ties—characterized not only cultural identity formation but also economic relations.

The very powers that divided Bilad al-Sham were forced to reflect on that region's continued weight. In France, economic and colonial circles in World War I intensified earlier calls for a French-controlled post-Ottoman Bilad al-Sham—and demanded unfettered access to all of it. Had not French capital for decades been invested up and down la Syrie?, asked groups like the chambers of commerce of Marseille (CCM) and of Lyon (CCL). Was not Syria therefore a Syrie française, glued to France by age-old historic ties? Although by 1918 those groups came to terms with the British presence in Bilad al-Sham, they continued referring to it as a region that ought to be as unified as possible. After all, Bilad al-Sham *was* a geographic unit, insisted the CCM-organized Congrès français de la Syrie in Marseille in 1919: an argument that in the summer of 1919 helped a CCM/CCL-sponsored mission to

Syria make their economic case for why a future French-ruled Syria, including Lebanon, should not be divided into statelets.[54]

Although this vision failed—Bilad al-Sham was divided; Syria, subdivided—French and British appreciation of Bilad al-Sham as a region did not fade. It continued to show in word, for instance in official geographical publications encompassing Bilad al-Sham, and in deed, in agreements about administrative coordination and economic matters. When a Franco-British team demarcated the border separating Lebanon and Syria from Palestine and Jordan in 1921–1922, it fully realized how easily territorial division could make life hard for people. As a French officer noted, "this delimitation has just cut into two a country that was totally unprepared for this division."[55]

The central problem was how to square Bilad al-Sham's considerable degree of economic integration with its political division. In 1921 France and Britain made a crucial decision. They turned Bilad al-Sham into a customs-free zone for all goods: those locally produced, those imported from outside and, possibly, processed, and those in transit. Crucially, then, post-Ottoman Bilad al-Sham "form[ed] one unit for economic purposes."[56] (Reality was somewhat more complex, as we will see.) France and Britain created that unit because they understood that "Palestine and Syria before the War were one territory with no Customs barriers." Even when French manufacturers protested that it was unfair to them that Palestinian goods entered Syria freely, the French authorities replied that the customs-free zone served "economic opportunity and the general interest. Hence, we are not planning to modify it, not even for one single item." In trade, Bilad al-Sham's integration continued after 1918.[57]

This persistence was facilitated by modest rail and extensive road expansion and by a technological coincidence: the postwar surge in the use of automobiles. Especially Britain expanded Ottoman-time railways. Already in 1918 / 1919, it finished extending the line it built in the war from Egypt to Palestine's south, to Lydda and Haifa, and by 1923 reopened some parts of the Hijaz line in Jordan. As for France, by 1921 it had rebuilt the Tripoli-Homs railway dismantled in World War I. More important, both powers invested in roads networks, building on already considerable Ottoman wartime expansions. In the French

Mandates all-weather roads grew, by one account, from 700 kilometers in 1919 to 2,900 kilometers in 1939, secondary roads from 600 kilometers to 6,800 kilometers. Besides the Ottoman-time Beirut-Damascus all-weather road, the other ones led from Ra's al-Naqura, on the border with Palestine, to Latakia and then eastward to Antioch and Aleppo, from Dir'a via Damascus and Homs to Aleppo, and from Tyre via the Shuf Mountains and Zahle to Ba'albek and Homs. That is, there were two north-south roads, along the littoral and in the interior, two east-west roads, in the north and center, and one southwest-to-northeast road. By one account, in British Palestine, there were 450 kilometers of all-weather roads in 1921, 1,247 kilometers in 1936, and 890 kilometers of dry-weather roads in 1929, 1,835 kilometers in 1936. In addition to the Ottoman-time Jerusalem-Jaffa road, the other ones led from Metula, on the Lebanese border, via Tiberias, Nazareth, Nablus, Jerusalem and Hebron to Beersheba, from Ra's al-Naqura via Acre, Haifa and the Jaffa-Tel Aviv region to Gaza, and from Acre to Safad, Haifa to Nazareth, and Jerusalem to the Jordan River. In other words, there were two north-south roads, along the littoral and in the interior, and three east-west roads, two in the north, one in the center.[58]

Especially in Lebanon and Palestine, cars made ample use of these expanded road networks.[59] Cabs connected Haifa with Beirut and Damascus from the early 1920s, for instance, and in 1926, a Beirut-Tripoli-Aleppo bus company was founded. Also, at the same time that railroad journeys became shorter, cars sped up travel, too. By 1925 a cab ride from Beirut to Haifa took four to five hours; before, it had been three to four days. Similarly, in 1928 road transport times between Beirut and Aleppo shrank with the opening of a new Aleppo-Lattakiyah motorway that extended the 1923 Lattakiyah-Tripoli road to Beirut. Although mechanical difficulties regularly forced cab companies to interrupt service, visitors contrasted prewar travel with the present "uninterrupted, dense motorized traffic in all cities and on all highways." This relative ease was reflected in that tourists to Palestine were routinely offered motor trips northward, for example to Damascus and Baalbek. Rail and car also brought the region closer to its neighbors. The expansion, northward to Lydda and Haifa, of the British wartime Kantara-Gaza railroad slashed traveling from Haifa to Egypt's Suez Canal to a mere ten hours.

Also, during the war and in its wake, France hoped to realize the prewar project of a French-controlled railroad from Syria to Iraq. It failed—but not quite. France and others believed that the car, not unlike the Hijaz Railway earlier in the last prewar decade, might soften the Suez Canal's deleterious impact on land transport from Iran and Iraq to the Mediterranean and westward. French authorities, by 1924 including High Commissioner General Maxime Weygand and the British consul in Damascus C. E. S. Palmer developed an active interest in this matter. In the 1930s, open competition would erupt; but for now, Palmer recognized that Paris had the upper hand. After all, the easiest routes to Iraq, still serving a few caravans, led through the deserts of French Syria, not via British Transjordan. But Palmer, too, had an ace up his sleeve. In early 1923, he asked the Nairn brothers to explore the possibility of a (Haifa-Beirut)-Damascus-Baghdad car service, knowing that a few people had already in 1922 smuggled, by car, gold from Damascus to Baghdad. A few trial runs were made and a French license and funding secured; a mail delivery contract with Iraq was signed and a powerful desert tribal leader paid; and in late 1923, Nairn started operating. Two years on, piggybacking on this and a few competing companies, the French and British authorities in Beirut and Baghdad concluded a transit trade agreement.[60]

However, such agreements and, more important, the 1921 Franco-British agreement to turn all of Bilad al-Sham into one single customs-free zone, did not mean that France and Britain relinquished their very own, independent economic policies. This had consequences. Their states developed differently, and their shared customs-free zone was composed of two sovereign units. But as economic interaction remained dense in, and because of, the Bilad al-Sham-wide customs-free zone, one imperial power's policy decisions often spilled over. This helped to shape economic claims and thus policy across the border. The imperially ruled nation-states could not be isolated from the region, and vice versa.[61]

One particularly spectacular spillover effect occurred in 1925–1926. It concerned the Syro-Lebanese reaction to Britain's decision, mainly due to Zionist pressure to support their budding manufacturing, to lower customs rates on some overseas raw material just as France was raising its rates from 15 percent to 25 percent. "Local interests protested bitterly. . . . The manufacturers had two grievances. Raw materials destined to local industry should be exempt from duty. Otherwise the Palestinian exemptions coupled with the free trade regime between the two countries would slowly choke local production. Conversely, the 25% duty was not high enough on certain manufactured products. Infant industries in Syria needed super-rates. Protest waxed more and more bitter. At length the All-Syrian Chambers of Commerce Congress met at Beirut and presented a comprehensive report on the tariff to [High Commissioner] M. Ponsot on May 16, 1928. For various reasons the protest bore fruit. M. Ponsot responded with the far-reaching arrêté No. 1970 of June 2, 1928." Consequently, "a decrease of duty on raw materials was particularly evident from 1928–1931. . . . [This] favored various industries."[62]

## Perceptions of the Bilad al-Sham-Wide Free Trade Zone

How did people in Bilad al-Sham see the customs-free zone and the regional economy in general? In the Yishuv, the (Jewish) Manufacturers' Association stated in a memorandum in 1927 that "previous to the war, Palestine was a constituent part of a big economic unit of the Turkish Empire and was economically closely bound up with some of its parts, particularly with Syria." It also acknowledged that "Palestine always had to depend on the good offices of neighbouring countries where there are important stocks of goods in existence (owing to better port facilities and advances [sic] commercial organization) and where the Palestine merchant and trader can buy goods as the need arises and can often rely on receiving credits."[63] This memorandum did not simply reflect past patterns. It addressed a burning question. In 1927 it became known that Britain and France were renegotiating the 1921 agreement. The British High Commissionership planned (since 1925) to raise customs on products that were more than 75 percent foreign in value or material, for instance textiles imported to Damascus, dyed, and reexported. While upholding the principle of regional economic unity, it sought to maximize sorely needed revenues and protect Palestine's fledgling industry. The Zionist reaction was a storm of indignation. Factory owners bombarded Jerusalem with memoranda like that above; workers threatened to strike; and the political leadership chimed in. Seen from today, this may be a surprise—though one that can tell us much about how region and nation-states became intertwined in the 1920s.[64]

In fact, the customs-free zone did not simply echo past regional economic integration. It actually bolstered that trend. In 1927 no Zionist sided in public with the High Commissioner. True, there had been some handwringing over the Syrian-Palestinian trade imbalance, and some merchants had specific reservations about the customs-free zone. Still, in 1927 there was public agreement on "how essential the Syrian market is to some of the Palestine Factories, particularly in the small textile trades: they were *established* under the existing Agreement by which the two Countries form one unit for economic purposes: some of them are specially working for this trade and the successful development of all of them depends on them having access on preferential terms to the Syrian consumers, who are three times as numerous as those of Palestine."[65] There was some hyperbole here. Zionists recognized that Syrian and Lebanese exports to Palestine were much higher than the reverse. By value, in 1921–1929 the trade ratio ranged from about 3:1 to 11:1 (only in 1922 was it 1:2), goods being mainly though not only agricultural: from Syria chiefly "cereals, animals and cloth" from Palestine "fruit, soap, hides, [and] skins." And whereas Palestine was, after an early dip, up there with Egypt, France, Turkey, and the United States as Syria and Lebanon's first (1925, 1926), second (1923, 1924, 1929), or at least third (1927, 1928) largest export destination, it was only the eleventh (1923), thirteenth (1924, 1927), fourteenth (1926, 1928), fifteenth (1925), or even sixteenth (1929) importer to Syria and Lebanon, a market cornered by France and Britain.[66]

Even so, in 1929 the Zionist Executive confirmed that the 1921 agreement had helped Jewish manufacturers. Palestine's exports indeed grew toward the end of the decade. (It was from 1927 to 1929 that the trade ratio turned 3:1.) From the mid-1920s, small-scale Jewish manufacturing started growing, eventually overcoming the 1926–1928 bump. And the textile sector that depended on Syria and Lebanon was from 1924 to 1927 "one of the most vigorous and rapidly growing industries."[67] In fact, its founders had decided to leave Europe and bet on Palestine partly because they knew they could sell their products customs-free throughout Bilad al-Sham. This, they appreciated doubly having experienced how the "erection of innumerable tariff barriers . . . was one of the principal causes of economic hardship" in postimperial Europe. (Many came from Poland, where some had worked in textile; more generally, postwar immigrants were less ideological than the prewar leftist second aliyah.) Cases like that of Erich Möller—the co-owner of a Czechoslovak spinning company who, emigrating to Palestine, planned to visit Beirut to "study the question of the outlet market"—illustrated that the customs-free zone did not simply reflect past integrative trends. Rather, it cemented them.[68]

The customs-free zone affected Bilad al-Sham's economic pecking order. Not only did Zionists believe the zone to help, or at least not to hurt too much, their young industries in the present. Prospects mattered, too. In the not-too-distant future, they hoped, the Yishuv might become the region's industrial center. No point, then, to tinker with the customs-free zone now. Once manufacturing had matured, one might revisit it. Until then "Syria is, and is likely to be much more valuable to Palestine as a consumer than dangerous as a competitor."[69]

This, in return, points to a fundamental shift. Like in identity formation so in the economy Bilad al-Sham was starting to turn into a region of separate yet fatefully intertwined nation-states. That one lived in and interacted with it was simply a given, and had fateful significance for one's nation-state. How one interacted with it: that was an entirely different question, one shaped by one's own interests and outlook. In the 1920s—years of comparative calm in Palestine and of sluggish growth in the Yishuv; years when many Syrians and Lebanese were focused, often violently, on their imperial rulers—many Zionists were guardedly optimistic about the possibility of a region-wide win-win economic situation.

Syrians, too, understood the economics of the intertwinement of nation-state and region. This showed already in their response to the customs-free zone arrangement in 1921. France and Britain initially intended to tax goods imported from outside Bilad al-Sham, or goods locally manufactured using foreign raw material, upon cross-border resale. They swiftly revised this opinion after loud protests, especially in Damascus. The result—the absolute customs-free arrangement—brought some relief to Syria. For as Damascus Chamber of Commerce vice president Lutfi al-Haffar underlined during the protests, in October 1921, there ought to be no customs inside "Syria from al-Arish," on the border to Egypt, "and the Hijaz in the south to Alexandretta and Anatolia in the north, and from Iraq in the east to the Mediterranean ports in the west."[70] This position persisted. And like in Palestine, it was thrown into relief in 1927 by the threat of an arrangement revision. The Damascus Chamber of Commerce protested again, declaring that a revision would "without doubt be a barrier in the path of Syria's industries and upset its trade with the neighboring region (*qutr*)." (France took it seriously, consulted with it, and blocked Britain's initiative. The new agreement, signed in 1929, did not substantially change the 1921 arrangement.)[71]

Syrian merchants and manufacturers favored a Bilad al-Sham-wide customs-free zone not simply for nostalgic reasons, but because it benefited them. Like before 1918, so during the 1920s, Syria was the manufacturing center of Bilad al-Sham, as well as of southern Anatolia, with strong ties also to eastern Iraq and Arabia. It had no real regional competitors yet—the Yishuv would become one only from the very late 1920s—and needed the customs-free zone as an outlet for the manufacturing base that it sought to modernize and expand. This was vital. A stronger economy was the "spirit of freedom and independence" that Syria was being denied.[72]

But while Syrians sought to muscle up their own economy to eventually break their French chains, they at the selfsame time saw their fortunes to be indissolubly tied to Bilad al-Sham. In this they were like the Zionists, just more so, because they had no other truly existential bond like the lifeline tying the Yishuv to the Jewish diaspora. Moreover, they did not distinguish between Syria's and Bilad al-Sham's good: "it is not in the interest of Palestine, which is part of Syria, and not in Syria's political and economic interest to erect the slightest customs barrier."[73] In this they were again like the Zionists, only that they talked of win-win with the confidence of a heavyweight, defining the region's interest as a function of their own. By contrast, the weaker Zionists asked how soon they could fully profit from their inescapable regional setting. "If we are to live we have to expand economically beyond the political frontiers of our poor little Erezisrael," is how Zionist Secretariat Trade and Industry Section head Nahum Thischby concluded a report on a study tour to Beirut and Damascus.[74]

But why exactly was this vital? Thischby provides one part of the answer. Palestine's 1,000,000 consumers—or even Syria's and Lebanon's 3,000,000—alone were a small market. This problem, to be sure, could be partially alleviated by selling goods abroad: Egypt remained a key market for all of Bilad al-Sham, maintaining its 8 percent prewar customs franchise until 1930, and agricultural goods—from Palestine chiefly oranges; grains from Syria—were sold overseas. But vexingly, post-Ottoman Turkey and Iraq had raised customs. And whereas sovereign states could tax Mandate imports at will, the League of Nations stipulated that Mandates had to tax imports from League member states and the United States equally. Although this Open Door free trade policy had an honorable veneer—to nix imperial exploitation—it meant that Mandate customs rates on manufactured imports were not very high. In return, this allowed industrialized countries to dump goods especially in the French part of Bilad al-Sham. Conversely, even Syria's relatively cheap labor was not cheap enough, and the Yishuv's comparatively well-trained workers not well-trained enough, to manufacture globally competitive goods.[75] In this situation, only a customs-free zone could even the odds: which explains the trust both Arabs and Jews put in it.

## The Economic Power and Limits of Beirut and of Its Interurban Ties

Having examined the socio-spatial restructuring of economic relations from the perspective of Bilad al-Sham—that is of how that region shaped, and was reshaped by, embryonic, imperially ruled nation-states and world economic forces—we now turn to look at the economy from the viewpoint of cities.

In Beirut, the postwar reintegration into the world market was not only a challenge. Import/export merchants profited here more than anywhere else in the region. "To say that Beirut is a trade city is like asserting that the day has 24 hours," wrote the newspaper *al-Haqiqa*. Indeed, as global trade expanded from 1918—though slower than before 1914—and as it reached its prewar volume by 1921, Beirut bounced back, too. From 1919 to 1921 its imports exploded almost tenfold. Until 1929, it basically remained a world trade port-city: a place good enough for Alfred Sursock to marry a European aristocrat and bring her there.[76]

Beirut also resumed a vigorous urban growth. Anxious to display their presence, the new French rulers widened streets to accommodate now motorized traffic and extended avenues and streetcar lines to mushrooming suburbs. Beirutis—whose number doubled from 1921 to 1932, reaching about 200,000—were busy, too, rebuilding neighborhoods and making late-Ottoman-times attractions ever livelier. Alfred Sursock finished a horse racing track in the Pine Park, to the city's south. And down town, the Place des Canons—now also called Place des Martyrs[77]—teemed with shoppers, moviegoers, café visitors, hotel guests, sailors from the adjacent port, and travelers using the many long-distance cabs and buses that arrived or departed from here. For Beirutis with deep pockets life was as sweet and Western as it got in Bilad al-Sham. Clothes from the Galeries Lafayette in Paris were on sale, "toujours de la nouveauté en stock;" classical Western concerts, often in hotels, were daily treats, and art exhibitions common; and the well-heeled and cultured held salons. Appetites did not get a raw deal, either, what with "la bonne charcuterie française, [L]es vins [et] liqueurs des meilleures marques" waiting for the city's "fins gourmets."[78]

Perhaps the finest, and certainly the richest, were Beirut's elite merchants, many of whom had survived the war. To be sure, several French trading companies and banks entered Beirut after 1918, and a number of merchants—some also arriving from smaller cities like Tripoli or Sidon—started working with them. But as the example of Alfred Sursock showed, those Beiruti merchants quickly regained self-confidence after 1918, helping to shape Beirut's atmosphere: "trade turns life into moving matter, perpetually stimulated by the great energizing force of competition." The stature of these merchants counted. As Sursock's interaction with Gouraud illustrated, French officials actively socialized with the Beiruti elite, so much so indeed that Beirut "occupied a special place within the French colonial world. . . . By involving themselves to such a degree in society life, French officials had helped to make it an opportunity for lobbying by their hosts."[79]

Beiruti elites' skill and power in dealing with France showed in that their city was the inevitable site for a 1921 French-Mandate-wide trade fair, simply called *Foire de Beyrouth*. It was subtly reflected, too, in a 1922 visit to Lebanon and Syria by a French economic delegation, including two Chambre de Commerce de Marseille representatives. Upon their return, their president sent letters of gratitude to his counterparts. Aleppo was a "grande ville" with an "excellent esprit"; Damascus he subtly patronized, applauding "your young assembly [that] already demonstrates a competence and activity full of promise." Aleppo's response, sent two months later, gently critiqued French trading habits; Damascus's, four months later, was long and flowery. The contrast to Beirut was like day and night. Marseille lionized it as a "grand centre commercial, intellectuel et administratif," and it was just as such that the Beirut Chamber of Commerce replied: immediately, hyper-efficiently—"votre estimée lettre du 7 Ct. Sub. N° 4360" were nine of merely seventy-five words—and with self-assured coolness.[80]

Beirut's businessmen did their best to defend their preeminence in a now divided Bilad al-Sham. They called Beirut the Bride of the East, while Jaffa was a more modest Bride of Palestine, and Haifa the Bride of the North. Tellingly, businesses in Palestine advertised in Bilad al-Sham's premier, Beirut-based business newspaper, *Le Commerce du Levant,* and the Beirut-based business guide *Dalil Lubnani-Suri* as a matter of course encompassed Palestine. Moreover, port Beirut handled two to three times the tonnage of Jaffa and Haifa. It also accounted for over three quarters of the French Mandate's external trade tonnage, and continued to stultify competitors. Its dominance was facilitated by French economic and strategic priorities: France, and the Beirut Port Company, steadily built up the port in the 1920s, also for the French navy.[81] By remaining Bilad al-Sham's biggest world trade hub, then, Beirut was supported by the sovereign. Although this was no novelty, France focused much more on Beirut than Istanbul: the Ottomans had tried protecting interior cities, too.

This fact showed not only in Beirut itself but also in the Beirut-Damascus interurban axis. Hence, a look is in order, first, at that axis, which we have met in Chapters 1 and 2. Staying on topic, we will then—before returning to cities—discuss two other interurban ties: between British Mandate Haifa and French Mandate Beirut and Damascus, respectively. The new Franco-British border's effect on those interurban ties and the latter's effect on economic realities on either side of that border: this twin process is a noteworthy dimension of transpatialization in the 1920s.

Mutually dependent though unequal before 1914, the Beirut-Damascus axis became more unequal in the 1920s, disadvantaging Damascus. Although France did invest in that city and although it continued growing, many there deplored France's neglect to protect the manufacturing that was crucial to it and to its relationship with Beirut. The latter showed in a thousand and one ways. When Beiruti and Damascene, and other Lebanese and Syrian, merchants and manufacturers convened to formulate demands vis-à-vis the French authorities, they did so as a matter of course in Beirut. Whenever the French army updated the telephone exchange in Damascus, phone calls to Beirut received a discount. And Damascus always had to beg for something. In 1923, its chamber of commerce applauded the addition of a passenger wagon to the Beirut-Damascus night freight train—but could not the mail be sent, too, please? The Syro-Lebanese border did not exist economically and was not demarcated—so could the border officials that France stationed anyway on the Beirut-Damascus highway at least stop mistreating voyagers? There were daily freight trains between Beirut and Damascus—so why did it often take two to three weeks for goods to transit from port Beirut to a newly set up Customs Office in Damascus? By the summer of 1923, the High Commissioner in Beirut had enough. He asked that "a final stop be put to these complaints" concerning transit and reaffirmed a letter by his Finance adviser, who had told the Damascene merchants that if they were not pleased they could do the work themselves in port Beirut by sending a representative.[82]

However, despite imperial support for Beirut, that city still was unable to turn preeminence into dominance. On the Beirut-Damascus interurban axis, not everything changed. In response to the High Commissioner's letter, Damascus's merchants searched for a Damascene candidate rather than asking a Beiruti for help. Also, their ad expressly looked for somebody who was at home in both Damascus and Beirut, reflecting that the two cities' merchants, while tight business partners, still tended to stick to their territory. Indeed, although Beirut was powerful, it and Damascus remained mutually dependent. When trade plummeted during the 1925–1927 revolt, Beirut's merchants suffered, too. And Damascene manufacturers' know-how, will to industrialize, and hunger for capital was not unattractive for Beiruti money. In 1925, Jamil Beyhum, representing Beiruti merchants, met Damascene merchants and manufacturers in Damascus to discuss possible investments.[83] Last, this mutual dependence with Damascus— Beirut's premier access to Bilad al-Sham's interior, and on to Iraq and Iran—was the most significant cause for Beirut's ability to dominate Lebanon. The Damascus-Beirut interurban tie molded the (Lebanese) nation-state's economic space, helping Beirut to be a grotesquely big head for a weakly body.

Another interurban link tied Haifa to Beirut. Late Ottoman Beirut had dominated the growing yet still small town that was part of its province from 1888 to 1918. (Also, many Haifawis, especially Christians, were originally from Lebanon or Syria.) And because Britain did not try to cut that tie, Arab Haifa's "leadership . . . looked towards Beirut or even Damascus" also in the 1920s. It was telling that Haifawis often still simply talked of "the north" when referring to events in Beirut. They remained connected also economically. Although Beiruti merchants like the Sursocks—who in the late 1800s had bought some land in Haifa and extensive lots near it, in the lower Galilee—sold some land, they kept much, also in Haifa, operating through their trusted agent, Maronite Salim al-Khuri, a scion of Haifa's richest family. Some Christian Lebanese, including Beirutis, continued coming to a city that for its religious mixity and openness was called *Umm al-Gharib* (Mother of the Stranger). Beirutis opened new businesses, too: a store by Beirut's famous Pharao family in 1920; a legal representative for a Beiruti firm in 1921; a Haifa-Beirut trade and transit office in 1925. And as early as 1921 the two cities' downtowns were linked by a daily cab service; ship connections continued unabated; and there was recurrent talk about a railroad line, which received Zionist support, too.[84]

## The Transnationalization of the Damascus-Haifa Economic Interurban Axis

Beirut had not been the only interurban tie of late Ottoman Haifa. Damascus had been the other principal one. From 1905, an Ottoman railway line connected the two cities, speeding up grain transports from the Hawran, Bilad al-Sham's breadbasket, to the Mediterranean and thence overseas. Haifawis even started calling the place where more and more Damascene merchants settled *Suq al-Shawwam,* the Damascenes' Market. After 1918 grain exports declined, but did not cease. More important, nongrain exports from Syria to Palestine, which as we saw earlier were extensive, came mostly via Damascus and often from Damascene manufacturers, and first to Haifa. Hence, it was not a surprise that Haifawis sometimes attended meetings by the Damascus Chamber of Commerce. Vice versa, when that chamber mentioned Palestinian merchants' publications, it referred to its Haifa counterpart. Moreover, Damascene merchants advertised their own trade and transit businesses and law offices in Haifa's *al-Karmal,* and "found a ready outlet in Haifa for Syrian exports, and various export firms, such as Saraqibi and Sba'i, opened branches in the city"; and "Haifa's Arab commercial community was enlarged during the 1920s by the advent of a substantial number of Damascene Muslim families." In return, *al-Karmal* informed its readers when Damascus newspapers were closed and reopened, and Haifa's "leadership . . . looked . . . even [toward] Damascus" for guidance. Given this two-way traffic, the Damascus-Haifa railway line remained well used—enough for an enterprising soul to open a restaurant in 1923 in Semakh Station, where the railway touched the southern tip of the panoramic Sea of Galilee.[85]

But it was not for the view that the restaurant was opened. It was for travelers, who had to spend some time in Semakh because it was the Palestinian-Syrian border station. The passport control office for the line was based here. Passing it required a passport from one's own government and a visa from one's neighbors. This was not the only hassle. Yes: Damascene merchants deemed the customs-free zone a "good" thing, indeed wanted it replicated for "Iraq and the Hijaz" and "Anatolia," with which trade conditions were "not good" and "very bad," respectively.[86] But trade was often an obstacle course. The customs-free zone did not mean no customs agents or customs policy. Bureaucrats ran customs warehouses in the large ports and in the interior cities Damascus and Aleppo, and were present also on road and railway border crossings like Semakh, bureaucratizing formerly less onerous trade and oftentimes vexing people. Customs policy was an even greater headache. France and Britain on and off found excuses to subvert the customs-free zone, raising customs on products or curtailing imports. This hurt merchants. In Haifa, British restrictions on reexporting (mainly Syrian) cereals, but also Zionist agricultural land purchases in the north, eventually meant that "[E]ven though a good number of [merchants] still operated in the city, by the end of the [1920s] they had to diversify their activities." In sum, the bureaucratic hoops and political-financial interests of the new, imperially ruled nation-states directly affected those economic interurban ties which, like that between Haifa and Damascus or even that between Damascus and Beirut, now straddled a border.[87]

The reverse happened, too. Damascus leveraged its tie to Haifa and more specifically its railway link, whose Palestinian bit was outside French control, against its imperial master. Because in the early 1920s railway freight prices in the French Mandate were high, by 1921–1922 Damascene merchants exported much wheat, and some other goods, not to Beirut but to Haifa—from where about half of the wheat was reexported to French Mandate ports. The French High Commissioner (HC) reacted. In 1923 he made the "Damas, Hama et Prolongement Co . . . [to] reduc[e] its freight rates by one-third," lowering the Damascus-Beirut price to 60 percent of the Damascus-Haifa price. Thereafter, whenever Damascene merchants had problems with Beirut, they nimbly insinuated that they again may make greater use of the Haifa route. Merchants elsewhere, for instance in Aleppo, lacked that weapon and continued paying high freight rates. Damascus's interurban tie to Haifa gave it not only some leverage over its imperial rulers, then.

It was a tactical advantage over Bilad al-Sham's other large interior trade city.[88]

## Haifa's Economic Rise at the Intersection of Nation-State, Region, and Empire

Having examined the economic aspect of transpatialization through the lens of interurban ties, let me now do so again through cities: Haifa, Aleppo, and Damascus.

In Haifa, change was in the air. Its growth, slow in the 1800s but gathering pace with the 1905 Haifa-Damascus railway, was boosted by Bilad al-Sham's division in 1918. Beirut lost its Ottoman-time province, and hence its ability to check rival ports in the part that after 1918 was in British Palestine. It started worrying about Haifa, and for good reason. While Haifa continued to be strongly tied to Beirut, its postwar detachment from Beirut cemented its rise. This situation was beautifully captured in Haifa's first history in Arabic, which appeared not by chance soon after the war, in 1922. While taking note of his city's long past the author, *al-Zuhur* newspaper editor Jamil al-Bahri, described it as a beacon of the present and future. "Haifa is a very modern city whose history returns, [linked to] progress and development, to the history of the establishment of the Hijaz Railway, that is not more than about twenty years," he started the section "Haifa's history." An "astoundingly speedy, palpable transformation" has made it "one of the most important Palestinian cities, nay one of the most commercially thriving Syrian cities, without however commercially upsetting Beirut, the only Bride of the East."[89]

Al-Bahri's deference to Beirut had the tongue-in-cheek undertone of an underling who is becoming a rival. Haifa was on the up and up, and he knew it. Having profited from the sacking of Acre by Ibrahim Pasha in 1830, and grown from about 2,000 to 20,000 inhabitants between 1850 and 1900, it doubled from 25,000 to 50,000 between 1922 and 1931. Immigration increased. For one thing, Arabs came, with thousands of non-Palestinian arrivals from Bilad al-Sham and from Egypt constituting a full quarter of all arrivals: a movement that, while to peak in the 1930s, was palpable already before. Indeed, since the mid-nineteenth century Haifa had resembled Beirut for its religious and socioeconomic mixity. Moreover, specifically in the 1920s the arrival "of a substantial number of Damascene Muslim families and smaller numbers of Lebanese Christians" fed Haifa's "antagonism against the hegemony of the Jerusalem leadership" in Palestine, for those Lebanese and Syrians "were even less inclined to follow [said] leadership." Haifa's strong northward orientation accentuated the persistence, in Palestine, of city-based political elites that did not merge into one nation-wide stratum.[90]

For another thing, mainly due to immigration Jews grew from a quarter of Haifa's population to a third between 1922 and 1931. This affected Haifa's Arabs. They were concerned by Zionism not only as a challenge to Palestine as a whole. They saw these Zionists as a local problem too: that a simple worker's "regular funeral procession" in 1926 was attended by an estimated 2,000 young workers was frighteningly impressive, for instance. Long-term trends were not less disconcerting. Jews benefitted disproportionally from new municipal infrastructural projects. Better organized than the Arabs, their neighborhoods—many new, and separate from Arab ones—profited most from laissez-faire British town planning. And Jews penetrated hitherto Arab trade sectors and launched industries that profited from changes in British customs policy. The Grands Moulins mill, Shemen, Nesher: they all radiated success.[91]

At the same time, these developments would truly radicalize especially Arab lower and lower middle classes only in the 1930s. Also, in the 1920s and indeed until the 1940s Haifa's municipality—Arab-Jewish under British tutelage—functioned better than any other mixed Palestinian city's, and cross-communal contacts abounded. And from the end of an economic slowdown, in the early 1920s, to the mid-1930s, "Arab merchants, both traditional and modern, managed to share in Haifa's general prosperity," indeed "diversified their lines of business and even initiated the import of novelties to the Arab market." This happened not the least because Haifa, small until the late 1800s and hence with a modest elite, became very socially mobile when it took off. Numerous people of modest background, many from outside Haifa, even from outside Palestine, became self-made men who were given a proper name: 'isamiyyun. The 1928 *Dalil* business guide listed thirty-four Arab *commissionaire* traders of a total of forty-two; twenty-nine Arab cereals merchants, of thirty; and eight Arab export-import merchants, of twenty-two. And Haifa's Islamic court records mentioned five new merchants in 1887–1898, seventeen in 1898–1919, but forty-two in 1920–1930. There were new landmarks, too. Hotels like the New Victoria, in 1923, were opened. Hotel Nassar, which was established before the war, felt impelled to rebrand itself Grand Hotel Nassar. In 1923 'Aziz Khayyat "built a four-storey office block—...a new departure for Haifa," next to a new Jewish commercial center in the expanding western part of Haifa's old main market. And as early as 1920 the Butaji family opened a large store for imported goods. In 1921, it expanded to Tiberias and Jaffa, in 1926 to Jerusalem: moves indicative of Haifa's widening horizons. These transcended Palestine. In 1926, an ad by manufacturers Karaman, Dik & Salti proclaimed that "people smoke *Uttuman wa-Mabruk* cigarettes from Tartus to the Sinai," that is across Bilad al-Sham. This new self-confidence was implicit in another ad, by the Windsor Hotel: it acted as an agent for "Nairn Transport Company" routes between "Haifa—Beirut—Baghdad," with "Buick automobiles travelling daily to Beirut around 10 A.M. or after the arrival of the train from Cairo."[92]

In fact, Haifa was taking off because its political detachment from Beirut allowed three geographical facts to work in its favor more than before. Haifa's topology—it lies on a bay—suits a port much better than Beirut and Jaffa. It also occupies a fairly central place along Bilad al-Sham's shore, certainly more central than its counterpart in Palestine, Jaffa, and as central as Beirut if one takes into account that Haifa enjoyed a direct railway connection to the Suez Canal and Cairo. And like Tripoli but again unlike Jaffa or Beirut, Haifa lies on the Mediterranean end of a west-east gap in Bilad al-Sham's north-south mountain chain, which gives it easy access to Bilad al-Sham's interior and eastward to Iraq. In sum, Haifa's position vis-à-vis the region improved.

But location is not everything. It can affect, but needs to tally, interests. In Mandate Haifa, the most powerful interests were those of the British Empire. Appreciating Haifa's advantages since the 1910s, Britain in the 1920s laid the groundwork for making it a "centre of communications" not only for Palestine and Bilad al-Sham but for imperial force projection in the Eastern Mediterranean. Palestine's Railway Authority was headquartered in Haifa, with Lebanese and Egyptians working there, too. The port was worked on. A key 1923 report recommending massive port construction was confirmed in 1927; new deep-water docks were built from 1929 and would be opened in 1933. Last but not least, an oil pipeline from Iraq was first discussed in 1927; the route was confirmed in 1930 / 1931; and oil would start flowing in late 1934.[93]

The effect that British imperial interests had on Haifa has been recognized by historians.[94] We may go further, though, and argue that through Haifa those interests affected also Bilad al-Sham, tightening its links to neighboring regions, most importantly Iraq and Egypt. Then again, one should question depictions of Britain as a free agent remaking Haifa. Britain had little choice, for it had limited alternatives. As much as making Haifa, its choice of Haifa—not unlike France's choice of Beirut—was made by Bilad al-Sham's existing geographical, political-economic, and infrastructural realities. Haifa combined a central position on the Eastern Mediterranean seaboard with a direct railway to Egypt, which mattered to Britain's navy. The city's local topology and access to Bilad al-Sham's interior were outstanding. And it profited from already existing Ottoman infrastructure investments, most important the Damascus railway, which had the bonus of competing with French Mandate Beirut. As Frederick Palmer, author of the decisive report on port modernization, determined, while expanding Jaffa's port was "desirable," Haifa's was "necessary."[95]

Haifa's privileged position relating to Bilad al-Sham's interior, to the Eastern Mediterranean and to Egypt had a fateful consequence. It gave the city leverage in its new nation-state space. Indeed, Haifa was a premier example of the double-sided process of transpatialization, in economic and strategic affairs, in the 1920s. As seen above, the new nation-state borders affected its relationship to Beirut and Damascus, and vis-à-vis Beirut allowed it to breathe. Vice versa, its privileged position in transnational fields, by giving it a leg up in Palestine, also helped to structure the economic space of this new nation-state.

Thus, when in late 1921 Palestinian merchants protested the first, limited Franco-British understanding on free trade in Bilad al-Sham, they met in Haifa rather than in the Mandate capital Jerusalem or in Jaffa, although the latter was more populous and its port busier than Haifa's in the 1920s. When during his tour of Palestine, Palmer met with Haifa's Arab Chamber of Commerce and the Arab mayor, the latter "was very emphatic in regard to the necessity for a port at Haifa as *the only place* capable of serving both Palestine and the interior to the east of the Jordan river. He was of [sic] opinion that, in time, the establishment of reasonably good harbor facilities would attract considerable trade from Damascus, the Hauran and the whole country east of the Jordan Valley, much of which was already connected by railways with Haifa." Similarly, al-Bahri believed that Haifa was "one of the most important Palestinian cities, nay one of the most commercially thriving Syrian cities" because it linked several worlds. His city "has become the port for the interior, like Damascus and the Hauran and especially the Hijaz, and the connecting point between these parts and the European world. . . . It will no doubt be amongst the greatest Mediterranean ports." On a related note, while some Haifawis like Butaji and Karaman, Dik, and Salti expanded to Jerusalem and / or Jaffa, mutual economic ties between Haifa's and central and southern Palestine's Arabs appear not to have been strong in the 1920s. Palestine's national economic space, while starting to fuse, was still divided into subunits. Jaffa was the port for Palestine's center and south and partly for central and southern Transjordan, Haifa for Palestine's north and for areas ranging from Transjordan via the Jawlan Heights to the southern Jabal 'Amil. (British neglect to improve the Jaffa-Haifa road until the 1930s did not help.) In an illuminating sample, a confidential set of files on nineteen Jaffawi merchants prepared by the French consul in Jaffa, the only Haifa connection was the representative of Karaman, Dik, and Salti.[96]

What about Haifa's Jews? On the one hand, they were firmly part of the nation-state-wide Yishuv. All who had Palestinian citizenship could vote for one of the many Yishuv-wide lists for the legislative assembly, the *Asefat ha-Nivharim*. Yishuv-wide organizations like the leftist labor union *Histadrut* operated in the city. And here as across the Yishuv, the Anglo Palestine Bank (APB) gave manufacturers loans. Also, Haifais participated in Yishuv-wide ethnic clubs; retail sellers had branches in various larger cities including Haifa; and Haifa's Hebrew Chamber of

Commerce, founded 1921, was in contact with the Zionist Executive headquartered in Jerusalem and met with other chambers there. As if to punctuate Haifa's integral part in the Zionist enterprise, the chamber head from 1922 to 1927, Shmuel Pewsner, was married to Lea Ginsberg, daughter of *Ahad ha-'Am,* the Russian-born founder of Cultural Zionism revered by Zionists worldwide; and already in 1905 Theodor Herzl had made Haifa the center of his utopian text *Altneuland.*[97]

On the other hand, Haifa's Jews benefited from the city's privileged position like its Arabs. Indeed, Jewish Haifa's case underlines an argument by historical geographers of Israel: modern Erets Israel as a national space did not appear whole cloth but was made. Moreover, it was not made in a homogeneous way.[98] This trait, scholars have shown for instance for Jewish Jaffa and Tel-Aviv and its surroundings, which in the 1920s became known as *merkaz ha-arets,* the country's center, demographically and economically.[99] What the case of Haifa adds to this argument is the weight of the regional framework: Haifa helped to make and shape modern Erets Israel also due to its position in Bilad al-Sham.

Indeed, the Yishuv's educated popular opinion and the Zionist Executive understood the strategic and economic importance of Haifa's excellent position vis-à-vis Syria and in the Eastern Mediterranean, and developed it as part of a Yishuv-wide view of economic progress.[100] As for Haifa's Jews, they made sure to toot their own horn. Like Haifa's Arabs, they called their hometown the City of Work—'*Ir ha-'Avodah,* in Arabic *Madinat al-'Amal,* a term used since the 1900s[101]—and '*Ir ha-'Atid,* the City of the Future, a term accepted across the Yishuv. And again like Haifa's Arabs, they used their city's extraordinary transnational position as leverage in the nation-state space. In economic matters related to Haifa's cross-border interior, in north Jordan, Jewish chambers of commerce often followed Haifa's lead. In one such case, powerful Jaffa-Tel-Aviv "found itself not enough competent to express its opinion and has decided to ask the opinion of the Haifa Chamber of Commerce": local knowledge mattered in the emerging Zionist nation-state. More important yet, when Palmer came to Haifa, the Jewish Haifa Chamber of Commerce's elite—besides Pewsner also one Muller and Nahum Wilbusch, the founder of Nesher—highlighted "the advantages of a port at Haifa as compared with Jaffa" for all of Palestine. They reasoned just like the Arab mayor, stressing that "such a port would also successfully compete with Beirut for the import trade of Damascus." Vice versa, Jewish Jaffa-Tel Aviv, which had lobbied Palmer, too—but unlike Haifa talked primarily about the port's importance for Jaffa-Tel Aviv itself—was displeased with Britain's choice of Haifa. Against most economists' opinion that tiny Palestine needed only one large port, many kept pushing for a Jaffa port expansion and a Tel Aviv jetty. Some even claimed— wrongly—that "the prospects of a port at Haifa are already diverting commercial initiative from Jaffa and Tel Aviv."[102]

### The Economic Fate of Transnationalized Hinterlands: Aleppo / Turkey and Damascus / Transjordan

If Haifa was one of Bilad al-Sham's towns that thrived most under the post-Ottoman circumstances, Aleppo was near the other end of the scale. After all, parts of its hinterland lay outside the Bilad al-Sham-wide customs-free zone, in eastern-central Turkey and northwestern Iraq. Then again, there are two sides to Aleppo's story that make it yet another distinct case of how old and new socio-spatial structures interacted and remolded each other in the 1920s.

Following the Franco-Turkish treaty of 1921, Turkey started imposing high customs to create its own national economic area. This was a "specially grievous blow" to Aleppo. France lacked leverage, indeed needed Turkey for quiet in northern Syria. It was telling that Ankara did not even ratify a customs treaty signed in 1922. A 1926 Good Neighbourly Agreement improved the situation somehow but was not renewed by Turkey in 1929. While deeply deplored by Damascus—which in questions of French customs duties and economic policies saw eye-to-eye, and was in contact, with Aleppo—this situation was worst for its north Syrian neighbor. "Let's stop having illusions," Selim Djambart, the head of Aleppo's Chamber of Commerce, told a high Mandate official in 1929. "The old commercial centre Aleppo, once the crossroad of caravans linking Orient and Occident, has died."[103]

This was true—and continued a process that, as Chapter 1 showed, had started in the nineteenth century. Even so, Aleppo was still the portal for massive Turkish and northern Iraqi exports into Syria. Thus, every year immense flocks of sheep, hundreds of thousands of heads, were traded through Aleppo. And there was a real silver lining, too. As a British report put it diplomatically, "In spite of the fact that the agreement concluded with Turkey is not fully working . . . trade is slowly finding its inevitable channels": smuggling was rampant on the about 900 kilometer long border, especially into Turkey. France closed both eyes, and Turkey was unable to suppress these activities. It did not have more knowledge of, or ties in, these border areas than Aleppine traders. A telling sign was that Ottoman-Turkish money continued to be used "for daily requirements" for years in Aleppo, more than in Damascus. And whatever export Damascus had effected into Anatolia before 1920 basically ceased. Its traders lacked their Aleppine counterparts' wherewithal, could not smuggle. However, not all Aleppine goods were smuggled equally well. European reexports apparently fared better, locally manufactured goods worse, partly because of rising Anatolian competition. Some Aleppine manufacturers turned south, to Egypt, also to Palestine, which raised some concerns in Damascus.[104]

While Aleppo's late-Ottoman hinterland was vulnerable to the Turkish nation-state and was held ransom to imperial French political and security consideration, its story is more complicated than that. Its late-Ottoman hinterland's social webs and economic ties, sturdy enough not to break under Turkish pressure, helped it to remain an autonomous economic pole inside the Syrian nation-state space: a pole both in contact and in competition with Damascus. The geoeconomic hierarchy of Bilad al-Sham's interior withstood Syria's birth.[105]

Not unlike Aleppo, Damascus continued turning inward, too, and kept doing what it had done since the late 1800s: penetrating its hinterland. A substantial part of that area now lay outside Syria, in Transjordan, which had belonged to Damascus Province. No matter: Damascus had "a hold on the trade of Transjordania and Northern Palestine." Transjordan was Syria's sixth export market from 1924 to 1928 and its eight in 1929, always ahead of Britain and often ahead of neighboring Iraq. This may appear strange, for Transjordan's population counted only half a million. It makes sense, though, if we see Transjordan not simply as a separate country but to a degree still as a part of Damascus's economic hinterland.[106]

Damascenes did not simply send goods to Transjordan. Like before 1918, so thereafter, some people moved there. One was Hasan al-Hamawi. Born 1900 in Hama, his parents soon moved to Damascus, where he trained as a baker. He left for Jordan in 1919, soon returned, then relocated again in 1925. Until 1926 he lived in Umm al-Ammad, next to the still small town of Amman, then moved north, to Mafraq, which then housed some British garrisons. There he got in touch with a few acquaintances in Damascus, who joined him to open a bakery. At some point, he branched out, started to send and sell wheat from the Hawran and from Irbid, in northern Jordan, to Amman. He became a family man, too. A sister in Damascus found him a neighbor's girl whom he married without having seen her. She joined him in Mafraq, where also other Damascenes, including members of the Tawila and Raja' trader families, had settled. And around 1937 they moved to Amman, where they settled down and opened a larger bakery, whose present owner, their son Marwan, told me their story.

Another migrant one was 'Umar Baalbaki. Born 1878 in Damascus into a family that traded and owned land, he had been sent by his father to Karak, in today's central-western Jordan, already sometime in the early 1900s. (Three other brothers were in Haifa, Beirut, and Aleppo.) He opened a shop, selling goods imported from Damascus. Around 1925, he married a Damascene girl who stayed in Damascus for a few more years until around 1930 they together moved to Amman. They bought a house near the area now known as the First Circle, furnishing it with local goods from Damascus and European goods from Haifa. Eventually, he got charitably involved in mosques and in the *Kulliyya Islamiyya* school; and immediately upon arriving, he opened a shop to sell goods from Damascus, though now also from Haifa and Jerusalem where he went for business trips, too. In Amman, however, his friends and fellow traders mostly were Damascenes from families acquainted already in Damascus.[107]

Not by chance, then, in Amman's "two principal merchants *suqs*, al-Riza and al-Sa'ada, most merchants [were] from Damascus." But here and in other cities like Salt and Karak, there also were native merchants and Palestinians, often Nabulsis. Moreover, Jordan became home also to Caucasian Cherkess whom Istanbul had sent there in 1878, to Armenians deported and stranded during World War I, and to Hijazis, Najdis, and others. In Amman, the Damascenes concentrated "in the city's east, near the merchants' market and Damascus Road." The richest, Damascenes as well as Palestinians mainly from Nablus, built in a "villa style, a residential model that had already spread in Lebanon, Syria and Palestine, where the building is an independent unit surrounded from all sides by a walled garden." Renters signed a contract that often named their ethnie—"the lessor [is] 'Ali Janikat Fallah, a Cherkess by extraction (*Charkasi al-asl*)," for instance—or their city. "The lessor is Kamal al-Batikhi, the Damascene, an Amman resident, the lessee *al-Hajj* 'Abd al-Qadir Abu Salih from Nablus, an Amman resident," read one; another, "the lessor is Hamid bin Naghawi from Amman, the lessee Salim bin Muhammad al-Ashqar from Damascus residing in Amman."[108]

*Sakin 'Amman,* an Amman resident, *qatin fi 'Amman,* residing in Amman: these labels are instructive. Amman was built by many different people who kept strong connections back home. Although fascinating, it is still looked down on by more established cities and in some ways keeps looking up to them. Thus, after I interviewed Marwan al-Hamawi in his large bakery's office, he made a business phone call and said of a batch of goods "baddi ahl al-sham kanu mabsutin": I want goods that would satisfy even Damascenes. Back in the interwar period, some Damascene women actually refused to stay in Amman and made their husbands return home—or so goes the story of why some families left Amman.[109]

Why, then, did so many stay? Particularly in the case of Damascenes, due to a forceful combination of push and pull. Hassan al-Hamawi and Sabri Tabba'a left Damascus partly because of political tensions and insecurity. Apparently, Tabba'a's shop in Damascus's Midhat Pasha Street and his house burned down at the start of the Syrian Revolt in 1925, perhaps a victim of the French bombardment that year. But they chose Jordan also because by the early 1920s it had been part of Damascus's hinterland for several decades. It still must have felt to them more like an extension of their city, Damascus, than a real abroad. Also, as it was not densely settled and expanding, it allowed them to get ahead. Its

Hashemite ruler Emir Abdallah—a brother of Emir Faisal, who from Damascus had ruled the first independent Arab state from 1918 to 1920, and himself a believer in a state in all of Bilad al-Sham—welcomed them with open arms. He needed them, indeed. Damascenes and other Arabs—some *qawmi* nationalists, others just hoping to get a leg up in life—came to work in Transjordan's small government and bureaucracy and in its armed force.[110]

The Transjordanian nation-state was still so embryonic in the 1920s that especially in trade it continued being part of the Damascene hinterland, with Nablus having its intersecting hinterland. Thus, it was Damascene and Nablusi merchants who founded the Amman Chamber of Commerce in 1923; and it was these two factions who competed with each other at times, for instance the early 1930s.[111] Just like Abdallah and Jordan's strongest tribal leaders found an equilibrium that shaped the emerging polity, the emir created mutually beneficial relationships with the richest or smartest merchants, Damascenes and Palestinians. A story—perhaps apocryphal; surely embroidered; definitely enlightening—may serve as an illustration. One day, Sabri Tabba'a's son Hamdi told me, Emir Abdallah (who, historians know, lived mainly on a moderate British subsidy) was running out of money. He gave an emissary a sword to be mortgaged in the traders' market. The emissary went from shop to shop, and eventually came to Tabba'a. A supporter of Faisal back in the day, the Damascene told him: "the sword of the Hashemites cannot be mortgaged." He went from friend to friend until he had collected 140 pounds, which he sent with the sword back to the emir. The rest is history: the emir invited him for an audience, and "since that my father did not leave this relation. . . . [H]e goes every day to the emir, to the diwan." There was "chemistry of both the two strangers, one coming from Hijaz, the other from Sham."[112]

## Inter-Imperial Administrative Cooperation and / as Regional Integration

Transnationalized late-Ottoman ties affected not only Bilad al-Sham's new nation-states but also its new imperial rulers. Although

Franco-British ties suffered systemically from open competition and diverging political outlooks, as historians have long shown, there was more to inter-imperial relations, certainly in Mandate Bilad al-Sham.[113] Here, cross-border movements forced officials—from High Commissioners down to European, Arab, and Jewish subordinates—into equally cross-border communication, even coordination. Crucial in its own right, this pattern was consequential, too. It tended to make people more visible to the state.[114] And it shows that because Bilad al-Sham was quite integrated in 1918, its division did not only, well, divide. By stimulating inter-imperial communication, it also created new region-wide ties. Even in administration, then, continuities existed to the late Ottoman period. But there were crucial changes. Administrative ties were not spun anymore within one Ottoman polity, but between two European imperial zones, and were structured by distinct imperial state interests.

Inter-imperial administrative communication tackled various challenges. A first set arose from the new border itself. Take local life. British and French border district officials sometimes received green light from their counterparts to cross the border in order to meet grandees involved in matters on their side. Further, the British High Commissioner in Jerusalem in 1925 "informed the French authorities that it was not proposed to raise any objection to the pursuit by Police Officers of Syria and the Lebanon of fugitives from justice who cross the frontier into Palestine." London agreed in principle but had concerns about sovereignty, where the devil is in the details. It asked pinpointed questions like "exactly how deep could incursions go," and insisted that captured fugitives be handed over to the sovereignly responsible police, which would hand them over to a judge, who would weigh extradition: meters of red tape enveloping the two sides.

The most momentous border-related issue concerned the local population. Regarding the central periphery, Britain and France understood that their new border cut across an integrated area, and that much local movement of goods and people would persist across a border that, while demarcated in 1921 / 1922, was not fenced up. Still, they were concerned about sovereignty. To solve this tension, they in 1926 signed a Good Neighbourly agreement. It upheld the status quo. It allowed inhabitants of the border districts of Acre and Safed in Palestine, Tyre, Marjayoun, and Hasbaya in Lebanon, and Quneitra in Syria "to cross the frontier freely and without a passport and to transport, from one side to the other of the frontier, their animals and the natural increase thereof, their tools, their vehicles, their implements, seeds and products of soil or subsoil of their lands, without paying any customs duties or any dues for grazing or watering or any other tax on account of passing the frontier and entering the neighbouring territory." But by its very nature, this agreement also put the status quo into a legal straightjacket. Moreover, French and British administrators soon started fiddling around with implementation. They introduced a shared laissez-passer system to try to better regularize free movement and tell local from nonlocal border-crossers. But the issuance of papers was sometimes interrupted; and as local peasants and bedouin regularly crisscrossed the border with cattle to find green pastures and plentiful waterholes, each side worried about veterinary diseases hitching a hike and spreading through its own, sovereign territory—a matter addressed in Chapter 4.[115]

A second set of challenges that required inter-imperial communication was regional. The key case, we have already encountered: Britain's and France's 1921 understanding about a region-wide customs-free trade zone. Another case was an extradition agreement. As High Commissioner Samuel explained in a letter to Secretary of State George Curzon, its roots reached back to the end of World War I, when British Palestine/ Transjordan, French Lebanon, and Arab Syria came to an agreement about "the delivery of fugitive offenders . . . based on the principle that the areas of Occupied Enemy Territory were administrative divisions of one country." After France occupied Syria in 1920, it and Britain consulted again, and in 1921 they signed a provisional agreement. It de facto excluded British and French subjects and, to forestall definitional disagreements and popular ire, de jure also political fugitives. Rather, it targeted regular criminals who indeed were regularly extradited in a multi-step process that involved the High Commissioners and a judge weighing the request. Within limits, then, acting French High Commissioner Robert de Caix's opinion—"close collaboration between the High Commissioners of Palestine and of Syria was desirable in the interests of both states"—became law: more red tape tying together British and French administrators.[116] Finally, epidemic diseases were another regional challenge requiring inter-imperial communication. For the 1920s, a pertinent example concerned Syria and Transjordan. Facing a bovine pest epidemic in early 1927, British and French authorities signed an agreement to temporarily close those countries' border to cattle. Related exchanges involved both High Commissioners, the British High Commissioner's representative in Amman, the French General Consul in Jerusalem, veterinary services, and intelligence services. The question of just when to reopen the border dragged on until 1928.[117]

Similarly, when Iraq suffered a cow typhoid outbreak in 1930, Lebanon and Syria temporarily halted cattle imports. That same year, Lebanon for a time hardened border sanitary precautions in reaction to a plague outbreak in Egypt. And locust attacks forced Syria and Turkey in 1931 to work on eradication, and animated various Middle Eastern countries including Lebanon, Syria, Palestine, and Egypt to convene anti-locust conferences in 1936 and 1938. Indeed, states not only in Bilad al-Sham but beyond reacted and interacted when faced by pests or epidemics that broke regional bounds. Administrative ties between states in Bilad al-Sham and various neighbors were strengthened.[118]

Thus, while inter-imperial communication inside Bilad al-Sham responded to specifically regional challenges, they also formed part of wider communications: some in the Middle East, others in the Mediterranean with ties to Europe, yet others global. Also, while some of these communications were new, others developed patterns initiated before 1914. And while European imperial administrations dominated such communications especially in the 1920s, already then these involved also other actors. As Chapter 4 will show, their weight would increase in the 1930s with the increased sovereign maneuver room of partly decolonized countries like Iraq and Egypt, with the latter's stepped-up use of the League of Nations as a public action arena, and with the League technical personnel's ability "to set the terms of debates over international questions."[119]

The third set of challenges was transregional (rather than border-related or regional) international, or less cumbersomely, international. It was about more than pests and epidemics, involving human beings like bedouin, too. To deal with issues as mundane as customary cattle raids and theft, and, more explosively, fatal consequences like murders, Britain and France in 1928 set up a regularly convening tribal confer- ence on the Syro-Jordanian border. These conferences were attended by officers and by leaders of tribes that seasonally moved back and forth across the border.[120] But tribes did not stick to Bilad al-Sham's confines. Some engaged in cattle raiding between Syria and Iraq and / or between the northern Hijaz, Transjordan, the southern Palestinian Negev Desert, and Egypt's Sinai Peninsula. As a matter of fact, they used the Palestine-Egyptian border—which, although demarcated, was not fenced and could not be crossed by police—as a screen behind which to disappear after cattle raids, mostly from the east into the Sinai and back. It was partly against this backdrop that Samuel's letter to Curzon discussing Franco-British extradition also suggested a similar treaty with Egypt. A first draft was drawn up in 1921; a provisional agreement became law the following year. But complaints persisted. In 1925, the Foreign Ministry of Egypt, which from 1922 had been a de jure independent nation-state though was still quite British-controlled, asked Palestine's High Commissioner to grant its police the same pursuit rights that France de facto already enjoyed. Palestine agreed; and after some diplo- matic back and forth, practice became law in 1929. Moreover, to facilitate catching bedouin raiders and other offenders, Palestine in 1926 resur- rected a late Ottoman police fort in Auja, a strategic spot for controlling movement from the Hijaz and Transjordan into the Negev and west- ward. It also proposed a police wireless network with Egypt and Tran- sjordan. An exploratory conference met in Cairo; in 1927, the wireless went on the air. Poor relative Transjordan bowed out, though it may have been connected through its Royal Air Force (RAF) station. The RAF, in fact, played a part in this story. Possessing Palestine's and Transjordan's only wireless network until 1926 and strongly present in British imperial hub Egypt, it was represented at the conference and its Cairo headquarters provided apparatuses for inspection. Thus, a mili- tary institution that helped connect British imperial possessions around the world became a blueprint for thickening administrative ties between British-ruled Bilad al-Sham and Egypt.[121]

Two other groups that caused administrators to strengthen ties not only in Bilad al-Sham but beyond were drug smugglers and communists.

Typically for imperial states' security concerns, law enforcement agencies were front and center also here. From 1918, British and Egyptian officials in Egypt became seriously concerned about narcotics with the smuggling of large quantities of heroin. Even by global standards, Egypt had become a heavy drug-consuming country. Heroin imports declined by 1930, but that drop was offset by a "marked increase" in the supply of Turkish and Levantine opium and hashish. These had remained prevalent even during heroin's heyday, but were now less tolerated than before 1914. Anglo-Egyptian authorities began to fight narcotics in the mid-1920s. At home, they stiffened drug-related penalties, imprisoned thousands, and urged European capitulatory countries to collaborate in their anti-drug war. Moreover, in February 1927, an Interior Ministry representative and the heads of the Palestinian police, the French Mandate Sûreté Générale, the Alexandria and Cairo city police, and the Egyptian Frontiers Administration and Coast Guard convened in Cairo and decided to tighten anti-narcotics intelligence coordination. That year still, regional list of smugglers started being shared and telegraphic communication codes were arranged for the interception of suspicious ships. And in 1929, "a catalogue of all important smugglers of hashish [was] compiled [by Egypt's Central Narcotics Intelligence Bureau (CNIB)] and copies [were] distributed to all [Egyptian] Preventive Services . . . as well as Palestine and Syria."[122] From 1929, the CNIB would also work with Turkish and European police forces.

Communism deeply worried French and British security services in and beyond the Mediterranean, too. Typically, in 1921 a British Ministry of Interior official in Egypt asked Palestine's Criminal Investigation Department (CID) to trace connections between communists there and in "Europe, Asia Minor, etc." Similarly, colonial lobbies like that in France saw an arc of "Bolshevist propaganda" extending from "the Pacific" across Asia to "the Mediterranean." For certain, ties between communists in Palestine, Egypt, and Syria / Lebanon *did* increase soon after they formed parties in the early 1920s. In Palestine—which in 1919 saw the Middle East's first Communist Party, a split from leftist Zionism—Jews helped communists to their north organize. From 1924 they tried to strengthen such ties also to comply with Moscow's demand for party

Arabization. Besides, from the mid-1920s dozens of Palestinians, Egyptians, Syrians, Lebanese, and Iraqis, together with other Asians, lived and studied under the same roof in Moscow's Communist University of the Toilers of the East.

Still, even Palestine had only a few hundred active communists. In fact, "the limited numerical strength of Communist parties in Arab territories bore no correlation to the degree of security service interest in their activities in the French and British empires." Their "internationalist dimension . . . suggested that . . . whatever their relative local weaknesses, their real strength lay elsewhere: in their appeal to colonial subjects to unite across imperial frontiers in opposition to European control." (Pan-Islamism elicited similar fears.) How serious communist activities were taken shows in that in the French Mandate, the elite Sûreté Générale rather than the regular police tracked communists. And, crucially, states collaborated. Palestine police initiated coordination with Egypt in 1925. In 1926 British Mandate, Anglo-Egyptian, and French Mandate police officials reached a formal agreement, soon joined by Iraq. And by 1927 all these forces regularly exchanged information on communists.[123]

Still, even between countries within the same imperial sphere, communication and coordination had limits. Often, each country primarily looked after its own interests.[124] A case in point was the "Z" list affair. In May 1921, following Arab-Jewish riots in Jaffa that started with an Arab attack triggered by a brawl between communist and leftist Zionist Jews, the CID hastily drew up a "Z" list of communist suspects, copying Egypt for urgent assistance. What followed was a tragi-comedy with a lesson attached. Some people were identified only by first or last names like "Dora" or "Goldman" which, an Immigration official jibed, are "so vague as to be practically useless." Other names like "Moshe Leib" were as common; accordingly, eager policemen in Kantara imprisoned people bearing similar names, for instance one Moses Lieber. Moreover, when two Z-listed suspects appeared in the shared Palestinian-Egyptian border station Kantara, Egypt waved them through, as their passports had been properly visa-stamped by Palestine. When Egyptian police arrested several people, CID mysteriously declared that the "Z" list "evidence is no longer available"; but soon thereafter, the list magically reappeared to justify—with a "guarantee[d] by the Jewish community in Cairo"—the deportation of one Moise Spector to Egypt. To British officials in Cairo, the lesson of all these inconsistencies was clear. Their counterparts in Jerusalem wanted to "wash their hands of [undesirables] and refuse to take them back, the Egyptian Government becom[ing] responsible for their maintenance, or their deportation to some other country, if that can be arranged."[125]

## Conclusion

The 1920s signaled the start of a second post-Ottoman stage of transpatialization. World trade, while recovering, was not in the same ship shape as before; the Ottoman Empire had died; new European overlords arrived and with them a new type of rule, the League of Nations Mandates; and Bilad al-Sham was divided. And yet, there was no total break. The 1920s were a transitional decade, an Ottoman twilight. Bilad al-Sham's nation-states were embryonic. Socio-spatial realities dating back to the mid-nineteenth century still echoed loudly.

Before World War I, first, the region's cities had become more tightly linked to outside worlds than before, including to global circuits of capital, culture, and migration. Still, they remained powerful makers and markers of identity. They were well-rooted; Istanbul somewhat protected some of them from the disadvantages of being incorporated into the world economy; and Istanbul also needed them and their elites, many of them notable families, as centers to project state territoriality through Bilad al-Sham. Transformed by the modern age, those cities also were the transformative places through which people in Bilad al-Sham lived that age. Second, to balance the pressures of world economy incorporation, cities sought to extract more resources from their hinterlands; and they linked up more strongly, creating a patchwork of various interurban links. As a result and third, the region as a whole, although not turning homogeneous, became more integrated culturally, economically, and in some ways administratively.

This threefold reality survived 1918. It molded Bilad al-Sham's new nation-states and their new European imperial rulers—and was remolded in return. This twin-sided process was fundamental to post-Ottoman transpatialization, most distinctly during its first phase, the 1920s. The urban hinterlands and interurban ties that now straddled a border were after 1918 transnationalized. Their functioning was affected by different countries' interests and policies. The region as a whole was similarly affected. At the same time, cultural, economic, and political contacts persisted within the region, within urban hinterlands, and along interurban axes. This deeply affected how Bilad al-Sham's new nation-states looked and felt like to their people and how they functioned. Put differently, late Ottoman urban, interurban, and regional socio-spatial realities that were transnationalized after 1918 vice versa actively transnationalized Bilad al-Sham's new countries from the moment the latter were born. This was true doubly because ties that had been transnational already before 1918 also persisted (in however changed forms), affecting the new countries.

Looking at this situation from the perspective of the region, one can point out three additional aspects. First, in the 1920s the region, while still a patchwork of cities and interurban ties, started to become an umbrella of nation-states, a trend that, however, would mature only in the 1930s. Put differently, the new conditions of the 1920s—the Ottoman Empire's death; European rulers' arrival; nation-states' birth; world trade's partial recovery—started affecting the very functioning of Bilad al-Sham. It was not an unchanging unit, not a geographically determined space. Second, the region's impact on new nation-states had a crucial upshot. Even in the postwar world of consolidating nation-states, those in Bilad al-Sham did not simply develop in isolation, but within a shared regional framework. This was, for one thing, because these countries and their cities, which a mere historical wink ago had belonged to one region in one empire, continued to interact. In this sense, the regional framework was the sum of its parts. For another thing, Bilad al-Sham's late-Ottoman integration was strong enough to persist after 1918. Here, the framework was more than the sum of its parts, had a life of its own. Its key manifestation points to a third issue: the sort of state territoriality exerted by the region's European rulers. France and Britain cooperated administratively to tackle cross-border movements and in 1921 created a Bilad al-Sham-wide customs-free zone, thereby reinforcing and indeed formalizing integration in the very region they had just divided. Last but not least, *qawmiyya* framed the region, including its nation-states, as an integral part of the wider world of Arabs. Even so, for Bilad al-Sham's *qawmiyyun,* their region was the center of their political actions and, to them, the heart of the world of Arabs, doubly because Egypt was less clearly part of that world than from the 1930s.

Studying the 1920s from the viewpoint of cities, four aspects in addition to those mentioned above are of interest. First, cities' hierarchy shifted again, in two ways. During World War I Bilad al-Sham's interior cities, especially Damascus and Aleppo, had done relatively well, temporarily reversing the nineteenth-century rise to dominance of coastal cities, but in the 1920s the tables were turned one more time. Furthermore, the balance of power among coastal and among interior cities changed. On the coast, Beirut, while rising again, did not quite return to its prewar dominance. The reasons were the only partial recovery of world trade, Bilad al-Sham's division, and the fact that this division benefited Haifa: situated in Palestine, that is outside Beirut's formal reach, it rose faster than in the last Ottoman decades. (By the 1930s, it would challenge Beirut.) Meanwhile, in the interior, Damascus did better than Aleppo, which was hit hard—though not as hard as it would be in the 1930s—when large swathes of its hinterland became part of Turkey.

Second, late-Ottoman urban developments forced European imperial rulers to make very specific choices—a pattern similar to the region's effect. Thus, France invested heavily in Beirut's infrastructure, and Britain, in Haifa. In return, this helped these cities' position within their respective nation-states, within the region, and beyond. The result was an intriguing quadrangular intertwinement of city, region, states, and world economic circuits. That is, those cities—and especially its elites—were able to leverage strength in one field, most particularly Bilad al-Sham and adjacent areas, to improve their position vis-à-vis European imperial rulers and within their country.

Third, a related set of quadrangular or triangular intertwinements structured how other cities positioned themselves within their new nation-states, a new reality which greatly challenged cities. This issue goes back to cities' transnational ties—the late-Ottoman regional or interurban ones that were transnationalized after 1918 as well as those that had been transnational already before 1918. After 1918, cities used those varied transnational ties—Damascus's function in the Islamic world, say, or many a city's deepened overseas ties through global circuits of culture and migration—to maximize their position within their nation-state space, materially and discursively. (By the 1930s, disagreement between different groups would grow louder as to how to position one's city.)

Fourth and last, the development noted in the last paragraph meant that cities—and their urban notable elites, who remained in the saddle politically after 1918—started to become nationalized, as it were, in the 1920s, again both materially and discursively. But this trend had a reverse side. From their very start, the new nation-states were imagined and politically and economically functioned not as homogeneous wholes, but as heterogeneous multi-urban ensembles riven with competition.

How did these dual, triangular and quadrangular intertwinements fare in the 1930s? This is the question to which we turn now.

## PRELUDE 4

# Hauranis Migrate to Palestine

> In the village of Saida the writer met a certain Haurani who had
> worked for three months in Palestine and had managed to save two
> pounds. He had worked as a porter in the Jaffa harbour and earned
> 40 mills a day. He spent 15 mills on food—lodging cost him nothing,
> since he slept in the open, either in the streets of Jaffa or near the
> port. He was deported by the Palestine Government but is already
> preparing to return back. The money he brought back with him is
> not enough for buying seeds but suffices to maintain his family for
> some time.

October 1934, Saida, in the southwestern Syrian province of Hauran.
Eliahu Epstein is shaken. He is no stranger to misery, mind you. He
survived a world war, the Russian civil war, and Soviet prison for
Zionist activism. Having immigrated to Palestine in 1925, he from 1931
covered the Great Depression years as a reporter for Reuters and for
Yishuvi papers based in Beirut, at whose American University he
studied Arabic and Arab history. He knew that his two-months-long
fact-finding mission to the drought-stricken Hauran for his new
employer, the Yishuv's para-state Jewish Agency, would be difficult.
Still . . .

In Saida, Epstein sees people surviving on "a baked mixture of
dhura and water which they eat once in two days . . . lest the village be
overtaken by famine once this sole gleaning from the drought-stricken
fields is consumed. About 80 percent of the villagers have no wheat or
barley and the happy few guard their treasure for the winter sowing.
The Government seems to have abandoned them to their fate." He
writes that the one hope is that the emigrants to Palestine, more than
half of the village's originally 780 inhabitants, according to the village
head, "will return with enough money to buy seeds for next year's

sowing. They possess no livestock since most of the animals perished or were sold at extreme low prices."[1]

Not all villages Epstein observes in the Hauran are as badly off. Of the 740 inhabitants of Sahem Julan, 550 are still there. But some villages are faring even worse. In Naime, only 120 of 550 villagers are left. In Ghazme, it is 22 out of 739, and the school, one of the Hauran's few, is closed because many children have died. At the railway station, Epstein "witnesse[s] a sight only too typical of prevailing conditions in the Hauran. As soon as the train drew into the station it was surrounded by a crowd of women and children shouting 'water, water' and begging the driver for the water from the engine."[2]

The Hauran "stands on a lower level than any other part of Syria. . . . [D]evoid of any natural defences, . . . [its] fertile plains . . . have attracted the invaders of all periods." From the late nineteenth century, Damascus fastened its grip on it. Backed by the Ottomans and later the French, Damascene merchants charged the Hauran's peasants 50–200 percent interest rates for grains for the next season and for "petty sums." The shopkeepers and most (and all high-ranking) officials in the Hauran were Damascenes.[3]

But the drought, which started in 1929 and would not let off for half a decade, pushed the Hauran to the brink. Damascus's merchants showed no pity. Caught in the Great Depression, they froze their credit lines. Moreover, when the Hauran's neighboring Druze dammed some jointly used creeks, the French cared little. They wanted to placate those whose fearlessness they had experienced in the 1925–1927 Syrian Revolt, but disregarded the Hauranis who were "in Syria . . . a synonym for cowardice." In Damascus, French and Syrian officials barely moved. While sending some water trains and drilling some wells, they had the Hauranis pay for the water and for gas and pumps.[4]

Emigration was the only way out. Of approximately 100,000 Hauranis, "during the spring and summer of 1934, some 25 to 30 thousand people left." Although Hauranis were not the only Arab labor migrants to Palestine—Egyptians came too, as did Transjordanians, and Lebanese especially from the south—by the 1930s they were most numerous. One in ten moved to Beirut or Damascus, the rest to Palestine.[5] This labor migration was not new. Hauranis had for decades cast around for work in Palestine. But the drought and the Great Depression turned a trickle into a flood. And although this movement had started in the late Ottoman period, when no border divided Palestine and Syria, that flood swamped the border, following the old trajectory from poor Hauran to up-and-coming Haifa.[6]

Although 1934 appears to have been the high tide of migration to Palestine, Epstein later estimated that in December 1936, about 6,000–8,000 Hauranis were permanently there, in addition to seasonal migrants and other non-Palestinian "illegal" migrants. Some Hauranis were employed by the British. Cheap, they helped trim the imperial budget. In early 1936, at the start of what would become the 1936–1939 Palestine Revolt, many replaced Palestinians striking in the port and municipal garbage collection. Others were employed by Arab peasants while some of the latter migrated to cities. In Yarka, a Druze village in northern Palestine, a parcel was called *Kaffat al-Hawarneh, the Lot of the Hauranis,* who, extremely poor, lived in stables; some dozen other Hauranis along with south Lebanese Shiis, came just for the olive harvest, earning half a Palestinian's wage. Also, Palestinian and Jewish orange grove owners, many on the coast, hired Hauranis for the harvest. So did the Dead Sea Potash Company, where hundreds worked on and off, living on "cigarettes and bread and margarina" and sending half of their minimal wage of six *grush* a day back home, as Abraham Hileli, a Jewish worker there in 1944–1945, remembers. But most Hauranis worked in cities. In Haifa, many did odd jobs. Zacharia Freilich, born in 1923, remembers that his mother walked down from the Hadar ha-Karmel neighborhood every Thursday to the main market; there, she'd hire a Haurani who moved with her through the market, putting her produce into a basket, which he then carried back up to Hadar ha-Karmel. And in Haifa as in Jaffa, Hauranis' largest employer was the port, where they bent their backs as porters. In 1934 and 1935, they and some Transjordanians accounted for two-thirds of all Arab port laborers, 1,200 men at peak times. And for Palestine as a whole, a census conducted in February 1936 registered 4,124 migrant workers.[7]

A statistic, an anonymous mass—this is all that the Hauranis were to Palestine's Jews and urban Arabs alike. There were no individuals, no Khalil Sakakinis, Rafiq Tamimis, or Alfred Sursocks. From 1930 to 1939, there were a total of twenty-eight entries on Hauranis in the leading Hebrew daily, *Davar,* and nine in another daily, *Doar Hayom.* The few notices that did appear were terse and told of petty theft—a watch here, a wallet there—or of work accidents or murders. "Yesterday, a Haurani porter in Port Haifa was crushed between two freight wagons." "In the village Zaita (Tulkarem), a murdered Haurani was found, with 15 stab wounds. His identity is undetermined. His killer has disappeared without a trace."[8]

Hauranis had no public face, but they did exist as arch-peasants, pure muscle, ranked below Palestine's urbanites and peasants. They were the butt of ditties. A known Arabic one in Haifa was "Ya Hurani ya fallah, ilhas tizi wen-l-miftah": "Hei Haurani, hei [you] peasant, lick my ass, where is [your] key," making fun of the homelessness of many Hauranis. And they were the victim of pranks, perhaps real, probably apocryphal, certainly reflective of how people saw them. "Two men from Zikhron Yacov come to Hamra Square in Haifa and, drinking a coffee, watch a British officer enter a government building. For one *qirsh,* they hire a Haurani to watch the officer's car, telling him it's their own. When the officer returns, the Haurani prevents him from getting into the car. A brawl ensues. Other Hauranis join in." Not by chance, in Syria *Hawrani* was a "byword for . . . general worthlessness," and in Hebrew *Horani* remains the archetype of a shabbily dressed man, as shown in the sketch in Figure P4.1 from a German Zionist periodical from 1936, depicting "an Arab from Haifa" and "porters from the Hauran."[9]

The persona of the Haurani was male, although some women joined their migrating husbands. The Haurani's poverty—his rags, sunburned face, bare feet—was truly outlandish (in the literal sense) and at the same time intimidating to some. A German Jewish woman who immigrated in the 1930s noted: "We came here by ship, to Haifa, and there were *Horaner* here in the port, and they bellowed . . . and we got startled and were afraid of them, because we were not used to such shouting! Later, I worked afternoons as a waitress in an ice cream parlor, and would return around midnight, and behind our house was the mountain . . . and I stormed up [the

Figure P4.1 "Araber in Haifa / Lastträger aus dem Hauran" [Arabs in Haifa / porters from the Hauran], sketch from the journal *Kinder-Rundschau* (1936).

hill to the house] . . . I was so afraid . . . [because of the] Horaner, yes, . . . they simply slept there on the mountain [ground] . . . they were very very poor." Similarly, German Jewish immigrant men wrote about their first day at work in port Haifa in 1937: "We come to the Kingsway and see the long row of black, muscled Hauranis who are walking towards the port. How numerous they are compared to our small group."[10]

Palestinian men—or rather, mostly Muslim peasants turned urban laborers—were anxious, too, though their fear was not about making it in a new country. It was about surviving amid a hardening Arab-Zionist conflict and making ends meet, which, despite Palestine's overall economic progress, became tougher. As early as 1932, the Palestinian Arab Laborers' Association in Haifa complained to the district commissioner that "fellahin and beduin from Syria and Transjordan . . . increase unemployment . . . and decrease wages. . . . [S]uch immigration should likewise be entirely stopped and strict legislation made . . ." Over the next few years, numerous similar complaints were heard from various quarters and newspapers in Haifa and elsewhere in Palestine. And in 1936, the British Port Haifa Manager punished Palestinian laborers who had participated in a nationwide strike in April by using non-Palestinian labor as leverage.

First, he hired more "dirt cheap" Hauranis and cheap Egyptians, and employed more Jews. By early 1937, he allowed some Palestinians back, but at significantly lower pay. He had been pressured by distinguished Haifawis and the national Arab Higher Committee, formed in April 1936; and the Palestine Revolt of 1936–1939 was underway.

Besides, middle- and upper-class Palestinians' attitudes toward non-Palestinian Arab laborers were shaped by their material interests and / or their definition of the national interest, rather than by the interests of Palestinian laborers. In 1935 and early 1936, the Port Manager employed non-Palestinian Arab labor also because merchants—Arabs and Jews—wanted porterage expenses to be minimal. And in May 1936—after the start of the nationwide strike and before some Palestinians were rehired in port Haifa in 1937—the Arab Higher Committee at first encouraged Britain to keep as many Hauranis as possible to prevent Jews from taking over Palestinians' jobs.[11]

For the British, then, the Hauranis were economically useful and posed few security problems. While there was talk in Haifa and in London about making entry into Palestine more difficult, not only on the Syrian border but also along the Jordan River, the latter was never realized, and the former only during the 1936–1939 revolt. After all, the only headache Hauranis created concerned petty crime and public health. In Haifa, some lived in tin hut slums, most near the port, in *Ard al-Raml,* together with thousands of Palestinian peasant-migrants, who were more numerous than the Hauranis. By the 1930s these slums had become an acute sanitary problem. In 1937, the British tried to evacuate 3,000 of the estimated 15,000–20,000 *Ard al-Raml* inhabitants. But this action barely made a dent. Rural-urban labor immigration was too massive.[12]

The loudest complaints about the Hauranis came from Zionists. It was not entrepreneurs who grumbled: Although responsive to pressure to hire Jews and pay them wages higher than for Palestinians, they also used Palestinians and cheap non-Palestinian Arab labor migrants, including the Hauranis. Rather, it was the Jewish Agency that from the early 1930s increasingly objected to their employment. These objections found a public forum during the British Peel Commission hearings, investigating the revolt in Palestine. In

December 1936, two high-ranking Jewish Agency Political Department officials testified: Epstein, who from 1934 was the Middle and Near East Section head, and Moshe Shertok (Sharett, who would serve as Israel's second prime minister from 1954 to 1955) who was department head.

Their remarks, and Zionist testimonies to the commission as a whole, show that to the Jewish Agency, the Haurani question was a sideshow to the Palestine drama and mattered because it could be a prop for two broader aims. The Haurani question could show that "it is an indefensible state of affairs in which the frontiers of Palestine are not effectively controlled." The Jewish Agency asked Britain to police the country's borders heavily and execute a stringent visa policy, even for Transjordanians who, as their country was legally part of the Palestine Mandate, should not have needed papers to enter Palestine. The Peel Commission found these requests unfeasible. In fact, the only time Britain tried to police a border strictly was during the 1936–1939 revolt, relating to Lebanon and Syria. Furthermore, Epstein and Shertok said Hauranis and other labor migrants ought to be in Palestine only in small, controlled numbers, and seasonally. This was not only because "the illicit infiltration from neighbouring countries [which] has, as one of its results, the undercutting of local labour and the lowering of the wage standards," but because Jews had the right, as per the Mandate Charter, to immigrate to Palestine and build a national home.[13]

The story of Haurani labor migration captures key features of the 1930s to be discussed in Chapter 4. Zionist and Palestinian attitudes show that the idea of the nation-state as a space to be delimited and protected was taking clear shape. Also, Palestine's economic fortune during the Great Depression, which attracted Syria's destitute Hauranis, illustrates that demographic-economic distinctions had grown among Bilad al-Sham's four nation-states. At the same time, the Hauran's marginality in Syria exemplifies that nation-state spaces remained deeply unequal. Damascus's grip on the Hauran illustrates that cities continued to matter. And Hauranis' concentration in Palestine's north shows that transnationalized interurban ties still structured nation-states' socioeconomic patterns. Indeed, as Bilad

al-Sham's nation-states matured, cities and transnationalized ties—
that is ties that until 1918 had been hinterland-wide, interurban, or
region-wide—did not simply become weaker. Rather, their interplay
with nation-states shifted. How, then, did transpatialization in the
1930s change relative to the 1920s? What continuities existed? And why
did Bilad al-Sham's nation-state movements mature as (however still
imperially ruled) nation-states in the 1930s; that is, why did the
Ottoman twilight end? These questions drive Chapter 4.

# 4

# TOWARD A REGION OF NATION-STATES
## 1929–1939

## Historical Context: Nation-State Movements, the Great Depression, and Imperial Geostrategy

By the late 1920s, the Ottoman twilight came to end. In a sense, this development was foretold: a regional chapter of a global story in which the nation-state became the most legitimate polity. But such teleology has its limits. After 1918, Bilad al-Sham's single-country nation-state (*watani*) movements did not evolve steadily. Around 1930, an extraordinary confluence of events and trends caused them to make a momentous leap.

Most important, by the late 1920s, after a decade-long build-up period, nation-state movements amassed more political power, and in some cases carried greater institutional and economic weight. France and Britain began to accept their demands to set the Mandates' discursive and institutional political agenda.[1] This was not independence—yet. But it transformed politics in what proved to be the start of a prolonged process of decolonization, in which nation-state movements solidified into nation-states.[2]

In Syria, the French victory of 1927 had been Pyrrhic and brought about a political change of heart in Paris. France started to accept as political interlocutors the Sunni urban elite notables, most of whose members had moderately backed the 1925–1927 revolt. When in

1927 / 1928 some notables formed the National Bloc (*Kutla Wataniyya*), France reluctantly chose to interact with it, for it was Syria's premier political formation and the address of Syrian nationalism. Two additional changes followed. One was parliamentary elections, in 1931. Although manipulated by the French—the Bloc received only sixteen of seventy deputies—their very existence showed that France was now playing the political game by mechanisms demanded by the nationalists. This had been unthinkable before—the 1928 elections to a Syrian National Constituent Assembly had been organized such that the nationalists boycotted them—and remained unimaginable in other French colonies. This was true also for the second change, the independence treaty that France offered Syria in 1933. (Syrians had cried murder when Britain granted Iraq independence light in 1930.) The French offer was too light; the Bloc rejected it. But again, the very act of granting independence showed that France had been forced to play by the Bloc's demands. This trend matured in 1936, when a new, leftist French government granted Syria a light independence treaty that was just good enough for the Bloc to accept. (In 1938 a new, right-wing French parliament refused ratification, though, for reasons explained below.)[3]

In Lebanon, France elected a parliament in 1929, the first since the establishment of the Lebanese Republic in 1926. It had limited powers. France still overwhelmingly shaped policies, indeed had slyly granted a parliament to deflect popular critique from itself. Although France was welcome as a protector by Lebanon's political dominant Maronite Christian elite, it closed the parliament in 1932 when politics became too nepotistic. Even so, and again as in Syria, the very act of opening a parliament showed that France believed it needed to heed demands for more political participation. Further, a new parliament was elected in 1934. On a related note, the first Sunni-Maronite contacts that would, in 1943, lead to a formula for Lebanese independence started in the early 1930s too. And in 1936, Lebanon, like Syria, was offered an independence treaty (which, though even more conditional than the Syrian one, was not ratified by the French parliament in 1938).[4]

In Transjordan, high politics were barely nationalist. But here, too, the late 1920s saw a turning point. In 1928 Emir Abdallah signed a treaty with Britain. While keeping him tied to London, it also helped him increase his hold, with British acquiescence, on the country in the 1930s.[5] In Palestine, Britain had already in the 1917 Balfour Declaration, which became an official part of the Palestine Mandate Charter, promised the Jews aid on the way to a vaguely defined future statehood. In consequence, the Zionist Executive had started functioning as a para-state institution already in the 1920s. But it underwent an expansion-cum-reorganization in 1929. As the Jewish Agency, it even more than before became the interlocutor for Palestine's British authorities.

Another cluster of developments around 1930 concerned the Zionist-Palestinian conflict. It was cemented by an event that was historic, all the more because it galvanized concern about Palestine across the Arab and Muslim world and especially in Bilad al-Sham, where it made thousands contribute to the 1936–1939 Palestine Revolt. That event was the Wailing / Buraq Wall riots of August 1929, in which Arabs reacted violently to breaches, from 1928 by some Jews, of a meticulous 1911 status quo agreement on rituals at the holy wall in Jerusalem. In one week, 133 Jews and 116 Arabs were killed and 570 were injured. The wall's symbolic importance had made it a deadly focal point for the conflict. It remolded politics. Spatial separation between Jewish and Arab communities deepened; Palestinian and Yishuvi security stances grew tougher; and mutual Arab-Yishuvi perceptions hardened. So did Arab perceptions of Britain—after Zionist lobbying, in 1931 London neutered its official postriot report, led by Sir John Hope-Simpson, which had recommended limiting Jewish immigration and land purchases. These developments peaked in the 1936–1939 revolt, which was a Palestinian stab at independence by force, just as Syria and Lebanon reached for independence (light) by treaty. In sum, in the 1930s much more than in the 1920s, Britain was not so much acting on, but rather reacting to, a pair of ever more opposed nation-state agendas and their political demands and logics.[6] Its policies meandered: in 1931, as just noted, and again in 1937, when the Peel Commission presented a partition plan, which London shelved in 1938 after massive Palestinian protests. Also, in 1939 London issued a White Paper restricting Jewish immigration and land purchases that, though rejected by many Palestinians as too little too late, was a British nod at their nationalist demands.[7]

Arab mass politics added to, but also complicated, the strengthening of *watani* movements. Mass politics opposed imperial rule with much greater force than notable politics. What began in the 1920s matured in the 1930s and had two socio-demographic roots: accelerating population growth and expanding secondary education, with educated middle class young people at their intersection. (Especially in Palestine, some peasants were radicalized, too, indeed were central to the 1936–1939 revolt; and in Palestine and Syria some workers were radicalized.) Although notables stayed on the top of the political game, they had to accommodate new forms of politics, including parties like the *Istiqlal* as well as scouts and Syrian paramilitary units. This was an uneasy arrangement. Young people willingly hit the streets to put pressure on the imperial rulers, but sometimes struck out on their own. Some also defended *qawmiyya* (pan-Arab nationalism), for instance in the *Istiqlal* Party, which did not always sit well with *watani* aspirations. Similarly, a first generation of native Jews, *sabras*, matured in the Yishuv: brash youngsters like Yigal Alon (1918–1980) or Yitzhak Rabin (1922–1995), whose archetype in the 1930s became the tiller of land with a rifle slung over the shoulder, head high.[8]

Such self-confidence owed much to the Yishuv's overall development. After flatlining in 1927–1928, Jewish immigration to Palestine recovered in 1929 and surged in 1932–1936. As European antisemitism worsened and America's doors were closing, the number of Jews in Palestine more than doubled between 1931 and 1936, from 174,610 to 384,078, and their proportion of the country's population leapt from 17 percent to 28 percent. As a result, Zionism's institutional and political gravitation point started to shift from Europe to Palestine. The Yishuv grew stronger, and it continued to purchase lands, further fueling the conflict with the Palestinians.[9] The material demands of this mass of people and the relative wealth of not a few immigrants (a good number from Germany), had drastic economic effects. Just when the Great Depression, "the most dramatic fall in the history of the world economy," caused global trade value to collapse by 60 percent from 1929 through 1932, Palestine's economy expanded until 1936. While that development was partly due to growing Arab citrus exports, profiting also some middle and upper class Palestinians, its main engine was the Yishuv's demographic-economic surge. Palestine's Jews benefited most. By contrast, Lebanon and Syria were severely hit by the depression. Imports and exports fell, tourism and overseas remittances dropped, and manufacturing and agriculture suffered.[10]

More broadly speaking, though, the depression affected all of Bilad al-Sham's countries, including Palestine. Not only countries overseas but also neighboring Egypt and Turkey raised tariffs. And the League of Nations' Mandate Open Door rule limited the Mandate powers' ability to raise tariffs effectively. In consequence, the regional customs-free zone that had been established in 1921, and which in 1929 was extended to 1939, became even more important to them than in the 1920s, and they looked at it more than before with their own nation-state interests in mind.

Why did not France, in 1938, ratify the independence treaties negotiated in 1936 with Syria and Lebanon? And why did Britain make concessions, however halfhearted, to Palestinian nationalism by shelving, in 1938, the Peel Partition Plan and by issuing the 1939 White Paper? The answer has to do with imperial geostrategy. In the 1930s, Germany, Japan, and Italy challenged the shaky postwar geostrategic status quo led by Britain and France. The challenge broke out in different areas, but merged and sped up midway through the decade. In 1935 / 1936 Italy, a rising Mediterranean power, struck southward, occupying Ethiopia. In 1936 Germany remilitarized the Rhineland province, next to France. And by 1937 Japan's rolling occupation of China caused open war.[11]

In the Mandates, France and Britain reacted in two ways. One was political. The 1936 Franco-Syrian and Franco-Lebanese treaties were meant to ensure quiet on the imperial front and to counter German, and especially Italian, propaganda and subversion. The nonratification in 1938 of the 1936 treaties, and the 1939 transfer of Syria's Alexandretta province to Turkey, reasserted full Mandatory control and secured Turkish neutrality in a looming world war. That is, France had a set geostrategy and ends, but flip-flopped on policy and means. The logic of ensuring political quiet also explains Britain's concessions, in 1938 and 1939, to Palestinians. It showed first in Egypt, though, the pivot of Britain's Mediterranean security disposition. Having hemmed and hawed for a good decade, in 1936 London signed an advanced autonomy treaty that made it give up its eyes and ears in Cairo ministries, among other things. In turn Cairo, which was afraid of neighboring Italian Libya, allowed London to strengthen its Egyptian bases.

The second reaction was strategic and infrastructural. Facing a worldwide "strategic abyss," Britain avoided tough calls. Still, a trend emerged. Because South Asia remained its premier colony and Japan its foremost naval rival, Britain turned to the United States for security in the Pacific. (Already in the 1920s Washington had, with some success, asked London to take distance from Tokyo.) In the Mediterranean Britain in 1936 started buttressing military installations including those that, arching from Alexandria to Haifa, protected the Suez Canal. This ensured the navy's wartime dispatch eastward to Asia—and was meant to simultaneously deter the Mediterranean challenger Italy, which at the same time was politically appeased to help focus on Germany and Japan. As for France, it had since long considered the western Mediterranean's south, that is North Africa, part of the defense of France proper, which was at the very center of its security doctrine. France's approach to Italy resembled Britain's—some military deterrence and political appeasement, to better focus on defending France against Germany. Relations were by and large fine until 1938, and tolerable until 1940. Still, specifically in the Mediterranean, France was from 1936 worried that a buildup of Italian air and naval bases would threaten not only the sea's west (and thence France and North Africa) but, from expanding Aegean bases, also the sea's east, and thence connections to French Southeast Asia. The need to protect an oil pipeline from Mosul to Tripoli that, in operation from 1934, provided France with 50 percent of its oil, only added to that worry and helped along the decision to build up military facilities, especially in port Beirut and Tripoli.[12]

## The Story to Come

Together, the above-noted changes—politically, the maturation of nation-state movements; economically, the Great Depression; and the strategically motivated French and British infrastructural build-up—impacted Bilad al-Sham in the 1930s.

Imperial infrastructural investments affected specific sites and helped to connect the region more strongly to the world near and far, furthering trends felt in the 1920s and rooted in the late Ottoman period. As crucial were two effects of the maturation, and hence the increasing distinctiveness, of nation-states in the 1930s.

First, Bilad al-Sham ceased to be mainly a patchwork region of cities, becoming principally an umbrella region for its nation-states. As the Hauranis's story in Prelude 4 illustrated, Lebanon, Syria, Palestine, and Transjordan matured in a shared regional framework rather than simply along separate tracks. This happened just as neighboring states underwent momentous political changes: Iraq reached quasi-independence in 1930/1932, and Egypt's very light independence of 1922 became more solid in 1936. (Saudi Arabia was independent from the start.) In consequence, Bilad al-Sham was more than before seen as part of the Arab world. But in return, this underlined the region's differences from other Arab areas—chiefly its fourfold division, the Zionist presence, and unabated imperial rule in the form of the Mandates.[13]

Second, the maturation of nation-states had an impact on their interaction with cities and with cities' transnational ties—those transcending Bilad al-Sham as well as those that before 1918 had been hinterland-wide, interurban, and region-wide. But this was not a zero-sum game. Cities and their transnational ties did not become less important but, to remain relevant, they "fit" themselves to their increasingly distinct nation-state. Further, the socio-demographic changes of the 1930s brought to the fore contentions among different groups about their respective city's identity. The interlinked socio-spatial intertwinements of the 1930s accentuated, but did not fundamentally alter, the pattern of the 1920s. This was a thick layer of change wrapped around a core of continuity: a distinct phase in the second, post-Ottoman stage of transpatialization, but not a new stage itself.

Like Chapter 3, this chapter follows a twofold structure. There is a section each on culture, on the economy, and on administration. And each section details the argument outlined above from the viewpoints, separately, of cities and of the region. This facilitates tracking continuities and changes relative to the 1920s.

## Urban Identities

As *watani* nationalisms matured politically and ideologically in the 1930s, cities became more pressed to define themselves vis-à-vis their nation-state spaces. To do so, they often used transnational ties. Moreover, while ignoring one's nation-space was out of the question, one had some choice in how to do so. And in the 1930s more clearly than in the previous decade, that choice differed from country to country. To represent that range of choices, this chapter will study four cities in three countries: Damascus (with a glance at Aleppo), Amman, Nablus, and Beirut.

## Damascus: Capital Effect and Transnational Ties

Damascus was Bilad al-Sham's city that in the 1930s like in the preceding decade positioned itself with greatest success as the center of its nation-state. Certainly, Aleppo was still Syria's other great city and, with Damascus the two were the twin centers of Syrian politics in the 1930s. Also, the two dominated media. In 1932, for instance, almost all of Syria's newspapers and periodicals were published in Damascus (23) and Aleppo (21), and from 1936 to 1938 each city was home to four of Syria's large dailies, selling between 3,000 and 4,000 copies. In 1951, an informal *Who's Who* listed almost two thirds of native Syrian personalities as having been born in either city.[14]

But in the same manual, Damascenes bested Aleppines by a factor of two. And Damascus indeed defined itself as the center of Syria. One demonstration of this civic pride is a manuscript on Damascus written in the 1930s by 'Abd al-'Aziz al-'Azma, a scion of a notable family. Born in 1856 and still loyal to the vanished Ottomans, his comments on the Old City's quarters with their alleys and doors that were closed at night and their watchmen, or his overly precise table of Damascus's seasons—"27 April: day of the last rain" and "27 October: first day of the southern wind" were just two of 49 similar entries—almost nostalgically stretched a hand out and back to a Damascus now disappearing. But his was still "a towering mountain" of a city. A city whose wondrous

Umayyad Mosque would always remain "among the world's oldest places of worship," and whose markets—"among the most outstanding of all the East," as even a foreign specialist acknowledged—easily trumped Aleppo's so "very narrow" ones. A city whose inhabitants were exemplary moral beings, and that was much more than itself, as the very structure of al-'Azma's writing shows: it swings back and forth between *Sham* the city and *Sham* the region, the former naturally the center of the latter.[15]

Damascus was not the only place in Syria that mattered, of course. *Thawrat Suriyya al-Wataniyya* for instance, *Syria's National Revolution,* a book published in Damascus on the 1925–1927 revolt by leading nationalist exile 'Abd al-Rahman Shahbandar (1880–1940), was about Syria's revolt as a whole and praised the rebellious Druze Mountains and other areas as much as Damascus. Still, Shahbandar assigned Syria's capital a particular role. It was the home base for men like him, nationalist leaders with nation-wide connections. This situation showed in realities, too. Take, again, the press. Damascus's *al-Ayyam,* founded in 1931 by the Bloc, was the most reliably nationalist organ together with other Damascus-based newspapers like *al-Qabas* and *Alif Ba'*. Besides, its 4,000 copies made it Syria's best-selling daily. This illustrated the long-term effect of Aleppo and Damascus ceasing to be equally ranked province capitals by 1918 and of Damascus becoming Syria's capital. Aleppo was nothing less than "the capital of the North," but also not more than that.[16]

New institutions were opened in Damascus, which in return reinforced Damascus's position. This feedback—the capital effect—sped up from the birth of the National Bloc in 1927 / 1928 and France's grudging acceptance of a Syria-wide nationalist political interlocutor with a center in Damascus. One result was that established bodies persisted, such as the Arab Academy of Science. Founded in 1919, it continued to function as a key center of research on Arab history and culture and on the Arabic language. While lionizing its own role in Syria's "scientific and literary renaissance," it ultimately remained focused on Damascus where fifteen of its twenty-two Syrian members lived in 1941. Other bodies were invigorated following the 1936 Syrian-French treaty—the obvious case was the Syrian government—or newly created, such as the Office

National Arabe de Recherche et d'Informations headed by Damascene National Bloc member Fakhri al-Barudi.[17]

The capital effect showed in Damascus's cityscape, too. From the first Syrian legislative election in 1928, plans started to be made for a parliament, which was built from 1932. Heavily referencing the Arab-Islamic past, including (Spanish) Andalusian and (Egyptian) Fatimid elements, it symbolically placed Damascus at Syria's center in the nationalist present as well as in the past. This impression was reinforced by the building, in 1936, of a national museum, which from 1920 had formed part of the Arab Academy of Science. It showcased pieces of monuments from across Syria. Some were pre-Islamic, many from Palmyra; others were Islamic, such as the Kasr el Her Umayyad castle of which a part was moved and reerected in Damascus. Further, Damascenes framed landmark infrastructural investments and events in their capital city as national events. In 1932 leading Bloc politician and merchant Lutfi al-Haffar, inaugurating the local 'Ain al-Fayha' water pipeline to Damascus, hailed it "the first national project." Similarly, in 1936 he dubbed a Damascus trade fair "a yardstick of . . . the nation's renaissance and vitality."[18]

The capital effect played out, last, in nationalism as action and ideology. For both, Damascus was a, and perhaps the, key arena in Syria.[19] Damascus was the center of operations for the best organized *qawmi* group, the League of National Action, which was founded in 1933 by about fifty *qawmiyyin* between the ages of twenty-five and thirty-four, most from Syria, Lebanon, and Palestine. Also, secondary schools in Damascus such as the *Tajhiz* and Syria's only university, also in Damascus, played a crucial role in politically mobilizing students. And on a different note, some non-Syrian authors with *qawmi* views published some of their work in Damascus. Nimr's *Ta'rikh Nablus* was one example; another was Shakib Arslan (1869–1946), who also lectured on *qawmiyya* at the Academy.[20]

Heightened nationalism blended with a continuing (but, due to non-Muslim French rule, marred) sense of Damascus's role as a transnational Muslim center. *Gharra'* and similar religious city schools (noted in Chapter 3) continued functioning. Also, from 1931 a new religious journal with a strong nationalist bent, *al-Rabita al-Islamiyya,* tried keeping Damascus on the map of wide-ranging contemporary Muslim Arab debates. While professing "no compulsion in religion" and taking note also of non-Muslim and non-Arab anticolonial activists such as Mahatma Gandhi, it focused on Islam worldwide and addressed the abolished Caliphate and other contemporary political-religious debates. Its mainly Syrian, often Damascene, authors excoriated foreign schools in Syria and beyond, be they missionary or secular. And they linked Islam to Arabness, describing Damascene contributor Jamil Bek al-ʿAzm as a leading Muslim scholar whose "books are of tremendous value to the Arab community," or proclaiming that "Islam will persist as long as Arabs persist."[21]

A similar concern about Damascus's role as a transnational Muslim center showed in the Arab Academy of Science's request, in 1938, for Arslan to assume its directorship. Born in the Mt. Lebanon to a noble Druze family, Arslan was until 1918 a fierce advocate of the Ottoman caliph-sultan as the political leader of the Islamic *umma,* hoping it would morph into an anticolonial community. In the 1920s he became the head of the Syro-Palestinian Congress' League of Nations office in Geneva, using the Swiss city as a spring-board to travel to and connect Arab and non-Arab Muslims from around the world. Arslan's pan-Islamism, and Arabs' weight in it, formed part of Islam's turn from merely a religion to a political community and civilization. Initiated by nineteenth-century thinkers like Muhammad ʿAbduh, in Damascus this trend showed also in *Jamʿiyyat al-Tamaddun al-Islami,* the Islamic Civilization Association, which was established in 1932 by Ahmad al-ʿAzma, a law student and scion of a leading Damascene notable family, and first directed by religious scholar Muhammad Hamdi al-Ustuwani. Last but not least, an illustrious event demonstrating Damascenes' assertion of their city's Islamic-religious-cum-Arab-national position at a time of foreign, non-Muslim occupation was the funeral, in 1935, of their preeminent religious scholar Muhammad Badr al-Din al-Hasani. Thousands thronged the streets, for al-Hasani had "stood out by this great title, the title *al-Muhaddith al-Akbar,* the greatest hadith scholar, not in Syria alone but in all countries of the Muslim World": an entity that was defined first as Arab—that is ranging "from Egypt to the Hijaz, from Iraq to far-away

Morocco"—although al-Hasani had taught students from India and Central Asia, too.[22]

## Amman: National and Regional Mosaic City

Amman experienced greater change than Damascus relative to the 1920s. When Circassian refugees settled Amman in the middle of the steppe in 1878, the only sound at this site's ancient Roman amphitheater was the howl of wild animals. With Amman's glory days long passed, the region's powerful or wealthy had no interest in Amman. But this also meant that no arrival was strong enough to really lord it over later arrivals. In return, Amman became an interesting place, despite the snubs of Cairo, Beirut, or Damascus, whose nights were faster and who possessed more gravitas. By the 1930s, Amman had grown into a small "mosaic" city. Peripheral and less developed yet hence also less unequal than the rest of Bilad al-Sham, it reflected *en miniature* Transjordan's nature and its role as a haven from violence between nationalists and European rulers that periodically shook the region.[23]

Amman's urban mosaic had a frame: the state. It had been the Ottomans who settled refugee-warriors from the Caucasus in Amman in 1878 and opened a Hijaz Railway station in 1905 and a municipality in 1909. This blazed a trail for Emir Abdallah. In 1922 he had made Amman his unofficial capital. Although larger and closer to Palestine, the town of Salt was less centrally located in the new Transjordanian polity. Meanwhile, Amman's municipality provided some oversight over the town's expansion, regulating rents, installing a water pipeline by 1929, and building roads, for example. But overall, the state frame was thin. Abdallah's Raghdan Palace, built in 1924, was modest, British-Jordanian army barracks were outside Amman in Marka, and civilian state buildings remained unpresuming.[24]

Amman itself gradually grew and diversified. From the early 1920s to 1930 it had doubled from under 5,000 to 10,000 inhabitants; and by 1941 had doubled again, reaching 22,000. Circassians were joined by Kurds, Armenians (some scattered by the Ottomans' wartime genocide), Turks, Najdis, Iraqis, and in the early 1930s a few Bukharis and

Iranians, among others. Large contingents arrived from Syria and Palestine, many from Damascus and Nablus. Some became Amman's mercantile and bureaucratic elite. Together they accounted for 45 percent and 27 percent, respectively, of Transjordan's nonnatives by 1936. Moreover, already in the 1920s, and especially after Amman officially became Transjordan's capital in 1928, people arrived from Karak and other Transjordanian towns, even from well-established Salt whose population was overtaken by Amman in the late 1930s. Bedouins from various Transjordanian tribes flocked to the capital, too: some were soldiers, others were civilians escaping the drought.

To be sure, Amman remained painfully aware of its size and nature. Some of its few hotels, looking up to the stars, offered "Baghdadi" and "Istanbuli" rooms, and the newspaper *al-Urdunn*'s "arrival" entries were eager to establish that Amman was not off the map of Arab intellectuals and other personalities. In fact, Amman had (and some say still has) an identity crisis because unlike Bilad al-Sham's other cities, it lacked an uninterrupted urban and hence sociocultural core, that is, because it was a true multi-national / ethnic / religious mosaic. This showed in Amman's extraordinarily decentralized neighborhood structure, which was made up of various Circassian quarters, the first bearing the distinctly non-Arab name *Shabsugh*; a Kurdish Quarter, *Mahallat al-Akrad*; a Foreigners' Quarter, *Mahallat al-Aghrab*; and a Migrants Quarter, *Mahallat al-Muhajirin*, among others. The mosaic quality was reflected in literature, too. In Adib Ramadan's *Aina al-Rajul, Where Is the Man*—an allegedly true story about a policeman's search for a brother who disappeared in Amman—that city was a stage for actors moving between Palestine, Transjordan, and Syria.[25]

But Amman was more than the sum of its parts. Because it was small *and* no community was fully dominant in the 1930s, its inhabitants shared central business and recreation amenities: a small set of markets; a few cafés like the Hamdan, Manshiyya, and Matilda; a central bathhouse; and for the few British and those on the up and up the Hotel Philadelphia, which bore Amman's Roman name. Although neighborhoods tended to be communal, hundreds of rental contracts show that property was let across ethnic and religious lines. Similarly, prospering Damascene as well as Nabulsi merchants lived in the same neighborhood, near the main market and the new Hussein Grand Mosque. Older Ammanis who remember an open city of "brotherhood" are not only waxing nostalgic, then. Amman gave birth to a civic spirit and urban form to Transjordan's multilayered nation-state in the making.[26] Last, from 1929 a naturalization law gave that process an official air. It is not only that in a year like 1930 a majority of newly naturalized Jordanians lived in Amman: people from across Bilad al-Sham and Turkey, as well as from Iraq, Arabia, Yemen, the Caucasus, Afghanistan, Tunisia, the Hadramawt, and Mauritania. More telling, in the 1930s more than before, nonnative Ammanis did not identify themselves in rental contracts—as many did in the 1920s—as *sakin fi 'Amman,* residing in Amman, and / or by their original town. Rather, many now chose "Jordanian," or "of Jordanian nationality," or simply "from Amman," as, in a 1936 contract, rich merchant Muhammad Sabri Tabba'a, the man who, as Chapter 3 showed, had arrived in the 1920s from Damascus.[27]

## Nablus: Contested Identity and the National Uses of Transnationalized Ties

My third and last case of a city's cultural development in the 1930s is Nablus, which illustrates the effects of the socio-demographic changes of the decade. As more peasants flocked to cities, as a modern middle class grew, and as a self-consciously young generation rose, city-dwellers increasingly challenged established elites' monopoly to define their city. Take the text written in the 1930s on Nablus, *Ta'rikh Jabal Nabulus wa-l-Balqa': Hawadith 'Ahd al-Iqta',* History of the Nablus Mountain and the Balqa': Events of the Feudal Period, which chronologically covered the time from the Crusades to 1861. Its gentleman-scholar author, Ihsan al-Nimr (1905–1985), was "a scion of a long-time ruling family in Nablus." This showed. His chapters, except those on general developments ordered Nablus's story by its leaders. Chapters 5, 6, and 7 were The Age (*'asr*) of Musa Bek, Ahmad Agha, and 'Abd al-Fattah Agha; Nablus's "golden age" of stability, wealth, morality, and knowledge was during The Age of the Nimrs (Chapter 3). As if to strengthen the message that

Nablus's established families mattered, Nimr called *Events of the Feudal Period*'s sequel *Feudal Civilization,* using a word for "progress" (*ruqiyy*) to characterize "feudal Nabulsi society." After all, it was under the rule of those families, "in the last five centuries," that Nablus "fulfilled . . . a momentous, glorious role in protecting Arabness and Sunniness," *'uru-biyya* and *sunniyya.* "Jabal Nablus' character emerged in this era," a single era persisting until today.[28]

However, buttressing Nablus's foremost families and the city's char-acter was more than a conservative move for Nimr. He sought to reaf-firm authority in a modern nationalist world in which nonelite social groups and parties, such as the Istiqlalists, challenged the elite's grip on its city's cultural meaning and politics. This adaptive strategy may have been facilitated by his education in an Ottoman school but also, from 1918, in a new Nabulsi nationalist establishment, the *Najah.* It became urgent because of the bloody events during which (and perhaps in reac-tion to which) he wrote, the three-year-long Palestine Revolt. Modern middle class and peasant men and women headed the revolt, and espe-cially the peasants despised notables almost as much as they hated the British and the Zionists.[29]

Nimr's subtly nationalist portrayal of Nablus and of its elite showed in his text, too. *Ruqiyy*—progress, to him the very trait of feudal Nabulsi society—was a key word also for the modern age. *'Urubiyya* and *sun-niyya* were neologisms that did to Arabs and Sunnis what *qawmiyya* did to people (*qawm*)—turning them into a unit of political action. And Nimr shared nationalists' concern about the impact of individual mo-rality on the collective. At the end of his book, he announced another book, *al-'Arabi al-Kamil (The Perfect Arab),* which would respect "today's ways" while "observing the principle that 'Islam is an everlasting religion.'"[30]

Up close, Nimr's notion of "protecting" Sunniness and Arabness was more nationalist-activist than conservative. He announced in the back matter of his first book a projected second sequel, to be titled *al-Hukm al-Ajnabi wa-l-Nidal al-Qawmi (Foreign Rule and National Struggle).* More subtly, "protecting" (*muhafaza* in Arabic) blended into resistance (*muqawama*). Mount Nablus's hills boasted watch towers that spotted approaching armies—Nimr's chosen example of enemy was foreign

Crusader, the "enemy who met resistance wherever he turned." (As it turns out, that enemy occupied Nablus twice . . . but that's another story.) As shrewdly, Nimr gave time a nationalist framing. The Israelites featured in his story—indeed had inhabited Nablus! This obviously posed a problem[31]—but Nimr found a solution. When Israelites inhabited Nablus, he said it had not been quite Nablus, but *Shakim,* in Hebrew *Shkhem.* Its "personality emerged" only in the last five centuries, and beforehand lacked any importance. And Nimr treated the Israelites in a one-page "Historical Introduction," which turned them into a *plus-quam-perfect,* a past before the past, absent in and irrelevant to Nablus's 500-year-long history.[32]

Nimr ardently loved his city, praising its natural bounty and plentiful water, even indicating the height of his hills in "*Nabulsi* ells." At the same time, he stressed its wider mooring, the "Arab East." Nablus's peers were "Aleppo, Baghdad, Mosul, and Damascus." The city mattered to that entire land, protecting the Arab East's "Sunniness, and *its* Arabness, and *its* mentality"—not only the city's own. Nablus's well-fortified, hilly position and reach made it "the heart of southern Syria."[33] This reflected historical reality. Even before the 1800s Nablus enjoyed close ties with the region's center, Damascus. Many of its merchants regularly visited the larger city; many clergymen trained there; and friendship and marriage ties linked the two. (Nablus entertained strong ties also with Cairo, but this city was further away and part of another region.) Nablus recognized Damascus as *the* center of its own region, Bilad al-Sham, and as the center of Sunni Islam and, since the 1910s, of *qawmi* nationalism. Not by chance, Nabulsis like Darwazeh more than Jerusalemites had, in Damascus in 1918–1920, advocated a Greater Syria-wide state when Faisal ruled Syria. Similarly, from the late 1920s Nablus was the only Palestinian home to a Syrian National Bloc branch. Nimr looked at his country from that angle as well. To him, "the Palestine Question" was "part of" the Sunni Arab "national struggle."[34]

Precisely because Nablus saw itself as more than simply a Palestinian city, it could punch above its weight. It played a larger role in Palestinian politics than its sagging fortune suggested. Many Nabulsis were emigrating, often to Haifa. Nablus's population—16,000 in 1922; 23,000 in 1945—was dwarfed by Jerusalem, Jaffa, and Haifa. And it was not

Palestine's capital. Nonetheless—or perhaps precisely for this reason—Nabulsis loved, and still love, to think of Jerusalemites as "taciturn and bound up in their own image of 'respectability,'" and viewed their city as Palestine's true center. For one, they defined their city as the southern geographical and political-ideological core of Bilad al-Sham *qua* region and *qua* Sunni Arab project—"the sister of Damascus," in the words of an article cited approvingly by nationalist Akram Zu'aytir in 1931. Moreover, Nablus was the largest Palestinian city without a Jewish presence. It was a hub of stalwart anti-British and anti-Zionist nationalism. It perhaps was even *the* hub—also because *Jabal Nabulus,* the Nablus Mountains, is hill country, which moreover has also been called *Jabal al-Nar,* Fire Mountain, after a bout of resistance to strengthened Ottoman rule following the Egyptian rule of the 1830s.[35]

Nablus was not the only such hub; Jaffa was another. Also, non-notable nationalists from Nablus were by no means active only there, but visited and often worked in other cities, and published in various newspapers. And not only did Nablus, too, have its politics of notables, but some of those notables were aligned with Jerusalemites.[36] Still, Nablus was, and presented itself as, staunchly nationalist, attracting like-minded people. It was Nabulsis who had opened the *Najah* school in 1918. Its Nabulsi head from 1922 to 1928, Darwazeh, had toured Palestine to lecture at youth and other nationalist clubs and to promote its guiding principle: He who demands independence, needs independent schools. In response, parents from across Palestine and from countries as far away as Morocco sent their children. They probably did so also because the American University of Beirut (AUB) accepted *Najah* graduates without an entrance exam, and perhaps, too, because *Najah* mixed Sunni Islam as religion, moral guide, and cultural identity with *qawmiyya*. Indeed, nation building happened not only in the classroom but in activities in which pupils were political subjects as much as educational objects. *Najahis* organized daily nationalist sing-ins, mixed with other schools' pupils, and enjoyed scouting, outings, football, and demonstrations.[37]

Outside *Najah*, too, Nabulsis practiced nationalism in defense of the nation's territory. In 1924 they had violently opposed a religious ceremony on nearby Mount Gerizim, to which Nablus's small Samaritan community, a Jewish offshoot, had invited regular Jews, and by the 1930s young people ritualistically threw stones at Jewish buses passing through. Indeed, in the 1930s Nablus played a leading role in Palestine's bottom-up political radicalization. Here, 1930 saw the formation of a Youngsters Block. In 1931, a meeting of 300 young politicians and an attendant demonstration, including women, pressured the notable-led Arab Executive into a more anti-British position. In 1932, most founders of the Arab Independence Party in Southern Syria, *Istiqlal,* were from Nablus. These men wished to integrate Palestine—as per the party charter "an Arab country and a natural part of Syria"—into a larger anti-imperialist and anti-Zionist Arab front, to "salvage[d] the [Palestinian] national, *watani,* cause from its wrong direction and [to] elevate [it] from its local and [notable] family objectives." In 1935, the Islamically inspired Izz al-Din al-Qassam—who, born in 1882 near today's Syrian Latakiyya, had worked among, and politically mobilized, the urban poor in Haifa—moved to the area between Nablus and Tulkarem to attack British forces, which however soon killed him and his followers. In 1935, too, Nablus organized the largest yearly protest thus far against the Balfour Declaration of 1917 at the day of its issuance, November 2. Delegates attended from across Palestine, and a call to action against Britain was issued. And in 1936, it was Nablus that first called for a nationwide strike which, immediately seconded by others, unleashed the Palestine Revolt—during which Nablus's rural area in the triangle with Tulkarem and Jenin became a rebel stronghold. Given this track record, it was not without justification that a nationalist call to action signed by hundreds of Nablusis and published in Palestine's newspapers in 1933 claimed that "since the dawn of the *watani* movement Nablus has always been a giant of nationalism, reliable in protecting [the nation]. In every national position, she bears the mark of true devotion; in every noble field she comes first and leads." Palestine recognized the city's rank. Following the 1935 anti-Balfour Declaration mass meeting, people from across Palestine declared their support of the Nablus declaration in newspapers. Leading Nablus-based nationalists like Zu'aytir were inundated by supportive telegrams. Soon thereafter Haifa's leading paper called Nablus "Palestine's capital."[38]

## Cultural Integration: Beirut as Bilad al-Sham's Gravitation
## Point for Education and Research

One field in which regional cultural relations intensified was higher education and research. Here, Beirut was the gravitation point. As Chapter 1
showed, that had been the case from the later nineteenth century, when
Beirut began to boast secondary schools and two colleges, the Université
de Saint Joseph (USJ) and the Syrian Protestant College (SPC, which
in 1920 was rechristened AUB).[39] After 1918, continued population in-
creases in Bilad al-Sham, a growing middle class, and the multiplication of states in need of skilled employees heightened the demand for
higher education. The Yishuv ran its secondary schools; other schools
were expanded or founded by nationalists in Palestine and Syria. Some
were opened by Britain, and France farmed out quite a number to private, often religious, bodies. But both imperial powers were tightfisted.
On the college level, too, offer trailed demand. Britain did not act, and
France's 1923 expansion of Damascus University, whose roots date
back to 1901, was insufficient. New Yishuvi institutions—Haifa's Tech-
nion, founded in 1924; Jerusalem's 1925 Hebrew University; the 1934
Weizmann Institute of Science in Rechovot, near Tel Aviv—did not
help. They served Jews and were too small even for their needs. Moreover, outside Bilad al-Sham, the Istanbuli option was eliminated by
the Ottoman Empire's fall. In Egypt, the Egyptian University, founded
in 1908 in Cairo, catered to Egyptians; the 1920 American University
of Cairo was small; and Alexandria University opened only in 1938.
And only few parents could afford to send children to Europe or the
United States.

As a result, Bilad al-Sham's increasing demand for college education
was mainly channeled to Beirut. The USJ played a minor role, AUB the
major role. USJ grew and became a French Mandate state school of
sorts; the French took to calling it l'Université française. Non-Lebanese
students continued being enrolled "at a significant level from 1920–
1940," reaching 50percent at the Medical Faculty in 1924–1953. But their
ratio had been higher before; most were Egyptians; and in most facul-
ties the non-Lebanese/Syrian percentage dropped, in Engineering, for
instance, to 19 percent. Postwar AUB grew, too. By 1940 it had twice as

many students as at its prewar peak in 1914, and it boasted new academic units. And it became, more than before, a school for Bilad al-
Sham, plus Iraq. In 1910, among living AUB graduates from the years
1871–1910, 27 percent had resided in Egypt and Sudan; 46 percent in
Syria, which presumably included Palestine; and 16 percent elsewhere
in the Ottoman Empire. By contrast, by 1931 and 1940, respectively,
Lebanese and Syrians (including local Armenians) were 51 percent and
54 percent of 1,525 and 1,992 students; Palestinians 18 percent and
19 percent; and Transjordanians 1 percent and 2 percent; Iraqis were
9 percent and 11 percent; Iranians 4 percent and 1 percent; and Egyptians in both years 3 percent. That is, in 1931, 70 percent, and in 1940,
75 percent of all AUB students were from Bilad al-Sham. Notes, in 1934,
by a former Iraqi Department of Education official and Palestine's
Director of Education, illustrated AUB's role in the region and to its east.
Because "there is as yet no Iraq University . . . Beirut acts as a magnet,"
remarked the first, and the second underscored that "no other institution in this part of the world offers the same opportunities of higher
education." Changes in the alumni organization echoed this sentiment.
In 1910 two of the three original SPC / AUB alumni offices had been in
Egypt, the third in Jerusalem. But by 1934 almost two-thirds, fourteen
of twenty-three offices, were spread across the four countries of Bilad
al-Sham: Beirut aside, in Tripoli, Sidon, and Zahleh; in Damascus,
Aleppo, Hama, and Homs; in Jerusalem, Jaffa, Haifa, Nazareth, and
Nablus; and in Salt. Six more were in the Middle Eastern cities of Tehran,
Baghdad, Mosul, Cairo, Alexandria, and Khartoum. And three were in
New York, Sao Paolo, and Buenos Aires.[40]

The transnational locations point to AUB's intensifying global connectivity, especially with the Americas, and also with Europe. In the
interwar period, successful émigrés and U.S. Protestants, and secular
U.S. donors, including John Rockefeller Jr., responded to AUB fund-
raising campaigns. AUB instructors from outside Bilad al-Sham were
almost all Americans, and U.S. and European researchers and professionals visited more frequently than before 1914. AUB's Lebanese
graduates continued a well-established pattern. Many migrated stayed
in touch with Lebanon, and some continued to come and go. Take
Philip Khuri Hitti (1886–1978). A Maronite peasant from the Mount

Lebanon, he graduated from SPC in 1908, received his PhD from Columbia University in Semitic languages in 1915, taught there until 1918, then returned to AUB. When in 1926 he crossed the Atlantic again westward, the AUB alumni journal *Kulliyyah* titled "Our Loss is Princeton's Gain," taking "consolation" because "distance does not in the least affect the ardor and loyalty of our beloved friend as regards his Alma Mater." And indeed, Hitti—a founder of modern Arab Studies in the United States until his retirement in 1954—remained involved in AUB affairs; in 1945, he would become the first Arab on AUB's board of trustees. Hundreds of AUB graduates stayed in touch elsewhere. The "Obituaries," "Marriages and Births," and "Miscellaneous" sections of a single *Kulliyyah* issue, in 1925, included news from people in, or on the way to or from, Zahle, Rio de Janeiro, Egypt, Jaffa, Bait Miri, Alexandria, Damascus, Jerusalem, Mansurah, Cairo, New York City, Tashkent, Tulkarem, Harbin, Manchuria, 'Abayh, Baghdad, Khartoum, Marjayoun, Syria / Egypt, Beirut / Switzerland, Beirut, Alexandria / United States, Addis Adeba, Venezuela / Vienna / Paris, Alay / Khartoum, Homs / Khartoum, and Lebanon / London. In 1931, another single news section included reports from "Peretz Cornfeld, B. A., from Johannesburg, Africa, [who] says that he is coming to Jerusalem and . . . intends to enter his son in our University," and from Dr. Jacob Michelin, Tel Aviv, visiting Beirut to see his friends, conduct medical business, and pay his annual alumnus fee at AUB.[41]

Beirut's, and particularly AUB's, weight was indeed felt even in the Yishuv. The latter was building its own educational and scientific infrastructure, and related links were almost all to Europe and the United States. But in what may be the best reflection of the region-wide force of Beiruti and especially AUB higher education, even the Yishuv entertained educational and some scientific contacts with Beirut and particularly with AUB.[42] Jews from the Yishuv likely formed a significant part of the 11 percent (1931) and 10 percent (1940) of AUB's students who were Jews. They were attracted by AUB's proximity to Palestine, by its educational quality, by instruction in English, the language of their own rulers, and by the British Mandate's recognition of AUB degrees. There also were a few active Jewish AUB alumni, though they were financially irrelevant to overall alumni affairs.[43]

Yishuvi Jews saw AUB as a place of research and knowledge, some-what beyond politics. In the fall of 1929, mere months after the bloody riots of August, alumnus Dr. Sarah Perelman, from Jaffa, attended an AUB medical conference. When in 1934 AUB invited Leon Roth, the Hebrew University Ahad Ha'am Chair in Philosophy, to lecture on Judaism, he "spoke of the cooperation of the Jews with the Arabs in serving the cause of science and learning during the rule of the Arabs" and underlined Judaism's belief in the "conception of the unity of God, the creator of the universe, the unity of mankind and the world's unity." And as late as 1951—three years after Israel entered its present-day state of war with Lebanon—Deborah Gershow, a 1924 AUB Nursery School graduate, sent the AUB Hospital a letter from Israel. Reporting without compunction to be the "chief secretary of the National Association of Israel nurses," she was "sorry to announce you that after 26 years I lost my pin of Graduation. I will be very thankful to you if you could send me an other pin [sic]."[44]

The sense that research and knowledge could exist alongside political disagreements was felt also at AUB. When AUB sociology professor Stuart Dodd edited a monumental bibliography of the Mandates, he decided to include a Hebrew fascicle and ask a Hebrew University librarian, A. Yaari, to edit it. B. Veicmanas, who lived in the Yishuv, wrote on 'Internal trade' for *Economic Organization of Palestine,* a volume edited by AUB economist Sa'id Himadeh with Dodd's backing. And Himadeh and other AUB professors were in contact with the economist Alfred Bonné. Educated in Munich, Bonné immigrated to Jerusalem in 1925 and in 1931 founded the Economic Archives for the Near East. Until 1935, it was housed at the Hebrew University. Its "double task was . . . establishing a central collection of economic material for the use of scientific research, and of supplying the public with reliable information." From 1935, when university funding dried up, it was subsidized by the Jewish Agency, which it advised. Still, Bonné understood it as a research body. From 1935 to 1937, it was visited by various AUB scholars, including Himadeh, Dodd, political science professor Ritcher, dean of School of Arts and Sciences Nicholy, and Social Science Research Section assistant Amin Himadeh, who gathered material for the volume on Palestine. To them and Bonné, it went without saying that they shared research interests. When in 1935, Bonné invited AUB economics professor George Hakim to contribute an article to the Archives' new quarterly, he underlined that the "post-war development of the Near East has created, in practically all the countries concerned, a number of major economic and social problems." (Hakim accepted.) And Dodd, preparing in 1936 his first visit of Bonné, wrote that "it is possible that our little Social Science Research Section here at the University, and your Institute, may cooperate in various ways in the future, at least to the extent of our not duplicating things which we discover you are doing."[45]

However, in the 1930s Jews' and Arabs' positions toward the Zionist/Palestine Question hardened. And now more than earlier, this question preoccupied people across Bilad al-Sham. Besides, for some students from across Bilad al-Sham and from Iraq and Egypt, AUB was an ideal place to live among fellow *qawmiyyin*, to reflect on *qawmiyya*, and to try to tackle Zionism. In this atmosphere, although in 1936 Himadeh invited Bonné to contribute a chapter to *Economic Organization of Palestine*, their collaboration faltered in 1937—fascinatingly, over the political "who" and "how" underpinning the scientific text. The two disagreed over the question of the hierarchy and hence legitimacy of different data sets produced by the Jewish Agency and by the Mandate government, and over formatting, that is over which paragraphs should be included in the body of the text, and which, in footnotes.[46]

## Cultural Integration:
### *Qawmiyya* and *wataniyya* vis-à-vis Bilad al-Sham

The second—and perhaps more significant—case of Bilad al-Sham's cultural integration, and its link to nation-states both within that region and adjacent to it, concerns the question of *qawmiyya* and of the relationship between distinct *watani* nation-state movements and the region. Here, changes relative to the 1920s were sharper than in higher education and knowledge production.

A good point to start this discussion is September 14, 1933. That day, Haifa was the scene of a gigantic funeral service, one so massive the city's population doubled. Six days earlier, in Berne, Switzerland, the Hashemite king Faisal had suddenly passed away. It was an early end for the man who had led the Arab Revolt from 1916 to 1918, ruled the first modern independent Arab country from Damascus in 1918–1920, been evicted by France to be made ruler of Mandate Iraq by Britain in 1921, and presided over Iraq's (conditional) independence in 1930. His body was transported by special train to Brindisi, Italy, and from there by the British warship *Dispatch* to Haifa. Here, Palestine's highest British officials and 100,000 Arabs from Palestine, Transjordan, Syria, Lebanon, and even from faraway Iraq gathered to pay him their last respects in a symbolic funeral. That same day a British Air Force plane, accompanied by an honor guard of seven other planes, flew him to Baghdad. On September 15, 100,000 people, mostly Iraqis, took their emotional leave of the tallest standard bearer of *qawmiyya*.[47]

*Qawmiyya*'s power and powerlessness, its past and its present, all were on display that week. Arab mourners came in droves—and yet it was Britain (which, despite its rather good relationship to the Hashemites, was seen by most Arabs as not much better than the French Empire) that brought the deceased king from Italy to Iraq. Another, generational contrast was visible during Faisal's funerals themselves. On the one hand, once more did a dynastic leader of *qawmiyya* stand out; the first generation of *qawmiyyin*—people educated in the late Ottoman Empire who had worked with Faisal and / or advocated *qawmiyya* in other ways—had another moment of glory, if a sad one; and people from many walks of life and religions mourned. In Jaffa for instance, the port's boatmen laid down their oars on September 14, the Orthodox Club "requested that radios and gramophones should not be played," "the people" asked the Municipality to name a new street after the late king, and Tel Aviv's Lodge of Solomon's Temple canceled a meeting.[48]

On the other hand, a new star shone brightly. To take again Jaffa, the Muslim Young Men's Association made it known it had not only renamed its school after Faisal but also sent "a delegation to Haifa to represent them in the funeral." Such energy was unsurprising. Youth organizations and mass politics spread in the 1930s in various Arab countries, including Egypt, Iraq, and as noted earlier Bilad al-Sham: *en miniature* in Transjordan; in Lebanon and Palestine; and in absolute numbers most impressively in Syria. By 1938, the Muslim Scouts of Syria—which in 1935 opened its ranks to minorities—had a staggering 38,000 members. Some youth groups involved the *Bloc*. In 1929, Damascene Fakhri al-Barudi founded the *Shabab Watani*, Nationalist Youth, as part of the tactic to strengthen the Bloc vis-à-vis France through street action; in 1936 the paramilitary Steel Shirts followed. Those moves paid off—almost too much so indeed. Young men and some women led anticolonialism with such force in the street that in instances like 1936, one is tempted to say that the tail wagged the dog.[49]

Moreover, for many young people, care for their country was paired with a surging interest in the Arab nation (*qawm*), which to them encompassed Bilad al-Sham, Iraq and Arabia, as well as Egypt in some eyes. (Many Egyptians in the 1930s were also increasingly seeing their country as a central part of a more and more broadly defined Arab world.[50]) Independence from imperialism for all Arabs was the objective of the young founding members of the League of National Action. *Tajhiz* pupils and Damascus University students were known for their *qawmi* critique of the Bloc, which tended to be too moderate for their taste. Scouts published papers that, like Beirut's *al-Kashshaf*, regularly featured *qawmi* articles. And from the late 1920s, they lived and breathed *qawmiyya* through cross-border tours and on camping trips that joined Syrians, Lebanese and Palestinians.[51]

One of those young *qawmiyyin*—with a brilliant mind, one less interested in hiking and camping, and more in writing—was Qustantin Zurayq. A Greek Orthodox born in 1909 in Damascus, he was educated at AUB, Chicago, and Princeton, received his PhD at twenty-one and became professor of history at his Beiruti alma mater. He was not your run-of-the-mill *qawmi*. "The Arab nation," he declared in his celebrated 1939 treatise *al-Wa'i al-Qawmi* (*National Consciousness*), "is stumbling about blindly, in intellectual chaos." Culpable were the "grandee intellectuals and literati." The old had no clue of how to "clearly distinguish between 'the Arab nation' and 'the Arab nations,' between 'Arabness,' 'the East,' and 'Islam.'" Zurayq did. (To sum it up, "every sound national renaissance . . . is based on three pillars" which need to be built consecutively, "national philosophy, national thought, and organization.") He went on to mentor student *qawmiyyin* until his death in 2000 and, always civil in deed, was universally respected. *Al-Wa'i al-Qawmi* was so successful in giving voice to the sentiment of a disillusioned generation that a second edition was printed after a few months. Meanwhile, Zurayq's attack on muddled brains involuntarily highlighted what was really muddled: reality.[52]

For no matter how logically one thought, "the Arab nation" and "the Arab nations," "Arabness," "the East," and "Islam," could not be neatly pigeonholed. Take nation versus nations. In the second decade after the Ottoman Empire's division, the new *watani* nation-states had developed a life of their own, acquired de facto legitimacy. Thus, although Syrian Edmond Rabbath upheld that "there is no Syrian nation, there is an Arab nation," he was knee-deep in *watani* politics, including the 1936 Franco-Syrian treaty negotiations. Even hardline *qawmiyyun* accepted *watani* realities. They ultimately thought in terms of "as well as," not "either or." Talking privately about a General Arab Congress that had met in 1931, Darwazeh for instance stated that it "reached a unanimous view that every [Arab] country should preserve its existence and thus a Federation would come into existence. None of the committee's members thought of unity."[53]

Moreover, neither the *qawmiyyuns*' political action space nor the *qawm*'s imagined space were homogenous. Rather, they had gravitation points. One was Iraq. The birthplace of many *qawmiyyin*, from 1921 the state of *qawmi* hero Faisal, and from 1930 / 32 quasi-independent, it was the single most powerful actor for *qawmiyya*. Another gravitation point was Bilad al-Sham. A minor reason was the (unfulfilled) *qawmi* plans of Transjordan's Abdallah. More vital, Bilad al-Sham connected Egypt, Arabia, and Iraq, and offered Arab Iraq strategic depth. Iraq sought out that depth to hedge against its sizeable non-Arab (Kurdish) minority and against Turkey and Iran, its two powerful non-Arab neighbors. Further, with Arabia independent, Iraq quasi-independent, and Egypt only loosely managed by Britain, *qawmi* anti-imperialists focused their attention on Mandate-ruled Bilad al-Sham, and were additionally fired up by Britain's protection of Zionism.[54]

Lastly, Bilad al-Sham's *qawmiyyun* closest political interactions were with one another—and never mind that Bilad al-Sham's countries' ties with Iraq and Egypt were tightening, and that the region's *qawmiyyun* wrote books such as *Our History, Told as Stories*, feting the nation's indivisibility. Thus, although the League of National Action sincerely promoted anti-imperialism and Arab unification, almost all of its founders were Syrians, Palestinians, or Lebanese, worked mostly in Syria, and focused on anti-French and anti-Zionist action. Moreover, *qawmiyyun* imagined Bilad al-Sham as a *qawmi* subspace. One example was the influential *qawmi* author George Antonius, who reportedly held "skeptical views regarding a broad Arab unity and stressed that only Bilad al-Sham from the Taurus Mountains to the Sinai Desert should be considered as the proper area."[55]

Another example was Rabbath. Doubtlessly, his Arab nation was *one*: an "undeniable social fact." It lived in "Arab Asia"—Bilad al-Sham, Arabia, and Iraq—which he called an area of "complete physical indivisibility," and it had been shaped and strengthened by Islam yet also— he was Christian—contained Christians, who were descendants of Arabs who had migrated from Arabia northward long before Islam. Hence, Arabia's Muslim warriors' seventh-century sweep up north was a "War of Liberation" from Constantinople that united "blood brothers." But as it turned out, "up north," that is Bilad al-Sham, was special—and so were, implicitly, the region's Christians. Bilad al-Sham "has always contributed with an undeniable intensity to the formation of political and cultural Arab nationalism (*Arabisme*)." It was the center of the first, Umayyad, Muslim dynasty; it fought the Crusaders; it helped "Arab heritage" to survive Mamluk and Turkish rule; and Lebanon usefully linked the Arab nation to the West.[56]

In sum, in the 1930s, Bilad al-Sham became more integrated into a nationally framed world of Arabs, and its meaning became more ideologically charged. In return, this highlighted its distinctiveness: its geographical centrality, fourfold territorial division, unabated imperial rule, and the Zionist challenge in its midst.

## The Great Depression and the Region as a Shared Competitive Framework for Nation-States' Economic Development

Perhaps even more than in cultural matters, Bilad al-Sham became an umbrella region for nation-states in economic affairs.

In the 1930s Palestine became more integrated with Syria and Lebanon, principally in trade, also regarding labor, and to a small degree in capital investment. Indeed, the economic development of the region's individual nation-states in the 1930s and the accompanying intensified economic nationalism of each cannot be analyzed in isolation. Even Jordan, least developed economically, became more interwoven with Syria and Palestine. And especially to Syria and Lebanon, the regional customs-free market (the agreement on which was formalized in 1929 and extended for a decade) became a lifeline.[57]

The initial cause was external. The Great Depression was closing off foreign markets, even in the Middle East. Egypt, in the 1920s a key export market for all countries of Bilad al-Sham, raised tariff walls in 1930; Turkey introduced an import contingent system in 1931; and Iraq refused to expand the 1925 transit trade agreement with the French Mandate to include regular trade. Also, League of Nation members and the United States exploited the League's Mandate Open Door economic rule to sell surplus products at minimal prices.[58]

But intensified economic interweaving was due to region-internal factors, too; moreover, these gave that region-wide process its shape. In the 1930s, Bilad al-Sham's nation-state economies became more different in some ways—but in other ways, more similar, too. Consequently, some interactions became more unequal—but overall more competitive, too. Basically, the region's economies become more integrated—but the terms of that process meant that the nation-states now saw the region principally as a competitive arena.

The Yishuv's fortunes made it the catalyst of Bilad al-Sham's stepped-up economic interweaving in the 1930s. It is not that it led that process; Lebanon and Syria were more active. Rather, two key unfolding differences between the Yishuv and Syria/Lebanon in the 1930s made the former a formidable consumer of goods: the explosion of its population from 174,610 to 384,078 in 1931–1936, and a 230 percent surge in its capital stock in 1932–1936.[59] More immigrants and even greater capital influx equaled rising wages and a rising average annual per capita income: more and wealthier consumers. While Palestine's exports grew 181 percent from 1932 to 1936—driven by oranges, mainly to Europe, 77 percent of exports by value in 1931–1939—imports grew 240 percent. By 1937 the value of imports was four times that of exports. Palestine had a serious trade deficit. But it paid. Or rather, the Jews did: 28 percent of Palestine's population by 1936, they bought 70 percent of imports. The per capita value of Palestine's imports, 39.7 gold U.S. dollars in 1935, dwarfed that of neighboring Turkey (2.6), Egypt (5.9), Iraq (5.9), and Syria / Lebanon (7.1). This differential was so massive that although Palestine's 1.3 million souls (1935) were eclipsed by Turkey's 16.2, Egypt's 15.9, Iraq's 3.6, and Syria / Lebanon's 3.3 million, the absolute value of its imports—51.6 million gold U.S. dollars—was topped only by Egypt (93.3) but was larger than Turkey's (41.6), Iraq's (21.1), and Syria's (23.4).[60]

This situation reverberated across Bilad al-Sham, all the more because Syria and Lebanon were not only pulled to Palestine, but pushed into it. There were internal Syrian / Lebanese push factors. Labor wages were lower than in Palestine. Agricultural production, though unable to attract major investments, remained steady. And growing investment capital, some tariff protection, and the need to balance out declining trade favored a modern import substitution industry—factories more than doubled from 400 to 900 between 1930 and 1939.[61] Further, the Great Depression hit Lebanon and Syria with force. To be sure, some tariff adjustments, especially in 1932, and growing capital—especially in Lebanon, often that of returning émigrés; and mainly in Syria, also through new, modern joint-stock companies—aided import substitution industries. Also, industrialists somewhat tackled foreign competition by depressing wages, not the least by hiring destitute Armenian World War I refugees. And from the mid-1930s the economy started to recover, benefiting mainly industry and trade, in Beirut also finance. However, from 1930 to 1937 real wages "in cities fell by half . . . [while] unemployment reached an estimated 30 percent." "Total imports . . . dropped by 50 per cent during the recession: from FF [Franc Français] 729 million in 1929 to FF339 million in 1936 [and] . . . exports decreased from FF 255 million in 1929 to FF156 million in 1934." Dropping tourism and remittances from overseas did not help. Neither did France's refusal to significantly change its economic policy. Unprotected, traditional handicraft manufacturing took an even bigger hit than in the 1920s, and agriculture languished.[62]

Together, those pull and push factors turned tiny Palestine from Lebanon and Syria's third-largest export market, in 1929 and 1930, into its largest, in 1931. Palestine's ratio of the value of all Lebanese-Syrian exports grew from 15 percent in both 1929 and 1930 to 25 percent (1931), 32 percent (1932), 40 percent (1933) and 38 percent (1934), hit a whopping 47 percent in 1935, then flattened out at 34 percent in 1936. Absolute value increased, too, from an average Palestinian Pound (£P) 955,794 between 1927 and 1933 to £P1,292,348 between 1934 and 1937, the lowest and highest figures being £P813,218 (1932) and £P1,401,484 (1936).[63] Syria and Lebanon exported raw and processed agricultural produce as well as manufactured products to Palestine. In 1934–1937, the top items were, in descending order, cloths, hard wheat, eggs, barley, shoes, wheat flour, cement, fresh fruit, leather, sweets, industrial olive oil, potatoes, furniture, and fresh vegetables. Regular French economic reports give an impression of what that trade meant week in, week out. Thus, in July 1935 forty Damascene fruit and vegetable merchants formed an association to intensify export to Palestine. Every day, they sent ten to twelve trucks laden with produce to Palestine, about 160 tons a week. To take another example, in September 1936 350 tons of fruits and vegetables and 80 tons of potatoes were exported every week. And Syrian / Lebanese products were cheap. Produce cost anywhere from 86 percent (potatoes) to 50 percent (cucumber), 38 percent (carrots), and 33 percent (eggplants) of the Yishuvi price in 1939. And the year before, a Jewish Agency report found that in Tel Aviv / Jaffa, Syrian cement cost 92 percent, chicken 83 percent, eggs 66 percent, artificial silk 50–57 percent, macaroni 48–74 percent, and shoes 23–68 percent of the local price.[64]

By contrast, Palestine's exports to Lebanon / Syria were stagnant until the later 1930s. They dipped from £P307,000 in 1929 to £P230,000 in 1932, and by 1936 regained £P310,000. During those eight years the export to import ratio averaged about 1:4, and Syria / Lebanon absorbed only 8.5 percent of Palestine's overall exports. Besides, Lebanon's cool mountain summer resorts attracted thousands of Palestinians and Jews, who transferred capital this way, too. In sum, during the 1930s, Palestine's and Lebanon's / Syria's economic profiles became more different in certain ways—which brought them closer.[65]

But in other ways, they became more alike. With Egypt raising tariff walls, Syria / Lebanon became Palestine's biggest Middle Eastern market, by far. In the first halves of 1936 and 1937, for instance, it led Egypt 4:1 and 8:1, Turkey 8:1 and 11:1, and Iraq 33:1 and 79:1, respectively. Also, from 1936 to 1937, Palestine's Syria / Lebanon-bound exports doubled to £P625,258, slightly less than half the reverse trade, an approximate ratio good until 1939. While from 1930 to 1939 77 percent of Palestine's exports was (mostly Europe-bound) citrus fruit, by 1934 Syria / Lebanon became Palestine's largest industrial products market, absorbing at least 25 percent of its exports. In fact, the Yishuv's economic take-off was boosted not only by citrus exports—which involved Arab as much as Jewish growers—but also by industrialization. Between 1929 and 1937, Jewish enterprises grew from 2,475 to 6,307, personnel from 10,968 to 27,260, invested capital from £P2,234,000 to £P12,700,000, and production value from £P2,510,000 to £P9,060,000.[66]

Because also Lebanese and Syrian industries were expanding, competition with the Yishuv stiffened. This was a new situation, and aggravated by Zionist-Arab tensions worsening across the region. As elsewhere around the world during the depression, the language of that competition was economic nationalism. At the same time, during the Great Depression more than ever, people in Bilad al-Sham appreciated being part of the region's customs-free zone. In sum, all wanted to have their cake and eat it, too. While armoring themselves, the Yishuv, Syria, and Lebanon aggressively pursued optimal access to the regional market. So did the Palestinians, but with a twist. Weakened, by the late 1930s they wanted the regional market also so that Syrian / Lebanese access to Palestine would help check the Yishuv.

## The Yishuvi-Syrian Competition from the Yishuvi Perspective

While firmly rooted in the pre–World War I era, Zionist economic nationalism peaked in the Depression-era 1930s.[67] The Zionists opined that Jews could teach Arabs "important [economic] lessons." They also stressed that economies needed some state planning, a view increasingly acceptable in developed capitalist countries. Meanwhile, their "national-economic ethos" started shifting from agriculture to industry. No doubt, agriculture still had stalwarts like Arthur Ruppin, the German Zionist and first head of the Palestine Office opened in Jaffa in 1908, whom we have encountered in the last three chapters. Also, agricultural output, settlements, and organization grew, and agriculture mattered to "economic independence." But belief in industry as the national economy's lead sector flourished. It showed as early as in the Zionist memorandum to the Hope-Simpson Enquiry into the 1929 riots. From the early 1930s, it was energized by the Yishuv's industrializing surge, which was put on display in Tel Aviv's 1932, 1934, and 1936 Levant Fairs, and which was promoted by the influential (Jewish) Manufacturers' Association of Palestine. Finally, in 1937 it became politically dominant. The head of the Jewish Agency, David Ben Gurion, did not put Ruppin in charge of representing the Yishuv's economic claims to the Peel Commission, but David Horowitz, who claimed that industrialization allowed Palestine to absorb vast numbers of immigrants.[68]

Centered on Palestine, too, was Zionist thinking about markets. With the Jewish population mushrooming, Palestine was an excellent lead market. As for the foremost non-Palestinian markets, they were overseas. Europe was the leading export destination for Palestine's principal export item, oranges. Also, resource-poor Palestine needed raw materials from overseas.[69]

Yet industrialists and Jewish Agency economists took great interest also in neighboring Egypt, Syria / Lebanon, Transjordan, and Iraq. Economic magazines such as *Meshek Shitufi, Pal News,* and the Jewish Agency's *Bulletin of the Economic Research Institute* continuously commented on them. The Jewish Agency regularly dispatched experts like Epstein or Ruppin on fact finding missions. The hope that the Yishuv might become the emerging Near Eastern manufacturing and trade center was crucial: it just had to use its capital, educated workforce, traffic infrastructure, neighbors' rising consumption, and its position astride Africa and Asia.[70]

This vision was rooted in the 1920s, but grew sharper in the 1930s; seemed somewhat more probable; and became more focused on Lebanon / Syria. Like before, the regional customs-free market offered export opportunities that were "essential for [the Yishuv's] industrial

production surplus" to come, as Jewish Agency economist Nahum Thischby noted in 1931. "Obviously, the economic future of the Yishuv in
particular and of all the country's inhabitants in general lies in the expanse of the outside markets, through suitable trade agreements, especially with the neighboring states. Small Palestine with its limited
market can under no circumstance exist as an economic unit." This was
just what Haifa industrialists told him in 1938: "there is great value in the
Syrian and Lebanese markets." And halfway through the decade, Horowitz underlined that already now, "Syria absorbs about 25% of the industrial exports of Palestine" and highlighted that the "technical minimum
of production . . . may be available on the joint Palestine-Syrian market,
while the Palestinian market itself would be too small." Most Jewish industrialists agreed. In a 1935 survey about the regional customs-free
agreement, 72 percent voiced satisfaction (11 percent abstained). In the
words of the Manufacturers' Association of Palestine (MAP) president
Arie Shenkar, "it is inconceivable to close us, . . . small Palestine," off
from Lebanon / Syria.[71]

However, from the Yishuv's view, its economic relationship with
Syria / Lebanon suffered from increasing material and ideological problems. By the mid-1930s, grumbling turned into protest. "For several past
years," declared Shenkar in his 1934 annual MAP address, "Syria has
been exporting to our country far more goods than she ever bought
from us. But since we are close neighbors, we believed that any barrier
or the closing of the borders was mutually disadvantageous. . . . However, we have recently ascertained that the people of Syria, particularly
of Damascus . . . fail to fully appreciate the great advantage which
this agreement gives them. . . . [They] have begun to discriminate
against the products of our country." The boycott of Yishuvi goods,
to be discussed later, was adding insult to the injury of substantial
Lebanese / Syrian exports to Palestine—which by the later 1930s was
decried, too, as unfair "social dumping," by the Jewish Agency and
Yishuvi producers. Lebanon and Syria, they found, exploited their social structure, that is low wages, to unload their goods on higher wage
Palestine.[72]

The affected producers belonged to various sectors including biscuits,
shoes, furniture, silk, cement, and agriculture. But not all complained.

In 1938, the Haifa-based Ata textile company insisted that "the markets of Syria and Lebanon are the best for most of the local [i.e., Palestine] industry"—which was true according to the statistics cited previously. Moreover, not everybody acted simultaneously. First producers spoke up. (They persisted throughout the decade.[73]) Then, in 1935, Britain joined in, keen for more customs revenues. It created a British-Arab-Jewish Palestine-Syrian Customs Agreement Revision Committee (CARC), which in 1937 submitted recommendations for how to revise the agreement once it expired in 1939. Finally, in 1937, the Jewish Agency started turning complaints into policy recommendations. Through 1939, it submitted a series of memoranda to the government, principally demanding the unilateral imposition of regular customs rates on certain Syro-Lebanese goods. (This was partially realized in the 1939 agreement renegotiation: being Lebanon / Syria's principal market, Palestine had leverage, and Britain had a fiscal interest.[74]) However, crucially, the Jewish Agency also adopted the CARC position it had helped develop: it did not want to abrogate the customs-free agreement per se. MAP agreed, demanding a treaty "revision" while insisting that "neither Palestine nor Syria are interested in a radical barring of the respective markets."[75] The Yishuv's economic nationalism was two-pronged, then: optimize access to the region while better defending its home.

Such an improved defense took the form, not the least, of the *totseret ha-arets* (domestic products) campaign. Rooted in the 1920s, that campaign was from the mid-1930s energized by producers, the Jewish Agency, the Merkaz le-maʿan Totseret ha-Arets, a body affiliated with the legislative Knesset Israel, and some gung-ho enforcers. It was the consumerist equivalent to ʿavoda ʿivrit, Jewish labor (of which the Yishuv's then leading party, MAPAI, was another key promoter). Both met with some success but also limits, fundamentally because Palestine's de facto sovereign was not the Jewish Agency, but Britain. Because the Jewish Agency lacked executive powers, and due to lukewarm British support and Arab products' cheap price, *totseret ha-arets* promoters acted in ways typical for nationalist economic actors under imperial rule—a few intimidated; many cajoled; all preached.[76]

Key targets were consumers and grocers. The former—especially women; even children—were courted by pervasive marketing and brochures including *The Housewife's Totseret ha-Arets [Guide]* and the *Totseret ha-Arets Guide,* which listed reliable grocers. The magazine of the grocers association encouraged *totseret ha-arets,* too, while revealing the difficulty of dealing with consumers and grocers with easy access to cheap "non-Jewish products." It complained that "the consumers ignore the importance of their purchases for the national economy as well as their household. This is true especially for the recent immigrants who need to be incessantly taught" by grocers. To them, it not only preached about "pure Jewish labor." It also promised that Jewish producers' modern (read non-Arab) technology, sophisticated marketing, and fixed supply and price would end up winning a loyal clientele.[77]

The objective of *totseret ha-arets* showed in the mottos of its consumer guides. "Consumer! The fate of the Hebrew industry is in your hands!" and "Buy *totseret ha-arets* and build your land with your own hands!" tied consumption to production, and both to nation-building. Put in the form of the image in Figure 4.1 (which is drawn from the perspective of the grocer who, on top, uses his clients' money to buy Hebrew goods, in the center, which then flow back into his store): together with Hebrew Labor and production, "Jewish" *consumption* was to create a separate and closed national economic circle. At the same time, sales to Palestinian consumers, which were not included in this drawing, were to be maintained.[78]

Also regarding *totseret ha-arets,* though, national and regional spheres were interwoven. *Totseret ha-arets* attacked not only Palestinian but also Lebanese / Syrian products. The publicly most visible target was foodstuffs, where the Jewish Agency and the agricultural cooperative *Tnuva* managed a forceful campaign. One front was vegetables. The reason was that in 1934–1936, Palestine's mushrooming population was fed not only by doubling Palestine's vegetable production but also by a 50 percent rise in imports figures. By 1936 the total value of vegetables sold amounted to £P500,000–600,000. About 10 percent of this sum, £P50–60,000, was Jewish produce; about 60 percent, £P300,000–400,000, was Arab Palestinian; and imports were worth £P150,000, about 30 percent. Of these, half—that is about 15 percent of the total—was Syrian / Lebanese.[79]

Figure 4.1  A sketch of the Hebrew economy, from the journal *Sokher ha-Makolet* (1937).

In 1936, this situation turned from annoying to dangerous in the eyes of the Yishuv. From April to October of that year, Palestinians went on a general strike, the first chapter of the 1936–1939 revolt. Throughout the revolt many tried, with some success, to block Palestinian purchases from Jews and mostly agricultural sales to them. Ironically, this made Jewish produce more competitive. It also boosted *totseret ha-arets*, which still targeted also Lebanon / Syria. Vice versa, Syrians, Lebanese, and Transjordanians supported the boycott; Damascus was most enthusiastic, but other cities acted as well. Damascene students threw busloads of vegetables destined for the Yishuv into the Barada River. Palestinian along with Lebanese and Syrian pro-Palestinian rebels attacked incoming lorries, burned their vegetables, and shot at their drivers. And in Beirut and Alexandretta, nationalists convinced stevedores to not load vegetables, eggs, and other produce onto Yishuv-bound ships. Palestine's 1936 vegetable import ratio fell to 29 percent.[80]

In 1937, Syrian / Lebanese exports resumed, though some still attempted to enforce the boycott.[81] Indeed, by that year many in the

Yishuv, including the Jewish Agency, had learned a lesson. More than before 1936, they did not simply *want* to produce more, they *had* to. Now, they demanded competitive tariffs on Syrian / Lebanese produce: to become less dependent. From late 1938 this view was reinforced by concerns about France curtailing Lebanon / Syria's exports to ensure wartime food security. While sharing those Yishuvi concerns, Britain felt that the Jewish Agency's approach was at present economically unsustainable. Indeed, although Yishuvi agricultural production grew steadily from 1937, by the spring of 1939 the Yishuv still imported 29 percent of its vegetables and 71 percent of its potatoes. The regional interpenetration of Palestine and Lebanon / Syria was too well-rooted historically and too well-established by postwar developments for any nation-state to close itself off from a regional competitor.[82]

## The Yishuvi-Syrian Competition from the Syrian Perspective

This was true regarding Syria, too. Exports to Palestine became vital for that country in the 1930s, and it continued perceiving itself as Bilad al-Sham's productive center. As a result, and because of increasing Arab-Zionist tensions, Syria acted against the steady expansion of Yishuvi manufactured exports to Syria. This paralleled the Yishuv's attempts to curb Syrian imports while keeping up its own exports—another sign that the two sides shared one regional framework. Likewise, Syria's attempts to curb Yishuvi imports were, it appears, as qualified a success as the Yishuv's reverse attempts. Methods were similar, too. Both Syria and the Yishuv pressured their respective imperial authorities, and *totseret ha-arets* was mirrored in Syria's "buy national" campaigns and in boycotts of Yishuvi products.

In the 1930s like in the 1920s, Syria's industrialists, most dealing in certain textiles and in other products like cement or conserves, defined themselves as Syria's productive leader. Although some, or their fathers, had started in handicrafts, and although they employed fewer laborers than handicraft manufacturers, they were up and coming, epitomizing industrial modernity and enjoying political clout as Bloc members. The importance of manufacturing showed in key declarations like the 1932 report of the Damascus Economic Conference. The 1936 Damascus trade fair displayed a range of manufactured products, showcasing some with prizes. And already in 1929, manufacturing was central to the Damascus Exposition and an attendant Industrial Economic conference—and orators and reporters called for its further strengthening.[83]

The latter also made manufacturing front and center of a broader national revitalization. The subtitle of a report on the 1929 Expo—"how can we become a living nation"[84]—said it all: independence from France was predicated on economics as much as on politics. Correspondingly they sharply rebuked the 1937 Exposition de Paris which, it was felt, did not grant the Syrian-Lebanese exhibition sufficient space. Already in the 1920s, some recognized that the economy mattered for Syria's anticolonial movement. But now, this understanding surged as import substitution industries rose and as industrialists and manufactured products exporters were among the leading Bloc members. These includes some of the greatest names Syria's economy, including Damascenese Lutfi al-Haffar, Faris al-Khuri and Shukri al-Quwatli and Aleppine Muhammad al-Za'im and 'Abd al-Rahman al-Kayyali. Indeed, manufacturers and exporters shaped Syria's economic nationalism. Chambers of commerce praised their members' nationalist standing and presumed street credit, exemplarily regarding the 1936 strike. Public stock companies like the Damascus cement factory sold its shares rapidly. And manufacturers were quite successful in diverting against French labor strikes that targeted them against France and that played an important role in economic demands on France.[85]

A principal demand was for France to convince neighbors other than Palestine and Transjordan to sign preferential trade agreements. Some Syrians made this their premier complaint indeed. Even at the peak of the depression al-Haffar insisted that Syria's troubles were rooted in the postwar division of a large area—reaching into southern Anatolia, Iraq, the Hijaz, even Egypt—of which Syria had been the manufacturing center and Egypt a crucial neighboring market. Doubly strong was the sense that Syria remained Bilad al-Sham's rightful economic master. This showed in telling details. A 1936 tourist map, for instance, focused on Syria and Lebanon but featured also Jerusalem; and in a 1930 Arab Academy of Science talk about "Bilad al-Sham's premier natural riches," a state official took Syria's perspective ("our land") while including Palestine and Jordan in his analysis.[86]

This approach also shaped Syria's reactions to the Yishuv's economic challenge. Thus, in 1934–1935 Damascene merchants and producers complained loudly about a wave of cheap Yishuvi textiles and confectionary. Some called on France to curb all Zionist imports. Others threatened to decamp to Palestine or Transjordan. In fact, two dozen merchants and producers opened branches there: a majority in Amman; ten also in Palestine, including two in Jerusalem, five in Haifa, and one in both Haifa and Jaffa.[87] This move related to one of the most persistent economic demands to the French authorities: to lower tariffs on raw materials imported for manufacturing to the level of British Palestine. Like in the 1920s, it highlighted an awkward fact. Bilad al-Sham's unified market was formed by two sovereign units, with policy decisions of one automatically spilling over into the other. No doubt, Syrian (and Lebanese) producers' and export merchants' long-standing protests about Palestine's better tariff in 1932 ended up convincing the French to lower tariffs. But protests continued, as we just saw. The French "are deaf," moaned an exasperated al-Haffar in 1933. Last, Syrians—and Lebanese—also called on France to combat the unregistered import of indigenous goods and the smuggling of foreign goods from Palestine, a result of differing tariffs.[88]

And then, there was boycott: a nationalist measure of mixed economic and political motives, containing various tactics, driven by multiple actors, with ups and downs but in some places quite endemic. The first large-scale call to boycott Yishuvi goods was triggered, it appears, by the Wailing Wall riots of August 1929. Soon, a reported tens of thousands of people demonstrated in support of Palestine in Beirut and Damascus; other cities like Aleppo and towns like Ehden, Lattakiyya, Tyre, and Amman voiced their protest, too; many sent aid; and some newspapers talked of a "nakba," a catastrophe. By September, Lebanese and Syrian papers had started to echo Palestinian calls to boycott "Zionist" goods and republished rumors, including one titled "Zionists poison Arab children."[89] In Damascus, this overlapped with the Damascus Fair's call for a national economic revitalization.[90]

The boycott soon petered out.[91] It was only in late 1933 and early 1934 that, according to *Commerce du Levant*, "a boycott of Yishuvi goods has lately been felt in Syria and especially Damascus," and that the Yishuv started paying attention and talking to the French, which agreed to underwrite counter-propaganda in the press.[92] Some Lebanese and Syrian merchants declared they would not attend Tel Aviv's 1934 Levant Fair. More crucial, when the MAP and the Jewish Agency sent Thischby to Damascus, he reported that Yishuvi goods were being boycotted there. It was in this context that MAP president Shenkar fumed that "the people of Damascus . . . openly boycott our goods." Two years on, the situation remained unchanged. "The Damascus people believe that they can continue to send into this country anything they wish, while, at the same time, continue to boycott our products," the MAP president complained. But although concluding with a dogged "we shall not agree to such presumptuousness," he conceded that "the present situation, for the time being, retards the demands for changes." After all, this was 1936: the start of the Arab revolt and the previously noted moves to boycott trade with the Yishuv.[93]

## The Palestinians: Between a Rock and a Hard Place

Palestinians heard the sirens of economic nationalism, too. In the 1930s, newspapers like *Filastin* became "buy Palestinian" advocates, and manufacturers' ads called consumption a nationalist act. "Those who purchase *Razi* matches, manifest their loyalty to national independence"; "Those who consume the cigarette *Sunduq al-Umma* [the Box of the People], save the land." Land possession was not only an economic resource but also an abstracted national symbol and a measure of collective will. With Zionist purchases ongoing, newspapers excoriated Palestinian sellers and their agents and exhorted readers with slogans like "He who has no land, has no nation." Last, various economic bodies were founded. Some sold shares to raise money to preemptively buy land; others encouraged an economic renaissance.[94]

And yet, Palestinians were trapped in a Mandate economic order that, as the tariff structure exemplified, favored the Yishuv. To make matters worse, in the 1930s they were outspent by Jewish capital imports. If in 1922 Jewish fixed reproducible capital equaled 17 percent of Palestine's total against their 76 percent (the government holding 7 percent), in the 1930s Jews overtook them, ending up with 52 percent against their 38 percent in 1947. No doubt, the rapid growth, in most of the 1930s, of Palestine's premier export cash crop, oranges, involved them as much as Jews, and the Yishuv's windfall profited some of them, including sellers of land whose value rose. After all, they and Jews lived in one country and were bound by manifold economic ties. Still, Jewish capital flowed into Jewish factories and purses, which with *totseret ha-arets* and *'avoda 'ivrit* started the establishment of an ethnic economy. Palestinians' economic nationalism stood on thinner legs. Actors were institutionally weaker and less coordinated; manufacturing expanded more slowly; and the urban modern middle class—the premier nationalist consumer—was poorer.[95]

Palestinians' economic nationalism was weaker also than Syrians'. In fact, Palestinians feared being out-competed by their neighbors to the north. In the mid-1930s, some protested against the Haurani migrants whose story was introduced in Prelude 4. Shoemakers and confectionary producers advocated tariffs. And when Britain founded CARC in 1935, its Palestinian and Jewish members both diagnosed a Syrian/Lebanese imports problem. More than that: in a 1935 CARC survey about attitudes toward the customs-free agreement, Palestinian manufacturers were three times more likely than Jews (62 percent against 17 percent) to support revisions. That same year, north Palestinian agricultural producers together with Yishuvi producers from the north and from Yehuda, with the Jewish Agency, sent CARC a joint letter demanding that competing Syrian/Lebanese produce be taxed. But not all was peace and harmony in CARC. In 1937 its Palestinian members demanded that cement, manufactured in the Yishuv and in Syria/Lebanon but not in Arab Palestine, be made cheaper by cutting Jewish laborers' wages, and that the Nesher Company should not produce more cement. CARC's Jewish representative found this irrelevant to CARC's mandate.[96]

It is not surprising then that in a joint body like CARC, economic questions such as labor costs and production rates were infused by the politics of the Zionist-Palestinian conflict and, overlapping, by the Yishuv's consolidation. Conversely, the intensified regionalization of that political dimension showed economically, too. We have seen increased Yishuvi-Syrian competition; boycott, which in many places was on and off but routinized in Damascus; *totseret ha-arets,* which targeted Syrian/Lebanese products; and tougher anti-Syrian Yishuvi thinking in the late 1930s.

Palestinians, too, played on that regional field. But unlike Syria and the Yishuv, they did so in an increasingly defensive role. While Palestinian chambers of commerce started biannual nationwide meetings in 1936—that is, tried to improve their position by cooperating more—Palestinians also increasingly relied on Syria/Lebanon to even out their disadvantage against the Yishuv. Especially in Haifa, a few bought shares in Damascus's joint stock company National Fruit Conserves, presumably because they lacked the financial and political capital to establish companies of such a size. More dramatically, from 1929 Palestinians initiated boycott calls that were picked up in Lebanon/Syria, and they warned Syrians and Lebanese about Yishuvi competition.[97]

Most crucially, the 1936–1939 revolt changed how many Palestinians thought about the region's economy. By 1938, they stopped calling for revisions to the regional customs-free agreement. The Arab Chamber of Commerce openly opposed a revision, which was Syria/Lebanon's position. This was "preposterous," exclaimed Jewish Agency economist Horowitz in 1939. Had not Palestinians themselves once demanded revisions? Had not their CARC members in 1937 signed revision recommendations? They had indeed. Still, their change of mind was not quite, as Horowitz asserted, a materially masochistic political knee-jerk reaction to Jewish calls for revision. Rather, it probably reflected an emerging conviction that between Syrian competition and sped-up Yishuvi ascendance due to a treaty revision, the former was the lesser evil, and might even check the latter. Palestinians embraced Bilad al-Sham for strategic depth even though they did not control the terms and would be hurt economically, which was happening anyway vis-à-vis the Yishuv. Thus, during the General Strike of 1936, the Arab Higher Committee called on Britain to keep as many Hauranis as possible in port Haifa to prevent Jews from taking over Palestinians' jobs. In 1938, Palestine's Arab chambers of commerce chose the regionally central economic journal *Commerce du Levant,* in Beirut, to oppose a treaty revision: Palestine/Transjordan and Syria/Lebanon "formed in the past a single economic unit, and despite their separation they have preserved that unity by maintaining free trade on the basis of the treaty presently in force." And when revision negotiations began in earnest in mid-1939, the same chambers chose *Filastin* to pressure the British government to stand down: "The public opinion is that the free trade between the two countries should be preserved as is. They form one economic unit, an economic unity which free trade preserved also after political division."[98]

### The Continued Heterogeneity of Nation-State Economic Spaces: The Central Periphery, Aleppo, and Damascus

Although the region's nation-states became more forceful, their economic spaces did not become homogenous. Three factors interplayed here. Neither the colonial states nor the colonized elites wanted or had the means to develop their nation-state-spaces equally. Further, social ties persisted inside cities' hinterlands and along equally well-established interurban lines that from 1918 straddled borders. And those by now transnationalized ties remained economically attractive—Lebanon/Syria and Palestine/Transjordan were different political economies, each with advantages and disadvantages that could be exploited or avoided by crossing the border. To illustrate the continued heterogeneity of nation-state economic spaces, three cases follow: Bilad al-Sham's central periphery and Aleppo's and Damascus's transnationalized hinterlands.

In Bilad al-Sham's central periphery, there was much legal trade, especially along the best macadamized roads, Haifa-Nakura-Tyre-Sidon-Beirut, Jerusalem/Haifa-Safed-Damascus, and Amman-Mafraq-Damascus. But there also was contraband, often from the British to the French Mandate zone, sometimes in reverse, along roads and narrower routes and on paths in the border zone. The zone's conditions facilitated contraband. The terrain was a hilly brush-land. Especially in the 1930s, army road expansions in the border zone benefited civilians, too. Also, most border-zone peasants lived modestly or were simply poor, and hence depended partly on smuggling to make ends meet. And they often trusted each other and could be fairly trusted. They operated between well-connected villages on either side of the border. This was the case especially for co-confessionalists, but by no means only among them. For instance, for most of the 1930s and in the 1940s Jewish settlers here had better relationship with their Arab neighbors than in the rest of Palestine, partly because the former were more isolated from the rest of the Yishuv, partly because nationalism was less active in the nationally peripheral border zone.

Smuggling paid off, for one, because there were illegal goods. The zone lay between the cannabis and opium poppy fields of Lebanon, Syria, and Turkey, and Egypt's narcotics consumers; hence, this contraband moved from the French into the British Mandate zone and from there to Egypt. Also, the increasingly diverging economies of Bilad al-Sham's countries created trade incentives, all the more because French customs rates were on average higher than British ones. Thus, in 1933 a combined Lebanese-Syrian Chambers of Commerce conference called south Lebanon a "center for vast smuggling" of overseas products via Palestine, pressuring France to lower import tariffs. Additionally, from the 1930s, inhabitants of the few Zionist settlements in the upper Galilee and local Lebanese, Syrian, and Palestinian smugglers brought into Palestine Jews both from Europe and from Lebanon and Syria. In conclusion, there was some irony to life in Bilad al-Sham's central periphery. On the one hand, each national bit was peripheral and marginalized in its own national economy. On the other hand, because these bits together formed a transnationalized transport crossroad, they received some relief. Then again, the partly semi- or illegal nature of trade also made its practitioners vulnerable.[99]

Aleppo's traders would have recognized this problem, though their social situation and geographical position differed greatly. Their city was incomparably larger, richer, and more widely connected than even the largest towns of the central periphery. But it faced a tough problem. It bordered not another colonial Mandate, but an independent state, Turkey, which protected its national economy in the 1930s with even greater determination than in the 1920s. Already in 1929, Aleppo's traders complained about Turkish trade restrictions and demanded stronger French action. They would continue to do so throughout the 1930s. To no avail. By 1936, a British report declared that "Local production in North Syria does not show by any means the same progress as the other regions of the country. . . . Customs barriers and other restrictions on trade now bar the way to those districts to the [Turkish] north which before 1914 looked to Aleppo for their supply of merchandise." Aleppo operated under the "conditions of [a] self-contained economy."[100]

Or did it? Well, there *was* economic activity in Aleppo. Two joint stock companies were launched in the 1930s (which, however, was fewer than the six of Damascus). And especially in the first half of the 1930s, when a drought hit central and southern Syria especially hard and Hawrani peasants fled to places like Palestine, northern Syrian grain helped feed the rest of the country, including Damascus. As for trade, historian Frank Peter has shown that smuggling to Turkey was "much larger than the official exchanges." France helped. It looked the other way, even helped Aleppines, and tried foiling Turkish counteraction, including commercial counter-espionage in Aleppo. Even Turkey helped, if indirectly. For its own commercial interests, it agreed to a railway line (opened in 1935) from Aleppo eastward to Iraq, running for long stretches along the Syrian-Turkish border. To be sure, the 1930s saw even illegal trade decrease compared to the 1920s, and its very composition changed. "A very large part of locally produced goods [could not] count on smuggling for their survival." The price difference to Turkey was too small. Even so, smuggling helped Aleppo to "preserve its function as a commercial entrepôt for southern Anatolia to a degree and [to] continue important business [transactions] by re-exporting European products."[101]

For Damascus, however, the 1930s sounded the death knell for any remaining trade with Turkey. (Conversely, Syria's exports to Palestine—much heavier than those to Turkey—were predominantly Damascene.[102]) The reason is telling. It was not simply raised Turkish tariffs, but Damascus's distance from the border, its very thin social network in Anatolia. This throws into relief Aleppo's qualified success, one that was apparent in its ability to remain the economic center for northern Syria and northwestern Iraq. Thus, when in 1935 Aleppine trader Mamarbachi founded a new camel import company and organized ties to northeastern Syrian Deir al-Zor, an official noted that "in the north, business is always done by this family" from Aleppo. In sum, in the 1930s even more than in the 1920s, nation-state forces on the relatively tough Syrian-Turkish border cut into and apart Aleppo's previous hinterland. Then again, the now transnationalized yet continuing social ties in Aleppo's old hinterland reduced the elbow room of nation-state actor Turkey; forced it into counteractions; were the underlying reason for Turkey agreeing to a railway and to trade; and gave colonial actor France a bit of economic breathing room in Syria's north.[103]

Damascus is a final example of a transnationalized hinterland. We have already seen how in the 1930s some Damascene producers and merchants threatened moving across the border, to Palestine or Transjordan. Some also tacitly reacted to French policy and to the devastating Great Depression. They opened branches in Amman. In a report that the French adviser to Syria's Agriculture and Commerce Ministry sent to the High Commissioner in 1935, he singled out three textile producers "of premier importance" in Damascus who had done so in 1932 and 1933, Haji Yassin Diab and Sons, Abdulwahab and Samadi, and Rushdi Baalbaki. He mentioned two other textile manufacturers, one, Hashim Yassin, from the Tabba'a family, and manufactured goods merchant Jawdat al-Bitar, adding that smaller shops—two confectionary shops and five individual confectionary workers—had permanently relocated to Amman. An attached statistic indicated that of all twenty-five Damascene traders and manufacturers who had opened a branch abroad from 1927 to 1934, only one had done so in the large country of Egypt, ten in Palestine, of which six in boomtown Haifa, but a whopping fourteen, including all large textile manufacturers, in the small city of Amman. Amman also boasted local representatives of Damascene establishments like the famous Conserve Factory, and was visited by known traders and manufacturers like Badr al-Din Diab.[104]

Such moves made sense, because British Transjordan's political economy and situation differed from French Syria's. As crucial, they were feasible, because Damascus was keeping strong social ties to this southern part of its area of economic influence. This also explains why more than twice as many producers and merchants—including all powerful ones—left for Amman than for Haifa. And this story involves a certain irony. On one side, the postwar transnationalization of Damascenes' old hinterland—its division and assignation to different nation-states—hurt. In the 1930s just as in the 1920s, Damascene merchants complained about this and, with Jordanians, about customs officials' violations of the customs-free rule. They feared rumors about the regional customs-free zone being canceled.[105] But on the other side, when one nation-state's economic policy and performance bested another's, that selfsame division paradoxically could become in part a remedy for the very disease that it was in the first place.

## Rising Nationalism, Falling World Trade, and the Peak of the Beirut-Haifa Competition

Rising nationalism and falling world trade affected also Beirut, which had owed its success from the mid-nineteenth century to a borderless Bilad al-Sham and expanding world trade. One effect was political. From 1936 to 1938, Lebanon and Syria had a spat over how to divide the hitherto shared customs receipts now that they had gained a modicum of independence. Led by Damascus, more populous Syria insisted on a fair share for its nation and, fed up particularly with Beirut, temporarily raised a customs barrier; Lebanon's capital insisted that "command[ing] the traffic of the principal [trade] routes . . . [gave] it a qualitatively advantageous position." A compromise was reached; but the spat would erupt with a vengeance following full independence in 1946, breaking the customs union in 1950. Second, rising nationalism and falling world trade affected trade. Although in the 1930s port Beirut's combined import and export tonnage remained about twice that of the sum total of the three next largest French Mandate ports (Alexandretta, Lattakiyyeh, and Tripoli), it suffered. From 567,000 metric tons, in 1929, it declined to 507,000 in 1930, inched up to 555,000 in 1933, then fell to 464,000 in 1934, to surpass the 1929 figure only in 1939, with 633,000. Exports fared even worse, crashing from 74,000 metric tons, in 1929, to 37,000, in 1932, where they flat-lined until climbing to 58,000 in 1936, then doubling to 110,000 in 1939. A third effect had to do with Beirut's overall economic profile. The protracted weakness of trade encouraged invest-

ments in modern import substitution industries. While contested—
some Beirutis insisted trade would always be their raison d'être—
industrialization shaped their city more than any other city in
Lebanon. Its "knitwear, hosiery, silk, cotton and wool textiles, leather,
shoes, processed foods, beverages, beer, alcohol products, soap, matches,
furniture, tiles, pipes, cement, nails, iron [and] metal works" factories
out-diversified Tripoli's "cotton-spinning, weaving, . . . cement, tile, pipe,
and soap." Home to Lebanon's highest, second highest, and fourth highest
capitalized factories, Beirut out-invested Tripoli, home to the third and
fifth, by almost 3:1. And according to a 1937 statistic, Beirut's industrial
workers out-numbered Tripoli's by more than 4:1.[106]

The abundance of cheap labor in Beirut—by one estimate, 60,000 immigrants from rural areas and towns in the years following 1929—caused
Beirut's population to surge to 200,000 in 1932. It also marked the
cityscape. No doubt, in neighborhoods like Ashrafiyya the middle and
upper classes continued living the good life portrayed in Chapter 3.
As a French guide noted at the peak of the Depression, in Beirut, "'society,' the ambiance, the 'salons' (there are even 'literary' ones where
writers are given a warm welcome)—in a word, life offers as many pos-
sibilities as the visitor may desire." And the city's largest square, the
downtown Place des Martyres, swarmed with shoppers, moviegoers,
and cabaret visitors, as well as café, restaurant, and hotel guests, and
pulsed with lights into the wee hours. But abundant, too, were tales of
social transgression, of rich youngsters lounging in dingy opium dens
and of well-heeled women moonlighting as prostitutes. From the
1920s and particularly during the Depression, the Place des Martyres
was home also to drug dealers, pickpockets, and prostitutes, after whom
the square's eastern flank was popularly called the *Suq al-Sharamit*
(Whores' Market). Put differently, Beirut's social divide was carved
into its very heart. Nearby, predominantly lower class and lower
middle-class neighborhoods such as Basta and Musaitbeh fell on hard
times during the Great Depression. And wrapped around Beirut, a
belt of shanti-neighborhoods was thickening with rural arrivals, roughly
divided by origin: Rmaylah, Furn al-Shubak, and Shiyyah, for instance,
absorbed mainly Maronites from the north and Mt. Lebanon, Druze
from the Shuf, and Shi'is from the south, respectively.[107]

The 1930s affected also Bilad al-Sham's other large port city, Haifa, if in even more complex ways than Beirut. It thrived economically, partly lifted by the Yishuv's surge. Port Haifa's combined import and export metric tonnage more than quadrupled from 1930 to 1939, from 236,000 in 1930, to 689,000 in 1934, and 995,000 in 1937. Declining to 794,000 in 1938, it bounced back to 996,000 in 1939. Export skyrocketed even faster, from 61,000 metric tons in 1930 to 100,000 in 1934, 296,000 in 1937, and 343,000 in 1939. Haifa's percentage of the total tonnage entered into Palestine grew, too, from 55 percent in 1932 to 76 percent in 1937. In 1934 it surpassed rival Beirut; and in 1935 it bested Jaffa by value (by tonnage already in 1930).

True, Jaffa continued to matter. A cultural hub and the economic center of Arab Palestine, it grew from 52,000 in 1931 (about two-thirds Muslim, one-sixth Christians, the rest Jews) to 94,000 in 1944 (about half Muslims, a third Jews, the rest Christians). Founded in 1909, Tel Aviv mattered even more by the 1930s. The First Hebrew City was recognized also by Arabs as the Yishuv's informal "capital," all the more because in 1934 Britain officially made it a city independent from Jaffa. Its population ballooned from 46,000 in 1931 to 160,000 in 1939: surpassing Jaffa, one-third of Palestine's Jews, and earning it a second moniker, "the White City," after the color of many of its new buildings. Also, in the 1930s, it remained not only the Yishuv's cultural hub but its manufacturing center as measured by factories: 294 against Haifa's 79 in 1930, 708 against 265 in 1937.[108]

Still, Haifa became Palestine's heavy industry center in the 1930s and the Yishuv's labor capital, *Haifa ha-Aduma* (Red Haifa). Capital investment in large factories like Nesher, Shemen, and Ata was twice Tel Aviv's total. Also, the influx of immigrant laborers caused Haifa's Jewish population to grow from about one-third of the city's overall 50,000 inhabitants, in 1931, to about one-half of 100,000, in 1939. They filled out mostly Jewish neighborhoods that had been founded in the 1920s, like Hadar ha-Karmel, and spilled over into Haifa's north, where five new labor suburbs collectively known as the Krayot were constructed.[109]

This development also brings out the complexity of Haifa's growth. Or more precisely, its unevenness. The Arab population grew more slowly than the Jewish and fell behind economically. On the one hand, modern middle-class employees and, especially until the mid-1930s but even thereafter, merchants and entrepreneurs continued to do well, populating historically central neighborhoods like Wadi Salib and Wadi Nisnas as well as newer quarters. Also, when a new avenue, Kingsway, was opened off the port in 1937, it attracted not only international companies and Jewish businesses but also "smaller-scale traders, port workers, and craftsmen, many of them from the Arab community." The Arab Haifa Chamber of Commerce moved there, and "many of Haifa's leading Arab merchant families also profited from the development of Kingsway and its surrounding" including Hamra Square, an "emerging commercial district." But on the other hand, even the well-off were hurt by the 1936–1939 revolt. And from the late 1920s, rural immigration swelled, creating a veritable underclass of proletariats many of whom, including Hauranis, squatted in the sprawling slum of Ard al-Raml. With so many hands looking for work, wages were stagnant and making ends meet was hard. That the partly Yishuv-driven construction boom cooled down from 1935 did not help; neither did the revolt. Symptomatic were developments in the port. Its traffic actually grew—in 1936 and 1937 also by attracting traffic from port Jaffa, on strike—but Palestinian workers had a tough time reclaiming their jobs after striking. In 1932, 58 Jews represented merely 10 percent of the port's workforce; but in 1937, 729 equaled 39 percent; and in 1939, 1,300 constituted 57 percent.[110]

## Intensified Imperial Investments and the Beirut-Haifa Competition

The Great Depression and nationalism were not the only factors affecting Beirut and Haifa in the 1930s, and rising chimneys and sprawling slums not their only common urban features. Imperial interests were at work, too: like in the last Ottoman decades and the 1920s, indeed even more so. Outstanding were infrastructural investments. In Beirut, an urban plan by the French Danger Brothers in 1931 recommended improving the port's and the city's regional rail and road connectivity. These measures were carried out and their effect was multiplied by work in the port, which inter alia built on a six-year Mandate-wide infrastructure plan that incoming High Commissioner Damien de

Martel issued in 1934. Having made sundry improvements to the port from the 1920s, by 1938 the French state and the French-majority Port of Beirut Company finished building deep-water docks, which served Beirut's French naval base, too. From 1928, Air Union-Lignes d'Orient hydroplanes connected Beirut to Marseilles, and in 1936 a small airport was opened, serviced by Air France as part of its France-Indochina route, by Egypt's Misrair, Poland's Lot, and Palestine Airways.[111]

In Haifa, an Irak Petroleum Company pipeline terminus opened in late 1934, complete with offices, port installations and, in 1939, a refinery. This set Haifa apart from Beirut. But otherwise, the imperial governments of those two cities developed their infrastructures similarly. From 1930, a new urban planning scheme was implemented. In 1933, Britain concluded a massive deep-water port construction project, started in 1929, which explains the port's massive growth and included a landfill on which Kingsway was built. From 1931, using Haifa's RAF aerodrome, British Imperial Airways linked Haifa with Alexandria and from 1932 with Baghdad. By 1935, the government had built a civilian airport that, while built "in anticipation of British imperial interest," connected Haifa to Cairo and Beirut by both Palestine Airways and Misrair. By 1937 the government also at last modernized Haifa's road to Jaffa / Tel Aviv. More important, in the 1930s "the government . . . worked hard to protect the existing railway network around Haifa as the epicenter of Palestinian transportation." Besides continuing to serve as the meeting points of the Damascus-Haifa and Haifa-Kantara railways and as Palestine Railway (PR) headquarters, Haifa got "its own railway workshops." Moreover, like in Beirut, infrastructures linked up. "An impressive road network [was built] in and around the downtown business centers"; the Irak Petroleum Company moved its hangars to the new airport; and a railroad track was laid straight up to the new ship quays to ease (un)loading.[112]

France and Britain invested in Beirut's and Haifa's transport and communication infrastructure in such similar a fashion because these two cities were hubs of their respective imperial interests in the Eastern Mediterranean. This was not new. In the 1920s Beirut had become the French Mandate capital and Haifa had caught Britain's eye (which was discussed in Chapter 3). But the 1930s witnessed three shifts. First, im-

perial investments became more intensive—infrastructure plans initiated in the later 1920s were realized along with new projects. Second, in
the case of oil, imperial authorities took all decisions on their own,
without consulting with locals. The reason was simple. Neither their national territories nor well-established colonies like India and Algeria
boasted noteworthy oil fields at the time, so access to oil elsewhere was
a matter of life or death for the British and French empires. In 1914, a
bullish British government bought the majority of the stocks of the
Anglo-Persian Oil Company (APOC), which after the war would turn
Iran into Britain's and its navy's leading oil supplier. Britain helped
APOC to 50 percent of the Turkish Petroleum Company (TPC, renamed
Irak Petroleum Company [IPC] in 1929; in 1928, APOC's share fell to
23.75 percent when Washington forced TPC to grant a U.S. consortium
that same share, with the Compagnie Française des Pétroles [CFP]
owning another 23.75 percent). In 1919 / 20, London browbeat Paris into
ceding the oil-rich Mosul province to British-ruled Iraq. In 1925 and
1931, Britain helped Iraq and TPC/IPC clinch two concession deals. It
insisted on the 1931 deal foreseeing a pipeline to Haifa despite the shorter
distance to the French-ruled Mediterranean coast. And in the late 1930s,
Britain built an eastward continuation of the Haifa-Irbid road that followed the pipeline from Irbid to Iraqi Rutbah whence it branched off to
Baghdad, and an Amman-Rutbah-Baghdad road, projects with as much
strategic as economic sense. While Haifawis were not discontent that
their city became an IPC pipeline terminus, London consulted neither
them nor other Zionists or Palestinians, and the sweeping legal and tax
concessions it granted the IPC were condemned as excessive. Similarly,
while nobody criticized the Baghdad roads, the one via Amman formed
part of a 1937 Palestine-Iraq transit trade agreement that London signed
without local consultation and that favored Iraq so clearly that both
Zionists and Palestinians soon protested. As for Paris, in exchange for
ceding Mosul and as a war compensation, it received the Deutsche Bank's
25 percent share of the TPC in 1920. In 1924, it transferred that share to
the CFP after initiating its foundation as a purely French company
safeguarding the country's oil needs; in the 1931 IPC-Iraq concession
deal, it secured its own pipeline; and that pipeline, which from 1935
covered a full 50 percent of France's oil needs, terminated—where? In

provincial Tripoli! Beirut's power cut no ice in the face of vital imperial interests, which dictated that the pipeline trajectory should be as simple as possible, that is cross through a break in Bilad al-Sham's north-south mountain chain east of Tripoli.[113]

The third shift in imperial infrastructural investments in the 1930s concerned reach. More than in the 1920s, Bilad al-Sham's French and British strategic hubs were part of both regional and worldwide imperial frameworks of action. Access to oil was only one reason. Another was that—as noted in the introductory section of this chapter—from the mid-1930s three challengers to the world's geopolitical status quo forced Paris and London to assign more strategic importance to the Mediterranean, including its eastern half. This area straddled the sea, air, and land lanes to imperial possessions in Asia, which were threatened by a resurgent Japan. Due to oil, the area played a role in France's continental strategy against Germany, as well as in Britain's navy. And it mattered for its own sake what with Italy challenging both French and British interests there.

France and Britain's increasing attention to the eastern Mediterranean materialized not only in Beirut and Haifa, though. The two empires also defended the pipeline routes. And wary of putting all eggs into one basket, they widened other cities' strategic reach. Most crucial, Tripoli's pipeline terminus received militarily protection and the city kept its airport. Similarly, Lydda—centrally located in Palestine, next to the country's largest urban conglomeration, Jaffa / Tel Aviv, and on the Jerusalem-Jaffa / Haifa-Kantara railroads crossing—got an airport in 1937, soon after an expansion of port Jaffa in 1934 / 35.

Wider reach was a reaction to more than geostrategic challenges. The Great Depression forced actors in Bilad al-Sham to develop trade wherever possible, even with Iraq and Iran. (However, this trade remained modest.) Although the Syrian Desert's north was easier to cross by car than its south, and the route Beirut-Damascus-Baghdad was shorter than Haifa-Mafraq / Amman-Baghdad, France did not build a road, unlike Britain. But otherwise, the two acted similarly, in fact competed. Take routes. Already in 1925 Nairn had tried out Haifa-Amman-Rutbah-Baghdad, which replaced Beirut-Damascus-Baghdad during the Syrian Revolt's peak and on which Britain was already "fixing one eye" according to the worried French. In 1927, France had granted Nairn (and a few soon defunct companies) customs privileges on the Damascus-Baghdad route. Two years later, France had made Nairn its chosen carrier in a Franco-Iraqi agreement, with Haim Nathaniel Nairn's Iraqi counterpart. Superbly organized and networked in Iraq, Nathaniel soon closed in. By 1932, he demanded Nairn's privileges. Partly for political reasons (a few Damascene companies were raising the same demand) France demurred. Nathaniel retaliated. Enticed by Britain, he switched his parcel service to the Amman route. Although the suspicious British refused to grant Nathaniel a monopoly, and although most passenger traffic continued through Damascus, the French sensed "grave danger." In 1935, with Nathaniel ever stronger, they yielded. Under the cover of a general decree, a specific "gentleman's agreement" was reached: Nairn's conditions were met in exchange for Nathaniel channeling more traffic through Damascus-Beirut than Amman-Haifa. Following the 1937 Palestine-Iraq trade deal, France feared Nathaniel may jump ship again, but he did not. Britain allowed no monopolies on the Haifa-Baghdad roads.[114]

The French and British Mandate authorities tried developing trade with their eastern neighbors through trade treaties and port facilities, too. And here, too, they competed. Already in 1925 France had signed a transit trade agreement with Iraq, stipulating a 0.5 percent transit customs rate. In 1930 it signed a transit trade treaty with Iran. And in 1932 it reduced the transit customs rate with Iraq to 0.1 percent, and signed a trade agreement with Turkey that, however, benefited the Mandates little if at all. The following year, port Haifa's deep-water docks opened, an event so momentous that the Palestine's Customs Office moved from capital Jerusalem to Haifa. Out-competed infrastructurally, France had to up the ante in another way. In early 1934, it carried out a measure first considered in 1929: a free port zone in Beirut, facilitating transit trade with Iraq and Iran. Small steps followed (in 1935, a new French-Iranian trade agreement lowered regular and transit customs rates and France and Iraq abolished transit customs) until the 1937 Palestine-Iraqi trade treaty marked another milestone. Among other measures, that treaty reacted to French action by mandating a Beirut-type free port in Haifa, managed by Iraqis. Fortunately for Beirut, by that time its own deep-water docks were near completion and from 1938 helped to close the gap to Haifa.[115]

Although French and British imperial interests were fundamental to expanding Beirut's and Haifa's reach and to tying Bilad al-Sham more firmly to Iraq and into wider imperial networks, they did not occur in a vacuum. As already noted, some infrastructures built in the 1930s had in the 1920s already been decided on (Haifa deep-water docks), planed (pipelines), or envisioned (Haifa-Amman-Baghdad route). Indeed, the focus on Beirut and Haifa meant that the imperial build-up moved along tracks laid in the late Ottoman period. Moreover, local and nation-state pressures mattered, doubly due to Franco-British competition. Masterful Nathaniel was the example par excellence. But also those who could not change routes, that is were married to one location, played the inter-imperial card. Beirut's mercantile elite—families like the Pharaons, the Bayhums, the Salams, many organized in the Chamber of Commerce led by the energetic Omar al-Daouk—pushed France hard to stay in the race with British Haifa, demanding appropriate infra-structural investments and economic measures.[116]

Meanwhile, in Haifa, the Jewish Agency and private Zionist entrepre-neurs, appreciative of the city's importance for British imperial planning, invested heavily. They "worked in close consultation with government planning," and "the Bay Area's transformation into the city's principal industrial zone was subsequently a Jewish-led process." Further, in the 1930s nongovernmental transport companies expanded their region-wide and transregional services from Haifa and Beirut. In Beirut, the bustling Place des Martyres was the arrival / departure station for most long-distance cabs and buses. In Haifa, Palmer Square, as well as Hamra Square, became busier, with cabs and buses serving not only Palestinian destinations but Jordan, Beirut, Damascus, and from 1935, through an *Egged* co-operative line, Baghdad.[117]

The intensified interest in economically connecting the Mediterra-nean via Bilad al-Sham eastward, that is in extending the region's reach, had a momentous effect. In the 1920s the two key conditions for Beirut's original rise from the mid-nineteenth century—an open world economy and a borderless Ottoman Arab East—had been fading. But in the 1930s an old-new socio-spatial framework was (re)built for Beirut and now also for Haifa. "Old" in that still, this framework connected economies in and beyond the Mediterranean to Bilad al-Sham, and in that already before the 1930s, it had had some contact with Iraq. "New" in that now, Haifa was a real player, intensifying its rivalry with Beirut; in that the Haifawi and Beiruti trade hubs were somewhat dividing Bilad al-Sham into a northern and southern zone; in that their reach into Iraq was strengthened; and, conversely, in that some Iraqi actors reached deeper into Bilad al-Sham. (Haifa would be cut off in 1948.) At the same time, Beirut's star would shine brighter than ever. In the 1940s–1960s, when Arabian petrodollars flowed and the Arab East's fledgling postindependence states still lacked some of Beirut's assets and ties, the old-new socio-spatial framework rooted in the 1930s would make the city an almighty trade, finance, consumerism, knowledge production, and air transport hub between the First World and the Arab countries east of Egypt.

## Inter-State Administrative Communication: Old and New International Dimensions

We now move on to administration, and specifically to three spaces of inter-state communication: international contexts transcending Bilad al-Sham's countries, inter-imperial Franco-British communication within Bilad al-Sham, and communication in the French-British Mandate border zone and its effects on that zone's inhabitants.

International contexts saw some continuity. Various international concerns persisted in the 1930s that had elicited similarly international administrative communication in the 1920s. One concern was tribes; another, diseases and pests.[118] A third was communists, an undiminished security risk in the eyes of anxious imperial and nation-state authorities, especially Iraqi and Egyptian. This perception was not entirely wrong. Communists did work across borders. Following the 1929 riots the Palestine Communist Party (PCP) affirmed, in its clandestine paper *Forois* (Forwards in Yiddish), that "We are on the eve of new great revolutions not only in Palestine but also in Egypt, Syria, and Iraq." More crucial, at a time when Moscow Communist International's

(Comintern) order to the PCP's Jewish leaders—'Hand over the leadership to Arabs'—started being effective, another order, issued in 1929, asked the PCP to tighten ties with Lebanese / Syrians and Egyptians. Delegations met secretly; in 1931, they convened and passed resolutions in Beirut. Also, some communists were full-time professionals who moved whenever told. Palestinian Najati Sidqi, a 1929 graduate of Moscow's Communist University of the Toilers of the East, from 1933 to 1936 clandestinely edited Comintern's newspaper *al-Sharq al-'Arabi* in Paris; then was called to Moscow; sent to the Spanish civil war and Algeria; and in 1937 asked to return to his leadership position in Palestine.[119]

Middle East communists were much weaker than the authorities believed, however, and few and far between. "The supreme irony . . . was that . . . nationalist [Arab] groups," distrusted particularly by France, "were instrumental in limiting the mass appeal of Communism. There was no fusion of Communism and anticolonial nationalism comparable to that achieved in Vietnam by the Indochinese Communist Party after 1931." But authorities continued fearing Communists, not the least precisely because they moved around. On the one hand, states tackled this challenge alone. The French War Ministry Section de Centralisation du Renseignement's "scrutiny of potential Communist subversion intensified" from 1930 to 1936, also in the Middle East. In Lebanon / Syria, the Sûreté Générale stayed on the ball, indeed ran faster than ever in the late 1930s. Cairo, too, remained concerned, and Baghdad started repressing the Iraqi Communist Party a mere year after its official birth in 1934. On the other hand, states also saw communism as a global challenge. The French colonial lobby's paper *Asie Française* routinely warned about Soviet and communist subversion across Asia. And typically, at the 1932 trial of Syrian / Lebanese Communist Party cofounder Khalid Bikdash and of Artin Madoyan, in Beirut, the attorney general pleaded for hard sentences: the only way to prevent communist uprisings spreading from French Indochina to the Levant, he argued. In this situation, it made sense to continue exchanging intelligence. And this is exactly what the police forces of Bilad al-Sham's Mandates, Egypt, and Iraq, as well as India and Britain (with Palestine and Egypt) did with unabated vigor in the 1930s.[120]

While there was some continuity in international administrative communication, two major qualitative shifts happened, too. One concerned colonized Middle Eastern countries. In the 1930s, particularly Iraq and Egypt gained more sovereign elbowroom. Thus, Bilad al-Sham's imperial authorities increased administrative communication with Iraq because Baghdad gained quasi-independence in the June 1930 Anglo-Iraqi Treaty, which stipulated that—foreign political and security affairs aside[121]—Britain would relinquish control. (Britain indeed meddled very little in the 1930s, and helped Iraq join the League of Nations in 1932, sealing the country's quasi-independence.) Hence, from 1930 Bilad al-Sham Mandate officials' Iraqi counterparts were not any more imperial British men but nation-state Iraqis. This has just been reflected in Iraq's—and Egypt's—increased role in fighting communism in the 1930s. Other nongeostrategic matters, old or new, now were handled more and more by nation-state officials, especially in Iraq but also in Egypt. Quasi-sovereignty showed in the stationing of Iraqi customs officials in port Haifa's Iraq transit zone, in the Franco-Iraqi transit trade agreements, and in the resulting flow of Franco-Iraqi bureaucratic communication. Its novelty was thrown into relief by the fact that in January 1930, mere months before the Anglo-Iraqi Treaty, a high-level bureaucratic discussion of the bourgeoning Iraqi-Bilad al-Sham motor traffic included not a single Iraqi.[122]

The second qualitative shift involved the League of Nations in Geneva: a place where increasingly sovereign ex-colonies lobbied with gusto. The main subject matter of this shift was noted in Chapter 3. From the mid-1920s, Anglo-Egyptian authorities combatted narcotics, principally heroin and hashish; 1927 saw the beginning of Egyptian-led international police cooperation involving also Palestine and Syria / Lebanon. Cooperation with central European and Turkish police forces cut heroin smuggling around 1930, so Egypt took better aim at Lebanon / Syria, for Egyptians' hashish was mostly from there. The Central Narcotics Intelligence Bureau, led by Englishman Russell Pasha but run mostly by Egyptians, and Egypt's government charged forward, and not only in the Middle East. Although Egypt joined the League only in 1937, it knew that narcotics worried also League bureaucrats and members including powerful Britain, and that France owed Geneva some accountability for Mandate Lebanon / Syria. Further, Egypt used the League to internationally shame Paris. In 1934, "repeated complaints . . . [and] strong reactions by the Société des Nations" bore fruit. The French Mandate authorities energized narcotics prosecution and created a Sûreté Générale anti-drug squad with a regional mandate. Anglo-Egyptian-French anti-narcotics cooperation peaked in 1937–1938, including French attempts to eradicate hashish and anti-traffic campaigns including systematic information exchanges, extraditions, coordinated actions, and Egyptian undercover operations on French Mandate territory. This was indicative of the international climate becoming conducive to ex-colonies asserting their sovereignty internationally, through inter-state ties and the League. In result, in the 1930s Bilad al-Sham's Mandate countries were increasingly tied into various international networks of administrative communication.[123]

## Inter-State Administrative Communication: In Bilad al-Sham and in the Central Periphery

In Bilad al-Sham as a whole, administrative communication remained inter-imperial, for unlike Iraq and Egypt, the Mandate countries did not gain more sovereignty. One example was the continued use of the provisional Franco-British extradition agreement signed in 1921; another, the monthly Franco-British-overseen tribal court meetings for offenses committed by nomads living in Syria and Trans-Jordan, a system that was regularized in 1929, a year after its birth. Together with other steps, such as the 1929 Franco-British decision to extend the regional customs-free zone agreement by a decade, this highlights that persistent cross-border movements of goods and people continued to require inter-imperial administrative communication.[124]

This was true, too, for Bilad al-Sham's inner border zone, the central periphery. Small, it lends itself to an account of how everyday life was affected by inter-imperial administrative communication and by how communication was structured by sovereign state interests. Recall that in 1926 Britain and France signed a Good Neighbourly Agreement that, as quoted in Chapter 3, permitting inhabitants of the border districts of

Acre, Safed, Tyre, Marjayoun, Hasbaya, and Quneitra "to cross the frontier freely and without a passport." At first glance, crossing the border seemed routine. Dahir Madi, born 1939 in Marjayoun, "remember[s] that there was no border. There was, each kilometer, a block, a stone, painted white." Even the decision, following the 1926 agreement, to make laissez-passers mandatory to tell local from nonlocal border-crossers, and the order that the border be crossed only at multiple customs points, seemed undramatic. In southern Lebanon for instance, these travel documents could be obtained at minimal cost. Karim Isbir Salamah, born in 1923, remembers receiving his papers without hassle in Marjayoun where he lived. More important, locals, including seasonal bedouin, could—and most did—cross the border between its few customs posts paperless. Naziha Farhat, born 1936 in the town of Bint Jbeil, west of Marjayoun, recalls poor Palestinian women bringing the daily catch from the Sea of Galilee to her town. Some landowners like the Farhats, also from Bint Jbeil, owned lands in northern Palestine. And some peasants tilled fields across the border. Abu Rafiq Sabeq, born 1907 in the now Israeli border village of Hurfesh, put it as follows: "Fish ikhtilaf kan, kull wahad biyruh 'al ardathu [There was no distinction, everyone went to his field]." Besides, in what really was a periphery, border forces normally were light.

Still, the laissez-passer system did affect people. Bedouin who had seasonally lived in the border zone fell outside the law. Sedentary locals were touched, too, if more subtly. Also, laissez-passer issuance was often interrupted in practice. Worse, the border, though barely visible and enforced, reinforced socioeconomic inequalities. Locals without travel permits were vulnerable to situations in which the state *was* present. In fact, lack of a permit signaled lack of social connections necessary to deal with such situations. ID controls per se were the least problem. More trying was abuse of power, and undocumented peasants were more likely to be arrested than were people of local importance, who regularly got away with serious offenses. Ali Abd al-Hassan Awadeh, born 1921 in Khiam, remembers that in 1943 south Lebanese notable Ahmed al-Assad assisted Bikaa Valley landowner-politician Sabri Hamadeh in convincing Palestinian customs to wave through a cargo of hashish, which miraculously "sar saman [became animal fat]."

Although the Good Neighbourly Agreement implicitly promised that the border would not change locals' life, it created a glass ceiling.[125]

Reality differed from text on paper, especially whenever the state faced an extraordinary situation. For instance, as border-zone peasants crisscrossed the border with cattle to find pastures and waterholes, veterinary administrators worried about infectious animal diseases. When detecting an epidemic, they suspended the relevant parts of the 1926 agreement. This happened in 1930 and 1938, and from December 1931 to at least July 1933. While herders continued to cross the border, they now were sent back when caught, and sometimes their animals were confiscated for a while.[126] This was particularly damaging in the early 1930s, when the draught devastating Bilad al-Sham's interior plagued also the central periphery, if less drastically. Eventually, some inhabitants protested. In May 1933 the head of the south Lebanese village of Meiss contacted the Services Spéciaux political officer, insisting on the "customary right" to graze animals in Palestinian Khalsa and Bouzieh. Captain May agreed. He first had to receive green light from Beirut, though, which he did in late May. Still, the border was not reopened. The French veterinary service dug in its heels; Britain's consul in Beirut told the French HC that water was scarce in Palestine, too; and on the border some Lebanese and Palestinian customs officials objected to allowing animals to cross, for epidemic and water scarcity reasons, respectively. (Palestinian peasants agreed.) By mid-July, the French veterinarians relaxed—having been invited to Palestine, they verified that the 1931 epidemic had abated, something their British counterparts had asserted—and later that month the French HC intensified his pressure on Jerusalem. More than two months had passed since Meiss's request, and no solution been found yet. French and British bureaucrats had to communicate. And both, including low-level Arab officials on the border, anxiously protected sovereign interests.[127]

The story had an epilogue. Back in May, Captain May had asked Meiss (and other villages) to prepare a detailed list of their herds. Else, how could an official be sure whether an animal was from the border zone, and from this or that side of the border? Perhaps building on this idea, in January 1934 a Franco-British agreement determined that

Whereas it is necessary to regulate by agreement certain questions of veterinary sanitary control in respect of the movement of certain animals in the Sub-Districts of Acre and Safad and the Kazas of Tyre, Marjayoun, Kuneitra, and Hasbaya.

1. The Syrian, Lebanese, and Palestinian owners of farms within the[se] Sub-Districts . . . shall be allowed to pass freely with their animals across the frontier with a view of proceeding to any of their respective lands; Provided

(a) that each owner or his herdsman accompanying the animals is in possession of an identity card of approved form establishing that his village of origin is one of the villages within the Sub-Districts of Acre and Safad or the Kazas of Tyre, Marjayoun, Kuneitra and Hasbaya entitled to benefit from the provisions of the Bon Voisinage Agreement, and indicating the number of animals of each kind (cattle, sheep, goats, horses, mules, donkeys, and camels); and that

(b) Each animal is marked by a metal ribbon bearing the letter 'S' in the case of Syrian and Lebanese animals and the letter 'P' in the case of Palestinian animals, securely attached to its right ear.

2. Identity cards shall be issued by the Officer des Services Speciaux [sic] in the case of Syria and the Lebanon, and by the District Officers of Safad or Acre in the case of Palestine in the form scheduled to this agreement.[128]

Donkey IDs? This is comical. Until, that is, one considers that this agreement further chipped away at the normalcy implied in the 1926 Good Neighbourly Agreement. Thus, the 1930s accentuated a pattern set in the 1920s. Inter-imperial reactions to an extraordinary situation, an epidemic, lastingly added to the bureaucratization of ordinary life. The sovereign state concerns that structured inter-imperial communication had reached the point of territorializing, indeed nationalizing, animals.

More of the same followed. From 1936 to 1939, many Lebanese, Syrians, and Transjordanians were stirred by the Palestine revolt. These feelings were given voice by known Damascene singer Muhi al-Din Bidawi. One ode began, "Listen, oh Easterner, son of my country / Listen to Palestine which demands aid and support / To deliver her from the cruel enemy, from the criminal Jew."[129] Many hundreds, perhaps thousands, joined the revolt and / or intensified arms smuggling (some for money, too). To reach Palestine, most crossed the Lebanese-Syrian-Palestinian border zone southward; and rebels at times retired northward for rest, refuge, or treatment. This two-way traffic transformed life in the border zone. Britain, with some French assistance, militarized it, and from 1937, Britain sought to intensify security coordination with France. Its main demand was for France to better secure its side of the border, and it asked for permission for British troops to pursue rebels into French Mandate territory and to execute identity controls on the Syrian leg of the Damascus-Haifa railway. Paris by and large cooperated on the first point.[130] It sometimes sent British troops intelligence about smugglers and fighters passing the border. And it agreed to host neutral and pro-British Palestinians seeking refuge from rebels. This cooperation was hoped to help secure London's support of Paris in its dealings with Ankara, and more broadly reflected the cautious Franco-British geostrategic rapprochement of the late 1930s. But Paris did not bend over all the way. Fearing unrest, it refused to extradite wanted Palestinian rebels and leaders like Haj Amin al-Husayni, another British demand. And citing its sovereignty, it declined to grant Britain pursuit or identity control rights.[131]

Britain often executed such operations anyway, brushing off French protests. In fact, while intensifying security cooperation with France, it honed its own anti-insurgency tools. Its sovereign concerns about territorial control were increasingly written in blood. Its tactics became more brutal, including torture and executions. On the border, it deployed planes and artillery and stationed more soldiers and policemen; in 1937 it built police forts and a road parallel to the border to facilitate operations; and from 1938 it mined most of the Lebanese-Palestinian border and with Zionist aid built a barbed-wire fence along it. This was the so-called Tegart Wall, named after Charles Tegart, a high-ranking British police officer who came to Palestine in 1937 to bring his expertise in repressing nationalists, infamous in India, to bear on the revolt.[132]

Rebels in Palestine and their supporters across the border reacted. They made heavier use of the Syrian-Palestinian border; blew up some mines along the Lebanese-Palestinian border; used cutters to destroy parts of the fence; damaged the border road; and echoing state rule, in January 1939 some rebels in Bint Jbeil made a vain stab at imposing their own border laissez-passer.[133] In fact, rebels often sought to impose their own rule—courts, taxes, and all. Hence, while some peasants became rebels, and while probably a majority supported the revolt and helped it occasionally, many were increasingly trapped between the hammer of rebel demands and the anvil of British counterinsurgency.[134]

The latter was both more brutal and more consequential. While meant to keep out arms and rebels, the fence affected all locals.[135] Although it had a dozen gates, peasants with fields across the border had to walk much longer, or simply could not cross. Tohme Maghzal, born 1928 in Kafr Bir'im, Palestine, remembers that their gate was opened only twice or thrice a day. "Al-zira'a khirbet. . . . Kanet fitra ktir sa'be [Agriculture was damaged. . . . It was a very hard period]." The gates also caught the locals between the rebels and the British, one demanding aid, the other retaliating. From the start of fence construction, in June 1938, Lebanese peasants complained to the Services Spéciaux. France requested five additional gates; Britain refused. (Zionists, too, had problems reaching their few fields in Lebanon—but mainly due to Arab resistance.) Lastly, like Britain's and France's reaction to the 1931–1933 epidemic, Britain's actions of 1936–1939 were not quite undone after life returned to its ordinary course. Its demands for identity control rights on the Syrian leg of the Haifa-Damascus train continued, and the border forts stayed put. So did the fence—although by 1940 most of it had been dismantled by locals, who sold its precious metal.[136]

## Conclusion

The 1930s differed enough from the 1920s to make them a distinct phase in the post-Ottoman stage of transpatialization. One development was economic: Bilad al-Sham's countries felt the Great Depression. Lebanon and Syria were hit hardest. And while the Yishuv thrived due to the surge of moneyed European immigrants, rising customs barriers around the world affected it, too. Another development concerned geostrategy. Britain and France invested more in transportation and communication infrastructures because Italy challenged them in the Mediterranean, because Franco-British trade competition to Iraq hardened, and because an Iraqi oil pipeline to the Mediterranean was opened. The most momentous development, however, was that Bilad al-Sham's single-country (*watani*) nation-state movements matured as nation-states. Although still imperially ruled, around 1930 they started to set their respective country's political agenda, and their economic and institutional importance grew. (Arab Palestine partook of this trend, though less successfully than others.) A prolonged process of decolonization in the A Mandates had begun.

Cities, their hinterlands and interurban ties, and the region continued to matter. Certainly, like before they were remolded by (nation- and empire-) state territoriality and by the world economy. But in return, they molded both. Beirut and Haifa, which had risen to prominence before nation-states and European empires arrived in Bilad al-Sham, channeled and attracted trade and imperial investments—just as in the 1920s, indeed, more so. Also, city hinterlands that were transnationalized after 1918 (i.e., came to straddle a new border) continued to affect people and policies on either side of the border. And while Bilad al-Sham's nation-states grew more distinct, they matured not simply in isolation but under a shared regional umbrella—doubly because they traded more within their customs-free zone as customs barriers rose around the world.

Relative to the 1920s, these processes of mutual molding and remolding were characterized by various changes, but also by continuities. As in the 1920s, cities had to position themselves within their nation-states, and used—in a fascinating triangulation—their transnational links to prove their national relevance. The latter process, a nationalization (of sorts) of cities, continued having a reverse side. Nation-states continued to be heterogeneous, multi-urban spaces, accentuating patterns rooted in the 1920s. As nation-states matured in the 1930s, cities were more compelled than before to prove their national value; and as nation-states grew more distinct, cities adapted in ways that were more

distinct than before, too. Accentuation: this characterized also the region. *Qawmiyya* existed in the 1930s as in the 1920s. But its adherents
tended to be more zealous, younger, more numerous, and more inclined
to see Egypt as Arab than before. And although they continued seeing
Bilad al-Sham as an integral part of the world of Arabs, that region was
their political gravitation point in both word and deed.

A more pronounced change relative to the 1920s concerned administrative cooperation. As Iraq and Egypt became more independent in the
1930s, officials from the Bilad al-Sham's Mandates started to interact
with them much more than before. Further, they did so more often
than before in an international arena outside the Middle East, at the
League of Nations in Geneva. Another pronounced change was nation-
states' greater focus on the Bilad al-Sham-wide customs-free zone. This
resulted not only in greater economic integration, but also in more
competition, especially between Syria and the Yishuv, which had become the region's strongest polities. A sharp accentuation concerned
Beirut's economic profile. The 1930s saw the final demise—following a
crisis already in the 1920s—of that city's late Ottoman-time global-
regional positioning, one based on a borderless Arab East and relatively
unfettered world trade. In result, and due to British investment, Haifa
became a much more dangerous rival than in the 1920s. But simultaneously, Beirut's tighter Iraqi ties, which were greatly helped by French
infrastructural investments, became a basis for another type of positioning that would mature in the 1940s–1960s, making Beirut the hub
between a by then U.S.-centered world trade and the Arab East and
Arabia. Beirut and Haifa in the 1930s, then, remained part of an intricate
quadrangular relationship. They leveraged their urban position in the
region with respect to their European imperial rulers, and exploited
that success to maximize their position in their nation-state.

How did the changed conditions of World War II affect the situation
summed up above? This is the question to which we turn now.

## PRELUDE 5

# Eliahu Rabino's War

Three men. A single group really, for all three are striking the same pose. It looks as if their suits are the same color and cut. Did they ask a tailor to fashion identical suits? Or is this photograph a practical joke? We can't know. What's certain is that the three are posing. They face the camera. They are relaxed and sure of themselves; there even is a hint of humor here.

Figure P5.1 Eliahu Rabino (right), Yasha (Yaacov) Rabino (left), and an unidentified Lebanese businessman in Beirut, early World War II. Courtesy of Shmuel Rabino, Haifa.

This photograph (Figure P5.1) shows an unidentified Lebanese businessman, and to his left and right, two brothers, the Haifa vegetable and fruit traders Eliahu and Yasha (Yaacov) Rabino. It was taken in early World War II in Lebanon, and is included in an album of the Rabinos'

work life. The album is slim. Many life-shaping events are undocumented. There are no images of the brothers' arrival from Russia's
Crimean peninsula to Jaffa in 1920, for instance, or of how Eliahu
subsequently tends fields in nearby Zikhron Ya'akov and Zaronia.
Neither does the album document his move with his wife Katia, née
Manto, and their baby son Shmuel to Haifa around 1927, nor the store he
opens there with a brother-in-law in the Arab produce market, which
he quits after the 1929 riots. But then starts a string of pictures of Eliahu
and his brother Yasha, his new partner, as they "move up in the world" in
Haifa. They are busy at work, neatly dressed year round, usually in tie
and pressed trousers, in winter donning hat and coat, too. In Figure P5.2,
we see them on the sidewalk of their new vegetable and fruit store in the
Jewish Commercial Center near Hamra Square.

Figure P5.2  Eliahu Rabino (right) and Yasha (Yaacov) Rabino in front of their
vegetable and fruit store in Haifa, 1930s. Courtesy of Shmuel Rabino, Haifa.

The album also includes photographs from abroad: The brothers'
vegetable and fruit import business is thriving. A few pictures show
Eliahu in Cairo, where the Rabinos work with the influential
Egyptian Jewish trader Isaac Vaena. One picture is taken in 1934;
others, during World War II, like the one in Figure P5.3, which

Figure P5.3  Eliahu Rabino (right) and a guide in Cairo, World War II.
Courtesy of Shmuel Rabino, Haifa.

features Eliahu with a guide relaxing after work in a lush park in Cairo, a flower inserted into his lapel.

Another wartime snapshot (Figure P5.4) catches Yasha walking down a snowy Istanbul street at the side of Monia (Moshe) Kuris, whose family is also originally from the Crimea like the Rabinos. Kuris and the brothers have been working together since the early 1930s.[1]

Figure P5.4  Yasha Rabino (left) and Monia (Moshe) Kuris
in Istanbul, World War II. Courtesy of Shmuel Rabino, Haifa.

In yet another photograph (Figure P5.5), taken in or just before
World War II, are Eliahu, an employee, Salzman, and a Tel-Aviv
wholesale merchant named Harubi, in a café in Lebanon. Around
1940, the Rabinos open an office in Beirut, run by a man of useful
connections, Eli Braun, a son of the rabbi of Sidon.

And then there is the photograph of the matching pose at the café
with the Lebanese businessman, with which we began. Reviewing it
again, alongside the others taken abroad during the war, the sociable
composure it radiates seems normal, though the times are anything
but. The horribly brutal war surely frightens these men. But life is not
quite bad. Business continues, not only in Palestine but beyond; not
only in Bilad al-Sham but in places as varied as Egypt and Turkey.

Figure P5.5  Eliahu Rabino (left), an employee, Salzman (middle), and
Tel-Aviv wholesale merchant Harubi (right), in a café in Lebanon, World War II.
Courtesy of Shmuel Rabino, Haifa.

The man who allowed me to copy these pictures told me the
Rabinos' story. In 2010, I interviewed Eliahu's son Shmuel in his and
his grandson's office in Haifa's Vegetables and Fruit Wholesale
Market. Shmuel was eighty-six yet sharp. He joined the family business in 1945 but knew information back to the mid-1930s. At the core
of his narrative was a personal and family success story. To be sure, he
noted Yishuvi-wide endeavors like the *Totseret ha-Arets* campaign,
mentioned in Chapter 4, and talked about British action during the
Palestine Revolt. British soldiers, with the Hagana and a family guard,
accompanied lorries importing Syrian / Lebanese produce from the
border at Ra's al-Naqura to Haifa. Also, when Britain occupied
pro-German Vichy-ruled Lebanon and Syria in the summer of 1941,
trade connections were invigorated. But what truly mattered to
Shmuel was the "drive" of his father Eliahu; his father's bonds to his
father-in-law Moshe and to his brother Yasha; and the sense that these
businessmen were not slaves to money but nurtured "family [and]
friends" and appreciated "culture [and] art," going on tours, sub-
scribing to orchestras, and enjoying the theater.

Why were the Rabinos' private vegetable and fruit imports successful enough for Shmuel to assert that in Haifa "we were not smaller, perhaps bigger" than Tnuva, the Yishuv's mightiest agricultural cooperative? Because, Shmuel Rabino said, his pragmatic father and uncle worked with everybody. They bought produce from private Jewish and Palestinian farmers, imported from the United States, Holland, Cyprus, Egypt, and bought most of their vegetables from Lebanon and Syria via Beirut. (While remembering Vaena and Braun, two Jews, Shmuel had forgotten the Lebanese partners' names.) He was a patriot, too. He joined the Hagana in 1942—the entire Yishuv at this point was alarmed about a possible German invasion of Palestine and the annihilation of its Jews—and recounted how in 1948, during Israel's war of independence, the Rabinos acceded to a Hagana request to smuggle arms under a cargo of onions from Egypt through Italy to Palestine.

Talking of Beirut, Shmuel affirmed that the Rabinos and their Beiruti partners had "ties of friendship [and] full trust" and insisted "this is legitimate." His views reflected an implicit transnational sense of social belonging: "If [these traders] have the status of a great distinguished merchant, then he [they] honor also another great distinguished merchant."He believed "the Kuris Rabino business" succeeded because "in any situation [it] adapted to a changing reality." During the 1936–1939 revolt, this meant expanding Lebanese-Syrian business. After the Israeli-Arab borders closed in 1948, it entailed branching out into Israeli agriculture while continuing imports from overseas. In between, during the Second World War, it required nurturing extant business with Egypt and Lebanon and Syria and honing the social relationships that underpin business.[2]

The Rabinos' relatively normal life and business trips during the war point to a crucial fact about World War II in the Middle East. Here, the years from 1939 to 1945 were not catastrophic, certainly not if compared with Europe and East Asia. Some people—including the Rabinos, merchants from the Zionist Yishuv—indeed traveled around the entire Middle East. Why did this happen? How did this specific fact and the specific economic and political conditions of war change transpatialization? And what were continuities from the 1930s? These questions drive Chapter 5.

# 5

# EMPIRE REDUX

## 1939–1945

### Historical Context: The Middle East in World War II

World War II was not catastrophic in the Middle East. This had three reasons.[1] First, open warfare lasted only three years, from 1940 to 1943, was mostly limited to North Africa and the southern Mediterranean Sea, and cost relatively few lives. In the largest battle, between the Italian-German Axis and British-led troops at the northwestern Egyptian town of El Alamein in late October / early November 1942, there were "only" about 45,000 casualties—soldiers killed, wounded, missing, or captured—a fraction of the mindboggling 2,000,000 casualties at the Battle of Stalingrad that lasted from August 1942 to February 1943. Most military casualties in Middle East battles were non-Arabs; so were most soldiers, Algerians aside. Moreover, unlike in Europe and East Asia, there were neither mass massacres nor sustained strategic bombing campaigns claiming untold civilian lives.

Warfare was restricted in the Middle East and North Africa because that theater was ultimately a periphery of World War II. As peripheries go, it was central, to be sure. The British Suez Canal base was strategically vital, Palestine protected its northern flank, and hence, tens of thousands of troops were massed here. The Middle East and North Africa, with India, was the hinge between the war's European and Asian theaters—one the Anglo-American Allies were determined to hold.

And until the summer of 1943, when Allied troops landed in Sicily, North Africa was British prime minister Winston Churchill's and U.S. president Franklin D. Roosevelt's only frontal fight on land against Hitler. Still, that theater was a periphery. The two mightiest of the three Axis aggressors, Germany and Japan, launched their key campaigns and were ultimately defeated not here, but in Europe and the Western Pacific. Although Italy and Germany challenged Britain and the United States in North Africa and General Erwin Rommel nearly broke through from Libya to Egypt in the summer of 1942, Axis forces proved to be too weak to prevail.[2]

Second, a World War I-style famine did not recur. Some people died of hunger, mainly in the Gulf, and many had to tighten their belts, but massive economic interventionism headed off serious deprivations. World War II was empire redux in the sense that (British Empire) state territoriality peaked. Britain expanded road, rail, port, and communication infrastructures, and, with some U.S. officials, in 1941 established the Middle East Supply Center (MESC). From its Cairo headquarters and through constant visits, the MESC ran a single Middle East / North Africa-wide economic-administrative area of production, exchange, and consumption. One of the war's most far-flung markets, at its zenith it encompassed approximately 100,000,000 people in twenty territories, including non-Arab Malta, Cyprus, Iran, Somalia, Eritrea, Ethiopia, and in some regards also Turkey. It sought and succeeded to "free shipping space needed for military supplies" and "minimize the inevitable civilian hardships caused by the sharp [wartime] reduction of overseas import." Britain spent massively on provisions, on agricultural schemes, and on import substitution industry factories employing hundreds of thousands of workers especially in key cities in Egypt and Palestine but also elsewhere. The cost was immense. By 1945 Britain's debt in the Middle East was "no less than one-sixth of [its] war debt to the USA."[3]

A last reason for the noncatastrophic nature of World War II in the Middle East was Britain's determination to keep the region calm politically. London backed some moderate pan-Arab (*qawmi*) and some nation-state (*watani*) aspirations. True, in Egypt, Britain firmed up its political position for strategic reasons; and in May 1941, it reoccupied

Iraq following a pro-German coup d'état. But matters differed in the four countries of Bilad al-Sham. Britain's occupation of Lebanon and Syria in Operation Exporter in June / July 1941—it was concerned when Vichy France, a German ally, took control in 1940; and alarmed when Axis aircraft flying to Iraq in May 1941 used Syria to refuel—had far-reaching political consequences. Britain's Beirut-based mission head for Lebanon and Syria, Sir Edward Spears, refused to allow anti-Vichy leader Charles de Gaulle's Free French troops to reassert Mandate rule even though London had let them enter Lebanon / Syria during Operation Exporter. Spears even helped Lebanese and Syrian nationalists gain conditional independence from France in 1943; full independence would come in 1946, after the withdrawal of the last French and British troops.[4]

In Transjordan, Emir Abdallah fostered his already close relationship with London, preparing the ground for independence in the wake of the war, in 1946. And in Palestine, Britain limited Jewish immigration and land purchases in the 1939 White Paper that was meant to placate the Palestinians, as noted in Chapter 4. Although many Palestinians deemed this too little too late, they did not take up arms again after the end of the 1936–1939 Palestine Revolt. All of Bilad al-Sham's Arab countries, then, made political gains during the war, some substantial, others very moderate. Simultaneously, the Yishuv made economic gains and enjoyed some military cooperation with Britain, especially from 1944. (Politically, the para-state Jewish Agency [JA], rather alienated from Britain's Palestine policy, used the strategic opening provided by the war to shift from "evolutionary" to more aggressive, "revolutionary" nation-state building. In 1942 JA head David Ben Gurion led the Biltmore Program declaration, officially calling for a Jewish state, which would be born in 1948.[5]) Last but not least, regarding *qawmi* aspiration, from 1943 to 1945, Britain facilitated the birth of a moderate initiative, the Arab League, in which Lebanon, Syria, Iraq, Transjordan, Saudi Arabia, Yemen, and Egypt were full members. Although the league was not a federation, let alone a unified state, it showcased *qawmi* bonds, and confirmed Egypt's rise as the political gravitation point of a slowly crystallizing Arab state system.[6]

## The Story to Come

Wartime conditions, including peak (British Empire) state territoriality not only in the countries of Bilad al-Sham but across the Middle East, interplayed in complex ways with the accentuated build-up of nation-states and with their cities and the regional framework. Thus, like the 1920s and the 1930s, the years 1939–1945 formed a distinct phase in the second, post-Ottoman stage of transpatialization. However, the very range of developments relative to the 1930s was wider than in the 1930s relative to the 1920s. The war years saw the accentuation of processes that had been well underway in the 1930s, but also sharper changes and basic continuities relative to the preceding decade. Overall, various aspects of the region—Franco-British administrative relations within it; the cultural-geographic framing of the region; its weight as an economic zone—underwent considerable if not pervasive change. Cities saw more continuity, though with new twists, shaping urban identity within their respective nation-states as well as cities' economic position. Overall, cities that did economically well in the late 1930s did particularly well in the war, because the manna of peak (British imperial) state territorialization was most concentrated there. World War II did not simply help Bilad al-Sham's nation-states reach for independence, but furthered the concentration of wealth and power in a handful of cities in each of those countries.

## The Franco-British Administrative Relationship

Franco-British relations, especially during their longest and most important wartime phase, 1941–1945, saw considerable changes, but also a few continuities. To understand this development, one has to appreciate how the war changed the Franco-British balance of power.

Most fundamental was the fact that France, but not Britain, succumbed to Germany in 1940. In Lebanon and Syria, this meant that during Britain's Operation Exporter in 1941 and thereafter until 1945, de Gaulle's Free French forces greatly depended on Britain. The Free French budget was small, the British troop presence large, and material supplies remained scarce and were reliant on British assistance. Britain's Cairo headquarters opened a large administrative mission in Beirut, which created an "ill-defined and dangerous duality of authority" politically and economically.[7] The mission's head until December 1944, Spears, was incensed by de Gaulle's posturing in Europe and Africa after France's defeat in mid-1940 and, in mid-1941, by the general's flip-flopping Levantine policy. In Operation Exporter, de Gaulle had his Levantine representative Georges Catroux promise independence to Lebanon and Syria, but reversed himself in post-ceasefire talks with Britain. By late 1941, Spears—a life-long Francophile, perfect Francophone, and early admirer of the general whom he had in June 1940 personally flown from under the nose of the Vichy government-in-the-making in Bordeaux to London—had become an obdurate de Gaulle hater, and an avid supporter of Lebanese and Syrian nationalists. Dismayed, the Foreign Office in London demanded softer "tunes," but to little avail. Spears was the man on the ground who was accepted by Britain's officers in Cairo, a headstrong "rogue" with little patience for diplomacy, and a personal friend of Churchill to boot. De Gaulle was not less of a character; he had been imbued with a sense of historical mission since his youth.

Larger-than-life personalities were only one reason for the antagonistic Franco-British relations in Lebanon and Syria. De Gaulle's grandstanding was a realpolitik need in his eyes—to uphold French status and power in the long term, in the face of the defeat against Germany. Moreover, there was a long history of Franco-British rivalry, of a nagging French recognition of being weaker, and of a French belief, not quite untrue, that "Perfidious Albion" was willing to subvert it. This shaped wartime perceptions. The Free French believed Spears's behavior reflected a deviously masked Foreign Office policy masterminded from London, an impression fueled by British Secret Service dealings the French got wind of. In return, they ignored Zionist arms smuggling from Lebanon and Syria to Palestine, and some for a short time even spread anti-British propaganda, which Britain in turn read as French ingratitude. In sum, tensions reflected a transformed political-military balance. The fact that Free France returned to Lebanon and Syria on British tanks, that thousands of British soldiers and administrators were stationed there, that supplies were organized through the Anglo-

American MESC, and most fundamentally that Britain dominated all four countries of Bilad al-Sham from 1941, would have affected Franco-British ties even if de Gaulle and Spears were the best of friends. As Spears put it, "all their [i.e., Lebanon and Syria's] needs, sugar, rice, textiles, etc. had been provided through the M.E.S.C. and the whole French organisation, including their armed forces, had been entirely dependent on the British." The ultimate demonstration of that dependence came in May 1945. From the liberation of Paris in August 1944 until that month, the Europeanists in the British Foreign Office had insisted that to build an all-important postwar alliance with Paris, the latter's Levantine interests had to be respected. Thus, in December, Churchill withdrew his protection from Spears, who resigned. But in May 1945, de Gaulle went too far. French troops killed hundreds in anti-French demonstrations in Syria. Britain, its credibility among Arabs hanging in the balance, was shocked into action. Churchill gave France an ultimatum to withdraw its forces to barracks; a bitter but weak de Gaulle gave in.[8]

Still, even in these hard times France and Britain somehow had to—and sometimes did openly—deal with each other. This was true particularly in 1939 / 1940, the first year of the war in which previous cooperation basically continued. In November 1939, Britain and France finalized their revision of the Greater-Syria-wide customs zone agreement. An amicable agreement replaced the previous customs-free principle with a new policy in which a number of goods exchanged were now taxed, if below the rate for non-Mandate goods. From the summer of 1940 to the summer of 1941, however, when Vichy ruled Mandate Syria and Lebanon, relations soured. Britain's embargo of the Mandates to exert political pressure on its Vichy rulers suspended administrative cooperation with France. But by December 1940, British diplomats in Beirut recommended loosening the embargo. In March 1941, London agreed. Lebanon and Syria were too close to Britain's core possessions in Egypt and Palestine to be allowed to veer out of control. Some areas of cooperation remained from 1941 to 1945. Although inter-imperial administrative cooperation had disappeared, for Britain now was the ultimate power also in French Syria and Lebanon, some cooperation existed in these two countries. The perhaps most important field was the Joint Supply Council for Lebanon and Syria. Unlike the Anglo-American

MESC, it included French representatives, too, as well as Syrians and Lebanese. British Spears Mission officials, who as a rule were fiercely critical of France, described exemplary cooperation: "On the whole our aims . . . are the same."[9]

## Urban Identities: Continuity with a Twist

As countries reached for independence (Lebanon, Syria, Transjordan) or further consolidated or planned for independence (the Yishuv, Palestine), cities had to prove their relevance to the nation-state, as they had done in the 1930s. As before, too, cities stressed transnational ties to demonstrate that they mattered in their nation-state spaces and beyond. And again as before, they did so in distinct ways, though in some cases with a new twist, because distinctions between the nation-states deepened as independence came within reach. This development will be tracked by looking at four cities in three countries: Tripoli, Beirut, Tel Aviv, and Damascus, with a glance also at Aleppo.

## Tripoli

Tripoli was stuck in a nation-state, Lebanon, that made little sense to it, for it had strong ties to Bilad al-Sham's interior, especially Damascus. In the late 1930s, though, Tripolitans had started accepting Lebanon as somehow separate from Syria—a development that unfolded further in World War II. Tripolitans were engaged in the political process of Lebanon becoming independent in 1943, indeed somewhat more than their political engagement in the later 1930s. But precisely for this reason, they also continued to doggedly assert their city's stature vis-à-vis Lebanon's capital, Beirut.

Situated on the Mediterranean end of a west-east gap in Bilad al-Sham's north-south mountain chain, Tripoli had easy access to the region's interior. Founded in the fourteenth century B.C., it had oftentimes been a busy port, a provincial (Ottoman) or independent (Crusader, Mamluk) capital, or part of a Damascus-centered (Umayyad, Abbasid) administrative unit. However, as part of changes analyzed in Chapter 1, in 1864, it lost its own province and was integrated into Damascus's province, called *Wilayat Suriya*. In 1888, it was transferred to the new province of Beirut. And in 1918, it was attached to Lebanon, that is detached from Bilad al-Sham's interior, Syria, even more than in 1888. Given Tripoli's deep connections to the interior, this was bad. Worse, Lebanon pivoted around Beirut, and was conceived as Christian. Thusly defined, these changes hurt Tripoli's stature, trade, and identity.

Throughout the interwar decades Tripolitans reacted by affirming their ties to the majority-Sunni Syrian interior: a perfect example of a city's use of (after 1918) transnationalized ties to maximize its position vis-à-vis its nation-states. This entailed a defense of Sunni Islam: Tripoli was devout and from the 1930s had an Islamic Educational College. Further, many Tripolitans were ardent *qawmiyyun* (pan-Arab nationalists). *Qawmiyya* was framed as nonsectarian national home for Christians but it also overlapped with Sunni sensibilities. Tripoli had its own Sunni *qawmi* scouts—from the 1930s the paramilitary *Shabab Watani*, who resembled the Syrian National Bloc's Iron Shirts, and from 1941 a branch of Lebanon's Sunni Najjada. In addition, many Tripolitans demanded Lebanon's unification with Syria. Urban leaders (*zu'ama'*; sg., *za'im*) who did not do so, such as the Jisrs and the Muqaddams, lost influence; and a number of youth pursued their higher education in the interior, mostly in Damascus. (These developments were similar to those in Nablus in the 1930s—the question of who may talk for the city intensified as middle classes and some workers were becoming more educated.) Tripoli's tight connection to Syria showed also in that three out of eight Sunni Lebanese founding members of Syria's National Bloc, in 1927, were Tripolitans, among them 'Abd al-Hamid Karami.[10]

In October 1936, a Sunni Lebanese conference was convened at the same time as the 1936 Franco-Lebanese independence treaty negotiations in Paris, described in Chapter 4. These, following similar Franco-Syrian negotiations, had a fateful consequence. A Syro-Lebanese federation, rather than unity, was accepted by Syria's realpolitik National Bloc and by some Lebanese Sunni *zu'ama'*. Particularly Beirutis such as Salim Salam, 'Umar Daouk, and 'Umar Beyhum felt that their capital city had little to fear, and were overall more influential than their Tripolitan counterparts. At first, Karami and another Tripolitan notable, Abd al-Latif Bisar, went along. But the idea was too toxic in Tripoli, especially among the city's combative youth, who stood out in country-wide protests, mainly by Sunnis, against the treaty in the fall of 1936. The *Shabab Watani* declared, "Oh Arab people, the nation (*watan*) has a covenant, and kept it, [and] Tripoli's wish for unity is that of all of Syria, and part of the Arabs' great cause, a just cause." A strike poster exclaimed, "Oh noble Tripolitan people, since the dawn of the *watani* movement until today you have struggled . . . while . . . in Beirut, the delegation has formed for negotiating the Franco-Lebanese treaty." However, by early 1937 Tripoli came around. A ministerial delegation from Beirut traveled north to call on and honor *za'im* Karami's mansion. Tripoli felt it had lost a battle—the independence treaty—but not the war, for after all, Lebanon was not really independent. And when in 1938 the French parliament refused to ratify the 1936 Franco-Lebanese treaty, Tripolitans felt that the federation with Syria may yet be interpreted expansively, as unity.[11]

The pattern set in the late 1930s persisted in World War II. But there was a twist: Now more than then, Tripolitans embraced the adage "when you can't beat them, join them"—"them" being Lebanon's independence, which entailed separating from Syria. At the same time, Tripolitans tenaciously tried to contain Beirut's dominance, an endeavor for which they continued to take advantage of their transnationalized Syrian connections.

The context of their political behavior was the fortune of Lebanon's and Syria's nationalists. Although the war had started inauspiciously for the nationalists following the 1941 British occupation they, as noted earlier, quickly built excellent relations with Spears, who systematically undercut French reassertions of power.[12] By the summer of 1943 de Gaulle's Free French representative in Lebanon and Syria, Catroux, was forced to allow elections. In Lebanon, nationalists won. Soon thereafter, Beiruti Sunni leader Riad al-Sulh made an oral agreement with a new ally, Maronite Bishara al-Khoury. This Christian-Muslim National Pact had roots in late Ottoman Mount Lebanon and in the Mandate, and crystallized two more recent developments. Politically, from the mid-1930s, most Sunnis acquiesced to Lebanon's separation from Syria and to a certain Western affinity. Vice versa, more and more Maronites accepted Lebanon to be an Arab country rather than a Christian French protectorate. And economically, Beirut's commercial-financial elite families, Sunnis and Christians alike, appreciated the advantage of keeping ties to both the West and to the *mashriq*.[13]

Tripoli's *zu'ama'* were unhappy with the tone of the National Pact, however. It was too Lebano-centric and Beirut-centric for their taste. But like in 1937 they fell in line, participating in a last stand-off with France, in November 1943. When that month, now-Prime Minister al-Sulh, backed by now-president al-Khoury, suppressed all mention of the Mandate in Lebanon's constitution, Free French troops arrested dozens of nationalists, including leaders such as Tripolitan Karami from cities other than Beirut. The subsequent protests—in Tripoli and all of Lebanon—forced France to release the prisoners and to accept Lebanon's independence.[14]

Over the following years, events in Tripoli and its *zu'ama'*'s role in Lebanese politics underlined the city's persistent self-regard—but also its painful limits imposed by a dominant Beirut. In the fall of 1944, during Lebanon-wide protests against galloping inflation and Beirut's (partly true, partly imagined) responsibility, Tripoli's *Shabab Watani* saw their city as the spear-point of a *watani* struggle. "Issued from the heart of Tripoli's population," its members declared to "join rank with the Lebanese people to condemn this despotic wave of inflation," for which the government in Beirut was responsible. Shortly after Karami became Lebanon's second prime minister in January 1945, he grew frustrated. His attempts to loosen the power of Beirut's political and mercantile elites, for instance by giving trade quotas to Tripolitans, was torpedoed time and again, with al-Sulh a mastermind in the capital's press and officialdom. Also, most Beiruti Sunni leaders refused to accept a non-Beiruti like Karami as a peer, that is as Lebanese prime minister material. Even a friend of his, Beiruti Christian banker and politician Henri Pharaon, in 1945 noted that he still "appears more Syrian than Lebanese." Karami resigned in August 1945.[15]

In the immediate postwar period, Tripoli continued to be the so-called capital of the North—second to Beirut, but only to it. In the wake of Karami's funeral five years after the war, in 1950, the Karamis extolled their power—and by extension asserted Tripoli's weight—by

Figure 5.1  A photograph of 'Abd al-Hamid Karami's empty chair, surrounded by Beiruti
notables, at the moment of his death in 1950. N. Imam, *al-Sahafi al-laji' Nur al-Din al-Imam
yuqaddim dhikrat al-za'im 'Abd al-Hamid Karami* (Beirut: N. Imam, 1951).

asking a Tripolitan, Nur al-Din Imam, to compose a book on the funeral. He delivered. He waxed lyrical about how Tripoli had paid its
respect—and made the capital Beirut omnipresent as number two, always behind Karami's Tripoli. He included a photo, taken in the American University hospital the moment Karami's death is announced, that
centers on a symbolically empty chair around which sits and stands,
jam-packed, the crème de la crème of Sunni Beirut (Figure 5.1).

He highlighted that al-Sulh, at that point again Lebanon's Prime
Minister, attended not only Karami's funeral but also the third day com-
memoration, and he listed all other Beiruti government and community
leaders attending the rites. Tellingly, non-Beiruti Lebanese politicians
(including other Tripolitan *zu'ama'*) were barely mentioned, while Syrian
politicians attending were listed in great detail. What mattered to Tripoli
was its stature vis-à-vis Beirut, and one of its best weapons in the arsenal was its still strong, transnationalized link to Damascus. Meanwhile, the funeral procession was declared an official national event: for

not only Beirut but also Tripoli, and certainly a notable like Karami, could represent the entire nation-state if need be. In front, two Lebanese flags were carried by two youngsters. Next walked two dozen groups such as the scouts and a women's delegation, Christians and Druze. Second-last was the family. Last came the government led by the president, the same al-Khoury who later that day extolled Karami as the man who had "buttress[ed] [Lebanon's] sovereignty and independence and strengthen[ed] the National Pact and sign[ed] the Arab League pact and [Lebanon's] United Nations membership."[16]

The upshot of all this was not only a display of the Tripolitan Karami's importance to all of Lebanon, including Beirut, but—paradoxically—a highly symbolic acceptance of Lebanon and of its capital. The very fact that Beirut had to be present for Tripoli to feel truly important was the ultimate proof of the capital's dominance in Lebanon.

## Beirut

Indeed, this dominance continued unabated during the war. Beirut's decades-old administrative, commercial, and cultural centrality made it the obvious choice as Britain's headquarters in Lebanon and Syria. That it remained Lebanon's capital after independence, in 1943, only added to its weight. Consuls became ambassadors, and foreign luminaries now could be fêted in the city by a Lebanese government. At the same time, especially richer and well-connected Beirutis still saw their city not simply as a national capital, but more important as a regional and global player. The pattern set already in the nineteenth century, and tweaked yet not changed after 1918, persisted.[17]

No doubt, "the horizons of the world were closed" during the war, as influential banker, politician, author, and *Le Jour* newspaper owner Michel Chiha put it in a talk in 1942. Some previously imported goods disappeared or became expensive; and most crucial, the working classes suffered from runaway inflation. Yet Beirut protected its status as a media, education, consumerism, and culture heavyweight. It was the home of thirty-five out of forty-nine (70 percent) of all Lebanese newspapers and periodicals launched from 1939 to 1945. In the fall of 1943, the Lebanese Fine Arts Academy opened, with branches in music, painting, and architecture, and featuring teachers as renowned as Michel Ecochard, a French city planner formerly in Damascus. The following year, the expanding Muslim *Maqasid* school hired additional teachers. Department stores such as ABC stayed in business—its ads reading "you find all what you need in the ABC stores." Sellers of luxury goods survived, too: Persian carpet sellers continued to praise their incoming products, "Isfahani, Kashani, Tabrizi, and others." And when in October 1943 one Mrs. Jbaili let Beirut's well-heeled "elegant women" know, in a newspaper ad, that she had reopened her hair salon Henri Quatre after returning from her summer holidays, she was not alone. In the summer of 1944, for instance, almost 50,000 vacationers traveled in a single week from Beirut to mountain resorts overlooking the capital. Back in the city, people of reasonable means enjoyed life not much less than before the war. New private sports clubs opened their doors. Beirut continued to expand, adding not only 450,000 square meters of newly paved "roads and sidewalks [but also] public gardens . . . in various neighborhoods." Cafés and cinemas such as the Hollywood and the Roxy flourished, screening mainly Egyptian and American movies. And the Cairo-based Syrian-born film and music star Farid al-Atrash visited to give concerts in the winter of 1943, at the same time as adored Egyptian belly dancer and cinema actress Tahiya Karioka.[18]

In fact, Lebanon was too small for Beirut even during World War II. This was reflected in how leading Beirutis saw themselves in the world. Take Chiha and Pharaon, two Christians related by blood, marriage, and since their fathers' generation by the *Banque Pharaon et Chiha*. They held complementary perspectives on Beirut's position in the war. On the one hand, Lebanon was on their mind. After all, it was becoming independent, a process in which both Chiha and Pharaon were involved. Typically, Chiha's 1942 talk was titled "Liban d'aujourd'hui" (Lebanon today). It addressed national challenges, including sectarianism, and drew attention to Lebanon's global position. Chiha argued that already in Antiquity the Phoenicians had embodied Lebanon's centrality in the world—from cities on the Lebanese littoral, they had traveled the Mediterranean. He insisted that "situated at the meeting point of three continents, we [Lebanese] are obviously an ideal bridgehead." On a related note, speaking more than one language, including "magnificent Arabic," was vital: Lebanon *had* to be "bi-lingual (even tri-lingual, if possible)" to thrive and link "Orient [and] . . . Occident."[19]

On the other hand, in a collection of short daily reflections, Chiha neither analyzed the pains of regular Lebanese nor commented on everyday national politics. In dozens of entries, Lebanon featured only as beautiful nature: as "sea and mountain" which to "neglect would be a failing of our soul," or as the place where "the snow turns pink and the mountain a dark amethyst-violet" "after a business day."[20] Beirut mattered more than Lebanon. In an entry called "Voyages," for instance, it connected to cities like Calcutta and countries like Burma and China. But this also showed that to Chiha, Beirut's value lied not simply in itself, but in being the place from which he joined the world, or more precisely, the place in which he could be in the world at large—that of business and of a West-centric universal culture. This perspective was not new. As Chapter 1 explained, Beirut had been Bilad al-Sham's principal entry point for anything Western from the mid-1800s, and the region's cultural-educational gravitation point. What was noteworthy about the persistence of this perspective in 1939–1945 was that Beirut's country, Lebanon, became independent, and that a world war was raging. While Chiha was clear-eyed about both—he noted that the times had passed when "*all* history was the History of France"—he then doubled down, asserting that even now France's "spiritual forces" remained unbroken. Not by chance, he wrote in French and his references were European—Mozart and Beethoven, Larivière, Philippe de Valois and Eduard III. And despite Europe's very own insane war, the antidote to the nascent "machine age" he bemoaned was the civilization, art, and literature of the Old Continent and in particular of France.[21]

Although most elite Beiruti Sunnis (and some Christians) would have disagreed with Chiha's ostentatious Franco-centrism, they, too, embraced Beirut's centrality. Like Chiha, they saw Beirut as their pied-à-terre in the world. Born in Alexandria, Pharaon was educated in Beirut, France, and Switzerland, then returned to Beirut to work in the family's far-flung business; in 1922 he brought to Beirut his fiancée, Nawali Kassar, the daughter of a merchant from Jaffa whom he had met on her family's tennis court; and throughout his life he was fascinated by Arab racehorses and by Byzantine, Arab, and Islamic art. Even during World War II he regularly visited Syria where he met and befriended sellers; and he arranged his home and life such that he experienced those Arab / Islamic worlds in Beirut. To him his city was the connecting point par excellence between "West" and "East," between economic-financial circuits and the Arab-Islamic world and past. Thus, he groomed a premier racehorse stable and for decades, and throughout the war, managed Beirut's racetrack that Alfred Sursock had built in the late 1910s. And his home, a virtual museum of antiquities, he rebuilt continuously from 1929 through the war years to the 1960s, using materials collected during his Syrian travels.[22]

## Tel Aviv

In the 1930s and World War II, there was a city in the Yishuv that started to approach Beirut's cultural energy: Tel Aviv. There was no competition between the two cities, however. Founded in 1909, Hebrew Tel Aviv was smaller than Beirut, counting 160,000 inhabitants in 1939 and 190,000 in 1944. Moreover, it could not challenge the globally networked and Arab city of Beirut for the position of Bilad al-Sham's ultimate culture, education, and media center. But it also chose not to do so, for it fashioned itself a distinctive place in its nation-state space much more than Beirut did. Even so, like Beirut, it insisted that its identity was linked to and part of modern, secular, Western culture; that it hence was a dynamic city of the world more than simply of its own national environs; and that this gave it an edge in those environs. In fact, because Tel Aviv—unlike any other city examined in this book—had no past, no time-honored space of its own to boast, it itched to be part of the world, to prove its relevance through its worldliness, during the war not less than before.

This showed, for one thing, in how Tel Aviv set itself apart from other places in Palestine. The city associated what it perceived as negative traits—ugliness, disorder, underdevelopment—with other places. Two sets of places to be precise: Jewish and Arab, an example par excellence of how Zionism tackled Jewish Selves as much as it defined itself vis-à-vis Gentile Others. Especially from the 1936 Arab Revolt but in essence from 1909, Tel Aviv "could develop its own contrary urban identity" in relation to "dirty," "violent," "unmodern" Arab Jaffa. From the 1930s, when it grew dramatically, it feared also so-called Levantinization, chaos. Moreover, as journalist Bar Drora asserted, Jewish "Jerusalem, Hebron, Tiberias, Haifa, etc.—each one of these cities has a history of thousands of years. . . . [In] Tel Aviv, not a single house stood thirty years ago, but this graceful woman already has her history—the history of relentless venture, of renewal and novelty, day after day." To be sure, Tel Avivians often feared that the characteristics of such Arab and Jewish cities—unmodern subversions of proper Zionist life à la Tel Aviv—affected their very own city, too. The municipality and other Tel Avivians tried to better manage unsupervised children, prostitutes visible especially now that thousands of Allied soldiers were stationed in and around the wartime city, Arab sellers and peddlers and Mizrahi Jews, as well as the (Eastern European) Ashkenazi men who jaywalked or women who dried clothes, underwear and all, on their apartment façade's washing line.[23]

Despite these concerns about appearances and identity, Tel Avivians fervently believed their city was making a distinctive contribution to the Yishuv. Take its coat of arms. It is drawn with waves in the foreground from the viewpoint of a sea-borne immigrant. In the background is the gate to the Promised Land. And it is topped by a "Beacon of Light to the Diaspora," as town clerk Yehuda Nedivi put it. This tallied with Jewish-only Tel Aviv's self-image as "the First Hebrew City". From the late 1920s various Zionist parties and organizations, like the Histadrut, made Tel Aviv their headquarters, and the city's massive municipal operations made it a "miniature National Home" in mayor Meir Dizengoff's words. From the late 1930s through World War II to 1950, Tel Aviv steadily became the Yishuv's de facto capital. It was home to the General Headquarters of the Jewish Agency's military, the Hagana, which was established semi-secretly in 1939. Here, too, from 1948–1950, were the Asefat ha-Nivharim legislative and to the Zionist Organization executive, otherwise in Jerusalem.[24]

Tel Aviv's positive self-image was that of a city clean and proper, secular modern, driven by commercial, manufacturing, and architectural ingenuity, and lively and joyous on top—the place for a distinctive, European-style bourgeois Zionist dream. Tel Avivians, just like city dwellers of other cities in Bilad al-Sham, if in a distinct way, tooted their own horn. Tel Aviv's "shops [are] full, the bank queues alive, the stream of people in the streets . . . endless," Nedivi boasted in 1941, and his inventory of glories included 10 secondary schools, 37 primary schools, and 38 kindergartens, almost all municipal and teaching 20,000 pupils, the Herzliah College, most Yishuvi publishing houses, all major Hebrew dailies, numerous periodicals, theatres, and the Palestine Orchestra, which "has already been privileged to play under the conductorship of world-masters such as Toscanini, Dr Malcolm Sargent, Weingartner and others."[25]

Around the same time, in 1940, artist Noah Berezovsky found another way of displaying Tel Aviv—the real way, as a commentator asserted. The way that unearths "the hidden something . . . that is specific precisely" to Tel Aviv: drawings of its "personalities, entrepreneurs, writers, artists." Berezovsky produced a book of 154 individual drawings, with short bios attached, most of men, a few of women. For good measure, he added 150 miniature drawings of all journalists of the newspapers Davar, Haaretz, and Ha-Boker, of the actors of the Ha-Bima and Ha-Matate theaters, and of the musicians of the Palestine Orchestra. Remarkable was not simply the quantity of Tel Aviv's crème de la crème; or that Berezovsky described these men's and women's work as vital for the entire Yishuv; or that to Berezovsky, an inhabitant of a city lacking the historic buildings of a city such as Jerusalem, it made sense to portray his city through its personalities. Remarkable, too, and reflective of the secular bourgeois culture setting the tone in Tel Aviv, was that neither rabbis in kaftans nor pioneers in khakis made it into Berezovsky's collection. Except the Labor movement Davar journalists and a handful others, men wore ties and jackets. A few, such as Ha-Boker's Gavriel Tsifroni, smoked a pipe. And Ha-Bima codirector and actor Hanna Rovina, the Minsk-born "First Lady of Hebrew Theater," even sported bejewelled earrings.[26]

Ha-Bima, in fact, was a striking example of how Tel Aviv constructed itself as the pioneer of an urbane, secular Zionism open to the world. If the theater's language of choice, Hebrew, was a cultural-ideological statement, its history illustrated the global character of Zionism. Its origins dated back to 1912 in Polish (then Russian) Białistok; it took off in Moscow in 1918; moved to New York in 1926; and split in 1928 when some members left for Tel Aviv—where they performed a few plays in Yiddish, too. Furthermore, when from 1935 to 1945 Berlin-trained Hungarian Jewish architect Oskar Kaufman built the theater's lasting home, it was in the same clean, modernist International Style that he had used for theater constructions in Berlin and Vienna: a style whose *Bauhaus* version was on display in hundreds of other edifices in 1930s Tel Aviv.

For Jews, Tel Aviv's worldly energies even showed in the most terrible dimension of World War II: the Holocaust. Jews who made it out of Europe were stunned by Tel Aviv's wartime "tranquility and hedonism." This did not mean that Europe was not on Tel Avivians' mind. On June 5, 1944, for instance, thousands crowded into and around Tel Aviv's Great Synagogue after the Chief Rabbinate had declared "a day of fasting and mourning . . . for the destruction of the Jewry of Hungary, the last remnant of European Jewry. . . . During the saying of psalms, the blowing of the Shofar, and the Memorial prayer, crying and wailing tore the sky open and rent hearts, especially when [people] sat on the ground for the Mourning prayers." It was a moment of catharsis for men and women who were not only helpless but removed from Europe by an entire sea, the same Mediterranean at whose beach they swam and sunbathed with abandon. It was against this background of a however tragic normalcy that Ashkenazi Chief Rabbi Amiel half admonished, half implored them: "And again we congregate *en masse,* to scream and forewarn, cry and lament. . . . And when you ask, what use is all this . . . one needs to answer that we come first and foremost to cure ourselves from the most dangerous disease that has infected us, the disease of paralysis. . . . Even as we read every day about the annihilation, Heaven Forbid, of myriads, of hundreds, thousands, and millions of our brothers, of our own flesh and blood, among us normalcy reigns supreme": *'olam ke-minhago noheg.*[27]

Amiel's cri de coeur reflected in the most heart-rending way possible that interwar cultural self-views and practices persisted in World War II. From here, from his *'olam ke-minhago noheg,* it is hard to simply move on. Still, the reality remains that Tel Aviv's wartime experience was part and parcel of a region-wide pattern. This will now be explored through one last case, Damascus, with a glance at Aleppo. Like the other cities, Damascus experienced basic continuity relative to the 1930s with a particular twist.

## Damascus and Aleppo

As Syria was reaching for independence, and as Damascus remained its capital, the capital effect analyzed in Chapters 3 and 4 persisted. After all, it was in Damascus that fateful political decisions were taken on behalf of Syria. An instance was the nationalists' move, in Syria's parliament, to strike the French Mandate from Syria's constitution in late 1943. Similarly, anti-French demonstrations in Syria were often best organized, and for the French most sensitive, in Damascus. In May 1945, the capital saw the fiercest clashes in Syria between demonstrators and French forces whom de Gaulle used in order to try (in vain) to make Syria and Lebanon sign a special treaty with France. And in an act of violence which was also symbolic, and which indicated that French Brigadier-General François Oliva-Roget too appreciated Damascus's capital effect, he had his artillery target the parliament building and his soldiers ransack it and slaughter all its guards.

Despite the significance of Damascus, Aleppo continued carrying weight in Syria, too. It boasted about the same number of leading newspapers as Damascus. Self-confident pupils of one of its principal secondary schools, the nationalist *Tajhiz,* published a periodical that addressed classmates not only in their school but in all of Syria. And Aleppo's National Bloc politicians asserted themselves, again falling out with their Damascene counterparts. In fact, following World War II, the National Bloc would split into a Damascus-centered National Party that was foreign-politically oriented southward, to Saudi Arabia and Egypt, and an Aleppo-centered People Party looking eastward, to Iraq. Back during the war, when the two cities' ties were shaky but not yet broken and France was not yet expelled, the Damascene notable, National Bloc leader, and eventual first Syrian president Shukri al-Quwatli woed Aleppo. When he went on a national tour in in May 1943, he made sure to first honor Aleppo. There, he started a speech full of praise: "I am surrounded by the extraordinary elite of the personalities of this noble city . . . amongst brethren who have stood in defense of their country's cause." He continued by implying equality with Damascus, telling his audience that "on this journey I bring to Aleppo greetings from your brothers in Damascus," and vowing that he wished to "meet all you [brothers] . . . and exchange opinions."[28]

But then, at the peak of his speech, his pitch subtly changed. "It over-joys me to announce that the past differences are over," he affirmed, and insisted, quite the father of the nation, that becoming independent "re-quires sacrifice and fighting individual egoism . . . for the sake of public egoism." Moreover, he of course felt at home most in Damascus, and in particular in his own neighborhood, Shaghur. In a speech there two months after his Syria tour, the horizontal vocabulary of Aleppo—talk of a "burden shared" by Damascenes and Aleppines, and by other Syrians—was out. In was the splicing of capital city and nation, of which al-Qauwatli thought in concentric circles: "I am a son not only of this neighborhood, I am a son of Damascus including all its neighbor-hoods, its different quarters and houses, I am a son of Syria, and I am a son of the Arabs," he intoned. And when he added "oh brothers," he meant it, for he had just "thank[ed] the people of this quarter and this city, because they stand shoulder to shoulder and talk with one voice; and behind this, behind this harmony and this unity, they aim for nothing but the uplift of their nation, its strengthening, and its sovereignty." Here, there was no trace of "individual egoism."[29]

The Muslim world continued to be a vital reference point for Dama-scenes during the war. The Gharra' schools remained open; *al-Rabita al-Islamiyya,* the religious journal with a strong Arab nationalist bent, still appeared; and Islamic texts continued to be published. Some au-thors, like 'Abd al-Fattah al-Imam, a scholar and comanager of the Damascene Islamic Civilization Association, published Quran exe-geses; others wrote anthologies of poems praising the Prophet Mu-hammad. Muhammad Jamal al-Din Malas explained their "ben-efit . . . [as] emulating [the prophet], being perfumed by his character, seeking to increase one's love for him"—intentions that were manifest in the opening stanza of the first poem in his anthology: "*ya ashraf khalq wa-ya ajall nabi'/ ma mithluka fi sa'ir khaliqat al-insan*" (oh most illustrious of creatures, oh most sublime prophet / you have no equal amongst humans).[30]

If Malas chose this poem for its directness, the Muslim Spanish provenance of its author, Ibn al-Hakim al-Andalusi, also exemplified that Damascus still framed itself as a central place in the Muslim world at large. Malas embodied this situation. The title page of his anthology introduced him as "a servant of Islam in India, China, and Java." It was to those parts—and to Iraq, Kuwait, and Bahrain, presumably vis-à-vis Shiis, and to Japan—that he, in 1929, had been inspired to travel and work by his teacher and preeminent scholar, Muhammad Badr al-Din al-Hasani. Moreover, back in Malas's anthology, a long introduction was penned by a group of scholars from one of the world's leading religious schools, Cairo's al-Azhar.[31]

Also new biographies continued to emphasize Damascus's importance in the Muslim world. Take *Rawd al-Bashar fi A'yan Dimashq fi al-Qarn al-Thalith 'Ashar,* a biography of Damascene notables deceased between 1786 and 1882 by Muhammad Jamil al-Shatti, the city's mufti of the (Sunni) Hanbali school. It resembled the biography parts of Muhammad al-Hisni's *Muntakhabat al-Tawarikh li-Dimashq* (see Chapter 3) in that it asserted Damascus's centrality in the Muslim World.[32] Al-Shatti did not only provide city-centered information, which often simply pointed back to Damascus's role in the Muslim world. He also boasted that Damascene scholars were impressive enough to work in other cities: thus, in 1786 Isma'il Effendi Katibzadih became judge in the Holy City of Medina. Damascus also retained extraordinary students like 'Abd al-Rahman al-Kuzbari, born in Damascus in 1771, "whose shoes nobody could fill"; and attracted famous foreigners like the Kurdish Sufi Khalid al-Naqshabandi, who lived there in the early 1800s. Furthermore, al-Shatti's original intention had been to compile a biography collection in which Damascus would rub shoulders with Cairo, its principal peer, and with Nablus and Homs, two cities tightly linked to it, while paying some attention also to Yemen, the Hijaz, Iraq, Aleppo, Hama, and Tripoli. It was only after thirty-six years of on-and-off work, in 1941, when that plan turned out to be too ambitious, that he zoomed in on Damascus. Or more precisely: on *"our* city Damascus," a quote which brings us full circle, indicating that the primary audience of *Rawd al-Bashar* was Damascenes.[33]

Another book published in World War II, *Dimashq: Madinat al-Sihr wa-l-Shi'r,* loved to love its city, too. Its very title praised *Damascus: City of Charm and Poetry.* And its author, Muhammad Kurd 'Ali, whom we have met in previous chapters, asserted his native town's geographic and historical centrality. "Due to its proximity to the Arabian Peninsula, Iraq, the Jazira [the river plane in today's northeastern Syria and northwestern Iraq], and Egypt, Damascus was a trading city that connected East and West," he stated. And the title page of his book read the verse "*Lawla Dimashq la-ma kanat Tulaitila/wa-la sahat bi-Bani al-Abbas Baghdan*" (without Damascus there would have been no Toledo/and Abbasid Baghdad would not have bloomed), referring to Muslim Spain and to Islam's second dynasty.[34]

But unlike al-Shatti, Kurd 'Ali wrote for the present. His book's longest section was "the political history of Damascus." It took pride in Syria's and Lebanon's independence, in 1943; commented on the ongoing negotiations about an Arab League; and featured a regional capital effect. The line "Arab countries started negotiations about forming a unity between Egypt, *al-Sham,* Iraq, and the Arab Peninsula," made Damascus not only Syria but also Greater Syria, playing on *al-Sham*'s double meaning. Given that Kurd 'Ali had authored a monument to the region, *Khitat al-Sham,* this was not surprising, though still striking for the postindependence year 1944. But truly eye-opening was how the above quote ended: "and if this wish is realized, which Damascus ardently desires, then she will become, after Cairo, the second capital of this unity, mediating between the Arab regions."[35]

Syria's leading, Damascene statesmen were receptive to Cairo, not the least to use it to balance out the still-present French. Intellectuals seconded them. Kurd 'Ali's *Dimashq* addressed not Damascenes, as al-Shatti's *Rawd al-Bashar,* but Arabs and particularly Egyptians. Besides calling Cairo the first Arab capital, the verse he selected for his title page, "Without Damascus," was by an Egyptian—Ahmad Shawqi, *Amir al-Shu'ara',* the Prince of Poets, who in 1926 had responded to the French repression of the Syrian Revolt with another poem, titled "Dimashq"—and his book was printed by a Cairene press, Matba'at al-Ma'arif.

## Bilad al-Sham's Declining Cultural Importance and
## Growing Arab Connectivities

Bilad al-Sham continued to change in 1939–1945, as it had done in the interwar decades when it had transformed from a patchwork region of cities to an umbrella region of nation-states. During World War II, this umbrella became less relevant as two processes took place. The region's nation-states reached for independence, and various Arab countries became yet more strongly tied together transnationally. As nation-states became more deeply grounded within the Arab world—which from the mid-1940s became a more current term, *al-ʿalam al-ʿarabi*[36]—the postcolonial Arab state system started to crystallize. In both processes Bilad al-Sham's nation-states were directly involved, country by country, rather than in a mediated regional form. This was a distinct change relative to the 1930s.

*Qawmiyya,* pan-Arab nationalism, had existed decades before World War II, and from the 1930s many Arabs saw Egypt as part of a wider Arab political arena. Still, the conditions and experience of World War II—the short-termed decrease of massive commercial and cultural ties to Western Europe and increase of trade and infrastructure; the independence of additional Arab states and the resultant dawn of an independent Arab state system, helped along by French weakness and British toleration; and the centrality of Egypt to the British-controlled Middle East—had a cumulative effect. Arabs drew yet a bit closer; the Egyptian state flexed a realpolitik *qawmi* muscle, mainly by promoting a league of Arab states; and Egypt became more central culturally.[37]

Kurd ʿAli's *Dimashq* illustrated this trend also by being part of a new book series, *Iqraʾ*, Read!, which was founded by Ahmad Amin, *Matbaʿat al-Maʿarif*'s editor, in 1943, a few years after cheap paperback series like Penguin and Pocket Books were launched in the British Empire and in the United States. The series was supervised by Taha Husayn, a leading Egyptian intellectual. In the preface to the inaugurational book, Husayn's own *Ahlam Shahrazad*, he surmised that Amin had chosen the name *Iqraʾ* because it was God's well-known Quranic imperative to Muhammad. Distinctly nontraditional, though, was the figure "*Iqraʾ*" that adorned the title page of Husayn's (and Kurd ʿAli's) book. Its letters were shaped in ninety-degree angles rather than calligraphic curves, composing a clean, modernist-looking square. Husayn's preface was pointedly contemporary as well. Due to advances in "civilization" and "democracy," he stated, "reading has become a universal right for everybody, nay a definitive duty for everybody." "There is nothing like reading to make people think, express themselves, and exercise their citizenship." The "short, straight, cheap books" of *Iqra'* would help to realize this idea. They would do so for "the Arab peoples"—from Cairo, it went without saying. Husayn's broad audience signified a shift from his landmark 1936 work *Mustaqbal al-Thaqafa fi Masr, the Future of Culture in Egypt,* a public intellectual intervention in Egyptian affairs. But this was a slight shift, for *Mustaqbal* had declared that Egypt could and should become the Arabs' cultural and educational leader. Husayn's note on *Iqra'* just projected his Egypto-centrism more plainly into the Arab world.[38]

Snippets of letters to the publisher reprinted in the back pages of Kurd 'Ali's *Dimashq* suggested that Arab readers appreciated the Cairene *Iqra'* initiative. But shining through them, too, was the theme "unity in multiplicity." The publisher started with quotes from Egypt, five in number; then came one from Sudan, two from Palestine, one from Transjordan, two from Syria and Lebanon, and two from Iraq. An Egyptian hailed the series "an enormous *qawmi* capital"; an Iraqi attested it to have "brought the praiseworthy [act of] reading closer to the sons of Arabness, *abna' al-'uruba.* Long live Egypt, and long live its literati." And a Syro-Lebanese snarked, "in the series *Iqra'* I expected to read how literature in Egypt has turned business," but then acknowledged that "reality taught me better." Arabs were growing closer, and Egypt's importance as an Arab leader grew. Still, sub-*qawmi, watani,* identities were persisting. And in Bilad al-Sham's countries, those identities were basically no longer mediated through a shared regional setting, but were formulated country by country.[39]

The intensifying Arab connectivity of the countries of Bilad al-Sham was the perhaps principal, but not the only, transnational trend unfolding in World War II. Bonds between people in Bilad al-Sham's countries and overseas diasporas, noted in past chapters, formed another trend.[40] Yet another, internal to Bilad al-Sham, was the resumption of a connection that had faded in the late 1930s, between Lebanese, principally Beirut-based, individuals and institutions and Zionist institutions in Palestine such as the Economic Research Institute (ERI) in Jerusalem that was comanaged by Alfred Bonné and cosponsored by the Zionist Organization. In 1940, Bonné met with Beiruti "journalists and people working at AUB." In 1943, he met with Tripoli's leading industrialist Georges Arida, discussing postwar Arab state federation and customs-free zone plans then under discussion by Arab states and by some in the Yishuv, including Bonné; with AUB economics professor George Hakim; with the (Jewish) editor of Beirut's *Commerce du Levant,* Tawfiq Mizrahi; and through him with the (unidentified) Beirut Chamber of Commerce vice president, an open anti-Zionist, as Bonné noted. In 1945, he met with officials from the Intérêts Communs, the Beirut-based Syro-Lebanese Customs-and-Budget commission, who agreed to permanently exchange economic data. That year, too, Bonné hosted *Commerce* journalist Émile Sailhoun at the ERI, for research.[41]

These contacts were a complex affair. On the one hand, some Beirutis opposed Zionism, and Bonné reported back to the Zionist Organization, which of course had clear political interests at heart. On the other hand, the two sides shared an interest in Greater-Syria and Arab-wide economic questions and policy, and had an awareness of living in the same place. In that sense, their contacts formed part of a longer arc, traced in Chapters 3 and 4, of the Yishuv situating itself within the region and of Beirutis feeling confident and cosmopolitan enough to engage Zionists.

## The Concentration of Economic Power and Bilad al-Sham's Decline

Economic development and the relationship between the region and its nation-states echoed the cultural developments of the 1939 to 1945: the regional umbrella mattered less than in the 1930s. The two principal reasons were Britain's 1940–1941 embargo of Vichy-ruled Syria and Lebanon, and, more important, its creation, in 1941, of a Middle East-wide market transcending Bilad al-Sham. Moreover, extensive economic British investments benefited many in Bilad al-Sham, but mostly those who already had most—and had been developed most—at the start of the war. Of Bilad al-Sham's four countries, the Yishuv did best. Within each country, the cities that had been economically most powerful in 1939 did best. And in many cities, it was the individuals best placed in 1939 who earned most. Put differently, peak (British empire) state territorialization of World War II did not simply intersect with and help nation-state formation, but turned it into a socio-spatially more concentrated process.

## The Yishuv Triumphant

As we saw in Chapter 4, already in the late 1930s Yishuvi manufacturing exports to Lebanon and Syria had started growing. In 1939, this trend was cemented by the Franco-British revision of the 1929 regional trade agreement, canceling disadvantages, to Palestine, about which especially Zionists had complained from the mid-1930s. The war sped up this development. When trade between Palestine and Lebanon / Syria resumed in 1941, the two had switched places. Although the overall region-wide trade volume slightly contracted during the war, Palestine's exports to Lebanon / Syria almost tripled between 1938 and 1944, from 36,000 to 101,000 tons.[42] Among Middle Eastern exporters, Palestine developed a real grip on Lebanon and Syria. If already in 1938 Palestine's exports to Lebanon and Syria were 33 percent larger than Egypt's and Iraq's and almost 60 percent larger than Turkey's, in 1944 those figures had ballooned to about 600 percent, 620 percent, and 1,100 percent.[43] Moreover, Palestine's expanding manufacturing base, which during the war faced almost no peace-time Western and Japanese competition, allowed it to increase its export into MESC countries up to eighty times the prewar level.[44] Still, in absolute figures, Lebanon and Syria remained Palestine's premier Middle East export market, worth LP1,431,488 in 1945.[45] By contrast, because France from 1939 to 1940, Vichy until 1941, and Britain until 1945, feared shortages in Lebanon and Syria, they not only massively expanded key manufacturing and agricultural sectors, but also kept most goods at home. In result, Lebanese-Syrian exports plunged between 1938 and 1944—to Palestine from 101,000 to 21,000 tons.[46]

Regarding overall trade, in Lebanon and Syria "Allied trade policy . . . reduced import volume on average by 24 per cent between 1939 and 1945 over 1935–8, and export volume by 71 per cent from 1942 to 1945 over 1935–8." And "by 1943, Middle Eastern countries furnished almost 90 per cent of total Syro-Lebanese imports, compared with 23 per cent in 1938; nearly 97 per cent of Syro-Lebanese exports were sold within the Middle East in 1943, compared with 37 per cent in 1938."[47] As for Palestine, plummeting world trade at first cut its nonoil imports from LP14.6 million in 1939 to LP12.3 million in 1941. It recovered to LP20.2 million in 1943 and LP31.2 million in 1945, with British colonies, the United States, and Britain constituting more than three quarters in 1945.[48] Regular exports first fell, too, from LP5.1 million in 1939 to a low of LP2.1 million in 1941, but then rose to LP7.4 million in 1943 and to LP14 million in 1945. But most crucial were the "invisible exports" to the British army, principally manufactured goods and some services and agricultural products. These exploded from LP2.6 million in 1939 to LP20.7 million in 1941, peaked at LP31.5 million in 1943, and still stood at LP24.3 million in 1945. This was a whopping "76 percent of the value of all goods and services exported in 1941 . . . and an average of 59 percent in the remaining war years."[49]

These numbers were reflected in the expansion of Yishuvi factories in response to British wartime demand: from 1,556 in 1937 to 2,120 in 1943. The Yishuv illustrated that the strongest manufacturing centers, in 1939, profited most during the war. Factories were concentrated in Haifa and Tel Aviv, with the former persisting as the center of the largest factories. In 1937, Haifa had 265, Tel Aviv 708, and Tel Aviv's vicinity 98 factories, equaling 17 percent, 46 percent, and 7 percent of the Yishuv's total, respectively—70 percent in all. By 1943 these numbers had risen to 289 (14 percent), 1,286 (61 percent), and 141 (7 percent)—82 percent.[50]

The British Empire gave the Yishuv, and especially Tel Aviv and Haifa, such a lift because, fighting an all-out war for its very survival, it wanted as great "a bang for the buck" as it could get and as quickly as possible. Though it invested in Palestinian manufacturing, it dealt even more with people whose economic (and political) demands it had given preferential treatment in the 1930s, who possessed a more educated work force, and who were technologically more advanced: that is, with Yishuvi manufacturers. While tens of thousands of Arabs and Jews found employment in British-run or British-financed factories and installations from 1940, and while Arab entrepreneurs profited, too, Jewish industrialists were best off. "Between 1940 and 1946, some LP12 million were invested in Jewish-owned industrial enterprises in Palestine, almost double the total for the entire 1930s. [And] British and Allied military expenditures in Palestine for goods ranging from clothing to processed food products to ammunition, for construction and for maintenance and repair services . . . reached some LP12 million in 1943."[51]

This development facilitated the Yishuv's consolidation as a nation-state in the making, a process that showed also in the expansion of Yishuvi manufacturing and exports in the MESC area. This expansion was manifested not only in cold numbers, but in specific business deals, in how the Yishuv presented itself, and in individuals' and Jewish Agency debates about the Yishuv's role in the region during the war and in the postwar future. In one example, in late 1944 unnamed Yishuvi "capitalists" were financing a new Lebanese conserve factory, to be established together with Mitri and Basil Chami, from Beirut, and to be operated with machinery allegedly smuggled from Palestine. Around the same time, George Arida's Tripolitan textile factory had hired a new manager, Mr. Mannheimer, who "through his excellent knowledge of spinning machinery [had] improved the production by 25%."[52]

As for exports, a particularly important case was the construction and service operations of Solel Boneh (Pave and Build), a construction and civil engineering company founded in 1921 as a branch of the Histadrut, the Yishuv's principle, powerful Labor Union. In wartime Iraq, it was a contractor for the then mainly British-managed Iraq Petroleum Company. In Lebanon and Syria, it worked with Britain from 1941 until 1946. Here, one reason for its success was that in 1941–1942 Free France prevented Syrians and Lebanese from being employed by the British Army. In fact, Catroux opposed Solel Boneh, too, but failed. Immediately following the British occupation, in July 1941, Solel Boneh teamed up with a Beiruti player of ample connections, influence, and capital in Lebanon and Syria: Albert Pharaon. Together, they formed Pharaon-Solel Boneh Engineers and General Contractors. British forces chose Solel Boneh because it had worked with and for the government in Jerusalem from 1921. In fact, in Palestine Britain had expanded its use of Solel Boneh's services immediately after the start of the war, in 1939. The resulting trust mattered doubly at this point, the summer of 1941, because Britain was frantically planning and building a defense scheme against a possible German push via Turkey and Lebanon and Syria / Palestine down to Egypt. From various offices, headquarters in Damascus and Beirut, and with Jewish specialists from Palestine, Solel Boneh built, among other installations, roads in Lebanon and Syria, army workshops in Rayak airport, various buildings in Tripoli and Damascus, a hospital in Asfuriyyeh, near Sidon, and as late as the fall of 1945, British army barracks near Damascus.[53]

The Yishuv's economic empowerment in the region was echoed in its self-confidence. We witnessed this, quasi-metaphorically, in the relaxed posture of the Rabino brothers (see Figure P5.1). It was manifest, too, on official occasions like the opening, in Cairo in August 1941, of the Palestine Government Industrial Exhibition. Initiated by Jerusalem's British rulers to market Palestine to the high command in Cairo and to Egyptian importers, that exhibition showcased Palestinian manufactured products and was attended by a powerful Palestinian, Rashid Hajj Ibrahim, Haifa Chamber of Commerce head. However, he was outnumbered by a dozen Jewish entrepreneurs, including the heads of the Haifa and of the Tel Aviv / Jaffa (Jewish) Chambers of Commerce, and by top-level Jewish Agency officials like Eliezer Hoofien. The story was the same with journalists: one Palestinian; half a dozen Jews. The Yishuv and its press took great pride in their industry's wartime surge and did their best to promote it. Jewish Agency economists and Yishuvi manufacturers regularly published English articles for British eyes, feeding into long-held imperial visions of Yishuvi usefulness. In 1941 they even launched a new magazine, *Palestine and the Middle East*. In the "Home Front" section, an interview with Jewish Agency treasurer Eliezer Kaplan carried the subtitle "Palestine undaunted and unbroken [and] ready for full war effort." Economist K. Mendelsohn declared tiny Palestine to have a "significant place in the planned war economy" of the empire. And an interview with Palestine Manufacturers Association president Arie Shenkar titled "Industry's war service: Palestine as Middle East industrial arsenal."[54]

Accompanying such self-presentation were debates about the Yishuv's role in the Middle East. Regarding Bilad al-Sham, the 1939 Franco-British customs treaty revision was in principle a good starting point, judged Jewish Agency economist David Horowitz in 1940. But he also held that extraordinary war conditions had undercut some of the new treaty rules. Palestine suffered from French Lebanon and Syria's currency devaluation, and some Syrian "social dumping" still irked. Then again, from late 1940 to mid-1941 Britain's embargo on Vichy Lebanon and Syria greatly reduced trade and rendered moot the question of an extension of the 1939–1940 treaty. And from 1941 to 1945, Yishuvi manufacturing and exports soared, unobstructed by the northern neighbors.[55]

By 1944, with peace on the horizon, the Jewish Agency's Trade and Industry Department peered into the postwar future. Together with representatives of all Yishuvi economic branches, it created a forum to prepare positions for possible, British-led postwar trade negotiations with Arab countries, especially Lebanon and Syria. "We do not know when, and under which political circumstances, [such] negotiations . . . will take place, but hence we are duty bound to use the time and define our trade demands." A few hardnosed individuals advocated ending all special relations with Arab states. Tel Aviv economist A. Markus attacked as baseless the belief that these relations would remain the Yishuv's main noncitrus export market after the war. And no matter how low tariffs for imports into (Jewish) Palestine, "social and nationalist snobbism" guaranteed that Syria and other Arab countries would turn their back as much as possible on Yishuvi goods. Time would prove him right. From its birth in 1945, the Arab League called for a boycott of Yishuvi goods. Syrians and Lebanese were particularly active in this regard, seeking to reverse the Yishuv's penetration of their domestic markets. Vice versa, the Yishuv was averse to allowing Arab goods to dominate its market.[56]

The conclusion of the Jewish Agency-led forum differed from Markus's opinion, though. It planned to ask Britain to put teeth into the 1939 trade treaty in future negotiations. A "change . . . is absolutely necessary," it determined, and called for regular tariffs for imported manufactured Syrian / Lebanese goods. In its eyes the economic region of yore was dying. But dead: this, it was not. Indeed, it ought not be. The Jewish Agency still desired preferential access to Syria and Lebanon and was willing to grant them some preferred access in return. However, it wanted a new treaty to treat its two signatories differently. Unlike the 1939 treaty, not the same types of goods ought to profit from reduced or canceled tariffs: "citrus fruit and some manufactured goods" from Palestine versus "some agricultural goods and raw materials" from Lebanon and Syria.[57]

Thus, the Jewish Agency saw the Yishuv's future in the region as an industrial center for mainly agricultural Arab countries and was determined not to let Syrian (and Lebanese) manufacturers get in the way. This was a new variation—a Wallersteinian-type core-periphery arrangement—of an endeavor that we saw already in the 1930s: to have one's cake and eat it, too, to seek open access to the market of one's neighbors in Bilad al-Sham while regulating their access to one's own. This view had, in fact, taken root before 1944.[58] In 1942 the Jewish Agency-sponsored Economic Research Institute produced a position paper about a possible future Palestine-Syrian-Iraqi customs unit. It argued that given the wartime surge in Yishuvi production and exports to its neighbors, especially Lebanon and Syria, a customs federation should again be considered. Although "Britain will be [Palestine's] first or second" export market after World War II just like before, the changes induced by the war meant that now, "Palestine can expand its import of raw and semi-raw products from [Syria and Iraq] not insubstantially [and] . . . supply [Syria and Iraq] with manufactured products better than before the war."[59]

It is true, confidence was accompanied by concern about the negative effects of a federation, also regarding Syrian / Lebanese agricultural exports. As Chapter 4 showed, this matter had preoccupied Yishuvi officials and agriculturalists already in the 1930s, mainly for political-economic reasons of autarky and, from 1936, for reasons of food security. And as Prelude 5 showed, traders like Rabino and Kuris continued to import Syrian / Lebanese produce during the war. Indeed, this issue continued coming up in papers and Jewish Agency debates until late 1941. This was the case doubly because produce prices were rising, and with them calls for more agricultural imports, and because Yishuvi agriculture expansion had sped up from late 1939. The stakes were higher now. Thus, in January 1941, when Britain signaled it may reconsider its embargo of Vichy Lebanon and Syria, Jewish Agency economists Horowitz affirmed that "the continuation of the campaign for greater agricultural self-sufficiency is vital for the food supply of this country. . . . A resumption of imports from Syria on a broad scale at dumping prices . . . would lead to a total breakdown of the price structure of several important products of agriculture. . . . The heavy blow given to Palestine's mixed farming would be out of all proportion to both the relatively small gain arising from the decrease in the cost of living and to the danger involved in making the supply of the country entirely dependent on the resources of another country."[60]

But ultimately, Horowitz was more confident. His booklet from November 1943, *Postwar Reconstruction,* was echoed by the Jewish Agency forum's positions in 1944. Horowitz discussed the pros and cons of a state interventionist, Keynesian postwar policy (he was mainly in favor); insisted that Palestine would need to become more competitive; and asserted that a trend toward "regionality" may continue in the postwar Middle East, with Palestine in a central position. Building on that last point, he concluded by placing the Yishuv at the forefront for a better Middle East, as part of the solution to the problem of humankind's postwar development. "The problem of [the Middle East]: the agrarian question, the low standards of life, sweated labour, ruthless exploitation, the rule of the money-lender and land-owners, backwardness and technical retrogression, all of them can only be solved by a great impulse coming from new and dynamic forces not inherent in the social and economic life of the Middle East. Economic conditions are changeable, they are not static and stagnant but dynamic and fluctuating: 'Freedom from want' in this area is tantamount to rapid development and economic and social transformation."[61]

## Arab Palestine: Running to Stay in the Same Place

Even as it appears to the Arabs in this land that they are [enjoying] all-round welfare and abundant prosperity, we see the

truth hidden beneath this fake gold. . . . The reality appears
naked and [it is] not how we would love it to be. . . . The greatest
catastrophe is happening in the [form of the] occupation of our
national Arab polity for no other sin than us being Arabs. The
traditional policy of the Mandatory government has put the
Arabs and their country in strange economic conditions in its
[own] ways and evil in its thoughts. And the Zionist conspiracy
to kill the Arabs in their [very own] home is coming true, real-
izing the untrue, baseless dream about the establishment of a
Jewish state in this country, not only a national home![62]

This was not a nationalist activist firing up a crowd, but the Textiles
Executive Committee of the Arab Conference for Palestine, addressing
the British authorities. The year was 1944. Half a decade had passed
since the war started. Palestinians in general and entrepreneurs and
merchants in particular were doing well, but only if compared to their
prewar situation, not relative to the Yishuv. This was the Palestinians'
supreme economic problem during the war. The Textiles Executive
Committee's related complaint was as long as an arm. It listed various
manifestations: government price setting, import quotas, employment rates, and more; named Jews high up in the government's light
industry section: Esher, Strauss, Frankfurter, and others; and called
that section's structure "three-class": on top the "dominant" British,
just beneath them the "ruling" Jews, and on the bottom the "working"
Arabs.[63]

Palestinians understood that they again were left behind in their own
country. The Textiles Executive Committee was not the only body to
complain about Britain's economic policies. Individuals as prominent
as Hajj Ibrahim or the retailer Emile Boutagy, and many others, had
raised their voice already before 1944, and not only about the matters
raised by the Textiles Executive Committee. Merchants complained
about Britain allocating wartime import licences on the basis of a merchant's trade volume from mid-1938 to mid-1939. This systemically dis-
advantaged Palestinians, for during these years the revolt had dislocated
their economy. The overall situation was irksome enough for merchants
to declare a one-day strike on May 18, 1944. And continuing a prewar

pattern, they tried to strengthen their position in Palestine by recruiting other Arabs and Muslims. Thus, in 1944 they sent copies of a set of demands to the High Commissioner, to the governments of Egypt, Iraq, Saudi Arabia, Yemen, Syria, Lebanon, Transjordan, Turkey, and Iran.[64]

Then again, peak wartime (British empire) state territorialization further crystallized Palestine as a nation-state in the making. It was not simply that Palestinians' absolute economic situation did improve considerably compared to the 1936–1939 Palestine Revolt. But also, annually thousands of businessmen made trips to the near abroad, especially Egypt and Lebanon and Syria. Bank deposits rose in the second half of the war (in two Arab banks, from LP2.5 to 4 million between mid-1943 and mid-1944, by another LP1 million in other banks). The capitalization of existing manufacturing and trade companies such as the Riad Building Company and Haifa's National Cigarette Company increased. And new companies mushroomed, some small, others with considerable capital like the Jaffa Yarn Importation Company and the Jaffa Textiles Importation Company. Moreover, while entrepreneurs outside Haifa, Jaffa, and Jerusalem protested about being under-represented in Palestine-wide economic associations, the World War II bonanza led to a few new factories being established in places like Nablus, Beisan, and Majdal, near Gaza.[65]

The war's effect on Palestine as a nation-state in the making—never mind that it was short-circuited in 1948—showed also in a reaction, by Palestinian entrepreneurs, to the 1936–1939 Palestine Revolt: they improved nation-wide ties and coordination. Not only did Palestine's chambers of commerce meet at biannual conferences (which they had done from 1936), but also, a number of new Palestine-wide trade companies and traders unions were formed. Before 1939, there had been one for textiles; now others followed, for instance for coffee and for tea. To be sure, Jaffa, Haifa, and Jerusalem dominated Palestine's economy. Also, the entrepreneurs and traders of one city still stuck together strongly. When in 1944 the Arabia Insurance Company, which planned to do business from Egypt to Iraq, was founded and headquartered in Jerusalem, three quarters of its initial 46,450 shares were held by Jerusalemites, who formed exactly half of the company's thirty initial shareholders. And as many shareholders were from Damascus and Lebanese

Baalbek as from Bethlehem and Nablus: one each. But seven were from Jaffa and three from Haifa, which with Betlehem and Nablus made twelve—which was almost as many as Jerusalemites.[66]

## Jordan: Amman Ascendant

Another one was from Amman. This was not surprising. A key economic development in wartime Transjordan was the "consolidation of the merchant class."[67] And also in Transjordan, economic developments were concentrated in some places more than in others, with Amman profiting more than others. The consolidation of Transjordan's, and especially Amman's, merchant class meant more intense contact with larger centers like Jerusalem, as the case of Arabia Insurance Company showed. (Also, Jerusalem's Chamber of Commerce now gained representatives from Mafraq.) More crucially, especially in Amman manufacturing increased, including of macaroni and starch, processing Transjordan's ample grain harvests: an accentuation of a process dating back to the 1930s. But perhaps most crucially, mainly in Amman a number of trading companies were founded, one capitalized with the considerable sum of LP100,000. In fact, the war sharpened the advantage Amman had started to enjoy already in the late 1930s, when Iraq-Palestine trade relations thickened and a new road was built between the two countries via Amman. With overseas trade waning and Middle East-wide trade waxing in 1939–1945, Transjordan and especially its capital became even less of a backwater and more of an intersection for goods flowing between four important regions: Iraq, Syria, Palestine, and the Arabian Peninsula.[68] Amman's geographically central position was expedient for smuggling, too, which was a godsend for Jordanian merchants. Some merchants profited also from Transjordan's grain exports becoming strategic. And especially the powerful ones gained from the way imports for domestic consumption were organized. The British-approved quota system assigned specific import quotas to individual traders, a system in use also elsewhere in Bilad al-Sham and beyond in the Middle East and North Africa during World War II.[69]

One of the most successful traders was Sabri Tabba'a, the Damascene who had settled in Amman in the 1920s and established a personal friendship with Emir Abdallah that decade. Tabba'a made a fortune during the war and used it to further cement his socio-political position. His success, and that of other Ammani merchants, was cemented by Emir Abdallah's relationship with Britain going from good to better. In the war, a real "partnership, even if it was an unequal one," matured between London and Amman. This was partly the doing of the new Resident, affable Alec Kirkbride, and the result of increased employment through war-related public works and through the expansion of the Arab Legion. Most important, though, it was due to Abdallah's ultimate loyalty to Britain even in 1940–1941, when Berlin's star was rising and London's fortune looked dire.[70]

## Syria: Damascene Power and an Aleppine Renaissance

If in Transjordan, the wealthy merchants of the capital city of Amman were significantly richer than their counterparts in any other city, Syria's wartime economy was a bit more complex. Britain tried to expand agriculture not the least by experimental stations in, and expansion of, areas beyond the agricultural areas surrounding Damascus and Aleppo: in the old agricultural region Homs as well as in the fertile Jazira, in Syria's east. Put differently, in Syrian agriculture, the war did bring about a certain change, which in the postwar period would speed up, especially with large-scale agriculture in the Jazira.[71]

But most important, Syria's wartime economic experience was polarized. Aleppo and Damascus fared by far best. Given Aleppo's travails in the 1930s, this signaled a sharp change, perhaps the greatest change among the cities. Aleppo profited from British investments and from the war flinging open the border to southern Anatolia, a part of Aleppo's hinterland of yore, access to which Turkey had tried to seal in the 1930s. Turkey, under tremendous economic pressure because of the war, joined the MESC trade exchange and production region and opened up its southern border. As a result, Aleppo temporarily became more of a trade center again, doubly because Iraq and Iran, to its east, were part of the MESC area, too. Further, manufacturing expanded in Aleppo, if less than in Damascus.[72] A fascinating case was manufacturers working with raw silk and wool. They grew because of Vichy France's and then Britain's domestic import substitution industry policy, and because their silk and wool attracted other Europeans: German agents and Swiss company representatives, both operating from Turkey. As the Syrian-Turkish border was long, and as Aleppines wanted maximum profit and were willing to smuggle, those Germans and Swiss had considerable success early on. But Britain was unwilling to accept this situation. It was determined to isolate German-ruled Europe, which included preventing Switzerland from selling on certain goods to its German neighbor. To do so with success, though, Britain found itself forced to raise the so-called fair silk and wool price. Anything else was out of the question given Syria's uncontrollable border with Turkey and the competitive prices that the Germans and Swiss were willing to pay.[73]

Damascus profited from the capital effect during the war. Here, there was no sharp change as in Aleppo, but basic continuity. This situation had many faces. For political reasons, the Syrian government and British supplies of essentials somewhat favored Damascus. On a related note, Damascus, like Aleppo, was a prime location for Vichy and especially British subsidized import substitution industry factories.[74] This choice "unleashed a phase of accumulation of capital that from 1945 would be invested *inter alia* in the significantly expanding industrial sector" of early postcolonial Syria. As for trade, in 1943, the city's chamber of commerce remarked with somewhat embarrassed satisfaction that Damascus was afloat with all sorts of goods (including some from India and Africa[75]). Even in the hard year 1940 / 1941, Damascus's chamber of commerce did well enough to afford a new building. Moreover, once the British occupation of 1941 had reopened Syria, Damascene merchants again visited neighboring Palestine, some also Egypt, by the dozens, mainly to import goods back home. Although the chamber clamored that they worked ethically, they, as industrialists, made immense profits, partly through quota monopolies. Also, many teamed up and used official connections—appealing to personalities all the way up to Quwatli—to prevent a special war profit tax. Damascene merchants were also attuned to overseas developments that may affect them in the postwar future. They took note of the 1944 Bretton Woods conference. Not unlike the Yishuv, they were already in the last war years looking ahead, beyond the region, to the world. Closer to home, they had, from independence in 1943, minor spats with Lebanon over questions of economic policy. And back in 1943 they reacted not only with joy but also with nervousness to Lebanon's declaration of independence. This event accentuated the question of how, or indeed whether, independent Lebanon and Syria would be able to keep their unified customs zone, a question that had exploded into a mini-crisis in the late 1930s and that in 1950 would lead to the dissolution of the union.[76]

## Beirut: Wartime Profits and the Dawn of a Second Golden Age

In Lebanon, the city that profited more than others from the war was Beirut. Its status as Bilad al-Sham's economically strongest city— maintained in the 1930s, though dangerously challenged by Haifa— persisted in 1939–1945. Toward the war's end this dominance was sharpened. It is true, Tripoli did not do badly either. Its oil refinery was working overtime, and both Vichy French and British industrial policy benefited factories such as those producing textiles, like Arida's, or a large sugar factory near Tripoli. In fact, in manufacturing, Tripoli, with Beirut, was an example of the rule that the war benefited those most who already had most by 1939. But in trade, this same rule meant that Tripoli did much worse than Beirut. In this crucial sense, Tripoli's wartime economic experience continued an interwar pattern. When Karami was Prime Minister in 1945, he tried to address this problem, secure more contracts also for his city's merchants, and raise serious war profit taxes. But many of Beirut's merchants / politicians, including Sulh, who had access to Beirut's press, torpedoed him. In fact, Lebanon's independence, in 1943, increased not simply the government's power, for instance in assigning quotas, but also the power of rich, well-connected merchants many of whom sat in government, as even high government officials like the head of the anti-inflation office Adel Hamdan affirmed in protest in 1944.[77]

Thus, Beirut secured being the trade hub for exports / imports with Palestine, which was Lebanon's key regional trade partner during World War II, and hence also the destination of manifold visits even by highest-ranking Beiruti financiers and merchants such as Michel Chiha or Nicolas Trad. Moreover, the city's merchants, already before the war well-capitalized and well-networked in the region and overseas, were at the height of the war perfectly placed to exploit leftover legal or illegal overseas trade, principally with merchants in Britain and the United States. Further, from 1944 Beiruti traders rode the wave of resuming world trade, doing business with various countries: this was the dawn of a second Beiruti golden age, lasting until the mid-1970s, after the first, late Ottoman one. The Swiss vice consul in Beirut reported that the very resourceful (*débrouillard*) Jean Fattal was finding various ways to import Swiss pharmaceutical products. However, the most re-munerative connections—connections much stronger than before the war—were with the United States, the world's largest and by now most powerful economy. Already in March 1941, for instance, the Kettaneh family—which had imported U.S. cars since the 1920s, selling them as far afield as Tehran—succeeded in obtaining licenses to export fifty-four tons of Syrian wool to the United States. Three years later, the Spears Mission noted that the same family had "made a 'fortune from illegal U.S. imports.'" They were not alone. Other Beiruti traders profit from the U.S. connection, too.[78]

Such cases point to another fact. Just like Beirut's trade outstripped other Lebanese cities, a smallish group of Beiruti merchants and finan-ciers profited more than others from the war. Less wealthy Beiruti mer-chants time and again complained that the government burdened them with the same war profits tax as rich merchants, and that the latter were using their influence to monopolize trade quotas. Lacking political in-fluence, they protested in vain. Adding insult to injury, newspapers af-filiated with merchants / politicians claimed that profits at any rate were not very high.[79]

Beirut's less wealthy merchants may have found a sympathetic ear in the peripheral north and south of Lebanon that Bishara al-Khoury toured in the fall of 1945. While honoring the president, villagers also presented him with long lists of complaints and demands. In south Lebanon, Maghdusha wanted roads, drinking water, and a girls' school—and that just for starters. In Qasimiyya, Sa'id Ibrahim Fiaz lamented as al-Khoury sat at lunch with south Lebanese grandee 'Adil Osseiran: "Have not you seen this crowd, dressed in garments older than the war?" And when al-Khoury reached Nabatieh, the small Communist Party branch insisted on an entire development plan for Lebanon's south. The underdevelopment of Lebanon's south "maims" the country as a whole, it insisted, and is shameful as the country is "the pioneer of the entire Arab East culturally, developmentally, and overall."[80]

All this was perfectly justified. But the rich merchants and politicians of Lebanon's capital were living in a world of their own—literally. In October 1944 Beirut's Chamber of Commerce received an invitation from the U.S. ambassador to send three delegates to a major international trade conference in Washington. And in November, when German submarines were still on the hunt in the Atlantic, Camille Chamoun, a parliamentarian, attended the Convention on International Civil Aviation in Chicago. The juxtaposition of southern Lebanese mired in poverty and trans-Atlantic Beirutis intimated that socio-spatial inequalities and interrelations inside, between, and beyond Bilad al-Sham's nation-states would outlive the war.[81]

## Conclusion

Two key developments marked World War II in the countries of Bilad al-Sham. First, in 1941–1945 (British Empire) state territoriality peaked. Britain created an area of imperial rule and, with the United States, of economic interaction and investment not only in that region but far beyond, in an area ranging from Iran, in the east, to Ethiopia, in the south, to Libya, in the west. That area arose due to preemptive British occupations (e.g. of Iraq, Syria / Lebanon, and Iran in 1941) and because Britain compensated plunging world trade. The area endured because the Allies kept the Axis out of the Middle Eastern heartland and in

1943 chased it from North Africa. And that area had a reasonably "good" war. Many fewer soldiers than in Europe or Asia-Pacific were killed; warfare barely touched civilians; and deprivations were overall bearable.

The second key wartime development in Bilad al-Sham was that its countries reached for independence. Lebanon and Syria succeeded in 1943 with British support. Transjordanian Emir Abdallah's steadfast loyalty to Britain paved the way for independence in the war's aftermath, in 1946. Palestinians fared least well. Their only real gain was the 1939 British White Paper limiting Jewish immigration—but they were materially better off than in the late 1930s. And the Yishuv enjoyed sturdy economic relations with Britain; and used the war to adopt, in 1942, a more openly assertive approach to state building. Except for this last case, all others happened basically because Britain sought to keep Bilad al-Sham's countries content and calm. Peak state territoriality helped to accentuate the build-up of nation-states.

This dynamic differed sufficiently from that of the 1930s to make 1939–1945 a distinct phase in the post-Ottoman stage of transpatialization. Certainly, there were basic continuities relative to the previous phase, most importantly in the relationship between cities and nation-states. The former still had to prove their significance within the latter, and still often did so by using transnational ties; conversely, the latter were still imagined and experienced as multi-urban heterogeneous rather than homogeneous places. However, there were noteworthy twists, too, relative to the 1930s. As Bilad al-Sham's four countries became more distinct, city-nation-state relationships in each became ever more distinct from the others. Also, some cities' identities experienced a twist: Damascus for instance looked to Cairo with somewhat greater intensity than before. But perhaps most important, peaking state territorialization was of greatest material benefit to the cities that had been strongest in 1939. In each of Bilad al-Sham's nation-states, World War II helped to further concentrate wealth and power.

Changes and accentuations of extant processes were as important as continuities with twists. Franco-British relationships certainly changed. As Britain ruled not only Palestine and Transjordan but also Lebanon and Syria from 1941, it needed to cooperate less with France. A mix of accentuations and real changes characterized the field of cultural affinities. On the one hand, *qawmiyya* advanced relative to the 1930s and 1920s, when it had already been in formation. In the years 1939–1945 almost all Arabs inhabited a single area of (British) rule; also, the Arab League was formed (with Britain's accord); and Egypt became a more central player in the Arab world. (It helped that it was Britain's wartime headquarters.) On the other hand, Bilad al-Sham's role in this process was not an accentuation of a previous pattern, but rather saw a substantial change. The region became less of an umbrella, less important as a mediating layer between the Arab world and the distinct nation-states. Not only were the latter reaching for independence. But as a group they became politically less distinct from neighbors Egypt and Iraq, which in the 1930s had been more autonomous (Egypt) or independent (Iraq) than any imperially ruled country of Bilad al-Sham. Economically, too, Bilad al-Sham lost in importance, another rather substantial change relative to the 1930s. In 1939, the region-wide customs-free zone agreement was renewed, but in a weakened form. In 1940–1941, Britain embargoed Vichy-ruled Lebanon and Syria. And in 1941, the region's countries became part of Britain's incomparably larger, unified Middle Eastern economic area that reached from Iran in the east, to Ethiopia in the south, to Libya in the west. The nation-state in the making in Bilad al-Sham that profited most from this area was the Yishuv. As Britain needed speedy economic expansion to balance plunging world trade imports into the area, it invested heavily in what by the late 1930s was a relatively advanced manufacturing economy.

The economic change / continuity balance sheet of cities differed quite significantly from the 1930s. Wartime conditions, including Britain's deepening presence, interplayed in complex ways with the building-up of nation-states. All cities were touched by the war and suffered some degree of deprivation, but in some, economic performance changed much more than in others. The difference from the 1930s was most striking in Aleppo and Amman. In both, merchants profited from the war's new geoeconomic situation, in Aleppo because access to Turkey became much easier, in Amman because it turned into a more important trade crossroad. Damascus and Tripoli experienced more continuity relative to their position in the 1930s. So did Beirut—but with a crucial twist. Toward the war's end, Beirut began to function as the intermediary between now U.S.-centric world trade and multiple Arab countries to its east: one part of the story to which we will now turn in the Postscript.

# THE MORE THINGS CHANGE
## 1945–2017

How did the socio-spatial processes shaping the Middle East from the mid-nineteenth to the mid-twentieth century develop thereafter? This question underlies the Postscript. While analyzing disentanglements and entanglements between Israel, Jordan, Lebanon, Syria, and the Palestinians, however, this chapter differs from the others. It is shorter and not based on primary source research. That is, it is suggestive rather than scholarly. It forms part of this book because historians may want to suggest how an analysis of the past relates to the present. Not to make policy recommendations—the present is too complex issues- and politics-wise for that—but to offer a background framework for thinking about the present.[1]

### The Disentanglement of Nation-States

Following World War II, decolonization matured in the Middle East, having started around 1930 and borne first fruit in 1943 in the de jure independence of Lebanon and Syria. Both gained full independence in 1946. So did Jordan. Israel followed in 1948—and was immediately invaded by its Arab neighbors and Iraq. A Palestinian-Yishuvi civil war, from 1947, became the inter-state 1948 War. In its course, half of the 1.4 million Palestinians were expelled and fled: their *nakba* (catastrophe), the reverse side of Israel's *'atsmaut* (independence), which sealed and radically worsened the statelessness of those whom the British Mandate did not formally recognized as a people with sovereign political rights.[2]

The new nation-states' disentanglement continued during and following their independence. From 1945, especially Lebanese and Syrians resumed boycotting Yishuvi goods, in reaction to the unfolding drama in Palestine and because the wartime growth of imports from the Yishuv posed a threat. In parallel, Zionist organizations resumed attempts to minimize some imports from neighboring countries. Regular Israeli-Arab diplomatic and commercial relations stopped in 1948. From 1946, Lebanon and Syria discussed how to manage their Mandate-era customs union. By 1950, the die was cast, the union dead: the two countries' economic profiles and interests diverged too much. Finally, in 1951 King Abdallah of Jordan was assassinated, the single most influential advocate between the 1920s and the late 1940s of a pan-Arab (*qawmi*) state in Greater Syria.[3]

These disentanglements had roots. Lebanese and Syrians had fought over their customs union already in the late 1930s. They, Zionists, and Palestinians had never quite followed Abdallah's *qawmi* ambitions. Boycotting Zionist goods had started in the 1920s. And Zionist thought about (voluntary) Palestinian (self-)transfer dated back to the pre–World War II period before becoming a militarily enforced practice in the 1948 War.[4] In sum, the disentanglements of the early postwar years reflected and further crystallized the resilience of the four post-Ottoman polities.

Those disentanglements have endured since the late 1940s. The four polities have resisted lasting unification or territorial change. Consider the polity that was Mandate Palestine. True, it changed form. Its official successor, Israel, whereas de jure present in all of Mandate Palestine until 1948 in the form of the Yishuv, possessed 77 percent of that territory by 1949. But in 1967 it occupied, among other areas, the Gaza Strip, Egyptian-ruled from 1948, and the West Bank, Jordanian-ruled from 1948. Ever since, it has exercised ultimate control over these two areas. The years 1949–1967 look increasingly like the exception to the rule that the polity of Israel / Palestine has in international law and / or on the ground been one, and Yishuv / Israeli dominated, for the last century.

Moreover, this situation is bound to continue. Over half a million settlers in the West Bank aside, Israel—the stronger side—has politically moved to the right in the past fifteen years, is under no serious international pressure to implement a two-state solution (yet?), and is wary to make concessions that might bring peace but also endanger its security given the continued "anarchic nature of the Middle East regional subsystem."[5]

Consider, too, the fate of Syria's 1958 unification with Gamal Abdel Nasser's Egypt. What started in joy for a majority of Syrians ended three short years later in discontented secession.[6] A slew of other unification plans, many involving Egypt and / or Iraq, never matured, if they were ever intended to.[7] And the most recent unification plan that really was serious—ISIS's disparagement of the Arab East's states as illegitimate, purely Western creations, and its initial success to link up Iraqi and Syrian conquests—has received vigorous political-ideological and military pushback. As for Lebanon and Syria, they never reestablished a customs union; and although Syria occupied over half of Lebanon from 1976 through 2005, partly by invitation, the two did not merge. The Palestinians have managed to sustain and even deepen a national identity in the face of exile and Israeli domination.[8] And in Jordan, Abdallah's successors, kings Hussein and Abdallah II, rarely if ever pursued his pan-Arab aspirations, and in 1994 the country, like Egypt in 1979, made the ultimate step to full recognition of the region's political division by signing a peace treaty with Israel.[9]

## The Persistent Importance of Cities

In parallel to the disentanglements of Greater Syria's states, however, cities have continued to matter after independence. To be sure, their social structures have changed. Perhaps most important, the notable elites that had, in different family constellations, been dominant in many cities from the seventeenth century and that first Ottomanized themselves, in the nineteenth century, and after 1918 nationalized themselves, declined in most cities by the 1950s / 1960s. Also, transnationalized interurban ties and hinterlands have become less influential as the postcolonial nation-states have grown deeper roots. Moreover, some established cities have lost ground. Haifa for instance was cut off its hinterland in 1948 and dropped off the map as Beirut's competitor, and the Jordanian city of Salt, which until about 1930 was larger than Amman, became a wallflower when the capital city's growth speeded up after World War II.

At the same time, new urban concentrations have emerged. Some Palestinian refugee camps acquired city traits, and state-led economic development, for example in Syria's Euphrates Valley, Israel's Negev Desert and Jordan's Red Sea, turned peripheral towns like Raqqa, Beersheba, and Aqaba into cities. Also, almost all cities in the region, like in the rest of the global south, have been boosted by population growth and rural emigration. And crucially, some interurban ties that are rooted in prewar if not premodern times still bind people together. Think of the sheer volume of Damascenes who have relocated to Beirut and Amman since 2011, or of the importance of Sunni Tripoli for Sunni Homs before the latter was retaken by the Syrian regime in 2015.

Perhaps most crucially, cities have remained key places of societal action and national identity construction in postcolonial politics. This carries on the nationalization of cities in the 1920s–1940s. After independence like during Mandate rule, political contestation has often crystallized most visibly in specific cities. Consequently, the latter were elevated to nationwide symbols. In Syria, from 1976 to 1982 and from 2011 to 2015 Homs became a bastion of antiregime resistance, latterly called the Capital of the Revolution.[10] Across Greater Syria, the refugee camp city best materializes the supreme Palestinian nationalist trait: *sumud*. "Steadfastness" showed in the resistance to the Israeli army in Ain al-Hilweh, adjacent to the Lebanese city of Sidon in the summer of 1982, and in the spring of 2002 in the West Bank refugee camp of Jenin, which was rechristened Jeningrad. A final example is Nablus, which was a nationalist bastion during the Mandate. Israel did not conquer it in 1948. Although Nabulsis had no hand in this—it was part of the "collusion across the Jordan" between Israel and Transjordan, which divided most of Palestine—it did mean that they stayed put and nationalism survived. In result, following the Six-Day War of June 1967, in which Israel occupied the West Bank, Palestine Liberation Organization (PLO) cadres including Yassir Arafat selected it as their West Bank headquarters. They failed: Most Nabulsi nationalists then were of pan-Arab persuasions which, with Israeli counterinsurgency, made Arafat escape to Jordan. But soon Palestinian nationalism was reascendant, and Nablus moved to the forefront of intermittent Palestinian resistance to Israel's occupation. This was most notable in the two intifadas, 1987–1993 and 2000–2005. In the latter, Nablus was where the Israeli army imposed a quasi-total curfew for a particularly long stretch, over seventy days, in the fall of 2002. And in April of the same year, after suicide bombers killed around 130 Israelis in "black March," Palestinians in Nablus's old city fought an Israeli attack in what was the intifada's second-most deadly battle, after Jenin's refugee camp. Eighty Palestinians and four Israelis died.[11]

## Beirut

Li-Beirut, min qalbi salamun li-Beirut / wa-qubalun li-l-bahri wa-l-buyut / li-sakhratin ka-annaha wajhu bahharin qadimin / hiya min ruhi al-sha'bi khamrun, hiya min / 'araqihi khubzun wa-l-yasamin / fa-kaifa sara ta'muha ta'ma narin wa-dukhanin.

To Beirut, from my heart a greeting to Beirut / and kisses to the sea and to the houses / to a rock, like an old sailor's face / she is wine from the people's soul, she is / the bread and Jasmine of its sweat / so how has her taste turned fiery and ashen.[12]

"So how has her taste turned fiery and ashen": like nobody else did Lebanese national treasure Fairuz captured people's bewilderment about Beirut's fall from glory. No doubt, when she sang her famous "Li-Beirut" in 1993, the city was rising to a new day. Although in the 1975–1991 civil war it had lost considerable substance, some networks and infrastructures stood ready for a reboot. Its knight on a white horse, Saudi-made billionaire Rafic Hariri, moved not to his native Sidon but to Beirut to help renew it. Bank doors were swinging open. Construction cranes were rising, as so often benefiting primarily the (newly) rich and powerful. And since, short wars and long crises notwithstanding, Beirut has again become a cultural, media, and financial destination not only for Lebanese but for many people, especially Arabs, beyond small Lebanon.[13]

Still, Beirut is not able to fully compete with rising global cities in the Gulf like Dubai.[14] The "taste" of which Fairuz sang was fullest from the mid-1940s to the early 1970s. During that time, Beirut was a truly extraordinary example, in the Middle East, of the continuing relevance of cities in the age of (early) postcolonial nation-state building. Rooted in its first golden age, the nineteenth century, and in its greater opening to Iraq from the 1930s, it experienced a second golden age—now as a particular type of global city. It became a high-intensity, laissez-faire go-between for two sets of actors: early postimperial Western finance, corporate, and Cold War state actors who wished to manage the oil business, sell goods, and gather information; and nation-state and private actors from across the Arab East and Arabian Peninsula. Only recently independent, these nation-states and economies were still fledgling and for a time still needed Beirut as their trade, finance, consumption, knowledge production, and air transport hub: their principal port to the world.

## Continued Regional Entanglements

Another trend that was visible in some ways in the nineteenth century but in a more integral way in the 1930s and especially 1940s, has only grown stronger: Greater Syria's cultural incorporation into the Arab world at large.[15] Indeed, traits that are still recognizably Greater Syriawide today have narrowed to, primarily, food and a distinct set of Arabic dialects—and even these have become less specific due to ballooning interaction with other Arab regions and the globe.[16]

At the same time, the region has continued to matter, in at least three ways. In the 1940s-1960s, it was what could be called a state formation region. After their independence, Syria, Jordan, and Lebanon had persisting affinities and shared a regional position: all were sandwiched be-

tween Iraq and Egypt, from the late 1940s to the 1960s the two dominant poles of an unstable Arab state system.[17] In 1958–1959, an explosion
of domestic sociopolitical and regional inter-state tensions that had built
up for a decade triggered state formation surges in Jordan, Lebanon, and
in Syria, which united with Egypt. These surges happened simultaneously.
They had the same goal, to stabilize societies and better counteract
neighbors' meddling. And they involved similar means, including socioeconomic plans and strengthened security forces, which rendered
state apparatuses more alike into the 1960s. In sum, although each state
acted autonomously, the surges together formed a single, region-wide
process.[18]

Greater Syria also became the Palestine Question region. Because it
had grown more tightly knit from the late Ottoman period, in 1948 Palestinians did not just flee any or everywhere. Most turned to their closest
neighbors: closest to walk or drive or sail to, and to return home from,
initially a real hope of many; closest in that Palestinians knew them
best; and closest because of all Arabs, those neighbors had taken most
interest in the unfolding conflict in Palestine already in the interwar
period. Relatively few Palestinians went to Egypt, Iraq, or Saudi Arabia.
Most came to Jordan, Syria, and Lebanon. As a result, the question *of*
Palestine and the struggle *for* it have been unfolding *in* Greater Syria.

There are qualifications. From the 1950s until the Six-Day War, most
Palestinians' beacon of hope was Nasser, pan-Arab hero and Egypt's
president; hundreds of thousands have migrated on, many to the Gulf,
others to the West; and when the Palestinian national movement was
revitalized in 1967, it went global, recently again in new forms including
the Boycott, Divestment, and Sanctions movement that is keeping Palestine a worldwide cause.[19]

At the same time, an overwhelming majority of Palestinians—about
90 percent—live in Israel, the West Bank and Gaza, Jordan, Syria, and
Lebanon. Except for 1982–1994, countries in the region have been the
PLO's / Palestinian Authority's (PA) headquarters. And sometimes the
region works as a unit of immediate political action, Palestine or Palestinian refugee-related matters in one country spilling over into others.
When Jordan expelled the PLO in 1971, the organization succeeded to
make Lebanon its new center; from the late 1960s to the early 1980s, the

PLO used Jordan and/or Lebanon to mount cross-border incursions into Israel; and since the 1990s, the fate of PA-Israeli ties sometimes reverberates through Palestinian camps and neighborhoods across the region.

Israeli action is another factor that makes Greater Syria the Palestine Question region. Already in the 1930s and 1940s, most of the Yishuv's attempts at political rapprochement outside Palestine and most of its then puny intelligence gathering there targeted Transjordan, Syria, and Lebanon. One reason was that of all Arab countries, those three were most tied to the struggle over Palestine. The *nakba* reinforced that situation. The resulting concentration of Palestinians in Jordan, Syria, and Lebanon, together with their latent or open challenge to Israel—including intermittent cross-border attacks from the early to mid-1950s and from the mid-1960s to early 1980s—is one reason why the Jewish state has always trained a considerable proportion of its armed and intelligence-gathering might on these three neighbors. However, the weak Palestinians have never posed an existential threat to Israel. If at all, such a threat came from powerful states: Egypt, until the late 1960s; Iraq, including its nuclear program, from the late 1970s to 1981; and recently Iran and its nuclear program.

Last, Greater Syria has become a core security region. Since the late 1960s especially Israel's, and until the 2011 civil war also Syria's, geostrategic security demands have transcended their own borders.

In the 1950s–1960s, the Jewish state did not actively define Greater Syria as a core security region. Its overwhelming concern was Nasser's Egypt, outside the region. Iraq shared no border with Israel, Palestinians were barely active, Lebanon was a military midget, a covert channel existed to Jordan, and Syria was a minor nuisance. Syria, while on and off, especially in 1958, meddling in Lebanon and Jordan, did not claim Greater Syria as its core security region, either. It too did not feel the need: Israel was focused on Egypt, and Lebanon and Jordan posed no threat. And it could not: its military was weak and its politics instable, and as noted the Arab state system was until the 1960s dominated by Egypt and Iraq.

Then came the Six-Day War. Soon, much changed. Occupying Egypt's Sinai Peninsula, Gaza, West Bank, and Syria's Golan Heights in six days, Israel proved to be a powerhouse. In 1970, Syrian feebleness ended with the rise to power of air force general Hafiz al-Asad, who seriously challenged Israel in the 1973 October War. And Egypt, having shocked Israel in that same war and turning from a Soviet partner into a U.S. client, was able to bring Israel to the negotiation table. By 1974 Syria remained Israel's only serious neighboring threat, although to the east, Iraq, and later Iran, were becoming more serious concerns, too.

Israel has reacted to this mixture of might, opportunities, and threats by trying to make Greater Syria its core security region. It has done three things. First, it has sought to cordon off the region to any external Middle Eastern military competitor. In the region's southwest, its 1979 peace treaty with Egypt partly demilitarized the Sinai. Regarding the east, Jordan, it in the 1970s communicated to Iraq that any armed crossing into Jordan would be a casus belli; and the 1994 peace treaty "preclude[es] the stationing of potentially hostile foreign troops on Jordanian soil . . . In essence, Jordan serves as a buffer between Israel and less friendly "outer ring" countries of the Persian Gulf."[20] In the northeast, as of 2016 Israel is determined—and directly talking with Russia—to minimize Iran's presence in post–civil war Syria.[21]

Second, Israel has intervened militarily within the region since the late 1960s much more frequently and forcefully than before. The original reason was that Greater Syria is the Palestine Question region and that the PLO became a serious actor after the Six-Day War. In 1967–1970 Israel fought PLO guerillas centered in western Jordan. Especially after Jordan evicted the PLO to Lebanon in 1971, the focus switched. The most massive Israeli actions were Operation Litani in south Lebanon in March 1978 and the 1982 invasion of Lebanon up to Beirut: a move welcomed by some Maronites. It ended in the PLO's eviction to Tunis and the establishment of a security zone in south Lebanon, evacuated only in 2000. Israel's air force still regularly flies surveillance sorties over Lebanon, and since 2013 sporadically attacks shipments of advanced missiles from Syria to Hezbollah, against which Israel kept the south Lebanese security zone in 1982–2000 and which it fought in a month-long war in 2006.

Third, Israel has sought to keep a precarious balance of power with Syria, while maintaining military superiority. When Syrian tanks penetrated northern Jordan in 1970, just before Asad came to power, Israel signaled it would react. (Syria withdrew.) The 1974 Israeli-Syrian Separation of Forces agreement following the 1973 War stipulated limited Syrian troop concentrations on the Golan. When Syria entered the Lebanese civil war in 1976, Israel set red lines—just south of the Beirut-Damascus highway—whose trespassing would, and did, trigger an armed response. And in 2007, Israel bombarded a Syrian nuclear reactor under construction.

From the early 1970s, Syria saw Greater Syria as a core security region, too. And it too did three things, mirroring Israel. First, it deepened its relationship with an external patron, the USSR, and since 1980 has nurtured an alliance with Iran. Second, it started to act militarily within the region. In 1976, a year after the outbreak of the Lebanese civil war, its troops intervened following a Christian invitation, staying in Lebanon's northern half until the 2005 Cedar Revolution forced it to withdraw. Third, it has sought to deter and blunt Israel's might. Its external relationships with the USSR and Iran (and help by Saudi Arabia until the 2000s) were key in this regard; related, in the 1970s–1980s Syria rather vainly pursued military parity with Israel. In the 1980s, it drew red lines in Lebanon for the invading Israeli forces, reacting when Israel crossed them. The 1974 Separation of Forces agreement stipulated limited Israeli troop concentrations on the Golan; and while keeping that border quiet, Syria used Palestinian proxies in the 1970s–1980s to wage small cross-border attacks, from Lebanon, into Israel. Finally, it has allowed Iran to funnel aid through its territory to Hezbollah in order to keep Israel busy in Lebanon rather than squarely focused on Syria.

In a sense, this precarious, competitive *dance-à-deux* has been a replay of the Yishuv's and Syria's geoeconomic regional competition in the 1930s. Then again, since the 1970s that competition has been geostrategic. The players have been independent, their means more powerful, and the stakes higher. And the geostrategic threats to, and opportunities for, Israel and Syria have since their independence gone far beyond the region and encompassed other Middle Eastern countries including Egypt, Ethiopia, Saudi Arabia, Iran, Iraq, and Turkey.

# Coda

The fact that from the 1940s nation-states became disentangled while at the same time Bilad al-Sham remained an entangled region, shows also in how people judge the past. I became aware of that matter during interviews conducted for this book. Whereas I was fascinated by stories of objects and persons moving between and beyond Palestine, Transjordan, Syria, and Lebanon, elderly women and men I met found them most often all but normal. An example took place in Marjayoun, a town in south Lebanon, in the summer of 2008. I visited Cecil Hourani, the brother of the late historian Albert Hourani, who welcomed me in his family's beautiful, cool stone house. After talking in his living room, we took a peek at his lush garden, then walked to the kitchen for a glass of water. And there it was: the oldest-looking fridge I had ever seen. I was curious. "When did you get this fridge?" "In the early 1950s; the family imported it through Haifa," Hourani answered.[22] Intrigued, I later inquired whether other Marjayounis possessed such a model. As it turned out, they do.[23] Hourani found his fridge quite ordinary.

It is doubly telling, then, that he and many other interviewees understood stories of moving objects and people in widely different ways. To most Israelis, their local significance was eclipsed by the rise of a self-consciously national Zionist community, a process sharpened after 1948 by political isolation from the Arab world. The eyes of Shulamit Yaari, born in 1920 in the Jewish settlement of Metula, on the Lebanese border, glittered when she described to me the Beiruti "patent leather shoes with buttons" that her better-off childhood girlfriends received at Jewish high holidays. She also recalled with amusement how a Palestinian Arabic teacher she had as an adult commented on her Lebanese accent. Still, she is an Israeli through and through; already thirteen years before the establishment of Israel in 1948, a formative experience of her life was moving to Tel Aviv, where she trained as a school teacher for Jewish children.[24] A different view of connections between the post-Ottoman states, one held especially by Arab city dwellers, also younger ones, inscribes them into what they see as a unitary, quasi national Greater Syrian region. A daughter of Fayez Nasrallah, a man born in 1930 in the southern Syrian village of Izra who from 1945–1948 had worked in the Palestinian port city of Jaffa, called me from Homs after I had talked to her father in the southern Syrian city of Suweida to insist that he "is an example for how people from everywhere in Bilad al-Sham moved around. It was one country (*bilad*)."[25] By contrast, Arabs who grew up on a rural border often remembered cross-border connections as part and parcel of one area that was the definite locus and focus of their lives. Tannus Salim Sayyah, born 1932 in the southwestern Lebanese village of Alma Sha'ab, talked of *qaraba* (closeness) to neighboring Palestinian villages like Bassa. This closeness was existential as much as spatial, nourished by marriages and friendships, economic transactions and cross-border land holdings in his account.[26]

The thoughts and memories of women and men like Cecil Hourani, Shulamit Yaari, Fayez Nasrallah, and Tannus Salim Sayyah bring us back from the postindependence era of this Postscript to the times central to this book. The following Conclusion pulls together my account's narrative strings and picks up conceptual issues that I broached first in the Introduction.

# CONCLUSION

This book has argued that the formation of the modern Middle East, and of the modern world more broadly, can be conceived as a process of transpatialization. Cities, regions, states, and global circuits reconstituted and transformed each other much more thoroughly and at a much faster rhythm than before in history.

In the Middle East from the mid-nineteenth to the mid-twentieth century, this inherently multi-dimensional process unfolded in two stages. From the viewpoint of the region of Bilad al-Sham and its cities, the first stage had three principal facets: cities' continued though recalibrated weight, strengthening interurban ties, and increasing regional integration. A wondrous illustration of the first facet was Khalil Sakakini's New York dreams of Jerusalem, mentioned in Prelude 1. Homesick, Sakakini dreamed of walking to his hometown on a telegraph wire and magically flew with his parents back and forth between Jerusalem and New York, and his friend Dawud caught a train that swept him from Jerusalem into the universe. Jerusalem was everything to Sakakini. It was his heart, his home, his *watan*. But now more radically than ever, that *watan* was not self-confined. Rather, it was the place through which Sakakini lived the world—a globalizing modern world with fast-paced novel technologies and a changing culture.

Part and parcel of this globalizing world was intensifying, now clearly Eurocentric economic circuits. The different position of Bilad al-Sham's cities in those circuits created significant variations. On the coast, particularly Beirut and Jaffa grew bigger fast, and so did their economic, cultural, and administrative influence. No more were they sleepy shadows of the interior cities of Damascus and Aleppo. In turn, the latter relatively speaking lost ground to Beirut, though they grew demographically, too. And whereas especially Beirutis were becoming quite quintessential capitalists who cared little for their city's fabric and without blinking razed the old to make place for the new, Damascenes and Aleppines were more married to their city's structures.

From about the 1850s, the transformation of the Ottoman state gave Istanbul a greater say in cities. This was not a zero-sum game, however. The center's gain was not provincial cities' loss. Rather, like in other states around the world at the time this was a new game, modifying center-province relationships. Bilad al-Sham's cities lost their earlier decision-making autonomy vis-à-vis Istanbul, but in return became regional centers of the Ottoman state's intensified territoriality, of a deepened projection of state power into the region. This modification benefited firstly urban notable elites, who survived the transition from the early modern to the modern period by becoming more Ottomanized. Economically, nonelite urban classes did not fare too badly either, though. This was not the least because in the late nineteenth century Istanbul sought to harden in particular Bilad al-Sham's interior cities against European encroachment. Indeed, cities continued to matter as centers of power, profit, and culture not only because they were age-old, or because they had been self-governing in the seventeenth and eighteenth centuries, or because Istanbul projected power through them—but also because Istanbul for long resisted European imperialism in its Asian provinces and tempered the impact of the Eurocentric world economy.

This pattern showed also in how cities "actively reacted" in their rural-tribal hinterlands and in interurban ties to their incorporation into the now Eurocentric world economy. The Ottoman state's pacification of tribes and new land laws helped urban merchants to penetrate their respective hinterland more thoroughly. Also interurban ties intensified. Key axes tied coastal cities to interior cities, most important Beirut to Damascus and Jaffa to Jerusalem. While these axes channeled trade with Europe, and while their transport infrastructure was partly financed by European capital, the cities greatly benefited, too. Especially merchants were involved in setting them up and used them to tighten interurban social ties, with little competition from European traders. Partly, this was an outcome of coastal cities' increased power in world economic circuits and of interior cities' deep roots and resulting staying power. But also here a crucial role was played by the Ottoman state, which sought to limit European political-mercantile encroachment and to deepen its own footprint in Bilad al-Sham. This helped strengthen urban actors' control of their respective interurban axis; also, Ottoman-self-financed infrastructural works multiplied those axes, buffering yet another coastal-interior axis, between Damascus and Haifa, and an interior axis, between Aleppo and Damascus. These two traits distinguished Bilad al-Sham's cities significantly from colonial cities. The Ottoman state's continued sovereignty and its resultant stance vis-à-vis Eurocentric global economic actors mattered for how Bilad al-Sham's cities and interurban ties developed in the late Ottoman period.

During that time, Bilad al-Sham was reshaped, too. It became more integrated, a more tightly knit multi-city patchwork region. This process had a gravitation point: Beirut. Becoming a world trade port city enriched Beirut and made it the region's premier secular educational center. Recognizing this fact and giving in to Beiruti pressure, Istanbul granted the city its own province in 1888, a step that helped to administratively reorganize Bilad al-Sham. Still, Beirut did not become all-powerful. Interior cities like Damascus and Aleppo were too well-established; some coastal cities like Jaffa and Alexandretta were at a sufficient distance from Beirut; and other coastal cities, especially Haifa, left Beirut's shadow by the early twentieth century with help from Istanbul.

Bilad al-Sham's tighter integration had a cultural dimension. Having long provided an elastic geographical meta-identity for its inhabitants, it now became the framework for a new, national type of geographical imagining. This was not a wholesale transformation but a shift, with a new meaning grafted on top of an older one. Further, some intellectuals appropriated for Bilad al-Sham the old European term Syria, Suriya. This development formed part of a rise, in many places around the world and also in the Ottoman Empire, of a national sort of spatial identity formation. Indeed, Bilad al-Sham was framed as part of a global ensemble of national spaces. However, in Bilad al-Sham that development was not politicized. At a time of European imperialism, almost everybody in Bilad al-Sham accepted the Ottoman Empire as their best or even only political bet.

Bilad al-Sham / Suriya, then, illustrates not only how older geographical frameworks were retooled in modern times. It also underscores the complexity, especially in the nineteenth century, of "nationalism:" a catch-all term for a variety of situations ranging from culturalist proto-nationalism, via nationalism within a still accepted imperial unit, to attempted and successful nation-state formation. The case of Bilad al-Sham indicates that even proto-national identity formations shared traits with more manifestly nationalist ones. A good example was the question of belonging. In Bilad al-Sham, the bedouin for example found themselves on the outside and now were seen less socio-ethnically and more in a racialized way. If the quote from Butrus al-Bustani (see Chapter 1)—bedouin are to Beirut what "cannibalistic Africans" are to Paris—is any indication, then the bedouin were seen as too shifty and shifting to fully fit into modern-time Bilad al-Sham.

The three primary facets of the first, Ottoman stage of transpatialization—cities' continued though recalibrated weight; strengthening interurban ties; and increasing regional integration—after 1918 powerfully shaped the region's four new nation-states, their new rulers, and a reviving world trade. In turn, cities, interurban ties, and the region were again reshaped. This double process was at the basis of transpatialization during its second, post-Ottoman stage. Far-reaching changes set that stage apart from the first one. World trade was less influential a factor, especially in the 1930s-1940s. Also, there now were not one but four states in the region; these were not empires but nation-states; and they were until the 1940s ruled by European empires. But there were continuities, too. State territoriality did not change radically. And the notable urban elites that had risen in the late seventeenth century, and been part of the Ottoman state's nineteenth-century transformation, persisted after 1918. Moreover, the two stages shared an important trait. Both started with a transitional phase that formed part of a global juncture. One phase was the transition from the early modern to the modern age, which in Bilad al-Sham occurred in the

1830s / 1840s. The other was the transition, in the 1920s, from what some historians have called the long nineteenth century ending with World War I—when European empires were at their peak, the world economy was Eurocentric and relatively unbound by borders, and nationalism rising—to the incipient crystallization of an international system of nation-states after the war.

After World War I, the region's new nation-states were not internally homogeneous, but conglomerates of various cities and their hinterlands and interurban ties, some of which—now straddling borders—were transnationalized. Put differently, Bilad al-Sham's new nation-states were from their birth urbanized, while vice versa cities were being nationalized. "More nation-state" did not mean "less city," then. There was no zero-sum game. Rather, after 1918 urbanites felt a pressing need to prove their city's relevance for the new nation-state.

To survive in this competition, different cities—and sometimes different social groups within a city—used different tactics. New capital cities held the best cards. One, which was tracked in Chapters 3 through 5, revealed a capital effect: Because Damascus was Syria's capital, it became the locus of more and more institutions and personalities, which in turn reinforced its sense of being the country's uncontested center. Other large cities reacted in kind. In Syria, Aleppo called itself "capital of the north"; Tripoli did the same in Lebanon; and Nablus' unbending nationalism earned it the moniker of Palestine's capital. Cities expressed their position within the new nation-state space in more inventive ways, too. In Palestine, Arab and Hebrew Haifa were busy being the City of Work, *Madinat al-'Amal/ 'Ir ha-Avoda,* and Arab Jaffa and Haifa feted themselves, respectively, as *'Arus Filastin* and *'Arus al-Shumal,* the Bride of Palestine and the Bride of the North, in particular the former term having been in use before 1918.

To assert their place within their nation-state some cities also "went above its head," as it were, stressing their role in broader, transnational worlds. Beirut lionized its role as a port city within the world economy and in a globalizing culture. Similarly, Tel Aviv waxed lyrical about its hyper-modern European bourgeois urbanity. Another set of cities—from big ones like Aleppo to small ones such as Sidon—underscored their standing in the world of Islam. Yet others, like Nablus or Hums, extolled their standing with Bilad al-Sham. On a related note, for people from Bilad al-Sham who had emigrated overseas, their old hometown became a metaphorical and often literal reference and entrance point to their new nation-state, from which one could try to tighten connections in the new capital. As Chapter 3 showed, while Humsis in Sao Paolo felt Syrian, they did so through a privileged connection with their old hometown.

Finally, cities exploited interurban links that now straddled a border—in other words were transnationalized within the region—to institutionally or economically improve their position within their new nation-state. Damascus played off its rail link to Haifa, in British Palestine, against the French, forcing them to keep freight prices on the Damascus-Beirut railroad low. Another example was the continued move of Nabulsis and Damascenes to Amman, the capital of Transjordan. While the separation of Bilad al-Sham's cities into four different colonial nation-states made their conditions diverge, they all faced the same challenge: how to maximize their position within the new nation-state. Some did so in ways that underlined if not reinforced continuous linkages between the four post-Ottoman states.

Socio-spatial intertwinements involving cities were interlinked with intertwinements involving the region. On the one side, the new nation-states' existence and their different experiences and structures meant that the region's perhaps most salient post-Ottoman development was its maturation, by the 1930s, as an umbrella region for its nation-states. Symptomatically, even though writers continued to refer to the region, they always also commented on, and in this sense fundamentally re-signed themselves to, the region's new divisions. The four countries were starting to move along distinct tracks.

But those tracks ran in parallel and were interlinked. This was the other side of Bilad al-Sham becoming an umbrella region for its nation-states. It showed in the shifting mental mapping of the region, in the stress on *Suriya al-Tabi'iyya* (Natural Syria), that is on the presumed geographic unity of the region. Moreover, the region's increased integration, in the late Ottoman period, after 1918 forced the hand of the new imperial rulers. They set up a region-wide customs-free zone, signed agreements about region-wide matters such as extradition, and cooperated administratively. It was not that the British and French loved each other. But they understood that they had to be in permanent contact. Together with certain infrastructural investments, especially in roads, and with the advent of the automobile, this created a curious situation. Having divided Bilad al-Sham, France and Britain unwittingly yet actively helped to keep its different parts quite close together.

This process involved nation-state actors. Politically and even more economically, many of them wanted to have their cake and eat it, too. They were protective of their increasingly distinct national interests, trying to limit political interventions and imports from neighboring countries. But simultaneously, each country treated the others as its natural outlet of goods and, in some cases, as an object of political interests. It was not that nation-state actors clearly distinguished between the national and the regional. Rather, these two were blurred. Especially in the 1920s and 1930s, the region was a space of preferential access, a place with which people in the four states identified themselves more than, say, with Turkey, Egypt, or Iraq. Hence, it also became a zone of competition. There are interesting comparisons to be made here, for example, to how after World War II French African colonies—and their imperial rulers—did not quite think in binary terms of nation-state versus everything else. Rather, as Frederick Cooper has recently showed, multiple actors weighed various combined solutions, including federal ones. The case of Bilad al-Sham's nation-states underscores not only that modern nation-states are a very big family, but also that this family is not clearly bounded. Rather, it elastically relates to other forms of state formation.[1]

Moreover, especially from the 1930s the region was more than before seen as part of a larger Arab world, doubly because the latter term became politicized. Not unlike in the relationship between cities and nation-states, this was not a zero-sum game. "More Arab world" did not equal "less region," certainly not in the 1930s. Rather, Bilad al-Sham became framed in new ways. A central dimension concerned pan-Arab nationalism, qawmiyya. On the one hand, its advocates, qawmiyyun, posited the existence of one Arab space and hence the need for one state, from the 1930s increasingly also including Egypt. On the other hand, qawmiyyun in Bilad al-Sham were more closely linked to each other than to Iraq and Egypt, and many mentally mapped "their" region as the very heart of the Arab world. However, by World War II the Bilad al-Shami umbrella became less important to the region's countries. This was because the entire Arab Middle East and various neighbors were ruled as an integrated area by the wartime British Empire; because independence came in reach for Bilad al-Sham's countries; and because the contours of the postcolonial Arab state system by now showed clearly. More than before, elites and commoners understood their respective country directly as part of the Arab world, rather than living under an intermediary regional umbrella. And more than before, the non-Bilad al-Shami country of Egypt was central to that Arab world.

Finally, the region was increasingly linked to other worlds. Those linkages were ruled by various logics. Besides *qawmiyya,* one was the fast expanding international arena centered on the League of Nations, in Geneva. Mandate powers France and Britain were de jure accountable for their actions to the League, and increasingly sovereign ex-colonies like Iraq and Egypt used the League as an arena to exert political and publicity pressure on others states. For example, Egypt shamed France into action against narcotics trafficking also in the Mandates in the 1930s. Another linkage concerned Beirut and its up-and-coming rival, Haifa. These two cities profited from—and their elites demanded—a serious French and British imperial expansion of transport infrastructures. Geoeconomically, both empires wished to improve their Mandates' access to Iraq and Iran, and geostrategically, both wanted to link the Mandates more tightly into evolving empire-wide transport and communication structures. In result, especially for Beirut the 1930s was a turning point. While World War I had destroyed the empire-state, free trade world in which it had experienced a first golden age, the developments of the 1930s were a first step toward a second golden age that would wax in the later 1940s and wane only in the early 1970s.

In the Introduction to this book, I offered a first set of conceptual observations about transpatialization. I now pick up that thread, starting with two notes on sources. First, looking at the region itself, actors in Beirut and the Yishuv produced more sources than others. This is hardly a surprise given their power. More noteworthy is that Beirut and the Yishuv have produced different source mixes. While all post-Ottoman nation-states developed a government apparatus, the Zionist

Executive/Jewish Agency may have been the largest. The resulting institutional archive, together with the records of chambers of commerce for instance in Tel Aviv and Haifa, are more voluminous than anything accessible in neighboring countries. By contrast, the city of Beirut stands out for the number and impact of its newspapers. Covering the region and beyond, many were read wide and far. Beirut produced another type of noninstitutional archive, too—that holding private papers of big merchants like Alfred Sursock, whom we met in Prelude 3—and nonstate institutional archives, for instance that of the American University of Beirut. However, although source mixes differ, their contents overlap and link up. Sources produced by a nation-state or by a city-based body, to take two examples, are not limited to a nation-state or a city. This is not simply because their actors are also interested in nonnation-state or noncity matters. It is because the very nature of nation-states and cities, and of their actors, is not fixed, but emerges in interaction with other sociospatial fields. Consequently, the sources underlying this book echo its conceptual argument about transpatialization.

My second note is related to the first. Both the Middle Eastern archives and the British and French colonial archives I consulted tend to cover core areas of nation-states more than peripheries. It was in order to balance out that effect that this book has dedicated considerable space to the central periphery, the border zone straddling Lebanon, Israel, Syria, and Jordan. Studying that area, I used not only archives but also oral history: open-ended interviews in which, skirting political topics and contemporary affairs, I asked concrete questions about everyday life up to the 1940s. The more people I talked to, the more I appreciated how oral history can question or help nuance a state archive's official perspective. A good example concerns women and men on the move. It was only after many interviews that I came to really understand what I conveyed in Chapter 4. Although the border zone was porous and many locals made do without a laissez-passer, state regulations still affected how people who were poor and not well-connected could move: at greater risk, with fewer goods, and via more arduous routes.

My next observation concerns socio-spatial intertwinements that, seen as a bundle, constitute the overall heuristic phenomenon of transpatialization in a given period. The first noteworthy point is that not only two socio-spatial fields—cities and the state, say, or the region and global circuits—were intertwined, but often three or four. Examples have abounded in this book, like cities using their transnational weight to assert themselves within the nation-state. From 1918, Damascus celebrated its stature in the Muslim world also with an eye toward its position in Syria. Nablus sought to draw level with Jerusalem, the capital of Mandate Palestine, by positing its own historical centrality in Bilad al-Sham's southern half. And Beirut was a truly urbanimperial-regional-global place before 1918—and would not have bounced back from the shock of Bilad al-Sham's post-Ottoman division if France had not, for its own reasons, invested in its traffic infrastructure and in infrastructures also to a transregional destination, Iraq. Moreover, triangular and quadrangular intertwinements were not simply structures, but showed in people's lives. The man at the center of Prelude 3, Alfred Sursock, negotiated French state connections on the social arena that was the city of Beirut all while staying in touch with former Ottoman officials and driving a far-flung business by investing in enterprises across Bilad al-Sham and beyond.

Intertwinements of socio-spatial fields often looked like the proverbial coin that has two sides. Post-Ottoman cities' nationalization, their inhabitants' endeavor to reframe themselves as nationally important, went hand in hand with the urbanization of post-Ottoman national spaces, that is with their constitution, from the very start as multiurban spaces. Moreover, multiple intertwinements evolved together. Some formed a knot, as it were. Post-Ottoman cities' continued transnational links were integral to the twin process of nationalizationurbanization. And these proverbial knots appeared in tandem. Thus, cities' recalibrated weight, strengthening interurban ties, and increasing regional integration happened simultaneously and were together central to the Ottoman stage of transpatialization.

One appreciates the very texture of one intertwinement best by focusing on it alone. A taster was the note, in Chapter 1, on Sidon. This small city continued to matter to inhabitants like Ahmad 'Arif al-Zain, who loved to love its history and its citrus products and their smells, who right there experienced shifts in the Ottoman state structure like the 1908 Young Turk Revolution, and whose journal *Kawthar* appealed to and was shaped by readers in Istanbul, Cairo, and Sao Paolo. The sheer breadth and interconnectedness of socio-spatial changes, by contrast, shows most clearly when one studies how multiple intertwinements unfolded together. Thus, the story of al-Zain's Sidon is linked to strengthening interurban ties—to how that city became subordinate to Beirut—and to Bilad al-Sham's fastening region-wide integration, which was illustrated in *Kawthar*'s appeal to readers across the region.

Next, a note is in order about the term "socio-spatial field," which I have used on several occasions throughout this book. Field is an alternative for scale, a term that, problematically, tempts us to think "vertically," upward and downward, from the local via the regional and national and imperial up to the global and back. This is confusing, for the world is not a high rise where global floors scrape the sky, stacked on top of imperial floors, which lord it over national floors that in turn grind local floors down into the dust. A sense of hierarchy persists even if we think of scales as, for instance, "concentric circles," or "rungs on a ladder," or pieces of a "matryoshka doll."[2] To make matters worse, one all too quickly thinks of scales as empirical places (some presumably just global, others local, say) and adopts a "zero-sum conception of spatial scale" (where the loss of one scale, say the global, is the win of another, say the nation-state): fallacies identified by geographers such as Doreen Massey and by social scientists such as Neil Brenner.[3] Historians have seconded them. Pierre-Yves Saunier has criticized "a *scalar* conception that suggests human societies, polities, activities and nonhuman factors are organised into levels that go from the local to the global, through the national, with each one fitted into the other according to some *pyramidal* structure." Similarly, Michael Müller and Cornelius Trop have argued that "it is simply not possible to distinguish arbitrarily between an 'inner-space' of the nation or the territorial state and an 'outer space' of interaction; in reality, people always acted in multiple geographical realms, and experienced and perceived space accordingly."[4] Field trumps scale because it is a better way to heuristically represent the multiplicity noted by Müller and Trop, or the reciprocal intertwinements of cities, regions, states, and global circuits studied in this book.

Studying such intertwinements, this book has concentrated on cases involving Bilad al-Sham and its cities. On a related note, the perspective from which I have studied the multi-dimensional heuristic process of transpatialization has been that of the region of Bilad al-Sham and of cities. Rather than being this book's methodological *unit* of analysis, however, the region of Bilad al-Sham is the *pivot* of analysis. The difference is real, not semantic. This book has treated the region not as homogeneous, but as constituted by various elements such as transnationally networked cities and inter-urban ties; not as clearly delimited in form, but as historically and contextually changing; and not as a sealed box, but as shaped in interplay also with outside fields. Internally, at its edges, and vis-à-vis the outside, the region is not a given. In short, my *methodological* use of the region as a pivot has followed this book's central *conceptual* claim: of transpatialization as the mutually constitutive intertwinement of cities, regions, states, and global circuits.[5]

Another point highlighted first in this book's Introduction was diachronic features of transpatialization. One feature was that socio-spatial intertwinements in one phase affect later phases, rather than being replaced by an entirely new set of intertwinements.[6] This point may be expanded on here. As Chapter 3 argued, following World War I the four new nation-states and British and French imperial interests were superimposed on and cut across Bilad al-Sham, interurban ties, and cities' hinterlands. Damascus's late Ottoman hinterland for instance came to lay, besides in southern Syria, also in northcentral Jordan, northeastern Palestine, and southeastern Lebanon. This also meant that previously region-wide, interurban, and hinterland ties did not simply vanish into thin air after 1918. Rather, they were transnationalized, which in turn had a transnationalizing effect on the new nation-states and on their imperial rulers' policies.

This observation matters also for how we think of the transnational. Interested historians often study transnational *situations*: how particular transnational, cross-border relationships work in a given period or even at a given moment. Further, most focus on transnational ties that are, or in as far as they are, contemporaneous with nation-states or emerge after nation-states. By contrast, examples like Damascus's transnationalized hinterland demonstrate that sometimes we can understand the complexity and functioning of a transnational situation better when we track it through time. To properly gauge why, in

Chapter 3, Damascenes Hasan al-Hamawi and Sabri Tabbaʿa moved to Amman in the 1920s, we have to see why by the late nineteenth century Damascus was penetrating its hinterland as far south as central Jordan. In short, it makes sense to study not only the transnational, not simply a situation, but transnationalization: a diachronic process by which existing socio-spatial ties are made transnational and in turn have a transnationalizing structuring effect on a nation-state from its inception.

As I stated earlier, my research of transpatialization has been written from the perspective of a region and of cities. This choice has usefully delimited the book and provided its chapters with a unified structure. A total history of all transpatialization patterns written from all perspectives would be a messy encyclopedia, not a history. This being said, other perspectives are possible. In the remainder of this Conclusion I take this book for a spin, shifting to the perspective of state territoriality and state formation.

This perspective is timely. The last few years have witnessed a reassertion, certainly in word but also in deed, of the nation-state. This is happening most manifestly in Western countries, and has led, for instance, to Brexit and to Donald Trump's election as president of the United States. Exceptions notwithstanding, this process does not reverse or stop globalization. It does, however, geographically redirect, restructure, and recategorize—including illegalize—certain transnational flows. Further, far right-wingers do not think of their respective country in isolation. Their project, the strengthening of nation-state territoriality and sovereignty, is firmly global. It just is not *liberal* global, or to use a more apt term for the post–World War II United States, it is not "nationalist globalism."[7] One takes joy in another's success: Trump in Brexit, for instance. Certainly in Europe, far right-wingers think, act, and interact across borders. Think of their parties making common cause in the European Parliament in Strasbourg. And they imagine their respective nation-state as part of a Western civilization, and believe that this civilization needs to be globally bolstered. Consider, to take a gruesome example, the professed fascist Norwegian mass murderer Anders Behring Breivik's manifesto, *2083: A European Declaration of Independence*.

The perspective of state territoriality and state formation is scholarly relevant, too. Scholars have been eagerly engaging with texts like Charles Maier's now classic "Consigning the Twentieth Century to History: Alternative Narratives for the Modern Era," published in 2000. And since the end of the Cold War and the dissolution of the Soviet Union, multitudes of historians have pored over the question of how empire state formations have been, and are, related to nation-state formations.[8]

Maier argued that a key trait from the 1860s to the 1970s, making those decades a period, was the rise of territorially intrusive, intensive states. This new type of state territoriality "emphasized that national power and efficiency rested on the saturation of space inside the frontier." In response, as I noted in the Introduction, some historians argued that state territoriality grew in interplay with, if not in response to, globalization. On a related note, in a recent *AHR* Conversation whose starting point was Maier's text, Manu Goswami argued that territoriality is not "something amenable to a 'rise and fall' metric" and not limitable to the state.[9]

It is in this context that one should see this book's point that regions and cities shaped, and were reshaped by, state territoriality. This held especially for the two most obvious changes concerning the state: the transition to a more territorialized and societally interventionist Ottoman Empire in the middle third of the nineteenth century, and the replacement of the Ottoman state by European-ruled Mandates in the 1920s. In both cases, uneven socio-spatial structures in one period helped shape the next. Britain and France found themselves compelled to concentrate means of state territoriality—infrastructures and troops, to name but two—in Haifa and Beirut, which rapidly rose from the late nineteenth century, and became Bilad al-Sham's central port city from the mid-nineteenth century, respectively. The accelerating integration, in the late Ottoman period, of region-wide ties later forced the British and French Mandate states into systemic region-wide cooperation. And a last example, in the rural border zone shared by Syria, Lebanon, Palestine, and Transjordan, Britain and France signed a Good Neighbourly Relations Agreement in 1926. Recognizing the zone's connectivity, that agreement created a transnational zone in the sense that the two Mandate state powers' territoriality and sovereignty stretched beyond their mutual border, and overlapped.

Another way of thinking about the channeling of socio-spatial structures from one state to its successor state is that it creates a double effect. First, it helps explain why, within a state's borders, territoriality is highly uneven, "thicker" in some parts than others. Thus, France maintained the Ottoman-time Beirut-Damascus infrastructural link due to its continued importance for Syria and Lebanon's place in the world economy after World War I. At the same time, state territoriality is reshaped by new developments. A case in point is the effect of the Palestine Revolt on the central periphery. From 1936 to 1939, British troops radically, unilaterally, and with some permanent effects reinterpreted the Good Neighbourly Relations Agreement by pursuing armed Arabs into French Mandate territory and conducting identity checks there, too. A previously thin layer of territoriality became thicker. Crucially, this meant not only that Britain reinforced the border with a wall-like structure, but also that it systematized its presence beyond that border. Still, the 1926 agreement remained in place at the time.

This last point serves as a stepping-stone for a side note. Not unlike different layers of different periods of capitalist accumulation—diagnosed with insight by Marxisant geographers like Neil Smith—territoriality is layered. Different periods and projects leave sediments, as it were, in the landscape of the territorial exercise and maintenance of power. Hence, territoriality is not simply "thicker" in some places than others. It is variedly layered, too. This is because practices of territoriality take on material form for a wide range of reasons. While "capital is continuously invested in the built environment in order to produce surplus value and expand the basis of capital itself," modern territorial states invest and change the built environment to legitimate themselves, and / or to provide infrastructures that facilitate business, and / or to provide security to an area, that is, for symbolic, economic, and / or political-strategic reasons, among others. In addition, for reasons including "pork," self-legitimation, and the immense variety of infrastructural tasks many modern states perform, old if not outdated material forms of territoriality are often kept up. By contrast, capital is much more creatively destructive, "continually withdrawn from the built environment so that it can move elsewhere and take advantage of higher profit rates." As a consequence, capital affects territory at a much faster rhythm and more radically than the state, which often has to accept, create, and maintain many more, and many more different, territoriality sediments.[10]

Returning to the double effect created by the channeling of socio-spatial structures from one state to its successor, the second effect—the other side of the same coin, really—is that these layers do not necessarily stop at borders. To be sure, materialized manifestations of state territoriality are most often visible within a state's own territory. But there are enough exceptions for that presumed "rule" to be bent, if not broken. Certainly since the interwar period, and in some ways from the later nineteenth century, there has been much international cooperation in and through institutions like the League of Nations, a point related to Glenda Sluga's *Internationalism in the Age of Nationalism*. Further, the stronger a state, the more readily it projects its territoriality beyond its borders. In the case of the United States, think of the world-enveloping web of Cold War and post–Cold War military bases. Consider, too, the material manifestations of Jenifer Van Vleck's U.S. *Empire of the Air* emerging, in Latin America, from the interwar period. And going back to the late nineteenth century, take the stationing of U.S. border control officers in Canadian ports, a move that, "although . . . infringing on British (and Canadian) sovereignty . . . London welcomed [because it] helped to reduce the number of undesirable immigrants."[11]

The Middle East, too, illustrates that a state's assertion of territorial power can be materially felt far beyond its borders. When Syria and Iraq nationalized parts of their economy in the 1950s and 1960s, a transnational ripple effect ensued, most manifestly in Beirut. Because Beirut had been Bilad al-Sham's dominant port city from the mid-nineteenth century, and started to seriously link up with Iraq from the 1930s, thousands of Syrians and Iraqis moved their capital along well-oiled, long-established networks to banks in the capital of Lebanon, which in 1956 passed an extremely strict bank secrecy law. Some even moved themselves, helping to create new neighborhoods like Badaro. Action in Damascus and Baghdad impacted—if indirectly, and via societal actors—Beirut's built environment. The postwar rise of oil production in Saudi

Arabia and Kuwait showed, too. From 1956 to 1966, two-thirds of Gulf oil surplus revenues flowed to Beirut. Seven banks in 1945 became ninety-three in 1966, many in the neighborhood of Hamra, helping to expand and change its structure.[12]

Money and people flowed from Arab states to Beirut and helped change its urban face as well because Beirut from the 1940s to the 1970s was a particular kind of—laissez-faire, pre-1970s neoliberal—global city. It linked international trade, finance, communication, transport, and knowledge circuits with multiple recently decolonized countries in the Arab East and Arabian Peninsula. Fledgling countries still needed Beirut's international links and vice versa—actors from outside the region still needed it for easy access to recently decolonized countries. For our purpose, what matters is that this development did not unfold in a state-free space. Beirut's rise was embedded within an international system dominated by the United States. And U.S. state territoriality had material manifestations in that city, too, if again mostly indirectly. Washington had had little political interest in the Middle East before World War II, but during the Cold War it was determined to protect the region's oil from the Soviet Union. It was under this powerful protective umbrella that U.S. oil companies expanded their operations on the Arabian Peninsula; invested heavily in the construction of the Trans-Arabian Pipeline from Saudi Arabia to Sidon, south of Beirut; and in Beirut opened administrative headquarters that were soon followed by U.S. banks like Chase Manhattan, which used the city as their Middle East-wide "observation post," and by other U.S. and Western businesses.[13]

I now turn to state formation, and specifically to the question of the relationship between empire- and nation-state formations, which as noted earlier has attracted the interest of many a historian in the past quarter century.[14] Most agree that the former did not lead neatly to the latter, and that in consequence the two are not by necessity mutually exclusive. My first point regarding this matter relates to a major qualitative shift in international administrative communications that included Bilad al-Sham's Mandate powers in the 1930s. That shift involved the League of Nations in Geneva, where Egyptian officials played an intricate lobbying game. This happened from the late 1920s, long before

Egypt became a League member in 1937; it did not regard high politics but narcotics, treated in a technical commission of the League; and it involved high British Egyptian police officials like Russell Pasha but also Egyptians, who dominated Egypt's Central Narcotics Intelligence Bureau. Policy-wise, Egypt used the League's worries about narcotics to put pressure on a sovereign country, France.

Equally important, Egypt used the League politically: As an international arena to maximize—to test and stretch and expand—partial sovereignty *before* it became quasi-independent in 1936. This point builds on Susan Pedersen's argument that the League, although an imperial creation, also became an international arena for political claim making for colonized people. Egypt's claim making differed from A Mandate subjects', for instance. Egyptian government officials had access to and dealings with a League commission, in effect affirming their state's partial sovereignty and seeking to extend it. By contrast, Syrian or Palestinian societal actors tried to send missives to Geneva and used lobbyists who, like Shakib Arslan, lived there but did not have regularized access to the League. But one may also see the two as being placed alongside each other on a continuum, each seeking to use the League to move on that continuum. On one end were fully sovereign states, most in Western Europe and America. Next came colonies that, though still under de facto imperial control, were early after World War I given more autonomy, like Egypt in 1922. (Britain called this independence.) These were followed by the A, B, and C Mandates, in this order. Finally, on the other end of the continuum were colonies whose subjects had no regularized access to the League whatsoever.[15]

This brings me to my second point. I have omitted one category of countries in the above list: the Eastern and Southeastern European states that gained independence before World War I, seceding from the Ottoman Empire, or following the dismemberment of the Austro-Hungarian Empire and Russia's and Germany's territorial contraction. These states were the ones profiting from the Wilsonian Moment and the willingness of the dominant Versailles Conference and League founding member states to internationally recognize them. But these League members treated Eastern and Southeastern Europe as a region filled with problem children, too, forcing its states to legally accept minority protection regimes as a precondition for international recognition and League membership. The first bilateral state League treaty was signed with Poland in 1919 and served as a model for later ones.[16]

Seen from this perspective, the distance between the ex-Ottoman A Mandate states and the Eastern and Southeastern European states starts to look less drastic. This was not colony versus nation-state, but colony "plus" versus nation-state "minus." That was the case not only because neither the A Mandates nor Eastern and Southeastern European states were fully independent. But also because minority protection regimes were in principle meant to remain in place, while the A Mandates were promised independence at some point in time. Further, there was the issue of political self-representation. In 1919, the Syrian General Congress, whose members came from across Bilad al-Sham, resolved that "considering the fact that the Arabs inhabiting the Syrian area . . . are by no means less developed than the Bulgarians, Serbians, Greeks, and Roumanians at the beginning of their independence, we protest against Article 22 of the Covenant of the League of Nations, placing us among nations in their middle stage of development which stand in need of a mandatory power." Put differently, the congress was not against Mandates per se—just not for Arabs, for they were in the same category as the ex-Ottoman Europeans. Next, postwar minority protection regimes were rooted in a prewar practice related to the Ottoman Empire's contraction: in the 1870s, Serbia, Montenegro, and Romania were recognized by the European powers under the condition that they would issue legally binding minority protection guarantees. Last, when the majority Arab A Mandate Iraq joined the League in 1932, it too was forced to accept a minority protection regime, that is it was inserted into the same category as all Southeast and Eastern European nation-states, including Turkey.[17]

The upshot of the above is that we may group European ex-Ottoman states, European ex-German / Austro-Hungarian / Russian states, and the ex-Ottoman A Mandates into one single historical category: polities that emerged from the contraction and collapse of Western Eurasian empires. Put differently, we may see the A Mandates, which became formally independent in the mid- to late 1940s, not as early cases of the post–World War II wave of decolonization of African and Asian colonies of West European empires, which is how they are normally categorized by historians of decolonization.[18] Rather, they were the tail end of a long wave of decolonization that started before World War I, with the existential problems of West Eurasian empires.

This view is supported, in addition to the five points above, with a point I made in Chapter 4. In the A Mandate states, decolonization did not simply happen in the 1940s. It started at the end of the 1920s. Iraq became independent in 1930, and at the same time the other A Mandates' nation-state movements—the Lebanese, Syrian, and Zionist; in a less formal way the Palestinian, and also the Transjordanian—garnered enough political and / or economic weight to effectively cajole France and Britain into beginning to accept their demands to set the Mandates' discursive and institutional political agenda. Although this was not independence, the speed of this development reflects that politically the A Mandates formed the tail end of the self-same process that had peaked in Eastern and Southeastern Europe at most a decade earlier, and that in postimperial Russia was settled—contained—as late as 1926.[19]

Moreover, the dusk of the dissolution of Western Eurasian empires coincided with the dawn of decolonization in post–World War II Africa and Asia. And the A Mandate states were right there in the front row: together with political developments in 1930s India, for instance, and with the first somewhat serious French and British attempts to use socioeconomic development to restructure and better legitimize their colonies, also those in Africa, against rising socioeconomic and political demands. At this point, too, people in the A Mandates increasingly made transnational links, rooted in the 1920s, to Asian colonies like India and to politicians like Mahatma Gandhi. Still, around 1930 only the A Mandate clearly demanded independence; elsewhere, this was not yet the case. It was as if around 1930 the A Mandates were at a watershed, looking in two directions: back to where they had come from, an Ottoman universe that had been tightly related to Europe and that was now disappearing into the fog of the past; and forward, to what after World War II became known as the Third World.

Let me conclude with a glance forward to 2017. Since the 1970s and especially 1990s, globalization has been speeding up, but an economic slowdown caused by the 2008 recession has now linked up with cultural worries to produce new calls for the (re)assertion of nation-states. In parallel, in the past two decades cities have again become more manifestly powerful; some are even creating new domestic and international networks. Regions are being reinvented and reconfigured, also across state borders, whether violently, as recently by the Islamic State, or peacefully, as in Europe. States are adjusting domestically, and they are recalibrating bilateral ties, multinational organizations like the European Union, and worldwide international cooperations. Last but not least, the exercise of power by dominant states is becoming more complex and contested with China's rise, Russia's renewed aspirations, and the United States' domestic travails, to name only three recent developments.

In sum, we seem to be experiencing again—like in the 1920s—a transitional phase: a time of confusion in which we may wish to take a hard look back, to a not-so-distant past, to analyze where we are and to ponder where we may be going.

# ABBREVIATIONS

| | |
|---|---|
| AAS | *Asian and African Studies* |
| AF | *Asie française* |
| AHR | *American Historical Review* |
| ASQ | *Arab Studies Quarterly* |
| BEO | *Bulletin d'études orientales* |
| BERI | *Bulletin of the Economic Research Institute* |
| BJMES | *British Journal of Middle Eastern Studies* |
| BPES | *Bulletin of the Palestine Economic Society* |
| CL | *Commerce du Levant* |
| CEH | *Contemporary European History* |
| CSSAME | *Comparative Studies of South Asia, Africa and the Middle East* |
| CSSH | *Comparative Studies in Society and History* |
| ED | *Economic Data* |
| GG | *Geschichte und Gesellschaft* |
| HC | *History Compass* |
| HJ | *Historical Journal* |
| HM | *History and Memory* |
| IHR | *International History Review* |
| IJMES | *International Journal of Middle East Studies* |
| ILR | *International Labour Review* |
| IS | *Israel Studies* |
| JAH | *Journal of American History* |
| JESHO | *Journal of Economic and Social History of the Orient* |
| JGH | *Journal of Global History* |

| | |
|---|---|
| JICH | *Journal of Imperial and Commonwealth History* |
| JIS | *Journal of Islamic Studies* |
| JMEH | *Journal of Modern European History* |
| JPS | *Journal of Palestine Studies* |
| JQF | *Jerusalem Quarterly File* |
| JUH | *Journal of Urban History* |
| JWH | *Journal of World History* |
| MAMM | *Monde Arabe Maghreb-Machrek* |
| MES | *Middle Eastern Studies* |
| MESAB | *Middle East Studies Association Bulletin* |
| MHR | *Mediterranean Historical Review* |
| MMIA | *Majallat al-Majmaʿ al-ʿIlmi al-ʿArabi* |
| MS | *Meshek Shitufi* |
| MT | *Misʾhar ve-Taʿasiyah* |
| MW | *Muslim World* |
| NN | *Nations and Nationalism* |
| NSGTD | *al-Nashra al-Shahriyya li-l-Ghurfa al-Tijariyya fi Dimashq* |
| PME | *Palestine and the Middle East* |
| PP | *Palestine Post* |
| RI | *al-Rabita al-Islamiyya* |
| RIPE | *Review of International Political Economy* |
| RMMM | *Revue des Mondes Musulmans et de la Méditerranée* |
| SM | *Sokher ha-Makolet* |
| TS | *Theory and Society* |
| WA | *Weltwirtschaftliches Archiv* |
| WI | *Die Welt des Islams* |
| ZDP | *Zeitschrift des deutschen Palästinavereins* |
| ZG | *Zeitschrift für Geschichtswissenschaft* |

# NOTES

## Introduction

1. The term "Middle East" became widely used only after World War II. See Michael Bonine, Abbas Amanat, and Michael Gasper, eds., *Is There a Middle East? The Evolution of a Geopolitical Concept* (Stanford, CA: Stanford University Press, 2012).

2. I chose the term "transpatialization" for two reasons. Two other terms I toyed with, "transnationalization" and "cross-territorization," were too strongly associated with one reference point, the nation and (state) territoriality, respectively. Hence, they did not adequately denote varied intertwinement patterns. Moreover, the term "transpatialization," while not well known, has been used before, in a way rather close to, though not identical with, my use. I thank the graduate students of a Basel University workshop who in November 2015 disabused me of the idea of using cross-territorization. In the ensuing discussion, we arrived at the term transpatialization and then found out that it had already been used, however en passant; see, e.g., Christiane Harzig and Dirk Hoerder, *What Is Migration History?* (Cambridge: Polity, 2009), 113.

3. Sebastian Conrad, *What Is Global History?* (Princeton, NJ: Princeton University Press, 2016), 118, 135. Similarly, Margrit Pernau, *Transnationale Geschichte* (Göttingen: UTB, 2010), 19, states that "we need empirical studies that treat their benchmarks [Bezugsgrössen] flexibly;" and Arif Dirlik, "Performing the World," *JWH* 16 (2005): 391, affirms that "the radical challenge of transnational history itself lies in its conjoining of the supranational and the sub-national." See also Ronald Robertson, "Glocalization: Time-Space and Homogeneity-Heterogeneity," in *Global Modernities,* ed. Mike Featherstone, Scott M. Lash, and Roland Robertson (London: Sage, 1995), 25–44, who posited "the simultaneity and the

interpenetration of what are conventionally called the global and the local" (30); and explained that nowadays the local is not autonomous but reframed through interplay with global trends.

4. Quote: Dominique Chevallier, "Consciences syriennes et représentations cartographiques à la fin du XIX et au début du XX siècles," in *The Syrian Land in the 18th and 19th Century: The Common and the Specific in the Historical Experience,* ed. Thomas Philipp (Stuttgart: Steiner, 1992), 4. See also Lamia Shehadeh, "The Name of Syria in Ancient and Modern Usage," in *The Origins of Syrian Nationhood: Histories, Pioneers and Identity,* ed. Adel Beshara (London: Routledge, 2011), 17–21; and Fruma Zachs, *The Making of Syrian Identity: Intellectuals and Merchants in Nineteenth-Century Beirut* (Leiden: Brill, 2005), 246–249.

5. Hans Wehr, *A Dictionary of Modern Written Arabic* (Beirut: Libraire du Liban, 1980), 72. See also Shehadeh, "Name of Syria," 17–20.

6. Muhammad Kurd 'Ali, "Min al-faiha' ila al-shahba,' " *Muqtabas* 6 (1911): 687.

7. Quotes: Arnon Groiss, "Communalism as a Factor in the Rise of the Syria Idea in the 1800s and early 1900s," in Beshara, *Origins of Syrian Nationhood,* 39; and Chevallier, "Consciences Syriennes," 4.

8. For the general relevance of cities in Islamic civilization, see Edmund Bosworth, "Editor's Introduction," in *Historical Cities of the Islamic World* (Leiden: Brill, 2007), xi; Renata Holod, Attilio Petruccioli, and André Raymond, "Introduction," in *The City in the Islamic World,* ed. Salma Jayyusi (Leiden: Brill, 2008), 1:xviii; and, magisterial, Paul Wheatley, *The Places Where Men Pray Together: Cities in Islamic Lands, Seventh through the Tenth Centuries* (Chicago: University of Chicago Press, 2001). For the importance of cities in eastern "Mediterranean civilisations" from Antiquity, see André Raymond, *Grandes villes arabes à l'époque ottomane* (Paris: Sindbad, 1985), 11.

9. Weberian views—based on Max Weber, *The City* (Glencoe: Free Press, 1958 [German, 1921])—that Islamic, unlike Western European, cities lacked self-governing mechanisms have long been refuted; so have been Orientalist arguments about one clearly identifiable "Islamic city." See Ira Lapidus, *Muslim Cities in the Later Middle Ages* (Cambridge: Harvard University Press, 1967); and Albert Hourani, "Introduction," in *The Islamic City: A Colloquium,* ed. Albert Hourani and Samuel Stern (Oxford: Bruno Cassirer, 1970), 9–24 at 11. More recent critiques include Janet Abu Lughod, "The Islamic City," *IJMES* 19 (1987): 155–176; Nezar Alsayyad, *Cities and Caliphs: On the Genesis of Arab Muslim Urbanism* (New York: Greenwood Press, 1991); André Raymond, "Islamic City, Arab City," *BJMES* 21 (1994): 3–18; and Nora Lafi, "Ville arabe et modernité administrative municipale," *Histoire urbaine* 1 (2001): 149–167. For the Ottoman period, see Raymond, *Grandes villes arabes;* and Jane Hathaway, with contributions by Karl Barbir, *The Arab Lands under Ottoman Rule, 1516–1800* (New York: Pearson Longman, 2008), 138–168. For rural life, see ibid., 169–187.

10. For the key elements of direct Ottoman rule, see Raymond, *Grandes villes arabes,* 25–29. For socio-administrative structures like guilds, see ibid., 118–167. For the notables, see Hathaway, *Arab Lands,* 79–113, and the classic text by Albert Hourani, "Ottoman Reform and the Politics of Notables," in *Beginnings of Modernization in the Middle East,* ed. William Polk and Richard Chambers (Chicago: University of Chicago Press, 1968), 41–68. For the renegotiation of political relationships in the seventeenth century, see Bruce Masters, *The Arabs of the Ottoman Empire, 1516–1918* (Cambridge: Cambridge University Press, 2013), 17–18, 83–88.

11. Classics are J. Gallagher and R. Robinson, "The Imperialism of Free Trade," *Economic History Review,* New Series 6, no. 1 (1953): 1–15; Eric Hobsbawm, *The Age of Capital, 1848–1875* (New York: New American Library, 1979); and Hobsbawm, *The Age of Empire, 1875–1914* (London: Weidenfeld and Nicolson, 1987). See also Steven Topik and Allen Wells, "Commodity Chains in a Global Economy," in *A World Connecting, 1870–1945,* ed. Emily Rosenberg (Cambridge, MA: Belknap Press of Harvard University Press, 2012), 593–814 (with focus on both the European center and truly global commodity chains); Giovanni Arrighi, "The Global Market," *Journal of World-System Research* 5 (1999): 218–227; Arrighi, *The Long Twentieth Century: Money, Power, and the Origins of our Times* (London: Verso, 1994) (a political economic take on capitalism); Jürgen Osterhammel, *The Transformation of the World: A Global History of the Nineteenth Century,* trans. Patrick Camiller (Princeton, NJ: Princeton University Press, 2014), esp. "Pax Britannica," 450–460; "Paths of Economic Development and Underdevelopment," 658–666; and "Capitalism," 667–672. See also John Darwin, *The Empire Project: The Rise and Fall of the British World System, 1830–1970* (Cambridge: Cambridge University Press, 2009), 23–304 (the empire as a "world-system," ibid., xi, which was as much driven by economic and technological globalization as it structured and policed the world).

12. Quote: Charles Bright and Michael Geyer, "World History in a Global Age," *AHR* 100 (1995): 1045–1046. For territoriality, see Charles Maier, "Consigning the Twentieth Century to History: Alternative Narratives for the Modern Era," *AHR* 105 (2000): 807–831; Charles Maier, "Leviathan 2.0: Inventing Modern Statehood," in Rosenberg, *A World Connecting,* 29–282; and Osterhammel, *Transformation,* 405–406, 572–633. For the Ottoman Empire, see Maurus Reinkowski, *Dinge der Ordnung. Eine vergleichende Untersuchung über die osmanische Reformpolitik im 19. Jahrhundert* (Munich: Oldenbourg, 2005); Şükrü Hanioğlu, *A Brief History of the Late Ottoman Empire* (Princeton, NJ: Princeton University Press, 2008); and François Georgeon, *Abdülhamid II* (Paris: Fayard, 2003). One may usefully compare the complexity of modern Ottoman state territoriality with the limits and conditions of late nineteenth-century European imperial expansion: Tony Ballantyne and Antoinette Burton, "Empires and the Reach of the Global," in Rosenberg, *A World Connecting,* 301. The term "Arabism" was coined by Ernest Dawn, "From Ottomanism to Arabism," *Review of Politics* 23 (1961): 378–400.

13. Osterhammel, *Transformation,* 58; Christopher Bayly, *The Birth of the Modern World, 1780–1914* (Malden, MA: Blackwell, 2004), 23–120. For the Ottoman Empire as a whole, see Ali Yaycıoğlu, *Partners of Empire. The Crisis of the Ottoman Empire in the Age of Revolutions* (Stanford, CA: Stanford University Press, 2016).

14. Quotes: Jean-Luc Arnaud, "Modernization of the Cities of the Ottoman Empire (1800–1920)," in Jayyusi, *City in the Islamic World,* 2:974; and Bruce Masters, "Review Essay," *JUH* 34 (2007): 161, who talks of cities in other regions, too. For urbanization around the world, see Osterhammel, *Transformation,* 241–321. For the Ottoman Empire, see Stefan Weber, *Damascus: Ottoman Modernity and Urban Transformation (1808–1918),* 2 vols. (Aarhus: Aarhus University Press, 2009); and Meropi Anastasiadou, *Salonique, 1830–1912. Une ville ottomane à l'âge des Réformes* (Leiden: Brill, 2000). For Europe, see Andrew Lees and Lynn Hollen Lees, *Cities and the Making of Modern Europe, 1750–1914* (Cambridge: Cambridge University Press, 2007), including ch. 8, "Imperial and Colonial Cities." For a continent that scholars for a long time rarely associated with urbanization, Africa, see Catherine Coquery Vidrovitch, *Histoire des villes d'Afrique noire* (Paris: Albin Michel, 1993), also on the pre-modern period.

15. Compare Daniel Headrick, *The Tentacles of Progress: Technology Transfer in the Age of Imperialism, 1850–1940* (New York: Oxford University Press, 1988).

16. Although declining relatively, those cities experienced urban growth, too. The term "regional gravitation point" is inspired by Fernand Braudel, *Civilization & Capitalism, 15th–18th Century,* trans. Siaìn Reynolds (New York: Collins, 1983), 2:27, arguing that "the world-economy always has an urban center of gravity."

17. For the war, see M. Talha Çiçek, *War and State Formation in Syria: Cemal Pasha's Governorate During World War I, 1914–1917* (New York: Routledge, 2014); and Hasan Kayalı, "Wartime Regional and Imperial Integration of Greater Syria during World War One," in *The Syrian Land: Processes of Integration and Fragmentation,* ed. Thomas Philipp and Birgit Schäbler (Stuttgart: Steiner, 1998), 295–306. More broadly, see Eugene Rogan, *The Fall of the Ottomans: The Great War in the Middle East* (London: Allen Lane, 2015); Leila Fawaz, *A Land of Aching Hearts: the Middle East in the Great War* (Cambridge: Cambridge University Press, 2014); and Michael Reynolds, *Shattering Empires: the Clash and Collapse of the Ottoman and Russian Empires, 1908–1918* (Cambridge: Cambridge University Press, 2011).

18. For continuities versus changes post-1918, see James Gelvin, "Was There a Mandate Period? Some Concluding Thoughts," in *The Routledge Handbook of the History of the Middle East Mandates,* ed. Cyrus Schayegh and Andrew Arsan (London: Routledge, 2015), 420–432. For the League, see Susan Pedersen, *The Guardians: The League of Nations and the Crisis of Empire* (Oxford: Oxford University Press, 2015).

19. See Adam Tooze, *The Deluge: The Great War and the Remaking of Global Order, 1916–1931* (London: Allen Lane, 2014); Peter Gatrell, "War after War: Conflicts, 1919–1923," in *Blackwell Companion to the First World War,* ed. John Horne (Oxford: Blackwell, 2010), 558–575; and Robert Gerwarth and Erez Manela, "The Great War as Global War: Imperial Conflict and the Reconfiguration of World Order, 1911–1923," *Diplomatic History* 38, no. 4 (2014): 787. Regarding Europe, Eric Hobsbawm remembers in his memoirs a transitional rather than totally new 1920s. Conversely, leading German historian Wolfgang Mommsen diagnosed the war as "the fatal crisis of old bourgeois Europe"; and in his historical works Hobsbawm agreed, pointing also to the effects of the Russian Revolution. Wolfgang Mommsen, "Der Erste Weltkrieg und die Krise Europas," in *"Keiner fühlt sich hier mehr als Mensch . . . ,"* ed. Gerhard Hirschfeld et al. (Essen: Klartext, 1993), 27. Eric Hobsbawm, *Interesting Times: A Twentieth-Century Life* (London: Allen Lane, 2002); Eric Hobsbawm, *The Age of Extremes: A History of the World, 1914–1991* (London: Michael Joseph, 1994). See also Enzo Traverso, *A feu et à sang. De la guerre civile européenne, 1914–1945* (Paris: Stock, 2007).

20. This periodization parallels, though is not driven by all, the same factors as those applied for Europe in Tooze, *Deluge.* See also the emphasis, by Robert Bocye, *The Great Interwar Crisis and the Collapse of Globalization* (Basingstoke: Palgrave, 2009), on the late 1920s / early 1930s as a twin economic *and* political-(strategic-diplomatic) crisis in Europe and beyond.

21. Cyrus Schayegh, "The Mandates and / as Decolonization," in Schayegh and Arsan, *Routledge Handbook of the History of the Middle East Mandates,* 412–419.

22. Ibid.

23. For *qawmiyya* in the 1930s, the locus classicus is Yehoshua Porath, *In Search of Arab Unity, 1930–1945* (London: Frank Cass, 1986). See also Adeed Dawisha, *Arab Nationalism in the Twentieth Century: From Triumph to Despair* (Princeton: Princeton University Press, 2003), 49–106.

24. For Britain, see Martin Wilmington, *The Middle East Supply Center* (Albany: State University of New York Press, 1971). For the League, see Porath, *Arab Unity.* For Beirut, see Samir Kassir, *Beirut,* trans. M. B. DeBevoise (Berkeley: University of California Press, 2010).

25. Edward Soja, "The Socio-Spatial Dialectic," *Annals of the Association of American Geographers* 70 (1980): 207–225.

26. Lara Putnam, "To Study the Fragments / Whole: Microhistory and the Atlantic World," *Journal of Social History* 39 (2006): 620, has rightfully stated that "the nation-states remains the *default* frame of reference" for historians (emphasis added).

27. Themes include migrations, human rights, environmental degradation, energy, economic globalization, "the possibility of shared emotions," "themes of cultural

encounters and networks," racism and anti-racism, NGOS, and war; see Akira Iriye, *Global and Transnational History: The Past, Present, and Future* (New York: Palgrave Macmillan, 2013), 48 and 52 (quotes), 36–68. Conceptually incisive primers are Pierre-Yves Saunier, *Transnational History* (New York: Palgrave Macmillan, 2013) and Pernau, *Transnationale Geschichte,* 36–131; see also Matthias Middell and Katja Naumann, "The Writing of World History in Europe from the Middle of the Nineteenth Century to the Present: Conceptual Renewal and Challenge to National Histories," in *Transnational Challenges to National History Writing* (New York: Palgrave Macmillan, 2013), 54–139. For geographical areas, see Matthias Middell and Katja Naumann, "Global History 2008–2010: Empirische Erträge, konzeptionelle Debatten, neue Synthesen," *Comparativ* 20 (2010): 93–133, a statistical analysis of 512 book reviews, conference announcements and conference reports posted from 2008–2010 on the internet listserv geschichte.transnational, which found that 37 percent treated various interactional zones, 32 percent world regions, 24 percent nation-states, 3 percent oceans and seas, and another 3 percent cities. A similar geographical profile emerges from bibliographies in Peter Stearns, *Globalization in World History* (London: Routledge, 2010), 123, 156–157, and in Jürgen Osterhammel and Niels Petersson, *Globalization: A Short History* (Princeton: Princeton University Press, 2005), 153–170, 171–180.

28. Middell and Naumann, "Global History 2008–2010," 99, have stated that "some speak of entangled history, others of shared or connected history, some try [their hand at] cultural exchange or interculturality, some call the result hybridization or entanglement (*Verflechtung*), others again seek to understand histoire croisée." For an overview of methods and for an excellent bibliography, see Pernau, *Transnationale Geschichte,* 36–84, 155–166; see also Agnes Arndt et al., "Europäische Geschichtsschreibung zwischen Theorie und Praxis," in *Vergleichen, Verflechten, Verwirren? Europäische Geschichtsschreibung zwischen Theorie und Praxis* (Göttingen: Vandenhoeck & Ruprecht, 2010), 11–32, esp. 15. For *histoire croisée,* see Werner and Zimmermann, "Beyond Comparison: Histoire Croisée and the Challenge of Reflexivity," *History and Theory* 45 (2006): 30–50. Also, some transnational historians originally trained in non-Western countries have argued that from a southern perspective the transnational may be analyzed as "translocal," for the initial absence of a 'nation' does not mean the absence, too, of so-called transnational connections; see Ulrike Freitag and Achim von Oppen "Introduction: 'Translocality': An Approach to Connection and Transfer in Area Studies," in *Translocality: The Study of Globalizing Processes from a Southern Perspective* (Leiden: Brill, 2010), 1–21. Similarly, see Jürgen Osterhammel, "Transnationale Gesellschaftsgeschichte: Erweiterung oder Alternative?" *GG* 27 (2001): 469; Albert Wirz, "Für eine transnationale Gesellschaftsgeschichte," *GG* 27 (2001): 491.

29. Pierre-Yves Saunier and Akira Iriye, "The Professor and the Madman," in *The Palgrave Dictionary of Transnational History* (New York: Palgrave, 2009), xviii. Similarly, see David Thelen, "The Nation and beyond: Transnational Perspectives on United States Historiography," *JAH* 86 (1999): 967.

30. For "umbrella," see Bernhard Struck et al., "Introduction: Space and Scale in Transnational History," *IHR* 33 (2011): 573, also 579, 581n6. For "angle" and "perspective," see Saunier and Iriye, "Professor," xx.

31. Quotes: Middell and Naumann, "Global History 2008–2010," 98; and Philipp Gassert, "Transnationale Geschichte," 10, Version: 2.0, in Docupedia-Zeitgeschichte, October 29, 2012, http://docupedia.de/zg. See also Kiran Patel, "Transnational History," pt. 4, 2010, www.ieg-ego.eu/en.threads/theories-and -methods/transnational-history. Some call that consensus slightly "wooly"; see Patricia Clavin, "Defining Transnationalism," *CEH* 14 (2005): 433.

32. However, in some parts of Europe, their medieval autonomy was eroded already in the early modern period, as Charles Tilly, *Coercion, Capital, and European States, AD 990–1990* (Cambridge: Blackwell, 1990), has shown looking at the interplay between state coercion and city capital, and as urban historians have detailed: see Yann Lignereux, *Lyon et le roi. De la "bonne ville" à l'absolutisme municipal (1594–1654)* (Seyssel: Champ Vallon, 2003).

33. Quotes: Lees and Lees, *Cities*, 281, 1–2. Three of many fascinating studies include Pierre-Yves Saunier, *L'esprit lyonnais: XIXe-XXe siècle: genèse d'une représentation sociale* (Paris: CNRS, 1995); David Harvey, *Consciousness and the Urban Experience: Studies in the History and Theory of Capitalist Urbanization* (Baltimore, MD: Johns Hopkins University Press, 1985); and Peter Fritzsche, *Reading Berlin 1900* (Cambridge, MA: Harvard University Press, 1996). Conceptually insightful is Bernard Lepetit, "La ville: cadre, objet, sujet," *Enquête* 4 (1996), http://enquete .revuews.org/663. A classic is Asa Briggs, *Victorian Cities* (London: Odham's Press, 1963).

34. Quotes: Osterhammel, *Transformation*, 244, 244. See also ibid., 241–264. Cities were central also in earlier periods of globalization (see Braudel, *Civilization & Capitalism*, 2:27) and later (see John Friedmann, "The World City Hypothesis," *Development and Change* 17 [1986]: 69–83; and Saskia Sassen, *The Global City* [Princeton, NJ: Princeton University Press, 1991]).

35. Programmatic statements about the city's multidimensionality and entwinement with other spaces have come principally from sociologists and geographers. See Manuel Castells, *The Rise of the Network Society,* 2nd ed. (Malden, MA: Blackwell, 2000), 407–459; Saskia Sassen, *Cities in a World Economy,* 4th ed. (London: Sage, 2012); Michael Timberlake and Xiulian Ma, "Cities and Globalization," in *The Blackwell Companion to Globalization,* ed. George Ritzer (Malden, MA: Blackwell, 2007), 254–2711; Allen Scott and Michael Storper, "The Nature of Cities: The

Scope and Limits of Urban Theory," *International Journal of Urban and Regional Research* 39 (2014): 1–15; and Doreen Massey, "A Global Sense of Place," in *Reading Human Geography,* ed. Trevor Barnes et al. (London: Arnold, [1991] 1997), 315–323. U.S. urban historians used to be less interested in these larger questions (see Bruce Stave, "A Conversation with Charles Tilly," *JUH* 24 [1998]: 205), but see the classic by Kenneth Jackson, *Crabgrass Frontier: The Suburbanization of the United States* (New York: Oxford University Press, 1985); Samuel Hays, "From the History of the City to the History of the Urbanized Society," *JUH* 19 (1993): 3–25; and Vivian Bickford-Smith, "Introduction: The Case for Studying Cities and Nationalisms," *JUH* 38 (2012): 855–861. Further, historians have historicized nation-state formation by looking at localities. Peter Sahlins, *Boundaries: The Making of France and Spain in the Pyrenees* (Berkeley: University of California Press, 1989), has studied the premodern and modern history of the Spanish-French border to demonstrate how local forces and spaces helped shape nation-states; and Alon Confino, *The Nation as a Local Metaphor: Württemberg, Imperial Germany, and National Memory, 1871–1918* (Chapel Hill: University of North Carolina Press, 1997), has studied how from 1870 the German term *Heimat*—approximately, 'homeland'—turned into an intermediating concept between a rising German-wide nationalism and local collective identities.

36. Peregrine Horden and Nicholas Purcell, "The Mediterranean and 'the New Thalassology,'" *AHR* 111 (2006): 735; Peregrine Horden and Nicholas Purcell, *The Corrupting Sea: A Study of Mediterranean History* (Oxford: Blackwell, 2000); Peter Burke, "Towards a Comparative History of the Modern Mediterranean, 1750–1919," *JWH* 23 (2012): 907–939; K. N. Chaudhuri, *Trade and Civilisation in the Indian Ocean: An Economic History from the Rise of Islam to 1750* (Cambridge: Cambridge University Press, 1985); David Igler, *The Great Ocean: Pacific Worlds from Captain Cook to the Gold Rush* (New York: Oxford University Press, 2013); and Donna R. Gabaccia and Dirk Hoerder, eds., *Connecting Seas and Connected Ocean Rims* (Leiden: Brill, 2011). A classic is Fernand Braudel, *The Mediterranean and the Mediterranean World in the Age of Philip II,* 2 vols., tr. Siàin Reynolds (New York: Harper and Row, 1972–1973 [French, 1949]).

37. John Beckett, *Writing Local History* (Manchester: Manchester University Press, 2007), 128–130; David Hey, "Local and Regional History: Modern Approaches," in *Oxford Companion to Family and Local History,* 2nd ed. (Oxford: Oxford University Press, 2010), 66–73; John Allen et al., *Rethinking the Region: Spaces of Neo-Liberalism* (London: Routledge, 1998), 1–3; and Tim Cresswell, *Geographic Thought: A Critical Introduction* (Chichester: Wiley-Blackwell, 2013), 59. For changing twentieth-century geographical thought about the region, see ibid., 61–75; and Paul Claval, *Histoire de la Géographie* (Paris: Presses Universitaires de France, 1996), 97–115.

38. For Europe, see Ulrike von Hirschhausen and Kiran Klaus Patel, "Europe-anization in History: an Introduction," in *Europeanization in the Twentieth Century: Historical Approaches,* ed. Martin Conway and Kiran Klaus Patel (New York: Palgrave Macmillan, 2010), 1–18; Arnd Bauerkämpfer, "Wege zur europäischen Geschichte," in Agnes Arndt et al., *Vergleichen, Verflechten, Verwirren,* 33–60; Philipp Ther, "Comparisons, Cultural Transfers, and the Study of Networks: Toward a Transnational History of Europe," in *Comparative and Transnational History: Central European Approaches and New Perspectives,* ed. Heinz-Gerhard Haupt and Jürgen Kocka (New York: Berghahn Books, 2009), 204–225; and Rumen Daskalov and Tchavdar Marinov, eds., *Entangled Histories of the Balkans,* 2 vols. (Leiden: Brill, 2013). For East Asia, see Sebastian Conrad and Prasenjit Duara, *Viewing Regionalisms from East Asia* (Washington, DC: American Historical Association, 2013); R. Bin Wong, "Entre monde et nation: les régions braudeliennes en Asie," *Annales* 56 (2001): 5–41; and Rick Fawn, "Regions and Their Study," in *Globalising the Regional, Regionalising the Global* (Cambridge: Cambridge University Press, 2009), 5–34. For the Sahara, see Ghislaine Lydon, *On Trans-Saharan Trails: Islamic Law, Trade Networks, and Cross-Cultural Exchange in Nineteenth-Century Western Africa* (Cambridge: Cambridge University Press, 2012); James McDougall, "Frontiers, Borderlands, and Saharan / World History," in *Saharan Frontiers,* ed. James McDougall and Judith Scheele (Bloomington: Indiana University Press, 2012), 73–92; and Judith Scheele, *Smugglers and Saints of the Sahara: Regional Connectivity in the Twentieth Century* (Cambridge: Cambridge University Press, 2012).

39. Quote: Bauerkämpfer, "Wege zur europäischen Geschichte," 34. See also Ther, "Comparisons," 214; Karl Schlögel, *Die Mitte liegt ostwärds* (Munich: Hanser, 2002); Martin Conway and Kiran Patel, eds. *Europeanization in the Twentieth Century: Historical Approaches* (New York: Palgrave Macmillan, 2010); and Daskalov and Marinov, *Entangled Histories of the Balkans.* A classic on space is Henri Lefebvre, *The Production of Space* (Oxford: Blackwell, 1991 [French, 1974]); Lefebvre, *State, Space, World: Selected Essays,* ed. Neil Brenner et al. (Minneapolis: University of Minnesota Press, 2009). See also Nigel Thrift, "Space: The Fundamental Stuff of Geography," in *Key Concepts in Geography,* ed. Nicholas Clifford et al., 2nd ed. (London: Sage, 2009), 85–96.

40. Quotes: Arno Strohmeyer, "Historische Komparatistik und die Konstruktion von Geschichtsregionen: der Vergleich als Methode der historischen Europaforschung," *Jahrbuecher fuer Geschichte und Kultur Suedosteuropas* 1 (1999): 47; and Stefan Tröbst, "Introduction: What's in a Historical Region?" *European Review of History* 10 (2003): 173, 173. "Accordingly, this term differs from intra-state and inter-state micro-regions like, e.g., 'Occitania' or 'Bavaria' and 'Bessarabia' or 'Alemania,' as well as from macro-regions like continents, world-systems,

civilisations or hemispheres—'Europe,' 'sub-Saharan Africa' or 'Southeast Asia' belonging in this category," (ibid.).

41. Holm Sundhaussen, "Die Wiederentdeckung des Raumes: Über Nutzen und Nachteil von Geschichtsregionen," in *Südosteuropa. Von vormoderner Vielfalt und nationalstaatlicher Vereinheitlichung*, ed. Konrad Clewing and Oliver Jens Schmitt (Munich: Oldenbourg, 2005), 18.

42. Strohmeyer, "Geschichtsregionen," 47.

43. Western Europeans have developed such mental map stereotypes about the Balkans. For an illuminating exchange around the issue of mental map / historical region, see Maria Todorova, *Imagining the Balkans* (New York: Oxford University Press, 1997); Holm Sundhaussen, "Europa balcanica. Der Balkan als historischer Raum Europas," *GG* 25 (1999): 626–653; and Maria Todorova, "Der Balkan als Analysekategorie," *GG* 28 (2002): 470–492 [English as Todorova, "The Balkans as Category of Analysis," in *Annäherungen an eine europäische Geschichtsschreibung*, ed. Gerald Stourzh (Vienna: Verlag der österreichischen Akademie der Wissenschaften, 2002), 57–83]; Sundhaussen, "Wiederentdeckung des Raumes." Finally, Todorova, "Analysekategorie," 480, stated that she did not think that the Balkans is an invention or a fiction, a point towards which her book tended. (Also, in Todorova, "Spacing Europe: What is a Historical Region?," *East Central Europe/L'Europe du Centre-Est* 32 (2005): 59–78, she proposed a new heuristic device, "historical legacy," as a way, it appears, to bridge between the overtly constructivist approach of *Imagining the Balkans* and what Torodova considers the reification of the historical meso-regions as proposed by Sundhaussen, Strohmeyer, and others.)

44. Sundhaussen, "Wiederentdeckung des Raumes," 23.

45. Quotes: Maier, "Twentieth Century," 807, 808, 814, 819–820.

46. Jean Quataert, "Constructing Narratives," September 11, 2000, www.historycooperative.org/phorum/list.php=3ff=3d10; Peter Groenewald and Tim te Pas, "Territoriality," September 18, 2000, www.historycooperative.org/phorum/list.php=3ff=3d10. Maier respectfully demurred regarding the former comment and was agnostic about the latter.

47. Quote: Matthias Middell and Katja Naumann, "Global History and the Spatial Turn," *JGH* 5 (2010): 149. See also Sebastian Conrad, *Globalization and the Nation in Imperial Germany* (Cambridge: Cambridge University Press, 2010); and, for the contemporary period, Nick Bisley, *Rethinking Globalization* (London: Palgrave, 2007), 56–81.

48. Quotes: Bayly, *Birth*, 1. It is precisely this dialectic—whose cause is the West-centric nature of globalization from the early nineteenth century to the later twentieth century—that distinguished modern globalization from premodern globalization. To be sure, certainly from the sixteenth century there were global

connections. But Bayly's dialectic did not exist; besides, events in one corner of the world often did not affect other corners, and if they did, then much more slowly than in the nineteenth century. Different views about when globalization started are outlined in Stearns, *Globalization*.

49. Osterhammel, *Transformation*, xx. For differences all having to be of the same sort, see, e.g., Cyrus Schayegh, *Who Is Knowledgeable, Is Strong: Science, Class, and the Formation of Modern Iranian Society, 1900–1950* (Berkeley: University of California Press, 2009). See also Robertson, "Glocalization."

50. Quotes: Bayly, *Birth*, 2; and Caroline Douki and Philippe Minard, "Histoire globale, histoire connectées: un changement d'échelle historiographique?" *Revue d'Histoire Moderne et Contemporaine* 54, no. 4 bis (supplément 2007): 8.

51. Quote: Osterhammel, *Transformation*, 907. See also ibid., 907–919.

52. See also, e.g., Valeska Huber, "Multiple Mobilities. Über den Umgang mit verschiedenen Mobilitätsformen um 1900," *GG* 36 (2010): 317–341; Middell and Naumann, "Global History and the Spatial Turn."

53. Overviews include James Gelvin, *The Modern Middle East: A History*, 4th ed. (New York: Oxford University Press, 2015), 180–195; Gudrun Krämer, *A History of Palestine: From the Ottoman Conquest to the Founding of the State of Israel*, trans. Graham Harman and Gudrun Krämer (Princeton: Princeton University Press, 2008); Tom Segev, *One Palestine, Complete: Jews and Arabs under the British Mandate* (New York: Holt, 2001); James Gelvin, *The Israel-Palestine Conflict* (Berkeley: University of California Press, 2005); Ilan Pappé, *A History of Modern Palestine: One Land, Two Peoples* (Cambridge: Cambridge University Press, 2006); Benny Morris, *Righteous Victims: A History of the Zionist-Arab Conflict, 1881–1999* (New York: Knopf, 1999); Anita Shapira, *Israel* (Waltham, MA: Brandeis University Press, 2012); Kamal Salibi, *The Modern History of Lebanon* (London: Praeger, 1965); Fawwaz Trabulsi, *A History of Modern Lebanon* (London: Pluto, 2007), William Harris, *Lebanon: A History, 600–2011* (Oxford: Oxford University Press, 2012), 147–276; Philip Robins, *A History of Jordan* (Cambridge: Cambridge University Press, 2004); Kamal Salibi, *The Modern History of Jordan* (London: I. B. Tauris, 1993); Philip Khoury, *Syria and the French Mandate: The Politics of Arab Nationalism, 1920–1945* (Princeton: Princeton University Press, 1987).

54. But see Gelvin, "Was There a Mandate Period?," for a sustained discussion of continuities and changes and, related, periodization.

55. While historians have critically questioned dominant (pan)-Arab (*qawmi*), Zionist, and Turkish narratives' claim that their nations are ancient and their political independence projects clearly predated 1918, tracing the cultural and proto-political roots of post-1918 nationalism is the principal Ottoman topic of relevance to post-Ottoman historians. Moreover, the question of nationalism

exercises also historians of late Ottoman Bilad al-Sham. They turn around the question of the nature of Arab nationalism at that time and place and its relationship to Ottoman nationalism, refuting *qawmi* claims about the Arab nation's pre-1918 modern political maturation, exploring cultural and proto-political roots. And they study other national ideas or movements. For views of the Ottomans in Bilad al-Sham, see Maurus Reinkowski, *Filastin, Filistin und Eretz Israel* (Berlin: Schwarz, 1995); Beshara Doumani, "Rediscovering Ottoman Palestine: Writing Palestinians into History," *JPS* 21 (1992): 5–28; Wajih Kawtharani, "Nationalist Thought and the Vision of the Ottoman Period during the First Half of the 20th Century: the Example of Lebanon," in *Ottoman Past and Today's Turkey,* ed. Kamal Karpat (Leiden: Brill, 2000), 253–271; Ulrike Freitag, *Geschichtsschreibung in Syrien, 1920–1990* (Hamburg: Deutsches Orient-Institut, 1991), 124–126. For nationalisms in the late Ottoman Bilad al-Sham, see Michelle Campos, *Ottoman Brothers: Muslims, Christians and Jews in Early Twentieth-Century Palestine* (Stanford, CA: Stanford University Press, 2011); Zachs, *Syrian Identity;* and Carol Hakim, *The Origins of the Lebanese National Idea, 1840–1920* (Berkeley: University of California Press, 2013). For both Palestine and areas beyond, see Julia Phillips Cohen, *Becoming Ottomans: Sephardi Jews and Imperial Citizenship in the Modern Era* (New York: Oxford University Press, 2014).

56. Quote: Charles Tripp, *The Power and the People: Paths of Resistance in the Middle East* (Cambridge: Cambridge University Press, 2013), 220. For how writing nationalist historiography helped building nation-states during the interwar period, see Zachary Lockman, *Comrades and Enemies: Arab and Jewish Workers in Palestine, 1906–1948* (Berkeley: University of California Press, 1996), 1–10; and Tarif Khalidi, "Palestinian Historiography: 1900–1948," *JPS* 10 (1981): 59–76. For the complex example of Lebanon, featuring different interpretations, see Axel Havemann, *Geschichte und Geschichtsschreibung im Libanon des 19. und 20. Jahrhunderts* (Würzburg: Ergon, 2002), 163–175; and Kamal Salibi, *A House of Many Mansions: The History of Lebanon Reconsidered* (Berkeley: University of California Press, 1988). For an ethnography of nation making in Jordan, see Andrew Shryock, *Nationalism and the Genealogical Imagination: Oral History and Textual Authority in Tribal Jordan* (Berkeley: University of California Press, 1997). Historiographic inquiries include Max Weiss, "The Historiography of Sectarianism in Lebanon," *HC* 7 (2009): 141–154; James Reilly, "Past and Present in Local Histories of the Ottoman Period from Syria and Lebanon," *MES* 35 (1999): 45–65; Raymond Hinnebusch, "Modern Syrian Politics," *HC* 6 (2008): 263–285; and Freitag, *Geschichtsschreibung.* For a country neighboring Bilad al-Sham, Egypt, see Yoav Di-Capua, *Gatekeepers of the Arab Past: Historians and History Writing in Twentieth-Century Egypt* (Berkeley: University of California Press, 2009). For modern Arab historiography in general, see Birgit Schaebler, "Writing the Nation in the Arabic-

Speaking World, Nationally and Transnationally," in *Writing the Nation: A Global Perspective,* ed. Stefan Berger (Basingstoke: Palgrave Macmillan, 2007), 179–196. For global patterns, see Stefan Berger and Chris Lorenz, eds., *Nationalizing the Past: Historians as Nation Builders in Modern Europe* (Basingstoke: Palgrave Macmillan, 2010); Christopher Hill, *National History and the World of Nations: Capital, State, and the Rhetoric of History in Japan, France, and the US* (Durham, NC: Duke University Press, 2008); and Dominic Sachsenmaier, *Global Perspectives on Global History: Theories and Approaches in a Connected World* (Cambridge: Cambridge University Press, 2011).

57. Porath, *Arab Unity;* Adeed Dawisha, *Arab Nationalism in the Twentieth Century: From Triumph to Despair* (Princeton: Princeton University Press, 2003); Bassam Tibi, *Arab Nationalism: Between Islam and the Nation-State* (Houndsmills, Basingstoke: Palgrave Macmillan, 1990); Malik Mufti, *Sovereign Creations: Pan-Arabism and Political Order in Syria and Iraq* (Ithaca, NY: Cornell University Press, 1996); William Cleveland, *The Making of an Arab Nationalist: Ottomanism and Arabism in the Life and Thought of Sati' al-Husri* (Princeton: Princeton University Press, 1971); and William Cleveland, *Islam against the West: Shakib Arslan and the Campaign for Islamic Nationalism* (London: Saqi, 1985). Polemical is Daniel Pipes, *Greater Syria: The History of an Ambition* (New York: Oxford University Press, 1990).

58. Mandate-wide frameworks of historical analysis are Cyrus Schayegh and Andrew Arsan, "Introduction," in *The Routledge History Handbook of the Middle East Mandates,* 1–23; Schayegh, "The Mandates and/as Decolonization"; Nadine Méouchy and Peter Sluglett, "General Introduction," in *The British and French Mandates in Comparative Perspectives* (Leiden: Brill, 2004), 1–20; Peter Sluglett, "Les mandats/the Mandates," in ibid., 103–128; Rashid Khalidi, "Concluding Remarks," in ibid., 699–700; and David Fieldhouse, *Western Imperialism in the Middle East, 1914–1958* (Oxford: Oxford University Press, 2006). See also Thomas Philipp and Christoph Schumann, "Introduction," in *From the Syrian Land to the State of Syria and Lebanon* (Würzburg: Ergon, 2004), 1–2. Keith Watenpaugh, *Being Modern in the Middle East: Revolution, Nationalism, Colonialism, and the Arab Middle Class* (Princeton: Princeton University Press, 2006), 10, explicitly rejects "nationalist and imperialist definitions of the historical and political bounds of [interwar] Aleppo." And Tariq Tell, *The Social and Economic Origins of Monarchy in Jordan* (New York: Palgrave, 2013), 15, remarks that the existing literature has "underplayed . . . tensions . . . between local loyalties and nation-building during Mandatory rule." Transborder and local contexts include Asher Kaufman, *Contested Frontiers in the Syria-Lebanon-Israel Region* (Washington, DC: Woodrow Wilson Center Press, 2014); Cyrus Schayegh, "The Many Worlds of Abud Yasin," *AHR* 116 (2011): 273–306; and various chapters in *Routledge History*

*Handbook of the Middle East Mandates,* including Toufoul Abou-Hodeib, "Sanctity across the Border: Pilgrimage Routes and State Control in Mandate Lebanon and Palestine," 383–394. For individuals, see Laila Parsons, *Fawzi al-Qawuqji and the Fight for Arab Independence, 1914–1948* (New York: Hill and Wang, 2016); Juliette Honvault, "Instrumentalisation d'un parcours singulier: La trajectoire mandataire de l'emir Adil Arslan," in *British and French Mandates,* 345–360. For the continued relevance of regional ties after independence, see Cyrus Schayegh, "1958 Reconsidered: State Formation and Cold War in the Early Post-Colonial Arab Middle East," *IJMES* 45 (2013): 421–443.

59. Andrew Arsan, *Interlopers of Empire: The Lebanese Diaspora in Colonial French West Africa* (New York: Oxford University Press, 2013); Ilham Khuri-Makdisi, *The Eastern Mediterranean and the Making of Global Radicalism, 1860–1914* (Berkeley: University of California Press, 2010); Stacy Fahrentold, "Sound Minds in Sound Bodies: Transnational Philanthropy and Patriotic Masculinity in al-Nadi al-Homsi and Syrian Brazil, 1920–32," *IJMES* 46 (2014): 259–283; and Christoph Schumann, "Nationalism, Diaspora and 'Civilisational Mission': The Case of Syrian Nationalism in Latin America between World War I and World War II," *NN* 10 (2004): 599–617. See also Keith Watenpaugh, "The League of Nations' Rescue of Armenian Genocide Survivors and the Making of Modern Humanitarianism," *AHR* 115 (2010): 1315–1339. A classic is Albert Hourani, ed., *The Lebanese in the World* (London: Tauris, 1992). Oliver Schmitt, *Levantiner. Lebenswelten und Identitäten einer ethnokonfessionellen Gemeinschaft im osmanischen Reich im „langen 19. Jahrhundert"* (Munich: Oldenbourg, 2005), links up Ottoman, Mediterranean, and European worlds. On the contemporary period, see, for instance, Leïla Vignal, ed., *The Transnational Middle East* (London: Routledge, 2017); and Fariba Adelkhah, *Mille et une frontière de l'Iran* (Paris: Karthala, 2012).

60. Jens Hanssen, Thomas Philipp, and Stefan Weber, "Introduction," in *The Empire in the City: Arab Provincial Capitals in the Late Ottoman Empire* (Würzburg: Ergon, 2002), 1–25. Monographs include Leila Fawaz, *Merchants and Migrants in Nineteenth-Century Beirut* (Cambridge: Cambridge University Press, 1983); Jens Hanssen, *Fin de Siècle Beirut: The Making of an Ottoman Provincial Capital* (Oxford: Oxford University Press, 2005); Weber, *Damascus;* Linda Schatkowski Schilcher, *Families in Politics: Damascene Factions and Estates of the 18th and 19th Centuries* (Wiesbaden: Harasowitz, 1985); Beshara Doumani, *Rediscovering Palestine: Merchants and Peasants in Jabal Nablus, 1700–1900* (Berkeley: University of California Press, 1995); Ilan Pappé, *The Rise and Fall of a Palestinian Dynasty: The Husaynis, 1700–1948* (Berkeley: University of California Press, 2010); and Johann Büssow, *Hamidian Palestine: Politics and Society in the District of Jerusalem, 1872–1908* (Leiden: Brill, 2011).

61. For hinterlands, see Doumani, *Palestine*. On the eighteenth and nineteenth centuries, see Abdul-Karim Rafeq's oeuvre, especially on Damascus, e.g., "City and Countryside in a Traditional Setting," in Philipp and Schäbler, *The Syrian Land*, 295–332. Port cities have attracted world-systems analysis historians. As classic collection is the journal issue *Review* 16 (1993), including studies of Beirut, Izmir, Patras, Salonica, and Trabzon. For the regional setting, see the brilliant James Reilly, "Regions and Markets of Ottoman Syria: Comparisons and Transformations," *Chronos* 10 (2004): 111–144, on which Chapter 1 draws heavily, and Philipp Thomas, "Bilad al-šam in the Modern Period," *Arabica* 51 (2004): 401–418. For regions beyond Bilad al-Sham, see Gad Gilbar, "The Muslim Big Merchant-Entrepreneurs of the Middle East, 1860–1914," *Welt des Islams* 43 (2003): 1–36; Faruk Tabak, "Local Merchants in Peripheral Areas of the Empire," *Review* 11 (1988): 179–214. General, and broad Ottoman, overviews include Roger Owen, *The Middle East in the World Economy 1800–1914* (London: Methuen, 1981); and Donald Quataert, "The Age of Reforms," in *An Economic and Social History of the Ottoman Empire,* ed. Halil Inalcık (Cambridge: Cambridge University Press, 1997), 2:759–944.

62. Arieh Saposnik, "'. . . Will Issue Forth from Zion?': The Emergence of a Jewish National Culture in Palestine and the Dynamics of Yishuv-Diaspora Relations," *Jewish Social Studies* 10 (2003): 151–184; Yair Wallach, "Rethinking the Yishuv: Late-Ottoman Palestine's Jewish Communities Revisited," *Journal of Modern Jewish Studies* (2016), DOI:10.1080/14725886.2016.1246230; and Lockman, *Comrades and Enemies*, 1–10. A critique showing in how far his 'relational' approach went too far is Deborah Bernstein, *Constructing Boundaries: Jewish and Arab Workers in Mandatory Palestine* (Albany: State University of New York Press, 2000).

63. For political relations, see Laura Zittrain Eisenberg, *My Enemy's Enemy: Lebanon in the Early Zionist Imagination, 1900–1948* (Detroit: Wayne State University, 1994); Avi Shlaim, *The Politics of Partition: King Abdullah, the Zionists, and Palestine, 1921–1951* (New York: Oxford University Press, 1998); and Gali Levi, "Masekhat ha Maga'im ha-Mediniim bein ha-Sokhnut ha-Yehudit be-Erets Israel we-ha-Gush ha-Leumi be-Suriah" (MA thesis, Tel Aviv University, 2005).

64. My approach thus forms part neither of post-Zionist nor post-post-Zionist historiography, for both focus squarely on the Yishuv/Israel. See Assaf Likhovski, "Post-Post-Zionist Historiography," *IS* 15 (2010): 1–23; for further literature, see ibid., 2n6–7.

65. "Culture" is used as a shorthand for a range of practices and framings that affect and reflect how people made sense of their place in the world: their mental maps, collective identities, and ideological formations, including *qawmi* and *watani* nationalisms and affinities.

66. For the idea of the "historical probe" and its methodological underpinning, see Dietmar Rothermund, "Unsichere Transaktionen in globalen Lebensläufen," in *Globale Lebensläufe,* ed. Bernd Hausberger (Vienna: Mandelbaum Verlag, 2006), 283. To think with Jill Lepore, "Historians Who Love Too Much: Reflections on Microhistory and Biography," *JAH* 88 (2001): 129–144, my historical probes are not biographical but microhistorical.

### Prelude 1. Khalil Sakakini Has a Dream

Epigraph: Khalil Sakakini, *Yawmiyyat Khalil al-Sakakini* (Ramallah: Markaz Khalil al-Sakakini al-Thaqafi, 2003), 1:95–96.

1. For an overview of the stay, see Salim Tamari, "A Miserable Year in Brooklyn," *JQF* 17 (2003): 19–40, including a mention of dreams: 34, 36.
2. Khalil Sakakini, *Yawmiyyat,* 1:202, 111, 95.
3. Ibid., 1:96.
4. Quotes: ibid., 1:63, 75, 76. For a detailed description of the relationship and Sultana Abdo, see Tamari, "Brooklyn," 122–123.
5. Sakakini, *Yawmiyyat,* 1:95, 186, 67–68, 73 (sweetheart); ibid., 116, about his meeting with Dawud in Jaffa.
6. Ibid., 1:95, 73. For emigration statistic, see Kemal Karpat, "The Ottoman Emigration to America," *IJMES* 17 (1985): 185. For the saying, see Hanna Hardan Khuri, *al-Akhbar al-Shahiyya 'an al-'Iyal al-Marj'ayuniyya wa-l-Timiyya* (Beirut: Matba'at al-Zaman, 1955), 94; compare Henri Lammens, *al-Rihla al-Suriyya fi Amirka al-Mutawassita wa-l-Janubiyya* (Beirut: al-Matba'a al-Katulikiyya, 1894), 3: "Thousands of inhabitants of this land [Syria] are looking to the American continent, for it has become to every one of them virtually a father, mother, brother, sister, or [other] relative."
7. Melhem Elias, "Hotel du Syrie," *Lisan al-Hal,* December 28, 1899, 3; see also "I'lan," *Lisan al-Hal,* December 5, 1899, 4. Promising "free stay for the poor," Elias highlighted the relative poverty of many immigrants. See also Dr. Bollamir, "Passage à Marseille de l'émigration syrienne vers les Amériques" (1901), ML4.2.7.3.1./01, Archives of the Chambre de Commerce et d'Industrie de Marseille, France.
8. Tamari, "Brooklyn," 27–28. For "Syrian restaurants" in New York around that time, see also Thomas Ricks, *Turbulent Times in Palestine: The Diaries of Khalil Totah, 1886–1955* (Jerusalem: Institute for Palestine Studies, 2009), 124. For the *Titanic,* see Leila Salloum Elias, "The Impact of the Sinking of the *Titanic* on the New York Syrian Community of 1912," *ASQ* 27 (2005): 75.
9. Tamari, "Brooklyn," 28.
10. Sakakini quote: ibid., 28. For the apartment, see ibid., 25. For friends, see Sakakini, *Yawmiyyat,* 2:237. For Totah, see Ricks, *Times,* 120, 124, 167, 205. For Elias's quotes, see Elias, "Hotel."

## 1. Rise of an Urban Patchwork Region

1. Quotes: Bruce Masters, *The Arabs of the Ottoman Empire, 1516–1918* (Cambridge: Cambridge University Press, 2013), 17; and Margaret Meriwhether, *The Kin Who Count: Family and Society in Ottoman Aleppo, 1770–1840* (Austin: University of Texas Press, 1999), 20, 66. For center-province relationships, see Masters, *Arabs*, 83–88; Ali Yaycıoğlu, *Partners of the Empire: The Crisis of the Ottoman Order in the Age of Revolutions* (Stanford, CA: Stanford University Press, 2016); and Albert Hourani, "Ottoman Reform and the Politics of Notables," in *Beginnings of Modernization in the Middle East: The Nineteenth Century*, ed. William Polk and Richard Chambers (Chicago: University of Chicago Press, 1968), 41–68. Case studies include Meriwhether, *Kin;* Heinz Gaube and Eugen Wirth, *Aleppo: historische und geographische Beiträge zur baulichen Gestaltung, zur sozialen Organisation und zur wirtschaftlichen Dynamik einer vorderasiatischen Fernhandelsmetropole* (Wiesbaden: Reichert, 1984); Karl Barbir, *Ottoman Rule in Damascus, 1708–1758* (Princeton, NJ: Princeton University Press, 1980); Linda Schatkowski-Schilcher, *Families in Politics: Damascene Factions and Estates of the Eighteenth and Nineteenth Centuries* (Wiesbaden: Steiner, 1985); the wide-ranging work by Abdul-Karim Rafeq, e.g., "City and Countryside in a Traditional Setting: The Case of Damascus in the First Quarter of the Eighteenth Century," in *The Syrian Land in the 18th and 19th Century: The Common and the Specific in the Historical Experience*, ed. Thomas Philipp (Stuttgart: Steiner, 1992), 295–332; Beshara Doumani, *Rediscovering Palestine: Merchants and Peasants in Jabal Nablus, 1700–1900* (Berkeley: University of California Press, 1995); Thomas Philipp, *Acre: The Rise and Fall of a Palestinian City, 1730–1831* (New York: Columbia University Press, 2001); and Ilan Pappé, *The Rise and Fall of a Palestinian Dynasty: The Husaynis, 1700–1948* (Berkeley: University of California Press, 2010). See also Antoine Abdel Nour, *Introduction à l'histoire urbaine de la Syrie ottomane (XVIe–XVIIIe siècles)* (Beirut: Librairie Orientale, 1982); Thierry Bianquis, "Cités, territoires et province dans l'histoire syrienne médiévale," *BEO* 52 (2000): 207–219. For city-centered historiographic traditions, see Sami Dahan, "The Origin and Development of the Local Histories of Syria," in *Historians of the Middle East*, ed. Bernard Lewis and Peter Holt (London: Oxford University Press, 1962), 108–117.

2. Quotes: Maurus Reinkowski, *Dinge der Ordnung. Eine vergleichende Untersuchung über die osmanische Reformpolitik im 19. Jahrhundert* (Munich: Oldenbourg, 2005), 285 (applying a term coined by Michael Mann that is also deployed in Eugene Rogan, *Frontiers of the State in the Late Ottoman Empire: Transjordan, 1850–1921* [Cambridge: Cambridge University Press, 1999], 3), 284; and Donald Quataert, *The Ottoman Empire, 1700–1922* (Cambridge: Cambridge University Press, 2000), 63. For the statistics, see ibid., 62–63. Other introductions include

Şükrü Hanioğlu, *A Brief History of the Late Ottoman Empire* (Princeton, NJ: Princeton University Press, 2008); François Georgeon, *Abdülhamid II* (Paris: Fayard, 2003); and, for pre-*tanzimat* changes, Christine Philliou, *Biography of an Empire: Governing Ottomans in an Age of Revolution* (Berkeley: University of California Press, 2011).

3. Quote: James Gelvin, *The Modern Middle East* (New York: Oxford University Press, 2005), 73. European balance of power politics—that is, Britain's and France's aversion of an excessively strong Russia—mitigated these losses, but only until the late 1870s. And although thereafter Germany became Istanbul's partner, it was not committed enough to nix continuing Ottoman territorial losses. Britain's conquest, Egypt, had basically been independent from Istanbul since the early nineteenth century.

4. For the geostrategic context and impetus for state reforms, see Michael Reynolds, *Shattering Empires: The Clash and Collapse of the Ottoman and Russian Empires, 1908–1918* (Cambridge: Cambridge University Press, 2011). For Istanbul as one of several reforming empires, see Jane Burbank and Frederick Cooper, *Empires in World History* (Princeton, NJ: Princeton University Press, 2010), 331–368; see also Selim Deringil, *The Well-Protected Domains: Ideology and the Legitimation of Power in the Ottoman Empire, 1876–1909* (London: I. B. Tauris, 1998).

5. Jürgen Osterhammel, *The Transformation of the World: A Global History of the Nineteenth Century*, trans. Patrick Camiller (Princeton, NJ: Princeton University Press, 2014), 58.

6. These changes were partly driven by the empire-wide 1864 Province (*Vilayet*) Law and had political as well as economic motives. Political motives concerned the *mutasarrifiyya*s. Istanbul wished to assert more direct control: in one, east of Aleppo around the interior town of Deir al-Zor in 1854, to better control the desert bedouin; and in two others, in Mount Lebanon in 1860 and from Jerusalem to the sea, including Jaffa, in 1872, to preclude greater European interventionism. Economic motives reflected the decline of old littoral heavyweight Sidon and its northern counterpart Tripoli, which in 1864 were incorporated into a province now called Suriya centered on Damascus, and the rise of Beirut, from 1888 the capital of a new province. See Lamia Shehadeh, "The Name of Syria in Ancient and Modern Usage," in *The Origins of Syrian Nationhood: Histories, Pioneers and Identity,* ed. Adel Beshara (London: Routledge, 2011), 22–23; Butrus Abu-Manneh, "The Establishment and Dismantling of the Province of Syria, 1865–1888," in *Problems of the Modern Middle East in Historical Perspective,* ed. John Spagnolo (Reading, UK: Ithaca Press, 1992), 7–26; Leila Fawaz, *Merchants and Migrants in Nineteenth-Century Beirut* (Cambridge: Harvard University Press, 1983); Jens Hanssen, *Fin de Siècle Beirut: The Making of an Ottoman Provincial Capital* (Oxford: Oxford University Press, 2005); Engin Akarli, *The Long Peace: Ottoman Lebanon, 1861–1920* (Berkeley: University of California Press, 1993); Johann Büssow, *Hamidian*

*Palestine: Politics and Society in the District of Jerusalem, 1872–1908* (Leiden: Brill, 2011).

7. For an overview, see Eugene Rogan, *The Arabs* (New York: Basic Books, 2011), 75–81. For an example, Palestine, see Gudrun Krämer, *A History of Palestine* (Princeton: Princeton University Press, 2008), 71–100.

8. Quote: Elizabeth Thompson, "Ottoman Political Reform in the Provinces: the Damascus Advisory Council in 1844–1845," *IJMES* 25 (1993): 472. Magisterial is Marc Aymes, *A Provincial History of the Ottoman Empire: Cyprus and the Eastern Mediterranean in the Nineteenth Century* (London: Routledge, 2014). Case studies include Randi Deguilhem, "Centralized Authority and Local Decisional Power: Management of the Endowments in Late Ottoman Damascus," in *The Empire in the City: Arab Provincial Capitals in the Late Ottoman Empire,* ed. Jens Hanssen, Thomas Philipp, and Stefan Weber (Würzburg: Ergon, 2002), 219–234; Martha Mundy, "*Qada*'Ajlun in the Late Nineteenth Century," *Levant* 28 (1996): 77–95. For similar takes, see Rogan, *Frontiers;* Reinkowski, *Ordnung;* Ussama Makdisi, "Ottoman Orientalism," *AHR* 107 (2002): 768–796; Hanssen, *Beirut;* Fawaz, *Merchants;* Stefan Weber, *Damascus: Ottoman Modernity and Urban Transformation (1808–1918)* (Aarhus: Aarhus University Press, 2009); Schatkowski-Schilcher, *Families;* Philip Khoury, *Urban Notables and Arab Nationalism: The Politics of Damascus, 1860–1920* (Cambridge: Cambridge University Press, 1983); Philip Khoury, "The Urban Notables Paradigm Revisited," *RMMM* 55–56 (1990): 215–228. Conceptual notes to this regard include Jens Hanssen, Thomas Philipp and Stefan Weber, "Introduction," in *The Empire in the City: Arab Provincial Capitals in the Late Ottoman Empire* (Würzburg: Ergon, 2002), 19; and, already in 1968, Hourani, "Notables," 43. For notable composition changes, see Adel Manna, "Continuity and Change in the Socio-Political Elite in Palestine during the Late Ottoman Period," in Philipp, *Syrian Land,* 69–89.

9. See Edhem Eldem, *French Trade in Istanbul in the Eighteenth Century* (Leiden: Brill, 1999). Joel Beinin, *Workers and Peasants in the Modern Middle East* (Cambridge: Cambridge University Press, 2000), 22–23. For a general overview of the eighteenth century, see Quataert, *Ottoman Empire,* 37–53. For a much broader view of economic Eurocentrism not predating the late eighteenth century, see Kenneth Pomeranz, *The Great Divergence: China, Europe, and the Making of the Modern World Economy* (Princeton, NJ: Princeton University Press, 2000).

10. Economic European inroads in the Ottoman Empire started on the western Turkish littoral already from the 1810s.

11. John Darwin, *The Empire Project: The Rise and Fall of the British World System, 1830–1970* (Cambridge: Cambridge University Press, 2009), esp. 23–304; Giovanni Arrighi, "The Global Market," *Journal of World-System Research* 5 (1999): 217–251 at 218–227. By the 1890s, Germany started to challenge the British Empire, but did not replace it.

12. For an overview, see Donald Quataert, "The Age of Reforms," in *An Economic and Social History of the Ottoman Empire,* ed. Halil Inalcık with Donald Quataert (Cambridge: Cambridge University Press, 1997), 2:759–944, esp. "Overview of the Nineteenth Century," "Transportation," and "Commerce," 761–777, 798–823, and 824–842; Roger Owen, *The Middle East in the World Economy 1800–1914* (London: I. B. Tauris, 1981).

13. Quotes: Beinin, *Workers and Peasants,* 46; and Arrighi, "Global Market," 219. For the 1838 treaty, see Reşat Kasaba, *Ottoman Empire and the World Economy: The Nineteenth Century* (Albany: State University of New York Press, 1988), 55; Şevket Pamuk, *The Ottoman Empire and European Capitalism, 1820–1913* (Cambridge: Cambridge University Press, 1987), 18–21. For prices, see Charles Issawi, *The Fertile Crescent, 1800–1914: A Documentary Economic History* (New York: Oxford University Press, 1988); Kostas Vergopoulos, "La grande dépression européenne et la crise d'Orient, 1875–1900," *Review (Fernand Braudel Center)* 11 (1988): 231–249.

14. For the interior, see Gad Gilbar, "The Muslim Big Merchant-Entrepreneurs of the Middle East, 1860–1914," *Welt des Islams* 43 (2003): 1–36; Faruk Tabak, "Local Merchants in Peripheral Areas of the Empire," *Review* 11 (1988): 179–214; Doumani, *Palestine;* Sherry Vatter, "Militant Journeymen in Nineteenth-century Damascus," in *Workers and Working Classes in the Middle East,* ed. Zachary Lockman (Albany: State University of New York Press, 1994), 1–20; Louise Schilcher, "The Grain Economy of Late Ottoman Syria and the Issue of Large-Scale Industrialization," in *Landholding and Commercial Agriculture in the Middle East,* ed. Çağlar Keyder and Faruk Tabak (Albany: State University of New York Press, 1991), 173–195; as well as Owen, *Middle East.* Regarding the Ottoman Empire as other parts of the world, world systems historians have studied port cities, see *Review* 16 (1993), with contributions inter alia on Beirut, Izmir, Patras, Salonica, and Trabzon, and esp. Çağlar Keyder, Eyüp Özveren, and Donald Quataert, "Port Cities in the Ottoman Empire: Some Theoretical and Historical Perspectives," 519–558. See also Çağlar Keyder, "Port Cities in the Belle Epoque," in *Cities of the Mediterranean from the Ottomans to the Present Day,* ed. Biray Kolluoğlu and Meltem Toksöz (London: I. B. Tauris, 2010), 14–22. For a focus on Ottoman agency, see Brant Downes, "Constructing the Modern Ottoman Waterfont" (PhD diss., Stanford University, 2008). For the Suez Canal, see Valeska Huber, *Channelling Mobilities: Migration and Globalisation in the Suez Canal Region and Beyond, 1869–1914* (Cambridge: Cambridge University Press, 2013).

15. Quote: Kasaba, *Ottoman Empire,* 55. See also Quataert, "Age of Reforms," 889; Deniz Kılınçoğlu, "The Political Economy of Ottoman Modernity: Ottoman Economic Thought during the Reign of Abdülhamid II (1876–1909)" (PhD diss., Princeton University, 2012), chaps. 2, 4; Mahmoud Haddad, "Ottoman Economic Nationalism in the Press of Beirut and Tripoli (Syria)," in *The Economy as an*

*Issue in the Middle Eastern Press,* ed. Gisela Procháska-Eisl and Martin Strohmeier (Berlin: LIT, 2008), 75–84; Jens Hanssen, "'Malhamé-Malfamé': Levantine Elite and Transimperial Networks on the Eve of the Young Turk Revolution," *IJMES* 43 (2011): 25–48.

16. For rural hinterlands economic function—"respon[ding] to local shortfalls (grain), or for specialized products"—see James Reilly, "Regions and Markets of Ottoman Syria: Comparisons and Transformations," *Chronos* 10 (2004): 112. Channeling is incisively developed by Reilly, e.g., ibid., 131.

17. For the Franco-British Istanbul-headquartered *Banque Impériale Ottomane,* see Christopher Clay, "The Origins of Modern Banking in the Levant," *IJMES* 26 (1994): 589–614; other than Beirut (1863), Damascus (1875) and Aleppo (1893), the other twelve branches in Bilad al-Sham opened between 1904 and 1914; all together amounted to one-sixth of all branches: ibid., 610. After 1908, the CUP had local branches, but it, too, was headquartered in Istanbul. One family, which partly worked in trade, that branched out were the Baalbakis in Damascus, which in the early twentieth century sent four sons to Beirut, Aleppo, Karak, and Haifa: author, interview with Muhammad Tahsin Baalbaki (born 1940, Damascus), June 28, 2011, Amman, Jordan.

18. Quote: Reilly, "Regions," 139 (emphasis added).

19. Some have called it "proto-national": Fruma Zachs, *The Making of Syrian Identity: Intellectuals and Merchants in Nineteenth-Century Beirut* (Leiden: Brill, 2005), 1.

20. An early instance was *al-Jam'iyya al-Suriyya li-l-'Ulum wa-l-Funun,* which a few Westerners and Beirutis opened in Beirut in 1847: Butrus al-Bustani, *al-Jam'iyya al-Suriyya li-l-'Ulum wa-l-Funun* (Beirut: Dar al-Hamra', [1847] 1990), 71. For an analysis, see Zachs, *Syrian Identity,* 137–145; hers is the principal study of the making of a Syrian Arabist proto-national identity from the 1840s, focusing on the coast and on Christians, with attention also to the supportive effect of state Ottoman action (ibid., 86–125) and to the role of U.S. Protestant missionaries (ibid., 126–154). Certainly by the late nineteenth century, also Muslims used the term Suriya as well as Suriyyun, Syrians. An example is travelogues by Egyptians like 'Abd al-Rahman Sami, *Safar al-Salam fi Bilad al-Sham* (Cairo: Matba'at al-Muqtataf, 1892), 5, 6, 9, 19, 22, 24; and Muhammad 'Abd al-Jawwad al-Qayati, *Nafhat al-Basham fi Rihlat al-Sham* (Cairo: Matba'at Jaridat al-Islam, 1901), 23, 149. Researchers have successively added actors and places to Arabism. An overview is Rashid Khalidi, "Ottomanism and Arabism in Syria before 1914: A Reassessment," in *The Origins of Arab Nationalism,* ed. Rashid Khalidid et al. (New York: Columbia University Press, 1991), 50–69. Key texts include Ernest Dawn, "From Ottomanism to Arabism," *Review of Politics* 23 (1961): 378–400; Albert Hourani, *Arabic Thought in the Liberal Age, 1798–1939* (Cambridge: Cambridge University

Press, 1983), 286–287; Hassan Kayalı, *Arabs and Young Turks: Ottomanism, Arabism, and Islamism in the Ottoman Empire, 1908–1918* (Berkeley: University of California Press, 1997); Eliezer Tauber, *The Emergence of the Arab Movements* (London: Frank Cass, 1993); James Gelvin, *Divided Loyalties: Nationalism and Mass Politics in Syria at the Close of Empire* (Berkeley: University of California Press, 1998). For a global focus, though on another project, leftism, see Ilham Khuri-Makdisi, *The Eastern Mediterranean and the Making of Global Radicalism, 1860–1914* (Berkeley: University of California Press, 2010), who focuses on Beirut, Alexandria, and Cairo as part of broader intellectual-political networks. Andrew Arsan, *Interlopers of Empire: The Lebanese Diaspora in Colonial French West Africa* (London: Oxford University Press, 2013), ch. 7, concerns another global connection, the political universe of Lebanese in Africa, though in the interwar period.

21. Quote: Zachs, *Syrian Identity*, 94. For Beirut/Mount Lebanon, see Asher Kaufman, *Reviving Phoenicia: The Search for Identity in Lebanon* (London: I. B. Tauris, 2004), 21–54; Carol Hakim, *Origins of the Lebanese National Idea, 1840–1920* (Berkeley: University of California Press, 2013). For proposed federalization, see Zachs, *Syrian Identity*, 103–104.

22. For Damascus, see Dawn, "Ottomanism"; Kayalı, *Arabs and Young Turks*, passim; and Itzchak Weismann, *Taste of Modernity: Sufism, Salafiyya and Arabism in Late Ottoman Damascus* (Leiden: Brill, 2001), 9, 310–316. For Ottoman loyalties, see Michelle Campos, *Ottoman Brothers: Muslims, Christians, and Jews in Early Twentieth-Century Palestine* (Stanford, CA: Stanford University Press, 2011); Samuel Dolbee and Shay Hazkani, "'Impossible Is Not Ottoman': Menashe Meirovitch, 'Isa al-'Isa, and Imperial Citizenship in Palestine," *IJMES* 47 (2015): 241–265; Yuval Ben-Bassat, "Rethinking the Concept of Ottomanization: The Yishuv in the Aftermath of the Young Turk Revolution of 1908," *MES* 45 (2009): 461–475. For the Young Turks, see Kayalı, *Arabs and Young Turks*; Şükrü Hanioğlu, *Preparation for a Revolution: The Young Turks, 1902–1908* (Oxford: Oxford University Press, 2001).

23. Quote: Yoav Di-Capua, "Nahda: The Arab Project of Enlightenment," in *The Cambridge Companion to Modern Arab Culture*, ed. Dwight Reynolds (Cambridge: Cambridge University Press, 2015), 54–74. See also Stephen Sheehi, *Foundations of Modern Arab Identity* (Gainesville: University Press of Florida, 2004); Dagmar Glass, "Creating a Modern Standard Language from Medieval Tradition: The Nahda and the Arabic Academies," in *The Semitic Languages*, ed. Stefan Weninger et al. (Berlin: De Gruyter Mouton, 2011), 835–844. For Bustani's role, see Albert Hourani, "Bustani's Encyclopaedia," *JIS* 1 (1990): 111–119; Paul Sheehi, "Inscribing the Arab Self: Butrus al-Bustani and Paradigms of Subjective Reform," *BJMES* 27 (2000): 7–24; Dagmar Glass, "Reorganizing and Disseminating Knowledge during the Nahda: Bustani's *Encyclopédie arabe* Revisited," in *Islamica: Studies in Memory*

*of Holger Preissler (1943–2006),* ed. Andreas Christmann et al. (Oxford: Oxford University Press, 2009), 101–118; and John Jandora, "Al-Bustani's Da'irat al-ma'arif," *Muslim World* 76 (1986): 86–92.

24. For the roots of those events in political and economic changes dating back to the 1840s, for the role of local (Muslim and Druze versus Christian), Ottoman, and (mainly French) European actors, and for effects on the formation of sectarianism, see Ussama Makdisi, *The Culture of Sectarianism: Community, History, and Violence in Nineteenth-Century Ottoman Lebanon* (Berkeley: University of California Press, 2000). See also Leila Fawaz, *An Occasion for War: Civil Conflict in Lebanon and Damascus in 1860* (London: I. B. Tauris, 1994).

25. The first book including the term Suriya—Khalil al-Khuri's *Kharabat Suriya*—appeared in Beirut the same year as *Nafir Suriya:* Zachs, *Syrian Identity,* 177–179. Moreover, Muslims also beyond Bilad al-Sham used not only Suriya but also *watan* for that region: Sami, *Safar al-Salam fi Bilad al-Sham,* 9, 19, 22, 24.

26. Quotes: Butrus al-Bustani, *Nafir Suriya* (Beirut: Dar Fikr li-l-Abhath wa-l-Nashr, [1860–1861] 1990), 9, 18–19, 22. For a similar view of the pernicious effect of unchecked religious tensions, see Shahin Makaryus, *Hasr al-Litham 'an Nakabat al-Sham* (Cairo: n.p., 1895), 5, analyzing the 1860–1861 events.

27. Both quotes: al-Bustani, *Nafir Suriya,* 21. For *awtan,* see ibid., 14.

28. Both quotes: Butrus al-Bustani, *Muhit al-Muhit* (Beirut: s.n., 1870), 2:2265. The encyclopedia is Butrus al-Bustani, *Da'irat al-Ma'arif* (Beirut: n.p., 1881), 5:744–752 (Beirut); ibid. (1883), 7:135–143 (Aleppo); 7:216–219 (Homs); 7:278–279 (Haifa); ibid., (1884), 8:1–29 (Damascus). Other authors used the city entries of the encyclopedia, and it contained numerous entries also about leading urban families: see Ahmad 'Arif al-Zain, *Ta'rikh Saida* (Sidon: 'Irfan, 1913), 16; Hourani, "Bustani," 118.

29. For the former, see, e.g., Jurji Yanni, *Ta'rikh Suriya* (Beirut: al-Matba'a al-Adabiyya, 1881), 7, which also calls Filastin a part of Suriya—ibid., 7, 11—just like Lebanon: ibid., 12.

30. Quote: Khairallah Khairallah, *La Syrie* (Paris: Ernest Leroux, 1912), 2. See also, e.g., Iqlimis Yusuf Dawud, *Kitab al-Qusara* (Beirut: al-Matba'a al-Adabiyya, 1887), 2; Makaryus, *Hasr,* 4. On a related note, Dawud, *Kitab,* passim, Makaryus, *Hasr,* 4, and Yanni, *Ta'rikh Suriya,* 5, like Khairallah mentioned Palestine's Roman and Jewish past. This link between the use of the term Palestine and greater attention to that past is addressed by a doctoral thesis in the making by Zachary Foster at Princeton University that bears the working title "A History of 'Palestine.'"

31. Dawud, *Kitab,* 17 (first quote), 2, 17; Yanni, *Ta'rikh Suriya,* 304 (second quote), 7, 11, 12; Henri Lammens, *al-Mudhakarat al-Jughrafiyya fi al-Aqtar al-Suriyya* (Beirut: al-Matba'a al-Katulikiyya, 1911), 29 (third quote; emphasis added). On Lammens, see Asher Kaufman, "Henri Lammens and Syrian Nationalism," in Beshara, *Origins of Syrian Nationhood,* 108–111; Kamal Salibi, "Islam and Syria in the

Writings of Henry Lammens," in Lewis and Holt, *Historians of the Middle East,* 330–342.

32. Yanni, *Ta'rikh Suriya.* For umam, see ibid., 4–7. For Yanni, see also Zachs, *Syrian Identity,* 180. His attention to cities was the rule. As ibid., 177, 179, shows, in al-Khuri's 1860 *Kharabat Suriya,* "The 'Syrian sites' of Greater Syria are arranged according to the importance of their cities and these cities' histories in pre-Islamic times are presented"; and Ilyas Matar, *al-'Uqud al-Durriyya fi al-Mamlaka al-Suriyya* (Beirut: n.p., 1874) had two parts, "a general introduction to the region and its features . . . [and] Syria's important cities in terms of history and geography."

33. All quotes: Khairallah, *Syrie,* 5.

34. Quotes: Lammens, *Mudhakarat,* 31, 30, 30. For the same list, see Kaufman, "Lammens," 111, using Henri Lammens, *La Syrie. Précis historique* (Beirut: Imprimérie Catholique, 1921). An author other than Khairallah drawing on Lammens was Bulus Nujaym: Kaufman, "Lammens," 114.

35. For the geographical determinism of Lammens and of contemporaries like Bulus Nujaym, see Kaufman, "Lammens," 110, and Kaufman, *Phoenicia,* 46.

36. Quotes: Lammens, *Mudhakarat,* 30, 31; Henri Lammens, "La Syrie et son importance géographique," *Revue des questions scientifiques* 55–56 (1904): 448; Lammens, *Syrie,* 2; and Lammens, *Mudhakarat,* 31. For Providence and "God's plan" showing in Syria's geography, see Lammens, "Syrie," 421, 425.

37. Quote: Lammens, *Syrie,* 1. Similar is Lammens, "Syrie," 449.

38. Quotes: Lammens, *Mudhakarat,* 7, 22, 8, 23, 26, 9. These views were recurrent: Makaryus, *Hasr,* 3, 4, called Syria "a seat of civilization" and "the natural link between West and East."

39. All quotes: Lammens, *Syrie,* 5. Similar is Lammens, "Syrie," 419. For Lammens's anti-Muslim sentiments, see Kaufman, "Lammens," 108. He studied early Islam intensely, though.

40. Quotes: Lammens, *Mudhakarat,* 33; and Lammens, *Syrie,* 10, 10. For the Umayyads, see ibid., 7–8.

41. Quotes: Makaryus, *Hasr,* 4; Philippe Pelletier, "La grande divergence à résorber: l'Orient et l'Occident vus par Élisée Reclus," in *Élisée Reclus—Paul Vidal de la Blache,* ed. Jean-Paul Bord et al. (Paris: Harmattan, 2009), 174; and the subtitle of an earlier work by Élisée Reclus, *La Terre. Descriptions des phénomènes de la vie du globe* (Paris: Hachette, 1869–1870). For Reclus's influence on Lammens, see Kaufman, "Lammens," 111–112, which however focuses on Reclus "provid[ing] Lammens (and Syrian nationalists) with a geographic theory of Syria as a distinct territorial entity." See also Kaufman, *Phoenicia,* 46–47, for Bulus Nujaym's reception of Reclus as a geographical determinist. Reclus (1830–1904) received the prestigious French Gold Medal of the Paris Geographical Society in 1892 for his work. However,

unless Paul Vidal de la Blache, he did not majorly influence geography in France, for he was an anarchist, which affected his life and formed his style. He was banned from France in 1872 and died in Belgium; and wrote for a broad audience and quite poetically, keeping scholarly footnotes to a minimum. See Richard Lafaille, "En lisant Reclus," *Annales de la Géographie* 98 (1989): 445–459; Federico Ferretti, *Élisée Reclus: pour une géographie nouvelle* (Paris: CTHS, 2014).

42. All quotes: Lammens, *Mudhakarat,* 29. See also ibid., 30.

43. Quote: Arnon Groiss, "Communalism as a Factor in the Rise of the Syria Idea in the 1800s and early 1900s," in Beshara, *Origins of Syrian Nationhood,* 39. The major exception regarding political independence was Naguib Azoury's *Le réveil de la nation arabe* [*The Arab Nation's Awakening*], published in French in French exile in 1905. It gained next to no traction, and became relevant to Arab nationalists only after World War I.

44. Quotes: Ahmad 'Arif al-Zain, "Rabi' Saida," *al-'Irfan* 1 (1909): 109–110; and al-Zain, *Ta'rikh Saida,* 135, referencing "Toma Efendi Kayyal in volume seven of year six of the journal *al-Mashriq.*" For economic matters and Beirut's rise, see Talal al-Majdhub, *Ta'rikh Saida al-Ijtima'i* (Beirut / Sidon: al-Maktaba al-'A-sriyya, 1983), 162–209, 186, 189–190.

45. Quotes: Eugen Wirth, "Damaskus-Aleppo-Beirut," *Die Erde* 97 (1966): 106; Sami, *Safar al-Salam fi Bilad al-Sham,* 52; and Muhsin al-Amin, "Jabal 'Amil wa-Talab al-'Ilm," *al-'Irfan* 1 (1909): 592. For Damascus, see also Muhammad Kurd 'Ali, *Ghutat Dimashq* (Damascus: Matba'at al-Taraqqi, 1949). More generally, Reilly, "Regions," 112, speaks of the "green belts surrounding major Syrian towns."

46. Al-Zain, *Ta'rikh Saida,* 135. Sidon's continued hold on its hilly hinterland, and continued connection to Damascus: al-Majdhub, *Ta'rikh Saida al-Ijtima'i,* 186. Citrus exports: ibid., 191; Reilly, "Regions," 119–121. Damascus apricot export: K. K. Handelsministerium, *Berichte der k.u.k. österr.-ung. Konsularämter über das Jahre 1902* (Vienna: n.p., 1904), B:VIII.10, 3:3. Agriculture as largest sector: Donald Quataert, "Agriculture," in Inalcık with Quataert, *Economic and Social History of the Ottoman Empire,* 843.

47. Quotes: al-Zain, *Ta'rikh Saida,* 108, 109, 107. He did not mention Sidon's synagogues. For a new take on folk religion that pays much attention to the countryside, introducing the notion of 'agrarian religion,' see James Grehan, *Twilight of the Saints: Everyday Religion in Ottoman Syria and Palestine* (Oxford: Oxford University Press, 2014).

48. Both quotes: al-Zain, *Ta'rikh Saida,* 124; see also ibid., 110–111. For Americans, see also *Historical Sketches of the Missions under the Care of the Board of Foreign Missions of the Presbyterian Church* (Philadelphia: n.p., 1890). I thank Ellen Fleischmann for this reference. For *Maqasid* association and schools, see al-Tamimi and Bahjat, *Wilayat Beirut* (Beirut: Iqbal, 1917), 1:160.

49. Al-Tamimi and Bahjat, *Wilayat Beirut,* 1:155, also 159–160 for education.

50. Quote: ibid., 1:133. (The text relates this sentence as a quote.) For the sayings, see Aharon Geva-Kleinberger, *Die arabischen Stadtdialekte von Haifa* (Wiesbaden: Harrassowitz, 2004), 3–4. For Tripoli, see John Gulick, *Tripoli, a Modern Arab City* (Cambridge: Cambridge University Press, 1967), 27–30.

51. For Aleppo, see Meriwhether, *Kin,* 66. For marriage ties, see also Judith Tucker, "Marriage and Family in Nablus, 1720–1856," *Journal of Family History* 13 (1988): 165–180. For the changing fortunes of local elite families, see Ruth Roded, "Ottoman Service as a Vehicle for the Rise of New Upstarts among the Urban Elite Families of Syria in the Last Decades of Ottoman Rule," *AAS* 17 (1983): 63–94; Manna, "Continuity and Change."

52. Quotes: al-Zain, *Ta'rikh Saida,* 123; and al-Zain, "Murur 'Am 'ala Tahrir al-Dawla al-'Uthmaniyya," *al-'Irfan* 1 (1909): 401. For other cities' celebrations, see Weber, *Damascus,* 1:42; Wasif Jawhariyya, *al-Quds al-'Uthmaniyya fi al-Mudhakkirat al-Jawhariyya,* ed. Salim Tamari (Beirut: Mu'assasat al-Dirasat al-Filastiniyya, 2003), 1:108; "Qarar al-baladiyya sarf thaman ziyyanat yawm nashr al-dustur al-'uthmani" (1908) 27/5/117, Nablus Municipal Archive, Palestine (hereafter, NMA). For the 1912 deputies for example, see http://coursesa.matrix.msu.edu/~fisher/hst373/Meclis-iMubasan1912.htm.

53. For Aleppo, see Muhammad Raghib al-Tabbakh, *I'lam al-Nubala' bi-Ta'rikh Halab al-Shahba'* (Aleppo: Dar al-Qalam al-'Arabi bi-Halab, 1923–1926 [1988]), 7:390. For Salt, see Hani al-'Amad, *Ahsan al-Rabt fi Tarajim Rijalat min al-Salt* (Amman: al-Bank al-Ahli, 2007), 153. For Palestine generally, see 'Adil Manna', *A'lam Filastin fi Awakhir al-'Ahd al-'Uthmani* (Jerusalem: Jam'iyyat al-Dirasat al-'Arabiyya, 1986), 63, 70, 71, 85, 167, 309. For Safad, see Muhammad al-'Abidi, *Safad fi al-Ta'rikh* (Amman: Jam'iyyat 'Ummal al-Matabi' al-Ta'awuniyya, 1977), 186; Mustafa Abbasi, "The 'Aristocracy' of the Upper Galilee," in *Ottoman Reform and Muslim Regeneration,* ed. Itzchak Weismann and Fruma Zachs (London: Tauris, 2005), 171. For Nablus, see Mahmoud Yazbak, "Nablusi Ulama in the Late Ottoman Period," *IJMES* 29 (1997): 78, finding that of forty-seven Nabulsi ulama from 1850–1900, nineteen studied in Cairo, fourteen in Damascus, eight in Istanbul, and six in Nablus. See also al-Qayati, *Nafhat al-Basham fi Rihlat al-Sham,* 8, 58, 79, 81, 95–97, 110.

54. For clashes with bedouin, see Gottlieb Schumacher, *The Jaulân* (London: R. Bentley and Son, 1889), 57–58. For a broader discussion of the Ottomans' policy toward and use of refugees, see ibid., 108–116. For Jordan, see Rogan, *Frontiers,* 72–76. For Tscherkess, see Jawdat Nashkho, *Ta'rikh al-Tshirkiss* (Amman: Lajnat Ta'rikh al-Urdunn, 1995), esp. 39–60, and Kemal Karpat, *Studies on Ottoman Social and Political History* (Leiden: Brill, 2002), 647–675. See also Algerian refugees in Damascus, the Galilee, and a few other cities, discussed in Pierre Bardin, *Al-*

*gériens et Tunisiens dans l'Empire Ottoman de 1848 à 1914* (Paris: Éditions CNRS, 1979).

55. For wall paintings, see Stefan Weber, "Images of Imagined Worlds: Self-Image and Worldview in Late Ottoman Wall Paintings in Damascus," in *Empire in the City*, 145–171. For the SPC's regional scope, see Abdul Latif Tibawi, "The American Mission in Beirut and Bustani," *St Antony's Papers* 16 (1963): 137–182. For newspapers, see "Akhbar Mahaliyya," *Lisan al-Hal*, March 23, 1900, 2, and March 31, 1900, 2. For bureaucrats, see *Man Huwa fi Suriya 1951* (Damascus: Maktab al-Dirasat al-Suriyya wa-l-ʿArabiyya, 1951), 364, entry on ʿAbd al-Rahman Jalani who worked in Aleppo, Beirut, Damascus, Kirkuk, Deir al-Zor, Tripoli, and Beirut, settling in Damascus in 1918, and ibid., 293–294, entry on Jamil al-Dahhan who worked in Ankara, Izmir and Libya as well as in Damascus, Jerusalem and Aleppo; and Muhammad Adib Al Taqi al-Din al-Hisni, *Muntakhabat al-Tawarikh li-Dimashq* (Damascus: al-Matbaʿa al-Haditha, 1928), 2:851, on Muhammad Pasha, of the Damascene Yusifiyya family, who exercised official functions in Damascus, Acre, Balqa, Tripoli, and Hama. For students in Istanbul, see Tauber, *Emergence*. (One instance was the Literary Club, founded in 1910 and presided over by a Shiite from today's southern Lebanon; another, the secret *al-Fatat,* first envisioned in 1908 by two students from Nablus and Damascus.) See also Fawzi al-Qawuqji, *Mudhakkirat Fawzi al-Qawuqji: 1912–1932* (Beirut: Dar al-Quds, 1975), 11–12.

56. ʿUmar al-Salih Barghuti, *al-Marahil* (Beirut: al-Muʾassasa al-ʿArabiyya li-l-Dirasat wa-l-Nashr, 2001), 119–120, an autobiography written in the third person.

57. Quotes: Jade Tabet, ed., *Beyrouth: Portrait de ville* (Paris: Institut Français d'Architecture, 2001), 8, quoting a Macmillan guidebook from 1901; and al-Bustani, *Nafir Suriya,* 64.

58. For a list of secondary schools, see Jens Hanssen, "The Birth of an Education Quarter," in *History, Space, and Social Conflict in Beirut. The Quarter of Zokak al-Blat,* ed. Hans Gebhardt et al. (Beirut: Ergon, 2005), 148. Especially on the Bustani-SPC competition, see Aleksandra Kobiljski, "Un modèle américain? Les collèges protestants de Beyrouth et Kyoto, 1860–1975," *Monde(s)* 6 (2014): 171–193.

59. Barghuti, *Marahil,* 118.

60. Quote: Ami Ayalon, *The Press in the Arab Middle East* (New York: Oxford University Press, 1995), 50; see also 31–39. Dagmar Glass, "Von Mirʾat al-ahwal zu Tamarat al-Funūn," in *Amtsblatt, vilayet gazetesi und unabhängiges Journal: die Anfänge der Presse im Nahen Osten,* ed. Anja Pistor-Hatam (Frankfurt am Main: Peter Lang, 2001), 29–45; Elizabeth Holt, "Serialization and Silk. The Emergence of a Narrative Reading Public of Arabic in Beirut, 1870–1884" (PhD diss., Columbia University, 2009), esp. ch. 1. For material culture and consumption, see Toufoul Abou-Hodeib, *A Taste for Home: The Modern Middle Class in Ottoman*

*Beirut* (Stanford, CA: Stanford University Press, 2017); Khuri-Makdisi, *Eastern Mediterranean.* For merchants, see Gerhard Höpp, "Kultur und Kommerz im 19. Jahrhundert: Beziehungen libanesischer Geschäftsleute zur Nahda," in *Entwicklung durch Reform: Asien und Afrika im 19. Jahrhundert* (Berlin: Akademie Verlag, 1991), 101–108; Fruma Zachs, "Cultural and Conceptual Contributions of the Beiruti Merchants to the Nahda," *JESHO* 55 (2012): 153–182. For *Thamarat al-Funun,* see Ayalon, *Press,* 37.

61. Quotes: Dagmar Glass, "Die *Masa'il*-Kolumne in *al-Muqtataf,*" in *Presse und Öffentlichkeit im Nahen Osten,* ed. Christoph Herzog et al. (Heidelberg: Orient-verlag, 1995), 61, quoting Philip Hitti, *Lebanon in History* (London, 1957), 466; and Jandora, "Al-Bustanī," 87. See also Ayalon, *Press,* 39–46, 51–62; Ayalon, *Reading Palestine: Printing and Literacy, 1900–1948* (Austin: University of Texas Press, 2004), 81. For non-Arab intellectuals, see Kamran Rastegar, *Literary Modernity between the Middle East and Europe* (London: Routledge, 2007); Khuri-Makdisi, *Eastern Mediterranean.*

62. Ayalon, *Press,* 50. For the number of shawwam in Egypt, see Egypt, Ministère des Finances, Direction des Statistiques, *Annuaire statistique de l'Egypte, 1910* (Cairo: Imprimérie Nationale, 1910), 3. I thank Angelos Dalachanis for this source.

63. Filib di Tarrazi, *Ta'rikh al-Sihafa al-'Arabiyya* (Beirut: al-Matba'a al-Adabiyya, 1933), 4:25–73.

64. Quote: Eliezer Tauber, "The Press and the Journalist as a Vehicle in Spreading National Ideas in Syria in the Late Ottoman Period," *WI* 30 (1990): 163. For the list, see ibid., 165. For *Kawthar,* see *Kawthar* (1911): 41–42, 87, 131–132, 184–185, 234, 281.

65. See e.g. "Harakat al-Intikhabat," *al-Muqtabas,* February 10, 1912, 1, quoting various Ottoman papers; or "Lutfi Fikri," *Filastin,* February 14, 1912, 2, quoting *Lisan al-Hal.* For characteristics of the newspapers, see Ayalon, *Reading Palestine,* 59; Tauber, "Press," 172–173.

66. Ibid., 163–177; ibid., 170, calls *al-Mufid* a particularly influential paper. *Al-Mufid* led the pack perhaps also because it staunchly opposed the CUP; it indeed had ties to the clandestine *al-Fatat.*

67. For Barghuti Sr.'s Beiruti acquaintances, see Barghuti, *Marahil,* 118. For publication numbers, see Di Tarrazi, *Sihafa,* 4:9–15. For Damascus, see ibid., 4:43–45; Tauber, "Press," 165; *Kawthar* (1911): 41–42, 87, 131–132, 184–185, 234, 281. For *Filastin* and Nablus, see "Akhbar Mahaliyya," *Filastin,* August 16, 1911, 3; "Haifa—'an al-Mufid," *Filastin,* July 19, 1911, 2; "Qarar sarf thaman jaridatai Beirut wa-l-Iqbal" (1907), 27/3/115, NMA; "Qarar saraf badal ishtirak al-baladiyya bi-jaridat al-Haris al-beirutiyya" (1912) 27/8/211, NMA.

68. Butrus al-Bustani, "Fi Madinat Beirut," in *al-Jam'iyya al-Suriyya li-l-'Ulum wa-l-Funun,* 72.

69. Quote: ibid., 72. See also Fawaz, *Merchants*, 30–31, 80–81, 84.

70. Leila Fawaz, "The Changing Balance of Forces between Beirut and Damascus in the Nineteenth and Twentieth Centuries," *RMMM* 55–56 (1990): 211. For demographics, see Fawaz, *Merchants*, 48–49. See also Tabak, "Local Merchants," 199; Fruma Zachs, "Commerce and Merchants under Amīr Bašīr II," *Oriente Moderno* 86 (2006): 61–63; Axel Havemann, "Die Entwicklung regionaler Handelszentren und die Entstehung eines Händlertums im Libanongebirge des 19. Jahrhunderts," *WI* 22 (1982): 51–60. Mount Lebanon Christians, some merchants from Zahle and Dayr al-Qamar, had resettled in Beirut since 1840.

71. For the road, see Fawaz, *Merchants*, 67–68. For geography, see Downes, "Waterfont," 134–135, 166–167; Wirth, "Damaskus-Aleppo-Beirut," 167.

72. Politically the mountain remained independent, becoming a *mutasarrifiyya* in 1861/1864.

73. Quotes: Owen, *Middle East*, 160, 157. See also Alexander Schölch, "Zum Problem eines aussereuropäischen Feudalismus," *Peripherie* 5–6 (1981): 110–114. For the *mutasarrifiyya*, see Akarli, *Long Peace*.

74. Julius Zwiedinek von Südenhorst, *Syrien und seine Bedeutung für den Welthandel* (Wien: Hölder, 1873), 12. Ernest Weakley/British Parliamentary Board of Trade, *Trade with Syria* (London: His Majesty's Stationery Office, 1911), 27, called Beirut "the commercial capital of Syria and Palestine."

75. For trade statistics, see Issawi, *Fertile Crescent*, 154–155; K. K. Handelsministerium, *Berichte der k.u.k. österr.-ung. Konsularämter über das Jahre 1907* (Wien: Verlag des k.k. österreichischen Handelsmuseums, 1908), B:VIII.5, 3:1.

76. For overall imports and exports, see Issawi, *Fertile Crescent*, 154–155, 157. (Imports: Beirut: 1,158,000 [1872], 1,698,000 [1906]; Jaffa: 138,000 [1873], 660,000 [1906]. Exports: Beirut: 699,000 [1872], 1,020,000 [1906]; Jaffa: 247,000 [1873], 500,000 [1906].) For ships, see K.u.K. Handelsministerium, *Berichte der k.u.k. österreichisch-ungarischen Konsularämter über das Jahr 1903* (Vienna: Verlag des k.k. österreichischen Handelsmuseums, 1905), B:X.7, 3:33. See also Weakley, *Trade*, 113–114. For demographics, see Wirth, "Damaskus-Aleppo-Beirut," 105, 125.

77. Quote: Wirth, "Damaskus-Aleppo-Beirut," 171; the second quote translates a quote, in ibid., 171, of R. Thoumin, *Géographie humaine de la Syrie centrale* (Tours: n.p., 1936), 325. For the city description, see Baedeker, *Palästina und Syrien* (Leipzig: n.p., 1900), 308–309; Haddad, "Economic Nationalism," 76–78; Samir Kassir, *Beirut*, trans. M. B. DeBevoise (Berkeley: University of California Press, 2010), 206–219.

78. Weakley, *Trade*, 28. For an example, Nablus, see Doumani, *Palestine*, 74.

79. Quote: subtitle of Hanssen, *Beirut* (who focuses more on the role of local merchant elites). For Istanbul's interest in maritime issues, including port Beirut, see Downes, "Waterfont." For Beirut's active municipality, see Malek Sharif, *Imperial*

*Norms and Local Realities: The Ottoman Municipal Laws and the Municipality of Beirut (1860–1908)* (Würzburg: Ergon, 2014).

80. Quote: Weakley, *Trade,* 28. For Egypt, see ibid., and the case of the Sursock family, discussed below.

81. Quotes: K. K. Handelsministerium, Berichte 1902, 3:B:VIII, p. 21, 22, 21; and Weakley, Trade, 28.

82. Quote: Jacques Thobie, *Intérêts et imperialisme français dans l'empire Ottoman (1895–1914)* (Paris: Imprimérie nationale, 1977), 165. See also ibid., 174. For broader contexts, see Steven Topik and Allen Wells, "Commodity Chains in a Global Economy," in *A World Connecting, 1870–1945,* ed. Emily Rosenberg (Cambridge: Belknap Press of Harvard University Press, 2012), 642–652; Daniel Headrick, *The Tentacles of Progress. Technology Transfer in the Age of Imperialism, 1850–1940* (New York: Oxford University Press, 1988).

83. This draws on Thobie, *Intérêts,* 164–177, 211–218, as well as on Downes, "Waterfront," and on Hanssen, *Beirut;* however, the latter two play down, respectively up, local conditions. For the port, this draws also on May Davie, "Flux mondiaux, expressions locales," *Chronos* 3 (2000): 139–172.

84. Quote: Vincent Cloarec, "L'entente cordiale et la question syrienne, 1904–1918," *Relations internationales* 93 (1998): 16. See also Thobie, *Intérêts,* 211–218; Rashid Khalidi, "The Economic Partition of the Arab Provinces of the Ottoman Empire before the First World War," *Review* 11 (1988): 251–264. A well-told, though top-heavy, account of the German side is Sean McMeekin, *The Berlin-Baghdad Express* (Cambridge: Harvard University Press, 2010), pt. 1.

85. Fawaz, *Merchants,* 94.

86. Quotes: ibid., 92–93. For Palestine holdings, see Alexander Schölch, *Palästina im Umbruch, 1856–1882* (Stuttgart: Steiner, 1986), 106–108. For the statistics of one case, Nazareth, see Asʻad Mansur, *Taʾrikh al-Nasira* (Cairo: Matbaʻat al-Hilal, 1924), 287–288. An interesting parallel case is Jens Hanssen, "'Malhamé-Malfamé': Levantine Elite and Transimperial Networks on the Eve of the Young Turk Revolution," *IJMES* 43 (2011): 25–48.

87. "Cher Alfred, il me tarde de te voir. Quand comptes-tu venir? N'as-tu pas assez de cette vie fatiguante que tu me mènes, je crois qu'il est déjà temps que tu reviennes faire ta retraite à Beyrouth. Le nouvel an a déjà passé . . .": L. Sursock to Alfred Sursock, Beirut, January 1, 1914; document #7046/1, Sursock Archives, Phoenix Center for Lebanese Studies, Université de Saint Esprit, Kaslik, Lebanon (hereafter, SA/PCLS). For Alfred Sursock's position in high Ottoman social and governmental circles, see e.g. soirée invitation, [French] Président du Conseil Ministre de l'Intérieur to Alfred Sursock, Honorary Secretary at the Turkish Embassy in Paris, Paris, March 1, 1902, document #6875, SA/PCLS; Pera, Istanbul, Sports Club membership, 1904, document #7790, SA/PCLS; or Abdulrahman to Alfred

Sursock, Beirut, December 7, 1905, document #6870, SA / PCLS, asking him to intercede on his behalf with a high Ottoman official.

88. For statistics, see Issawi, *Fertile Crescent*, 155, 157. (Jaffa: import: 1,313,000; export: 745,000. Beirut: import: 2,175,000; export: 631,000.) For the Damascus-Acre / Haifa railway, see Juni Mansur, *al-Khatt al-Hadidi al-Hijazi: Ta'rikh wa-Tatawwur Qitar Dir'a-Haifa* (Jerusalem: Mu'assasat al-Dirasat al-Maqdisiyya, 2008).

89. Thobie, *Intérêts*, 168–169.

90. Quote: James Reilly, "Damascus Merchants and Trade in the Transition to Capitalism," *Canadian Journal of History* 27 (1992): 3. See also ibid., 3–4; Rafeq, "City and Countryside," 295–332, esp. 307, 328; Reilly, "Regions," 117–118; Antoine Abdel Nour, "Le réseau routier de la Syrie ottomane," *Arabica* 30 (1983): 169–189.

91. This analysis draws on Reilly, "Damascus Merchants," 1–14; Abdul-Karim Rafeq, "The Impact of Europe on a Traditional Society: the Case of Damascus, 1840–1870," in *Économie et sociétés dans l'empire ottoman*, ed. Jean-Louis Bacqué-Grammond and Paul Dumont (Paris: Editions CNRS, 1983), 420–422.

92. Quote: Linda Schatkowski Schilcher, "Violence in Rural Syria in the 1880s and 1890s," in *Peasants and Politics in the Modern Middle East*, ed. Farhad Kazemi and John Waterbury (Miami: Florida International University Press,, 1991), 51. See also Schatkowski Schilcher, "Grain Economy." Grain exports were already energized by rising European demand during the French Revolution and the Napoleonic Wars.

93. Quote: von Südenhorst, *Syrien*, 89. An Arab voice was Nu'man al-Qasatli, *Kitab al-Rawda al-Ghanna fi Dimashq al-Fayha'* (Beirut: s.n., 1879), analyzed in Abdul-Karim Rafeq, "Social Groups, Identity, Loyalty, and Historical Writing in Ottoman and Post-Ottoman Syria," in *Les arabes et l'histoire créatrice*, ed. Dominique Chevallier (Paris: Presses de l'Université de Paris-Sorbonne, 1995), 88–89.

94. For artisans, see Donald Quataert, "Ottoman Handicrafts and Industry in the Age of European Industrial Hegemony, 1800–1914," *Review* 11 (1988): 169–178. A specific analysis that also is attentive to politics is Vatter, "Journeymen"; see also James Reilly, "From Workshops to Sweatshops: Damascus Textiles and the World Economy in the Last Ottoman Century," *Review* 16 (1993): 199–213. For Ottoman action, see Faruk Tabak, "Local Merchants," 203. For a related case of Istanbul helping a city vis-à-vis European economic actors, see Elena Frangakis-Syrett, "Capital Accumulation and Family Business Networks in Late Ottoman Izmir," *International Journal for Turkish Studies* 21 (2015): 61, showing that Istanbul helped Izmir maintain rivalries between Europeans to "acquire better terms for the same or other project(s)."

95. Honorable life in Damascus: Leila Hudson, "Investing by Women or Investing in Women? Merchandise, Money, and Marriage and the Formation of a Prenational Bourgeoisie in Damascus," *CSSAME* 26 (2006): 108. An architectural-*cum*-historical

survey is Weber, *Damascus*. See also Jean-Luc Arnaud, *Damas: urbanisme et architecture, 1860–1925* (Arles: Sindbad, 2006). For an analysis of a new sense of (political, prenationalist) publicness, see Leila Hudson, "Late Ottoman Damascus," *Critique* 15 (2006): 151–169. For differences to Beirut (and to Aleppo), see also Wirth, "Damaskus-Aleppo-Beirut."

96. Quote: Reilly, "Merchants," 22. Exceptions include the families mentioned in al-Hisni, *Muntakhabat*, 2:884, 902, 909, a source that Reilly (and other historians) uses, too.

97. For the continued strength—but also regional/imperial spatial focus—of merchants from the region's interior, mostly Muslims, see also Gilbar, "Muslim Big Merchant-Entrepreneurs," and Tabak, "Local Merchants." Compare global analyses of persisting Asian merchant networks, including Claude Markovits, *The Global World of Indian Merchants, 1750–1914* (Cambridge: Cambridge University Press, 2000).

98. Muhammad Saʿid al-Qasimi, *Qamus al-Sinaʿat al-Shamiyya* (Damascus: Dar Talas, 1988), 322, 349, 417–418, a source other historians have used, e.g., Leila Hudson, *Transforming Damascus: Space and Modernity in an Islamic City* (London: I. B. Tauris, 2008).

99. Quotes: al-Qasimi, *Qamus*, 322, 322, 123. For "near cities," see ibid., 123, 349.

100. For spreading beyond the *ʿAsruniyya*, see ibid., 123. For trading with or living as trader in Beirut, see al-Hisni, *Muntakhabat*, 875 (twice), 880, 884, 888, 891, 894, 907, 909, 910. (All entries cover people living from the late nineteenth century.) About half of these Damascenes trading with or in Beirut also traded with, or had a family member trading with, other Ottoman centers: ibid., 875 (a brother in Istanbul), 880 (a brother in Izmir), 888 (first in Istanbul), 907 (also trading with the Hijaz, and with a brother in Medina). Moving to Beirut for other purposes: ibid., 828, 840, 875, 900, 901. For the Beyduns, see ibid., 904, but see also the Beyhums in Fawaz, *Merchants*, 96–97. For Istanbul, see al-Hisni, *Muntakhabat*, 875, 888, 889, 890, 896, 902.

101. Reilly, "Damascus Merchants," 16. Also Weakley, *Trade*, 32; Tabak, "Local Merchants," 201.

102. Reilly, "Damascus Merchants," 15–18, 25; Sarah Shields, "Interdependent Spaces: Relations between the City and the Countryside in the Nineteenth Century," in *The Urban Social History of the Middle East, 1750–1950*, ed. Peter Sluglett (Syracuse: Syracuse University Press, 2008), 52–57, for landownership and taxation of urbanites in rural regions. For security, see Rogan, *Frontiers*. For specific cases, see Riccardo Bocco, "État et tribus bédouins en Jordanie, 1920–1990" (PhD diss., Institut d'études politiques de Paris, 1996), 49–106; Marwan Hanania, "From Colony to Capital: A Socio-Economic and Political History of Amman, 1878–1958" (PhD diss., Stanford University, 2010), chaps. 1–3. For the caravan trade, see Hind

Abu al-Sha'r, *Ta'rikh Sharq al-Urdunn fi al-'Ahd al-'Uthmani* (Amman: al-Lajna al-'Ulya li-Kitabat Ta'rikh al-Urdunn, 2001), 388; Muhammad Kurd 'Ali, "Rihla ila al-Madina al-Munawwara," *Muqatabas* 7 (1912): 505–525.

103. Quotes: Reilly, "Damascus Merchants," 21; and Hind Abu al-Sha'r, *Irbid wa-jiwaruha (nahiyyat Bani 'Ubayd), 1850–1928* (Amman: Bank al-A'mal, 1995), 380. See also ibid., 381–388; Abu al-Sha'r, *Ta'rikh,* 382. An example of how conditions in particular villages either facilitated or complicated purchases is Mundy, "'Ajlun," 83. For Salt, see al-'Amad, *Salt,* 99, 140; Jurj al-Dawud, *al-Salt wa-Jiwaruha* (Amman: Jami'at Al al-Bayt, 2009), 611.

104. Quote: Dawud, *Salt,* 594. For the Al-Bisharat, see Ra'uf Abu Jabir, *Al al-Bisharat* (Amman: n.p., 2008), 33–34, 36, 39, 106. For other cases, see al-'Amad, *Salt,* 25, 70, 80, 92, 181–182; and author, interview with Hassan Mango, Amman, June 29, 2011, whose grandfather Khalil had moved from Nablus to Salt in the late nineteenth century. For Irbid, see Abu al-Sha'r, *Irbid,* 379, 383. For the Nablus municipality, see "Tilighrafat" (1908), 27 / 4 / 181 and 27 / 4 / 194, NMA; "Masrufat taslih wa-ta'mir qayiq nahr al-Urdunn" (1892), 27 / 1 / 408, NMA. Secondary literature includes Doumani, *Palestine,* 74 (about pressure by Beiruti and Damascene merchants); Gad Gilbar, "Economic and Social Consequences of the Opening of New Markets: the Case of Nablus, 1870–1914," in Philipp, *Syrian Land,* 281–291; Eugene Rogan, "Moneylending and Capital Flows from Nablus, Damascus and Jerusalem to *Qada'* al-Salt," in Philipp, *Syrian Land,* 239–260.

105. Wirth, "Damaskus-Aleppo-Beirut." For Aleppo's role in the premodern world economy, see Gaube and Wirth, *Aleppo,* 8–17, 223–247.

106. For settling tribes, see Gaube and Wirth, *Aleppo,* 262. For northern Anatolia's re-orientation, see ibid., 261. For Damascus, see Wirth, "Damaskus-Aleppo-Beirut," 106–111. For Aleppo as a steppe city and its consequences in the late nineteenth century, see ibid., 110; Gaube and Wirth, *Aleppo,* 262–266.

107. Quote: Schölch, *Palästina,* 74. See also May Davie, *Beyrouth et ses faubourgs (1840–1940)* (Beirut: CERMOC, 1996), 141; Ruth Kark, *Jaffa* (Jerusalem: Ben-Zvi, 1990), 141n34, 151, 230–238; Mark LeVine, *Overthrowing Geography: Jaffa, Tel Aviv, and the Struggle for Palestine, 1880–1948* (Berkeley: University of California Press, 2005), 35, 55; Muhammad Tarawneh, *Qada' Yafa fi al-'Ahd al-'Uthmani* (Karak[?]: M. S.Gh. al-Tarawinah, 2000), 477–502; Schölch, *Palästina,* 124; "Beirut, 'an Jara'idiha," *Filastin,* July 17, 1911, 2, "Beirut," *Filastin,* August 30, 1911, 3; Noha Tadros Khalaf, *Les mémoires de 'Issa al-'Issa* (Paris: Karthala, 2009), 123, 134.

108. Quote: Louis Lortet, *Syrie d'aujourd'hui* (Paris: Hachette, 1884), 363 (quoted in LeVine, *Geography,* 32), calling it "one of the most comprehensive guides to Greater Syria of the period." For population increase, see Ruth Kark, "The Contribution of the Ottoman Regime to the Development of Jerusalem and

Jaffa, 1840–1917," in *Palestine in the Late Ottoman Period,* ed. David Kushner (Jerusalem: Ben-Zvi, 1986), 47. (However, although remaining much smaller, neighboring littoral Haifa grew as fast as Jaffa, and "only in the first decades of the twentieth century is there a an evident tendency for a rise in the proportion of the coastal population above that of the inland towns": Ruth Kark, "The Rise and Decline of Coastal Towns in Palestine," in *Ottoman Palestine, 1800–1914,* ed. Gad Gilbar [Leiden: Brill, 1990], 74.) For surface, see Kark, "Contribution," 46. (In *dunam* [919 square meters in the late Ottoman Empire]: Jaffa: 108 and 1,550; Jerusalem: 699 and 4,130.) For imports / exports, see Tarawne, *Yafa,* 393–403; Kark, *Jaffa,* 263, 265; Schölch, *Palästina,* 76–88, Doumani, *Palestine,* 15. For immigration, see Kark, *Jaffa,* 142, 159. Haim Gerber, "Modernization in Nineteenth-Century Palestine: The Role of Foreign Trade," *MES* 18 (1982): 250–264, and Schölch, *Palästina,* buried the argument that Palestine's economic growth was initiated by German Templers or the Yishuv.

109. For European capital, see Thobie, *Intérêts,* 158; Frédérique Schillo, "Les commerçants français en Palestine pendant la période ottoman (1842–1914)," in *De Bonaparte à Balfour,* ed. Dominique Trimbur and Ran Aaronsohn (Paris: Editions CNRS, 2001), 133–155. For Istanbul's role, see Kark, *Jaffa,* 204–238; Tarawne, *Yafa,* 480–484; 'Arif al-'Arif, *Ta'rikh al-Quds* (Cairo: Dar al-Ma'arif, 1951), 118. The road, in a bad state for years, was constantly usable only from the 1880s: Mordechai Eliav, *Britain and the Holy Land, 1838–1914: Selected Documents from the British Consulate in Jerusalem* (Jerusalem: Ben-Zvi, 1997), 234.

110. In 1858 an exploratory Templer committee visited Jaffa. They built Sarona, near Jaffa, in 1871, three years after their first successful settlement, in Haifa in 1868; settlements in Jerusalem, near Lydda, near Sarona, and in the Galilee followed. For overviews, see Alex Carmel, *Die Siedlungen der württembergischen Templer in Palästina 1868–1918* (Stuttgart: Kohlhammer, 1973), and, more recent, Schölch, *Palästina;* Yossi Ben Artzi, *Mi-Germania le-Erets ha-Kodesh* (Jerusalem: Ben-Zvi, 1996); Mahmoud Yazbak, "Templars as Proto-Zionists? The German Colony in late Ottoman Haifa," *JPS* 28 (1999): 40–54.

111. For the Jewish population, see Kark, *Jaffa,* 154. For interactions between old and new Yishuv, see Abigail Jacobson, "Jews Writing in Arabic: Shimon Moyal, Nissim Malul and the Mixed Palestinian / Eretz Israeli Locale," in *Late Ottoman Palestine,* ed. Yuval Ben-Bassat and Eyal Ginio (London: I. B. Tauris, 2011), 165–182.

112. Quotes: Leon Pinsker, *Auto-Emancipation* (1882), reproduced in Arthur Herzberg, *The Zionist Idea* (Philadelphia: Jewish Publication Society, 1997), 184, 193. For introductions, see James Gelvin, *The Israel-Palestine Conflict* (Cambridge: Cambridge University Press, 2007), 46–75; Gideon Shimoni, *The Zionist Ideology* (Hanover: University Press of New England for Brandeis University Press, 1995). A classic is Walter Laqueur, *A History of Zionism* (New York: Schocken, [1972] 2003).

113. Arthur Ruppin, *Arthur Ruppin: Memoirs, Diaries, Letters* (New York: Herzl, 1971), 89. See also Hanna Ram, *Ha-Yishuv ha-Yehudi be-Jaffo be-ʻEt ha-Hadasha* (Jerusalem: Karmel, 1996), 90–99, 168–210; Nachum Gross, "The Anglo-Palestine Company," in *Ottoman Palestine, 1800–1914*, ed. Gad Gilbar (Leiden: Brill, 1990), 219–253. For neighboring settlements, see Yuval Ben-Bassat, "Proto-Zionist— Arab Encounters in Late Nineteenth-Century Palestine," *JPS* 38 (2009): 42–63; Arieh Saposnik, *Becoming Hebrew: the Creation of a Jewish National Culture in Ottoman Palestine* (New York: Oxford University Press, 2008).

114. For shipping problems, and Ruppin's imports from Beirut, see Ruppin, *Memoirs*, 93, 99. For interest in Beirut, see "Konservierung von Früchten zum Export in Syrien," *Palästina* 1 (1902): 87; "Syrische Bahnen. Beirût-Damaskus," *Altneuland* 1 (1904): 24; "Beirût (Syrien). Handelsbericht für das Jahr 1902," *Altneuland* 1 (1904): 181–185. For SPC, see Howard Bliss to Arthur Ruppin, Beirut, 1916, Arthur Ruppin personal collection (A107/566), Central Zionist Archives, Jerusalem, thanking for the condolence letter Ruppin had sent at the occasion of the death of Howard's father Daniel. For Ben-Gurion, see Shabtai Teveth, *Ben-Gurion* (Boston: Houghton Mifflin, 1987), 62. For Chelouche, see Teveth, *Parashat Hayai 1870–1930* (Tel Aviv: Babel, 2005), 56–66. For the importance of the region and of understanding its economy, see Alfred Nossig, "Über die Notwendigkeit von Erforschungsarbeiten in Palästina und seinen Nachbarsländern," *Palästina* 1 (1902): 6–9; Lazar Pinkus, *Palästina und Syrien: Untersuchungen zur Wirtschaftspolitik* (Geneva: Verlag der Zionistischen Monatshefte, 1903) including D. Pasmanik, "Vorrede," xv–xix; Davis Trietsch, "Die Nachbarsländer," *Altneuland* 2 (1905): 184–199; O. Warburg, "Syrien als Wirtschafts- und Kolonisationsgebiet," *Altneuland* 3 (1906): 33–43, 65–77, 109–116. For Sursock land sales, see, e.g., "Bi-la ʻUnwan," *al-Karmal*, November 16, 1920, 1; "al-Buyuʻ fi Marj Ibn ʻAmir," *al-Karmal*, July 30, 1924, 1.

115. "Akhbar al-Jihhat," *Filastin*, July 19, 1911, 2–3, July 26, 1911, 2–3, August 2, 1911, 2–3, August 5, 1911, 2–3, August 9, 1911, 2–3, August 16, 1911, 2–3, August 19, 1911, 2–3, and August 23, 1911, 3.

116. "Akhbar Shatta," *Filastin*, July 19, 1911, 3, and July 26, 1911, 2.

117. "Nablus—li-Mukatibina," *Filastin*, July 26, 1911, 2; "Ghazza—li-Mukatibina," *Filastin*, August 2, 1911, 3; "al-Ludd—li Murasilina," *Filastin*, August 19, 1911, 3; "al-Quds—li-Murasilina," *Filastin*, July 19, 1911, 2–3. For references to other newspapers, see "Haifa—ʻan al-Mufid," *Filastin*, July 19, 1911, 2, "al-Sham," *Filastin*, August 19, 1911, 3 (from *al-Muqtabas*), "Haifa," *Filastin*, August 30, 1911, 3 (from *al-Karmal*). For Jerusalem, see "Akhbar Mahaliyya: ʻAdliyyat al-Quds," *Filastin*, August 19, 1911, 3, "Akhbar Mahaliyya: ʻAin Kerem," *Filastin*, August 23, 1911, 3.

118. For the church bell, see Eliav, *Britain*, 233. For the economy, see Schölch, *Palästina*, 111–134; Schölch, "Jerusalem in the Nineteenth Century," in *Jerusalem in History*, ed.

Kamil Asali (New York: Olive Branch, 1990), 235. For the effect of the railway, see Eliav, *Britain,* 279. For pilgrims and European interests in Jerusalem, see Schölch, *Palästina,* 47–73; Issam Nassar, *European Portrayals of Jerusalem* (Lewiston: Edwin Mellen, 2006). For European competition, see Eliav, *Britain,* 136–139, 175–177, 178–180.

119. Quote: Ruppin, *Memoirs,* 90. For Jews marrying in, and moving to, Jerusalem, see Büssow, *Palestine,* 158–159. For ideology / agriculture, see Gershon Shafir, *Land, Labor, and the Origins of the Israeli-Palestinian Conflict, 1882–1914* (Cambridge: Cambridge University Press, 1989); Oz Almog, *The Sabra: The Creation of the New Jew* (Berkeley: University of California Press, 2000).

120. Quote: Teveth, *Ben-Gurion,* 63. See also ibid., 71. For Ben-Gurion in Jerusalem, see also Teveth, *Zikhronot* (Tel Aviv: 'Am 'Oved, 1971), 49–50. For Ruppin in Jerusalem, see his *Memoirs,* 91–92, 96–97. For the demographic outflux from Jerusalem to Jaffa, see Kark, *Jaffa,* 142. For small businesses in Jerusalem and Jaffa, see, e.g., "Krugliakov," *Ha-Tsvi,* September 10, 1914, 4. For ads for Jaffa stores and institutions, see, e.g., "Beit Sokhnut Librecht et Lapin," *Ha-Tsvi,* November 28, 1890, 4; "Beit Miskhar Amzalek be-Yafo," *Ha-Tsvi,* September 26, 1897, 1; "Ha-Gimnasia ha-'Ivrit Jafo," *Ha-Tsvi,* December 14, 1908, 1.

121. Büssow, *Palestine,* 144, 146. However, in another Muslim neighborhood, Shaykh Jarrah, Jaffa's percentage was lower: ibid., 164.

122. For Jerusalem's cultural scene, see Jawhariyya, *Mudhakkirat,* 1:79, 108, 133, 148; Ayalon, *Reading Palestine.* For races, see Issam Khalidi, "The coverage of sports news in "Filastin" 1911–1948," *JQF* 44 (2010): 46. For Sakakini buying a press in Jerusalem, see Tadros Khalaf, *Mémoires,* 134.

123. Khalil Sakakini, *Yawmiyyat Khalil al-Sakakini* (Ramallah: Markaz Khalil al-Sakakini al-Thaqafi, 2003), 1:351–352; Tadros Khalaf, *Mémoires,* 138–139.

124. Najib al-Khuri Nassar, *al-Sihiuniyya* (Haifa: al-Karmal, 1911), 3. Nassar also embraced the empire as a framework for action: "Today our government is constitutional, and constitutional governments belong to the people"; ibid., 63. This was doubly interesting given that from 1908–14 also the Yishuv believed that Zionists best worked under Istanbul's umbrella. For Nassar, see also Campos, *Ottoman Brothers,* 158–165. For Ottomanism, see ibid.; Dolbee and Hazkani, "'Impossible Is Not Ottoman'"; Ben-Bassat, "Ottomanization." For the roots and nature of Palestinian proto-nationalism, see Rashid Khalidi, *Palestinian Identity: The Construction of Modern National Consciousness* (New York: Columbia University Press, 1997); and an incisive conceptual note in Pappé, *Husaynis,* 19. For Zionist-Arab relations, see Jonathan Gribetz, *Defining Neighbors: Religion, Race, and the Early Zionist-Arab Encounter* (Princeton, NJ: Princeton University Press, 2014); Yuval Ben Bassat, "Local Feuds or Premonitions of a Bi-National Conflict?" (PhD diss., University of Chicago, 2007); Neville Mandel, *The Arabs and Zionism be-*

*fore World War One* (Berkeley: University of California Press, 1976). For relations in Jerusalem, see Abigail Jacobson, *From Empire to Empire: Jerusalem between Ottoman and British Rule* (Syracuse: Syracuse University Press, 2011); Ruth Kark and Joseph Glass, "The Valero family," *JQF* 21 (2004): 27–40; Jawhariyya, *Mudhakkirat,* 1:20, 74.

125. Quote: Ben-Gurion, *Zikhronot,* 22. For the immediate departure for Petah Tikvah, see David Ben-Gurion to his father, Jaffa, September 7, 1906, reprinted in *Igerot David Ben Gurion,* ed. Yehuda Erez (Tel Aviv: 'Am 'Oved, 1971), 1:69.

126. Quotes: Amy Marcus, *Jerusalem 1913* (New York: Viking, 2007), 76, 77. For Jerusalem's notables, see Manna, "Continuity and Change"; Pappé, *Husayinis,* 13–15. For Jerusalemites' anti-Zionism, see ibid., 115, 120–121; Schölch, "Jerusalem," 243–244. For Tel Aviv, see LeVine, *Geography.* For *Filastin* and Zionism, see Tadros Khalaf, *Mémoires,* 135–137, 140–141. For free copies, see Rashid Khalidi, "Anti-Zionism, Arabism and Palestinian Identity: 'Isa al-'Isa and *Filastin,*" in *Configuring Identity in the Modern Arab East,* ed. Samir Seikaly (Beirut: AUB Press, 2009), 86. For the Jaffa riot, see Eliav, *Britain,* 275–255, 347–350; for the Jaffa protest, see Campos, *Ottoman Brothers,* 220.

127. Michael Bracy, "Building Palestine: 'Isa al-'Isa, *Filastin,* and the Textual Construction of National Identity, 1911–1931" (PhD diss., University of Arkansas, 2005), 67, quoting *Filastin,* July 15, 1911, 1 (emphasis added). For contemporaries' terminology, see Büssow, *Palestine,* 5, mentioning documents in "Arabic, Ottoman Turkish, Hebrew and several European languages." Regarding the local/national, compare Alon Confino's *The Nation as a Local Metaphor: Württemberg, Imperial Germany, and National Memory, 1871–1918* (Chapel Hill: University of North Carolina Press, 1997), and Celia Applegate, *A Nation of Provincials: The German Idea of Heimat* (Berkeley: University of California Press, 1990). Ilan Pappé, *A History of Modern Palestine* (Cambridge: Cambridge University Press, 2004), 13, goes further, emphasizing the need to study mini-societies below or astride national narratives. As for the *mutasarrifiyya,* it is telling that its deputies to the 1908 Ottoman parliament came from Jerusalem (2) and Jaffa (1): al-'Arif, *Ta'rikh al-Quds,* 121. For the *mutasarrifiyya* as Palestine, see Büssow, *Palestine,* 5.

128. Geographical outlines include Ernest Masterman, *Studies in Galilee* (Chicago: University of Chicago Press, 1909), 11–33; Muhsin al-Amin, *Khitat Jabal 'Amil* (Beirut: Matba'at al-Insaf, 1961), vol. 1, 47–52; Schumacher, *Jaulân,* 9–11.

129. Shmuel Feiglin, *Zikhronot Ish Metula* (Haifa: self-published, 1954), mem aleph.

130. Quotes: Hanna Hirdan al-Khuri, *al-Akhbar al-Shahiyya 'an al-'Iyal al-Marj'ayuniyya wa-l-Timiyya* (Beirut [?]: Matba'at al-Zaman, 1955), 356, 402, 426. See also ibid., 357, 414. For Beiruti and Saidawi merchants' land purchases, see Sabrina Mervin, *Un réformisme chiite: ulémas et lettrés du Gabal 'Amil, actuel Liban-Sud, de la fin de l'Empire ottoman à l'indépendance du Liban* (Paris: Karthala,

2000), 42. Marjayouni merchants also bought land, often in the Upper Galilee: see Mustafa Bazzi, *Jabal ʿAmil wa-Tawabuʿuhu fi Shimal Filastin* (Beirut: Dar al-Mawasim, 2002), 141–242. For trading with bedouins, see Schumacher, *Jaulân*, 53–54; Iris Agmon, "Shivtei ha-Beduim be-ʿEmek ha-Hula ve-ʿEmek Beit Shean be-Shalhei ha-Shilton ha-ʿUthmani," *Kathedra* 45 (1987): 94–97.

131. Quote: author, interview with Fayek Hourani (b. 1938, Marjayoun, to Saʿad), September 12, 2008, Beirut. For the 1900 list, see Khuri, *Akhbar,* 315–321. See also ibid., 425–427; author, interview with Jamal Abu Murad (b. 1946, in Marjayoun, to Ilias Abu Murad), September 10, 2008, Marjayoun; Abbasi, "'Aristocracy,'" 173–174 (on Safad); Mustafa Bazzi, *al-Takamul al-Iqtisadi baina Jabal ʿAmil wa-Muhitihi al-ʿArabi, 1850–1950* (Beirut: Dar al-Mawasim, 2002), 429–497 (on Jabal Amil); and Schumacher, *Jaulân*, 208 (on Marjayouni and Quneitra).

132. For general information on Marjayoun, see *Salnamih-yi vilayet-i Beyrut 1908* (Beirut: Vilâyet Matbaası, 1908), 259–260. For Marjayouni families, see Khuri, *Akhbar,* 335, 412, 422, 426, 493. Marjayounis were not exceptional. Some Safadis originated from Damascus (Abbasi, "'Aristocracy,'" 171); some bedouins arrived in the 1830s from Egypt with Ibrahim Pasha (Walter Zenner, "Aqiili Agha: The Strongman in the Ethnic Relations of the Ottoman Galilee," *CSSH* 14 [1972]: 178–179); and Christians in Nazareth traced their origins back to the Hawran and to Lebanon (Mansur, *Taʾrikh al-Nasira,* 205). For Shadid, see Anthony Shadid, *House of Stone* (Boston: Houghton Mifflin Harcourt, 2012). For Marjayounis (and other Lebanese) migrating to West Africa, see Arsan, *Interlopers of Empire.*

### Prelude 2. Rafiq al-Tamimi and Muhammad Bahjat Make a Tour

Epigraph: Rafiq al-Tamimi and Muhammad Bahjat, *Wilayat Beirut* (Beirut: Iqbal, 1917), 1:5.

1. This mission came against the background of ʿAzmi himself having inspected the sub-provinces (*liwaʾ*) Nablus and ʿAkka in late 1915: see "Safar al-Wali," "Aʿmal Hadrat al-Wali," and "Qudum al-Wali," *al-Ittihad al-ʿUthmani,* October 26, 1915, 3; November 17, 1915, 3; and November 20, 1915, 3. For the inadequacy of *salnamih*s, see al-Tamimi and Bahjat, *Wilayat Beirut,* 1:5. For an analysis of *Wilayat Beirut* as a document of Ottoman Orientalism, see Avi Rubin, "Ha-Mizrah Davar Ehad ve-ha-Maʿarav Davar Aher?," *Jamaʾa* 7 (2001): 54–81.

2. For Turkish, see al-Tamimi and Bahjat, *Wilayat Beirut,* 2:215. For roads, see ibid., 1:65, 66, 90. For cities, see ibid., 1:134; 2:176–177. For "You," see ibid., 2:138, 142, 147.

3. Ibid., 2:140, 146.

4. Ibid., 1:5, 93, 127; 2:180. This is a main theme in Rubin, "Mizrah."

5. Ibid., 2:188.

6. Ibid., 1:176.

7. Ibid., 1:131–134; 2:200, 209–210.

8. Quotes: ibid., 2:171, 193. See also ibid., 2:199, 205.

9. Quotes: G. Bergsträsser, "Tagebuch der wissenschaftlichen Reise von Major Trautz und Prof. Dr. Bergsträsser nach Syrien und Palästina, Frühjahr 1918," 70 (see also 76), Nachlass Friedrich Trautz, N508/108, Bundesarchiv Freiburg i.B., Germany (hereafter, BArch), and Anhang #10, 10, Nachlass Friedrich Trautz, N508/108, BArch. Trained before 1914, Bergsträsser spent the entire war in the Ottoman Empire and thereafter would receive various academic posts in Germany until his untimely death in 1933.

## 2. Crucible of War

1. For various aspects of World War I being global like no war before, see Hew Strachan, "The First World War as a Global War," *First World War Studies* 1 (2010): 3–14; Oliver Janz, "Einführung: Der erste Weltkrieg in globaler Perspektive," *GG* 40 (2014): 147–159; Gerard de Groot, *The First World War* (New York: Palgrave, 2001); John Morrow, *The Great War: An Imperial History* (London: Routledge, 2004); Eric Brose, *A History of the Great War* (New York: Oxford University Press, 2010).

2. Şevket Pamuk, "The Ottoman Economy in World War One," in *The Economics of World War One*, ed. Stephen Broadberry and Mark Harrison (Cambridge: Cambridge University Press, 2005), 112. For a wartime reading of Ottoman economic developments, see the German economist in Istanbul G. Herlt, "Kriegswirtschaft in der Türkei," *WA* 8 (1916): 466–476; 9 (1917): 107–112, 285–288; 11 (1917): 145–154; and 13 (1918): 183–190.

3. This approach drew on the famous 1883 work *Das Volk in Waffen* (*The Nation in Arms*) by German Field-Marshall Colmar Freiherr von der Goltz (1843–1916); following the defeat of 1877–1878, Goltz had reorganized the Ottoman army; from 1915–1916 he helped repel a British attack on central Iraq, where he died of typhus. For 1914 not as a break but as a continuation of a series of wars, see Robert Gerwarth and Erez Manela, "The Great War as a Global War: Imperial Conflict and the Reconfiguration of World Order, 1911–1923," *DH* 38 (2014): 787; Najwa al-Qattan, "Safarbarlik: Ottoman Syria and the Great War," in *From the Syrian Land to the States of Syria and Lebanon*, ed. Thomas Philip and Christoph Schumann (Beirut: Ergon, 2004), 165; Abdallah Hanna, "The First World War According to the Memories of 'Commoners' in the Bilad al-Sham," in *The World in World Wars: Experiences, Perceptions and Perspectives from Africa and Asia*, ed. Heike Liebau et al. (Leiden: Brill, 2010), 303.

4. Feroz Ahmad, "War and Society under the Young Turks, 1908–1918," *Review* 11 (1988): 267, argues that the wartime state "mobilized . . . all its resources, human

and material." For military reform, see Handan Akmeşe, *The Birth of Modern Turkey: The Ottoman Military and the March to World War One* (London: I. B. Tauris, 2005); Mehmet Beşikçi, *The Ottoman Mobilization of Manpower in the First World War* (Leiden: Brill, 2012). For prewar sociopolitical contexts, see Eyal Ginio, "Mobilizing the Ottoman Nation during the Balkan Wars (1912–1913)," *War in History* 12 (2005): 156–177; Nadir Özbek, "Defining the Public Sphere during the Late Ottoman Empire," *MES* 43 (2007): 795–809. For the use, already in 1912–1913, of the term *safarbarlik*, also in reference to the Balkan War, see Hanna, "First World War," 303. For an example, see Siham Tergeman, *Daughter of Damascus* (Austin: University of Texas at Austin Center for Middle Eastern Studies, 1994), 166. For German-Ottoman relations, see Ulrich Trumpener, *Germany and the Ottoman Empire, 1914–1918* (Princeton, NJ: Princeton University Press, 1968).

5. "Nebenkriegsschauplatz": Freiherr von Hammerstein-Gesmold, "Persönliche Aufzeichnungen über den Einsatz des Inf. Rgts. Nr. 146 und des Asien-Korps in Palästina" (12.1.1918–Nov. 1918), 4, N309 / 17, Bundesarchiv Freiburg i.B., Germany (hereafter, BArch). The German *Armee-Zeitung Jildirim*, published in 1918 in Damascus, talked of Bilad al-Sham as the "most remote and southern-most front of this world war": ibid., May 19, 1918, 1. Gerhard Wiegand, *Halbmond im letzten Viertel. Briefe und Reiseberichte aus der alten Türkei von Theodor und Marie Wiegand 1895 bis 1918* (Munich: Bruckmann, 1970), 233 (letter to his wife, Damaskus, February 24, 1917), talked of "periphery."

6. Keith Watenpaugh, *Being Modern in the Middle East: Revolution, Nationalism, Colonialism, and the Arab Middle Class* (Princeton, NJ: Princeton University Press, 2006), 122. Spearheaded by the Hashemite rulers of Mecca and Medina, the idea of an independent Arab state was "the backwards-oriented utopia of an Arab Caliphate coexisting with the aspirations of a modern nation building" (Bassam Tibi, *Arab Nationalism* [New York: St. Martin's Press, 1990], 21, quoted in Hassan Kayalı, *Arabs and Young Turks: Ottomanism, Arabism, and Islamism in the Ottoman Empire, 1908–1918* [Berkeley: University of California Press, 1997], 215n38). And the British-supported revolt they started in 1916 was "a convergence of dynastic ambition and strategic exigency" (ibid., 16). This diplomatic, and related political and geostrategic, issues have been of greatest interest to both Western and Arab historians of the Ottoman World War I. An overview is Charles Smith, "The Historiography of World War One and the Emergence of the Contemporary Middle East," in *Middle East Historiographies*, ed. Israel Gershoni et al. (Seattle: University of Washington Press, 2006), 39–69. See also Jonathan Schneer, *The Balfour Declaration* (New York: Random, 2010). For a critique of the Arab-nationalist inspired historiographic focus, see Kayalı, *Arabs and Young Turks,* 3. A focus especially of British / imperial accounts is military history: see David Bullock, *Allenby's War: The Palestine-Arabian Campaigns, 1916–1918* (London: Blandford,

1988); Kristian Coates Ulrichsen, *The Logistics and Politics of the British Campaigns in the Middle East, 1914–1922* (New York: Palgrave, 2010); Priya Satia, *Spies in Arabia: the Great War and the Cultural Foundations of Britain's Covert Empire in the Middle East* (Oxford: Oxford University Press, 2008). New excellent overviews are Eugene Rogan, *The Fall of the Ottomans: The Great War in the Middle East* (London: Allen Lane, 2015); and Leila Fawaz, *A Land of Aching Hearts: The Middle East in the Great War* (Cambridge: Harvard University Press, 2014).

7. See "The Balfour Declaration," BBC News, November 29, 2001, http://news.bbc.co
   .uk/2/hi/in_depth/middle_east/israel_and_the_palestinians/key_documents
   /1682961.stm.

8. The casualty figures are computed from an exceedingly well documented Wikipedia page, https://en.wikipedia.org/wiki/World_War_I_casualties. I adopted maximum numbers wherever there was a range. Using the same source, the ratio of Ottoman military casualties to total population (7 percent) was lower than in France (14 percent), Germany (10 percent), and Austria-Hungary (10 percent), though higher than in the United Kingdom (6 percent) and Russia (4 percent). For knowledge of the nature of the European war, see the section "Tilighrafat al-Harb" of almost every World War I issue of *al-Ittihad al-'Uthmani*. In "al-Harb al-Markaziyya," *al-Ittihad al-'Uthmani*, November 7, 1915, 1, a journalist wrote that "[I]n earlier times armies clashed face to face. . . . But now defensive war has developed to a horrifying degree" in Western Europe including "trenches . . . barbed wire, . . . dug-in artillery and mines." Similarly, see "Sadd Hadidi Jadid," *al-Ittihad al-'Uthmani*, December 9, 1915, 1. Following the war, Muhammad Kurd 'Ali, *Khitat al-Sham* (Beirut: Dar al-'Ilm li-l-Malayin, [1925] 1970), 3:135, noted that "in truth, there was no serious warfare in Syria." (See also "Appendix: Reverend George Curtis Doolittle, *Pathos and Humor of the War Years in Syria* [Sidon, 1920]" in Nicholas Ajay, "Mount Lebanon and the Wilayah of Beirut, 1914–1918: The War Years" [PhD diss., Georgetown University, 1973], 267, noting that "Syria saw little or nothing of the real war.") For Gaza, see Oberst Freiherr Kress von Kressenstein, "Überblick über die Ereignisse an der Sinaifront," *Zwischen Kaukasus und Sinai* 1 (1921): 31–41; Werner Steuber, *"Jildirim": Deutsche Streiter auf heiligem Boden* (Oldenburg: Stalling, 1925), 23. The only Ottoman front remotely comparable to Western Europe was the Dardanelles where in 1915 Ottoman logistical advantage, topographical superiority, well-prepared artillery and tactical readiness resulted in static warfare and British defeat.

9. In March and April 1917 two British attacks on Sinai's northeastern exit, around Gaza, failed. A high-ranking officer who worked under Jamal Pasha for two years, Freiherr von Kress, "Achmed Dschemal Pascha," *Zwischen Kaukasus und Sinai* 3 (1923): 18, attested that the commander of Bilad al-Sham, Jamal Pasha, "had a very

strongly developed sense of reality." Thus, in 1917 Jamal resisted Enver's pressure to attack well-defended British positions in Gaza (ibid., 18–20).

10. Kayalı, *Arabs and Young Turks*, 192.

11. The CUP envisioned a "state-based patriotism" "akin to the French example": Kayalı, *Arabs and Young Turks*, 9. This fits into a more global picture of "nation-statization": Christophe Charle, *La crise des sociétés imperiales* (Paris: Seuil, 2001), talks of "nationalized *sociétés imperiales*." (In the Ottoman case, from 1913 this had an Islamist note which, however, focused on Turks' and Arabs' shared *political* fate in the face of Western imperialism.) For Jamal Pasha as a state builder, see M. Talha Çiçek, *War and State Formation in Syria: Cemal Pasha's Governorate during World War One, 1914–1917* (New York: Routledge, 2014). Hasan Kayalı, "Wartime Regional and Imperial Integration of Greater Syria during World War One," in *The Syrian Land: Processes of Integration and Fragmentation*, ed. Thomas Philipp and Birgit Schäbler (Stuttgart: Steiner, 1998), 296, argues that "Cemal's actions were consistent with the broader political and ideological goals of the Ottoman government during and just before World War One," centering on "a comprehensive program aimed at developing the Syrian infrastructure."

12. Hauptmann Merkel, "Die deutsche Jildirim-Etappe," *Zwischen Kaukasus und Sinai* 1 (1921): 108, also shows how the German army constructed a partly parallel transport system using trucks. Transport through Anatolia was no less easy, and no less deplored: see Deutscher Militär-Bevollmächtiger bei der Kaiserlichen Botschaft in Konstantinopel to General Mertz von Quirnheim, Istanbul, November 14, 1917, N242/4, BArch.

13. Quote: Sa'id Himadeh, *The Economic Organization of Syria* (Beirut: AUB Press, 1936), 178. See also 'Ali al-Hasani, *Ta'rikh Suriya al-Iqtisadi* (Damascus: Matba'at Bada'i' al-Funun, 1924), 243–244. A postwar description is Steuber, "Jildirim," 71–103 ("Im Kraftwagen durch Syrien und Palästina"). During the war, construction cost the lives of untold undernourished and overworked soldiers slaving away in "labor battalions." For impressions, see Wiegand, *Halbmond*, 190 (letter to his wife, road to Jerusalem, October 20, 1916), 224 (letter to his wife, Maan, January 4, 1917). However, some railway lines, for example Tripoli-Homs, were stripped, partly for use in other places, partly to preclude enemy use from 1917–1918: see Fritz Grobba, *Die Getreidewirtschaft Syriens und Palästinas seit Beginn des Weltkrieges* (Hannover: Heinz Lafaire, 1923), 101.

14. Willhelm Feldmann, *Reise zur Suesfront* (Weimar: Kiepenheuer, 1917), 80, reporting on a trip with Jamal Pasha made in 1916.

15. Kayalı, "Integration." For a postwar explanation of his wartime behavior, see Djemal Pascha, *Erinnerungen*, 298–312.

16. Quotes: Feldmann, *Reise*, 82; and Max Übelhör, *Syrien im Krieg* (Berlin: Deutsche Verlags-Anstalt, 1917), 39, 11, 43. See also von Kress, "Djemal Pascha," 21–22, on

the pasha's non-war-relevant urbanist undertakings (which baffled von Kress). After the war, Ahmed Djemal Pasha, *Erinnerungen eines türkischen Staatsmannes* (Munich: Drei Masken Verlag, 1922), 305, noted that he had thought of his plans as relevant also for the postwar period. For Ruppin, see Arthur Ruppin, *Syrien als Wirtschaftsgebiet* (Berlin: Kolonial-Wirtschaftliches Komitee, 1917).

17. For war as more than battles, see "Maslahatuna al-Wataniyya," *al-Ittihad al-'Uthmani,* December 3, 1915, 1. There were sustained attempts already during the war to link the inhabitants of Bilad al-Sham more strongly than before to the empire's center. Besides the use of Turkish, which see below, popular exhibitions and talks, partly by Arab Muslim grandees who had visited Istanbul and the northern warfronts, brought to the region knowledge of Ottoman power, most impressively victories on the Dardanelles against Britain. See "Die Dardanellen in—Damaskus," *Armee-Zeitung Jildirim,* May 27, 1918, 6; "Khutbat Mufti al-Balda," *al-Ittihad al-'Uthmani,* December 9, 1915, 3; "Khutbat al-Mufti," *al-Ittihad al-'Uthmani,* December 11, 1915, 3; "al-Wafd al-Beiruti," *al-Ittihad al-'Uthmani,* December 16, 1915, 3. There also were German information posts, also about Ottoman military exploits, in main cities: see "Muqtataf al-Akhbar fi Dimashq," *al-Ittihad al-'Uthmani,* October 14, 1915, 4; "Muqtataf al-Akhbar fi Yafa," *al-Ittihad al-'Uthmani,* October 28, 1915, 3; Nadim al-Sayyid, *Ta'rikh Halab al-Musawwar* (Aleppo: Shu'a' li-l-Nashr wa-l-'Ulum, 2011), 471–472.

18. "Muwazzafun Lubnaniun," *al-Ittihad al-'Uthmani,* March 12, 1915, 2; "Ta'iin," *al-Ittihad al-'Uthmani,* October 3, 1915, p. 3; "Ila Tarablus," *al-Ittihad al-'Uthmani,* October 14, 1915, 3.

19. Quotes: Feldmann, *Reise,* 81, relating the pasha's words; and "Muwazzafu al-Sikka al-Hadidiyya wa-l-Lugha al-Rasmiyya," *al-Ittihad al-'Uthmani,* February 4, 1915, 2.

20. For ads for private instruction in Beirut, see "Ta'lim al-Lugha al-Turkiyya," *al-Ittihad al-'Uthmani,* October 1, 1915, 4; "al-Lugha al-Turkiyya," *al-Ittihad al-'Uthmani,* November 12, 1915, 4. For the thirty-one schools, see "al-Ma'arif fi Lubnan," *al-Ittihad al-'Uthmani,* November 4, 1915, 3. For other schools, see Kayalı, "Integration," 302–303; Übelhör, *Syrien,* 8, 37; Khalil Sakakini, *Yawmiyyat* (Ramallah: Markaz Khalil al-Sakakini al-Thaqafi, 2003), 2:248–249. On another note, in World War I the state also sped up women's organization. In late 1915 a Women Welfare Association in Damascus was founded in a ceremony attended by Jamal Pasha's wife, who continued being involved in this "great national project." See "al-Jam'iyya al-Khairiyya li-l-Nisa' fi Dimashq," *al-Ittihad al-'Uthmani,* November 19, 1915, 4. A similar committee existed in Beirut: see "Jam'iyyat al-Sayyadat al-Suriyyat li-Tashghil al-Fuqara'," *al-Ittihad al-'Uthmani,* March 22, 1915, 2. Jamal Pasha was a known supporter of women rights in Istanbul before 1914 and in the war put Halide Edib Hanum, a known woman education

activist, in charge of *Bilad al-Sham*'s female secondary schools: see Übelhör, *Syrien,* 37; Halidah Adib, *Memoirs of Halidé Edib* (New York: Century, 1926). Also, not unlike European countries, women worked in nondomestic positions, reportedly 10,000 in army production jobs in Damascus alone in 1916: see Feldmann, *Reise,* 27.

21. Quote: Von Kressenstein, "Achmed Dschemal Pascha," 15. For Arab indignation, see Wiegand, *Halbmond,* 236 (letter to his wife, Damascus, March 11, 1917); Salim Tamari, *Year of the Locust: A Soldier's Diary and the Erasure of Palestine's Ottoman Past* (Berkeley: University of California Press, 2011) (analyzing wartime diaries); Abigail Jacobson, "Negotiating Ottomanism in Times of War," *IJMES* 40 (2008): 69–88. For negative wartime perception of Jamal Pasha, see, e.g., Youssef Mouawad, "Jamal Pacha, en une version libanaise," in *The First World War as Remembered in the Countries of the Eastern Mediterranean,* ed. Olaf Farschid et al. (Beirut: Ergon, 2006), 425–446.

22. The most successful ones dealt with aliments, most importantly wheat. See "al-Hinta fi Lubnan," *al-Ittihad al-'Uthmani,* October 2, 1915, 3; "Sharikat Mushtara al-Hinta fi Tarablus al-Sham," *al-Ittihad al-'Uthmani,* December 30, 1915, 3. For other commodities, see for instance this ad for Nabulsi soap sold in Beirut, "Sabun Nabulsi 'al," *al-Ittihad al-'Uthmani,* October 3, 1915, 4. On a related note, in Beirut "a number of German import firms became army contractors": see Johann Strauss, "The Disintegration of Ottoman Rule in the Syrian Territories as Viewed by German Observers," in *The Syrian Land,* 314.

23. Al-Qattan, "Safarbarlik," 163–173; Hanna, "First World War," 299, 309.

24. Quote: Wiegand, *Halbmond,* 224 (letter to his wife, Maan, January 4, 1916). For the famine, see Linda Schatkowski-Schilcher, "The Famine of 1915–1918 in Greater Syria," in *Problems of the Modern Middle East in Historical Perspective,* ed. John Spagnolo (Reading, UK: Ithaca Press, 1992), esp. 229–230; Zachary Foster, "Can the Locust Speak? Greater Syria during World War One," unpublished paper, 2012, argues that a massive locust attack in 1915 / 1916 turned hunger into famine. Exact statistics of victims of the famine and famine-related diseases do not exist. Kurd 'Ali, *Khitat al-Sham,* 3:135, speaks of "at least . . . three hundred thousand"; Schatkowski-Schilcher, "Famine," 239, of a maximum of 500,000.

25. Wiegand, *Halbmond,* 250 (letter to his wife, Beirut, May 18, 1917); Dr. Range, "Wanderfahrten in Galiläa," *Zwischen Kaukasus und Sinai* 2 (1922): 108. See also Ajay, "Mount Lebanon and Beirut," "Appendix 1. B: Interview with Mister Shahadi Sasin Mu'allim," 8; and "D: Interview with Mr. Halīm Mūsa Ashqar," 18. Also, under extreme circumstances especially poor urban dwellers—for example, some Beirutis—wandered to surrounding villages to scavenge for food: see ibid., "Appendix 1. A: Interview with Mister Shakir Naṣṣar," 3; and "D: Interview with Mr. Halīm Mūsa Ashqar," 20. For movement to the hinterland, see Nail Abu

Shaqra, "al-Ghala' wa-Atharuhu fi Mihnat al-Harb al-'Alamiyya al-Ula," in *Lubnan fi al-Harb al-'Alamiyya al-Ula*, ed. Antoine al-Qassis (Beirut: Manshurat al-Jami'a al-Lubnaniyya, 2011), 1:31–32; Shakib Arslan, *Sira Dhatiyya* (Beirut: Dar al-Tali'a, 1969), 166; Rafiq al-Tamimi and Muhammad Bahjat, *Wilayat Beirut* (Beirut: Iqbal, 1917), 2:140; Schilcher, "Famine," 230.

26. For broad conceptual notes, see Christoph Schumann, "Individual and Collective Memories of the First World War," in *The First World War as Remembered in the Countries of the Eastern Mediterranean,* ed. Olaf Farschid et al. (Beirut: Ergon, 2006), 247–263; Elizabeth Thompson, *Colonial Citizens: Republican Rights, Paternal Privilege, and Gender in French Syria and Lebanon* (New York: Columbia University Press, 2000), 16–38. For the 1920s, see Samuel Dolbee, "Seferberlik and Bare Feet: Rural Hardship, Cited Dreams, and Social Belonging in 1920s Syria," *JQ* 51 (2012): 21–35. For the entire twentieth century, see Fruma Zachs, "Transformations of a Memory of Tyranny in Syria," *MES* 48 (2012): 73–88. Christian Lebanese have been the toughest critics of the Ottomans, claiming they planned to starve them for being pro-French, an accusation as false as understandable given the Armenians' fate: see Bishara Bawari, *Mudhakkirat Bishara Jirjis al-Bawari 'an Arba' Sini al-Harb* (Beirut: n.p., 1926 [originally published in New York's *al-Huda* newspapers in 1921]); Antun Yamin, *Lubnan fi al-Harb* (Beirut: al-Matba'a al-Adabiyya, 1919); Faruq Hiblis, "Hadith al-Maja'a fi Safarbirlik baina al-Watha'iq al-Rasmiyya wa-l-Dhakira al-Sha'biyya," in *Lubnan fi al-Harb*, 1:191–218. For general Arab accusations of Turkish oppression, see Salim Tamari, "The Great War and the Erasure of Palestine's Ottoman Past," in *Transformed Landscapes,* ed. Camille Mansour and Leila Fawaz (Cairo: AUC Press, 2009), 105–135; Maurus Reinkowski, "Late Ottoman Rule over Palestine: Its Evaluation in Arab, Turkish and Israeli Histories, 1970–90," *MES* 35 (1999): 66–97.

27. Mouawad, "Jamal Pacha."

28. "Humor. Deutsch-Türkisches Lexikon für K.d.O. (Kenner des Ostens)," *Beilage der Mitteilungen des Bundes der Asienkämpfer* 3 (March 1, 1920): 4.

29. For the Armenians, see Wiegand, *Halbmond*, 202 (letter to his wife, Damascus, November 2, 1916); 210 (from his travel diary, Amman, December 9, 1916); 220 (from his travel diary, Wadi Musa, December 17, 1916). Feldmann, *Reise*, 27, reported that in Damascus the army employed 2,500 Armenian women besides 7,500 Muslim women. For soldiers, see Hikmet Özdemir, *The Ottoman Army, 1914–1918* (Salt Lake City: University of Utah Press, 2008); Jan Zürcher, "Between Death and Desertion: The Experience of the Ottoman Soldier in World War One," *Turcica* 28 (1996): 235–258. For the timing of enlistment in Lebanon, see Ajay, "Mount Lebanon and Beirut," 138, 147–153. Wali's threat: "Ila al-Junud al-Farin," *al-Ittihad al-'Uthmani*, October 30, 1915, 3. For deserters caught and bands, see

"Qatl Farari," *al-Ittihad al-ʿUthmani,* October 3, 1915, 3; "ʿIbra li-l-Farin," *al-Ittihad al-ʿUthmani,* October 5, 1915, 3; "Mask Ashqiyyaʾ," *al-Ittihad al-ʿUthmani,* October 27, 1915, 3. For Nassar, see Raja Shehada, *A Rift in Time: Travels with My Ottoman Uncle* (London: Profile Books, 2010), 196.

30. For fear, see Yosef Eliyahu Chelouche, *Parashat Hayay* (Tel Aviv: Babel, 2005), 200. For the *mutasarrif* of Jerusalem's and Jamal Pasha's reasoning about the evacuation, see Siegfried Hoofien to [Richard] Lichtheim [working for the World Zionist Organization in Istanbul], Jerusalem, April 8, 1916 [*sic.* Correct: 1917], Z3/81/1, Central Zionist Archives, Jerusalem (hereafter, CZA). Some Zionists even believed that the order to evacuate Jaffa signaled the start of Armenian-like deportation-and-murder: see Report about letter, Poʿalei Zion to Secretariat of the Socialist Conference in Stockholm, May 21, 1917, Z3/81, CZA.

31. At the same time, Jamal Pasha also distrusted Zionist aspirations for more autonomy. Besides executing the few members of NILI, a small pro-British Zionist spy ring, he for example forced Ruppin to move to Istanbul in 1916. Quotes: letter of introduction, Kaiserlich Deutsches Generalkonsulat Jerusalem, November 23, 1915, A107/631, CZA; and Siyahat-waraqasi #748, A107/631, CZA. For contacts between Jamal Pasha and Zionists, see also "Report about a meeting on 28 May 1917 in Jerusalem," in telegram #25, Dr. Thon to Auswärtiges Amt, Z3/81, CZA. Those contacts were reinforced by many officials being nationals of Istanbul's principal ally, Germany, and by German representatives helping Zionist-Ottoman communications: see Arthur Ruppin to (Zionist) Zentralbüro, Istanbul, October 29, 1917, Z3/84, CZA. For Jaffa Hebrew Gymnasium students enrolled in an officers' course in Istanbul, see: list, March 22, 1917, Z3/77, CZA. For Ben Gurion, see Anita Shapira, *Ben-Gurion:Father of Modern Israel,* tr. Anthony Berris (New Haven: Yale University Press, 2014), 36–40.

32. Feldmann, *Reise,* 24.

33. Damascus becoming Bilad al-Sham's administrative center meant that for certain military-related matters people were forced to make a trip there. Thus, "al-Wathaʾiq wa-Rusum Ashabiha fi Dimashq," *al-Ittihad al-ʿUthmani,* November 10, 1915, 3, ordered all people exempt from service to report within fifteen days to Damascus to be issued new papers. See also Ajay, "Mount Lebanon and Beirut," "Appendix 1. E: Interview with Dr. Raʾif Abī al-Lamʿ," 31. For Beiruti paper's references to Damascus, see, for example, "Manʿ Muhakama wa-Luzum Muhakama," *al-Ittihad al-ʿUthmani,* October 9, 1915, 3, regarding *al-Muqtabas.* For reports, see section on Beirut below. For the Armee-Zeitung, see "Feld-Buchhandlung der Armee-Zeitung Jildirim," *Armee-Zeitung Jildirim,* August 12, 1918, 4.

34. Quote: Feldmann, *Reise,* 28. See also Übelhör, *Syrien,* 9. For the cereal situation, see Grobba, *Getreidewirtschaft.* He was the German official responsible for food procurement, especially wheat, in Jerusalem and Damascus.

35. Quote: Arthur Ruppin to Zionistisches Aktionskommittee Berlin, Istanbul, May 26, 1917, 3, Z3 / 81, CZA. For the attack, see von Kress, "Achmed Dschemal Pascha," 18–20. (However, in 1914–1915 Jamal thought he could conquer Egypt.)

36. For Jamal Pasha's arrival, see Arslan, *Sira Dhatiyya*, 136–137, and "Safar Wali Beirut ila Dimashq," *al-Ittihad al-'Uthmani*, December 8, 1914, 2. For *walis'* and *mutasarrifs'* regular travels to Damascus, see "A'mal Hadrat al-Wali," *al-Ittihad al-'Uthmani*, November 17, 1915, 3; "Safar al-Wali," *al-Ittihad al-'Uthmani*, January 3, 1916, 3; "Wali Halab," *al-Ittihad al-'Uthmani*, January 7, 1916, 4; Grobba, *Getreidewirtschaft*, 61, about a meeting of all *walis* with Jamal Pasha in April 1917. For advisers, see Wiegand, *Halbmond*, 198. For Ruppin, see Grobba, [handwritten diary of] "Reise nach Syrien," 3, November 27, 1915, A107 / 631, CZA.

37. For travels, see Feldmann, *Reise*, 79, whose delegation accompanied Jamal Pasha to Aley, Beirut, Jerusalem, the Dead Sea, and Jaffa, besides Damascus; Arslan, *Sira Dhatiyya*, 167–169. For telegrammed orders, see "al-Dhakhira fi Suriya: Barqiyya Jadida," *al-Ittihad al-'Uthmani*, January 3, 1916, 1; "Qa'id al-Jaysh," *al-Ittihad al-'Uthmani*, December 9, 1914, 2.

38. Quotes: Übelhör, *Syrien*, 8, 11. For Beirut, see "Beirut al-Jadida," *al-Ittihad al-'Uthmani*, December 2, 1915, 1; "Tariqan Jadidan," *al-Ittihad al-'Uthmani*, December 22, 1915, 3. For Damascus, see "Sharikat al-Kahraba' wa-l-Nuqud fi Dimashq," *al-Ittihad al-'Uthmani*, December 23, 1915, 3; "Islah Dimashq," *al-Ittihad al-'Uthmani*, January 15, 1916, 3.

39. Kayali, "Integration," 302. For an overview, see also Übelhör, *Syrien*, 8–16. Jamal Pasha also had a particular interest in the collection of information on, and the renovation of, old Islamic and Ottoman buildings, showering 150,000 German Mark on the Damascene Sultan Selim Mosque alone: see Kayalı, "Wartime," 301–302, and Wiegand, *Halbmond*, 198–199, for the mosque, whose Ottoman builder had conquered Egypt, which may help explain Jamal's fascination with him.

40. Quote: Sakakini, *Yawmiyyat*, 2:252. For other mentions of the avenue, see ibid., 2:248, 252, 257, 267, 280, 312, 320.

41. "Fahrendes Volk in Damaskus," *Armee-Zeitung Jildirim*, August 8, 1918, 4; "Damaszener Rummel," *Armee-Zeitung Jildirim*, July 8, 1918, 8; "Maulbeerenernte," *Armee-Zeitung Jildirim*, June 20, 1918, 4; "Spaziergang durch die Gärten von Damaskus," *Armee-Zeitung Jildirim*, June 17, 1918, 8. Cafés: Sakakini, *Yawmiyyat*, 2:287, 306.

42. Quote: Günther Popp, "Türkei, Palästina, Ägypten (Meine Erlebnisse nach Briefen an meine Angehörigen)," 15, Damaskus, 23.5.1918, MSG2 / 4437, BArch. For 1914, see "Al-Nazihun ila Dimashq," *al-Ittihad al-'Uthmani*, November 13, 1914, 3; "Fuqara' al-Muhajirin al-Beirutiyyin fi Dimashq," *al-Ittihad al-'Uthmani*, November 25, 1914, 2 (however, especially in winter some returned to warmer Beirut:

"Ruju' al-Nazihin," *al-Ittihad al-'Uthmani*, December 11, 1914, 2). For 1916, see Schilcher, "Famine," 239; and Nicola Ziadeh, "A First-Person Account of First World War One in Greater Syria," in *The First World War as Remembered in the Countries of the Eastern Mediterranean*, ed. Olaf Farschid, Manfred Kropp, and Steven Dähne (Wüzburg: Ergon, 2006), 269. For 1917, see Schilcher, "Famine," 241; compare Sarah Ben-Re'uben, *Nashim 'Ivriot be-Damesek* (Jerusalem: Ariel, 2010), 32, on one Dvasha Ehrlich. (Hunger worsened in Damascus by 1917 because the Ottoman authorities' attempts to increase grain production had failed, because the number of refugees, including a reported 16,000 Armenians, and of soldiers in the city was peaking, and because the government had to supply also the Hijaz.) For an overview of factors in 1918, see "Bericht von Konsul Graf Schulenburg vom 16.3.1918," in Anlage 6: Akten des Konsulats Damaskus, in Anhang 11, Nachlass Trautz, N508/108, BArch.

43. Sakakini, *Yawmiyyat*, 2:262, also 239, 260–261, 286–288.

44. Quote: ibid., 2:228–229. For provenance, see ibid., 2:237, 250, 253, 236, 337. Regarding exile, by no means all were sent to Damascus. For Jerusalem and Anatolia, see Arslan, *Sira Dhatiyya*, 147–154, 185–186; for Ankara, see Sakakini, *Yawmiyyat*, 2:226, 307.

45. In order: Sakakini, *Yawmiyyat*, 2:267, 259, 205, 290, 307, 226, 215, 263, 204, 216, 345, 239, 271, 303. For Jaffawi Jews, see Yaron Harel, "'Mi-Khurban Yafo Nivnet Dameseq.' Ha-Mifgash bein Golei Erets Israel le-Kehilat Dameseq ve-Totsaoteha," *Tsion* 61 (1997): 183–207. See also Ben-Re'uben, *Nashim*, which like Harel focuses not on ties to Arab Damascus but on the Jewish community/Yishuvi dimension, here especially women: ibid., 6. For al-'Alami, see "Khalil Sakakini's Ottoman Prison Diaries: Damascus (19017–1918)," tr. Jennifer Peterson *JQF* 20 (2004): 23n12.

46. Sakakini, *Yawmiyyat*, 2:261.

47. However, on the coast, too, troop levels were higher than until 1914.

48. Howard Bliss historic diary, May 13, 1917, folder AA2.3.3.1.2., Nickoley Bliss Collection, AUB Archives and Special Collection, Beirut, Lebanon (hereafter, AUBASC). For Ottoman troop levels, see Ajay, "Mount Lebanon and Beirut," 30–62. For Arwad and the introduction of money, see Yigal Sheffy, *British Military Intelligence in the Palestine Campaign, 1914–1918* (London: Frank Cass, 1998), 81; Ajay, "Mount Lebanon and Beirut," "Appendix IV. The private papers of Father Būlus 'Aqil," 170–176.

49. Quote: Private papers of Father Būlus 'Aqil," section "Abstract," 1. See also ibid., 138–182.

50. Quote (an announcement): "Akhbar Dimashq," *al-Ittihad al-'Uthmani*, November 16, 1914, 3, the names referring to the French controlled Société Ottomane du Chemin de fer Damas—Hamah et Prolongements. The move to Damascus happened in December: see "Naql al-Sikka al-Hadidiyya," *al-Ittihad al-'Uthmani*, De-

cember 17, 1914, 2. For restrictions of civilian freight, see Merkel, "Die deutsche Jildirim-Etappe." An example is "Qatar al-Sikka al-Hadidiyya," January 24, 1915, 2. For trains, see "Ijazat al-Sikka al-Hadidiyya," *al-Ittihad al-'Uthmani*, November 19, 1914, 2; "Min al-Sikka al-Hadidiyya," *al-ittihad al-'Uthmani*, December 26, 1914, 2; "Masir al-Qatar," *al-Ittihad al-'Uthmani*, March 28, 1915, 2; also, e.g., "Baina Beirut wa-Tarablus," *al-Ittihad al-'Uthmani*, November 25, 1914, 2. For postal services, see "Barid Dimashq," *al-Ittihad al-'Uthmani*, February 12, 1915, 2.

51. Quote: "Shukr al-Beirutiyyin ila Ikhwanina al-Dimashqiyyin," *al-Ittihad al-'Uthmani*, November 9, 1914, 2. See also "Mas'alat al-Tahin," *al-Ittihad al-'Uthmani*, November 14, 1914, 3; "'Asharat Fakunat Tahin li-Beirut," *al-Ittihad al-'Uthmani*, April 5, 1915, 2.

52. As early as November 1914, a reported 1,700 people mostly from Beirut had sought subsistence in Damascus. See "Iwa' al-Muhajirin fi Dimashq," *al-Ittihad al-'Uthmani*, November 11, 1914, 1; Howard Bliss historic diary, May 21, 1917. For schools, see "al-Madaris al-Beirutiyya fi Dimashq," *al-Ittihad al-'Uthmani*, November 23, 1914, 3.

53. For success, see "Naql Madrasat al-Tibb min Dimashq ila Beirut," *al-Ittihad al-'Uthmani*, November 23, 1915, 1. For an attempt (concerning the *Dar al-Mu'allimin* and the *Maktab Sultani*), see "Maktab al-Huquq," *al-Ittihad al-'Uthmani*, November 26, 1915, 3. Regarding the SPC, the only major hiccup was the (Ottoman) "map affair": American consul Edelman, Damascus, to Howard Bliss, Beirut, February 1, 1916, p, folder AA2.3.2.18.1, Howard Bliss Collection, AUBASC.

54. For the SPC, see Howard Bliss historic diary, February 9, 1917. For Iranians, see Houchang Chehabi, "An Iranian in First World War Beirut: Qasem Ghani's Reminiscences," in *Distant Relations: Iran and Lebanon in the Last 500 Years* (London: I. B. Tauris, 2006), 120–135. For the list, see "Min Shu'bat Akhd al-'Askar," *al-Ittihad al-'Uthmani*, October 26, 1915, p. 4. (The remaining 30 percent were distributed as follows: 5: Hama, Jaffa, and Nablus; 4: Athens; 3: Acre, Sidon, and Tyre; 2: Damascus and Haifa; 1: Aleppo, Egypt, Hasbaya, Hirmil, Homs, Iskandariyya, Jerusalem, Trablus, and Zahle.)

55. For avenues and castle plan, see Übelhör, *Syrien*, 8. For the pine forest (and quote), see undated historical outline, document #8038, Sursock Archives, Phoenix Center for Lebanese Studies, Université de Saint Esprit, Kaslik, Lebanon (hereafter, SA / PCLS). For the (1915) rental agreement between Alfred Sursock and Beirut Municipality, see document #8044, SA / PCLS. The racetrack was finished soon after the British occupation of Beirut with British army help: see document #8038, SA / PCLS.

56. Howard Bliss historic diary, May 22, 1917.

57. Quote: ibid (emphasis added). For the medal, see document #7780, SA / PCLS. For Sursock's life before 1914, see Chapter 1.

58. G. Bergsträsser, "Tagebuch der wissenschaftlichen Reise von Major Trautz und Prof. Dr. Bergsträsser nach Syrien und Palästina, Frühjahr 1918," 69 (Beirut, 3 April [1918]), Nachlass Friedrich Trautz, N508 / 108, BArch. For the deal, see "Anlage 24e: Bericht über die wirtschaftliche Lage in Damaskus im März und April 1918 und über grosszügige Getreideverträge türkischer Beamten und Offiziere. Vom 27.4.1918 von Oberleutnant Dr. Grobba," 6–7, in Anhang 11, Nachlass Friedrich Trautz, N508 / 108, BArch. Ibid., 7, adds that "the wali of Syria, Tachsim Bey, concluded [another] contract . . . with a trade consortium from Tripoli, Beirut and Damascus." For other deals, see Schilcher, "Famine," 239, 245, mentioning Sursock's deal, too; and Grobba, *Getreidewirtschaft*, 68, on an even more profitable deal.

59. Michel to Alfred Sursock, Istanbul, July 5, 1918, 1, document #6839 / 1, SA / PCLS; see also document #24226, SA / PCLS. The Sursocks continued staying in touch with Jamal until his assassination, by an Armenian, in 1922: see Azmi Pasha to Alfred Sursock, Berlin, January 11, 1920, document #7104, SA / PCLS, mentioning the "letter you have sent to Madame Djémal Pacha."

60. A Paris-educated francophone, Jamal responded in French, "and you, are you also afraid of me?" "Yes, Excellency, though I have a clean conscience," the German parred: Wiegand, *Halbmond*, 198 (Theodor Wiegand to his wife, Damascus, November 1, 1916).

61. Quote: Chelouche, *Parashat Hayay*, 200. Lebanese: Ajay, "Mount Lebanon and Beirut," "Appendix 1.D: Interview with Mr. Ḥalīm Mūsa Ashqar," 22.

62. Wiegand, *Halbmond*, 266 (letter to wife, Damascus, December 8, 1917).

63. Grobba, *Getreidewirtschaft*, 67. Sakakini, *Yawmiyyat*, 2:306. See also ibid., 2:263, 264, 292, 307 about the necessity of solving problems through personal access to officials.

64. Quote: Von Kress, "Achmed Dschemal Pascha," 17. For corruption, see Grobba, *Getreidewirtschaft*; Anlage 24e, Anhang 11, Nachlass Friedrich Trautz, N508 / 108, BArch; also Sakakini, *Yawmiyyat*, 2:255. For the effect of food procurement policies from 1914, see Grobba, *Getreidewirtschaft*, 17–18, 52–53, 58, 66–67. Regarding planning, an exception was the forced agricultural labor law passed in early 1917, which however had only limited and temporary effects: see ibid., 53, 58. For a comparison with Germany, see ibid., 16–17; G. Herlt, "Kriegswirtschaft in der Türkei," *WA* 13 (1918): 190. For complaints about inadequate planning, see Ajay, "Mount Lebanon and Beirut," "Appendix: Doolittle, *Pathos and Humor of the War Years in Syria* (1920)," 255–261 (ch. 8, "The Turk Tries to Regulate Things"). However, in late 1917 Damascus succeeded in organizing a massive bread rationing program for 74,000–80,000 people: see Grobba, *Getreidewirtschaft*, 78. Also, Beirut in early 1915 the government started selling wheat at fixed low prices to people, through neighborhood heads (*mukhtars*): see 'Abd al-Latif al-Haris, "al-Awda' al-Iqtisadiyya wa-l-Maliyya fi al-Dawla al-

'Uthmaniyya wa-l-Muqata'at al-Lubnaniyya (1914–1918)," in *Lubnan fi al-Harb*, 1:175.

65. Ajay, "Mount Lebanon and Beirut," "Appendix 1. U: Interview with Mr. and Mrs. Bayard Dodge," 117 (also on Homs). For Transjordan, see Grobba, *Getreide-wirtschaft*, 72. For the correlation between grain deliveries and food prices, see "Mas'alat al-Tahin," *al-Ittihad al-'Uthmani*, December 21, 1914, 2; "Suq al-Hajiat," *al-Ittihad al-'Uthmani*, March 17, 1915, 2; "Ghala' al-Tahin," *al-Ittihad al-'Uthmani*, March 30, 1915, 2.

66. Simun 'Abd al-Masih, "Al-Mas'ala al-Zira'iyya wa-Ma'sat 'Harb al-Ju' fi Mutasar-rifiyat Jabal Lubnan," in *Lubnan fi al-Harb*, 2:521–560; Melanie Tanielian, "The War of Famine" (PhD diss., University of California, Berkeley, 2012).

67. Thus, Father Bulus 'Aqil, who smuggled money through Arwad into Lebanon, wrote hair-raising descriptions: see Ajay, "Mount Lebanon and Beirut," "Appendix I: Texts of Interviews with Eyewitnesses," and "Appendix IV," 168–226. In Beirut, the president of the Syrian Protestant College, Howard Bliss, wrote that "the daily sights along the streets seem like a dream—like a horrible nightmare." "The[y] . . . are no less horrible than those in the mountains. We see children running after dogs to take bones away from them and then fight among themselves to determine who shall gnaw the bone. . . . Children actually go down the street hunting through animal dung to find grains of undigested barley and eating to satisfy their pangs of hunger. It is amazing how tenaciously the human being clings to life": see Howard Bliss historic diary, February 15, 1917. These reports also need to be read as documents meant for the Allies and for Church officials outside Lebanon, however.

68. Quote: Ajay, "Mount Lebanon and Beirut," "Appendix 1. J: interview with Dr. Nabih Shab," 53–54. In interviews that historian Nicholas Ajay conducted in the 1960s nobody addressed rumors—some perhaps true—about man's ultimate taboo: to eat his fellow man. Still, this taboo was so horribly powerful that some interviewees circled around it with wary half-silences. "Death by starvation was very common. . . . People who ordinarily were law-abiding turned to robbery in order to get food. No murders, just food or money to get food," noted one. Another stated that "The crime rate increased but there was no killing. All the people, soldiers and civilians, committed crimes for food or for money to buy food." See ibid., "Appendix 1. B: interview with Mr. Shahadi Sasin Mu'allim," 9; and "Interview with Mr. Halim Musa Ashqar," 18.

69. Quote: Ajay, "Mount Lebanon and Beirut," "Interview with Mister Shahadi Sasin Mu'allim," 12. See also ibid., "Anonymous Interview," 47. *Mukhtars* played crucial implementing roles too (see ibid., 47; and al-Haris, "Awda'," 175).

70. Bergsträsser, "Tagebuch," 105–107 (May 4, [1918], in the Bikaa Valley). For working with local grain merchants, see Schilcher, "Famine," 237–239; Arslan, *Sira Dhatiyya*, 163–164, 167–168.

71. Quote: Sakakini, *Yawmiyyat*, 2:311. See also ibid., 2:227, 260, 249. For patriarchate, see ibid., 2:234, 260, 262, 278, 309. Levine: ibid., 2:267, 309. For Khalidi and Jawhariyya, see ibid., 2:269.

72. Ibid., 2:261, 287, 305, 316, 319.

73. Ibid., 2:296 (letter), 238, 344.

74. Excellent on this aspect is Nadim Bawalsa, "Sakakini defrocked," *JQF* 42 (2010): 5–25, who calls Sakakini "an admirer of things western, specifically, education, science, philosophy, and even a western brand of national consciousness": ibid., 7.

75. Quote: Sakakini, *Yawmiyyat*, 2:230. For dreams, see ibid., 2:216, 241, 236, 257, 267. For *ghurba*, see ibid., 2:230. For food, see ibid., 2:269.

76. Ibid., 2:233, 237. Bawalsa, "Sakakini," 14, shows, too, that Jerusalem remained a key reference point for Sakakini.

77. Quotes: Sakakini, *Yawmiyyat*, 2:356, 271, 344. For Syria and Palestine, see also ibid., 2:352.

78. All quotes: ibid., 2:366, where he also remarks that "an *umma* (community) with [men] of their [his friends] like will not die." See Bawalsa, "Sakakini," 8–12, critiquing ahistorical "Palestinian" readings.

79. For military functions, see Hilmar Kaiser, *At the Crossroads of Der Zor. Death, Survival and Humanitarian Resistance in Aleppo, 1915–1917* (Princeton, NJ: Gomidas, 2002), 13. For the Second Army, see Grobba, *Getreidewirtschaft*, 69.

80. Both quotes: Kaiser, *Crossroads*, 13.

81. Quotes: Watenpaugh, *Being Modern*, 42; and Kamil al-Ghazzi, *Nahr al-Dhahab fi Ta'rikh Halab* (Aleppo: al-Matba'a al-Maruniyya, 1924), 3:579. See ibid., 578, on his critical appraisal of Armenians' own actions. For Armenians in Aleppo 1915–1917, see Kaiser, *Crossroads*. Key accounts in European languages include Beatrice Rohner, *Die Stunde ist gekommen. Märtyrerbilder aus der Jetztzeit* (Frankfurt am Main: Orient, 1920); John Minassian, *Many Hills Yet to Climb: Memoirs of an Armenian Deportee* (Santa Barbara: Jim Cook, 1986). For an analysis, see Ronald Grigor Suny, *"They Can Live in the Desert but Nowhere Else": A History of the Armenian Genocide* (Princeton, NJ: Princeton University Press, 2015).

82. Rising prices and hunger: "Getreidebericht von Konsul Rössler vom 28.4.1917," in Anlage 2: Akten des Konsulats Aleppo über die landwirtschaftliche Produktion im Gebiet des Vilajets, in Anhang 11, Nachlass Friedrich Trautz, N508/108, BArch, identifying natural factors and transport limitations as the main reasons for rising food prices. Death toll: Grobba, *Getreidewirtschaft*, 83.

83. "Anhang 10," 12, Nachlass Friedrich Trauz, N508/108, BArch.

84. Another reason was a clement rain season. Quote: Anlage 3: "Der Handel in Aleppo, nach mündlichen Mitteilungen von Herrn Kirchner," in Anhang 11, Nachlass Friedrich Trautz, N508/108, BArch. For Rössler, see "Getreidebericht von Konsul Rössler vom 28.4.1917," in Anlage 2: Akten des Konsulats Aleppo über

die landwirtschaftliche Produktion im Gebiet des Vilajets, in Anhang 11, Nachlass Friedrich Trautz, N508/108, BArch. For the logistics officer, see "Bericht des Intendanturrats Brown bei der deutschen Etappeninspektion Jildirim über die Versorgung der Etappeninspektion Aleppo, vom 6.4.1918," in Anlage 2: Akten des Konsulats Aleppo über die landwirtschaftliche Produktion im Gebiet des Vilajets, in Anhang 11, Nachlass Friedrich Trautz, N508/108, BArch.

## Prelude 3. Alfred Sursock Keeps Busy

Epigraph: G. Fakhr, "Rapport sur le parc," Beirut, December 1, 1919, 3, to Alfred Sursock, document #8082, Sursock Archives, Phoenix Center for Lebanese Studies, Université de Saint Esprit, Kaslik, Lebanon (hereafter, SA/PCLS).

1. This does not equal endorsement of ideological uses, e.g. by the Syrian Social Nationalist Party, founded in Beirut in 1932.

2. For Britain, see Elizabeth Monroe, *Britain's Moment in the Middle East (1914–1971)* (Baltimore: Johns Hopkins University Press, 1981), esp. 11–12, 18–19, 51–52; John Darwin, "An Undeclared Empire: the British in the Middle East, 1918–39," *JICH* 27 (1999): 161; Glen Balfour-Paul, "Britain's Informal Empire in the Middle East," in *The Oxford History of the British Empire*, vol. 1: *The Twentieth Century*, ed. Wm Roger Louis and Judith Brown (Oxford: Oxford University Press, 1999), 490. Oil in Iran and Iraq played a role too: Darwin, "Empire," 160–163. For France, see Rajnarayan Chandavarkar, "Imperialism and the European Empires," in *The Short Oxford History of Europe: Europe 1900–1945*, ed. Julian Jackson (Oxford: Oxford University Press, 2002), 147 (on strategic interests in the Mediterranean); Stephen Roberts, *The History of French Colonial Policy, 1870–1925* (London: Frank Cass, 1963), 591–592; Martin Thomas, *The French Empire between the Wars: Imperialism, Politics and Society* (Manchester: Manchester University Press, 2005), 6–9 (uncertainty about French strategy and the colonies' part); Jacques Thobie and Gilbert Meynier, *Histoire de la France colonial* (Paris: Pocket, 1991), 2:465–467 (colonial lobby).

3. More on the Mandate system in Chapter 3. Full confirmation of the A Mandates came in 1922. That year, too, Transjordan was administratively separated from Palestine, though still part of that Mandate. Borders were fully recognized only in 1924, the last problem being Turkey's recognition of Syria's border.

4. "Magic City" may also have referred to the 1893 Chicago World's Fair's Magic City.

5. Historical outline of the park construction, undated but written earliest in 1919, document 8038, SA/PCLS (judging by the content clearly written by a family member or somebody aligned with it).

6. In letter, Alfred Sursock to Michel Sursock, Beirut, September 20, 1918, document #8694, SA/PCLS, he asked him to write Azmi in Istanbul from time to time,

which likely signifies that he himself considered staying in contact with Azmi worthwhile.

7. Document #7104, SA / PCLS.

8. Azmi Pasha contacted others, too, e.g. Omar Beyhum; Azmi Pasha to Alfred Sursock, Berlin, February 13, 1920, document #5521, SA / PCLS.

9. Document #7105, SA / PCLS. In letter, Azmi Pasha to Alfred Sursock, November 30, 1922, [n.p.], document #7109, SA / PCLS, Azmi thanks for 10,000 francs. Compare Azmi Pasha to Alfred Sursock, Istanbul, December 31, 1923, document #7106, SA / PCLS.

10. Quote: Document #7104, SA / PCLS. The other two letters are Azmi Pasha to Alfred Sursock, Berlin, February 10, 1920, document #5522, SA / PCLS; Document #7105, SA / PCLS. Compare Michel to Alfred Sursock, France, March 3, 1919, document #6838, SA / PCLS, stating that "the Emir Schekib [Arslan] is in Bern. Azmi Badri Bey, Aleppo's ex-vali & Jamal [Pasha] are in Munich." For the wives, see postcard, Seniha [Ismet Pasha's wife] to Alfred Sursock [Carlton Hotel, Cannes, France], Partenkirchen, February 10, 1920, document #24207, SA / PCLS; letter, Seniha to Sursock, Munich, December 23, 1919, document #24208, SA / PCLS. Sursock also kept buildings in Turkey: "Rapport sur les propriétiés de Mersine et Tarsous en litige," [n.d.], document #8185, SA / PCLS.

11. Note, document #1554, SA / PCLS. (The note is undated but must have been sent in the fall of 1919.)

12. Various people continued thinking of detaching Beirut from Lebanon, and / or about a smaller, purely Christian Lebanon focused on Beirut with easy trade access to all of Syria. (The Syro-Lebanese) Correspondence d'Orient to Alfred Sursock, Paris, September 2, 1922, document #6810, SA / PCLS, shows that by 1922 Sursock definitely wanted the latter while suggesting that he may still have envisioned the former, too. As for Europe, negotiations about free cities resulted in the Free State of Fiume, between Italy and Yugoslavia from 1920 to 1924, and the Free City of Danzig, between Germany and Poland, from 1920 to 1939.

13. Alfred Sursock, "Note sur un programme d'action économique en Syrie et au Liban," January 1924, Paris, document #7020, SA / PCLS. For the centrality of the sewage contract, see "Note générale," 5, document #7024, SA / PCLS. SGFO: besides Sursock and one Moussalli, from Beirut, its founding members were French investors and engineers: "Note sur la création d'une société immobilière et de travaux publics en Syrie," Paris, October 6, 1923, document #7009, SA / PCLS; "Note générale sur les affaires en Syrie," document #7024, SA / PCLS.

14. See "Transport Nairn," document #7010, SA / PCLS. Sursock tried to mount an independent company that, he hoped, could be fused with the Nairn Transport Company: HC Weygand to Alfred Sursock, Beirut, April 8, 1924, document #6823, SA / PCLS. See Norman Nairn to Alfred Sursock, Beirut, April 9, 1924, document #6828-3, SA / PCLS, for Nairn's interest in an investment by Sursock, who how-

ever passed away soon thereafter. Also, Sursock kept land not only in Mersin and Alexandria but throughout Greater Syria coastal region, mostly in Beirut as well as in Tyre, Mount Lebanon, Jaffa, Haifa, and in extended agricultural areas of northwestern Palestine. See "Traduction d'un acte de dévolution successorale," Beirut, June 21, 1924, document 8851, SA/PCLS; declaration of the 1,145 individual Beiruti real estates owned by Sursock's widow, Maria Theresa Serra de Cassano, in July 1925 in République libanaise, al-dawa'ir al-'iqariyya, reçu Nº 500, Beirut, March 5, 1931, document #8359, SA/PCLS; Gudrun Krämer, *Geschichte Palästinas* (Munich: Beck, 2002), 287.

15. Quote: "Exposé de la Société Générale Française d'Entreprises et des Travaux Publics (section d'Orient)," 2, n.d. [February 1924], document #8761, SA/PCLS. See also official letter of appointment, SGFETP to Alfred Sursock, Paris, 18 March 1924, document #8762, SA/PCLS. Sursock was open to, and pursued, non-French investors, too. Since his 1920 marriage with an Italian, he also tightened contacts with Italian companies, which he tried to interest in investing in the SGFO: Alfred Sursock to Raphaele Pompei, Directeur Général de I.N.C.L.E (Rome), Paris, January 19, 1924, document #8697, SA/PCLS (referring to another name of the SGFO, the Crédit Immobilier d'Orient); "Note," 7, document #7009, SA/PCLS. And he answered positively to an inquiry by Egyptians about investing in his branch of the SGFETP: Alfred Sursock to Jean Bustros, Beirut, April 26, 1924, document #7806, SA/PCLS.

16. Henri Gouraud to Alfred Sursock, Paris, March 6, 1922, document #176, SA/PCLS, Gouraud hoping that Sursock's society would not only engage in real estate construction, a field in which Sursock was particularly interested. Quote: Sursock, "Note," 1, document #7020, SA/PCLS.

17. Vlado Sursock to Alfred Sursock, Marseille, 1921, document #6785, SA/PCLS; Alfred Sursock to Michel Sursock, Beirut, June 25, 1919, document #8691, SA/PCLS; telegram draft, document #8733, SA/PCLS (it is undated but its topic means it can only have been written in 1923; it is unsigned but it is included in Alfred Sursock's private papers and its handwriting looks identical to Sursock's handwriting); "Communication de Mr. Alfred Sursock à la Commission des Affaires Extérieures du Sénat," February 7, 1924, 1, document #8673, SA/PCLS. Regarding the prewar era, Sursock had started developing connections as a secretary at the Ottoman embassy in Paris and as the treasurer of the Ligue Franco-Ottomane. See soirée invitation, [French] Président du Conseil Ministre de l'Intérieur to Alfred Sursock, Honorary Secretary at the Turkish Embassy in Paris, Paris, March 1, 1902, document #6875, SA/PCLS; Ligue Franco-Ottomane to Alfred Sursock, Paris, July 14, 1909, document #169, SA/PCLS.

18. 1918: Note, Alfred Sursock to Emir Faisal, 1918, Document #7831, SA/PCLS; also Isabelle Bustros to Alfred Sursock, undated [though clearly written immediately following the Anglo-French occupation of Beirut], document #7128, SA/PCLS.

1919: Comité Central Syrien to Alfred Sursock, Paris, March 25, 1919, document #7131, SA/PCLS; Chekri Ganem to Alfred Sursock, Paris, January 27, 1920, document #7120, SA/PCLS. 1921: Gouraud to Sursock, Aley, October 22, 1921, document #171, SA/PCLS.

19. Invitations to the proclamation of Le Grand Liban, September 1, 1920, documents #155 and #156, SA/PCLS; Henri Gouraud to Alfred Sursock, Paris, January 9, 1922, document #167, SA/PCLS; letter and dinner invitation, Henri Gouraud to Madame Alfred Sursock [n.p., Beirut or Aley], July 22, 1921, document #168, SA/PCLS.

20. Letter to Alfred Sursock, Paris, September 15, 1923, document #7787, SA/PCLS.

21. As noted in Chapter 1, an interesting parallel case is Jens Hanssen, "'Malhamé-Malfamé,'" *IJMES* 43 (2011): 25–48. Related, see Malte Rolf, "Einführung: Imperiale Biographien," *GG* 40 (2014): 5–21.

### 3. Ottoman Twilight

1. Quote: Albert Hourani, *Arabic Thought in the Liberal Age, 1798–1939* (Cambridge: Cambridge University Press, 1983), 286. In the past two decades or so, historians have increasingly questioned *qawmi* hegemony and Arab homogeneity, and taken a greater interest in *watani* nationalisms. Overview: Gelvin, "Modernity and Its Discontents," *NN* 5 (1999): 73; case study: Peter Wien, "Preface: Relocating Arab Nationalism," in a special issue on Arab nationalism, *IJMES* 43 (2011): 203–204. Historians have declared primordialism dead, and most are constructivists, with a few arguing that some premodern collectivist traits were folded into nationalism. All this amounts to a "'polycentric' or 'peripheral' perspective on nationalism, ... attending to [its] numerous regional, confessional, generational and socio-spatial forms": Israel Gershoni and James Jankowski, "Introduction," in *Rethinking Nationalism in the Arab Middle East* (New York: Columbia University Press, 1997)," xiv; see also James Gelvin, "'Arab Nationalism': Has a New Framework Emerged?," *IJMES* 41 (2009): 10–12. For Greater Syria-wide nationalism and/or state projects, see Najla' Sa'id Makawi, *Mashru' Suriyya al-Kubra* (Beirut: Markaz Dirasat al-Wahda al-'Arabiyya, 2010), 51–76; Muhannad Salhi, *Palestine in the Evolution of Syrian Nationalism (1918–1920)* (Chicago: Middle East Documentation Center, 2008); Meir Zamir, "Faysal and the Lebanese Question, 1918–1920," *MES* 27 (1991): 404–426; Philip Khoury, "Divided Loyalties? Syria and the Question of Palestine, 1919–1939," *MES* 21 (1985): 324–348; Zachary Foster, "Arab Historiography in Mandate Palestine" (MA thesis, Georgetown University, 2011), 36–43. For *qawmiyya*, see Birgit Schaebler, "From Urban Notables to 'Noble Arabs': Shifting Discourses in the Emergence of Nationalism in the Arab East, 1910–1916," in *From the Syrian Land to the States of Syria and Leb-*

*anon,* ed. Thomas Philipp et al. (Beirut: Ergon, 2004), 175–198; Nur Masalha, "Faisal's Pan-Arabism, 1921–33," *MES* 27 (1991): 679–693 at 679–683; Ernest Dawn, "The Formation of Pan-Arab Nationalism in the Interwar Period," *IJMES* 20 (1988): 67–91; Hourani, *Arabic Thought,* 294–295; Nadine Méouchy "Les nationalistes arabes de la première génération en Syrie (1918–1928)," *BEO* 47 (1995): 109–128.

2.  For the Yishuv, see Dan Horowitz and Moshe Lissak, *Origins of the Israeli Polity: Palestine under the Mandate* (Chicago: University of Chicago Press, 1978); Anita Shapira, *Land and Power: The Zionist Resort to Force, 1881–1948* (Stanford, CA: Stanford University Press, 1992); Yosef Gorny, *Zionism and the Arabs, 1882–1948: A Study of Ideology* (Oxford: Clarendon, 1987); Itamar Rabinovich and Jehuda Reinharz, eds., *Israel in the Middle East: Documents and Readings* (Waltham, MA: Brandeis University Press, 2008), 571–572 (demographics). For Arab Palestine, see Ann Lesch, *Arab Politics in Palestine, 1917–1939: The Frustration of a Nationalist Movement* (Ithaca, NY: Cornell University Press, 1979); Gudrun Krämer, *A History of Palestine* (Princeton, NJ: Princeton University Press, 2008), 199–215; Ilan Pappé, *The Rise and Fall of a Palestinian Dynasty: The Husaynis, 1700–1948* (Berkeley: University of California Press, 2010); Muslih, "Rise," 180; Henry Laurens, "La vie politique palestinienne avant 1948," *MAMM* 159 (1998): 12–27. For Lebanon, see Asher Kaufman, *Reviving Phoenicia: The Search for Identity in Lebanon* (London: I. B. Tauris, 2004); Kaufman, "Lammens and Syrian nationalism," in *Origins of Syrian Nationhood,* ed. Adel Beshara (New York: Routledge, 2011), 108–122; Carol Hakim, *The Origins of the Lebanese National Idea* (Berkeley: University of California Press, 2013), esp. 213–260; Kais Firro, "Lebanese Nationalism versus Arabism," *MES* 40 (2004): 1–27. For nationalism in Syria, see, James Gelvin, *Divided Loyalties: Nationalism and Mass Politics in Syria at the Close of Empire* (Berkeley: University of California Press, 1998); Philip Khoury, *Syria and the French Mandate: The Politics of Arab Nationalism, 1920–1945* (Princeton, NJ: Princeton University Press, 1987); Muhammad Muslih, "The Rise of Local Nationalism in the Arab East," in *The Origins of Arab Nationalism,* ed. Rashid Khalidi et al. (New York: Columbia University Press, 1991), 167–185; Keith Watenpaugh, "Middle-Class Modernity and the Persistence of the Politics of Notables in Inter-War Syria," *IJMES* 35 (2003): 257–286. For Transjordan, see Mary Wilson, *King Abdullah, Britain, and the Making of Jordan* (Cambridge: Cambridge University Press, 1987); Philip Robins, *A History of Jordan* (Cambridge: Cambridge University Press, 2004), 16–34; Yoav Alon, *The Making of Jordan: Tribes, Colonialism and the Modern State* (London: I. B. Tauris, 2007), 37–83; Joseph Massad, *Colonial Effects: The Making of National Identity in Jordan* (New York: Columbia University Press, 2001); Tariq Tell, *The Social and Economic Origins of Monarchy in Jordan* (New York: Routledge, 2013).

3. Michael Adas, "Contested Hegemony: The Great War and the Afro-Asian Assault on the Civilizing Mission Ideology," *JWH* 15 (2004): 31–63; Erez Manela, *The Wilsonian Moment* (Oxford: Oxford University Press, 2007); Rajnarayan Chandavarkar, "Imperialism and the European Empires," in *The Short Europe History of Europe: Europe, 1900–1945*, ed. Julian Jackson (Oxford: Oxford University Press, 2002), 147–150. For France, see also Claude Liauzu, *Histoire de l'anticolonialisme en France* (Paris: Armand Colin, 2007), 123–174.

4. Quotes: Peter Shambrook, *French Imperialism in Syria, 1927–1936* (Reading, UK: Ithaca Press, 1998), 1; and Norrie MacQueen, *Colonialism* (New York: Longman, 2007), 56. B Mandates were in Africa; C Mandates, in the Pacific.

5. Benjamin Gerig, *The Open Door and the Mandates System* (London: Allen & Unwin, 1930), 154–157, 160–161, 180; Norman Burns, *The Tariff of Syria, 1919–1932* (Beirut: American Press, 1933), 132–140. For French finance interests, see, e.g., United Kingdom and Jane Priestland, eds., *Records of Syria* (Slough: Archive Editions, 2005), 2:768, 787.

6. Quotes: Véronique Dimier, "'L'internationalisation' du débat colonial: rivalités franco-britanniques autour de la Commission permanente des Mandats," *Outre-mers* 336–337 (2002): 334, 334, 337. For the League, see Susan Pedersen, *The Guardians: The League of Nations and the Crisis of Empire* (Oxford: Oxford University Press, 2015).

7. For conceptual reflections on the Palestine charter, see Rashid Khalidi, *The Iron Cage: The Story of the Palestinian Struggle for Statehood* (Boston: Beacon, 2006), 9–22; Gudrun Krämer, *Geschichte Palästinas* (Munich: Beck, 2002), 195–208; Nadine Picaudou, "Les Arabes comme catégorie du discours mandataire britannique en Palestine," in *Temps et espaces en Palestine,* ed. Roger Heacock (Beirut: IFPO, 2008), 235–245.

8. Quotes: Pierre Rondot, *L'expérience du Mandat français en Syrie et au Liban, 1918–1945* (Paris: Pedone, 1948), 15; and Pierre Bonardi, *L'imbroglio syrien* (Paris: Rieder, 1927), 27. For French-British differences, see Peter Sluglett, "Les mandats / the Mandates," in *The British and French Mandates in Comparative Perspectives,* ed. Peter Sluglett and Nadine Méouchy (Leiden: Brill, 2004), 103–128. For the French administration, see Pierre Amory, *Le régime administratif au Liban* (Lyon: Bosc Frères, 1934). For minorities, see Benjamin White, *The Emergence of Minorities in the Middle East: The Politics of Community in French Mandate Syria* (Edinburgh: Edinburgh University Press, 2011); Max Weiss, *In the Shadow of Sectarianism: Law, Shi'ism, and the Making of Modern Lebanon* (Cambridge: Harvard University Press, 2010); Nadine Méouchy, "La réforme des jurisdictions religieuses en Syrie et au Liban (1921–1939)," in *Le choc colonial et l'Islam,* ed. Pierre-Jean Luizard (Paris: Découverte, 2006), 359–382. For North Africa, see Henry Laurens, "Synthèse de conclusion. Le Mandat français sur la Syrie et le Liban," in

*France, Syrie, et Liban, 1918–1946,* ed. Nadine Méouchy (Damascus: IFEAD, 2002), 411–412.

9. France raised its rate nominally from 11 percent to 15 percent in 1924 and to 25 percent in 1926, but it effectively stayed around 15 percent while slightly increasing in time: see Burns, *Tariff,* 124–125, 177–178. Like France, Britain used customs "as a major fiscal tool" but "mov[ed] from the Ottoman *ad valorem* to specific duties": see Jacob Metzer, *The Divided Economy of Mandatory Palestine* (Cambridge: Cambridge University Press, 1998), 182.

10. For the economy, see also Caroline Gates, *The Merchant Republic of Lebanon: Rise of an Open Economy* (London: I. B. Tauris, 1998), 20–33; Metzer, *Divided Economy,* 3–5. For self-serving claims, see "Speech delivered by the Right Hon. Sir H. Samuel," July 1920, in *Political Diaries of the Arab World. Palestine and Jordan,* vol. 1: *1920–1923,* ed. Robert Jarman (Slough: Archives Edition, 2001), 4–5, 7, 4; Comte R. de Gontaut Biron, *Sur les routes de Syrie après neuf ans de Mandat* (Paris: Pon, 1928), i; Raymond O'zoux, *Les états du Levant sous Mandat français* (Paris: Larose, 1931), x. For wider imperial influences, see Edmund Burke, "A Comparative View of French Native Policy in Morocco and Syria, 1912–1925," *MES* 9 (1973): 175–186. For security, see Martin Thomas, *Empires of Intelligence: Security Services and Colonial Disorder after 1914* (Berkeley: University of California Press, 2008); Daniel Neep, *Occupying Syria under the French Mandate* (Cambridge: Cambridge University Press, 2012); Jean-David Mizrahi, *Genèse de l'État mandataire* (Paris: Publications de la Sorbonne, 2003); Michael Provence, *The Great Syrian Revolt and the Rise of Arab Nationalism* (Austin: University of Texas Press, 2005). For reliance on societal actors, see Esther Möller, *Orte der Zivilisierungsmission: Französische Schulen im Libanon 1909–1943* (Göttingen: Vandenhoeck & Ruprecht, 2013); Jennifer Dueck, *The Claims of Culture at Empire's End: Syria and Lebanon under French Rule* (Oxford: Oxford University Press, 2010); Erica Simmons, ed., *Hadassah and the Zionist Project* (Lanham, MD: Rowman & Littlefield, 2006). For grassroots-elites-authorities triangles, see Weiss, *Sectarianism.* For authorities-elite interactions, see Elizabeth Thompson, *Colonial Citizens: Republican Rights, Paternal Privilege, and Gender in French Syria and Lebanon* (New York: Columbia University Press, 2000), esp. 39–57; Kais Firro, *Inventing Lebanon. Nationalism and the State under the Mandate* (London: I. B. Tauris, 2003), 71–125, Khoury, *Syria;* Khalidi, *Iron Cage,* 31–64; Krämer, *Palästina,* 235–238; Alon, *Jordan,* 4–7, 61–83.

11. "Muqaddama," "al-Mas'ala al-Suriyya wa-l-Qadiyya al-Sahiuniyya," "Mahalliyya," and "Harakat al-Bawakhir," all in *Mir'at al-Sharq,* September 17, 1919, 1, 2, 4, 4.

12. For the last point, a source-rich outline that also looks at the late Ottoman period is Foster, "Historiography," 36–43. Regarding the port, other local newspapers, too,

reported only their cities' own movements. For Haifa, see, e.g., "Sharikat al-Bawakhir al-Khadiwiyya," *al-Karmal*, January 15, 1921, 4; "al-Misajiri Maritim," *al-Karmal*, September 23, 1922, 4.

13. "Filastin fi 'Am," October 8, 1919, 4; "Murasalat," November 12, 1919, 2; "Murasalat," November 26, 1919, 2 (including Karak, now in Jordan), all in *Mir'at al-Sharq.*

14. "Mas'alat Suriya," October 15, 1919, 3; "Mahalliyya," October 15, 1919, 4; "Akhbar al-Jihhat," October 1, 1919, 3, all in *Mir'at al-Sharq.*

15. "Akhbar Suriya," November 5, 1919, 3; November 19, 1919, 3; and December 3, 1919, 3; "Akhbar al-Sham," December 17, 1919, 4, all in *Mir'at al-Sharq.* On a different though related note, *Mir'at al-Sharq* reprinted news from Syrian and Egyptian papers—"Akhbar Suriya," December 3, 1919, 3; "Qalat al-Muqattam," September 17, 1919, 3—and included news on Turkey in the section *Akhbar Uruba*, European news: "Turkiya," November 12, 1919, 3; November 19, 1919, 3.

16. "Mahalliyya," October 15, 1919, 4, and "Ja'ana min al-Nadi al-'Arabi," December 10, 1919, 4, both in *Mir'at al-Sharq.* Similarly, in the early 1920s Haifa's *al-Karmal* used *mahalliyya* for *qawmi* issues like the Syrian National Congress as well as for Palestine-wide events such as various towns' support of a delegation to the 1921 British conference in Cairo: "Mahalliyya," *al-Karmal*, March 5, 1921, 2, and March 18, 1921, 2–3.

17. Both quotes: Kamil al-Ghazzi, *Nahr al-Dhahab fi Ta'rikh Halab* (Aleppo: al-Matba'a al-Maruniyya, 1924), 3:613 (the book included references to Aleppo's wider hinterland). For Jamal's 1914 order, see ibid., 3:564. For the pipeline, see "Anlage 1: Antwort von Konsul Rössler auf einen Fragebogen der 'Zentralauskunfts-stelle für Auswanderer' für deutsche Schulen im Ausland, Februar 1917," in Anhang 11, Nachlass Friedrich Trautz, N508/108, Bundesarchiv Freiburg i.B., Germany.

18. Muhammad Raghib al-Tabbakh, *I'lam al-Nubala' bi-Ta'rikh Halab al-Shahba'* (Aleppo: Dar al-Qalam al-'Arabi bi-Halab, [1923–1926] 1988), 1:28, 29, written mostly before 1914 (ibid., 1:24). Like al-Ghazzi, Tabbakh included events and people in Aleppo's hinterland as a whole, not only in the city.

19. Quotes: Qustaki al-Humsi, *Udaba' Halab Dhawu al-'Athr fi al-Qarn al-Tasi'-'Ashar* (Aleppo: al-Matba'a al-Maruniyya, 1925), 154, 136, 137. For Aleppo as *watan*, see ibid., 90, 100, 112, 121.

20. "Sanatuna al-Tasi'a," *Hums*, May 27, 1923, 1 (including quote); "Qudum," *Hums*, September 13, 1923, 7; "Mahalliyya," *Hums*, June 16, 1923, 6; "al-Ab Sheikhu fi Hums," *Hums*, June 9, 1923, 6.

21. Muhammad Adib Al Taqi al-Din al-Hisni, *Muntakhabat al-Tawarikh li-Dimashq* (Damascus: al-Matba'a al-Haditha, 1927–1934), 822. For *watan*, see ibid., 821.

22. Quotes: ibid., 825 (on the Al al-Siyyid al-Ghuth 'Abd al-Qadir al-Jilani), 5. See also Al al-Yafi al-Akarim, with branches in Cairo, Damascus, Beirut, Jaffa and Gaza:

ibid., 828. For the al-Bakris and ʿUmaris, see ibid., 819, 823. See also Nadine Méouchy, "La presse de Syrie et du Liban entre les deux guerres," *RMMM* 95–98 (2002): 66; Nizar Abaza, *al-Shaykh ʿAli al-Daqr* (Damascus: Dar al-Fikr, 2010), 47, 96, 117–127; Muhammad al-Farfur, *al-Muhaddith al-Akbar* (Damascus: Dar al-Imam Abi Hanifa, 1986), 86–87, 91; Yusri Darkazinli, *al-Muhaddith al-Akbar* (n.p.: n.p., 1979), 97–98 (a list of students including only one Azhari), 117; Itzchak Weismann, "The Invention of a Populist Islamic Leader: Badr al-Din al-Hasani, the Religious Educational Movement and the Great Syrian Revolt," *Arabica* 52 (2005): 109–139.

23. Quotes: al-Tabbakh, *Iʿlam,* 7:398; 1:24, 24. See also Thomas Pierret, *Baas et Islam en Syrie* (Paris: Presses universitaires de France, 2011), 56–57. For background, see Itzchak Weismann, *Taste of Modernity: Sufism, Salafiyya, and Arabism in Late Ottoman Damascus* (Leiden: Brill, 2001).

24. Quotes: al-Humsi, *Udabaʾ,* 13, 171. See also ibid., 30, 48, 100, 111, 121, 151 (links to Egypt); 6, 8, 46–47, 60, 103, 121 (Lebanon); 8, 40, 55, 75, 89, 106, 148 (Istanbul); 18, 139, 140 / 44 / 53 (Paris and Marseille); 56, 106 (Baghdad); 128 (Mersin); 115 (Mecca); 8 (London). For Aleppo's continued Ottoman and Turkish ties, see Keith Watenpaugh, *Being Modern in the Middle East: Revolution, Nationalism, Colonialism, and the Arab Middle Class* (Princeton, NJ: Princeton University Press, 2006).

25. "Qudum," *Hums,* August 16, 1923, 7; August 19, 1923, 7; September 6, 1923, 7; September 13, 1923, 7; and September 15, 1923, 7. For the Americas, see "Qudum," *Hums,* August 26, 1923, 7; "Ihdaʾ al-Jarida," *Hums,* June 16, 1923, 7.

26. Quotes: "Akhbar," *MMIA* 1, no. 4 (1921): 125; and "Akhbar," *MMIA* 2, no. 3 (1922): 94. See also Issa al-Maʾluf, "al-Majamiʿ al-ʿIlmiyya fi al-ʿAlam," *MMIA* 1, no. 4 (1921): 97–105, and *MMIA* 1, no. 5 (1921): 147–154; "Naʿi mustashriqin," *MMIA* 1, no. 3 (1921): 92–95; Muhammad Kurd ʿAli, "al-ʿAdiliyya wa-l-Zahiriyya," *MMIA* 1, no. 2 (1921): 36–40; "Aʿdaʾ," *MMIA* 8, no. 1 (1928): 15–17 (statistic).

27. This interpretation especially of the way in which the above historical works were framed (though not necessarily their content) somehow differs from evaluations that see them purely as continuations of traditional local histories: Abdul-Karim Rafeq, "Syrian Historical Studies on Syria," *MESAB* 9 (1975): 1; Ulrike Freitag, *Geschichtsschreibung in Syrien 1920–1990* (Hamburg: Deutsches Orient-Institut, 1991), 135, 139. For Palestinian local histories, see Meir Litvak, "A Palestinian Past," *HM* 6 (1994): 50n15.

28. Quote: Issa al-Maʾluf, "Sada Aʿmal al-Majmaʿ," *MMIA* 2:2 (1922): 61. For activities, see "al-Taqrir al-Rabiʿ," *MMIA* 8, no. 1 (1928): 1–14. Statistic: "Aʿzaʾ," *MMIA* 8, no. 1 (1928): 15–17.

29. Muhammad Kurd ʿAli, *Muqaddamat Kitab Khitat al-Sham* (Damascus: Matbaʿat al-Batrirkiyya al-urtudhuksiyya, 1924), 2, 3, 3, 2. For an analysis, see Freitag, *Geschichtsschreibung,* 144–156.

30. Both quotes: al-Hisni, *Muntakhabat*, 2. Nami had to bend to French pressure by eventually including pro-French politicians in his government, but first chose some nationalists (whom France soon arrested). Also, until his dismissal in 1928 he actively, though in vain, pushed France to replace Mandate rule with a thirty-year friendship treaty with a united Lebanon and Syria, and demanded compensation for the victims of the 1925–1927 revolt.

31. Al-Tabbakh, *I'lam*, 1:24.

32. Quotes: al-Humsi, *Udaba'*, 155; and Freitag, *Geschichtsschreibung*, 66. For Academy members, see al-Humsi, *Udaba'*, 112, 119, 121, 155. For al-Humsi in Damascus, see ibid., 154–155. Thinking of Aleppo and Damascus as Syria's twin towers was common: see Gelvin, "Modernity and Its Discontents," 76–77, quoting an article in *al-'Asima*, May 7, 1919. Also *bona fide* nationalists thought that way: Muhammad Kurd 'Ali, *Khitat al-Sham* (Beirut: Dar al-'Ilm li-l-Malayin, [1925] 1969), 3:175, called the French occupation of Syria in 1920 "France's attack on the four cities," Damascus and Aleppo and the third and fourth largest cities, Homs and Hama. France's separation of Aleppo and Damascus, from 1920 to 1924, was an early example of the changing subdivisions of Syria in the 1920s and 1930s.

33. Both quotes: "Kulliyyat Hums al-Wataniyya," *Hums*, October 14, 1923, 3. (Hymn: second refrain.) See also the decision by Hashim al-Atasi, a premier Syrian nationalists in the 1920s, to continue living in his hometown Homs while keeping in close touch with other Syrian nationalists: M. Radwan Atassi, *Hashim Atasi* (Damascus: M. R. al-Atasi, 2005), 97–98.

34. Our eminent correspondent in the Brazilian [city of] Sao Paolo, "Sada al-mahjar," *Hums*, August 29, 1923, 4. (The celebration took place May 2, 1923.) On the club, see Stacy Fahrentold, "Sound Minds in Sound Bodies: Transnational Philanthropy and Patriotic Masculinity in al-Nadi al-Homsi and Syrian Brazil, 1920–32," *IJMES* 46 (2014): 259–283.

35. Typical is "al-Maqala al-Iftitahiyya," *Jaridat Sao Paolo*, August 5, 1920, 1. The same holds for Palestinian nationalism: see, e.g., "al-Nahda al-Wataniyya fi al-Mahajir," *al-Karmal*, October 22, 1921, 2; "Filastin fi al-Mahjar," *al-Karmal*, June 27, 1925, 2. For an analytical focus on the *mahjar* and Syria / Lebanon, see Maria del Mar Logrono Narbona, "The Development of Nationalist Identities in French Syria and Lebanon" (PhD diss., University of California Santa Barbara, 2007), esp. 99–198; Christoph Schumann, "Nationalism, Diaspora and 'Civilisational Mission,'" *NN* 10 (2004): 599–617.

36. Quotes: "Min Akhbar al-Sham," *Hums*, June 9, 1923, 1; "Sada al-Mahjar," *Hums* June 16, 1912, 2; and "Sada al-Mahjar," *Hums*, September 30, 1923, 4. See also the section "Rasa'il al-Mahjar" of *Ba'albak*, the newspaper of the Lebanese town of Baalbak, which featured hundreds of "Letters from the diaspora" and informed

which diaspora Ba'albakis had subscribed to the paper: e.g., "Rasa'il al-Mahjar," *Ba'albak,* March 1, 1928, 12, and November 11, 1928, 8.

37. Quote: all the below texts used this term. (Also, all addressed other physical geographic features like lakes or rivers.) For distinguishing features, see Khalil Totah and Habib Khuri, *Jughrafiyyat Filastin* (Jerusalem: Mu'assasat Ibn Rushd, 1923), 4; Sabri Sharif 'Abd al-Hadi, *Jughrafiyyat Suriya wa-Filastin al-Tabi'iyya* (Cairo: al-Matba'a al-Rahmaniyya, 1923), 4 (with a note on the title page indicating where in Nablus one can buy the book); Sa'id Sabbagh, *Jughrafiyyat Suriyya al-'Umumiyya al-Mufassala* (Sidon: Matba'at al-'Irfan, 1923), 21 (focusing more than others on the geological features, including the fault line). See also "al-Bilad al-'Arabiyya: Suriya," *al-Sharq al-'Arabi,* December 15, 1925, 3 (a Jordanian paper). See also George Samné, *La Syrie* (Paris: Bossard, 1920), 5–19, esp. 6, a member of the Francophile *Comité Central Syrien;* and Henri Lammens, *La Syrie: Précis historique* (Beirut: Imprimérie Catholique, 1921).

38. Sabbagh, *Jughrafiyya,* 28 (drawing); Totah and Khuri, *Jughrafiyya,* 10 (quote; emphasis added), also 13.

39. Quotes: Totah and Khuri, *Jughrafiyya,* 2, 1. For natural borders, see Totah and Khuri, *Jughrafiyya,* 1–2; 'Abd al-Hadi, *Jughrafiyya,* 2–3; Sabbagh, *Jughrafiyya,* 22; Adib Farhat, *Suriya wa-Lubnan* (Sidon: Matba'at al-'Irfan, 1924), 1; "al-Bilad al-'Arabiyya: Suriya," *al-Sharq al-'Arabi,* December 15, 1925, 3. Farhat's book was particularly popular, even in more peripheral parts of Greater Syria like Transjordan: "Suriya wa-Lubnan," *al-Sharq al-'Arabi,* November 5, 1923, 2.

40. For Turkey, see Totah and Khuri, *Jughrafiyya,* 2; also Kurd 'Ali, *Khitat al-Sham,* 1:9. For the Egypt-Palestine border of *Bilad al-Sham,* see Sabbagh, *Jughrafiyya,* 22; Farhat, *Suriya wa-Lubnan,* 1; "al-Bilad al-'Arabiyya: Suriya," *al-Sharq al-'Arabi,* December 15, 1925, 3.

41. Totah and Khuri, *Jughrafiyya,* 3, 13. Similarly, although 'Abd al-Hadi's book was called *Jughrafiyyat Suriya wa-Filastin al-Tabi'iyya,* it was ordered such that Palestine was clearly a part of Syria. See also Kurd 'Ali, *Khitat al-Sham,* 1:6, 8; 3:168.

42. Sabbagh, *Jughrafiyya,* 71; 'Abd al-Hadi, *Jughrafiyya,* 227; Farhat, *Suriya wa-Lubnan,* 131. (On a related note, authors cited nationalist reasons for their geography texts: Totah and Khuri, *Jughrafiyya,* unpaginated introduction; 'Abd al-Hadi, *Jughrafiyya,* ba, jim, waw; Sabbagh, *Jughrafiyya,* 1; Farhat, *Suriya wa-Lubnan,* ha.) For manmade factors, see Totah and Khuri, *Jughrafiyya,* 6, 21; 'Abd al-Hadi, *Jughrafiyya,* 239; 'Ali al-Hasani, *Ta'rikh Suriya al-Iqtisadi* (Damascus: Matba'at Bada'i' al-Funun, 1924), 289–290.

43. The text was first published in a German journal in 1916. For fieldwork, see Ruppin's two travel diaries, in German, in A107/631, Central Zionist Archives, Jerusalem (hereafter, CZA), and A107/632, CZA. For glowing reviews in German journals, see copies included in A107/631, CZA. Reference: Moshe Novomeysky,

*Industry in Palestine: Its Condition and Prospect* (Jaffa-Tel Aviv: Palestine Economic Society, 1924), 4. For Jamal Pasha, see note, Mr. Schmidt, Kaiserlich Deutsches Generalkonsulat, Jerusalem, November 23, 1915, A107 / 631, CZA. For correspondence, see Friedrich Freiherr Kress von Kressenstein to Ruppin, Hudsch, August 19, 1917, L2 / 411, CZA, and letters, Ruppin to Zentralstelle des Hamburger Kolonialinstituts, Jaffa, March 15, 1916, and to Deutsch-türkische Wirtschaftszentrale, Jaffa, March 20, 1916, L2 / 411, CZA. For a similarly German perspective, see Hans Fischer, "Wirtschaftsgeographie von Syrien," *ZDP* 42 (1919): 1–112; ibid., 1 on Germany's "vital interest," *Lebensinteresse*, "in Syria and in all of Turkey."

44. Both quotes: Arthur Ruppin, *Syria: An Economic Survey* (New York: Provisional Zionist Committee, 1918), 3. For zones, see ibid., 3–4. See also the Jaffan resident Léon Schulmann, "Handel und Verkehr in Syrien," *WA* 12 (1918): 189, 191 ("Palestine" as "southern Syria"), 173 (all of Syria being one "transit region").

45. For "development as one," see Nahum Wilbusch, "Aussichten der Industrie und Gewerbe in Palaestina," 1, Jaffa, December 1918, typed manuscript, A355 / 135, CZA (Wilbusch was an industrialist whose Nesher Company would become one of the Yishuv's most powerful producers); Novomeysky, *Industry*, 4 (Novomeysky developed the Palestine Potash Company). For transport, see Arthur Ruppin, "The Economic Development of Palestine, Past and Future," *BPES* 2 (1922): 13; "Ba-Mizrah ha-Karov," *MT* 4 (1925): 86; "Heifah ve-Beirut," *MT* 4 (1926): 113. For "the shared pool," see Wilbusch, "Aussichten," 4, 8, 37; Novomeysky, *Industry*, 14.

46. Quote: Kurt Grunwald, "Palästinas wirtschaftliche Entwicklung seit dem Kriege," *WA* 26 (1927): 49. For the question of markets, see Wilbusch, "Aussichten," 4, 39, 40, 42; Nahum Thischby, "Sikuie Ta'asiyat ha-Tekstil be-Erets Isra'el," *MT* 3 (1925): 470 (a leading Zionist Executive economist); Novomeysky, *Industry*, 12; Irit Amit, "Economic and Zionist Ideological Perceptions: Private Initiative in Palestine in the 1920s and 1930s," *MES* 36 (2000): 91, for Jewish capitalists wanting to invest in Palestine. For dominance, see Wilbusch, "Aussichten," 37, 39, 46; "Heifah ve-Beirut," 113; Y. Ziman, "Ha-Mis'har ha-Hitsoni shel Suriyah," *MT* 4 (1926): 151–153; "'Al ha-Perek," *MT* 4 (1926): 175.

47. Grunwald, "Palästina," 49. Yet another reason was the economic condition in Poland, from where almost half of all Zionist immigrants originated in the 1920s.

48. Quote: Wilbusch, "Aussichten," 3. See also ibid., 2, 4; Arthur Ruppin, *Der Aufbau des Landes Israel* (Berlin: Jüdischer Verlag, 1919), 292 (on Syria as well as Egypt as the Yishuv's future primary export markets); "Trade and Industry Department, Palestine Zionist Executive, Extract from a Memorandum Submitted to the Executive," *ED* 1 (1922): 1 (a Zionist Executive journal); Nahum Tischby, "Eretz Israel and the Jews overseas (written for the Bombay newspaper Zion Messenger)," *ED* 4 (1922): 1–3; Ruppin, "Economic Development," 17; Tishby, "Sikuie,"

470–471; "Ha-Ksharim 'im ha-'Olam ha-Hitsoni," *MT* 3 (1925): 12–13; "Heifah ve-Beirut," 113.

49. Ruppin, "Economic Development," 17. Similar: Wilbusch, "Aussichten," 2.

50. Kurd 'Ali, *Khitat al-Sham*, 1:8 (quote); Totah and Khuri, *Jughrafiyya*, 2, 4; 'Abd al-Hadi, *Jughrafiyya*, 63, 227–228; Sabbagh, *Jughrafiyya*, 48, 26.

51. Kurd 'Ali, *Khitat al-Sham*, 1:16 (quote); Totah and Khuri, *Jughrafiyya*, 3, 4; 'Abd al-Hadi, *Jughrafiyya*, ha; "al-Bilad al-'Arabiyya: Suriya," *al-Sharq al-'Arabi*, December 15, 1925, 6; Iliyas and Jurj Jad'un, *al-Dalil al-Lubnani al-Suri* year 5 (Beirut: Matba'at Jad'un, 1928), 5, a business *Who Is Who* that saw Greater Syria as a "meeting point of nations."

52. Or so the documents in 1/31 ('malaf al-zilzal'), Nablus Municipal Archive (hereafter, NMA), suggest. For Egypt, see telegram from Sa'd Zaghlul, received in Nablus July 17, 1927; information in a letter from Ashoura newspaper to Nablus, Cairo, July 12, 1927; information in note, Salem and Said Bazaraa, Cairo, July 16, 1927, all in 1/31, NMA. Other aspects of Egypt's ties to Syria: Ami Ayalon, *Reading Palestine: Printing and Literacy, 1900–1948* (Austin: University of Texas Press, 2004), 60; "Baina Masr wa-Suriyya," *NSGTD* (August–September 1925): 8–20 (a talk in Damascus by the Bank Masr president, Tal'at Bek Harb); "Li-l-Duktur Taha Hussein," *Ahrar Musawwara* April 21, 1926, 6 (an Egyptian intellectual's visit to Beirut); "Muhadarat Adib Masri 'an al-Adab al-Suri," *Ahrar* December 6, 1929, 3; Khalil Sakakini, *Filastin ba'd al-Harb al-Kubra* (Jerusalem: Matba'at Beit al-Maqdas, 1925), 32–33, 50; Lutfi Bek al-Haffar, "Yakdhabun wa-la Yastahhun," in *Dhikriyyat* (Damascus: Matabi' Ibn Zaydun, [1925] 1954), 81.

53. Documents in 1/31, NMA; "Li-Mankubi al-Zilzal," *al-Sha'b*, August 16, 1927, 2; "Lajnat Tawzi' al-Mi'at Alf Lira," *al-Sha'b*, August 23, 1927, 2; "Filastin," *al-Sha'b*, September 6, 1927, 2. The same pattern—Greater Syrian contributions to Palestine that however were smaller than those collected in Palestine itself—showed in donations sent to Jaffa following the 1921 unrests: "Le-Tovat Negu'ei ha-Bilbulim be-Yaffo," *Doar Hayom*, May 20, 1921, 3 (Damascus); "Ahli," *al-Karmal*, May 25, 1921, 2 (Beirut).

54. For World War I, see Firro, "Lebanese Nationalism versus Arabism," 3–4. Two examples are Chambre de Commerce de Marseille (hereafter, CCM), "Note sur la valeur économique de la Syrie intégrale," esp. 2, 12–14, Marseille, June 23, 1915; and Chambre de Commerce de Périgueux, "La question de la Syrie," October 4, 1915, both in MQ5.4./35, Archives de la Chambre de Commerce de Marseille, France (hereafter, ACCM). Congress: Clément Huart, "Les frontières naturelles de la Syrie," in *Congrès français de la Syrie* (Marseille: Secrétariat Chambre de Commerce, 1919), 2:139–144; Emmanuel de Martonne, "L'unité géographique de la Syrie," in ibid., 2:226–229. Mission: Paul Huvelin, *Que vaut la Syrie?* (Marseille: Secrétariat Chambre de Commerce, 1919). See also Simon Jackson, "'What Is Syria

Worth?' The Huvelin Mission, Economic Expertise and the French Project in the Eastern Mediterranean, 1918–1922," *Monde(s)* 4 (2013): 83–103.

55. Commandant Devaux, "Le Haouran et la frontière syro-palestinienne," March 1922, 19, paper written for the cours de perfectionnement tactique, Armée du Levant, box 2200, versement (hereafter, v.) 1, Mandat Syrie-Liban (hereafter, MSL), Archives du Ministère des Affaires Étrangères / Nantes (hereafter, MAE-Nantes). For the demarcation team, see Report, Colonel Paulet, head, French party to the Border Commission, Samakh, July 8, 1921, box 655, v.1 / MSL, MAE-Nantes, here regarding the Jawlan-Hula area. (Only the western Syrian-Jordanian border was demarcated.) For geographical publications, see Geographical Section of the Naval Intelligence Division, Naval Staff, Admiralty, *A Handbook of Syria (including Palestine)* (London: His Majesty's Stationery Office, 1920), esp. 9–12.

56. Quote: Memorandum, Economic Board for Palestine to the Under-Secretary of State, Colonial Office, London, August 22, 1927, 2, CO733 / 135 / 4, The National Archives, Kew, UK (hereafter, TNA). British Transjordan concluded a customs-free agreement with the French Mandate in 1923. See also Burns, *Tariff,* 69. Unlike maritime and railway transport, traffic by "caravan and lorry receives no *transit* immunity" (ibid., 70; emphasis added).

57. Quotes: Précis, minutes of meeting between Director of Customs, Excise, and Trade[,] Representatives of the Palestine Zionist Executive and Federation of Jewish Industries in Palestine, October 20, 1927, CO733 / 135 / 4, TNA; and Inspection générale des douanes to Chambre de Commerce de Marseille, Beirut, December 3, 1928, MQ.5.4. / 36, ACCM.

58. For rails and roads, see Fritz Grobba, *Die Getreidewirtschaft Syriens und Paläs-tinas seit Beginn des Weltkrieges* (Hannover: Orient-Buchhandlung Heinz Lafaire, 1923), 102–103; anonymous, *L'oeuvre française en Syrie et au Liban, 1919–1939* (Paris: Larose, 1939), 18–19; Sa'id Himadeh, ed., *The Economic Organization of Syria* (Beirut: AUB Press, 1936), 179; Sa'id Himadeh, ed., *The Economic Organization of Palestine* (Beirut: AUB Press, 1938), 304–305, 308. Partly to encourage use of its state railways, Britain invested less in roads than France; the Jaffa-Haifa road for instance was in a bad state until 1937. France and Britain in the 1920s also made steady improvements to various ports, firstly Jaffa, Haifa, and Beirut. (In the 1930s, massive port expansions would follow, and airports.) See Jacques de Monicault, *Le port de Beyrouth* (Paris: Librairie technique et économique, 1936), 41–42; Report collection, "Palestine: Correspondence 1925–1927 relating to the improvement of harbor facilities at Haifa and Jaffa," CO935 / 1 / 12, TNA.

59. In Lebanon there were approximately 1,000 cars by 1921; 3,700 in 1926, and 8,000 in 1931. See "Multiplication des automobiles," *AF* (January 1932): 35. In 1931, there was one car for every seventy-five people in Lebanon, a ratio six times that for Egypt, for instance. Palestine had 236 registered motor vehicles in 1923, 2,123 in

1926, and 3,186 in 1930. See Husni Sawwaf, "Transportation and Communication," in Himadeh, *Economic Organization of Palestine*, 332.

60. Quote: Hugo Herrmann, *Eine werdende Welt: Reiseeindrücke aus Palästina* (Prague: J. Flesch, 1925), 72. See also "Multiplication des automobiles," *AF* (January 1932): 35; Général Dolot, "Le Transsyrien de Tripoli a Baghdad," *Revue tunisienne* 131 (1919): 147–152; "Rennie Mac Innes, *Notes for Travellers by Road and Rail in Palestine and Syria* (London: H.B. Skinner, 1925), 53; "La commerce des automobiles dans le Levant," *AF* (March–April 1925): 125; Samir Kassir, *Beirut*, trans. M. B. DeBevoise (Berkeley: University of California Press, 2010), 273–274; "La route Lattaquié-Alep," *AF* (February 1927): 70; Daphna Sharfman et al., eds., *Teh 'al Mirpeset ha Kasino* (Haifa: Mishpaton, 2006), 181–182; Zvi Stahl, *Toldot ha-Tahbura ha-Tsiburit be-Erets Israel* (Tel Aviv: Yaron Golan, 1995), 33; *Almanach français, 1934: Beyrouth-Damas-Alep* (Beirut: n.p., 1934), 135; itinerary of "Special Mediterranean Cruise, January 29th to March 15th, 1925," AK436/5, CZA; "Conférence faite par le Général Weygand sur la Syrie," 1924, 1, 4H120, Service historique de l'Armée de terre, Vincennes, France (hereafter, SHAT); Service des Renseignements, "Rapport d'ensemble sur les possibilités et l'utilité qu'il y aurait de créer un service français de transports réguliers entre Damas Bagdad et Teheran," Beirut, January 15, 1924, 4H120 (Dossier 4), SHAT; John Munro, *The Nairn Way* (Delmar: Caravan, 1980), 35–51; D. McCallum and C. E. S. Palmer, "Report on reconnaissance by motor car from Beyrout via Damascus to Bagdad" (April 1924), box 702, v.1/MSL, MAE-Nantes; Sarrail to Foreign Ministry, Beirut, January 29, 1925, box 699, v.1/MSL, MAE-Nantes.

61. For different developments, see Simon Jackson, "Mandatory Development: The Political Economy of the French Mandate in Syria and Lebanon" (PhD diss., New York University, 2009); Smith, *Roots;* Jacob Norris, *Land of Progress: Palestine in the Age of Colonial Development, 1905–1948* (Oxford: Oxford University Press, 2013).

62. Burns, *Tariff,* 178–79, 180–81. For protests, see "al-A'mal Allati Qamat bi-ha al-Ghurfa al-Tijariyya," *NSGTD* (January–February 1928): 35, 47; "Entre la Syrie et la Palestine," *CL,* May 23, 1930, 1.

63. Memorandum, Manufacturers' Association to the (British) Director of Customs, Excise and Trade, 2, 14, Tel Aviv, July 21, 1927, CO733/135/4, TNA, underlining also the significant ties with Egypt (ibid., 14).

64. For British plan, see S. Pattison, "Memorandum. Palestine-Syria Customs Convention," Jerusalem, March 2, 1927, CO733/135/4, TNA. For Zionist reactions, see Chamber of Commerce of Jaffa and District to Southern District Commissioner, Jaffa, August 25, 1927, 31/0100, Tel Aviv Municipal Archive (hereafter, TAMA); Manufacturers' Association, Memorandum; Zionist Executive/Central Office to the Under-Secretary of State/Colonial Office, London, August 24, 1927, CO733/135/4, TNA.

65. Quote: Economic Board for Palestine, Memorandum, 2 (emphasis added). See also Manufacturers' Association, Memorandum, 8. For merchants' earlier reservations, see Aryeh Mehulal, *Heifah* (Haifa: n.p., 1995), 95 (the French Franc's devaluation making Syrian imports to Palestine cheaper in 1923); "Heifah," *Do'ar Hayom*, August 31, 1923, 8; Memorandum of meeting of Haifa industrialists interested in trade with Syria, Haifa, July 19, 1926, S1/624, CZA.

66. Quote: Burns, *Tariff*, 67. The data is the result of my calculation of data in ibid., 282–285 (1923 figures are estimates; Lebanon and Syria are combined).

67. Quote: Manufacturers' Association, Memorandum, 12. 1929 report: Zionist Executive, Trade and Industry Section, "The Market in Syria and Lebanon" (1929), S8/2153, CZA. For manufacturing growth and profile, see Nahum Gross, "Some New Light on the Palestinian Census of Industries 1928," *AAS* 13 (1979): 264–275.

68. Quotes: Manufacturers' Association, Memorandum, 2; and letter, anonymous to Farhi, Beirut, in German ("to be translated in Hebrew"), file "Syria and Lebanon until September 1930," KH4B/2120, CZA. Joseph Farhi was fascinating: a leading Beiruti Jew who called himself "a good Jew and 'Zionist'" and helped Zionist delegations, he also felt compelled, as he stated, to "fight Zionism" because, born in Damascus, "Palestine [was] an inseparable part of Syria" to him. Hans Kohn to Leo Kohn, Beirut, May 13, 1927, KH4/B/2122, CZA.

69. Quote: Economic Board for Palestine, Memorandum, 2. See also Memorandum of meeting of Haifa industrialists, 4 (argument by Thischby). For maturation, see Manufacturers' Association, Memorandum, 1. Tellingly, some Jews considered investing in Syrian industries. See A. Shenkar, "'Al Beit-Haroshet ha-Hadash le-Garbayyim be-Suriah," *MT* 6 (1928): 262.

70. Lutfi al-Haffar, "Ihtijaj Tujjar Dimashq," in *Dhikriyyat*, 39–40. For the 1921 protests, see ibid., 37–38; in Palestine: "al-Rusum al-Jumrukiyya," *al-Karmal*, September 28, 1921, 3; "al-Ijtima' al-Tijari," *al-Karmal*, December 7, 1921, 3. For a reference to the exchange of notes, see "Memorandum on Syria-Palestine Customs Agreement," October 7, 1927, CO733/135/4, TNA.

71. Quote: "al-Mufawadat," *NSGTD* (January–March 1928): 39. See also ibid., 39–64. For the persisting position, see Frank Peter, *Entrepreneurs de Damas: nation, impérialisme et industrialisation* (Paris: Harmattan, 2010), 190–191.

72. Quote: subtitle of al-Hasani, *Ta'rikh Suriya al-Iqtisadi*. The Damascus Chamber of Commerce journal made this point tirelessly, often quoting other newspapers: *NSGTD* (January 1922): 10–11; (January–February 1923): 2–3, 8–9; (May–June 1923): 23–26; (September–October 1923): 2–3; (November–December 1925): 2–4; (July–September 1927): 150–53. Burns, *Tariff*, 4n1, "visited many Syrian factories and [was] impressed on every occasion with the extraordinary enthusiasm of the Syrian people for local industry."

73. Al-Haffar, "Ihtijaj," 39.

74. Nahum Thischby, "Visit to Beyrouth and Damascus" (1925), 9, Z4/40287, CZA.

75. They tried. There were Yishuvi trade fairs in Europe to interest Jewish and non-Jewish European buyers and capitalists: "Ha-Ta'arukha ha-Nodedet shel Mis'har ve-Ta'asiyah," *MT* 3 (1925): 615. Subpar global competitiveness: Manufacturers' Association, Memorandum, 11.

76. Quote: "Harikat al-Tijara," *al-Haqiqa,* February 10, 1919, 2 For global trade, see Sandra Chirazi and Raphaël Menand, *Histoire de la mondialisation capitaliste* (Paris: Pantin, 2011), 2:14. Statistics are based on al-Hasani, *Ta'rikh Suriya al-Iqtisadi,* 311.

77. It was now also called Place des Martyrs because the political executions that were carried out in Beirut in World War I, took place here.

78. For demographics, see Kassir, *Beirut,* 85. The 1932 census of 161,382 Beirutis was an underestimation: see Helmut Ruppert, *Beyrouth* (Beirut: CERMOC, 1969), 33. For urban structure and culture, see Jade Tabet et al., *Beyrouth* (Paris: Institut Français d'Architecture, 2001), 13–19; "Galleries Lafayette," *L'Orient,* January 17, 1925, 3; "Royal Hotel," *L'Orient,* January 6, 1925, 3; Kirsten Scheid, "Necessary Nudes," *IJMES* 42 (2010): 203–230; "Carnet mondain," *L'Orient,* January 9, 1925, 2; "Au [sic] fins gourmets," *L'Orient,* January 28, 1925, 2; see also Kassir, *Beirut,* 279–326.

79. Quotes: "À nos lecteurs," *CL,* July 19, 1929, 1; and Kassir, *Beirut,* 314. For confidence, see "Ila al-Tujjar," *al-Haqiqa,* March 2, 1919, 2. For a merchants' roster, see "Ghurfat al-Tijara," *al-Haqiqa,* January 21, 1919, 2. For French companies, see May Davie, *Beyrouth et ses faubourgs (1840–1940): une intégration inachevée* (Beirut: CERMOC, 1996), 82–83.

80. Letters, CCM, to Aleppo, Damascus and Beirut Chambers of Commerce, all November 7, 1922, all in MQ5.4./35, ACCM. For responses, see letter, Chambre de Commerce d'Alep, January 27, 1923; letter, Chambre de Commerce de Damas, March 4, 1923; letter, Chambre de Commerce et d'Industrie, Beirut, November 23, 1922, all to CCM, all in MQ5.4./35, ACCM.

81. For the "bride," see Jad'un, *Dalil,* 3. Ads include "Elimeleh Sachs," *CL,* June 9, 1925, 3; "Hotel Allenby, Jerusalem" and "Hôtel Central 'Haïfa,'" *CL* June 26, 1925, 3. Statistics are for 1927–1929, using data in de Monicault, *Port,* 61, and Sawwaf, "Transportation," 337. For stultification, see Kassir, *Beirut,* 273. For ports other than Beirut, see Mas'ud Dahir, *Ta'rikh Lubnan al-Ijtima'i* (Beirut: Dar al-Farabi, 1974), 99–103; for an example, Tyre, see Hasan Diab, *Ta'rikh Sur al-Ijtima'i* (Beirut: Dar al-Farabi, 1988), 95. For Beirut's centrality to France, see Marwan Buheiry, *Beirut's Role in the Political Economy of the French Mandate* (Oxford: Centre for Lebanese Studies, 1986); Gates, *Merchant Republic,* 20–33. For Beiruti transport links, see Tabet, *Beyrouth,* 18–19. For port development in the 1920s, see de Monicault, *Port,* 41.

LL

82. Quotes: "A'mal," *NSGTD* (November–December 1923): 27, 28 (Arabic translations of the French letters). See also "Bayan," *NSGTD* (April–June 1928): 145–46; "Shikayat," "Qarar Raqm 1793," and "Li-Hadrat al-Ra'is," *NSGTD* (January–February 1923): 11, 14–15, and 17–19; "A'mal," *NSGTD* (September–October 1923): 18. For Damascus's development, see Jean-Luc Arnaud, *Damas: urbanisme et architecture, 1860–1925* (Arles: Actes sud-Sindbad, 2006). For Damascus's problems as a manufacturing center and related complaints, see Geoff Schad, "Colonialists, Industrialists, and Politicians: the Political Economy of Industrialization in Syria, 1920–1954" (PhD diss., University of Pennsylvania, 2001); Peter, *Entrepreneurs de Damas*. For the Damascus customs office, see United Kingdom, *Report on the Trade, Industry and Finance of Syria* (London: H.M. Stationary, 1922), 11.

83. For trade statistics, see Jad'un, *Dalil,* 59. For Beyhum, see "A'mal," *NSGTD* (March–April 1925): 31–34.

84. Quotes: May Seikaly, *Haifa: Transformation of a Palestinian Arab Society, 1918–1939,* 185; "al-Wahda al-Suriyya," *al-Karmal,* February 23, 1921, 3. For Khuri, see Seikaly, *Haifa,* 34. For businesses, see 'Ali al-Bawwab, *Mawsu'at Haifa al-Karmaliyya* (Amman: n.p., 2009), 1:635, 636; "Ila al-Tujjar," *al-Karmal,* April 20, 1921, 2; "Shirka Jadida," *al-Karmal,* June 17, 1925, 2. For transport, see "Utumubilat," *al-Karmal,* November 8, 1921, 3; "Heifah ve-Beirut," 113–14. For late Ottoman Haifa, see Mahmud Yazbak, *Haifa in the Late Ottoman Period* (Leiden: Brill, 1998).

85. Quotes: Seikaly, *Haifa,* 107, 185, 185. For Damascene merchants' particular strength, see Joseph Vashitz, "*Dhawat* and *'Iṣamiyyūn:* Two Groups of Arab Community Leaders in Haifa," *AAS* 17 (1983): 111. For Syria's as Damascus's export, see Peter, *Entrepreneurs de Damas,* 196; an example is United Kingdom, *Report 1922,* 9. For Damascene-Haifawi merchants' references and meetings, see "Filastin," *NSGTD* (April–June 1927): 113–114; "Mufawadat," *NSGTD* (January–March 1928): 47; "A'mal," *NSGTD* (March–April 1925): 32 (the same meeting attended by Beirut's Jamil Beyhum); notes, meeting of British Chief Justice with Haifa Chamber of Commerce, Haifa, March 29, 1924, 31–2855, TAMA. Ads include "Al-Sada 'Ata Alla Judkhar," *al-Karmal,* January 12, 1921, 6; "Maktab Muhama," *al-Karmal,* February 23, 1921, 3; "Jaridat Alib Ba," *al-Karmal,* October 11, 1921, 3; see also Joseph Vashitz, "Tmurot Hevratiot be-Yishuv ha-'Aravi shel Heifah be-Tkufat ha-Mandat ha-Briti," in *Kalkalah u-Hevrah be-Yamei ha-Mandat,* ed. Avi Bareli and Nahum Karlinsky (Sdeh Boker: Ha-Merkaz le-Moreshet Ben-Guryon, 2003), 396n13. For the restaurant, see "Mat'am," *al-Karmal,* June 23, 1923, 4.

86. For "travellers," see "Mat'am," *al-Karmal,* June 23, 1923, 4. Lutfi al-Haffar, "al-Azma al-Iqtisadiyya al-Hadira," *NSGTD* (July–August 1924): 4.

87. Quote: Seikaly, *Haifa,* 106. For passport and visa problems, see Jaffa and District Chamber of Commerce to Jaffa Assistant District Governor, Jaffa, February 12,

1924, 31 / 0067, TAMA. For customs police problems, see "Ahwaluna al-Iqtisadiyya," *NSGTD* (September–October 1923): 4–5 (Greater Syria); "Ibtida'," *NSGTD* 1 (1922): 15; and "A'mal," *NSGTD* (July–August 1924): 57 (Damascus customs office); "L'activité de la Chambre de Commerce d'Alep," *CL,* August 23, 1929, 1 (Aleppo); "'Al ha-Sedarim be-Veit ha-Mekhes ha-Yafoi," *MT* 3 (1925): 581 (Jaffa). For policy problems, see "A'mal," *NSGTD* (March-April 1923): 22 (Jordan); "Taqrir 180," *NSGTD* (March-April 1923): 52 (Palestine); "al-Mufawadat," *NSGTD* (January-March 1928): 41–43 (Palestine).

88. Quote: United Kingdom, *Report on the Trade, Industry and Finance of Syria* (London: H.M. Stationary, 1925), 15. For HC action, see also United Kingdom, *Report 1922,* 14. For the 1921–1922 exports via Haifa, see Grobba, *Getreidewirtschaft,* 108. For insinuation, see "A'mal," *NSGTD* (July-August 1924): 58. The same threat was made in 1938 during a fight, between (then more autonomous) Syrian and Lebanese governments, over their joint budget; see Palestine Railway General Manager to HC, Haifa, April 5, 1938, M60 / 49, ISA.

89. Quote: Jamil al-Bahri, *Tarihk Haifa* (Haifa: al-Maktaba al-Wataniyya, 1922), 1. For Beirut's worries, see Kassir, *Beirut,* 272–274.

90. Seikaly, *Haifa,* 185. For Arab immigration, see ibid., 31, 33, 50, 65, 107. For Haifa resembling Beirut, see ibid., 30.

91. Quotes: "Janazat 'Amil," *al-Karmal,* March 21, 1926, 6; Seikaly, *Haifa,* 69. See also ibid., 47–48, 57, 81–121. For separate neighborhoods, see Yossi Ben-Artzi, *Lahafokh Midbar le-Karmel: Hithavut ha-Karmel ke-Merhav Nivdal be-'Ir Me'urevet* (Jerusalem: Magnes, 2004).

92. Quotes: Seikaly, *Haifa,* 110, 111, 110; "Min Tartus," *al-Karmal,* September 5, 1926, 12; and "Windsor Hotel," *al-Karmal,* August 8, 1925, 4. For the municipality, see Tamir Goren, *Shituf be-Tsel 'Imut: 'Aravim we-Yehudim ba-Shilton ha-Mekomi be-Hefah be-Tkufat ha-Mandat ha-Briti* (Ramat Gan: Universitat Bar-Ilan, 2008). For cross-communal contacts, see Zachary Lockman, *Comrades and Enemies: Arab and Jewish Workers in Palestine, 1906–1948* (Berkeley: University of California Press, 1996); Vashitz, "Tmurot," 394, on the "civil society" in which Arabs and Jews met even though their "political societies" were distinct, even clashed. For *'isamiyyun,* see Vashitz, "*Dhawat.*" (However, social integration into Haifa was limited for recently arrived merchants and almost nil for poor immigrants. See Mahmud Yazbak, *al-Hijra al-'Arabiyya ila Haifa* [Nazareth: Maktabat al-Qabas, 1988], 129, 110.) For the *Dalil,* see Jad'un, *Dalil,* 465, 466, 469. For the informal count, see Bawwab, *Haifa,* 635–639 (with the Butaji shops the 1920–1930 number rises to 46). For hotels, see ibid., 642. For Butaji, see ibid., 639; "Akbar mahall fi Filastin," *al-Karmal,* May 25, 1921, 4; "Akhbar Mahallat Butaji," *al-Karmal,* December 12, 1926, 1.

93. Quote: Seikaly, *Haifa,* 72. For infrastructure, see ibid., 61, 72–74; Norris, *Land of Progress.*

94. For British agency, see Seikaly, *Haifa,* 72; Shim'on Stern, "Ha-Ma'avak 'al Hakamat Namal Heifah," *Kathedra* 21 (1981): 171. For the British imperial dimension, see Norris, *Land of Progress.* Also, for the role of nationalism in reshaping post-war Haifa, see Deborah Bernstein, *Constructing Boundaries: Jewish and Arab Workers in Mandatory Palestine* (Albany: State University of New York Press, 2000); David De Vries, *Ide'alizm ve-Byurokratiah: Shorsheha shel Heifah ha-Adumah* (Tel Aviv: ha-Kibuts ha-Me'uhad, 1999); Seikaly, *Haifa.*

95. Frederick Palmer, *Report on the Facilities of Harbour Provision for Palestine* (London: H.M. Stationary, 1923), 32. For British policy choice implicitly building on Ottoman policies, see also Norris, *Land of Progress.*

96. Quotes: Palmer, *Report,* 22 (emphasis added); and al-Bahri, *Haifa,* 1. For the 1921 meeting, see "al-Ijtima' al-Tijari," *al-Karmal,* December 7, 1921, 3. The Jaffawi merchants list, composed on June 4, 1929, is attached to MAE to CCM, Paris, December 9, 1929, MQ.5.4/21, ACCM. However, a few small Haifawi entrepreneurs moved to Jaffa, and Ramla and Lydda. See Seikaly, *Haifa,* 7.

97. For the APB, see Mehulal, *Heifah,* 54, 63, 96. For ethnic clubs, see "Mo'etset Yotsei Ukrainah," *Doar Hayom,* December 31, 1920, 3. For businesses, see "Ha-Ner," *Doar Hayom,* March 16, 1921, 4; "Krone Brauerei," *Doar Hayom,* August 12, 1924, 4; "Kaspi-Diskin-Kaplan," *Doar Hayom,* July 1, 1928, 1.

98. For historical geography, see Ruth Kark, ed., *The Land That Became Israel* (New Haven, CT: Yale University Press, 1989); Yehoshua Ben-Aryeh, *Erets be-Re'i 'Avrah* (Jerusalem: Magnes, 2001); Yossi Ben-Artzi, "The Contribution of Historical Geography to the Historiography of the Establishment of Israel," in *Making Israel,* ed. Benny Morris (Ann Arbor: University of Michigan Press, 2007), 147–177. Zionists did not walk in lockstep also in other ways. The principally central and Eastern European middle class immigrants of the 1920s (and 1930s) were less ideologically driven than the prewar leftist, mainly Russian second aliyah, and had more individual material interests: see Anita Shapira, *Israel* (Waltham, MA: Brandeis University Press, 2012), 103–118. And private businesses were more central to the Yishuv's development than earlier historians—absorbed with the politically and ideologically dominant Zionist institutions, with the left, and with collective agriculture that supposedly gave the "useless" diaspora Jew a real body and soul—had acknowledged. See Amit, "Perceptions," 84; Nahum Karlinky, *California Dreaming: Ideology, Society and Technology in the Citrus Industry of Palestine, 1890–1939* (Albany: State University of New York Press, 2005). For economic historiography, see Yacob Metzer, "Kalkalat Erets Isra'el be-Tkufat ha-Mandat," in *Kalkalah u-Hevrah,* 7–57.

99. Amiram Gonen, "Keitsad Kam 'Merkaz ha-Arets,'" in *Kalkalah u-Hevrah,* 439–488. Growing from a total of under 7,000 to 55,000 between 1922 and 1931, Jewish Jaffa-Tel Aviv overtook Jewish Jerusalem. It also became the Yishuv's economic

leader: not by chance, the (Jewish) Manufacturers' Association of Palestine was housed in Tel Aviv and its chamber of commerce was the Yishuv's most influential. The Jewish chambers of commerce defaulted to another's opinion in some national questions with Jaffa-Tel Aviv often playing a leading role: see, e.g., Chamber of Commerce Jaffa and District to Chamber of Commerce Jerusalem, Jaffa, September 10, 1924, and Chamber of Commerce Jerusalem to International [sic] Chamber of Commerce Jaffa, Jerusalem, May 14, 1924, both in 31/2855, TAMA. A Yishuv-wide General Association of the Jewish Merchants of Palestine would be founded only in 1938 and immediately contested by local chambers: see General Association of the Jewish Merchants of Palestine to the Jaffa-Tel Aviv Chamber of Commerce, Jerusalem, June 21, 1938, and Haifa Jewish Chamber of Commerce and Industry to Jaffa-Tel Aviv Chamber of Commerce, Haifa, August 22, 1938, both 31–2348, TAMA. In the 1920s, chambers existed in Tiberias, Jerusalem, Jaffa and Haifa, with at least the latter three having separate Arab and Jewish chambers. Arab Nablus, Gaza, and Ramallah, and Acre, Hebron, and Nazareth, had Arab chambers and traders associations, respectively. Chamber locations are listed in Palestine Government to all chambers, Jerusalem, March 21, 1924, 31/2855, TAMA; for the membership list, see letter and list, Jewish Haifa Chamber of Commerce to Jaffa-Tel Aviv Chamber of Commerce, Haifa, March 14, 1924, 31–2861b, TAMA.

100. For popular opinion and the Zionist Executive, see "Mi-Saviv le-Yamenu," *Doar Hayom,* May 31, 1920, 1; Seikaly, *Haifa,* 64.

101. Juni Mansour, *al-Khatt al-Hadidi al-Hijazi* (Jerusalem: Mu'assasat al-Dirasat al-Maqdisiyya, 2008), 149.

102. Quotes: (Jewish) Chamber of Commerce Jaffa to Chamber of Commerce Jerusalem, Jaffa, July 17, 1924, 31/0430, TAMA; Palmer, *Report,* 22–23; and Frederick Kisch, *Palestine Diary* (London: Gollancz, 1938), 114 (April 17, 1924, reporting opinions in Tel Aviv). For Haifa's role in Jordan, see also "Jumruk Haifa," *al-Urdunn,* August 3, 1926, 5. For the chambers' origins, see Yigal Drori, "Re'shitam shel Irgunim Kalkaliim," *Kathedra* 25 (1982): 108–109; Mehulal, *Heifah,* 20–21, 29, 51–56. For tooting Haifa's horn and *'Ir ha-'Atid,* see Yosef Ben-Shabat, "Sahar Haifa," *Doar Hayom,* January 16, 1920, 1, and Mehulal, *Heifah,* 149 (the term may have been coined in Britain). For Jaffa's lobbying, see Palmer, *Report,* 7–11.

103. First quote: United Kingdom, *Report 1922,* 5. See also Hasani, *Ta'rikh Suriya al-Iqtisadi,* 297; and, for analysis, Peter, *Entrepreneurs de Damas,* 200–201. The Djambart quote is included in "L'activité de la Chambre de Commerce d'Alep," *CL,* August 23, 1929, 1. The Franco-Turkish treaty followed France's withdrawal from Cilicia, in today's south-central Turkey, which it had occupied from 1918.

104. Quotes: United Kingdom, *Report 1925,* 11; and United Kingdom, *Report 1922,* 7. For an analysis of smuggling, see Peter, *Entrepreneurs de Damas,* 206–207. For sheep,

see "Le commerce du bétail en Syrie en 1924," box 861, v.1/MSL, MAE-Nantes. For Damascene concerns, see "al-Mansujat al-Wataniyya," *NSGTD* (January–March 1927): 18. However, even in 1935, when Turkey's border was more shut than even in the 1920s, Aleppo's and Alexandretta's combined part in Syria's exports to Palestine was only 16.5 percent. See Peter, *Entrepreneurs de Damas,* 196.

105. The continued different economic situation of Damascus was reflected in French reporting. See, e.g., Service économique et agricole, "Note sur la situation économique," Beirut, March 1926, box 861, v.1/MSL, MAE-Nantes. For a very useful map of cities' hinterlands in the late Ottoman period, see Peter, *Entrepreneurs de Damas,* 180.

106. Quote: United Kingdom, *Report 1925,* 11. The statistic is based on Burns, *Tariff,* 282–283. See also Abla Amawi, "The Transjordanian State and the Enterprising Merchants of Amman," in *Amman: ville et société,* ed. Jean Hannoyer and Seteney Shami (Beirut: CERMOC, 1996), 115.

107. Author, interview with Marwan al-Hamawi (born 1951, Amman), June 21, 2011, Amman; author, interview with Muhammad Tahsin al-Ba'albaki (born 1940, Damascus), June 28, 2011.

108. First three quotes: Hind Abu al-Sha'r and Nufan al-Sawariyya, *'Amman fi al-'Ahd al-Hashimi, 1916–1952* (Amman: Amanat 'Amman, 2002), 34, 34; and Talib al-Rifa'i and Raba al-Kan'an, *Buyut 'Amman al-Ula* (Amman: al-Jami'a al-Urdunniyya, 1987), introduction (no pagination). Last three quotes: extracts of 1928–1929 rental agreements reprinted in Muhammad Rafi', *Dhakirat al-Madina* (Amman: Markaz al-Husayn al-Thaqafi: 2002), 1:19, 13, 16. However, there was also reference to a "Syrian" and a "Palestinian": ibid., 20, 21.

109. Notes on, and interview with, al-Hamawi.

110. Tabba'a: author, interview with his son, Hamdi Tabba'a (born 1936, Amman), June 21, 2011, Amman.

111. Robins, *Jordan,* 45; Tell, *Jordan,* 78.

112. Interview with Tabba'a.

113. In the Middle East Mandate, London was more relaxed about Arab nationalism than Paris—it was interested in stability in British Palestine and Hashemite Transjordan—and pro-Hashemite and other Arab nationalists often crossed borders to take refuge, to the almost permanent chagrin of Paris. For such competition in the Mandates area, see, on World War I, David Fromkin, *A Peace to End All Peace: The Fall of the Ottoman Empire and the Creation of the Modern Middle East* (New York: Holt, 1989); on the interwar period, see Anne-Lucie Chaigne-Oudin, *La France et les rivalités occidentales au Levant* (Paris: Harmattan, 2006) (however, she also addresses cooperation: ibid., 265–268); and on World War II, see Aviel Roshwald, *Estranged Bedfellows: Britain and France in the Middle East during the Second World War* (Oxford: Oxford University Press, 1990). More

broadly regarding the Mandate system, see Pedersen, *Guardians,* e.g., ibid., 44, for the early 1920s. A classic on Franco-British competition in another region, Africa, is Prosser Gifford and Wm. Roger Louis, ed., *France and Britain in Africa: Imperial Rivalry and Colonial Rule* (New Haven, CT: Yale University Press, 1971). On a different note, as John Darwin, "An Undeclared Empire: The British in the Middle East, 1918–39," *JICH* 27 (1999): 159, and Henry Laurens, "Synthèse de conclusion," in *France, Syrie et Liban,* ed. Nadine Méouchy (Damascus: IFEAD, 2002), 409, have noted, imperial historians have been rather indifferent to the Mandates. For how plugging the postwar Middle Eastern case into the imperialism debate might affect both, see Yoav Alon, "Historiography of the Empire," in *Britain and the Middle East,* ed. Zach Levey and Elie Podeh (Brighton: Sussex Academic Press, 2008), 33–47.

114. This fact is illustrated in Chapter 4's section on the central periphery. As for inter-imperial communication, it can be linked to two sets of literature. One studies how local actors helped shape imperial governance. A synthesis is Colin Newbury, *Patrons, Clients, and Empires* (Oxford: Oxford University Press, 2003). Case studies are Richard Price, *Making Empire: Colonial Encounters and the Creation of Imperial Rule in Nineteenth-Century Africa* (Cambridge: Cambridge University Press, 2008); John Cell, "Colonial Rule," in *Oxford History of the British Empire,* ed. Judith Brown and Roger Louis (Oxford: Oxford University Press, 1999), 4:235 (the 1930s indigenization of British colonial services in South Asia). The other set concerns bilateral interimperial exchanges between imperial government (e.g., Véronique Dimier, *Le gouvernement des colonies, regards croisés franco-britanniques* [Brussels: Editions de l'Université de Bruxelles, 2004]; Pierre Singaravélou, "Les stratégies d'internationalisation de la question coloniale et la construction transnationale d'une science de la colonisation à la fin du XIX$^e$ siècle," *Monde(s)* 1 [2012]: 135–157]); bilateral inter-imperial diplomacy (e.g., Claire Hirshfield, *The Diplomacy of Partition: Britain, France, and the Creation of Nigeria, 1890–1898* [The Hague: Kluwer Boston, 1979]); bilateral inter-imperial security cooperation (e.g., Martin Thomas, *Britain, France, and Appeasement* [Oxford: Oxford University Press, 1996]), and the postwar multilateral quest for new security arrangements (Jeffrey Taliaferro et al., eds., *The Challenge of Grand Strategy: The Great Powers and the Broken Balance between the World Wars* [Cambridge: Cambridge University Press, 2012]). However, both sets are historiographically developed from an imperial or Great Power perspective.

115. First two quotes: Amery / Downing Street to HC Plumer / Jerusalem, London, November 26, 1925, 1, FO 141 / 508 / 5, TNA (paraphrasing a letter by Plumer). Third quote: *Agreement between Palestine and Syria and the Lebanon to Facilitate Good Neighbourly Relations in Connection with Frontier Questions* (London: H.M.

Stationary, 1927), 4. For laissez-passers and issuance interruptions, see, e.g., "'Ala al-Hudud," *al-Ahrar,* March 26, 1931, 5. For border-crossing officials, see report, Service des Renseignements, Kuneitra, January 11, 1928, box 1532, v.1/MSL, MAE-Nantes. It is unclear whether a Franco-British pursuance agreement was officialized. A 1926 draft is "An Ordinance to provide for the pursuit of fugitive offenders from Egypt and Syria," FO141/508/5, TNA.

116. Quotes: HC/Samuel to State/Curzon, Jerusalem, December 17, 1920, p. 1, FO141/441/6, TNA; and British Consulate General Beirut to HCs in Egypt, Mesopotamia, and Palestine, December 11, 1920, FO141/441/6, TNA. For Franco-British consultations (mainly concerning political fugitives), see ibid., attached "memo #1." For agreement enforcement, see Priestland, *Records of Syria,* 2:666.

117. French HC to French General Consulate in Jerusalem, January 5, 1927; French HC Ponsot to British HC Plumer, Beirut, December 6, 1927; Memo requesting opinion, French Intelligence Service (Service du Renseignments [SR]) to Veterinary Service, December 29, 1927; head of SR to HC, December 14, 1927, referencing an exchange between the SR office in Dir'a and the British HC representative in Amman; all in box 861, v.1/MSL, MAE-Nantes.

118. "Al-Ta'un al-Baqari fi al-'Iraq," *al-Ahrar,* September 3, 1930, 4; "al-Tadabir al-Sahhiyya 'ala al-Hudud," *al-Ahrar,* July 9, 1930, 4; "Mukafahat al-Jarad," *al-Ahrar,* June 11, 1931, 4; "Mu'tamar al-Jarad al-Duwali fi al-Qahira," *al-Ahrar,* February 7, 1936, 4; "Mu'tamar al-Jarad al-Duwali," *al-Ahrar,* September 14, 1938, 5.

119. Quote: Communication, Susan Pedersen to author, September 22, 2013. For pre-1914 roots, see Mark Mazower, *Governing the World. The History of an Idea, 1815 to the Present* (New York: Penguin, 2012), 3–115.

120. For tribal conferences, see entire box 554, v.1/MSL, MAE-Nantes. An example of a tribe moving across borders (and being socially affected by the post-1918 changes) is treated in Johann Büssow, "Negotiating the Future of a Bedouin Polity in Mandatory Syria," *Nomadic Peoples* 15 (2011): 68–92.

121. For extradition, see HC/Samuel to State/Curzon, 3; "Draft Agreement," Ministry of Justice, Cairo, February 20, 1921, FO141/441/6, TNA; "Provisional Agreement," printed in Egypt, *Supplément au Journal Officiel,* No. 112 du Jeudi, December 21, 1922. For pursuit, see Egyptian Ministry of Foreign Affairs to HC Egypt, Bulkeley, August 23, 1925, FO141/508/5, TNA; HC Palestine to HC Egypt, Jerusalem, October 22, 1925, FO141/508/5, TNA; Ministerial Arrêté No 35 re pursuance of fugitive offenders about the boundaries between Egypt and Palestine, July 17, 1929, FO141/508/5, TNA. (On a side note, as Egypt was only de jure independent since 1922, its foreign ministry had to send its request through Egypt's British High Commissioner. In this context, its reference to French rights was a

smart move to maximalize Egypt's sovereignty.) For Auja, see Report, HC/Jerusalem to Secretary of State for the Colonies, Jerusalem, April 29, 1926, FO141/508/5. For wireless, see HC Palestine to HC Egypt, June 29, 1926, FO141/508/5; conference report, December 15–18, 1926, Cairo, FO141/508/5; HC Palestine to HC Egypt, August 20, 1927, FO141/508/5.

122. Quotes: CNIB, *Annual Report, 1931* (Cairo: n.p., 1932), xv; and CNIB, *Annual Report, 1929* (Cairo: n.p., 1930), 18.

123. Quotes: Ministry of Interior to Palestine Police, Cairo, July 27, 1921, FO141/441/6, TNA, Henri Froideveaux, "L'agitation soviétique en Asie," *AF* (June 1925): 186; and Martin Thomas, *Empires of Intelligence: Security Services and Colonial Disorder after 1914* (Berkeley: University of California Press, 2008), 91, 73. For communists, see Suliman Bashear, *Communism in the Arab East, 1918–1928* (London: Ithaca, 1980), 23–89; Musa Budeiri, *The Palestine Communist Party, 1919–1948* (Chicago: Haymarket Books, [1979] 2010), esp. 1–44; Tareq Ismael, *The Communist Movement in the Arab World* (London: RoutledgeCurzon, 2005), 8–16; Najati Sidqi, *Mudhakkirat* (Beirut: Mu'assasat al-Dirasat al-Filastinyya, 2001), 29–69; "List of militant communists," 2–4 (including cross-border agents), attachment to A. Mavrogordato/CID to Chief Secretary, Jerusalem, March 25, 1930, CO733/189/4, TNA. For police coordination, see Bashear, *Communism,* 108; Thomas, *Empires,* 91; Secretariat of the Council of Ministers to HC/Iraq, Baghdad, August 28, 1927, and HC/Iraq to Secretary of the Council of Ministers, Baghdad, September 2, 1927, both in CO732/28/13, TNA.

124. Those limits highlight that the sprawling British Empire was not a centralized managed unit. See John Darwin, *The Empire Project: The Rise and Fall of the British World System, 1830–1970* (Cambridge: Cambridge University Press, 2009).

125. Quotes: Department of Immigration and Travel to C.I.D., Jerusalem, June 27, 1921; and Ministry of Interior to Chancery, Cairo, August 7, 1921, 4, 4, 2. See also HC/Cairo to HC/Jerusalem, June 25, 1921; DIT to HC/Civil Secretary, Jerusalem, July 11, 1921; all in FO141/441/6, TNA.

## Prelude 4. Hauranis Migrate to Palestine

Epigraph: Eliahu Epstein, "Report on Present Conditions in the Hauran. With Special Reference to the Migration Problem" (1935), 46–47, box A405/118, Central Zionist Archives, Jerusalem (hereafter, *CZA*).

1. Ibid., 37.

2. Ibid., 32–33. For famine conditions elsewhere in Syria, see "La famine," January 16, 1933, box 862, versement (hereafter, v.) 1/Mandat Syria-Liban (hereafter, MSL), Archives du Ministère des Affaires Étrangères, Nantes, France (hereafter,

MAE-Nantes); "L'avenir des nomads du desert de Syrie," *AF* 318 (1934): 77–79 (a tour by Epstein, under the aegis of the American University of Beirut, in 1934).

3. Quotes: Epstein, "Report," 12, 10.

4. Quote: ibid., 12. See also ibid., 29, 32, 33, 46, 45. (The Jewish Agency had an interest in the Hauran also because in 1891 Edmond de Rothschild had bought some land there with the intention, never realized, to settle Jews; in 1929/1930, he transferred the deeds to the Palestine Jewish Colonization Association.)

5. Quote: ibid., 44.

6. Ibid., 46; Palestine Royal Commission (Peel Commission), *Minutes of Evidence Heard at Public Sessions* (London: His Majesty's Stationery Office, 1937), 99 (witness: Eliahu Epstein). See Juni Mansour, *al-Khatt al-Hadidi al-Hijazi* (Jerusalem: Mu'assasat al-Dirasat al-Maqdisiyya, 2008), 147–150, for Syrians and for Haifa's closer connection to the Hauran from 1905; and see Zionist Executive Labor Department, "Comments on the number of non-Jewish unemployed people," 1, Jerusalem, 1929, S9/1040, CZA, for 1928–1929, when "hundreds" of Haurani laborers arrived, working as longshoremen in the port and doing odds and ends jobs in the city, "depressing daily wages in untrained jobs" and forming a super-proletariat.

7. Quote: author, interview with Abraham Hileli (b. 1929, Aleppo), April 7, 2010, Haifa. For 1934 as high tide and for the 1936 estimate, see Palestine Royal Commission, *Minutes*, 91, 96. For wages, see ibid., 98. (By 1935, mass emigration caused labor wages in the Hauran to double: see "Bulletin hebdomadaire agricole et économique," 1, July 13, 1935, box 863, v.1/MSL, MAE-Nantes.) See also "Be-Jaffo," *Davar*, June 8, 1936, 7; Ma'ayan Hess-Ashkenazi, "Ha-Hagira ha-'Aravit la-Sharon be-Tkufat ha-Mandat," *Kathedra* 116 (2005): 103–116; "Hurani Ratsah et Havero liad Haderah," *Davar*, January 30, 1935, 39, involving the police rounding up fifty Haurani in Hadera; author, interview with Shiriban bint Nimr Ziyad Abu Tarif (born 1932, Yarka, Palestine), Yarka, Israel, April 10, 2010 (I thank Yusri Khaizran for guiding me in Yarka); author, interview with Zacharia Freilich (born 1923, Haifa), April 13, 2010, Haifa; Haifa Labor Council, "Po'alim Yehudim we-'Aravim be-Namal Heifah, 1934–1938," box IV-250-27-2-319, Pinchas Lavon (Labor Party) Archive, Tel Aviv (hereafter, PLA); Report "Huranim," (1936), 1, box S90/774, CZA.

8. Quotes: "Haifa. Te'unah," *Doar Hayom*, January 8, 1935, 6; and "Hurani Harug," *Davar*, February 15, 1935, 1. Other newspapers items include "Lakakh et ha-Arnak le-'Eineiha," *Davar*, August 12, 1934, 7; "Hurani Ratsah;" "Shnaim Ohzim ba-Talit," *Doar Hayom*, February 7, 1935, 3; and ""Olim,'" *Davar*, March 14, 1937, 5.

9. Quote: Epstein, "Report," 12. For the ditty and the prank, see author, interview with Benny Nachshon (b. 1929, Haifa), April 10, 2010, Haifa. For the sketch, see *Kinder-Rundschau* 14 (1936): 3. I thank Viola Rautenberg for sharing this source.

10. Quotes: Viola Rautenberg, interview with Ilse B., November 1 and 8, 2009, Haifa; and "Wie wir Hafenarbeiter wurden," *Mitteilungsblatt der Hitachdut Olej Germania* (July 1938): 10. I thank Viola Rautenberg for sharing both sources. For Haurani women, see Epstein, "Report," 37.

11. Quote: "From a memorandum of the Arab Workers Association, Haifa, February 9, 1932," written by I. Asfour, legal adviser, box S90/774, CZA. See also Report "Huranim," 2; Memorandum "Hoser 'Avodah" (1936), 3, box S90/771, CZA; Port Haifa Manager to Department of Customs, Haifa, March 2, 1936, box M37/15, ISA; Director Department of Customs to Chief Secretary, Haifa, March 2, 1937, box M40/22, ISA; Haifa Port Manager to Director Department of Customs, Haifa, February 15, 1937, box M40/22, ISA. The port manager also wanted to prove that the state, which in July 1935 had taken over all port operations, was up to the task.

12. Palestine Royal Commission, *Minutes,* 94 (witness: Eliahu Epstein); High Commissioner Arthur Wauchope to Colonial Office, Jerusalem, June 1 and August 16, 1937, box CO733/351/1, The National Archives, Kew (hereafter, TNA); "Ha-Wa'adah ha-Yishuvit" (1936), 7, box 00090/6, 1820 ת.נ., Haifa Municipal Archive, Israel, shows that under pressure by the Arab-Jewish municipality, especially its Jewish members, the British tried to move *Ard al-Raml* inhabitants not to another site in Haifa, near Neve Sha'anan, but to Balad el-Sheikh, six kilometers away.

13. Quotes: Palestine Royal Commission, *Minutes,* 95, 93. However, there was another, useful side to the second aim. Massive Arab labor immigration, the Jewish Agency representatives asserted, is "one of the proofs that the [British] Government's estimates of absorptive capacity were . . . an under-estimate." It reinforced the Zionist demand that Britain issue more visas to Jews and ignore opposite Palestinian demands: ibid., 97.

### 4. Toward a Region of Nation-States

1. It bears recalling that in the late Ottoman era, in 1908–1914, Shawwam had enjoyed political emancipation including a constitution and parliamentary elections.

2. Cyrus Schayegh, "The Mandates and/as Decolonization," in *Routledge Handbook of the History of the Middle East Mandates,* ed. Cyrus Schayegh and Andrew Arsan (London: Routledge, 2015), 412–419. This also means that one can historiographically divide the A Mandate period into two distinct phases—the 1920s and the 1930s–1940s.

3. Overviews include Philip Khoury, *Syria and the French Mandate* (Princeton, NJ: Princeton University Press, 1987), 245–582; Peter Shambrook, *French Imperialism in Syria, 1927–1936* (London: Ithaca Press, 1998).

4. Overviews include Fawwaz Traboulsi, *A History of Modern Lebanon* (London: Pluto, 2007), 95–108; Meir Zamir, *Lebanon's Quest* (London: I. B. Tauris, 2000), 84–247.

5. Following the 1928 agreement and until 1933, Abdallah allowed a Transjordan National Congress (TNC) to convene. The TNC helped crystallize a "Hashemite Compact" between key social groups and Abdallah. Its "enduring contribution . . . was as a forum at which the competing interests between the state and leading socio-economic actors could be aired, managed, negotiated and ameliorated." Quotes: Tariq Tell, *The Social and Economic Origins of Monarchy in Jordan* (New York: Palgrave Macmillan, 2013), 12; and Philip Robins, *A History of Jordan* (Cambridge: Cambridge University Press, 2004), 40. Overviews include ibid., 35–52; Tell, *Origins*, 73–112; Mary Wilson, *King Abdullah, Britain, and the Making of Jordan* (Cambridge: Cambridge University Press, 1987).

6. For 1929 as the conflict's "Year Zero," see Hillel Cohen, *Year Zero of the Arab-Israeli Conflict, 1929* (Waltham, MA: Brandeis University Press, 2015)). The wall is revered by Jews and Muslims alike: the Quran says prophet Muhammad made a night-long ascent to heaven from what is the sole remnant of the Jewish Second Temple, which Rome destroyed in 70 A.D. and now is *al-Haram al-Sharif,* the Holy Precinct, to Muslims. In 1929, some Arabs saved Jews, but most Jewish victims fell at an Arab hand, mainly in three Old Yishuv cities, Hebron, Safed, and Jerusalem; and most Arab victims fell at the hand of the police, but some were harmed also by Jews, mostly in New Yishuv cities like Haifa and Tel Aviv. See Gudrun Krämer, *A History of Palestine: From the Ottoman Conquest to the Founding of the State of Israel* (Princeton, NJ: Princeton University Press, 2008), 224–237; Arieh Saposnik, "Wailing Walls and Iron Walls: the Western Wall as Sacred Symbol in Zionist National Iconography," *AHR* 120 (2015): 1653–1681; Charles Anderson, "From Petition to Confrontation: The Palestinian National Movement and the Rise of Mass Politics, 1929–1939" (PhD diss., New York University, 2013). For the Yishuv's evolving security ethos, see Anita Shapira, *Land and Power: The Zionist Resort to Force, 1881–1948* (Stanford, CA: Stanford University Press, 1992), 173–276.

7. For the 1936–1939 revolt, see Krämer, *Palestine,* 264–295. A classic is Yehoshua Porath, *The Palestinian Arab National Movement: From Riots to Rebellion* (London: Frank Cass, 1977). Some Zionist, crucially the head of the Jewish Agency, David Ben Gurion, tactically accepted the Peel Plan as a useful (though territorially to be expanded) step to independence: Yossi Katz, *Partner to Partition: The Jewish Agency's Partition Plan in the Mandate Era* (London: Frank Cass, 1998).

8. For sabras, see Oz Almog, *The Sabra: The Creation of the New Jew* (Berkeley: University of California Press, 2000). For mass politics, see Krämer, *Palestine,* 264–295 (the revolt); Zachary Lockman, *Comrades and Enemies: Arab and Jewish*

Workers in Palestine, 1906–1948 (Berkeley: University of California Press, 1996), esp. 148–265 (workers); Weldon Matthews, *Confronting an Empire, Constructing a Nation* (London: I. B. Tauris, 2006), esp. 44–74 (youth), 102–134 (the *Istiqlal* party); Christoph Schumann, *Radikalnationalismus in Syrien und Libanon: politische Sozialisation und Elitenbildung 1930–1958* (Hamburg: Deutsches Orient-Institut, 2001), esp. 192–229; Jennifer Dueck, *The Claims of Culture at Empire's End: Syria and Lebanon under French Rule* (Oxford: Oxford University Press, 2010), 183–228 (scouts); Keith Watenpaugh, *Being Modern in the Middle East: Revolution, Nationalism, Colonialism, and the Arab Middle Class* (Princeton, NJ: Princeton University Press, 2006), 255–298 (scouts). See also, on Egypt, Omnia El Shakry, "Youth as a Peril and Promise: the Emergence of Adolescent Psychology in Postwar Egypt," *IJMES* 43 (2011): 591–610.

9. For Yishuvi demographic data, see Itamar Rabinovich and Jehuda Reinharz, ed., *Israel in the Middle East: Documents and Readings* (Waltham, MA: Brandeis University Press, 2008), 571–572. For an overview, with a focus on immigration and its absorption, see Yoav Gelber, *Moledet Hadashah: 'Aliyat Yehudei Merkaz Europa u-Klitatam, 1933–1948* (Jerusalem: Ben Zvi, 1990). For land purchases, see Kenneth Stein, *The Land Question in Palestine* (Chapel Hill: University of North Carolina Press, 1984), 173–211. Land purchases accentuated, but were not the only reason for, the impoverishment of Palestinian peasants, more of whom now moved to towns where they "encountered social marginalization and often again abject poverty." Mahmoud Yazbak, "From Poverty to Revolt," *MES* 36 (2000): 94.

10. Quote: Geoffrey Wood and Forrest Capie, "Introduction," in *The Great Depression* (London: Routledge, 2011), 11. For the depression's causes, see ibid., 5; Harold James, "Economy," in *The Short Oxford History of Europe, 1900–1945*, ed. Julian Jackson (Oxford: Oxford University Press, 2002), 56. See also Robert Boyce, *The Great Interwar Crisis and the Collapse of Globalisation* (Basingstoke: Palgrave Macmillan, 2009), chs. 4–6; Ian Brown, ed., *Economies of Africa and Asia in the Inter-War Depression* (London: Routledge, 1989).

11. Jeffrey Taliaferro et al., eds., *The Challenge of Grand Strategy: The Great Powers and the Broken Balance between the World Wars* (Cambridge: Cambridge University Press, 2012), esp. Steven Lobell et al., "Introduction," 9–12, and Steven Lobell, "Britain's Grand Strategy during the 1930s," 147–170; Gerhard Weinberg, "How a Second World War Happened," in *A Companion to World War II*, ed. Thomas Zeiler et al. (Hoboken: Wiley-Blackwell, 2013), 1:13–28.

12. Quote: John Darwin, *The Empire Project: The Rise and Fall of the British World System, 1830–1970* (Cambridge: Cambridge University Press, 2009), 476. See also David Omissi, "The Mediterranean and the Middle East in British Global Strategy, 1935–1939," in *Britain and the Middle East in the 1930s*, ed. Michael Cohen and Martin Kolinsky (Basingstoke: Macmillan, 1992), 3–20; Martin Kolinsky, *Britain's*

*War in the Middle East* (New York: St. Martin's Press, 1999), 17–31, 93–103; Zamir, *Lebanon,* 180–183; Martin Thomas, *The French Empire between the Wars* (Manchester: Manchester University Press, 2005), 322–328; Massimiliano Fiore, *Anglo-Italian Relations in the Middle East, 1922–1940* (Surrey: Ashgate, 2010), focusing on Italian challenges.

13. The term "Arab World" itself, *al-'alam al-'arabi,* became current only from the mid-1940s. An influential Arab nationalist text of the 1930s, Georges Antonius, *The Arab Awakening: The Story of the Arab National Movement* (London: Hamish Hamilton, 1938), did not use the term, and "Arab" referred to the people of Bilad al-Sham and the Hijaz. However, see Syrian nationalist 'Abd al-Rahman Shahbandar, *al-Qadaya al-Ijtima'iyya al-Kubra fi al-'Alam al-'Arabi* (Cairo: Mattba'at al-Muqtattaf wa-l-Muqattam, 1936), 91, 95, including references to various Arab countries. Then again, most of his book's references concerned Syria.

14. Cyrus Schayegh, "'Who's Who in Syria?,'" *Middle East Critique* 20 (2011): 220; Shams al-Din al-Rifa'i, *Ta'rikh al-Sihafa al-Suriyya* (Cairo: Dar al-Ma'arif, 1969), 2:94, 118.

15. Quotes: 'Abd al-'Aziz al-'Azma, *Mir'at al-Sham* (London: Riyad al-Rayyis li-l-Kutub wa-l-Nashr, 1987), 30, 19, 48, 65; see also ibid., 96.

16. Quotes: Rifa'i, *Sihafa,* 2:102; and [Izz al-Din?] al-Tanukhi, "Athar al-Majma' fi Nahdat al-Sham al-'Ilmiyya wa-l-Adabiyya," *MMIA* 15, nos. 9–10 (1937): 379. See also 'Abd al-Rahman Shahbandar, *al-Thawra al-Suriyya al-Wataniyya* (Damascus: n.p., 1933), 34–36, 13–14; Rifa'i, *Sihafa,* 2:93, 95, 99–100, 102–104, 119, 122, 126.

17. Muhammad Tabbakh, "Dawr al-Kutub fi Halab Qadiman wa-Hadithan," *MMIA* 15, nos. 7–8 (1937): 299–310. See also "'Ahda'," *MMIA* 16, nos. 1–2 (1941): 4–5.

18. Quotes: Lutfi al-Haffar, *Dhikriyyat* (Damascus: Matabi' Ibn Zaydun, 1954), 1:233. See also ibid., 2:63; Samir Abdulac, "Damas: les années Ecochard," *Cahiers de la Recherche Architecturale* 11 (1982): 32–34; "Le musée de Damas," *Architecture d'aujourd'hui* 7, no. 3 (1936): 78–79; "L'urbanisme au Levant," *Architecture d'aujourd'hui* 16, no. 3 (1945): 119; Christel Braae, "The Early Museums and the Formation of the Publics," in *Middle Eastern Cities, 1900–1950,* ed. Hans Korsholm and Jakob Skoovgard-Petersen (Aarhus: Aarhus University Press, 2001), 123–125. The museum was built by Michel Ecochard, a young *Service des Antiquités* recruit who from 1932 restored numerous Syrian monuments, mainly in Damascus, and who was involved in city planning.

19. This was mirrored within Damascus, that is in its political cityscape: the Old City became less relevant. Philip Khoury, "Syrian Urban Politics in Transition: The Quarters of Damascus during the French Mandate," *IJMES* 16 (1984): 507–540; Haffar, *Dhikriyyat,* 1:226–229.

20. Khoury, *Syria,* 400–401, 410–412, 417–419; 'Abd al-Karim Rafiq, *Ta'rikh al-Jami'a al-Suriyya* (Damascus: Maktabat Nubil, 2004), 102–106, 154–170, 227–239; Shakib

Arslan, "Nahdat al-ʿArab al-ʿIlmiyya," *MMIA* 15, nos. 11–12 (1937): 415–443; Arslan, *al-Wahda al-ʿArabiyya* (Damascus: Maktabat ʿArafa, 1938). However, in the 1930s, Arslan published most of his books—like *Li-mada Taʾakhkhara al-Muslimun [Why Have the Muslims Fallen Back]* (Cairo: Matbaʿat al-Manar, 1930)—in Cairo.

21. Quotes: "La Ikrah fi al-Din," *RI* 1, no. 1 (1931): 14; editor's remark to article by Jamil Bek al-ʿAzm in *RI* 1, no. 1 (1931): 9; and Raghib al-ʿUthmani, "Yabqa al-Islam Ma Yabqa al-ʿArab," *RI* 1, no. 4 (1931): 123–127. See also "al-Islam min Nazar al-Zaʿim al-Hindusi Mahatma Gandi," *RI* 1, no.1 (1931): 24; Jamil Bek al-ʿAzm, "al-Imama wa-l-Khilafa," *RI* 1, no. 3 (1931): 84–90; Muhammad Saʿid al-ʿUrfi, "Min Aʿmal al-Mubashshirin," *RI* 2, no. 2 (1933): 124–129; Khoury, *Syria*, 608–609.

22. Quote: "Sheikh al-Muslimin," *al-Qabas*, June 30, 1935, 1. For Arslan, see Raja Adal, "Constructing Transnational Islam," in *Intellectuals in the Modern Islamic World*, ed. Stéphane A. Dudoignon et al. (London: Routledge, 2006), 176–210; William Cleveland, *Islam against the West* (Austin: University of Texas Press, 1985); and Götz Nordbruch and Umar Ryad, "Introduction: Toward a Transnational History of Islam and Muslims in Interwar Europe," in *Transnational Islam in Interwar Europe: Muslim Activists and Thinkers* (London: PalgraveMacmillan, 2014), 1–12. (Arslan's journal *La Nation Arabe*, published in France from 1930 to 1938, addressed especially Arab, but also non-Arab, Muslim concerns.) See also Johann Büssow, "Re-imagining Islam in the Period of the First Modern Globalization: Muhammad ʿAbduh and His *Theology of Unity*," in *A Global Middle East: Mobility, Materiality and Culture in the Modern Age, 1880–1940*, ed. Liat Kozma, Cyrus Schayegh, and Avner Wishnitzer (London: I. B. Tauris, 2014), 273–320.

23. Jean Hannoyer, "Amman, texte modèle, histoire rebelle?," in *Amman*, ed. idem and Seteney Shami (Beirut: CERMOC, 1996), 29, principally on postindependence Amman.

24. Hind Abu Shaʿr and Nufan al-Sawariyya, *ʿAmman fi al-ʿAhd al-Hashimi, 1916–1952* (Amman: Amanat ʿAmman, 2004), 8–11, 18–20, 105; Muhammad al-Kurdi, *ʿAmman* (Amman: Dar ʿAmmar, 1999), 114; Jane Hacker, *Modern ʿAmman: A Social Study* (Durham, NC: Durham Colleges in the University of Durham, 1960), 26–28, 31.

25. Quote: Hannoyer, "Amman," 26. See also Abla Amawi, "The Transjordanian State and the Enterprising Merchants of Amman," in *Amman*, ed. Jean Hannoyer, 115; Muhammad Rafiʿ, *Dhakirat al-Madina* (Amman: Markaz al-Husayn al-Thaqafi, 2002), 1:63; Abu Shaʿr, *ʿAmman*, 18–19, 42, 111; al-Kurdi, *ʿAmman*, 19–21, 104, 108, 183–218; Hacker, *ʿAmman*, 35, 41 (map), 57; Abd al-Rahman Munif, *Story of a City: A Childhood in Amman* (London: Quartet, 1996) (mainly for the 1940s); "Qudum Adib," *al-Urdunn*, September 22, 1935, 2 (Damascene Zaki al-Rajali), "Qudum Udaba," *al-Urdunn*, April 8, 1936, 2 (Beiruti Qustanti Zurayq; Jerusalemite Raʾif al-Khuri); Adib Ramadan, *Aina al-Rajul* (Damascus: n.p., 1940 [?]).

26. Quote: al-Kurdi, *ʿAmman*, 97 (similar: 102, 108, 109). For Amman as refuge, see ibid., 97, 115; Abu Shaʿr, *ʿAmman*, 19, 25; Rafiʿ, *Madina*, 62. For amenities, see Rafiʿ, *Madina*, 29, 115; al-Kurdi, *ʿAmman*, 99, 108.

27. Quotes: from multiple contracts reprinted in Rafiʿ, *Madina*, 185, 190, 191, 202, 203, 204, 206, 208, 211, 220, 229, and (Tabbaʿa) 205. For the naturalization list, see Abu Shaʿr, *ʿAmman*, 27–30.

28. Quotes: Beshara Doumani, "Archiving Palestine," *JQF* 36 (2009): 9; and Ihsan al-Nimr, *Taʾrikh Jabal Nabulus wa-l-Balqaʾ* (Damascus: Matbaʿat Ibn Zaydun, 1938), 113, 308, 8.

29. In his memoirs, Nimr claimed to have felt "strong zeal for Arab unity" and Salafi Islam; stated that he was actively involved in the Revolt, even had to flee to Amman and Damascus; but also reported "quarrelling" in 1929 with nonelite Nabulsi nationalists ʿIzzat Darwazeh, because Nimr wanted to confront only Britain, not "the Jews": Ihsan al-Nimr, *Mudhakkirat* (Nablus: n.p., 1970), 91, 44; also ibid., 48. He may have played up quarrelling because in 1970 Israel was already occupying the West Bank, including Nablus.

30. Quote: al-Nimr, *Taʾrikh*, 310, see also 9.

31. This problem was mirrored in other Palestinians' claim that Filastin was Arab, and counter-mirrored in Jewish texts excising non-Jews from Erets Israel. See Tarif Khalidi, "Palestinian Historiography: 1900–1948," *JPS* 10 (1981): 59–76.

32. Quotes: Al-Nimr, *Taʾrikh*, 36, 8, 10, see also 44, 309.

33. Quotes: ibid., 38, 8, 114, 8 (emphasis added), 8, see also 37–38, 113.

34. Quotes: ibid., 8. See also Krämer, *Palestine*, 257, 258; Beshara Doumani, *Rediscovering Palestine: Merchants and Peasants in Jabal Nablus, 1700–1900* (Berkeley: University of California Press, 1995); Yehoshua Porath, *The Emergence of the Palestinian-Arab National Movement, 1918–1929* (London: Frank Cass, 1974), 80–83.

35. Quotes: Akram Zuʿaytir, *Min Mudhakkirat Akram Zuʿaytir, 1909–1935* (Beirut: al-Muʾassasa al-ʿArabiyya li-l-Dirasat wa-l-Nashr, 1994), 1:340; and email in response to question by author, Dana Sajdi to author, November 29, 2013. For Nabulsi emigration and economy, see Mahmud Yazbak, *al-Hijra al-ʿArabiyya ila Haifa* (Nazareth: Maktabat al-Qabas, 1988), 90; Sarah Graham-Brown, "The Political Economy of the Jabal Nablus," in *Studies in the Economic and Social History of Palestine,* ed. Roger Owen (London: Macmillan, 1982), 88–176. For Nabulsi anti-Zionist action in the 1920s, see anonymous, "Nachklänge zum gehabten Erdbeben" (1927), AK436 / 9, Central Zionist Archives, Jerusalem (hereafter, CZA).

36. For Jaffa, see Ann Mosely Lesch, *Arab Politics in Palestine, 1917–1939: The Frustration of a Nationalist Movement* (Ithaca, NY: Cornell University Press, 1979), 106; ʿAwni ʿAbd al-Hadi, *Mudhakkirat* (Beirut, n.p., 2002), 163, 415; "Future of Arab Executive," *PP*, April 3, 1934, 2. For activities in other cities, see Zuʿaytir,

*Mudhakkirat,* 1:20, 26, 27, 33; Muhammad Darwazeh, *Mudhakkirat* (Beirut: Dar al-Gharb al-Islami, 1993), 1:528, 533.

37. Darwazeh, *Mudhakkirat,* vol. 1:522, 528, 533, 541–542; Zu'aytir, *Mudhakkirat,* 1:361.

38. Quotes: Zu'aytir, *Mudhakkirat,* 1:413, 402, 511; and "Nablus, 'Asimat Filastin," *al-Karmal al-Jadid,* February 15, 1936, 9. See also Darwazeh, *Mudhakkirat,* 1:588–590; "The wrong target," *PP,* May 14, 1933, 4; "Wadi Kabani," *PP,* March 9, 1933, 5; Zu'aytir, *Mudhakkirat,* 1:216, 359, 761–775; Lesch, *Palestine,* 105, 115; Krämer, *Palestine,* 256, 271, 274, 285; Ellen Fleischmann, *The Nation and 'Its' Women: The Palestinian Women's Movement, 1920–1948* (Berkeley: University of California Press, 2003), 121; "Arab Terrorists," *PP,* November 22, 1935, 9; "Da'wat Shaban Nablus," *al-Karmal al-Jadid,* November 2, 1935, 8; "Yawm 2 Nufimbir fi Nablus," *al-Karmal al-Jadid,* November 7, 1935, 3.

39. At the same time, though, the Ottoman state, Muslim associations, missionaries, and others opened secondary schools in cities across Bilad al-Sham, and Istanbul's state colleges attracted hundreds of Arabs, also from Ottoman Bilad al-Sham.

40. Quotes: Carla Eddé, *L'USJ* (Beirut: Presses de l'université Saint-Joseph, 2000), 32; and Stephen Penrose, *That They May Have Life* (New York: Trustees of the American University of Beirut, 1941), 214, 214 (quoting "AUB—Description of its Organization and Work" [1934], 45, 46). See also Penrose, *Life,* 128, 164, 331–333; "Registration," *Kulliyyah* 17, no. 3 (1931): 56–59; "Representatives," *Kulliyyah* 20, no. 3 (1934): 67; Eddé, *USJ,* 27. AUB's importance for the region is illustrated, too, by Nablus' *Najah* school concluding an agreement with AUB that allowed *Najah* pupils to enroll at the Beiruti college without an entrance examination: see Darwazeh, *Mudhakkirat,* 1:535.

41. Quotes: "Our Loss Is Princeton's Gain," *Kulliyyah* 13, no. 1 (1926): 24; and "Letter from Peretz Cornfeld," *Kulliyyah* 18, no. 2 (1931): 49. See also "Distinguished Visitors," *Kulliyyah* 17, no. 2 (1930): 44–45; "Obituaries etc.," *Kulliyyah* 12, no. 2 (1925): 51–53; and "Alumni News," *Kulliyyah* 18, no. 2 (1931): 51 (about Michelin). For an instance of Rockefeller support, see Cyrus Schayegh, "The Inter-war Germination of Development and Modernization Theory and Practice: Politics, Institution Building, and Knowledge Production between the Rockefeller Foundation and the American University of Beirut," *GG* 41 (2015): 649–684.

42. In parallel, there were Zionist-Maronite political ties. However, an official alliance never materialized. Even pro-Zionist Maronites understood that getting along with their Muslim compatriots—an approach that by 1943 would produce the informal National Pact—was a better long-term strategy than a non-Muslim axis with Palestine's Jews. See Laura Eisenberg, *My Enemy's Enemy: Lebanon in the Early Zionist Imagination, 1900–1948* (Detroit: Wayne State University Press, 1994), esp. 64, 97, 100.

43. For percentages of Jews at AUB, see "Registration"; Penrose, *Life,* 333. For contributions, see *Kulliyyah* 13, no. 2 (1926): 57 (Haifa); 15, no. 4 (1929): 106 (Jaffa; Haifa). In 1929, Mrs. Louis Cantor was elected an Alumnus official in the AUB Alumni Jerusalem branch, then headed by known Palestinian physician and ethnologist Tawfik Canaan: see "Nine Days in Palestine," *Kulliyyah* 15, no. 6 (1929): 167.

44. Quotes: "Modern Tendencies in Judaism," *Kulliyyah* 20, no. 3 (1934): 81–82; and Deborah Gershow to A.U.B. Hospital, n.p., December 5, 1951, box IV-208-1-6273, Pinchas Lavon (Labor Party) Archive, Tel Aviv. See also "Seventh Medical Conference," *Kulliyyah* 15, no. 8 (1929): 207; "Distinguished Visitors," *Kulliyah* 17, no. 1 (1930): 12 (Dr. and Mrs. Heinz Pflaum, Hebrew University). On a related note, Roth, "best remembered for his constant promulgation of the idea that reason was firmly linked to tolerance, . . . resigned his position in 1948 and returned to Britain because of the lack of condemnation of Jewish terrorism among the general Israeli population" (See Oona Ajzenstat, review of *Is There a Jewish Philosophy? Rethinking Fundamentals,* by Leon Roth, Humanities and Social Sciences Online, October 1999, www.h-net.org/reviews/showrev.php?id=3493).

45. Quotes: Alfred Bonné, "Memorandum" (1933), 1, A473/7, CZA; Bonné to Hakim, Jerusalem, August 12, 1935; and Dodd to Bonné, Beirut, February 10, 1936, both in A473/1, CZA. See also A. Yaari, ed., "Hebrew Fascicle," in *A Post-War Bibliography of the Near Eastern Mandates,* ed. Stuart C. Dodd (Beirut: AUB Press, 1932); B. Veicmanas, "Internal Trade," in *Economic Organization of Palestine,* ed. Sa'id Himadeh (Beirut: AUB Press, 1938), 343–384; Bonné, "Statement über die Lage des Wirtschaftsarchivs" (1935), A473/7, CZA; Himadeh to Bonné, Beirut, September 12, 1935, February 26, 1936, and December 31, 1936, and Dodd to Bonné, Beirut, July 7, 1936, all A473/1, CZA; Eisenberg, *Enemy,* 72. For the AUB Social Science Research Section, see Schayegh, "Inter-War Germination."

46. I infer Bonné's retraction from Himadeh saying that "according to your letter of June 28th, 1937, you are unable to agree to my reshaping the discussion": Himadeh to Bonné, Beirut, August 16, 1937, A473/1, CZA. See also Bonné to Vitales, Jerusalem, May 23, 1937, Himadeh to Viteles, Beirut, June 3, 1937, Himadeh to Bonné, Beirut, July 16, 1937, and Himadeh to Bonné, August 16, 1937, all in A473/1, CZA.

47. "100,000 Arabs Pay Homage to Feisal," *New York Times,* September 15, 1933, 12. For delegations from both Syria and Palestine congregating in Lydda to meet King Saud during a visit to Palestine, see "Emir Saud Arrives," *PP,* August 15, 1935, 5.

48. All quotes: "King Feisal Mourned," *PP,* September 14, 1933, 5.

49. Quote: "King Feisal Mourned," *PP,* September 14, 1933, 5. For Syria, see Khoury, *Syria,* 406–408, and Watenpaugh, *Being Modern,* 255–298. For Syria and Lebanon, see Dueck, *Claims,* 183–228. For Palestine, see Matthews, *Empire,* 44–74. For Transjordan, see Maan Abu Nowar, *The Development of Trans-Jordan, 1929–1939*

(Reading, UK: Ithaca Press, 2006), 184–187. For U.S.-European contexts, see Jon Savage, *Teenage. The Creation of Youth Culture* (New York: Viking, 2007), from the late nineteenth to the mid-twentieth centuries.

50. Israel Gershoni and James Jankowski, *Redefining the Egyptian Nation 1930–1945* (Cambridge: Cambridge University Press, 1995). An example was Taha Hussein, *Mustaqbal al-Thaqafa fi Masr* (Cairo: Matba'at al-Ma'arif wa-Maktabatuha, 1938), 519–533, a leading thinker of Egypt's nationhood and Euro-Mediterranean position, who however also emphasized Egypt's duty in fomenting Arab cultural cooperation.

51. Khoury, *Syria*, 400, 411; "Rihlat al-Kashshaf ila Dimashq," *al-Kashshaf* 1 (1927): 311–319, 372–378, 437–446; "Rihlat al-Kashshaf al-Muslim ila Halab-Mirsin," *al-Ahrar*, August 14, 1929, 6; "Rihlat al-Firqa al-'Abbasiyya ila al-Bilad al-'Alawiyya," *al-Kashshaf* 3 (1930): 307–309; Zu'aytir, *Mudhakkirat*, 1:263; "al-Ittihad Ruh al-Qawmiyya," *al-Kashshaf* 3 (1930): 414–419; Dueck, *Claims*, 199. Characteristically, the Beirut Scout Press printed the third edition of Akram Zu'aytir and Darwish Miqdadi, *Ta'rikhuna bi-Uslub Qasasi* [*Our History, Told as Stories*] (Beirut: n.p., [1st edition: Baghdad, 1935] 1939), a compilation of stories of the Arab nation's heroics. Not all *qawmiyyun* were youngsters, of course. The older *qawmi* generation, including many who had worked under Faisal in Damascus from 1918–1920 and decamped with him to Iraq, was active; indeed, some League of National Action founders had from the late 1920s, as students in Europe, been in contact with them. Conversely, not all youngster were *qawmiyyin*. Youth mobilization was common to most ideological, and some religious, groups. Syria for example featured a *Scout de France*, Christian paramilitary youth groups—in Aleppo, say, the Order of the White Badge—and the *Bloc*'s *watani* Nationalist Youth; some members of the small Lebano-Syrian communist party were youngsters, too.

52. Quotes: Qustantin Zurayq, *al-Wa'i al-Qawmi* 2nd ed. (Beirut: Dar al-Makshuf, 1940), 33, 22–23, 23, 21–22. The (relative) elder he singled out was the Egyptian Taha Hussein, whose famous *Mustaqbal al-Thaqafa fi-Misr*, ha, reflected the youth cult of the 1930s too, however: it was dedicated to university students and expressed the hope that they would be able to do for Egypt "what [their] elders had been unable to do."

53. Quotes: Edmond Rabbath, *Unité syrienne et devenir arabe* (Paris: Marcel Rivière, 1937), 33; and Taha al-Hashimi, *Mudhakkirat*, 2:40, quoted in Yehoshua Porath, *In Search of Arab Unity, 1930–1945* (London: Frank Cass, 1986), 149.

54. For Iraq, see Porath, *In Search of Arab Unity*, 1–3.

55. Quote: Ibid., 62, citing David Ben-Gurion, *My Talks with Arab Leaders* (Jerusalem: Keter, 1972). Given Ben-Gurion's own ideological position, his pronouncement should be taken with a large grain of salt, however. For the League of National Action, see *Bayan Mu'tamar al-Ta'sis li-'Usbat al-'Amal al-Qawmi*

*al-Mun'aqad fi Qarnayil 1933* (Damascus: n.p., n.d. [1933?]), 10–11, 26–27. The *qaw-miyyuns'* view finds its exact reverse in the Syrian Social Nationalist Party, which focused on Bilad al-Sham while counting areas beyond, specifically Iraq, as 'eastern' Syria: see Antun Sa'adah, *The Genesis of Nations [Nushu' al-Umam]* (Beirut: Department of Culture of the Syrian Social Nationalist Party, 2004 [Arabic, 1936]), 131, 186, 188, 191.

56. Quotes: Rabbath, *Unité*, 68, 65, 81, 81, 69, 70. See also Zu'aytir and Miqdadi, *Ta'rikhuna*. Further, in Syria' schools, a new history curriculum, in 1932, focused more heavily than before not only on the Arabs but on Bilad al-Sham, too: see Ulrike Freitag, *Geschichtsschreibung in Syrien* (Hamburg: Deutsches Orient-Institut, 1991), 128–130.

57. For an analysis, see Norman Burns, *The Tariff of Syria, 1919–1932* (Beirut: American Press, 1933), 68–74.

58. For neighbors' customs, see Frank Peter, *Les entrepreneurs de Damas: nation, impérialisme et industrialisation* (Paris: L'Harmattan, 2010), 193–210. A particularly painful case of non-Arab exports to the region was Japanese textile dumping. See Hiroshi Shimizu, "The Mandatory Power and Japan's Trade Expansion into Syria in the Inter-War Period," *MES* 21 (1985): 152–171; David Horowitz, *Aspects of Economic Policy in Palestine* (Tel Aviv: Hapoel Hazair, 1936), 29–41.

59. As Prelude 4 showed, despite expanding Hebrew Labor, the soaring Yishuv also attracted cheap Palestinian and non-Palestinian Arab labor.

60. Jacob Metzer, *The Divided Economy of Mandatory Palestine* (Cambridge: Cambridge University Press, 1998), 161–162; "Commerce extérieur," *CL*, September 24, 1937, 1; "Porte ouverte," *CL*, November 2, 1937, 2.

61. Zamir, *Lebanon*, 85; Carolyn Gates, *The Merchant Republic of Lebanon: Rise of an Open Economy* (London: I. B. Tauris, 1998), 26. See also Peter, *Entrepreneurs de Damas;* Geoff Schad, "Colonialists, Industrialists, and Politicians: the Political Economy of Industrialization in Syria, 1920–1954" (PhD diss., University of Pennsylvania, 2001).

62. Quotes: Elizabeth Thompson, *Colonial Citizens: Republican Rights, Paternal Privilege, and Gender in French Syria and Lebanon* (New York: Columbia University Press, 2000), 156; and Zamir, *Lebanon*, 85. See also Peter, *Entrepreneurs de Damas;* Schad, "Colonialists;" Gates, *Lebanon,* 24–29; 'Abdallah Hanna, *al-Haraka al-'Ummaliyya fi Suriyya va Lubnan, 1900–1945* (Damascus: Dar Dimashq, 1973), 124–129; Anonymous, "Working Conditions in Handicrafts and Modern Industry in Syria," *ILR* 29 (1934): 407–411; Catherine Coquery-Vidrovitch and Charles-Robert Ageron, *Histoire de la France coloniale* (Paris: Pocket, 1996), 3:27–50. For producers' protests, see "A'mal," *NSGTD* (1931): 103–109; "Taqrir," *NSGTD* (1932): 97–124; "Kalima li-Ra'is al-Ghurfa al-Tijariyya bi-Dimashq 'Arif Bik al-Halabuni," *NSGTD* (1934): 30–35. For Turkey and Egypt, see Dietmar Rothermund, *The*

*Global Impact of the Great Depression, 1929–1939* (London: Routledge, 1996), 75, 79.

63. The mushrooming volume of Palestine's overall imports shows also in the dropping ratio of (absolutely speaking rising) imports from Lebanon / Syria in Palestine's imports: while rising from 15 percent in 1929 and 1930 to 17 percent in 1931, it declined to 10 percent (1932), 8 percent (1933), and 7 percent (1934, 1935), then inched up to 10 percent in 1936 and 9 percent in 1937. For data, see "Échanges commerciaux," *CL*, June 22, 1937, 1; Peter, *Entrepreneurs de Damas*, 195; Government of Palestine, "Trade between Palestine and Syria, 1927–1937," 3, (February 1939), M51 / 26, Israel State Archives, Jerusalem (hereafter, ISA).

64. "Trade between Palestine and Syria, 1927–1937," 3; "Bulletin Hébdomadaire agricole et économique," July 13, 1935, 3, July 22, 1935, 2, and July 29, 1935, 2, box 863, versement (hereafter, v.1) / collection Mandat Syrie-Liban (hereafter, MSL), Archives du Ministère des Affaires Étrangères / Nantes, France (hereafter, MAE-Nantes), as well as September 10, 1936, box 864, v.1 / MSL, MAE-Nantes (the 160 tons included small exports to Transjordan); "La politique économique de la Palestine," *CL*, November 5, 1937, 2; Tnuva, report "Gidul Perot we-Yerakot," 5, (1937), S25 / 7378, CZA; Agricultural Workers Association (AWA), "Report on the tariff protection of Palestinian vegetables against Syrian imports," Kinnereth, January 13, 1939, M45 / 31, ISA; A. Marcus / Jewish Agency (hereafter, JA), research report, n.p., January 31, 1938, S54 / 327, CZA.

65. David Horowitz / JA, "Memorandum on the Palestine and Syrian trade agreement," October 1937, S54 / 200, CZA; Nahum Thischby (Jewish Agency [hereafter, JA] Trade and Industry department), memorandum to M. Brown (Secretary, Palestine-Syria Customs Agreement Revision Committee), October 10, 1937, 3, S54 / 200, CZA.

66. "Le développement du commerce de la Palestine," *CL*, October 5, 1937, 1; David Horowitz / JA, "Trade between Palestine and Syria" (August 1935), 7, CZA, S25–7377; Arie Shenkar, Manufacturers' Association of Palestine, to A. Kaplan / JA, Tel Aviv, November 7, 1935, S53 / 1288, CZA; David Horowitz and Rita Hinden, *Economic Survey of Palestine* (Tel Aviv: Economic Research Institute of the Jewish Agency for Palestine, 1938), 81.

67. The Yishuv's economic nationalism started under Ottoman rule in the sense that nonstate actors to advanced specifically Jewish agendas, which, however, were inscribed into an Ottoman imperial framework, as Chapter 2 and 3 showed. From the early 1880s, philanthropists like Baron Edmond de Rothschild underwrote First Aliyah (1882–1904) settlements like Rishon le-Zion. From the late 1900s the World Zionist Movement's Palestine Office under Arthur Ruppin used the Jewish National Fund and the Anglo-Palestine Company, a bank, to build Second Aliya (1905–1914) settlements like Degania. In the late 1910s, the arrival of a Big Power sympathetic to Zionism remolded actors, means and ends related to

economic nationalism. The British state, esteeming a Jewish-developed Palestine as a boon to its empire (Jacob Norris, *Land of Progress: Palestine in the Age of Colonial Development, 1905–1948* [Oxford: Oxford University Press, 2013]), assisted the Yishuv's nascent economy with policies including tariffs. Meanwhile, the now proto-state executive Jewish Agency deployed "national capital" to "operat[e] as a public sector," mainly buying agricultural land. With British state policy, this was "the major instrument . . . for the implementation of Zionist economic policy. . . . [T]he movement's economic aims were to create a national Jewish economy," which would develop Palestine as a whole and help build a state. Jacob Metzer, "The Concept of National Capital in Zionist Thought," *AAS* 11 (1977): 306. See also Barbara Smith, *The Roots of Separatism in Palestine: British Economic Policy, 1920–1929* (Syracuse: Syracuse University Press, 1993).

68. Quotes: Alfred Bonné, *Palästina: Land und Wirtschaft,* 2nd ed. (Leipzig: Deutsche Wissenschaftliche Buchhandlung, 1933), 271; Arie Krampf, "Reception of the Developmental Approach in the Jewish Economic Discourse of Mandatory Palestine, 1934–1938," *IS* 15, no. 2 (2010): 82; and Shlomit Mashkeh, "le-She'elat 'Atsma'utah shel Erets Israel," *MS* 4, nos. 2–3 (1936): 51–53 (title). See also Horowitz and Hinden, *Survey,* 9; Bonné, *Palästina,* 185; Arthur Ruppin, "Introduction," *BERI* 1, no. 1 (1937): 3; Ruppin, *Shloshim Shanot Biniyan be-Erets Israel* (Jerusalem: Shoken, 1937), 307, M33/22, ISA; the [Jewish] Manufacturers' Association of Palestine (hereafter, MAP), "Ha-Totsa'ot ha-Kalkaliot shel Yerid ha-Mizrah," *PN,* July 3, 1934, 3–4; Krampf, "Reception," 92–96; Abraham Ulitzur, *Ha-Hon ha-Le'umi u-Viniyan ha-Arets* (Jerusalem: Ha-Lishkah ha-Rashit shel Keren ha-Yesod, 1939). On Horowitz' industry-centered economic thought and its rise to dominance in the mid-1930s, see Arie Krampf, *Ha-Mekorot ha-Leumiim shel Kalkalat ha-Shuk* (Jerusalem: Magnes, 2015), 31–55.

69. [No first name] Froim, "'Totseret ha-Arets' we-ha-Sikuiim le-'Anafei Ta'asiyah Hadashim," *MS* 4, nos. 18–19 (1936): 275; Ruppin, *Shloshim Shanot,* 293; Horowitz and Hinden, *Survey,* 83; Mashkeh, "'Atsma'ut," 51.

70. Alfred Bonné, "Die Wirtschaftslage in Palästina" (1932), A473/1, CZA; Shlomit Mashkeh, "Matsavo we-Sikuiav shel Sahar ha-Huts ha-Erets-Israeli," *MS* 3, nos. 14–15 (1935): 244–251; Bonné, "Erets Israel we-ha-Mizrah ha-Karov," *MS* 4, nos. 16–17 (1936): 236–239; Froim, "'Totseret ha-Arets,'" 275; Ruppin, "[Journey to] Iraq" (1932), A107/286, CZA.

71. Quotes: JA memo, Nahum Thischby to Dr. Arlozoroff, 1, 3, Jerusalem, August 28, 1931, S25/7377, CZA; JA memo, Thischby to B. Joseph, November 24, 1938, S25/7378, CZA; David Horowitz, "Trade between Palestine and Syria," JA memo (1934), 7, 10, S25/7377, CZA; and Shenkar/MAP to A. Kaplan/JA, Tel Aviv, November 7, 1935, S53/1288, CZA.

72. Shenkar, MAP "Opening Address," 5, 6, Tel Aviv, September 26, 1934, M33/22, ISA; he used the word "boycott." For dumping, see Tnuva, "Gidul"; David Horo-

witz/JA, "Memorandum," 2, October 1937, S54/200, CZA; Froumine & Sons Ltd. to JA, Jerusalem, October 8, 1937, 2, S54/200, CZA.

73. Shenkar, Bi-Annual MAP address, October 1936, 9, M33/22, ISA; Jerusalem Union of Merchants to HC, Jerusalem, September 29, 1937, M46/13, ISA; Shenkar, MAP address, January 1938, 13, M33/22, ISA.

74. FO371/23278 and FO371/23279 (Syrian-Palestinian Customs Agreement 1939), The National Archives, Kew, UK (hereafter, TNA).

75. For the affected sectors, see Letter by Froumine; Horowitz/JA, "Memorandum," 2, 3; JA memo, Thischby to Shertok, Jerusalem, August 31, 1938, S25/7378, CZA; Thischby/JA to Adams/HC, Jerusalem, June 30, 1937, S25/7378, CZA; Tnuva, "Gidul"; 1939 AWA report. For Ata, see Ata to MAP, Haifa, October 12, 1938, S25/7378, CZA. For the CARC recommendations, see JA memorandum on Syro-Palestinian trade agreement revision, JA to HC, Jerusalem, November 7, 1938, S25/22390, CZA. For the JA, see ibid.; JA to HC, Jerusalem, February 23, 1939, S25/7378, CZA, mentioning also 1937 memos. For the MAP, see memorandum, MAP to HC economic advisor, April 10, 1938, quoted in MAP memo draft (n.d. [late 1938]), S25/7378, CZA.

76. For an overview, see Hisky Shoham, "'Buy Local' or 'Buy Jewish'?: Separatist Consumption in Interwar Palestine," *IJMES* 45 (2013): 469–489. For an account of success/failure, see Ha-Merkaz le-ma'an Totseret ha-Arets (MTA), *Din we-Heshbon 1936–1937* ([Jerusalem]: n.p., 1937).

77. "Wenige Zeilen," *SM* 9 (1939): 15; "Warum 'TNUVA'?," *SM* 4 (1937): 11.

78. Quotes: MTA, *Totseret ha-Arets le-'Ikeret ha-Bait* (n.p.: Hotsa'at ha-Merkaz le-ma'an Totseret ha-Arets, 1935), 2; and MTA, *Madrikh Totseret Erets Israel* (n.p.: Hotsa'at ha-Merkaz le-ma'an Totseret ha-Arets, 1936), 3. Image: *SM* 1 (1937): 4. For relevance of sales to Palestinians, see Z. Abramovitz, "Ha-Meshek ha-Yehudi we-ha-Tsarkhan ha-'Aravi," *MS* 8, nos. 11–12 (1940): 162–165.

79. "Local and Foreign Vegetables," *PP*, January 26, 1937, 11. For numbers, see also Tnuva, "Gidul," 1, 2; and, for an analysis from March 1936, Horowitz, *Aspects*, 55–68.

80. Quote: Tnuva, "Gidul," 2. See also "Vegetables Thrown into the River," *PP*, May 5, 1936, 12; "Palestine Riots Echo in Syria," *PP*, May 31, 1936, 6; "Food Cargo Held Up," *PP*, May 31, 1936, 7; "Syrians Attack Jewish Shipping," *PP*, June 7, 1936, 2; "The Rest of the Crime Sheet," *PP*, August 12, 1936, 5; "Awaiting Reinforcements," *PP*, September 22, 1936, 7.

81. By early 1937 Damascene merchants made another push, and in 1939 the *qawmi* paper *al-Jazira* regularly printed "boycott Zionist goods/fight its exports" slogan-ads. See "Boycottage," *CL*, January 1, 1937, 2; "Boycottage," *CL*, March 30, 1937, 1; and "Qata'u," *al-Jazira*, April 7, 1939, 4. Lebanese youth launched a respective call in 1939 and—another example—Jordanian merchants promised to use only port Jaffa for their transit goods. See "Khatar al-Bada'i' al-Sahiyuniyya,"

*al-Jazira,* March 14, 1939, 4; "Rasala al-Tujjar al-Urdunniyyin," *al-Urdunn,* July 30, 1939, 3.

82. "Production of Milk, Eggs and Vegetables on Jewish Farms," *BERI* 3, nos. 7–10 (1939): 164; "Wenige Zeilen," *SM* 10 (1939): 15; minutes, meeting between Horowitz and HC economic advisor Clauson, 2, February 22, 1939, S25/7378, CZA; memo "Trade and Politics," Shertok/JA to HC, 2, Jerusalem, July 4, 1939, S25/7378, CZA; CO323/1592/39, TNA (Palestine Food Supplies, Control, etc., 1938–1939).

83. "Taqrir," *NSGTD* (1932): 97–98; Arif al-Nakdi, "Muhasanat Iqamat al-Ma'rad," *NSGTD* 1936): 98–108; "Al-Nahda al-Sina'iyya fi al-Ma'amil al-Wataniyya," *al-Ahrar,* September 11 1929, 6 (a speech by Muhammad al-Za'im); "Ba'd Ma Ra'aitu fi Ma'rad Dimashq," *al-Ahrar,* September 14, 1929, 1; Haffar, *Dhikriyyat,* 1:144–147.

84. "Al-Ma'rad," *al-Ahrar,* September 21, 1929, 2. Similarly, see Lutfi Haffar, "Ihiya' al-Sana'i' al-Sharqiyya," *Qabas,* October 14, 1929, reprinted in *Dhikriyyat,* 1:155–159.

85. For economic nationalism, see Schad, "Colonialists," esp. 154–185, 283–312. For 1920s roots, see ibid., 282, 306. See also "Pavillon," *CL,* September 10, 1937, 1 (a critique from Beirut); "Wafah al-Wajih al-Siyyid 'Arif al-Halabuni," *NSGTD* (1937): 2–3; Haffar, *Dhikriyyat,* 2:159; "Hadith Ta'rikhi 'Azim," *NSGTD* (1936): 32–41; "Correspondence de Damas," *CL,* October 24, 1930, 1.

86. "Al-Ittifaq al-Tijari al-Jumruki baina al-Bilad al-Muntadaba wa-Masr," *NSGTD* (1930): 43–45; "A'mal," *NSGTD* 1931): 104; "al-Siyasa al-Jumrukiyya," *NSGTD* (1932): 99; "Nazra 'Amma hawla Wadi'at al-Bilad al-Iqtisadiyya," *NSGTD* (1934): 32, 37; al-Haffar, *Dhikriyyat,* 1:178, 200, 204, 249 (contemporary speeches and texts); "al-Sham, Bilad Siyaha," *NSGTD* (1936): 72; Mustafa Shahabi, "Ahamm Mawarid al-Tharwa fi Bilad al-Sham," *NSGTD* (1930): 23–45. Some Lebanese seconded Haffar's view: see "La Syrie, Carrefour commercial de l'Orient," *CL,* October 24, 1930, 1; "État économique de la Syrie et du Liban," *CL,* January 2, 1931, 1.

87. "Sakakir," *NSGTD* (1935): 54. (Indeed, by the mid-1930s Syria and Lebanon had become the leading export market for the Yishuvi confectionary factories Lieber and Elite. See "L'Industrie de Chocolat en Palestine," *CL,* November 12, 1937, 2, also reporting that Elite opened a store in Beirut.) "Bulletin Hébdomadaire économique et agricole" (August 18, 1934); Sûreté Générale (source Damas), "les commerçants et l'importation palestinienne," Beirut, December 5, 1934; Cabinet Politique, extrait du Bulletin Hébdomadaire, May 27, 1935; (French) Syrian Agriculture and Commerce Ministry advisor to HC, Damascus, February 18, 1935, 4; all in box 863, v.1/MSL, MAE-Nantes.

88. Quote: al-Haffar, *Dhikriyyat,* 1:255. For tariff protests, see "Rapport de la Chambre de Commerce de Damas sur le tarif douanier," *CL,* February 18, 1933, 1; "Nazra 'Amma," 35, 37; report, HC to French Foreign Ministry, Beirut, November 17, 1933, 5, box 863, v.1/MSL, MAE-Nantes. For anti-smuggling calls, see "La contrebande palestinienne en Syrie," *CL,* December 28, 1932, 2; "A'mal," *NSGTD* (1933): 31; "La

situation économique en Syrie," Damascus, May 8, 1934, 4, box 863, v.1/MSL, MAE-Nantes.

89. *Al-Ahrar,* September 27, 1929, 5.

90. "Thalathun Alfan Tatathaharun fi Dimashq," *al-Ahrar,* August 29, 1929, 1; "Mutha-hara fi Beirut," *al-Ahrar,* August 29, 1929, 4; "Waqʿ al-Hawadith fi ʿAmman," *al-Ahrar,* August 29, 1929, 4; "Ihtijajat," *al-Ahrar,* August 31, 1929, 4; Nida' Lajnat Beirut li-Muʿunat Filastin," *al-Ahrar,* September 7, 1929, 4; "Li-Beyik ya Filastin," *al-Ahrar,* September 28, 1929, 5 (Aleppo); "Nakbat Filastin," *al-Ahrar,* September 6, 1929, 5; "Qataʿu al-Bada'iʿ al-Sahiyuniyya," *al-Ahrar,* September 19, 1929, 5; "Ila Ashab al-Maʿamil al-Wataniyya," *al-Ahrar,* September 25, 1929, 5. Nakba/1948: Qunstantin Zurayq, *Maʿna al-Nakba* (Beirut: Dar al-ʿIlm li-l-Malayin, 1948).

91. For a fascinating critique (and exhortation), see Arslan, *Muslimun,* 18–19.

92. Quote: JA translation, into Hebrew, of a CL article published January 24, 1934, S25/7377, CZA. See also Customs/Excise/Trade to Chief Secretary/HC, February 9, 1934, M32/12, ISA.

93. Quotes: Shenkar, MAP address, 5, 6, Tel Aviv, September 26, 1934, M33/22, ISA; and Shenkar, MAP address, 9, October 14–15, 1936, M33/22, ISA. See also "Ha-ʿIton 'La Syrie' be-Beirut Metif Musar le-Mahrimei ha-Yerid be-Tel Aviv," *Palnews,* March 13, 1934, 4–5; "Economic Nonsense," *PP,* August 11, 1936, 10; Peter, *Entrepreneurs de Damas,* 196.

94. Quotes: Deborah Bernstein and Badi Hasisi, "'Buy and Promote the National Cause': Consumption, Class Formation and Nationalism in Mandate Palestinian Society," *NN* 14 (2008): 142, quoting *Filastin,* January 10, 1937; and "Man la Ard lahu la Watan lahu," *al-Karmal al-Jadid,* #1838 (1934), 16. See also "al-Samasira fi Qada' Beisan," *al-Karmal al-Jadid,* February 8, 1935, 4; "al-Shirka al-Ziraʿiyya," *al-Karmal al-Jadid,* February 8, 1935, 6; "Jamʿiyyat al-Nahda al-Iqtisadiyya al-ʿArabiyya," *al-Karmal al-Jadid,* March 28, 1936, 1.

95. For statistics, see Metzer, *Palestine,* 105.

96. Shenkar/MAP to A. Kaplan/JA, Tel Aviv, 3, November 7, 1935; Thischby/JA to Kaplan/JA, Jerusalem, January 6, 1936; Thischby/JA to Brown/CARC secretary, Jerusalem, October 10, 1937; all in S53/1288, CZA; Horowitz, memorandum "Trade and Politics," 3, attached to Shertok/JA to HC, Jerusalem, July 4, 1939, S25/7378, CZA (referencing pre-1936 Palestinian calls for a treaty revision).

97. "Actions," *CL,* August 16, 1932, 2; "Souscription," *CL,* August 30, 1932, 2; "Société des Conserves," *CL,* November 12, 1932, 2 (Lebanese, Iraqis, and others bought shares, too); article by a Palestinian merchant in *Ayyam,* quoted in "Extrait de la revue de presse arabe de Damas du 4/1/33," box 862, v.1/MSL, MAE-Nantes.

98. Quotes: Horowitz, "Trade and Politics," 4; "Initiative," *CL,* December 9, 1938, reprint included in S25/7378, CZA; and *Filastin,* June 9, 1939, Hebrew translation in S25/7378, CZA.

99. Quote: "Rapport du deuxième congrès des chambres de commerce des états sous Mandat français," pt. 2 ('le tariff douanier'), 4, box 717, v.1 / MSL, MAE-Nantes. For details, see Asher Kaufman, *Contested Frontiers in the Syria-Lebanon-Israel Region* (Baltimore, MD: Johns Hopkins University Press, 2014), 78–94; Cyrus Schayegh, "The Many Worlds of Abud Yasin, or: What Narcotics Trafficking in the Interwar Middle East Can Tell Us about Territorialization," *AHR* 116 (2011): 273–306, including files from the Mandate Legal Documents Collection, Historical Documents Collection (Markaz al-Watha'iq al-Ta'rikhiyya), Damascus, Syria. See also Malek Abisaab, *Militant Women of a Fragile Nation* (Syracuse, NY: Syracuse University Press, 2010).

100. Quote: UK Department of Overseas Trade / G.T. Havard, *Report on Economic and Commercial Conditions in Syria and the Lebanon* (London: His Majesty's Stationery Office, 1936), 21, 22. See also Mahmoud Hreitani and Jean-Claude David, "Souks traditionnels et centre moderne: éspaces et pratiques à Alep," *BEO* 36 (1984): 1–78; "al-Mu'ahadat," *al-Ahrar,* July 6, 1929, 4; "Tujjar Halab," *al-Ahrar,* July 6, 1929, 5; Burns, *Tariff,* 52–66;

101. Quotes: Peter, *Entrepreneurs de Damas,* 205, 206–207, 206 (emphasis added). See also Schad, "Colonialists," 261; "Bulletin hebdomadaire économique et agricole," March 5, 1935, 2, and July 13, 1935, 1, box 863, v.1 / MSL, MAE-Nantes; Havard, *Report,* 23. See also, for Aleppine contacts with Damascus, "Muqabalat Hadrat Ma'mur Iqtisad Halab," *NSGTD* (1933): 60–61.

102. In the combined Lebanese / Syrian exports to Palestine, Damascus accounted for a whopping 41 percent, Aleppo and Alexandretta together for 16.5 percent: see Peter, *Entrepreneurs de Damas,* 196.

103. Quote: Note, Services spéciaux, Deir al-Zor, September 26, 1935, box 863, v.1 / MSL, MAE-Nantes. See also Peter, *Entrepreneurs de Damas,* 207.

104. Quote: (French) Syrian Agriculture and Commerce Ministry advisor to HC, 2, Damascus, February 18, 1935, box 863, v.1 / MSL, MAE-Nantes. For the statistic, see ibid., 4. See also "Muhammad Hasan," *al-Urdunn,* February 25, 1937, 2; "Qudum Tajir Wajih," *al-Urdunn,* March 2, 1937, 2. 'Local' Jordanians and Palestinians also founded factories: see "Ma'amil fi Suwailah," *al-Urdunn,* June 5, 1937, 8, on (Cherkess?) Shams al-Din Sami (Gharanduqa?), among others.

105. "Mukatabat," *NSGTD* (1934): 44; "Bulletin hebdomadaire économique et agricole," Damascus, June 21, 1934, box 863, v.1 / MSL, MAE-Nantes; "Kitab Mudiriyyat Jamarik Sharq al-Urdunn li-l-Ghurfa al-Tijariyya fi Dimashq," *NSGTD* (1933): 86–87.

106. Quotes: "Séparation économique," *CL,* October 27, 1937, 1; and Gates, *Lebanon,* 27. See also "Muhafiz Dimashq," *Beirut,* January 12, 1937, 4; "Rusum al-Dukhuliyya," *Beirut,* July 15, 1938, 4; "L'avenir économique du Liban: Déclarations de Omar bey Daouk, president de la chambre de commerce et d'industrie de Beyrouth," *CL,*

December 22, 1937, 1–2; "A propos des déclarations de Omar bey Daouk au 'Jour': Commerce ou production? Un problème mal posé," *CL*, December 25, 1937, 1; Gates, *Lebanon*, 33; Souraya Kanaan Abi Fares, "Le commerce de Beyrouth (1920–1939)" (PhD diss., Paris IV, 1999), 419.

107. Quote: André Geiger, *Le Liban et la Syrie* (Grenoble: B. Arthaud, 1932), quoted in Samir Kassir, *Beirut*, trans. M. B. DeBevoise (Berkeley: University of California Press, 2010), 301. See also May Davie, *Beyrouth et ses faubourgs (1840–1940): Une intégration inachevée* (Beirut: CERMOC, 1996), 84–86; Kassir, *Beirut*, 290; Khalid al-Lahham, *Beirut fi al-Dhakira al-Sha'biyya* (Beirut: Sharikat Khalid al-Lahham, 1997), 1:147; Traffic de stupéfiant to Directeur, Beirut, March 12, 1936, box 6, v.1/MSL, MAE-Nantes; Directeur SG, "Renseignements"#473 i/9, Beirut, July 19, 1926, box 854, v.1/MSL, MAE-Nantes; "Ghaniyya wa-Dhat Ba'al," *al-Ahrar*, December 22, 1931, 4; Pierre Bonardi, *L'imbroglio syrien* (Paris: Rieder, 1927), 131, 136.

108. Quote: "al-Yahud 'Asimatuhum Til Abib," *al-Karmal al-Jadid*, February 8, 1936, 1. For all statistics in this and the previous paragraph, see A. Gertz, *Statistical Handbook of Jewish Palestine* (Jerusalem: Department of Statistics, Jewish Agency for Palestine, 1947), 220–221, 280. See also Maoz Azariahu, *Tel Aviv: Mythography of a City* (Syracuse, NY: Syracuse University Press, 2010), 63–65; Mark Levine, *Overthrowing Geography: Jaffa, Tel Aviv, and the Struggle for Palestine, 1880–1948* (Berkeley: University of California Press, 2005), 84–85.

109. Horowitz, *Aspects*, 141; May Seikaly, *Haifa: Transformation of a Palestinian Arab Society, 1918–1939* (London: I. B. Tauris, 1995), 47, 49, 86, 101–102.

110. Quotes: Norris, *Land of Progress*, 134, 135, 134. See also Seikaly, *Haifa*, 110–111; Bernstein, *Boundaries*, 148.

111. Gates, *Lebanon*, 31–32; Marlène Ghorayeb, "L'urbanisme de la ville de Beyrouth sous le mandat français," *RMMM* 73 (1994): 331, 334; Jacques de Monicault, *Le port de Beyrouth* (Paris: Librairie technique et économique, 1936), 41–42.

112. Four quotes: Norris, *Land of Progress*, 118, 112, 112; and Seikaly, *Haifa*, 67. See also Husni Sawwaf, "Transport and Communication," in Himadeh, *Economic Organization of Palestine*, 337.

113. For the previous two paragraphs, see J. H. Bamberg, *The History of the British Petroleum Company* (Cambridge: Cambridge University Press, 1994), 2:, 155–171, 174–179. Critiques: Alfred Bonné, "The Concessions for the Mosul-Haifa Pipeline," *Annals of the American Academy of Political and Social Science* 164 (1932): 124–126; David Horowitz, "La politique économique de la Palestine," *CL*, November 5, 1937, 2; speech by S. Natanson, Haifa Jewish Chamber of Commerce and Industry head, April 6, 1937, 5, M32/14, ISA. The 1928 agreement gave Dutch Shell 23.75 percent, too, and a private magnate, Calouste Gulbenkian, 5 percent.

114. Quotes: Services Économiques, "Route automobile Beyrouth-Baghdad," Beirut, March 13, 1926; HC representative Damascus to HC/Beirut, Damascus,

December 18, 1932; and "Note sur le transit Damas-Baghdad" (June 3, 1937), attached to HC/de Martel to French Foreign Ministry, Beirut, December 3, 1937, all in box 702, v.1/MSL, MAE-Nantes. See also "Beyrouth-Téhéran," *CL,* June 26, 1925, 1; "Rapport sur la question des transports vers l'Irak et la Perse," February 4, 1926, box 702, v.1/MSL, MAE-Nantes; a series of exchanges in the British HC in Jerusalem in 1933/1934, especially note #164, March 16, 1934, M86/48, ISA; Note, HC/Cabinet Politique, Beirut, September 8, 1934, box 703, v.1/MSL, MAE-Nantes; arrêté 221/LR, September 26, 1935, box 702, v.1/MSL, MAE-Nantes; Note, Affaires Économiques, Beirut, July 15, 1937, 3, box 702, v.1/MSL, MAE-Nantes.

115. Note, Service Politique for HC/Affaires Financières, Beirut, August 27, 1931, box 699, v.1/MSL, MAE-Nantes; "Mu'ahada Tijariyya," *al-Ahrar,* April 16, 1930, 4; "'Aqd Ittifaq Jumruki ma'a al-Bilad al-Turkiyya," *al-Ahrar,* December 12, 1932, 5; note 1772/D (July 5, 1929) mentioned in Douanes to HC/Bureau Diplomatique, Beirut, February 13, 1930, box 699, v.1/MSL, MAE-Nantes; "La direction de la Douane palestinienne," *CL,* January 4, 1933, 2; Peter, *Entrepreneurs de Damas,* 209; "Inauguration de la zone franche," *AF* 318 (1934): 97; "Tabadul al-Bada'i' bainana wa-baina Iran," *al-Ahrar,* August 13, 1935, 4; arrêté 90/LR, April 24, 1935, box 699, v.1/MSL, MAE-Nantes; HC to Ministère Étrangère, Beirut, December 3, 1937, box 702, v.1/MSL, MAE-Nantes.

116. The latter included tireless calls for lowering customs on finished goods, to combat smuggling from northern Palestine: see Economic Recovery Committee (ERC) to HC, 2, Beirut, March 28, 1935, box 863, v.1/MSL, MAE-Nantes; telegram, ERC to HC, Beirut, May 23, 1935, box 863, v.1/MSL, MAE-Nantes. A first success came already in 1934: see HC/Affaires Économiques, "Situation économique générale des Territoires sous Mandat français en 1934," 14, box 863, v.1/MSL, MAE-Nantes.

117. Both quotes: Norris, *Land of Progress,* 121. For Beirut, see the last endnote, as well as Douanes to HC/Bureau Diplomatique, Beirut, February 13, 1930, box 699, v.1/MSL, MAE-Nantes; "Ijtima' Iqtisadi fi al-Mufawadiyya," *al-Ahrar,* February 14, 1930, 4; "Commerce de transit," *CL,* September 13, 1932, 1; "Le port de Beyrouth menacé," *CL,* June 15, 1937, 1.

118. For tribes, see boxes 554, 565, 990, 995, v.1/MSL, MAE-Nantes. For diseases and pests, see "al-Ta'un al-Baqari fi al-'Iraq," *al-Ahrar,* September 3, 1930, 4; "al-Tadabir al-Sahhiyya 'ala al-Hudud," *al-Ahrar,* July 9, 1930, 4; "Mukafahat al-Jarad," *al-Ahrar,* June 11, 1931, 4; "Mu'tamar al-Jarad al-Duwali fi al-Qahira," *al-Ahrar,* February 7, 1936, 4; "Mu'tamar al-Jarad al-Duwali," *al-Ahrar,* September 14, 1938, 5.

119. Quote: in Palestine Police, "Secret Memorandum on recent activity of the Palestine Communist Party," 1930, 21, attached to Police to HC, Jerusalem, June 17, 1930, CO733/189/4, TNA. See also Martin Thomas, *Empires of Intelligence: Security Services and Colonial Disorder after 1914* (Berkeley: University of

California Press, 2008), 19; Sondra Rubenstein, *The Communist Movement in Palestine and Israel, 1919–1984* (Boulder, CO: Westview Press, 1985), 221–223; Najati Sidqi, *Mudhakkirat* (Beirut: Mu'assasat al-Dirasat al-Filastiniyya, 2001), 109–153; Khalid Bikdash, *al-ʿArab wa-l-Harb al-Ahliyya fi Isbania* (Damascus: n.p., 1937), including a chapter on Morocco, 71–78; Joseph Berger-Barzilai, *Ha-Tragediah shel ha-Mahapekhah ha-Sovietit* (Tel Aviv: ʿAm ʿOved, 1968), 13–89, on trips to Moscow in the 1920s. A recent attempt to splice local with Moscow-centered readings of interwar communist action is Joachim Häberlen, "Between Global Aspirations and Local Realities: the Global Dimensions of Interwar Communism," *JGH* 7 (2012): 415–437.

120. Quotes: Thomas, *Empires of Intelligence,* 93, 93. See also Martin Thomas, "French Intelligence-Gathering in the Syrian Mandate," *MES* 38 (2002): 5, 24; Johan Franzén, *Red Star over Iraq* (London: Hurst, 2011), 36–37; "Orientalisme révolutionnaire," *AF* 287 (1931): 54–58; "Extrémistes et communists en Syrie," *AF* 303 (1932): 308–309; "Les intrigues soviétiques en Extrême Orient," *AF* 306 (1933): 7–14; Niqula Shawi, *Tariqi ila al-Hizb* (Beirut: Dar al-Farabi, 1984), 288; Police to HC, Jerusalem, June 17, 1930, CO733/189/4, TNA; Palestine Police, "Secret Memorandum," 34.

121. The treaty's articles 1, 4, 5 gave Britain the right, respectively, to expect "full and frank consultation between [it and Iraq] in all matters of foreign policy which may affect their common interests": to militarily use Iraq's territory during a war; and to expect "the permanent maintenance and protection in all circumstances of [its] essential communications" and keep air bases; and according to annex clauses 1, 5, and 7, Britain could, respectively, keep some troops in Hinaidi and Mosul until 1935; instruct Iraq's military officers, supply their army, and advise them; and have its troops transit Iraq. Quotes: "Anglo-Iraqi Treaty (1930)," Wikipedia, last modified April 22, 2016, http://en.wikipedia.org/wiki/Anglo-Iraqi_Treaty_%281930%29.

122. For Iraq/League, see Susan Pedersen, "Getting out of Iraq," *AHR* 115 (2010): 975–1000. In that meeting, in January 1930, French Mandate officials, Damascus-based British diplomats, and a British Iraq official met in Damascus to discuss trans-desert motor traffic management. Their recommendations, which were implemented, included prescribed travel routes and times, laissez-passers, technical specifications for cars, and a direct wireless link between Baghdad, Rutbah, Damascus, and Amman Police for the continuous exchange of information about traffic-related problems: see "Procès verbal de la conférence syro-irakienne tenue à Damas les 22 et 23-I-30," box 702, v.1/MSL, MAE-Nantes, and "Conférence syro-irakienne sur le contrôle du traffic de la route Damas-Baghdad," box 703, v.1/MSL, MAE-Nantes.

123. Quote: SG, report #5679, Beirut, July 5, 1939, box 855, v.1/MSL, MAE-Nantes. See also Schayegh, "Territorialization," 296–299 (297n97 for details on police coordination).

124. In 1935, France and Britain even discussed regularizing the (provisional) extradition agreement of 1921: see "Draft Convention for the Extradition of Offenders," CO733/274/8, TNA. For tribal courts, see box 565, v.1/MSL, MAE-Nantes, e.g. Contrôle Bedouin, "Réglement des litiges entre nomades et entre nomades et sém dentaires de ces États de 1927 à 1932" (1932); see also box 955, v.1/MSL, MAE-Nantes. Related is CO733/205/12, TNA. Moreover, France and Britain in 1935 held a conference to discuss reopening the Hijaz Railroad south of Ma'an. See Jane Priestland, ed., *Records of Syria* (London: Archives Edition, 2005), 3:459–482; "Procès verbal de la conférence," 1935, box 52, v.2/MSL, MAE-Nantes. (The plan failed.)

125. Quotes: *Agreement between Palestine and Syria and the Lebanon* (London: H.M. Stationary, 1927), 4; author, interview with Dahir Madi (b. 1939, Marjayoun), September 9, 2008, Marjayoun; author, interview with Abu Rafiq Sabeq (b. 1907, Hurfesh), April 19, 2010, Hurfesh, Israel; and author, interview with 'Ali 'Abd al-Hassan Awade (b. 1921, Khiam), September 10, 2008, Khiam. (SAA, Brigade du Liban du Sud, "Rapport mensuel sur la contrabande," 2, February 28, 1945, Box 101, MAE-Nantes, mentions the same names in an almost identical story for 1945.) For laissez-passer issuance and interruptions, see, e.g., "'Ala al-Hudud," *al-Ahrar*, March 26, 1931, 5. For the other oral history sources, see author, interviews with Naziha Farhat (b. 1936, Bint Jbeil), September 12, 2008, Beirut; and with Muhammad Farhat (b. 1923, Barajit), September 12, 2008, Beirut. For identity card controls, see also "Mufattishiyyat al-Darak al-'Amma Tasdaru Taqriran," *Beirut*, September 16, 1936, 4; "Qadiyyat Ijtiaz al-Hudud," *al-Ahrar*, July 3, 1932, 4. "Mukhalafat Ittifaq al-Hudud," *al-Ahrar*, March 23, 1931, 5, complained that British refused to fully implement the 1926 treaty. "Jawazat al-Hudud," *al-Ahrar*, December 9, 1930, 2, informed the public that the HC reasserted valid *laissez-passers* according to the 1926 agreement and added regulations. The penalties foreseen opened the door for abuse; for a complaint, see, e.g., SS, Liban Sud, Bulletin d'information hébdomadaire #10, March 5–11, 1934, 8, box 1875, v.1/MSL, MAE- Nantes.

126. "Tawqif Ijazat al-Ru'a," *al-Ahrar*, December 24, 1930, 4; HC/Relations extérieures to HC's Lebanese government delegate, Beirut, September 15, 1933, box 857, v.1/MSL, MAE-Nantes; Conseiller administratif du Liban Sud (hereafter, CALS) to HC, Sidon, June 18, 1938, box 652, v.1/MSL, MAE-Nantes.

127. Mukhtar of Meiss to Services Spéciaux (SS), May 6, 1933; note, SS, Marjayoun, May 8, 1933; note, Service Général, Marjayoun, May 23, 1933; British General Consulate to HC, Beirut, June 30, 1933; note, Police Sanitaire Vétérinaire, Beirut, July 1, 1933; note, HC, Beirut, July 1, 1933; note, Police Sanitaire Vétérinaire, Beirut, July 11, 1933; HC/Cabinet Politique to French ambassador Jerusalem, Beirut, July 19, 1933; all in box 657, v.1/MSL, MAE-Nantes.

128. Note, SS, Marjayoun, May 8, 1933, box 657, v.1/MSL, MAE-Nantes; "Agreement between the territories of Syria and the Lebanon and Palestine to facilitate the movement of certain animals from one territory into the other for purposes of

grazing and watering," January 3, 1934, DO 118/69/5, TNA. The agreement had to be, and was, renewed yearly.

129. For translation to French, see "Traduction de [sic] chansons populaires," 2, attached to CALS to HC, Sidon, December 12, 1938, box 652, v.1/MSL, MAE-Nantes. (Seven hundred and eight copies were confiscated in Sidon in 1938.)

130. Already in 1936, France started to cement its border disposition to address "inexistent . . . surveillance": see Note, CALS, Sidon, February 22, 1936, 4, box 422, v.1/MSL, MAE-Nantes.

131. SS Kuneitra to SS Damascus, Kuneitra, December 19, 1937; information, CALS, Sidon, November 25, 1937, June 10, 1938; Compte rendu, Gendarmérie Libanaise, 3, June 5, 1938; British General Consul Beirut to Kieffer, Beirut, October 27, 1938; note, HC/Cabinet Politique, Beirut, June 7, 1938; président du conseil ministère de la défense nationale to Ministre des Affaires Étrangères, Paris, April 28, 1939; HC Syrian delegate to HC, Damascus, May 31, 1939; HC délégué général to Troupes du Levant commander, Beirut, September 3, 1938; HC/Cabinet Politique to Ministre des Affaires Étrangères, Beirut, June 7, 1938 (all documents in box 653, v.1/MSL, MAE-Nantes); two letters, HC/Cabinet Politique to French General Consul in Jerusalem, Beirut, January 16, 1939, and n.d. [January 1939], box 652, v.1/MSL, MAE-Nantes.

132. For the brushing off of protests, see Information, CALS, Sidon, November 19, 1938, and HC/Cabinet Politique to French Consul General Jerusalem, Beirut, January 16, 1939, both in box 652, v.1/MSL, MAE-Nantes. For brutal tactics, see Matthew Hughes, "The Banality of Brutality," *English Historical Review* 124 (2009): 313–354; Information, CALS, Sidon, November 26, 1938, box 652, v.1/MSL, MAE-Nantes, about Ulster Fusiliers' cold-blooded execution of peasants in Zouk el Tahtani and Naamé. For other measures (barbed wire fence construction and its mining and air force and artillery use), see Informations, CALS, Sidon, May 5, June 4, July 12, 19, 21, 1938, March 6, 1939, all in box 652, v.1/MSL, MAE-Nantes.

133. Note, SS, Kuneitra, October 9, 1938, box 653, v.1/MSL, MAE-Nantes; Note, "Trafic d'armes & de munitions de guerre," HC Syrian delegate to HC/Cabinet Politique, Damascus, October 24, 1938, box 652, v.1/MSL, MAE-Nantes; Informations, CALS, Sidon, June 16, 21, 24, August 31, 1938, all box 652, v.1/MSL, MAE-Nantes; Telegram, HC to MAE, Beirut, August 27, 1938, box 653, v.1/MSL, MAE-Nantes; Information, CALS, Sidon, January 6, 1939, box 652, v.1/MSL, MAE-Nantes; CALS to HC, Beirut, November 14, 1938, box 855, v.1/MSL, MAE-Nantes.

134. Informations, CALS, Sidon, May 3, 12, June 21, 24, November 19, 26, December 9, 1938, box 652, v.1/MSL, MAE-Nantes.

135. Information, 3, CALS, February 22, 1939, box 652, v.1/MSL, MAE-Nantes, quoting the Galilee district officer, said it indeed succeeded—but this may also be a sign of overall repression, that is fewer attempts to cross the border.

136. Quote: author, interview with Tohme Maghzal (b. 1928, Kafr Bir'im), April 28, 2010, Jish, Israel. Information, CALS, Sidon, June 18, 1938; British General Consul Beirut to French HC, Beirut, January 16, 1939; HC/Cabinet Politique to French General Consul in Jerusalem, Beirut, September 3, 1938; French General Consul in Jerusalem to HC, Jerusalem, October 7, 1938; Information, CALS, Sidon, February 22, 1939; British HC to French General Consul Jerusalem, Jerusalem, September 30, 1939; HC Syria Delegate to HC, Damascus, April 17, 1940; Douanes to Bureau Politique, Beirut, November 23, 1940; all in box 652, v.1/MSL, MAE-Nantes.

## Prelude 5. Eliahu Rabino's War

1. From Odessa, where they had been wholesale merchants, the Kurises moved to Jaffa in the early 1920s, and eventually opened a branch also in Jerusalem: author, interview with Shmuel Rabino (born 1924, Zaronia), April 15, 2010, Haifa.
2. Ibid.

## 5. Empire Redux

1. That the Middle East and North Africa (MENA) had a relatively "good" war is perhaps the reason why it is understudied and why there is no MENA World War II New Military History focusing on nonmilitary/diplomatic aspects. For an assessment of the latter, see Peter Paret, "The New Military History," *Parameters* 21 (1991): 10–18. For other theaters, see Thomas Zeiler, "Introduction," in *A Companion to World War II* (Hoboken, NJ: Wiley-Blackwell, 2013), 1:2; David Reynolds, "World War II and Modern Meaning," *DH* 25 (2001): 457–458.
2. For the war in MENA, see Gerhard Weinberg, *A World at Arms: A Global History of World War II* (Cambridge: Cambridge University Press, 2005), 348–362, 419–420, 431–447; Antony Beevor, *The Second World War* (New York: Weidenfeld & Nicolson, 2012), 374–386, 391–395, 410–416; Barbara Tomblin, "The Naval War in the Mediterranean," and Simon Davis, "The Middle East and World War II," both in Zeiler, *Companion to World War II*, 1:222–242, 278–295; Martin Kolinsky, *Britain's War in the Middle East: Strategy and Diplomacy, 1936–42* (New York: St. Martin's Press, 1999), 93–219; Keith Jeffrey, "The Second World War," in *The Oxford History of the British Empire,* ed. Judith Brown and Wm. Roger Louis (Oxford: Oxford University Press, 1999), 5:316–318. British naval operations knew a Mediterranean and an Indian Ocean command, the former headquartered in Alexandria and represented in Cairo, the latter represented in Cairo.
3. Quotes: Martin Wilmington, *The Middle East Supply Center* (Albany: State University of New York Press, 1971), 4; and Kolinsky, *Britain,* 189. British propositions

for Middle East self-sufficiency in the case of war dated back to 1938: ibid., 188. For Keynesianist state interventionism, see Robert Vitalis and Steven Heydemann, "Explaining State-Market Relations in the Post-War Middle East," in *War, Institutions, and Social Change in the Middle East,* ed. Steven Heydemann (Berkeley: University of California Press, 1999), 100–145. See also Davis, "Middle East"; Lizzie Collingham, *The Taste of War: World War Two and the Battle for Food* (New York: Penguin, 2011), 126–132.

4. For overviews, see Philip Khoury, *Syria and the French Mandate: The Politics of Arab Nationalism, 1920–1945* (Princeton: Princeton University Press, 1987), 583–618; Eyal Zisser, *Lebanon: The Challenge of Independence* (London: I. B. Tauris, 2000).

5. Both quotes: Anita Shapira, *Land and Power: The Zionist Resort to Force, 1881–1948* (Stanford, CA: Stanford University Press, 1992), 280. See also Kolinsky, *Britain,* 193–194. The Biltmore Program called the state a Commonwealth. For Transjordan, see Philip Robins, *A History of Jordan* (Cambridge: Cambridge University Press, 2004), 52–56.

6. Yehoshua Porath, *In Search of Arab Unity, 1930–1945* (London: Frank Cass, 1986), 185–196, 236–311; Michael Thornhill, "Britain and the Politics of the Arab League," in *Demise of the British Empire in the Middle East: Britain's Responses to Nationalist Movements, 1943–55,* ed. Michael Cohen and Martin Kolinsky (London: Frank Cass, 1998), 41–50. For the Arab state system after the war, see Bruce Maddy-Weitzman, *The Crystallization of the Arab State System, 1945–1954* (Syracuse, NY: Syracuse University Press, 1993).

7. Aviel Roshwald, *Estranged Bedfellows: Britain and France in the Middle East during the Second World War* (Oxford: Oxford University Press, 1990), 86.

8. This and the previous paragraph follows the analysis of Roshwald, *Estranged Bedfellows;* see also Meir Zamir, *The Secret Anglo-French War in the Middle East: Intelligence and Decolonization, 1940–1948* (Milton Park, Abingdon: Routledge, 2015). Quote: Spears to FO / Eden, Beirut, June 20, 1944, 6, FO371 / 40336, The National Archives, Kew (hereafter, TNA). See also Edward Spears, *Fulfilment of a Mission: The Spears Mission to Syria and Lebanon, 1941–1944* (Hamden: Archon, 1977), 174. A key French text is Georges Catroux, *Dans la bataille de la Méditerrannée* (Paris: Julliard, 1949).

9. Quote: Memo, British Legation Beirut, August 2, 1944, 5, FO371 / 40336, TNA. See also "An agreement to regulate the importation and exportation of goods between Palestine and Syria," Supplement 2 to the Palestine Gazette Extraordinary no. 966 of November 30, 1939; Telegram, Havard / British Legation Beirut to Ministry of Economic Warfare / London, Beirut, December 24, 1940, FO371 / 24595, TNA; Telegram, Ministry of Economic Warfare / London to HC / Jerusalem, March 19, 1941, FO892 / 80, TNA.

10. Nasri Sa'igh, 'Abd al-Hamid Karami (Beirut: Sharikat al-Matbu'at li-l-Tawzi' wa-l-Nashr, 2011), 188, 198–201; Bassam Sourati, "La ville contre l'État," *Bulletin de la Société Laguedocienne de Géographie* 20 (1986): 223–239; 'Abdallah Said, *Al al-Jisr fi Tarabulus* (Tokyo: Manshurat Ma'had al-Abhath fi Lughat wa-Thaqafat Asiya wa-Afriqiya, 2007), 101–166; Muhammad Darniqa, *al-Shaykh Nadim al-Jisr* (Tripoli: Dar al-Ma'arif al-'Umumiyya, 1992), 5–56; Salim Kabbara, *Tarabulus fi Dhakirat al-Watan,* ed. Tariq Ziada (Beirut: Dar al-Nahar, 2004), 69–74, 121–134.

11. Quotes: Sa'igh, *Karami,* 204–205, 206. For the 1936 conference and upshot, see Raghid Sulh, *Lebanon and Arabism* (London: I. B. Tauris, 2004), 45–46. For 1937, see Sa'igh, *Karami,* 214.

12. In 1939, steely new High Commissioner Maxime Weygand tightened the screws, suspending constitutional politics, stiffening censorship, and packing national-ists off into internal exile. His Vichy replacement, in June 1940, first stayed his course. But effective from early 1941, schemes by Vichy's German uber-masters and inflation, caused by hoarding and a partial British embargo, opened a po-litical window of opportunity. In Damascus, the National Bloc leader, the urban notable Shukri al-Quwatli, taunted the government as "not worthy its very name," and leveraging popular discontent for a general strike, Syrian nationalists forced France to install a cabinet that, however, was nonnationalist. Quote: Shukri al-Quwatli, *Shukri al-Quwatli Yukhatib Ummatahu* (Beirut: Markaz al-Watha'iq al-Mu'asira, 1970), 28.

13. For the National Pact, see Zisser, *Lebanon,* 25–67, esp. 57–67; and Michael Johnson, *Class and Client in Beirut: The Sunni Muslim Community and the Leba-nese State, 1840–1985* (London: Ithaca Press, 1986).

14. Ibid., 249, 262–309; Sourati, "Ville," 236.

15. Quotes: Sûreté aux Armées, "Information spéciale #3271," Tripoli, November 13, 1944, box 67, v.1 / MSL, Archives du Ministère des Affaires Étrangères, Nantes, France (hereafter, MAE-Nantes); and Note in Bishara al-Khuri, *Haqa'iq Lub-naniyya,* 2:21, quoted in Sa'igh, *Karami,* 319. (Unlike the Najjada, the Shabab refused to directly attack the government, though.) See also Sûreté aux Armées, "Information spéciale #3239," Tripoli, November 9, 1944, box 67, v.1 / MSL, MAE-Nantes; Sûreté aux Armées, "Information #311," Beirut, January 23, 1945, box 67, v.1 / MSL, MAE-Nantes; Note, "Cheikh Karamé," Beirut, August 7, 1944, box 76, v.1 / MSL, MAE-Nantes; Sourati, "Ville," 235; Fawaz Traboulsi, *A His-tory of Modern Lebanon* (London: Pluto, 2007), 115–118. Reprints of Najjada wartime posters underlining Tripoli's particularity are found in Kabbara, *Tarabulus,* 220–225.

16. Quote: Nur al-Din Imam, '*Abd al-Hamid Karami* (Beirut: N. Imam, 1951), 21, see also 1–21, photo opposite 12. One Tripolitan *zu'ama'* family that he ignored were

the Muqaddams. Allegedly provoked, Karami had shot one of them dead in 1935, and in 1948 clipped the entire family's wings in an armed confrontation over the honor to receive *qawmi* Tripolitan hero Fawzi al-Qawuqchi who was visiting his hometown after doing battle in Palestine.

17. For consuls and luminaries, see, e.g., "Qunsul Misr fi Beirut Yusbihu Waziran Mufawwadan," *al-Nahar,* October 13, 1943, 2; "Hiflatan 'ala Sharaf Huda Sha'rawi," *al-Nahar,* August 23, 1944, 2.

18. Quotes: Michel Chiha, *Liban d'aujourd'hui: 1942* (Beirut: Éditions du Trident, 1949 [1942]), 5; "ABC," *al-Nahar,* August 12, 1944, 2; "al-Sajjad al-'Ajami," *al-Nahar,* October 30, 1943, 2; "al-Sayyidat al-Aniqat," *al-Nahar,* October 29, 1943, 2; and Samir Kassir, *Beirut,* trans. M. B. DeBevoise (Berkeley: University of California Press, 2010), 286. See also Yusuf Daghir, *Qamus al-Sihafa al-Lubnaniyya* (Beirut: al-Maktaba al-Sharqiyya, 1978), 428–430 (of the fourteen non-Beiruti items, six were published elsewhere in Lebanon, six in South America, one in Palestine, and one in Cairo); "al-Akadimi al-Lubnaniyya li-l-Funun al-Jamila," *al-Nahar,* October 12 and 29, 1943, 2; "Talab Mu'allimin wa-Mu'allimat," *al-Nahar,* August 19, 1944, 2; "49,417 Rakiban," *al-Nahar,* August 18, 1944, 2; "Tadshin Mal'ab Riadi," *al-Nahar,* October 29, 1943, 2; "Sinima Huliwud" and "Sinima Ruksi," *al-Nahar,* both October 30, 1943, 2; "Lailatan Nadiratan," *al-Nahar,* December 12, 1943, 2.

19. Chiha, *Liban,* 16–17, 54, 55, 55.

20. Michel Chiha, *Essais* (Beirut: Éditions du Trident, 1950), 1:118–119. Not by chance did the author of a Lebanese history published following the war open by complaining about his compatriots' ignorance: Yusuf Mazhar, *Ta'rikh Lubnan al-'Amm* (Beirut: n.p., n.d. [late 1940s]), 1:3.

21. Chiha, *Essais,* 22, 15, 16, 35. See also ibid., 31, 86.

22. Simun 'Awwad, *Hinri Far'un Kama Rawa* (Antelias: Dar 'Awwad, 1999), 28–29, 35–37, 149. See also May Farhat, "A Mediterraneanist's Collection: Henri Pharaon's 'Treasure House of Arab Art,'" *Ars Orientalis* 42 (2012): 102–113. In 2006 Pharaon's house became the Robert Mouawad Private Museum.

23. Quotes: Barbara Mann, *A Place in History: Modernism, Tel Aviv, and the Creation of Jewish Urban Space* (Stanford, CA: Stanford University Press, 2006), 202; and Bar Drora, "Bar Drora," in *Pene Tel Aviv be-Karikaturot,* ed. Moshe Shainboym (Tel Aviv: Shainboym, 1940), 156. For the self-juxtaposition to Jaffa and to other Arab and Jewish cities in Palestine, see Mann, *Place,* 192–205; Mark Levine, *Overthrowing Geography: Jaffa, Tel Aviv, and the Struggle for Palestine, 1880–1948* (Berkeley: University of California Press, 2005); Deborah Bernstein, *Nashim ba-Shulayim: Migdar we-Le'umiyut be-Tel Aviv ha-Mandatorit* (Jerusalem: Ben-Zvi, 2008); Ya'acov Shavit and Gideon Biger, *Ha-Historiah shel Tel-Aviv* (Tel Aviv: Universitat Tel-Aviv, 2007), 2:15, 41; Maoz Azaryahu, *Tel Aviv: Mythography of a City* (Syracuse, NY: Syracuse University Press, 2007), 4, 9, 41, 43, 49, 58, 60, 61,

208–223; Anat Helman, *Young Tel Aviv: A Tale of Two Cities* (Waltham, MA: Brandeis University Press, 2010), 17, 35, 40.

24. Quotes: Yehuda Nedivi, "Tel Aviv. A Tour Conducted by Yehuda Nedivi, Town Clerk of Tel Aviv," in *Guide to Tel Aviv*, ed. Yehuda Nedivi et al. (Tel Aviv: Olympia, 1941), 19; and Azaryahu, *Tel Aviv*, 64, quoting Dizengoff in 1933. Tel Aviv's coat of arms also has a motto, "I will build thee and thou shall be built," taken from Jer. 31, 4.

25. Nedivi, "Tel Aviv," 27, 27, 25. See also Azaryahu, *Tel Aviv*, 39–40, 44–45; Helman, *Young Tel Aviv*, 39; Shavit and Biger, *Tel-Aviv*, vol. 2. For newspapers, see also the membership register *Association of Palestine Journalists* (Jerusalem: Association of Palestine Journalists, 1945), 14–15, showing that all eight Hebrew-language dailies were in Tel Aviv, only English-language *Palestine Post* in Jerusalem. (However, all foreign correspondents were based in the Mandate capital: ibid., 5–11.)

26. Quote: Y. W., "Galeriah shel Ishim," in *Karikaturot*, 158.

27. Quotes: Shavit and Biger, *Tel Aviv*, 2:20 (nonreferenced quote); and Tel Aviv Great Synagogue Religious Association, *'Al Shever Bat 'Ami* (Tel Aviv: s.p., 1944 [?]), 3, 4.

28. Quotes: al-Quwatli, *al-Quwatli*, 39–40. See also Shams al-Din al-Rifa'i, *Ta'rikh al-Sihafa al-Suriyya* (Cairo: Dar al-Ma'arif, 1969), 2:150–151; "Hawashi al-Hawadith," *Risalat al-Tajhiz bi-Halab* 1 (1941): 36.

29. Quotes: al-Quwatli, *al-Quwatli*, 40, 39, 59, 58–59. Similar: "Kalima," *NSGTD* (1943–1943): 41, 42, in which the Damascus Chamber of Commerce head, in an address honoring Quwatli as Syria's first president, as a matter of course first talked about the glory of this day for "Damascus," but then also underlined how all Syrian merchants have helped Syria politically and economically.

30. Quotes: Muhammad Jamal al-Din Malas, *al-Tuhfa al-Mardiyya fi Madih Khayr al-Barriyya* (Damascus: Matba'at Ibn Zaydun, 1940), 4, 21. See also 'Abd al-Fattah al-Imam, *al-Tafsir al-'Asri al-Qadim* (Damascus: al-Matba'a al-Sha'biyya, 1945).

31. Muhammad Jamal al-Din Malas, *Minhaj al-Yaqin fi Rihlat al-Sharq al-Aqsa li-Khidmat al-Din* (Damascus: s.p., 1947), 4–8; Malas, *Tuhfa*, 4–20.

32. *Rawd al-Bashar* resembled *Muntakhabat* also in form. Al-Shatti processed earlier compilations, opening most entries with a formula like 'x was biographed by y,' and affirming to have "followed as much as possible in the tracks of those who had put forward [these notables'] memory, relying on pure transmissions and true words," a method resembling that used by religious scholars like him in *Hadith*, transmitted stories about the Prophet: Muhammad Jamil al-Shatti, *Rawd al-Bashar fi A'yan Dimashq fi al-Qarn al-Thalith 'Ashar* (Damascus: Matba'at Dar al-Yaqza al-'Arabiyya, 1946), 3.

33. Quotes: al-Shatti, *Rawd al-Bashar*, 139, 3 (emphasis added), see also 113, 54, 80, 3. (In 1948, al-Shatti published a follow-up volume on notables deceased between

1883 and 1931, *Tarajim Aʻyan Dimashq fi Nusf al-Qarn al-Rabiʻ ʻAshar* [Damascus: Matbaʻat Dar al-Yaqza al-ʻArabiyya].)

34. Muhammad Kurd ʻAli, *Dimashq* (Cairo: Matbaʻat al-Maʻarif wa-Maktabatuha, 1944), 9, title page. Debates about the loss of *al-Andalus,* in 1452, to 'the Christians' had started intensifying among Arabs and Muslims with late nineteenth-century European imperialist expansion. For a contemporary study, see Jonathan Shannon, "Performing al-Andalus, Remembering al-Andalus: Mediterranean Soundings from Mashriq to Maghrib," *Journal of American Folklore* 120 (2007): 308–334.

35. Kurd ʻAli, *Dimashq,* 49.

36. This was due to various developments, chiefly the creation of the Arab League in 1945 and soon thereafter the unresolved Palestine Question and the 1948 War. The travelogue by Muhammad Thabit, *al-ʻAlam al-ʻArabi ka-ma Raʼaituha* (Cairo: Matbaʻat Mustafa al-Babi al-Halabi, 1945), "the Egyptian globetrotter" (al-rahhala al-misri: ibid., alif), which recounted travels from Iraq to Morocco and Spain, started by stating its context being the Egyptian-led creation of the League: ibid., haʼ. Similarly, American University of Cairo, *al-ʻAlam al-ʻArabi al-Yawm* (Cairo: AUC Press, 1946), reflected on the League: ibid., unnumbered page entitled al-ʻAlam al-ʻArabi al-Yawm, 12. In 1947, the monthly *al-ʻAlam al-ʻArabi* was founded in Cairo. And the 20 pages-long political poem by Mahmud Muhammad Sadiq, *Risalat al-Shiʻr al-Qawmi ila al-ʻAlam al-ʻArabi* (Cairo: Dar al-Maʻarif, 1949), 6–24, focused on Palestine, starting with "Palestine's martyrdom" and e.g. discussing the "fake [Zionist] statelet" ibid., 6, 23. On a related note, for initial political effects, see Michael Doran, *Pan-Arabism before Nasser: Egyptian Power Politics and the Palestine Question* (Oxford: Oxford University Press, 1999).

37. Porath, *Arab Unity;* Khoury, *Syria;* Israel Gershoni and James Jankowski, *Redefining the Egyptian Nation, 1930–1945* (New York: Cambridge University Press, 1995). See also Zisser, *Lebanon;* Doran, *Pan-Arabism;* Bruce Maddy-Weitzman, *The Crystallization of the Arab State System, 1945–1954* (Syracuse: Syracuse University Press, 1993).

38. Quotes: Taha Husayn, *Ahlam Shahrazad* (Cairo: Matbaʻat al-Maʻarif wa-Maktabatuha, 1943), pages 2, 1, 3 of the un-paginated Introduction. See also Husayn, *Mustaqbal al-Thaqafa fi Masr* (Cairo: Matbaʻat al-Maʻarif wa-Maktabatuha, 1938), 519–529; Albert Hourani, *Arabic Thought in the Liberal Age, 1798–1939* (Cambridge: Cambridge University Press, 1983), 324–340. For the changes in the intellectual sphere more broadly from the 1940s—the decline of the old *nahdawi* intellectuals—and into the 1960s, see Yoav di Capua, *Bad Faith: Arab Intellectuals, Decolonization, and Jean-Paul Sartre* (Chicago: Chicago University Press, forthcoming).

39. Letters reprinted in Kurd 'Ali, *Dimashq,* 154–155.

40. Andrew Arsan, *Interlopers of Empire: The Lebanese Diaspora in Colonial French West Africa* (Oxford: Oxford University Press, 2013), includes notes on the war years: 147, 162, 171, 173, 186; 160 and 197–198 on a landmark Lebanese travelogue of Africa based on a journey between 1938 and the early 1940s, Michel Hayik, *Fi Majahil Afriqiya* (Beirut: Matba'at Jaridat al-'Alam, n.d. [1952?]). In its preface, ibid., 4, Henri Gemayel praised it for showing how Lebanese emigrants were economically "active and constructive" as well as dedicated to "national, literary, and social objectives."

41. Quote: Alfred Bonné, "Secret. Impressions from my trip to Lebanon," Jerusalem, March 27, 1940, S90/843/1, Central Zionist Archives, Jerusalem (hereafter, CZA). See also Bonné, "Secret. Report on my trip to Lebanon," April 18, 1943, S90/850/1, CZA; Intérêts Communs to Alfred Bonné/ERI, Beirut, March 5, 1945, S90/859/2, CZA; Émile Seilhoun to Alfred Bonné, Beirut, March 25, 1945, S90/859/2, CZA; Bonné to Léon Mourad/Intérêts Communs, June 8, 1945, S90/859/2, CZA.

42. Transjordan's exports to Lebanon and Syria dropped from 2,500 tons (1938) to 1,000 tons (1944); reverse exports from 7,400 tons to 900 tons. In this entire paragraph, all figures are taken from, and all percentage calculations based on, Félix Rosenfeld, "Les échanges commerciaux entre la Syrie et le Liban et les autres pays du Proche Orient," *Économiste Européen,* November 25, 1945, 333 (tonnage figures), and D. Gurevich, *Statistical Handbook of Jewish Palestine 1947* (Jerusalem: Department of Statistics, Jewish Agency for Palestine, 1947), 251 (LP figures in current prices).

43. Would one include oil, though, Iraq's exports would be twice Palestine's.

44. Palestine's export growth rate to Lebanon and Syria—in Palestinian Pounds (LP) 350% from 1938 to 1945—was eclipsed by that to Turkey (2,200%), to Egypt (5,300%, including reexports of Iraqi oil pipelined to Haifa), and to Iraq (8,000%). Ibid.

45. Although 1945 exports to Egypt, LP5,382,287, beat those to Lebanon and Syria, they were lower without Palestinian Iraqi oil reexports. Iraq stood at LP670,059; Turkey at LP952,444. Ibid.

46. Exports to Turkey fell from 4,600 to 500 tons; to Egypt, from 20,800 to 15,900 tons; and from 78,700 to 56,000 tons to Iraq, a number that still allowed that country to overtake Palestine as Lebanon and Syria's premier Middle Eastern export market. Ibid.

47. Carolyn Gates, *The Merchant Republic of Lebanon: Rise of an Open Economy* (London: I. B. Tauris, 1998), 39, 40–41. Ibid. notes that imports from Europe and the USA collapsed from 67% of the total, in 1938, to 3% in 1943; exports there from 55% to 4%.

48. For numbers, see Nachum Gross and Jacob Metzer, "Palestine in World War II: Some Economic Aspects," in *The Sinews of War: Essays on the Economic History*

*of World War II,* ed. Geofrey Mills and Hugh Rockoff (Ames: Iowa State University Press, 1993), 77 (table 4.7; current prices). The Anglo-American percentage figures are based on Gurevich, *Handbook,* 250.

49. Gross and Metzer, "Palestine," 65. For figures, see ibid., 77, 64, 65 (current prices). See also David de Vries, *Diamonds and War: State, Capital, and Labor in British-Ruled Palestine* (New York: Berghan, 2010).

50. Gurevich, *Handbook,* 220–221. For Haifa, see also Jacob Norris, *Land of Progress: Palestine in the Age of Colonial Development, 1905–1948* (Oxford: Oxford University Press, 2013), 104, 111–112, 116–119; "The Industrial Position in Haifa Bay," *Palnews* 16 (April 24, 1941): 6; "Haifa's Industrial Undertakings," *Palnews* 17 / 18 (May 8, 1941): 8; for a Haifai proposing measures for further expansion, see Erwin Wittkowski, "Haifa als Industriestandort" (July 1941), S90 / 843 / 1, CZA. For Tel Aviv, see de Vries, *Diamonds;* Shavit and Biger, *Tel-Aviv,* 86; Levine, *Geography,* 90 (also for Jaffa). Factories in Jerusalem, Petah Tikva, and villages and communal settlements declined relatively and absolutely, from 229 (15%) to 199 (9%), from 53 (3%) to 51 (2%), and from 177 (11%) to 128 (6%), respectively: Gurevich, *Handbook,* 220–221.

51. Quote: Zachary Lockman, *Comrades and Enemies: Arab and Jewish Workers in Palestine, 1906–1948* (Berkeley: University of California Press, 1996), 267. See also ibid., 266–321; Gudrun Krämer, *A History of Palestine* (Princeton, NJ: Princeton University Press, 2008), 296–299; Issa Khalaf, *Politics in Palestine: Arab Factionalism and Social Disintegration, 1939–1948* (Albany: State University of New York Press, 1991), esp. 45–160; de Vries, *Diamonds and War,* 1–66; Sherene Seikaly, *Men of Capital: Scarcity and Economy in Mandate Palestine* (Stanford, CA: Stanford University Press, 2015).

52. Quote: H.R. Hill, "Report on Visit to Syria and Lebanon," 3, March 1945, FO922 / 378, TNA (Mannheimer was probably a Yishuvi Jew, for non-Jewish Germans would not have been allowed to work in a large factory, and from the late 1920s, considerable numbers of Czechoslovak and Polish Jewish emigrants to Palestine had been, and continued being, textile specialists). See also Sûreté aux Armées, "Information spéciale 2520," Beirut, October 6, 1944, box 30, v.1 / MSL, MAE-Nantes.

53. British Legation Beirut, note about "M. Massigli's Note to Mr. Duff Cooper," 5, Beirut, June 20, 1944, FO371 / 40336, TNA; Telegram, Francom Beirut to Free French Consul Jerusalem, Beirut, August 25, 1941, box 64, v.1 / MSL, MAE-Nantes; Australian Imperial Forces to Chef de la Sûreté Générale, Headquarters, August 21, 1941, box 64, v.1 / MSL, MAE-Nantes; Pharaon-Solel Boneh Engineers and General Contractors to Sûreté Générale, Damascus, November 24, 1941, box 64, v.1 / MSL, MAE-Nantes, including attached list of list of Yishuvi foremen and surveyors and other workers; "Rapport d'enquête. Objet: A. Pharaon et Solel-

boneh," July 1942, box 64, v.1 / MSL, MAE-Nantes; Sûreté aux Armées, "Informa-
tion," Beirut, October 10, 1945, box 64, v.1 / MSL, MAE-Nantes; Kolinsky, *Britain's
War,* 198–202; Shlomo Shva, *Derekh ba-Midbar: Sipuro shel Solel-Boneh* (Tel Aviv:
'Am 'Oved, 1976), 204–227.

54. "Arab Industries in Palestine," *Palnews* 36 (September 15, 1941): 6 (reporting an
Egyptian newspaper's interview with a Palestinian at the exhibition); "Erets
Israel be-Kahir," *Haaretz,* August 24, 1941, copy in 31–2788, Tel Aviv Municipal
Archive (hereafter, TAMA); HC to Tel Aviv and Jaffa Chambers of Commerce,
May 29, 1941, 31–2788, TAMA; interview with Shenkar, "Industry's War Service,"
*PME* 9, no. 14 (1942): 164–165; interview with Eliezer Kaplan, "Palestine in
Second War Year," *PME* 1, no. 13 (1941): 8–10; Dr. K. Mendelsohn, "Economic
Mobilization," *PME* 9, no. 13 (1941): 166–167; similar: David Horowitz, "War-
time Economic Policy. Key Points in Programme of Economic Defence," *PME* 2,
no. 13 (1941): 23–25. For the Yishuv's imperial usefulness, see Norris, *Land of
Progress.*

55. David Horowitz, "Memorandum on Trade Relations between Syria and Palestine," Tel Aviv, August 4, 1940, S90 / 843 / 1, CZA.

56. "Handelsvertrag Syrien-Libanon," 1, attached to Jewish Agency (hereafter,
JA), "Vorbereitungen der Handelsvertragsverhandlungen mit dem nahen Aus-
land," June 19, 1944, S8 / 2289b, CZA; A. Markus, "Ha-Heskem ha-Miskhari 'im
E"I—Suriah we-Levanon," 3, exposé for Shertok / JA, October, 19, 1944, S8 / 2289b,
CZA; Chamber of Commerce Tel Aviv-Jaffa, *Twentythird and Twentyfourth
Annual Report of the Committee, 1944 / 1945* (Tel Aviv: n.p., 1945), 88; Sûreté aux
Armées, "Information 4978," Beirut, December 12, 1945, box 30, v.1 / MSL, MAE-
Nantes; Sûreté aux Armées, "Information," Damascus, December 12, 1944, box
30, v.1 / MSL, MAE-Nantes; note on Lebanese newspaper excerpts protesting
against Zionist economic "domination" in Lebanon, Jerusalem, September 27,
1945, S90 / 859 / 2, CZA.

57. "Handelsvertrag," 4, 5.

58. On a related note, following the 1942 Biltmore Program demand for a Jewish state,
Judah Leon Magnes (1877–1948)—from his early years in the United States as pac-
ifist; coauthor, in 1925 in Palestine, of the founding document of the short-lived
binationalist Brit Shalom; and Hebrew University president 1935–1948—and a few
other individuals, including former Brit Shalom members, launched a new, tiny
binationalist group, Ihud (Unity). It called for a Arab-Jewish state as part of a
Arab Federation. Magnes had expounded such a position already in 1941 position
papers, which exceeded what Ben Gurion would have been ready to compromise
on even back in the 1930s, let alone now, and which most Arabs rejected, too, also
when they in 1943 started the talks that in 1945 led to the Arab League: *Palestine
and Arab Union* (Jerusalem: Be'ayot hay-Yom, 1941).

59. Quote: "Der Aussenhandel zwischen Palästina, Syrien, Irak unter dem Gesichtspunkt einer Zollfederation," 32, Jerusalem, May 1942, S90/616, CZA. See also Jenny Radt/ERI, "Wirtschafts- und Handelspolitik in den Beziehungen zwischen Palaestina und Syrien," March 1941, S90/231, CZA.

60. Quote: David Horowitz/ERI, "Trade with Syria and the cost of living in Palestine," 5, Tel Aviv, January 21, 1941, S90/223, CZA. See also "Aussenhandel," 32–33; JA, "Pratei-Kol shel Yeshivat ha-Wa'adah le-Yahasei ha-Miskhar 'im Ertsot Misrah ha-Tikhon," July 7, 1941, S90/843/1, CZA; Ha-Merkaz le-ma'an Totseret ha-Arets, *Madrikh Totseret ha-Arets* (Tel Aviv: Zvieli/Ha-Merkaz le-ma'an Totseret ha-Arets, 1940); Meir Livni, *Ha-Maavak she-Nishkakh* (Netanyah: Ekspres, 1990), 38–60 (on the agricultural side of totseret ha-arets).

61. David Horowitz, *Postwar Reconstruction* (Tel Aviv: Palestine and Middle East Magazine, 1943), 30, 32. The phrase "Freedom from want" was coined by U.S. president Franklin Roosevelt in 1941.

62. Textiles Executive Committee of the Arab Conference for Palestine to HC, 2, Jaffa, June 1, 1944, Chamber of Commerce file 1/36, Nablus Municipal Archive (NMA). For Palestinian merchants in the war, see especially Seikaly, *Men of Capital*; Khalaf, *Politics in Palestine*.

63. Textiles Executive Committee to HC, 3. Jews also complained about Britain refusing to involve them in all wartime administrative units. In 1943, a conference of Jewish traders and merchants in Palestine protested that "entrusting the administration of economic questions to officials alone . . . has proven highly detrimental to the maintenance of proper supplies to the country": First Conference of Jewish Importers and Traders, "Resolution," 1, Tel Aviv, March 31, 1943, M77/33, Israel State Archives, Jerusalem (hereafter, ISA). In fact, Britain resolved to keep *this* matter—import licences, prepared in each MENA territory, but approved or rejected by MESC in Cairo—in its own hands. Only the United States joined in, at the Cairo-level, in 1942; even Free France was kept out. For a very astute analysis of Palestine's economy, its actors, and their ultimate powerlessness in the face of British support of Zionism, which also looks at the war, see Seikaly, *Men of Capital*.

64. Rashid Hajj Ibrahim, welcome speech to the 13th Palestine Chambers of Commerce Conference, Haifa, December 5, 1942, Chamber of Commerce file 1/36, NMA; Emile Boutagy to Jerusalem British government, n.d. [November 1943?], Merchants' letters file (1942–1944) 7/36, NMA; Jerusalem Arab Chamber of Commerce, Yearly Report, May 31, 1943, 1, Chamber of Commerce file 1/36, NMA. 1938/39: Office of Executive Committee [of the] Conference of the Arab Chambers of Commerce of Palestine to HC, Jerusalem, January 4, 1940, M39/15, ISA; Jerusalem Chamber of Commerce annual report, March 31, 1944, 6, Chamber of Commerce file 1/36, NMA (concerning a 1943 Palestine Chambers

of Commerce Conference demand to the HC); Haifa Chamber of Commerce to HC, 4, Haifa, February 15, 1944, M65/15, ISA. Strike and letter abroad: Textiles Executive Committee of the Arab Conference for Palestine to the HC, 13.

65. "Travel to Neighboring Countries," *Palnews* 45 (November 27, 1941): 6; "The Development of the Arab Economic Sector in Palestine," *Palnews* 11/12 (March 26, 1943): 8; "The Arab Industry," *Palnews* 17/18 (middle of May, 1944): 3; "The Arab Economic Sector in Palestine Strengthens its Capital," *Palnews* 25/26 (middle of July 1944): 3; Tulkarem Chamber of Commerce to Executive Committee of the Arab Conference for Palestine, August 18, 1943, Executive Committee file 5/36, NMA, complaining, also on behalf of Acre, Nazareth and Gaza, against the "tyranny" of Jerusalem, Jaffa, and Haifa; Report, 13th Palestine Chambers of Commerce Conference, 4, December 5, 1942, Chamber of Commerce file 1/36, NMA (new chambers founded in Safed, Hebron, Tiberias, Jenin, and Tulkarem, demanding inclusion in the conference).

66. Rashid Hajj Ibrahim, welcome speech (regarding a Palestine-wide company); Jerusalem Arab Chamber of Commerce, Annual Report, March 31, 1943, 2, Chamber of Commerce file 1/36, NMA; initial shareholders' list, attached to "Manshur li-asdar asham fi Shirkat al-Ta'min al-'Arabiyya al-Muttahida" (July 1944), Chamber of Commerce file 1/36, NMA.

67. Quote: Abla Amawi, "The Consolidation of the Merchant Class in Transjordan during the Second World War," in *Village, Steppe and State: The Social Origins of Modern Jordan,* ed. Eugene Rogan and Tariq Tell (London: British Academic Press, 1994), 162.

68. This development also helped to cement the Ammani self-identification that commenced in the 1930s. Marwan Hanania, "From Colony to Capital" (PhD diss., Stanford University, 2010), 263; a wonderful example is the autobiographical Abd al-Rahman Munif, *Story of a City: A Childhood in Amman* (London: Quartet, 1996).

69. Besides Amawi, "Consolidation," see also Glubb to Kirkbride, Amman, March 23, 1943, FO922/99, TNA (compare, for 'Syrian' nomads, Buss to Jackson/MESC, February 15, 1943, FO922/99, TNA); Jerusalem Arab Chamber of Commerce, Annual Report, March 31, 1943, 2, Chamber of Commerce file 1/36, NMA; "The Arab Industry," *Palnews* 17/18 (middle of May 1944): 3; "Tahrib," *NSGTD* (1940–41): 9–10 (rampant smuggling between Syria and all its neighbors); author, interviews with Hamdi Tabba'a, June 21, 2011, Amman, and with Hassan Mango, June 29, 2011, Amman, on the crucial importance of the quota system.

70. Quote: Ron Pundik, *The Struggle for Sovereignty,* 33, quoted in Robins, *Jordan,* 53. Thus, although Britain declined to support yet another Bilad al-Sham plan by Abdallah—it feared that relations with other Arab countries would suffer—

by 1943 the kernel were planted for what by 1947/1948 would grow into a sturdy "Greater Transjordan policy," which identified Transjordan as Britain's most loyal ally in an area of the world, including the Suez Canal, that the British Empire wished to keep and that it and the USA feared might become a Soviet target in a Third World War. Quote: Ilan Pappé, "British Rule in Jordan, 1943–55," in *Demise of the British Empire*, 201. See also Robins, *Jordan*, 52–56.

71. See, e.g., Spears Mission/Economic Mission/Agricultural Office, "Agricultural progress: Syria. 27th. November, 1942—May 26th. 1943," FO922/99, TNA; "Summary of a report by Major G. Howard-Jones on British help to agriculture in the Levant states, 1941–43," FO922/99, TNA. For macro-economic data, including inflation, see Gates, *Lebanon*, which partially holds for Syria, too, and Paul Klat, "War Economic Policy in Syria and Lebanon" (MA thesis, American University of Beirut, 1944), 90–91.

72. Geoff Schad, "Colonialists, Industrialists, and Politicians" (PhD diss., University of Pennsylvania, 2001), 261, counts four joint-stock companies founded in Aleppo between 1939 and 1945, eight in Damascus.

73. "Taqrir," *NSGTD* (1940/41): 18; Memorandum, "Economic warfare objectives in Syria," annex IV, attached to letter, Spears/Beirut to Ministry of Economic Warfare/London, Beirut, April 3, 1942, FO892/142, TNA; "Syrian silk and wool. Notes on a conference at the Ministry of Economic Warfare 9th January 1942," FO892/116, TNA; Troutbach/Ministry of Economic Warfare to Eyres/Foreign Office, London, January 20, 1942, FO892/116. See also "Rapport de gestion 1943. IV: activités économiques," 9, Dossier Beirut/E2400#1000/717#89*, Schweizerisches Bundesarchiv, Berne (hereafter, SB), for the figure of CHF4,080,000 of imports from Syria/Lebanon, mainly wool, in 1942.

74. By no means all manufacturing branches thrived, though; as in Lebanon, some contracted, others even closed, often for lack of raw material and machinery. Gates, *Lebanon*, 46–50; Klat, "War Economic Policy," 55–59.

75. India was a supplier of the MENA economic region; and Ethiopia was part of that region, too, and Kenia an important supplier.

76. Quote: Frank Peter, *Les entrepreneurs de Damas: Nation, impérialisme et industrialisation* (Paris: Harmattan, 2010), 13. See also Schad, "Colonialists," 315, 331; Sûreté aux Armées, "Information 375," Lattakiyya, November 24, 1944, box 50, v.1/MSL, MAE-Nantes; "Taqrir," *NSGTD* (1942/43): 10; "Muqaddama," *NSGTD* (1940/41): 5; Sûreté Générale, "noms des commerçants syriens qui ont pris des titres de circulation pour la Palestine en date du I0-3-1942," Damascus, March 10, 1942, box 30, v.1/MSL, MAE-Nantes; "Kalima," *NSGTD* (1942/43): 42; Sûreté aux Armées, "Information du 8.I2.1944, Damas," box 50, v.1/MSL, MAE-Nantes; Sûreté aux Armées, "Information du 4.8.43, Damas," box 30, v.1/MSL, MAE-Nantes; Spears/Beirut to Tench/Foreign Office, August 12, 1944,

FO371/40336, TNA; "Ittifaq Britun Wuds," *NSGTD* (1944/45): 30–36; "Taqrir," *NSGTD* (1942/43): 11–12.

77. Gates, *Lebanon,* 37, 53; Sûreté aux Armées, "Information 311 du 23.I.1945," Beirut, box 67, v.1/MSL, MAE-Nantes; Sûreté aux Armées, "Information 1395," Beirut, April 13, 1945, box 30, v.1/MSL, MAE-Nantes; Sûreté aux Armées, "Information 2652 du 4.7.45.," Beirut, box 30, v.1/MSL, MAE-Nantes; Sûreté aux Armées, "Information spéciale 3029 du 7-11-1944, Beyrouth," box 76, v.1/MSL, MAE-Nantes; Sûreté aux Armées, "Information spéciale No 3157 du 14-11-1944, Beyrouth," 6, box 67, v.1/MSL, MAE-Nantes.

78. Two quotes: Letter, Swiss Vice Consul to Political Department Berne, Beirut, May 17, 1944, Dossier Transfer von Wahrenzahlungen/E2001E#1000/1572#921*, SB; and Gates, *Lebanon,* 39/161n20. See also "Qawafil al-Sikr wa-l-Ruz Taruddu ilaina min Filastin," *Ahrar,* October 31, 1940, 2; "Burtiqal," *Ahrar,* May 19, 1943, 2; Overland Trade Company to Nablus Chamber of Commerce, Beirut, October 8, 1942, Merchants' letters file (1942–1944) 7/36, NMA; announcement of a new Haifa-Beirut company, al-Sharika al-Sharqiyya li-l-Tijara wa-l-Wikalat, Haifa, February 15, 1944, Merchants' letters file (1942–1944) 7/36, NMA; Sûreté Générale aux Armées, "Etat nominatif des commerçants libanais et syriens qui se rendent en Palestine et Egypte," Beirut, March 9, 1942, box 30, v.1/MSL, MAE-Nantes, listing fifty-seven traders, including famous names like Michel Pharaon, Michel Chiha, Alexander Sursock, Nicolas Trad, all but four to Palestine; the ad "Kettaneh-distributor—Dodge Brothers, cars, trucks, & buses," *Ittila'at,* March 27, 1930, 2 (a Tehrani paper). For the rise of the United States, see Gates, *Lebanon*; Harpham/Spears Mission Beirut to Department of Overseas Trade/London, Beirut, October 28, 1944, FO371/40336, TNA.

79. Traboulsi, *Lebanon,* 115–118; Sûreté aux Armées, "Information 105 du 8.I.1945. Beyrouth"; Sûreté aux Armées, "Information 295 du 22.I.1945. Beyrouth"; Sûreté aux Armées, "Information du 17.2.1944. Beirut," Sûreté Générale aux Armées, "Information du 5.I.1943. Beirut"; and Sûreté Générale aux Armées, "Bulletin d'information spécial No 973/C.E.," Beirut, July, 17, 1942; all in box 30, v.1/MSL, MAE-Nantes.

80. Copy of speech by Sa'id Ibrahim Fiaz, October 27, 1945; Village Maghdusha, "Fakhamat Ra'is Jumhuriyyatina al-Lubnaniyya al-Mu'azam," October 25, 1945; "Biyan al-Hizb al-Shuyu'i al-Lubnani fi Nabattiyya ila Fakhamat Ra'is al-Jumhuriyya bi-Matalib al-Junub," [n.d. (1945)]; and a similar example of the Christian Lebanese nationalist *Kata'ib,* "Ihtijajat Mintaqat al-Junub," [n.d. (1945)]; all in Correspondence, part 2, box 7, folder 3, collection Riyyasat al-Jumhuriyya, Lebanese State Archive, Beirut.

81. "Ijtima'," *al-Nahar,* October 27, 1944, 2; "Mandubuna fi Mu'tamar al-Tiran," *al-Nahar,* November 4, 1944, 2.

Postscript

1. Related, see Jo Guldi and David Armitage, *The History Manifesto* (Cambridge: Cambridge University Press, 2014).

2. For the war itself, see Benny Morris, *The Birth of the Palestinian Refugee Problem Revisited* (Cambridge: Cambridge University Press, 2004).

3. "Replies to questions put forward by Mr. G. Cox," November 13, 1946, S90 / 897 / 2, Central Zionist Archives, Jerusalem (on the effects of the Arab boycott); "Pro-Palestinian Products," *Ha-Boker,* August 1, 1947, newspaper clip translated from Hebrew into English, M5210 / 1, Israel State Archives, Jerusalem (on Zionist action); Youssef Chaitani, *The Decline of Arab Nationalism and the Triumph of the State: Post-Colonial Syria and Lebanon* (London: I.B. Tauris, 2007), 54–73; Yehoshua Porath, *In Search of Arab Unity, 1930–1945* (London: Frank Cass, 1986).

4. For self-transfer, see Yossi Katz, *Partner to Partition: the Jewish Agency's Partition Plan in the Mandate Era* (London: Frank Cass, 1998), 85–110.

5. Abdel Monem Said Aly, Shai Feldman, and Khalil Shikaki, *Arabs and Israelis: Conflict and Peacemaking in the Middle East* (New York: Palgrave Macmillan, 2013), 446.

6. Elie Podeh, *The Decline of Arab Unity: The Rise and Fall of the United Arabic Republic* (Brighton: Sussex, 1999); James Jankowski, *Nasser's Egypt: Arab Nationalism and the United Arab Republic* (Boulder, CO: Lynne Rienner, 2002).

7. Malik Mufti, *Sovereign Creations: Pan-Arabism and Political Order in Syria and Iraq* (Ithaca, NY: Cornell University Press, 1996).

8. A detailed overview is Mark Tessler, *A History of the Israeli-Palestinian Conflict* (Bloomington: Indiana University Press, 2009).

9. On the principal exception to the rule that serious *qawmi* endeavors died with Abdallah, Jordan's short-lived 1958 union with Hashemite Iraq, which was meant to geostrategically balance the Egyptian-Syrian merger, see Avi Shlaim, *Lion of Jordan: The Life of King Hussein in War and Peace* (New York: Vintage Books, 2007), 156–162.

10. However, the Syrian regime's repression of the 1976–1982 revolt peaked in Hama, where it killed between 10,000 and 30,000 people.

11. Quote: Avi Shlaim, *Collusion across the Jordan: King Abdullah, the Zionist Movement, and the Partition of Palestine* (Oxford: Clarendon, 1988). For Nablus in the second intifada, see, Amnesty International, "Israel and the Occupied Territories: Shielded from Scrutiny: IDF Violations in Jenin and Nablus," November 4, 2002, 44, https://www.amnesty.org/en/documents/mde15/143/2002/en.

12. Fairuz, "Li-Beirut" (1993).

13. Franck Mermier, *Le livre et la ville: Beyrouth et l'édition arabe: essai* (Arles: Sindbad, 2005).

464    Notes to Pages 320–337

14. Ahmed Kanna, *Dubai, the City as Corporation* (Minneapolis: University of Minnesota Press, 2011); Marcia Inhorn, *Cosmopolitan Conceptions: IVF Sojourns in Global Dubai* (Durham, NC: Duke University Press, 2015).

15. A good contemporary example is the mediascape. See Ezzeddine Abdelmoula, *Al Jazeera and Democratization: The Rise of the Arab Public Sphere* (London: Routledge, 2015); Bruce Etling, John Kelly, Robert Faris, and John Palfrey, "Mapping the Arabic Blogosphere: Politics, Culture, and Dissent," in *Media Evolution on the Eve of the Arab Spring,* ed. Leila Hudson, Adel Iskandar, and Mimi Kirk (New York: Palgrave Macmillan, 2014), 49–74.

16. Catherine Miller, ed. *Arabic in the City: Issues in Dialect Contact and Language Variation* (London: Routledge, 2007); Mohamed Embarki and Moha Ennaji, *Modern Trends in Arabic Dialectology* (Trenton: Red Sea Press, 2011).

17. Bruce Maddy-Weitzman, *The Crystallization of the Arab State System, 1945–1954* (Syracuse, NY: Syracuse University Press, 1993).

18. Cyrus Schayegh, "1958 Reconsidered. State Formation and Cold War in the Early Post-Colonial Arab Middle East," *IJMES* 41 (2013): 421–443.

19. Paul Chamberlin, *The Global Offensive: The United States, the Palestine Liberation Organization, and the Making of the Post-Cold War Order* (Oxford: Oxford University Press, 2012); John Collins, *Global Palestine* (London: Hurst, 2011).

20. Abbas Kelidar and Asher Susser, "Jordan: Between Israel and Iraq," Washington Institute Policy Analysis, December 30, 1996, http://www.washingtoninstitute.org/policy-analysis/view/jordan-between-israel-and-iraq.

21. Barak Ravid, "Putin soheah 'im Netanyahu," *Haaretz,* February 24, 2016, http://www.haaretz.co.il/news/politics/premium-1.2862288.

22. Author, interview with Cecil Hourani (b. 1917, Manchester, UK), September 9, 2008, Marjayoun, Lebanon.

23. Phone conversation with Cecil Hourani, August 8, 2011.

24. Author, interview with Shulamit Yaari (b. 1920, Metula), April 7, 2010, Neve Efal, Israel.

25. Author, interview with Fayez Nasrallah (b. 1930, Izra', Syria), August 5, 2009, Suweida, Syria.

26. Author, interview with Tannus Salim Sayyah (b. 1932, Alma Sha'ab), June 5, 2007, Alma Sha'ab, Lebanon.

Conclusion

1. Frederick Cooper, *Citizenship between Empire and Nation: Remaking France and French Africa, 1945–1960* (Princeton, NJ: Princeton University Press, 2014).

2. Quotes: Andrew Herod, *Geographies of Globalization: A Critical Introduction* (Malden, MA: Wiley-Blackwell, 2009), 96, 97, 98. See also Andrew Herod et al., eds., *Geographies of Power: Placing Scale* (Malden, MA: Wiley-Blackwell, 2002).

3. Quote: Neil Brenner, "Global Cities, Glocal States," *RIPE* 5 (1998): 3. See also Doreen Massey, "A Global Sense of Place," in *Reading Human Geography,* ed. Trevor Barnes et al. (London: Arnold, [1991] 1997), 315–323; Saskia Sassen, "The Many Scales of the Global," in *The Postcolonial and the Global,* ed. Revathi Krishnaswamy et al. (Minneapolis: University of Minnesota Press, 2008), 82–93; Peter Taylor, "Regionality in the World City Network," *International Social Science Journal* 56 (2004): 361; and Taylor, "Embedded Statism and the Social Sciences," *Environment and Planning A* 28 (1996): 1917–1928.

4. Quotes: Pierre-Yves Saunier, "Learning by Doing: Notes about the Making of the *Palgrave Dictionary of Transnational History,*" *JMEH* 6 (2008): 171; and Michael Müller and Cornelius Trop, "Conceptualising Transnational Spaces in History," *European Review of History* 16 (2009): 612. On a related but distinct—because actor-centered—note, see the concept of 'transboundary formations' developed in Thomas Callaghy, Ronald Kassimir, and Robert Latham, eds., *Intervention and Transnationalism in Africa: Global+Local Networks of Power* (Cambridge: Cambridge University Press, 2001), showing how actors are systematically present on different scales, hence helping to link them up and to qualify their differences.

5. For a chapter-long methodological exercise of a set of transnational ties as a "circulatory regime" with a "catchment area" and "riverbeds," "tributaries," "slopes," and "flows," which the historian needs to methodologically order his inquiry, see Pierre Yves Saunier, *Transnational History* (New York: Palgrave Macmillan, 2013), 58–79.

6. Geographer Edward Soja would call this a "socio-spatial dialectic": while socio-spatial fields, in this case, are produced rather than simply naturally out there, once in place, they help structure the options available to people later on. Edward Soja, "The Socio-Spatial Dialectic," *Annals of the Association of American Geographers* 70 (1980): 207–225.

7. John Fousek, *To Lead the Free World: American Nationalism and the Cultural Roots of the Cold War* (Chapel Hill: University of North Carolina Press, 2000), 7.

8. Charles Maier, "Consigning the Twentieth Century to History: Alternative Narratives for the Modern Era," *AHR* 105 (2000): 807–831.

9. Quotes: Maier, "Consigning the Twentieth Century to History," 819; and Manu Goswami et al., "AHR Conversation: History after the End of History: Reconceptualizing the Twentieth Century," *AHR* 121 (2016): 1571. See also Peter Groenewald and Tim te Pas, "Territoriality," September 18, 2000, www.historycooperative.org /phorum/list.php=3ff=3d10; Sebastian Conrad, *Globalisation and the Nation in Imperial Germany* (Cambridge: Cambridge University Press, 2010); and Isabella Löhr and Roland Wenzlhuemer, "Introduction," in *The Nation State and Beyond: Governing Globalization Processes in the Nineteenth and Early Twentieth Century* (Heidelberg: Springer, 2013), 1–23.

10. Quote: Neil Smith, *Uneven Development: Nature, Capital, and the Production of Space,* 3rd ed. (Athens, GA: University of Georgia Press, [1984] 2008), 6.

11. Glenda Sluga, *Internationalism in the Age of Nationalism* (Philadelphia: University of Pennsylvania Press, 2013); Ruth Oldenziel, "Islands: The United States as a Networked Empire," in *Entangled Geographies: Empire and Technopolitics in the Global Cold War*, ed. Gabrielle Hecht (Cambridge: MIT Press, 2011), 13–42; Jenifer Van Vleck, *Empire of the Air: Aviation and the American Ascendancy* (Cambridge, MA: Harvard University Press, 2013). Quote: Tobias Brinkmann, "Introduction," in *Points of Passage: Jewish Transmigrants from Eastern Europe in Scandinavia, Germany, and Britain, 1880–1914* (New York: Berghahn, 2013), 14–15.

12. Samir Khalaf and Per Kongstad, *Hamra of Beirut: A Case of Rapid Urbanization* (Leiden: Brill, 1973); Helmut Ruppert, *Beirut: Eine westlich geprägte Stadt des Orients* (Erlangen: Palm & Enke, 1969); Samir Kassir, *Beirut*, trans. M. B. DeBevoise (Berkeley: University of California Press, 2010), 358.

13. Quote: "Note pour la direction Afrique-Levant. a/s Installations de banques américaines à Beyrouth," Paris, October 29, 1957, 1, box Liban LA 636 (1953–1959), direction Afrique-Levant, Archives du Ministère des Affaires Étrangères, La Courneuve, France.

14. Karen Barkey and Mark von Hagen, eds., *After Empire: Multiethnic Societies and Nation-Building: The Soviet Union and the Russian, Ottoman, and Habsburg Empires* (Boulder, CO: Westview Press, 1997); Hasan Kayal, *Arabs and Young Turks: Ottomanism, Arabism, and Islamism in the Ottoman Empire, 1908–1918* (Berkeley: University of California Press, 1997); Andreas Kappeler, *The Russian Empire: A Multiethnic History* (Harlow: Pearson Education, 2001); Gary Wilder, *The French Imperial Nation-State: Negritude and Colonial Humanism between the Two World Wars* (Chicago: University of Chicago Press, 2005); Joseph Esherick, Hasan Kayalı, and Eric Van Young, eds., *Empire to Nation: Historical Perspectives on the Making of the Modern World* (Lanham, MD: Rowman & Littlefield, 2006); Peter Zarrow, *After Empire: The Conceptual Transformatrion of the Chinese State, 1885–1924* (Stanford, CA: Stanford University Press, 2012).

15. Susan Pedersen, *The Guardians: The League of Nations and the Crisis of Empire* (New York: Oxford University Press, 2015).

16. Quote: Erez Manela, *The Wilsonian Moment: Self-Determination and the International Origins of Anticolonial Nationalism* (Oxford: Oxford University Press, 2007). The other countries were Czechoslovakia and the Kingdom of Serbs, Croats and Slovenes. The League insisted on similar treaties for Greece and Romania in return for their territorial expansion, and for countries who, or whose empires, had lost the war, Hungary, Austria, Bulgaria, and Turkey. Albania, the three Baltic states, and Iraq accepted minority protection obligations to join the League, too.

17. Quote: "Resolution of the Syrian General Congress at Damascus, 2 July 1919," reprinted in James Gelvin, *The Modern Middle East: A History*, 3rd ed. (New York: Oxford University Press, 2011), 227. For the prewar cases, see Carole Fink,

*Defending the Rights of Others: The Great Powers, the Jews, and International Minority Protection, 1878–1938* (Cambridge: Cambridge University Press, 2004), 37.

18. Dane Kennedy, *Decolonization: A Very Short Introduction* (Oxford: Oxford University Press, 2016); Jan Jansen and Jürgen Osterhammel, *Decolonization: A Short History* (Princeton: Princeton University Press, 2017).

19. Jonathan Smele, *The "Russian" Civil Wars, 1916–1926: Ten Years That Shook the World* (London: Hurst, 2014).

# ACKNOWLEDGMENTS

This book has been long in the making. I wrote most of it after arriving at Princeton University's Department of Near Eastern Studies (NES) in 2008. I came to share the department's genuine dedication to what makes area studies worthwhile, including the pursuit of non-Western languages, while being next door to Princeton's History Department. There, Jeremy Adelman introduced me to global and imperial historians; and Molly Green became a true colleague. So did, at NES, Michael Cook, Jonathan Gribetz, Bernard Haykel, Satyel Larson, Marina Rustow, Max Weiss, and Qasim Zaman. I learned more than I can possibly describe from them and my other colleagues about the Middle East. I also cherished my time with NES students like Nadirah Mansour and Lindsey Stephenson. Sharp-witted, they argued any standpoint with and against me, pushing me intellectually; and warm-hearted, they made me a better adviser. I was privileged to work alongside Qasim Zaman and Michael Cook; with Karen Chirik; and with Greg Bell, Nancy Coffin, Nilufer Hatami, and Amineh Mahallati. The latter four, pillars of the NES language program, cared for students in inspiring ways. As NES manager, Karen was my right arm and my left, as it were, when I directed Princeton's Near Eastern Studies Program. Who knows when this book would have appeared without her and the other NES staff members, Bill Blair, Angela Bryant, Linda Kativa, James LaRegina, Gayatri Oruganti, Judy Schedneck, and Tammy Williams. Coteaching with Michael turned out to be a master class for me: in distilling knowledge. Writing, I often recall him exhort examinees to "not waste words or embroider; once you have shown that you know what you are talking about, move on." And I was lucky to direct the NES Program, my first administrative charge, when the NES Department was led by Qasim's steady hand. I have learned a great deal from him.

Princeton was also a place for friendships. At NES, I deeply enjoyed M'hamed Oualdi's caustic wit and was treated to many negroni and lovely dinners by Lara

Harb and her husband, Fulvio Domini. Salute! At NES, too, I met Andrew Arsan, now at Cambridge. In 2013, we co-organized a conference on the Mandates and subsequently coedited a respective volume. All this made me deeply value him as a man equally kind and sharp. In Manhattan, James Delbourgo and Laura Kopp were always ready for an evening of laughter, in-flat badminton, and reminiscing about good ol' times in New York, where we had met in the late 1990s. Nearby, in Jersey City, lived Emmanuel Szurek and Muriel Cohen. Showing me a New Jersey I did not know—even though in running shoes sometimes!—was the least of all they did for me. Born and bred Parisians, they introduced me to many things French, including Parisian academia. And warm and welcoming to a fault, they continued seeing me after their return to France. Toward the end of my stay at Princeton I got to know and love Michael Laffan for countless games of pool ("Revenge!") and gin and tonics, and for dinners also with Vanita Neelakanta. And then, there is Antonis Hadjikyriacou. Soon after his arrival as a postdoctoral fellow, I learned to love him for his genuine care during long talks, for his deliberate, unhurried pace, his exquisitely simple food, and a deep passion for history and politics alike.

For much of my time in Princeton, Boston was a home, too. For all that was good and for truly formative years of my life, I deeply thank Naghmeh Sohrabi. I also became part of the circle of her loved ones, especially Afsaneh Najmabadi, Kanan Makiye and Walada Sarraf, and Ben Smith and Alison Morse. The generous Houchang Chehabi has supported my career since my graduate years. A true cosmopolitan—a tireless traveler and master of many languages—he is a formidable role model, too. And it has been a pleasure to reconnect with Kamran Rastegar and Dana Sajdi, fellow Columbia graduates, and to get to know their partners, Christine Bustany and Jim Bowley.

I came to Princeton from Beirut. From 2005 to 2008, I taught at the Department of History and Archaeology of the American University of Beirut (AUB). It was during those years that this book was born—though not in an archive. Rather, I developed a certain sense for places, for their ties and differences: the urban remnants of Beirut's many pasts; the splendor of pre-civil war Aleppo, which belied it not being a capital city; or stories by elderly south Lebanese about past links with northern Palestine. More broadly, my years in Beirut were a formative introduction to the Arab world. For this, a heartfelt thank you goes to AUB colleagues Abdul-Rahim Abu-Husayn, Nadia El-Cheikh, Hermann Genz, John Meloy, Hélène Sader, Helga Sedeen, Samir Seikaly, and Tarif Khalidi. They taught me a whole lot. I had a very good time in their midst, too: Daily ten o'clock coffee break! Christmas carols in the department corridor! Dinners at Sultan Ibrahim! And I could go on and on. Also at AUB, I would like to thank Kaoukab Chebaro, Samar Mikati-Kaissi, Nadine Knesevitch, Iman Abdallah, Kamilia Kassis, Mervat Kobeissi, and Abeer Mudawwar, all at Jafet Library's Archives and Special Collections. Firas Talhuk helped me collect newspaper articles.

Makram Rabah assisted me in obtaining travel permits for my first interview trips to southern Lebanon. And Hussein Abdulsater tried to whip my Arabic into shape. Last but not least, life in Beirut would not have been the same without friends I made, in particular Tamara al-Samerraie, Cynthia Zaven, and Peter Speetjens.

During my years at Princeton, I presented this book project at various universities: in Austin, Basel, the American University of Beirut, Berne, Brandeis, St. John's College at the University of Cambridge, the University of Crete in Rethymnon, the Graduate Institute in Geneva, the Hebrew University of Jerusalem, the City University of New York, New York University, the University of Pennsylvania, Princeton, Rutgers, the National University of Singapore, and Tübingen. Attendees provided crucial critique about details, order and presentation, and perspective, encouraging me to think hard about this project. So did language editor Frankie Wright; Michael Reynolds, Molly Greene, Andrew Arsan, On Barak, Antonis Hadjikyriacou, Pierre-Yves Saunier, and Yoav Di-Capua, who all read chapter drafts; anonymous readers for Harvard University Press; and Sharmila Sen, my editor at the Press, and assistant editor Heather Hughes. Although I started this book as an area studies historian, I eventually came to think about it, and about modern Middle Eastern history more broadly, as a fascinating vantage point from which to think about the world as a whole.

This endeavor required visiting archives and libraries. In Princeton, Boston, Nantes, Paris, Vincennes, London, Oxford, Freiburg im Breisgau, Berne, Geneva, Damascus, Amman, Beirut, Juniye, Jerusalem, Haifa, Tel Aviv, and Nablus, I could not have done my research without diligent staff members. I am deeply grateful to all the men and women who agreed to be interviewed for this project. In Palestine, I thank Sherene Seikaly and Salim Tamari for introducing me to the Nablus Municipal Archive. And I would like to warmly thank Yusri Hazran for arranging a first round of interviews in Israel.

For two decades and counting, Yoav Di-Capua has been a faithful friend. More times than I can count I tasted his skillful cooking and admired his love for coffee. "World's best cappuccino, anybody?" is how mornings start with him and his family: a promise always kept. He is my guide to intellectual history, Arab and otherwise, and a great critic of my texts. Most important, he listens when times are tough, and gives deeply reflected advice. Second to none as friends are Daniel Lüscher and Karin Schatzmann. In Bern with their sons Nicolas, Ludovic, and Tamino, they are a home away from home. For more than a quarter of a century now, they have given me a place to revel in life's joys, talk through sorrows, cook together, and just be. I am truly fortunate to have them.

An immense thank you goes to my Yeroushalmis. Being with them has created too many memories to recount: emptying Yossi and Tami's fridge (before they padlocked it!); drinking Carlsbergs and watching soccer at Kami and Judy's while learning about the finer points of Iranian history; at Albert and Idit's, engaging with my uncle's lovely silly humor; and so much more involving my other uncles and aunts, Sina,

Diana, and Ehsan, and my many cousins. Together with other members of the Schayegh-Yeroushalmi-Geula-Shoa-Naji tree of families that from the 1960s left Iran for many countries, they ground me. So does my family on my mother's side, Vroni and Hansueli Schmid and Susi and Fritz Marti, and their children—my cousins—and Ursula and Mohamed Fergui-Wernly and their children, who are always a treat to visit. Last but not least, late into the making of this book I had the deep pleasure of gaining new relations, the Nalbantians-Oundjians.

Both my parents, Christine and Masud, pushed beyond the harsh material constraints of their upbringing to build careers, a lasting relationship, and a family. They are not only wonderful parents but also role models. So is my sister, Leila. Together with my great brother-in-law, Daniel Saraga, she combines a stellar career with boundless dedication to her family. Seeing all of them never fails to nourish my soul. Their love and enthusiasm and energy, their resolve to keep me close even when I was far, and their joy upon learning I am returning to Europe are deeply touching.

I dedicate this book to the best of all nieces and nephews, Dalia and Leo, who give me more pleasure than they will ever know; and to my wife, Tsolin Nalbantian, with whom life is all I have always dreamed it might be.

# INDEX

Page numbers followed by *f* indicate figures.

World War II (*continued*)
and Aleppo, 290–294, 313;
culture, declining importance of
Bilad al-Sham, 294–296, 313;
economics, power after Bilad
al-Sham's decline, 296–297;eco-
nomics, in Arab Palestine,
303–306; economics, in Jordan,
306–307; economics, in Damascus and Aleppo, 307–309;
economics, in Beirut, 309–311,
314
World Zionist Organization, 78, 105,
152, 287, 296

Yaari, A., 221
Yaari, Shulamit, 325
Yanni, Jurji, 45–46
Yassin, Hashim, 245
Yehuda, Eliezer Ben, 82
Yemen, 4, 13, 213, 274, 292, 305
Yishuv: pre–World War I, 76–79,
81–85; during World War I, 101,
105–106, 396n31; in the 1920s, 132,

133 152–155, 156–164, 169, 170, 172,
175–177, 186–187, 422n9, 439n67; in
the 1930s, 196–198, 202–203, 206,
214, 218, 220–222, 225, 226–236,
238–239, 240, 243, 246–255,
262–263; during World War II,
266–271, 274, 276, 286–290, 296,
297–303; post–World War II,
315–316, 322, 324, 325. *See also*
Israel
Young Men's Association, 223
Youngsters Block, 217
Young Turk revolution (1908), 42,
52, 142, 336–337
Youth movements, in 1930s,
223–224, 437n51

Za'im, Muhammad al-, 237
Zionism / Zionists. *See* Yishuv
Zionist Executive, 11, 133, 154, 161,
176, 202, 334–335
"Z" list affair, 187–188
Zu'aytir, Akram, 216, 217
Zurayq, Qustantin, 224–225